Advances in Fixed Point Theory and Its Applications

Advances in Fixed Point Theory and Its Applications

Editor

Timilehin Opeyemi Alakoya

Basel • Beijing • Wuhan • Barcelona • Belgrade • Novi Sad • Cluj • Manchester

Editor
Timilehin Opeyemi Alakoya
Queen's University Belfast
Belfast
UK

Editorial Office
MDPI AG
Grosspeteranlage 5
4052 Basel, Switzerland

This is a reprint of articles from the Special Issue published online in the open access journal *Mathematics* (ISSN 2227-7390) (available at: https://www.mdpi.com/si/mathematics/Fixed_Point_Theory_Appl).

For citation purposes, cite each article independently as indicated on the article page online and as indicated below:

Lastname, A.A.; Lastname, B.B. Article Title. *Journal Name* **Year**, *Volume Number*, Page Range.

ISBN 978-3-7258-1875-4 (Hbk)
ISBN 978-3-7258-1876-1 (PDF)
doi.org/10.3390/books978-3-7258-1876-1

© 2024 by the authors. Articles in this book are Open Access and distributed under the Creative Commons Attribution (CC BY) license. The book as a whole is distributed by MDPI under the terms and conditions of the Creative Commons Attribution-NonCommercial-NoDerivs (CC BY-NC-ND) license.

Contents

About the Editor vii

Austine Efut Ofem, Jacob Ashiwere Abuchu, Reny George, Godwin Chidi Ugwunnadi and Ojen Kumar Narain
Some New Results on Convergence, Weak w^2-Stability and Data Dependence of Two Multivalued Almost Contractive Mappings in Hyperbolic Spaces
Reprinted from: *Mathematics* **2022**, *10*, 3720, doi:10.3390/math10203720 1

Adrian Nicolae Branga and Ion Marian Olaru
Generalized Contractions and Fixed Point Results in Spaces with Altering Metrics
Reprinted from: *Mathematics* **2022**, *10*, 4083, doi:10.3390/math10214083 27

Ali Turab and Norhayati Rosli
Study of Fractional Differential Equations Emerging in the Theory of Chemical Graphs: A Robust Approach
Reprinted from: *Mathematics* **2022**, *10*, 4222, doi:10.3390/math10224222 40

Timilehin Opeyemi Alakoya and Oluwatosin Temitope Mewomo
A Relaxed Inertial Tseng's Extragradient Method for Solving Split Variational Inequalities with Multiple Output Sets
Reprinted from: *Mathematics* **2023**, *11*, 386, doi:10.3390/math11020386 56

Arul Joseph Gnanaprakasam, Gunaseelan Mani, Ozgur Ege, Ahmad Aloqaily and Nabil Mlaiki
New Fixed Point Results in Orthogonal B-Metric Spaces with Related Applications
Reprinted from: *Mathematics* **2023**, *11*, 677, doi:10.3390/math11030677 82

Mohammad Al-Khaleel, Sharifa Al-Sharif and Rami AlAhmad
On Cyclic Contractive Mappings of Kannan and Chatterjea Type in Generalized Metric Spaces
Reprinted from: *Mathematics* **2023**, *11*, 890, doi:10.3390/math11040890 100

Zoran D. Mitrović, Abasalt Bodaghi, Ahmad Aloqaily, Nabil Mlaiki and Reny George
New Versions of Some Results on Fixed Points in *b*-Metric Spaces
Reprinted from: *Mathematics* **2023**, *11*, 1118, doi:10.3390/math11051118 110

Manoj Kumar, Pankaj Kumar, Rajagopalan Ramaswamy, Ola A. Ashour Abdelnaby, Amr Elsonbaty and Stojan Radenović
$(\alpha - \psi)$ Meir–Keeler Contractions in Bipolar Metric Spaces
Reprinted from: *Mathematics* **2023**, *11*, 1310, doi:10.3390/math11061310 119

Gunaseelan Mani, Salma Haque, Arul Joseph Gnanaprakasam, Ozgur Ege and Nabil Mlaiki
The Study of Bicomplex-Valued Controlled Metric Spaces with Applications to Fractional Differential Equations
Reprinted from: *Mathematics* **2023**, *11*, 2742, doi:10.3390/math11122742 133

Yuan Meng, Conghong He, Renhao Ma and Huihui Pang
Existence and Uniqueness of Non-Negative Solution to a Coupled Fractional q-Difference System with Mixed q-Derivative via Mixed Monotone Operator Method
Reprinted from: *Mathematics* **2023**, *11*, 2941, doi:10.3390/math11132941 152

Rattanakorn Wattanataweekul, Kobkoon Janngam and Suthep Suantai
A Novel Two-Step Inertial Viscosity Algorithm for Bilevel Optimization Problems Applied to Image Recovery
Reprinted from: *Mathematics* **2023**, *11*, 3518, doi:10.3390/math11163518 174

Monairah Alansari, Yahya Almalki and Muhammad Usman Ali
Czerwik Vector-Valued Metric Space with an Equivalence Relation and Extended Forms of Perov Fixed-Point Theorem
Reprinted from: *Mathematics* **2023**, *11*, 3583, doi:10.3390/math11163583 194

Isaac Karabo Letlhage, Deepak Khantwal, Rajendra Pant and Manuel De la Sen
The Stability and Well-Posedness of Fixed Points for Relation-Theoretic Multi-Valued Maps
Reprinted from: *Mathematics* **2023**, *11*, 4271, doi:10.3390/math11204271 208

Badriah Alamri
Solving Integral Equation and Homotopy Result via Fixed Point Method
Reprinted from: *Mathematics* **2023**, *11*, 4408, doi:10.3390/math11214408 221

Matlhatsi Dorah Ngwepe, Lateef Olakunle Jolaoso, Maggie Aphane and Ibrahim Oyeyemi Adenekan
An Algorithm That Adjusts the Stepsize to Be Self-Adaptive with an Inertial Term Aimed for Solving Split Variational Inclusion and Common Fixed Point Problems
Reprinted from: *Mathematics* **2023**, *11*, 4708, doi:10.3390/math11224708 240

About the Editor

Timilehin Opeyemi Alakoya

Timilehin Opeyemi Alakoya is a Research Fellow in the School of Mathematics and Physics at Queen's University Belfast, the United Kingdom. His current research interests include traffic and transportation system modelling, network analysis, optimization, and fixed-point theory applied in solving various real-world problems that arise in fields such as traffic modelling, medical science, and economics. Related areas of his research interests include numerical analysis, variational analysis, optimal control, dynamical systems, stochastic methods, and machine learning, among others.

Article

Some New Results on Convergence, Weak w^2-Stability and Data Dependence of Two Multivalued Almost Contractive Mappings in Hyperbolic Spaces

Austine Efut Ofem [1,*], Jacob Ashiwere Abuchu [1,2], Reny George [3,*], Godwin Chidi Ugwunnadi [4,5] and Ojen Kumar Narain [1]

1. School of Mathematics, Statistics and Computer Science, University of KwaZulu-Natal, Durban 4001, South Africa
2. Department of Mathematics, University of Calabar, Calabar P.M.B. 1115, Nigeria
3. Department of Mathematics, College of Science and Humanities in Al-Kharj, Prince Sattam Bin Abdulaziz University, Al-Kharj 11942, Saudi Arabia
4. Department of Mathematics, University of Eswatini, Private Bag 4, Kwaluseni M201, Eswatini
5. Department of Mathematics and Applied Mathematics, Sefako Makgatho Health Sciences University, Pretoria 0204, South Africa
* Correspondence: 222128007@stu.ukzn.ac.za (A.E.O.); renygeorge02@yahoo.com (R.G.)

Abstract: In this article, we introduce a new mixed-type iterative algorithm for approximation of common fixed points of two multivalued almost contractive mappings and two multivalued mappings satisfying condition (E) in hyperbolic spaces. We consider new concepts of weak w^2-stability and data dependence results involving two multivalued almost contractive mappings. We provide examples of multivalued almost contractive mappings to show the advantage of our new iterative algorithm over some exiting iterative algorithms. Moreover, we prove several strong $\triangle$-convergence theorems of our new algorithm in hyperbolic spaces. Furthermore, with another novel example, we carry out a numerical experiment to compare the efficiency and applicability of a new iterative algorithm with several leading iterative algorithms. The results in this article extend and improve several existing results from the setting of linear and CAT(0) spaces to hyperbolic spaces. Our main results also extend several existing results from the setting of single-valued mappings to the setting of multivalued mappings.

Keywords: weak w^2-stability; multivalued almost contractive mappings; multivalued mappings satisfying condition (E); data dependence; strong and $\triangle$-convergence

MSC: 05A30; 30C45; 11B65; 47B38

1. Introduction

In fixed point theory, the role played by ambient spaces is paramount. Several problems in diverse fields of science are naturally nonlinear. Therefore, transforming the linear version of a given problem into its equivalent nonlinear version is very pertinent. Moreover, studying various problems in spaces without a linear structure is significant in applied and pure sciences. Several efforts have been made to introduce a convex-like structure on a metric space. Hyperbolic space is one of the spaces that posses this structure.

In this paper, our studies will be carried out in the setting of hyperbolic space studied by Kohlenbach [1]. This notion of hyperbolic space is more restrictive than the notion of hyperbolic space considered in [2] and more general than the notion of hyperbolic space studied in [3]. Banach and CAT(0) spaces are well known to be special cases of hyperbolic spaces. Moreover, the class of hyperbolic spaces properly contains a Hilbert ball endowed with hyperbolic metric [4], Hadamard manifolds, $\mathbb{R}$-trees, and the Cartesian product of Hilbert spaces.

Definition 1. *A hyperbolic space $(Q, d, \mathcal{K})$ in the sense used by Kohlenbach [1] is a metric space (Q, d) with a convexity mapping $\mathcal{K} : Q^2 \times [0, 1] \to Q$ that satisfies*

(C_1) $d(\eta, \mathcal{K}(m, w, \xi)) \leq \xi d(\eta, m) + (1 - \xi) d(\eta, w)$;
(C_2) $d(\mathcal{K}(m, w, \xi), \mathcal{K}(m, w, v)) \leq |\xi - v| d(m, w)$;
(C_3) $\mathcal{K}(m, w, \xi) = \mathcal{K}(w, m, (1 - \xi))$;
(C_4) $d(\mathcal{K}(m, u, \xi), \mathcal{K}(w, v, \xi)) \leq (1 - \xi) d(m, w) + \xi d(u, v)$,

for all $m, w, u, v \in Q$ and $\xi, v \in [0, 1]$. A nonempty subset $\mathcal{J}$ of a hyperbolic space Q is termed convex, if $\mathcal{K}(m, w, \xi) \in \mathcal{J}$, for all $m, w \in \mathcal{J}$ and $\xi \in [0, 1]$.

Suppose $m, w \in Q$ and $\xi \in [0, 1]$, the notation $(1 - \xi)m \oplus \xi w$ is used for $\mathcal{K}(m, w, \xi)$. The following also holds for the more general setting of convex metric space [5]: for any $m, w \in Q$ and $\xi \in [0, 1]$, $d(m, (1 - \xi)m \oplus \xi w) = \xi d(m, w)$ and $d(w, (1 - \xi)m \oplus \xi w) = (1 - \xi) d(m, w)$. Consequently, $1m \oplus 0w = m$, $0m \oplus 1w = w$ and $(1 - \xi)m \oplus \xi m = \xi m \oplus (1 - \xi)m = m$.

The notion of multivalued contraction mappings and nonexpasive mappings using the Hausdorff metric was initiated by Nadler [6] and Markin [7]. The theory of multivalued mappings has several applications in convex optimization, game theory, control theory, economics, and differential equations.

Let Q be a metric space and $\mathcal{J}$ a nonempty subset of Q. The subset $\mathcal{J}$ is called proximal if for all $m \in Q$, there exists a member w in $\mathcal{J}$ such that

$$d(m, w) = \text{dist}(m, \mathcal{J}) = \inf\{d(m, s) : s \in \mathcal{J}\}.$$

Let $\mathcal{P}(\mathcal{J})$ denote the collection of all nonempty proximal bounded and closed subsets of $\mathcal{J}$, and $\mathcal{BC}(\mathcal{J})$ the collection of all nonempty closed bounded subsets. The Hausdorff distance on $\mathcal{BC}(\mathcal{J})$ is defined by

$$\mathcal{H}(\mathcal{W}, \mathcal{V}) = \max\left\{\sup_{m \in \mathcal{W}} d(m, \mathcal{V}), \sup_{w \in \mathcal{V}} d(w, \mathcal{W})\right\}, \forall \mathcal{W}, \mathcal{V} \in \mathcal{BC}(\mathcal{J}).$$

A point $m \in \mathcal{J}$ is called a fixed point of the multivalued mapping $\mathcal{G} : \mathcal{J} \to 2^{\mathcal{J}}$ if $m \in \mathcal{G}m$. Let $\mathcal{F}(\mathcal{G})$ denote the set of all fixed points of $\mathcal{G}$. A multivalued mapping $\mathcal{G} : \mathcal{J} \to \mathcal{BC}(\mathcal{J})$ is called nonexpansive if $\mathcal{H}(\mathcal{G}m, \mathcal{G}w) \leq \rho(m, w)$, for all $m, w \in \mathcal{J}$ and it is called quasi-nonexpansive if $\mathcal{F}(\mathcal{G}) \neq \emptyset$ such that $\mathcal{H}(\mathcal{G}m, \mathcal{G}q^*) \leq \rho(m, q^*)$, for all $m \in \mathcal{J}$ and $q^* \in \mathcal{F}(\mathcal{G}) \neq \emptyset$. In 2007, the notion of single-valued almost contractive mappings of Berinde [8] was extended to multivalued almost contractive mappings by M. Berinde and V. Berinde [9], as follows.

Definition 2. *A multivalued mapping $\mathcal{G} : \mathcal{J} \to \mathcal{BC}(\mathcal{J})$ is said to be almost contractive if there exist $\varrho \in [0, 1)$ and $L \geq 0$ such that the following inequality holds:*

$$\mathcal{H}(\mathcal{G}m, \mathcal{G}w) \leq \varrho d(m, w) + L \text{dist}(m, \mathcal{G}m), \forall m, w \in \mathcal{J}. \tag{1}$$

In 2008, Suzuki [10] introduced a generalized class of nonexpansive mappings, which is also known as condition (C), and further showed that the class of mapping satisfying condition (C) is more general than the class of nonexpansive mappings. In 2011, Eslami and Abkar [11] defined the multivalued version of condition (C) as follows.

Definition 3. *A multivalued mapping $\mathcal{G} : \mathcal{J} \to \mathcal{BC}(\mathcal{J})$ is said to satisfy condition (C) if the following inequalities hold:*

$$\frac{1}{2}\text{dist}(m, \mathcal{G}m) \leq d(m, w) \Rightarrow \mathcal{H}(\mathcal{G}m, \mathcal{G}w) \leq d(m, w), \forall m, w \in \mathcal{J}. \tag{2}$$

Very recently, García–Falset et al. [12] defined a new single-valued mapping called condition (E). This class of mappings is weaker than the class of nonexpansive mappings and stronger than the class of quasi-nonexpansive mappings. Recently, Kim et al. [13] defined the multivalued and hyperbolic space version of the class of mappings satisfying condition (E). The authors also established some existence and convergence results for such mappings.

Definition 4. *A multivalued mapping $\mathcal{G} : \mathcal{J} \to \mathcal{BC}(\mathcal{J})$ is said to satisfy condition (E_μ) if the following inequality holds:*

$$\operatorname{dist}(m, \mathcal{G}w) \leq \mu \operatorname{dist}(m, \mathcal{G}m) + d(m, w), \ \forall\, m, w \in \mathcal{J}. \tag{3}$$

The mapping $\mathcal{G}$ is said to satisfy condition (E) whenever $\mathcal{G}$ satisfies condition (E_μ) for some $\mu \geq 1$.

The studies involving multivalued nonexpansive mappings are known to be more difficult than the concepts involving single-valued nonexpansive mappings. For the approximation of fixed points of various mappings, iterative methods are well known to be essential. In recent years, several authors have introduced and studied different iterative algorithms for approximating fixed points of multivalued nonexpansive mappings as well as multivalued mappings satisfying condition (E) (see [13–18] and the references in them).

In 2007, Argawal et al. [19] introduced the S-iterative algorithm for single-valued contraction mappings. In 2014, Chang et al. [15] considered the mixed-type S-iterative algorithm in hyperbolic spaces for multivalued nonexpansive mappings as follows:

$$\begin{cases} m_1 \in \mathcal{J}, \\ w_k = \mathcal{K}(m_k, u_k, \eta_k), \quad k \in \mathbb{N}, \\ m_{k+1} = \mathcal{K}(u_k, v_k, \xi_k), \end{cases} \tag{4}$$

where $v_k \in \mathcal{G}_1 w_k$, $u_k \in \mathcal{G}_2 m$, $\{\xi_k\}$ and $\{\eta_k\}$ are real sequences in $(0,1)$.

In addition, in [13] Kim et al. considered the multivalued and hyperbolic space version of S-iterative algorithm for fixed points multivalued mappings satisfying condition (E) as follows:

$$\begin{cases} m_1 \in \mathcal{J}, \\ w_k = \mathcal{K}(m_k, u_k, \eta_k), \quad k \in \mathbb{N}, \\ m_{k+1} = \mathcal{K}(u_k, v_k, \xi_k), \end{cases} \tag{5}$$

where $v_k \in \mathcal{G} w_k$, $u_k \in \mathcal{G} m_k$, $\{\xi_k\}$ and $\{\eta_k\}$ are real sequences in $(0,1)$.

It is worth noting that the iterative algorithm (4) involves two multivalued mappings and the iterative algorithm (5) involves one multivalued mapping and the class of mappings considered by Kim et al. [13] is more general than the class of mappings considered by Chang et al. [15].

In 2019, Chuadchawnay et al. [20] studied the iterative algorithm (4) for common fixed points of two multivalued mappings satisfying condition (E) in hyperbolic spaces.

Very recently, Ahmad et al. [21] developed the hyperbolic space version of the F iterative algorithm [22]. The authors obtained some fixed point convergence results for single-valued mappings satisfying condition (E) and single-valued almost contractive mappings. Furthermore, they obtained data dependence and weak w^2-stability results for single-valued almost contractive mappings. At the same time, they also raised the following interesting open questions:

Open Question 1. *Is it possible to establish all the results of Ahmad et al. [21] in the setting of multivalued mappings?*

Open Question 2. *Is it possible to establish all the results of Ahmad et al. [21] in the setting of common fixed points?*

Remark 1. *It is worth mentioning that, as far as we know, there are no works in the literature concerning stability and data dependence results of mixed-type iterative algorithms for single-valued and multivalued mappings in hyperbolic spaces. Therefore, one of our aims in this article is to fill such gaps and hence give affirmative answers to the above Open Questions 1–2.*

It is well known that common fixed point problems have direct application with minimization problems [23].

Motivated and inspired by the above results, in this paper, we introduce the following mixed-type hyperbolic space version of the novel iterative algorithm considered in [24]:

$$\begin{cases} m_1 \in \mathcal{J}, \\ s_k = \mathcal{K}(m_k, u_k, \eta_k), \\ w_k = \mathcal{K}(u_k, t_k, \xi_k), \quad k \in \mathbb{N}, \\ p_k = h_k, \\ m_{k+1} = \ell_k, \end{cases} \tag{6}$$

where $\{\xi_k\}, \{\eta_k\}$ are real sequences in $(0,1)$ and $\ell_k \in \mathcal{G}_1 p_k, h_k \in \mathcal{G}_2 w_k, t_k \in \mathcal{G}_1 s_k, u_k \in \mathcal{G}_2 m_k$. We prove strong convergence theorems of the iterative method (6) for common fixed points of two multivalued almost contractive mappings. Next, we present some novel numerical examples to compare the efficiency and applicability of our new iterative algorithm (6) with many leading iterative algorithms in the current literature. Moreover, we study new concepts of weak w^2-stability and data-dependence results of (6) for two multivalued almost contractive mappings. Furthermore, we prove strong and $\triangle$ convergence results of (6) for common fixed points of two multivalued mappings satisfying the condition (E). We provide another example and with the aid of the example, we show the advantage of our iterative method (6) over some existing iterative methods in terms of rate of convergence. Our results give affirmative answers to the two above Open Questions 1 and 2 raised by Ahmad [21].

2. Preliminaries

A hyperbolic space $(\mathcal{Q}, d, \mathcal{K})$ is termed uniformly convex [5], if, given $s > 0$ and $\varepsilon \in (0, 2]$, there exists $\sigma \in (0, 1]$, such that for any $m, w, p \in \mathcal{Q}$,

$$d(\frac{1}{2}m \oplus \frac{1}{2}w, p) \leq (1-\sigma)s,$$

provided $d(m,p) \leq s, d(m,p) \leq s$ and $d(m,w) \geq \varepsilon s$. A mapping $\Theta : (0, \infty) \times (0, 2] \to (0, 1]$ which ensures that $\sigma = \Theta(s, \varepsilon)$ for any $s > 0$ and $\varepsilon \in (0, 2]$, is said to be a modulus of uniform convexity. The mapping Θ is termed monotone if for fixed ε, it decreases with s; that is, $\Theta(s_2, \varepsilon) \leq \Theta(s_1, \varepsilon)$, for all $s_2 \geq s_1 > 0$.

In 2007, with a modulus of uniform convexity $\sigma(s, \varepsilon) = \frac{\varepsilon^2}{8}$ quadratic in ε, Leustean [25] showed that CAT(0) space are uniformly convex hyperbolic spaces. This implies that the class of uniformly convex hyperbolic spaces are a natural generalization of both CAT(0) space and uniformly convex Banach spaces [5].

Next, we give the definition of $\triangle$-convergence. In view of this, we consider the following concept which will be useful in the definition. Let $\mathcal{J}$ denote a nonempty subset of the metric space $(\mathcal{Q}, d)$ and $\{m_k\}$ be any bounded sequence in $\mathcal{Q}$. For all $m \in \mathcal{Q}$, we define

- asymptotic radius of $\{m_k\}$ at m as

$$r_a(\{m_k\}, m) = \limsup_{k \to \infty} d(m_k, m);$$

- asymptotic radius of $\{m_k\}$ relative to $\mathcal{J}$ as

$$r_a(\{m_k\}, \mathcal{J}) = \inf\{r_a(\{m_k\}, m); m \in \mathcal{J}\}; \text{ and}$$

- asymptotic center of $\{m_k\}$ relative to $\mathcal{J}$ as

$$AC(\{m_k\}, \mathcal{J}) = \{m \in \mathcal{J}; r_a(\{m_k\}, m) = r_a(\{m_k\}, \mathcal{J})\}. \tag{7}$$

It is known that every sequence that is bounded has a unique asymptotic center with respect to each closed convex subset in Banach spaces and CAT(0) spaces. If the asymptotic center is taken with rest to $\mathcal{Q}$, then we simply denote it by $AC(\{m_k\})$.

The following lemma by Leustean [25] shows that the above property holds in a complete uniformly convex hyperbolic space.

Lemma 1 ([25]). *Let $(\mathcal{Q}, d, \mathcal{K})$ be a complete, uniformly convex hyperbolic space with a monotone modulus of uniform convexity Θ. Then, for any sequence $\{m_k\}$ that is bounded in $\mathcal{Q}$, it has a unique asymptotic center with respect to any nonempty closed convex subset $\mathcal{J}$ of $\mathcal{Q}$.*

Now, we further consider some definitions and lemmas that will be useful in proving our main results as follows.

Definition 5. *A sequence $\{m_k\}$ in $\mathcal{Q}$ is said to be $\triangle$-convergent to an element m in $\mathcal{Q}$, if m is the unique asymptotic center of every subsequence $\{m_{k_l}\}$ of $\{m_k\}$. For this, we write $\triangle - \lim_{k \to \infty} m_k = m$ and say m is the $\triangle$-limit of $\{m_k\}$.*

Lemma 2 ([23]). *Assume that $\mathcal{Q}$ is a uniformly convex hyperbolic space with the monotone modulus of uniform convexity Θ. Let $m \in \mathcal{Q}$ and $\{\vartheta_k\}$ be a sequence in $[d, e]$ for some $d, e \in (0, 1)$. Suppose $\{m_k\}$ and $\{w_k\}$ are sequences in $\mathcal{Q}$ such that $\limsup_{k \to \infty} d(m_k, m) \leq c$, $\limsup_{k \to \infty} d(w_k, m) \leq c$ and $\lim_{k \to \infty} d(\mathcal{K}(m_k, w_k, \vartheta_k), m) = c$ for some $c \geq 0$, and then we get $\lim_{k \to \infty} d(m_k, w_k) = 0$.*

Lemma 3 ([26]). *Let $\{\rho_k\}$ and $\{\phi_k\}$ be non-negative sequences for which one assumes that there exists a $z_0 \in \mathbb{N}$ such that, for all $z \geq z_0$, and*

$$\rho_{k+1} = (1 - \varphi_k)\rho_k + \varphi_k \phi_k$$

is satisfied, where $\varphi_k \in (0, 1)$ for all $k \in \mathbb{N}$, $\sum_{k=0}^{\infty} \phi_k = \infty$ and $\phi_k \geq 0 \ \forall k \in \mathbb{N}$. Then the following holds:

$$0 \leq \limsup_{k \to \infty} \rho_k \leq \limsup_{k \to \infty} \phi_k.$$

Definition 6 ([26]). *Let $\mathcal{G}, \tilde{\mathcal{G}}$ be two self-mappings on $\mathcal{Q}$. We say that $\tilde{\mathcal{G}}$ is an approximate operator of $\mathcal{G}$ if for all $\epsilon > 0$, we have that $d(\mathcal{G}m, \tilde{\mathcal{G}}m) \leq \epsilon$ holds for any $m \in \mathcal{Q}$.*

Definition 7 ([27]). *Two sequences $\{m_k\}$ and $\{w_k\}$ are said to be equivalent if*

$$d(m_k, w_k) \to 0, \text{ as } k \to \infty.$$

Definition 8 ([28]). *Let $(\mathcal{Q}, d)$ be a metric space, $\mathcal{G} : \mathcal{Q} \to \mathcal{Q}$ be a self-map and for arbitrary $m_1 \in \mathcal{Q}$, $\{m_k\}$ is the iterative algorithm defined by*

$$m_{k+1} = f(\mathcal{G}, m_k), \ k \geq 0. \tag{8}$$

Assume that $m_k \to q^*$ as $k \to \infty$, for all $q^* \in \mathcal{F}(\mathcal{G})$ and for any sequence $\{y_k\} \subset \mathcal{Q}$ which is equivalent to $\{m_k\}$, and we have

$$\lim_{k \to \infty} d(y_{k+1}, f(\mathcal{G}, y_k)) = 0 \implies \lim_{k \to \infty} y_k = q^*,$$

and then we say that the iterative algorithm (8) is weak w^2-stable with respect to $\mathcal{G}$.

Proposition 1 ([13]). *Suppose $\mathcal{G} : \mathcal{J} \to \mathcal{BC}(\mathcal{J})$ is a multivalued mapping satisfying condition (E), such that $\mathcal{F}(\mathcal{G}) \neq \emptyset$, and then $\mathcal{G}$ is a multivalued quasi-nonexpansive mapping.*

Lemma 4 ([13]). *Let $(\mathcal{Q}, d, \mathcal{K})$ be a complete uniformly convex hyperbolic space with a monotone modulus of uniform convexity Θ, and let $\mathcal{J}$ be a nonempty closed convex subset of $\mathcal{Q}$. Let $\mathcal{G} : \mathcal{J} \to \mathcal{P}(\mathcal{J})$ be a multivalued mapping which satisfies condition (E) with convex values. Suppose $\{m_k\}$ is a sequence in $\mathcal{J}$ with $\triangle - \lim_{k \to \infty} m_k = m$ and $\lim_{k \to \infty} \text{dist}(m_k, \mathcal{G} m_k) = 0$, then $m \in \mathcal{F}(\mathcal{G})$.*

Lemma 5 ([15]). *Let $(\mathcal{Q}, d, \mathcal{K})$ be a complete uniformly convex hyperbolic space with a monotone modulus of uniform convexity Θ and $\{m_k\}$ be a sequence which is bounded in $\mathcal{Q}$ such that $AC(\{m_k\}) = \{m\}$. Suppose that $\{u_k\}$ is a subsequence of $\{m_k\}$ such that $AC(\{u_k\}) = \{u\}$, and the sequence $\{d(m_k, u)\}$ is convergent, and then we have $m = u$.*

3. Convergence Results for Two Multivalued, Almost Contraction Mappings

Theorem 3. *Let $\mathcal{J}$ be a nonempty closed convex subset of a hyperbolic space $\mathcal{Q}$ and $\mathcal{G}_i : \mathcal{J} \to \mathcal{P}(\mathcal{J})$ (i=1,2) be two multivalued almost contraction mappings. Let $\mathscr{F} = \bigcap_{i=1}^{2} \mathcal{F}(\mathcal{G}_i) \neq \emptyset$ and $\mathcal{G}_i q^* = \{q^*\}$ for each $q^* \in \mathscr{F}$ $(i = 1, 2)$. Let $\{m_k\}$ be the sequence defined by (6). Then, $\{m_k\}$ converges to a point in $\mathscr{F}$.*

Proof. Let $q^* \in \mathscr{F}$. From (1) and (6), we have

$$\begin{aligned}
d(s_k, q^*) &= d(\mathcal{K}(m_k, u_k, \eta_k), q^*) \\
&\leq (1 - \eta_k) d(m_k, q^*) + \eta_k d(u_k, q^*) \\
&\leq (1 - \eta_k) d(m_k, q^*) + \eta_k \text{dist}(u_k, \mathcal{G}_2 q^*) \\
&\leq (1 - \eta_k) d(m_k, q^*) + \eta_k \mathscr{H}(\mathcal{G}_2 m_k, \mathcal{G}_2 q^*) \\
&= (1 - \eta_k) d(m_k, q^*) + \eta_k \mathscr{H}(\mathcal{G}_2 q^*, \mathcal{G}_2 m_k) \\
&\leq (1 - \eta_k) d(m_k, q^*) + \eta_k [\varrho d(q^*, m_k) + L \text{dist}(q^*, \mathcal{G}_2 q^*)] \\
&\leq (1 - \eta_k) d(m_k, q^*) + \eta_k \varrho d(m_k, q^*) \\
&= (1 - (1 - \varrho) \eta_k) d(m_k, q^*).
\end{aligned} \quad (9)$$

Because $0 \leq \varrho < 1$ and $0 < \eta_k < 1$, it follows that $(1 - (1 - \varrho) \eta_k) < 1$. Thus, (9) becomes

$$d(s_k, q^*) \leq d(m_k, q^*). \quad (10)$$

By using (6) and (10), we have

$$\begin{aligned}
d(w_k, q^*) &= d(\mathcal{K}(u_k, t_k, \xi_k), q^*) \\
&\leq (1 - \xi_k) d(u_k, q^*) + \xi_k d(t_k, q^*) \\
&\leq (1 - \xi_k) \text{dist}(u_k, \mathcal{G}_2 q^*) + \xi_k \text{dist}(t_k, \mathcal{G}_1 q^*) \\
&\leq (1 - \xi_k) \mathscr{H}(\mathcal{G}_2 m_k, \mathcal{G}_2 q^*) + \xi_k \mathscr{H}(\mathcal{G}_1 s_k, \mathcal{G}_1 q^*) \\
&\leq (1 - \xi_k) \varrho d(m_k, q^*) + \xi_k \varrho d(s_k, q^*) \\
&\leq (1 - \xi_k) \varrho d(m_k, q^*) + \xi_k \varrho d(m_k, q^*) \\
&\leq (1 - (1 - \varrho) \xi_k) \varrho d(m_k, q^*).
\end{aligned} \quad (11)$$

Because $0 \leq \varrho < 1$ and $0 < \xi_k < 1$, it follows that $(1 - (1-\varrho)\xi_k) < 1$. Thus, (9) becomes
$$d(w_k, q^\star) \leq \varrho d(m_k, q^\star). \tag{12}$$

Moreover, from (6) and (12), we have
$$\begin{aligned} d(p_k, q^\star) &= d(h_k, q^\star) \\ &\leq \operatorname{dist}(h_k, \mathcal{G}_2 q^\star) \\ &\leq \mathcal{H}(\mathcal{G}_2 w_k, \mathcal{G}_2 q^\star) \\ &\leq \varrho d(w_k, q^\star) \\ &\leq \varrho^2 d(m_k, q^\star). \end{aligned} \tag{13}$$

Finally, by (6) and (13), we have
$$\begin{aligned} d(m_{k+1}, q^\star) &= d(\ell_k, q^\star) \\ &\leq \operatorname{dist}(\ell_k, \mathcal{G}_1 q^\star) \\ &\leq \mathcal{H}(\mathcal{G}_1 p_k, \mathcal{G}_1 q^\star) \\ &\leq \varrho d(p_k, q^\star) \\ &\leq \varrho^3 d(m_k, q^\star). \end{aligned} \tag{14}$$

Inductively, we obtain
$$d(m_{k+1}, q^\star) \leq \varrho^{3(k+1)} d(m_0, q^\star).$$

Because $0 \leq \varrho < 1$, it follows that $\lim_{k \to \infty} m_k = q^\star$. $\square$

Next, we give examples of two multivalued almost contractive mappings that are neither contraction nor nonexpansive mappings. With the provided example, we also compare the efficiency of our iterative algorithm (6) with some existing methods.

Example 1. *Let $\mathcal{Q} = \mathbb{R}$ with the distance metric and $\mathcal{J} = [-1,1]$. Let $\mathcal{G}_1, \mathcal{G}_2 : \mathcal{J} \to \mathcal{P}(\mathcal{J})$ be defined by*

$$\mathcal{G}_1 m = \begin{cases} [0, \frac{m}{4}], & \text{if } m \in [-1, 0], \\ \{0\}, & \text{if } m \in (0, 1]; \end{cases}$$

and

$$\mathcal{G}_2 m = \begin{cases} [0, \frac{m}{8}], & \text{if } m \in [-1, 0] \\ \{0\}, & \text{if } m \in (0, 1]. \end{cases}$$

Because every nonexpansive mapping is continuous, we know that $\mathcal{G}_1$ and $\mathcal{G}_2$ are not multivalued nonexpansive mappings because of their discontinuity at $0 \in [-1,1]$ and hence, they are not multivalued contraction mappings. Next, we show that $\mathcal{G}_1$ is a multivalued almost contractive mapping. In view of this, we consider the following cases.

Case I: When $m, w \in [-1, 0]$, we have

$$\begin{aligned}
\mathscr{H}(\mathcal{G}_1 m, \mathcal{G}_1 w) &= \frac{1}{4}|m-w| \\
&\leq \frac{1}{4}|m-w| + \frac{4}{5}\left|\frac{3m}{4}\right| \\
&= \frac{1}{4}|m-w| + \frac{4}{5}\left|m-\frac{m}{4}\right| \\
&= \frac{1}{4}d(m,w) + \frac{4}{5}\text{dist}\left(m, [0, \frac{m}{4}]\right) \\
&= \frac{1}{4}d(m,w) + \frac{4}{5}\text{dist}(m, \mathcal{G}_1 m).
\end{aligned}$$

Case II: When $m, w \in (0,1]$, we have

$$\mathscr{H}(\mathcal{G}_1 m, \mathcal{G}_1 w) = 0 \leq \frac{1}{4}d(m,w) + \frac{4}{5}\text{dist}(m, \mathcal{G}_1 m).$$

Case III: When $m \in [-1, 0]$ and $w \in (0, 1]$, we have

$$\begin{aligned}
\mathscr{H}(\mathcal{G}_1 m, \mathcal{G}_1 w) &= \left|\frac{m}{4}\right| \\
&< \frac{1}{4}|m-w| + \frac{4}{5}\left|\frac{3m}{4}\right| \\
&= |m-w| + \frac{4}{5}\left|m-\frac{m}{4}\right| \\
&= \frac{1}{4}d(m,w) + \frac{4}{5}\text{dist}\left(m, [0, \frac{m}{4}]\right) \\
&= \frac{1}{4}d(m,w) + \frac{4}{5}\text{dist}(m, \mathcal{G}_1 m).
\end{aligned}$$

Case IV: When $m \in (0, 1]$ and $w \in [-1, 0]$, we have

$$\begin{aligned}
\mathscr{H}(\mathcal{G}_1 m, \mathcal{G}_1 w) &= \left|\frac{w}{4}\right| \\
&< \frac{1}{4}|m-w| + \frac{4}{5}|m| \\
&= |m-w| + \frac{4}{5}|m-0| \\
&= \frac{1}{4}d(m,w) + \frac{4}{5}\text{dist}(m, \{0\}) \\
&= \frac{1}{4}d(m,w) + \frac{4}{5}\text{dist}(m, \mathcal{G}_1 m).
\end{aligned}$$

From all the above cases, we have seen that $\mathcal{G}_1$ satisfies (1) for $\varrho = \frac{1}{4}$ and $L = \frac{4}{5}$.

Similarly, we can show that $\mathcal{G}_2$ satisfies (1) for $\varrho = \frac{1}{4}$ and $L = \frac{4}{5}$. Clearly, $\mathscr{F} = F(\mathcal{G}_1) \cap F(\mathcal{G}_2) = \{0\}$.

Now, for control parameters $\xi_k = \eta_k = \zeta_k = 0.65$, for all $k \in \mathbb{N}$ and starting point $m_1 = 1$, then by using MATLAB R2015a, we obtain the following Tables 1 and 2 and Figures 1 and 2.

Table 1. Convergence behavior of various iterative algorithms.

m_k	Mann	Ishikawa	Abbas	S	M	New
m_1	1.000000	1.000000	1.000000	1.000000	1.000000	1.000000
m_2	0.512500	0.433281	0.348068	0.170781	0.032031	0.003557
m_3	0.262656	0.187733	0.121152	0.029166	0.001026	0.000000
m_4	0.134611	0.081341	0.042169	0.004981	0.000033	0.000000
m_5	0.068988	0.035244	0.014678	0.000851	0.000001	0.000000
m_6	0.035357	0.015270	0.005109	0.000145	0.000000	0.000000
m_7	0.018120	0.006616	0.001778	0.000025	0.000000	0.000000
m_8	0.009287	0.002867	0.000619	0.000004	0.000000	0.000000
m_9	0.004759	0.001242	0.000215	0.000001	0.000000	0.000000
m_{10}	0.002439	0.000538	0.000075	0.000000	0.000000	0.000000
m_{11}	0.001250	0.000233	0.000026	0.000000	0.000000	0.000000
m_{12}	0.000641	0.000101	0.000009	0.000000	0.000000	0.000000
m_{13}	0.000328	0.000044	0.000003	0.000000	0.000000	0.000000
m_{14}	0.000168	0.000019	0.000001	0.000000	0.000000	0.000000
m_{15}	0.000086	0.000008	0.000000	0.000000	0.000000	0.000000

The reds show the point of convergence of various iterative methods.

Table 2. Convergence behavior of various iterative algorithms.

m_k	Noor	SP	Picard-Man	Picard-S	F	New
m_1	1.000000	1.000000	1.000000	1.000000	1.000000	1.000000
m_2	0.458320	0.134611	0.128125	0.042695	0.008008	0.003557
m_3	0.210058	0.018120	0.016416	0.001823	0.000064	0.000000
m_4	0.096274	0.002439	0.002103	0.000078	0.000001	0.000000
m_5	0.044124	0.000328	0.000269	0.000003	0.000000	0.000000
m_6	0.020223	0.000044	0.000035	0.000000	0.000000	0.000000
m_7	0.009269	0.000006	0.000004	0.000000	0.000000	0.000000
m_8	0.004248	0.000001	0.000001	0.000000	0.000000	0.000000
m_9	0.001947	0.000000	0.000000	0.000000	0.000000	0.000000

The reds show the point of convergence of various iterative methods.

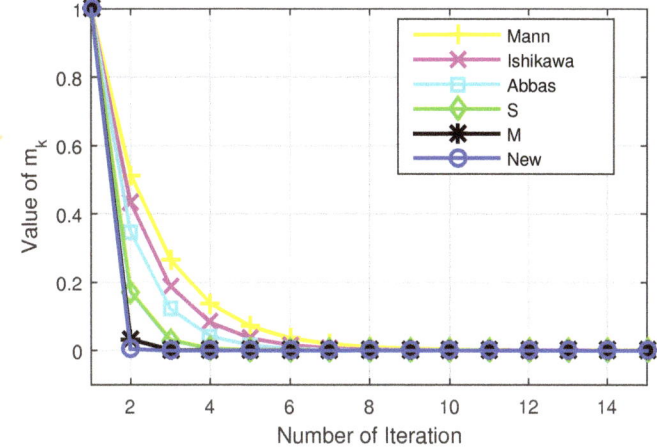

Figure 1. Graph corresponding to Table 1.

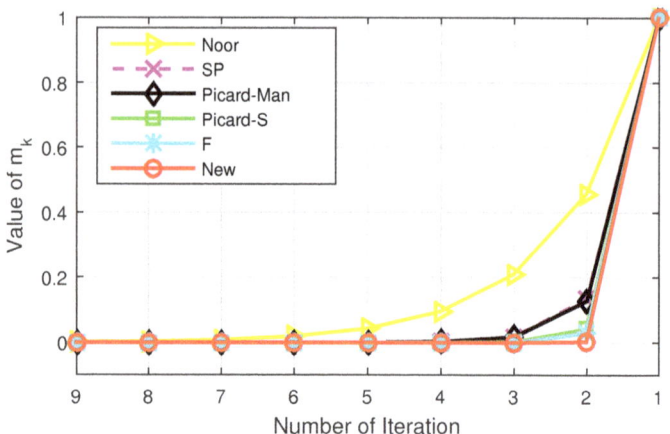

Figure 2. Graph corresponding to Table 2.

As seen in Tables 1 and 2 and Figures 1 and 2 above, it is very clear that our new iterative algorithm (6) converges faster to 0 than Mann [29], Ishikawa [30], Abbas [31], S [19], M [32], Noor [33], SP [34], Picard-Man [35], Picard-S [36], and F [22] iteration processes.

4. Weak w^2-Stability Results for Two Multivalued Almost Contractive Mappings

In this section, we first give the definition of w^2-stability involving two mappings in hyperbolic space. After this, we prove that our new iterative algorithm (6) is weak w^2-stable with respect to two multivalued almost contractive mappings.

Definition 9. *Let $(\mathcal{Q}, d, \mathcal{K})$ be a hyperbolic space, $\mathcal{G}_i : \mathcal{Q} \to \mathcal{Q}$ $(i = 1, 2)$ be two self-maps, and arbitrary $m_1 \in \mathcal{Q}$, $\{m_k\}$ be the iterative algorithm defined by*

$$m_{k+1} = f(\mathcal{G}_i, m_k) \ (i = 1, 2), \ k \geq 0. \quad (15)$$

Assume that $m_k \to q^\star$ as $k \to \infty$, for all $q^\star \in \mathscr{F} = \bigcap_{i=1}^{2} \mathcal{F}(\mathcal{G}_i)$ and for any sequence $\{x_k\} \subset \mathcal{Q}$ which is equivalent to $\{m_k\}$, we have

$$\lim_{k \to \infty} \epsilon_k = \lim_{k \to \infty} d(x_{k+1}, f(\mathcal{G}_i, x_k)) = 0 \implies \lim_{k \to \infty} x_k = q^\star.$$

Then we say that the iterative algorithm (15) is weak w^2-stable with respect to $\mathcal{G}_i$ $(i = 1, 2)$.

Theorem 4. *Suppose that all the assumptions in Theorem 3 are satisfied. Then, the sequence $\{m_k\}$ defined by (6) is weak w^2-stable with respect to $\mathcal{G}_1$ and $\mathcal{G}_2$.*

Proof. Suppose $\{m_k\}$ is the sequence defined by (6) and $\{x_k\} \subset \mathcal{J}$ an equivalent sequence of $\{m_k\}$. We define $\{\epsilon_k\} \in \mathbb{R}^+$ by

$$\begin{cases} x_1 \in \mathcal{W}, \\ c_k = \mathcal{K}(x_k, g_k, \eta_k), \\ b_k = \mathcal{K}(g_k, i_k, \xi_k), \\ a_k = f_k, \\ \epsilon_k = d(x_{k+1}, e_k), \end{cases} \quad k \in \mathbb{N}, \quad (16)$$

where $\{\xi_k\}, \{\eta_k\}$ are real sequences in $(0,1)$ and $a_k \in \mathcal{G}_1 a_k$, $f_k \in \mathcal{G}_2 b_k$, $i_k \in \mathcal{G}_1 c_k$, $g_k \in \mathcal{G}_2 x_k$.

Suppose $\lim_{k\to\infty} \epsilon_k = 0$ and $q^* \in \mathcal{F}$. From (6) and (16), we have

$$\begin{aligned}
d(s_k, c_k) &= d(\mathcal{K}(m_k, u_k, \eta_k), \mathcal{K}(x_k, g_k, \eta_k)) \\
&\leq (1-\eta_k)d(m_k, x_k) + \eta_k \mathcal{H}(\mathcal{G}_2 m_k, \mathcal{G}_2 x_k) \\
&\leq (1-\eta_k)d(m_k, x_k) + \eta_k \varrho d(m_k, x_k) + \eta_k L\mathrm{dist}(m_k, \mathcal{G}_2 m_k) \\
&\leq (1-(1-\varrho)\eta_k)d(m_k, x_k) + \eta_k Ld(m_k, q^*) + \eta_k L\mathrm{dist}(\mathcal{G}_2 m_k, q^*) \\
&\leq (1-(1-\varrho)\eta_k)d(m_k, x_k) + \eta_k Ld(m_k, q^*) + \eta_k L\mathcal{H}(\mathcal{G}_2 m_k, \mathcal{G}_2 q^*) \\
&\leq (1-(1-\varrho)\eta_k)d(m_k, x_k) + \eta_k Ld(m_k, q^*) + \eta_k L\varrho d(m_k, q^*) \\
&\leq (1-(1-\varrho)\eta_k)d(m_k, x_k) + \eta_k L(1+\varrho)d(m_k, q^*). \quad (17)
\end{aligned}$$

Because $0 \leq \varrho < 1$ and $0 < \eta_k < 1$, it follows that $(1-(1-\varrho)\eta_k) < 1$. Thus, (17) becomes

$$d(s_k, c_k) \leq d(m_k, x_k) + \eta_k L(1+\varrho)d(m_k, q^*). \quad (18)$$

By (6), (16), and (18), we obtain

$$\begin{aligned}
d(w_k, b_k) &= d(\mathcal{K}(u_k, t_k, \xi_k), \mathcal{K}(g_k, i_k, \xi_k)) \\
&\leq (1-\xi_k)\mathcal{H}(\mathcal{G}_2 m_k, \mathcal{G}_2 x_k) + \xi_k \mathcal{H}(\mathcal{G}_1 s_k, \mathcal{G}_1 c_k) \\
&\leq (1-\xi_k)[\varrho d(m_k, x_k) + L\mathrm{dist}(m_k, \mathcal{G}_2 m_k)] + \xi_k[\varrho d(s_k, c_k) + L\mathrm{dist}(s_k, \mathcal{G}_1 s_k)] \\
&\leq (1-\xi_k)[\varrho d(m_k, x_k) + Ld(m_k, q^*) + L\mathrm{dist}(\mathcal{G}_2 m_k, q^*)] \\
&\quad + \xi_k[\varrho d(s_k, c_k) + Ld(s_k, q^*) + L\mathrm{dist}(\mathcal{G}_1 s_k, q^*)] \\
&\leq (1-\xi_k)[\varrho d(m_k, x_k) + Ld(m_k, q^*) + L\mathcal{H}(\mathcal{G}_2 m_k, \mathcal{G}_2 q^*)] \\
&\quad + \xi_k[\varrho d(s_k, c_k) + Ld(s_k, q^*) + L\mathcal{H}(\mathcal{G}_1 s_k, \mathcal{G}_1 q^*)] \\
&\leq (1-\xi_k)[\varrho d(m_k, x_k) + Ld(m_k, q^*) + L\varrho d(m_k, q^*)] \\
&\quad + \xi_k[\varrho d(s_k, c_k) + Ld(s_k, q^*) + L\varrho d(s_k, q^*)] \\
&\leq (1-\xi_k)[\varrho d(m_k, x_k) + L(1+\varrho)d(m_k, q^*)] \\
&\quad + \xi_k[\varrho d(s_k, c_k) + L(1+\varrho)d(s_k, q^*)] \\
&\leq \varrho d(m_k, x_k) + L(1+\varrho)d(m_k, q^*) \\
&\quad + \xi_k \varrho d(s_k, c_k) + \xi_k L(1+\varrho)d(s_k, q^*) \\
&\leq \varrho d(m_k, x_k) + L(1+\varrho)d(m_k, q^*) \\
&\quad + \xi_k \varrho [d(m_k, x_k) + \eta_k L(1+\varrho)d(m_k, q^*)] + \xi_k L(1+\varrho)d(s_k, q^*). \quad (19)
\end{aligned}$$

By (6), (16), and (19), we obtain

$$\begin{aligned}
d(p_k, a_k) &= d(h_k, f_k) \\
&= \mathcal{H}(\mathcal{G}_2 w_k, \mathcal{G}_2 b_k) \\
&\leq \varrho d(w_k, b_k) + L\mathrm{dist}(w_k, \mathcal{G}_2 w_k) \\
&\leq \varrho d(w_k, b_k) + Ld(w_k, q^*) + L\mathrm{dist}(\mathcal{G}_2 w_k, q^*) \\
&\leq \varrho d(w_k, b_k) + Ld(w_k, q^*) + L\mathcal{H}(\mathcal{G}_2 w_k, \mathcal{G}_2 q^*) \\
&\leq \varrho d(w_k, b_k) + Ld(w_k, q^*) + L\varrho d(w_k, q^*) \\
&\leq \varrho d(w_k, b_k) + L(1+\varrho)d(w_k, q^*) \\
&\leq \varrho^2 d(m_k, x_k) + \varrho L(1+\varrho)d(m_k, q^*) \\
&\quad + \varrho^2 \xi_k[d(m_k, x_k) + \varrho \eta_k L(1+\varrho)d(m_k, q^*)] \\
&\quad + \varrho \xi_k L(1+\varrho)d(s_k, q^*) + L(1+\varrho)d(w_k, q^*). \quad (20)
\end{aligned}$$

By using (6), (16), and (20), we obtain

$$
\begin{aligned}
d(x_{k+1}, q^*) &\leq d(x_{k+1}, m_{k+1}) + d(m_{k+1}, q^*) \\
&\leq d(x_{k+1}, e_k) + d(e_k, m_{k+1}) + d(m_{k+1}, q^*) \\
&\leq \epsilon_k + d(e_k, \ell_k) + d(m_{k+1}, q^*) \\
&\leq \epsilon_k + \mathcal{H}(\mathcal{G}_1 p_k, \mathcal{G}_1 a_k) + d(m_{k+1}, q^*) \\
&\leq \epsilon_k + \varrho d(p_k, a_k) + L\text{dist}(p_k, \mathcal{G}_1 p_k) + d(m_{k+1}, q^*) \\
&\leq \epsilon_k + \varrho d(p_k, a_k) + L d(p_k, q^*) + L\text{dist}(\mathcal{G}_1 p_k, q^*) + d(m_{k+1}, q^*) \\
&\leq \epsilon_k + \varrho d(p_k, a_k) + L d(p_k, q^*) + L\mathcal{H}(\mathcal{G}_1 p_k, \mathcal{G}_1 q^*) + d(m_{k+1}, q^*) \\
&\leq \epsilon_k + \varrho d(p_k, a_k) + L d(p_k, q^*) + L\varrho d(p_k, q^*) + d(m_{k+1}, q^*) \\
&\leq \epsilon_k + \varrho^3 d(m_k, x_k) + \varrho^2 L(1+\varrho) d(m_k, q^*) \\
&\quad + \varrho^3 \xi_k [d(m_k, x_k) + \varrho^2 \eta_k L(1+\varrho) d(m_k, q^*)] \\
&\quad + \varrho^2 \xi_k L(1+\varrho) d(s_k, q^*) + \varrho L(1+\varrho) d(w_k, q^*) \\
&\quad + L(1+\varrho) d(p_k, q^*) + d(m_{k+1}, q^*).
\end{aligned}
\tag{21}
$$

By Theorem 3, $\lim_{k \to \infty} d(m_k, q^*) = 0$. Consequently, we have $\lim_{m \to \infty} d(m_{k+1}, q^*) = 0$. Moreover, by the equivalence of $\{m_k\}$ and $\{x_k\}$, we have $\lim_{m \to \infty} d(m_k, x_k) = 0$.
Thus, using (10), (12), (13), and by taking the limit of both sides of (21), we have

$$\lim_{k \to \infty} d(x_k, q^*) = 0.$$

Hence, our new iterative sequence (6) is weak w^2-stable with respect to $\mathcal{G}_1$ and $\mathcal{G}_2$. □

5. Data Dependence Results for Two Multivalued Almost Contractive Mappings

In this section, we show that our new iterative method (6) is data dependent with respect to two multivalued almost contractive mappings.

Theorem 5. *Let $\mathcal{J}$ be a nonempty closed convex subset of a hyperbolic space $\mathcal{Q}$ and $\mathcal{G}_i : \mathcal{J} \to \mathcal{P}(\mathcal{J})$ (i=1,2) be two multivalued almost contractive mappings. Let $\tilde{\mathcal{G}}_i : \mathcal{J} \to \mathcal{P}(\mathcal{J})$ (i=1,2) be two multivalued approximate operators of $\mathcal{G}_1$ and $\mathcal{G}_2$, respectively, such that $\mathcal{H}(\mathcal{G}_i m, \tilde{\mathcal{G}}_i m) \leq \epsilon$ (i=1,2) for all $m \in \mathcal{J}$. If $\{m_k\}$ is the sequence defined by (6) for two multivalued almost contractive mappings $\mathcal{G}_1$ and $\mathcal{G}_2$. Then, we define an iterative sequence $\{\tilde{m}_k\}$ as follows:*

$$
\begin{cases}
\tilde{m}_1 \in \mathcal{J}, \\
\tilde{s}_k = \mathcal{K}(\tilde{m}_k, \tilde{u}_k, \eta_k), \\
\tilde{w}_k = \mathcal{K}(\tilde{u}_k, \tilde{t}_k, \xi_k), \quad k \in \mathbb{N}, \\
\tilde{p}_k = \tilde{h}_k, \\
\tilde{m}_{k+1} = \tilde{\ell}_k,
\end{cases}
\tag{22}
$$

where $\{\xi_k\}$, $\{\eta_k\}$ are real sequences in (0,1) such that $\frac{1}{2} \leq \xi_k \eta_k$ and $\tilde{\ell}_k \in \tilde{\mathcal{G}}_1 \tilde{p}_k$, $\tilde{h}_k \in \tilde{\mathcal{G}}_2 \tilde{w}_k$, $\tilde{t}_k \in \tilde{\mathcal{G}}_1 \tilde{s}_k$, $\tilde{u}_k \in \tilde{\mathcal{G}}_2 \tilde{m}_k$. If $\mathscr{F} = \bigcap_{i=1}^{2} F(\mathcal{G}_i) \neq \emptyset$, $\mathcal{G}_i q^* = \{q^*\}$ for each $q^* \in \mathscr{F}$ (i = 1, 2), $\tilde{\mathscr{F}} = \bigcap_{i=1}^{2} F(\tilde{\mathcal{G}}_i) \neq \emptyset$ and $\tilde{\mathcal{G}}_i \tilde{q}^* = \{\tilde{q}^*\}$ for each $\tilde{q}^* \in \tilde{\mathscr{F}}$ (i = 1, 2) such that $\tilde{m}_k \to \tilde{q}^*$ as $m \to \infty$, and we have

$$d(q^*, \tilde{q}^*) \leq \frac{11\epsilon}{1 - \varrho},$$

where ϵ is a fixed number.

Proof. From (6) and (22), we have

$$
\begin{aligned}
d(s_k, \tilde{s}_k) &= d(\mathcal{K}(m_k, u_k, \eta_k), \mathcal{K}(\tilde{m}_k, \tilde{u}_k, \eta_k)) \\
&\leq (1 - \eta_k) d(m_k, \tilde{m}_k) + \eta_k d(u_k, \tilde{u}_k) \\
&\leq (1 - \eta_k) d(m_k, \tilde{m}_k) + \eta_k d(u_k, \mathcal{G}_2 \tilde{m}_k) + \eta_k d(\mathcal{G}_2 \tilde{m}_k, \tilde{u}_k) \\
&\leq (1 - \eta_k) d(m_k, \tilde{m}_k) + \eta_k \mathcal{H}(\mathcal{G}_2 m_k, \mathcal{G}_2 \tilde{m}_k) + \eta_k \mathcal{H}(\mathcal{G}_2 \tilde{m}_k, \tilde{\mathcal{G}}_2 \tilde{m}_k) \\
&\leq (1 - \eta_k) d(m_k, \tilde{m}_k) + \eta_k \varrho d(m_k, \tilde{m}_k) + \eta_k L \operatorname{dist}(m_k, \mathcal{G}_2 m_k) + \eta_k \epsilon \\
&\leq (1 - (1 - \varrho)\eta_k) d(m_k, \tilde{m}_k) + \eta_k L d(m_k, q^\star) + \eta_k L \operatorname{dist}(\mathcal{G}_2 m_k, q^\star) + \eta_k \epsilon \\
&\leq (1 - (1 - \varrho)\eta_k) d(m_k, \tilde{m}_k) + \eta_k L d(m_k, q^\star) + \eta_k L \mathcal{H}(\mathcal{G}_2 m_k, \mathcal{G}_2 q^\star) + \eta_k \epsilon \\
&\leq (1 - (1 - \varrho)\eta_k) d(m_k, \tilde{m}_k) + \eta_k L d(m_k, q^\star) + \eta_k L \varrho d(m_k, q^\star) + \eta_k \epsilon \\
&= (1 - (1 - \varrho)\eta_k) d(m_k, \tilde{m}_k) + \eta_k L (1 + \varrho) d(m_k, q^\star) + \eta_k \epsilon. \quad (23)
\end{aligned}
$$

From (6), (22) and (23), we have

$$
\begin{aligned}
d(w_k, \tilde{w}_k) &= d(\mathcal{K}(u_k, t_k, \xi_k), \mathcal{K}(\tilde{m}_k, \tilde{u}_k, \xi_k)) \\
&\leq (1 - \xi_k) d(u_k, \tilde{u}_k) + \xi_k d(t_k, \tilde{t}_k) \\
&\leq (1 - \xi_k)[d(u_k, \mathcal{G}_2 \tilde{m}_k) + d(\mathcal{G}_2 \tilde{m}_k, \tilde{u}_k)] \\
&\quad + \xi_k [d(t_k, \mathcal{G}_1 \tilde{s}_k) + \eta_k d(\mathcal{G}_1 \tilde{s}_k, \tilde{t}_k)] \\
&\leq (1 - \xi_k)[\mathcal{H}(\mathcal{G}_2 m_k, \mathcal{G}_2 \tilde{m}_k) + \mathcal{H}(\mathcal{G}_2 \tilde{m}_k, \tilde{\mathcal{G}}_2 \tilde{m}_k)] \\
&\quad + \xi_k [\mathcal{H}(\mathcal{G}_1 s_k, \mathcal{G}_1 \tilde{s}_k) + \mathcal{H}(\mathcal{G}_1 \tilde{s}_k, \tilde{\mathcal{G}}_1 \tilde{s}_k)] \\
&\leq (1 - \xi_k)[\varrho d(m_k, \tilde{m}_k) + L \operatorname{dist}(m_k, \mathcal{G}_2 m_k) + \epsilon] \\
&\quad + \xi_k [\varrho d(s_k, \tilde{s}_k) + L \operatorname{dist}(s_k, \mathcal{G}_1 s_k) + \epsilon] \\
&\leq (1 - \xi_k)[\varrho d(m_k, \tilde{m}_k) + L d(m_k, q^\star) + L \operatorname{dist}(\mathcal{G}_2 m_k, q^\star) + \epsilon] \\
&\quad + \xi_k [\varrho d(s_k, \tilde{s}_k) + L d(m_k, q^\star) + L \operatorname{dist}(\mathcal{G}_1 s_k, q^\star) + \epsilon] \\
&\leq (1 - \xi_k)[\varrho d(m_k, \tilde{m}_k) + L d(m_k, q^\star) + L \mathcal{H}(\mathcal{G}_2 m_k, \mathcal{G}_2 q^\star) + \epsilon] \\
&\quad + \xi_k [\varrho d(s_k, \tilde{s}_k) + L d(s_k, q^\star) + L \mathcal{H}(\mathcal{G}_1 s_k, \mathcal{G}_1 q^\star) + \epsilon] \\
&\leq (1 - \xi_k)[\varrho d(m_k, \tilde{m}_k) + L d(m_k, q^\star) + L \varrho d(m_k, q^\star) + \epsilon] \\
&\quad + \xi_k [\varrho d(s_k, \tilde{s}_k) + L d(s_k, q^\star) + L \varrho d(s_k, q^\star) + \epsilon] \\
&= (1 - \xi_k) \varrho d(m_k, \tilde{m}_k) + (1 - \xi_k)[L(1 + \varrho) d(m_k, q^\star) + \epsilon] \\
&\quad + \xi_k \varrho d(s_k, \tilde{s}_k) + \xi_k [L(1 + \varrho) d(s_k, q^\star) + \epsilon] \\
&= (1 - \xi_k) \varrho d(m_k, \tilde{m}_k) + (1 - \xi_k)[L(1 + \varrho) d(m_k, q^\star) + \epsilon] \\
&\quad + \xi_k \varrho [(1 - (1 - \varrho)\eta_k) d(m_k, \tilde{m}_k) + \eta_k L(1 + \varrho) d(m_k, q^\star) + \eta_k \epsilon] \\
&\quad + \xi_k [L(1 + \varrho) d(s_k, q^\star) + \epsilon] \\
&\leq \varrho [1 - (1 - \varrho)\xi_k \eta_k] d(m_k, \tilde{m}_k) + L(1 + \varrho) d(m_k, q^\star) + \epsilon \\
&\quad + \varrho \xi_k \eta_k L(1 + \varrho) d(m_k, q^\star) + \varrho \xi_k \eta_k \epsilon \\
&\quad + \xi_k L(1 + \varrho) d(s_k, q^\star) + \xi_k \epsilon. \quad (24)
\end{aligned}
$$

From (6), (22), and (24), we have

$$\begin{aligned}
d(p_k,\tilde{p}_k) &\leq d(h_k,\tilde{h}_k)\\
&\leq d(h_k,\mathcal{G}_2\bar{w}_k) + d(\mathcal{G}_2\bar{w}_k,\tilde{h}_k)\\
&\leq \mathcal{H}(\mathcal{G}_2w_k,\mathcal{G}_2\bar{w}_k) + \mathcal{H}(\mathcal{G}_2\bar{w}_k,\tilde{\mathcal{G}}_2\bar{w}_k)\\
&\leq \varrho d(w_k,\bar{w}_k) + L\mathrm{dist}(w_k,\mathcal{G}_2 w_k) + \epsilon\\
&\leq \varrho d(w_k,\bar{w}_k) + Ld(w_k,q^\star) + L\mathrm{dist}(\mathcal{G}_2 w_k,q^\star) + \epsilon\\
&\leq \varrho d(w_k,\bar{w}_k) + Ld(w_k,q^\star) + L\mathcal{H}(\mathcal{G}_2 w_k,\mathcal{G}_2 q^\star) + \epsilon\\
&\leq \varrho d(w_k,\bar{w}_k) + Ld(w_k,q^\star) + L\varrho(w_k,q^\star) + \epsilon\\
&= \varrho d(w_k,\bar{w}_k) + L(1+\varrho)d(w_k,q^\star) + \epsilon\\
&\leq \varrho^2[1-(1-\varrho)\xi_k\eta_k]d(m_k,\tilde{m}_k) + \varrho L(1+\varrho)d(m_k,q^\star) + \varrho\epsilon\\
&\quad + \varrho^2\xi_k\eta_k L(1+\varrho)d(m_k,q^\star) + \varrho^2\xi_k\eta_k\epsilon\\
&\quad + \varrho\xi_k L(1+\varrho)d(s_k,q^\star) + \varrho\xi_k\epsilon + L(1+\varrho)d(w_k,q^\star) + \epsilon. \quad (25)
\end{aligned}$$

From (6), (22), and (25), we obtain

$$\begin{aligned}
d(m_{k+1},\tilde{m}_{k+1}) &\leq d(\ell_k,\tilde{\ell}_k)\\
&\leq d(\ell_k,\mathcal{G}_1\tilde{p}_k) + d(\mathcal{G}_1\tilde{p}_k,\tilde{\ell}_k)\\
&\leq \mathcal{H}(\mathcal{G}_1 p_k,\mathcal{G}_1\tilde{p}_k) + \mathcal{H}(\mathcal{G}_1\tilde{p}_k,\tilde{\mathcal{G}}_1\tilde{p}_k)\\
&\leq \varrho d(p_k,\tilde{p}_k) + L\mathrm{dist}(p_k,\mathcal{G}_1 p_k) + \epsilon\\
&\leq \varrho d(p_k,\tilde{p}_k) + Ld(p_k,q^\star) + L\mathrm{dist}(\mathcal{G}_1 p_k,q^\star) + \epsilon\\
&\leq \varrho d(p_k,\tilde{p}_k) + Ld(p_k,q^\star) + L\mathcal{H}(\mathcal{G}_1 p_k,\mathcal{G}_1 q^\star) + \epsilon\\
&\leq \varrho d(p_k,\tilde{p}_k) + Ld(p_k,q^\star) + L\varrho(\ell_k,q^\star) + \epsilon\\
&= \varrho^3[1-(1-\varrho)\xi_k\eta_k]d(m_k,\tilde{m}_k) + \varrho^2 L(1+\varrho)d(m_k,q^\star) + \varrho^2\epsilon\\
&\quad + \varrho^3\xi_k\eta_k L(1+\varrho)d(m_k,q^\star) + \varrho^3\xi_k\eta_k\epsilon\\
&\quad + \varrho^2\xi_k L(1+\varrho)d(s_k,q^\star) + \varrho^2\xi_k\epsilon + \varrho L(1+\varrho)d(w_k,q^\star)\\
&\quad + \varrho\epsilon + L(1+\varrho)d(p_k,q^\star) + \epsilon. \quad (26)
\end{aligned}$$

Because $0 \leq \varrho < 1$ and $0 < \xi_k,\eta_k < 1$, then (26) yields

$$\begin{aligned}
d(m_{k+1},\tilde{m}_{k+1}) &\leq [1-(1-\varrho)\xi_k\eta_k]d(m_k,\tilde{m}_k) + L(1+\varrho)d(m_k,q^\star)\\
&\quad + \xi_k\eta_k L(1+\varrho)d(m_k,q^\star) + \xi_k\eta_k\epsilon\\
&\quad + L(1+\varrho)d(s_k,q^\star) + L(1+\varrho)d(w_k,q^\star)\\
&\quad + L(1+\varrho)d(p_k,q^\star) + 4\epsilon. \quad (27)
\end{aligned}$$

Because $\frac{1}{2} \leq \xi_k\eta_k, \forall k \geq 1$, it implies that $1 \leq 2\xi_k\eta_k, \forall k \geq 1$. Thus, (27) becomes

$$\begin{aligned}
d(m_{k+1},\tilde{m}_{k+1}) &\leq [1-(1-\varrho)\xi_k\eta_k]d(m_k,\tilde{m}_k) + 2\xi_k\eta_k L(1+\varrho)d(m_k,q^\star)\\
&\quad + \xi_k\eta_k L(1+\varrho)d(m_k,q^\star) + \xi_k\eta_k\epsilon\\
&\quad + 2\xi_k\eta_k L(1+\varrho)d(s_k,q^\star) + 2\xi_k\eta_k L(1+\varrho)d(w_k,q^\star)\\
&\quad + 2\xi_k\eta_k L(1+\varrho)d(p_k,q^\star) + 9\xi_k\eta_k\epsilon.\\
&\leq [1-(1-\varrho)\xi_k\eta_k]d(m_k,\tilde{m}_k) + (1-\varrho)\xi_m\eta_k \times\\
&\quad \frac{\left\{\begin{array}{c} 2L(1+\varrho)d(m_k,q^\star) + L(1+\varrho)d(m_k,q^\star) + \epsilon\\ +2L(1+\varrho)d(s_k,q^\star) + 2L(1+\varrho)d(w_k,q^\star)\\ +2L(1+\varrho)d(p_k,q^\star) + 9\epsilon \end{array}\right\}}{1-\varrho}. \quad (28)
\end{aligned}$$

Therefore, (28) can be written as

$$\rho_{k+1} = (1 - \varphi_k)\rho_k + \varphi_k \phi_k,$$

where

$$\rho_{k+1} = d(m_{k+1}, \tilde{m}_{k+1}),$$
$$\varphi_k = (1 - \varrho)\xi_k \eta_k \in (0,1),$$

and

$$\phi_k = \frac{\left\{\begin{array}{l} 2L(1+\varrho)d(m_k, q^*) + L(1+\varrho)d(m_k, q^*) + \epsilon \\ +2L(1+\varrho)d(s_k, q^*) + 2L(1+\varrho)d(w_k, q^*) \\ +2L(1+\varrho)d(p_k, q^*) + 9\epsilon \end{array}\right\}}{1-\varrho} \geq 0.$$

From Theorem 3, we know that $m_k \to q^*$ as $k \to \infty$ and by the hypothesis $\tilde{m}_k \to \tilde{q}^*$ as $k \to \infty$, then applying Lemma 3, we obtain

$$d(q^*, \tilde{q}^*) \leq \frac{11\epsilon}{1-\varrho}.$$

□

6. $\triangle$-Convergence and Strong Converges Results for Two Multivalued Mappings

In this section, we establish $\triangle$-convergence and strong convergence theorems of our new iterative algorithm (6) for common fixed points of two multivalued mappings satisfying condition (E). Throughout the remaining part of this article, let $(\mathcal{Q}, d, \mathcal{K})$ denote a complete uniformly convex hyperbolic space with a monotone modulus of convexity Θ and let $\mathcal{J}$ be a nonempty closed convex subset of $\mathcal{Q}$.

Theorem 6. *Let $\mathcal{J}$ be a nonempty closed convex subset of $\mathcal{Q}$ and $\mathcal{G}_i : \mathcal{J} \to \mathcal{P}(\mathcal{J})$ $(i = 1, 2)$ be two multivalued mappings satisfying condition (E) with convex values. Let $\mathcal{F} = \bigcap_{i=1}^{2} F(\mathcal{G}_i) \neq \emptyset$ and $\mathcal{G}_i q^* = \{q^*\}$ for each $q^* \in \mathcal{F}$ $(i = 1, 2)$. Let $\{m_k\}$ be the sequence defined by (6). Then, $\{m_k\}$ $\triangle$-converges to a common fixed point of $\mathcal{G}_1$ and $\mathcal{G}_2$.*

Proof. The proof will be divided into the following three steps:

Step 1: First, we show that $\lim_{k \to \infty} d(m_k, q^*)$ exists for each $q^* \in \mathcal{F}$. By Proposition 1, we know that $\mathcal{G}_i$ $(i = 1, 2)$ are multivalued quasi-nonexpansive mappings. Therefore, for all $q^* \in \mathcal{F}$ and by (6), we obtain

$$\begin{aligned} d(s_k, q^*) &= d(\mathcal{K}(m_k, u_k, \eta_k), q^*) \\ &\leq (1 - \eta_k)d(m_k, q^*) + \eta_k d(u_k, q^*) \\ &\leq (1 - \eta_k)d(m_k, q^*) + \eta_k \text{dist}(u_k, \mathcal{G}_2 q^*) \\ &\leq (1 - \eta_k)d(m_k, q^*) + \eta_k \mathcal{H}(\mathcal{G}_2 m_k, \mathcal{G}_2 q^*) \\ &\leq (1 - \eta_k)d(m_k, q^*) + \eta_k d(m_k, q^*) \\ &= d(m_k, q^*). \end{aligned} \quad (29)$$

Again, from (6) and (29), we have

$$\begin{aligned}
d(w_k, q^\star) &= d(\mathcal{K}(u_k, t_k, \xi_k), q^\star) \\
&\leq (1 - \xi_k) d(u_k, q^\star) + \xi_k d(t_k, q^\star) \\
&\leq (1 - \xi_k) \text{dist}(u_k, \mathcal{G}_2 q^\star) + \xi_k \text{dist}(t_k, \mathcal{G}_1 q^\star) \\
&\leq (1 - \xi_k) \mathscr{H}(\mathcal{G}_2 m_k, \mathcal{G}_2 q^\star) + \xi_k \mathscr{H}(\mathcal{G}_1 s_k, \mathcal{G}_1 q^\star) \\
&\leq (1 - \xi_k) d(m_k, q^\star) + \xi_k d(s_k, q^\star) \\
&\leq (1 - \xi_k) d(m_k, q^\star) + \xi_k \varrho d(m_k, q^\star) \\
&= d(m_k, q^\star).
\end{aligned} \qquad (30)$$

From (6) and (30), we have

$$\begin{aligned}
d(p_k, q^\star) &= d(h_k, q^\star) \\
&\leq \text{dist}(h_k, \mathcal{G}_2 q^\star) \\
&\leq \mathscr{H}(\mathcal{G}_2 w_k, \mathcal{G}_2 q^\star) \\
&\leq d(w_k, q^\star) \\
&\leq d(m_k, q^\star).
\end{aligned} \qquad (31)$$

Finally, by (6) and (31), we have

$$\begin{aligned}
d(m_{k+1}, q^\star) &= d(\ell_k, q^\star) \\
&\leq \text{dist}(\ell_k, \mathcal{G}_1 q^\star) \\
&\leq \mathscr{H}(\mathcal{G}_1 p_k, \mathcal{G}_1 q^\star) \\
&\leq d(p_k, q^\star) \\
&\leq d(m_k, q^\star).
\end{aligned} \qquad (32)$$

This implies that the sequence $\{d(m_k, q^\star)\}$ is non-increasing and bounded below. Thus, $\lim_{m \to \infty} d(m_k, q^\star)$ exists for each $q^\star \in \mathscr{F}$.

Step 2: Next, we show that

$$\lim_{k \to \infty} \text{dist}(m_k, \mathcal{G}_i m_k) = 0, \text{ for all } i = 1, 2. \qquad (33)$$

From Step 1, it is established that for all $q^\star \in \mathscr{F}$, $\lim_{k \to \infty} d(m_k, q^\star)$ exists. Let

$$\lim_{k \to \infty} d(m_k, q^\star) = \gamma \geq 0. \qquad (34)$$

If $\gamma = 0$, then we get

$$\begin{aligned}
\text{dist}(m_k, \mathcal{G}_i m_k) &\leq d(m_k, q^\star) + \text{dist}(\mathcal{G}_i m_k, q^\star) \\
&\leq d(m_k, q^\star) + \mathscr{H}(\mathcal{G}_i m_k, \mathcal{G}_i q^\star) \\
&\leq d(m_k, q^\star) + d(m_k, q^\star) \\
&= 2 d(m_k, q^\star) \to 0 \text{ as } k \to \infty.
\end{aligned}$$

Hence, $\lim_{k\to\infty} \text{dist}(m_k, \mathcal{G}_i m_k) = 0$, for all $i = 1, 2$. If $\gamma > 0$, Now from (29), (30), (31) and (32), we have

$$\limsup_{k\to\infty} d(s_k, q^*) \leq \gamma; \quad (35)$$

$$\limsup_{k\to\infty} d(w_k, q^*) \leq \gamma; \quad (36)$$

$$\limsup_{k\to\infty} d(p_k, q^*) \leq \gamma; \quad (37)$$

and

$$\limsup_{k\to\infty} d(\ell_m, q^*) \leq \gamma. \quad (38)$$

Consequently, we obtain the following inequalities

$$\limsup_{k\to\infty} d(u_k, q^*) \leq \limsup_{k\to\infty} \mathcal{H}(\mathcal{G}_2 m_k, \mathcal{G}_2 q^*)$$
$$\leq \limsup_{k\to\infty} d(m_k, q^*) = \gamma; \quad (39)$$

$$\limsup_{k\to\infty} d(t_k, q^*) \leq \limsup_{k\to\infty} \mathcal{H}(\mathcal{G}_1 s_k, \mathcal{G}_1 q^*)$$
$$\leq \limsup_{k\to\infty} d(s_k, q^*) \leq \gamma \quad (40)$$

and

$$\limsup_{k\to\infty} d(\ell_k, q^*) \leq \limsup_{k\to\infty} \mathcal{H}(\mathcal{G}_2 p_k, \mathcal{G}_2 p_k)$$
$$\leq \limsup_{k\to\infty} d(p_k, q^*) \leq \gamma. \quad (41)$$

By using (6) and (34), we have

$$\gamma = \lim_{k\to\infty} d(m_{k+1}, q^*) = \lim_{k\to\infty} d(\ell_k, q^*)$$
$$\leq \lim_{k\to\infty} \mathcal{H}(\mathcal{G}_1 p_k, \mathcal{G}_1 p_k)$$
$$\leq \lim_{k\to\infty} d(p_k, q^*)$$
$$= \lim_{k\to\infty} d(h_k, q^*)$$
$$\leq \lim_{k\to\infty} \mathcal{H}(\mathcal{G}_2 w_k, \mathcal{G}_2 q^*)$$
$$\leq \lim_{k\to\infty} d(w_k, q^*)$$
$$= \lim_{k\to\infty} d(\mathcal{K}(u_k, t_k, \xi_k), q^*).$$

From Lemma 2, we obtain

$$\lim_{k\to\infty} d(u_k, t_k) = 0. \quad (42)$$

Again, from (6) we get

$$d(m_{k+1}, q^*) = d(\ell_k, q^*)$$
$$\leq \mathcal{H}(\mathcal{G}_1 p_k, \mathcal{G}_1 q^*)$$
$$\leq d(p_k, q^*),$$

this yields
$$\gamma \leq \liminf_{k\to\infty} d(p_k, q^\star). \tag{43}$$

By (22) and (43), we have
$$\lim_{k\to\infty} d(p_k, q^\star) = \gamma. \tag{44}$$

Now, by using (6), we obtain
$$\begin{aligned} d(p_k, q^\star) &= d(h_k, q^\star) \\ &\leq \mathcal{H}(\mathcal{G}_2 w_k, \mathcal{G}_2 q^\star) \\ &\leq d(w_k, q^\star), \end{aligned} \tag{45}$$

which yields
$$\gamma \leq \liminf_{k\to\infty} d(w_k, q^\star). \tag{46}$$

From (36) and (46), we have
$$\lim_{k\to\infty} d(w_k, q^\star) = \gamma. \tag{47}$$

From (6) and (42), we have
$$\begin{aligned} d(w_k, q^\star) &= (\mathcal{K}(u_k, t_k, \xi_k), q^\star) \\ &\leq d(u_k, q^\star) + \xi_k d(t_k, u_k), \end{aligned}$$

which gives
$$\gamma \leq \liminf_{k\to\infty} d(u_k, q^\star). \tag{48}$$

By using (39) and (48), we have
$$\lim_{k\to\infty} d(u_k, q^\star) = \gamma. \tag{49}$$

In addition,
$$\begin{aligned} d(u_k, q^\star) &\leq d(u_k, t_k) + d(t_k, q^\star) \\ &\leq d(u_k, t_k) + \mathcal{H}(\mathcal{G}_2 s_k, \mathcal{G}_2 q^\star) \\ &\leq d(u_k, t_k) + d(s_k, q^\star), \end{aligned}$$

implies that
$$\gamma \leq \liminf_{k\to\infty} d(s_k, q^\star). \tag{50}$$

From (35) and (50), we obtain
$$\lim_{k\to\infty} d(s_k, q^\star) = \gamma. \tag{51}$$

Finally, by (6), we obtain
$$\lim_{k\to\infty} d(s_k, q^\star) = \lim_{k\to\infty} d(\mathcal{K}(m_k, u_k, \eta_k), q^\star) = \gamma. \tag{52}$$

Now, due to (34), (39), (52), and Lemma 2, we have

$$\lim_{k\to\infty} d(m_k, u_k) = 0. \tag{53}$$

Because $\mathrm{dist}(m_k, \mathcal{G}_2 m_k) \leq d(m_k, u_k)$, we get

$$\lim_{k\to\infty} d(m_k, \mathcal{G}_2 m_k) = 0. \tag{54}$$

On the other hand, by (6) and (53), we have

$$d(s_k, m_k) = d(\mathcal{K}(m_k, u_k, \eta_k), m_k) \leq \eta_k d(m_k, u_k), \tag{55}$$

and

$$\begin{aligned}
\mathrm{dist}(s_k, \mathcal{G}_1 s_k) &\leq d(s_k, t_k) \\
&= d(\mathcal{K}(m_k, u_k, \eta_k), t_k) \\
&\leq (1-\eta_k) d(m_k, t_k) + \eta_k d(u_k, t_k) \\
&\leq (1-\eta_k)[d(m_k, u_k) + d(u_k, t_k)] + \eta_k d(u_k, t_k).
\end{aligned} \tag{56}$$

Now, by using (42) and (53), we have

$$\lim_{k\to\infty} \mathrm{dist} d(s_k, \mathcal{G}_1 s_k) = 0. \tag{57}$$

Because $\mathcal{G}_1$ satisfies condition (E), we obtain

$$\begin{aligned}
\mathrm{dist}(m_k, \mathcal{G}_1 m_k) &\leq d(m_k, s_k) + \mathrm{dist}(s_k, \mathcal{G}_1 m_k) \\
&\leq d(m_k, s_k) + \mu \mathrm{dist} d(s_k, \mathcal{G}_1 s_k) + d(s_k, m_k) \\
&\leq 2d(u_\gamma, w_\gamma) + \mu \rho(w_\gamma, M_1 w_k).
\end{aligned}$$

By (53), (55), and (57), we have

$$\lim_{k\to\infty} \mathrm{dist}(m_k, \mathcal{G}_1 m_k) = 0. \tag{58}$$

Hence, $\lim_{k\to\infty} \mathrm{dist}(m_k, \mathcal{G}_i m_k) = 0$, $i = 1, 2$.

Step 3: Finally, we show that the sequence $\{m_k\}$ is $\triangle$-convergent to a point in $\mathscr{F}$. In view of this, it suffices to show that

$$\mathcal{K}_\triangle(\{m_k\}) = \bigcup_{\{u_k\} \subset \{m_k\}} \subset \mathscr{F} \tag{59}$$

and $\mathcal{K}_\triangle(\{m_k\})$ has only one point. Set $u \in \mathcal{K}_\triangle(\{m_k\})$. Then a subsequence $\{u_k\}$ of $\{m_k\}$ exists such that $AC(\{u_k\}) = \{u\}$. From Lemma 1, a subsequence $\{v_k\}$ of $\{u_k\}$ exists such that $\triangle - \lim_{k\to\infty} v_k = v \in \mathcal{J}$. Because $\lim_{k\to\infty} \mathrm{dist}(v_k, \mathcal{G}_i v_k) = 0$ $(i = 1, 2)$, by Lemma 4, we know that $v \in \mathscr{F}$. By the convergence of $\{d(u_k, v)\}$, then from Lemma 5, we obtain $u = v$. This implies that $\mathcal{K}_\triangle(\{m_k\}) \subset \mathscr{F}$. Now, we show that the set $\mathcal{K}_\triangle(\{m_k\})$ contains exactly one element. For this, let $\{u_k\}$ be a subsequence of $\{m_k\}$ with $AC(\{u_k\}) = \{u\}$ and $AC(\{m_k\}) = \{m\}$. We have already seen that $u = v$ and $v \in \mathscr{F}$. Conclusively, by the convergence of $\{d(m_k, q^*)\}$, then by Lemma 5, we obtain $m = v \in \mathscr{F}$. It follows that $\mathcal{K}_\triangle(\{m_k\}) = \{m\}$. This completes the proof. □

Next, we establish some strong convergence theorems.

Theorem 7. *Let $\mathcal{J}$ be a nonempty closed compact subset of $\mathcal{Q}$ and $\mathcal{G}_i : \mathcal{J} \to \mathcal{BC}(\mathcal{J})$ $(i = 1, 2)$ be two multivalued mappings satisfying condition (E) with convex values. Let $\mathcal{F} = \cap_{i=1}^{2} F(\mathcal{G}_i) \neq \varnothing$ and $\mathcal{G}_i q^* = \{q^*\}$ for each $q^* \in \mathcal{F}$ $(i = 1, 2)$. Let $\{m_k\}$ be the sequence defined by (6). Then $\{m_k\}$ converges strongly to a point in $\mathcal{F}$.*

Proof. For all $m \in \mathcal{J}$ and $i = 1, 2$, we can assume that $\mathcal{G}_i$ is a bounded closed and convex subset of $\mathcal{J}$. By the compactness of $\mathcal{J}$, we know that $\mathcal{G}_i$ is a nonempty compact convex subset and bounded proximal subset in $\mathcal{J}$. It follows that $\mathcal{G}_i : \mathcal{J} \to \mathcal{P}(\mathcal{J})$. Thus, all the assumptions in Theorem 6 are performed. Hence, from Theorem 6, we have that $\lim_{k \to \infty} (m_k, q^*)$ exists and $\lim_{k \to \infty} \text{dist}(m_k, \mathcal{G}_i m_k) = 0$, for each $q^* \in \mathcal{F}$ and $i = 1, 2$. By the compactness of $\mathcal{J}$, we are sure of the existence of a subsequence $\{m_{k_i}\}$ of $\{m_k\}$ with $\lim_{k \to \infty} m_{k_i} = \chi \in \mathcal{J}$. By using condition (E) for some $\mu \geq 1$ and for each $i = 1, 2$, we have

$$\begin{aligned}\text{dist}(\chi, \mathcal{G}_i \chi) &\leq \text{dist}(\chi, m_{k_i}) + \text{dist}(m_{k_i}, \mathcal{G}_i \chi) \\ &\leq \mu \text{dist}(m_{k_i}, \mathcal{G}_i m_{k_i}) + 2d(\chi, m_{k_i}) \to 0 \text{ as } k \to \infty.\end{aligned}$$

This shows that $\chi \in \mathcal{F}$. By the strong convergence of $\{m_{k_i}\}$ to χ and the existence of $\lim_{k \to \infty} d(m_k, \chi)$ from Theorem 6, it is implied that the sequence $\{m_k\}$ converges strongly to χ. □

Theorem 8. *Let $\mathcal{J}$ be a nonempty closed compact subset of $\mathcal{Q}$ and $\mathcal{G}_i : \mathcal{J} \to \mathcal{BC}(\mathcal{J})$ $(i = 1, 2)$ be two multivalued mappings satisfying condition (E) with convex values. Let $\mathcal{F} = \cap_{i=1}^{2} F(\mathcal{G}_i) \neq \varnothing$ and $\mathcal{G}_i q^* = \{q^*\}$ for each $q^* \in \mathcal{F}$ $(i = 1, 2)$. Let $\{m_k\}$ be the sequence defined by (6). Then $\{m_k\}$ converges strongly to a point in $\mathcal{F}$ if and only if $\liminf_{k \to \infty} \text{dist}(m_k, \mathcal{F}) = 0$.*

Proof. Suppose that $\liminf_{k \to \infty} \text{dist}(m_k, \mathcal{F}) = 0$. From (32), we have $d(m_{k+1}, q^*) \leq d(m_k, q^*)$ for all $q^* \in \mathcal{F}$. It follows that $\text{dist}(m_{k+1}, \mathcal{F}) \leq \text{dist}(m_k, \mathcal{F})$. Therefore, $\lim_{k \to \infty} \text{dist}(m_{k+1}, \mathcal{F})$ exists and $\lim_{k \to \infty} \text{dist}(m_{k+1}, \mathcal{F}) = 0$. Thus, there exists a subsequence $\{m_{k_r}\}$ of the sequence $\{m_k\}$ such that $d(m_{k_r}, t_r) \leq \frac{1}{2^r}$ for all $r \geq 1$, where $\{t_r\}$ is a sequence in $\mathcal{F}$. In view of (32) we obtain

$$d(m_{k_{r+1}}, t_r) \leq d(m_{k_r}, t_r) \leq \frac{1}{2^r}. \tag{60}$$

By using (60) and the concept of triangle inequality, then we get

$$\begin{aligned}d(t_{r+1}, t_r) &\leq d(t_{r+1}, w_{k_{r+1}}) + d(w_{k_{r+1}}, t_r) \\ &\leq \frac{1}{2^{r+1}} + \frac{1}{2^r} < \frac{1}{2^{r-1}}.\end{aligned}$$

It follows clearly that $\{t_r\}$ is a Cauchy sequence in $\mathcal{J}$ and moreover, it is convergent to some $p \in \mathcal{J}$. Because for all $i = 1, 2$,

$$\text{dist}(t_r, \mathcal{G}_i p) \leq \mathcal{H}(\mathcal{G}_i t_r, \mathcal{G}_i p) \leq d(p, t_r)$$

and $t_r \to p$ as $k \to \infty$, it is implied that $\text{dist}(p, \mathcal{G}_i p) = 0$, and hence, $p \in \mathcal{F}$ and $\{m_{k_r}\}$ strongly converges to p. Because $\lim_{k \to \infty} d(m_k, p)$ exists, it is implied that $\{m_k\}$ converges strongly to p. □

Theorem 9. *Let $\mathcal{J}$ be a nonempty closed compact subset of $\mathcal{Q}$ and $\mathcal{G}_i : \mathcal{J} \to \mathcal{BC}(\mathcal{J})$ $(i = 1, 2)$ be two multivalued mappings satisfying condition (E) with convex values. Let $\mathcal{F} = \cap_{i=1}^{2} F(\mathcal{G}_i) \neq \varnothing$ and $\mathcal{G}_i q^* = \{q^*\}$ for each $q^* \in \mathcal{F}$ $(i = 1, 2)$. Let $\{m_k\}$ be the sequence defined by (6). Assume* that there exists an increasing self-function f defined on $[0, \infty)$ such that $f(0) = 0$ with $f(l) > 0$ for all $l > 0$ and $i = 1, 2$, and we have

$$\text{dist}(m_k, \mathcal{G}_i m_k) \geq f(\text{dist}(m_k, \mathcal{F})).$$

Then, the sequence $\{m_k\}$ converges strongly to a point in $\mathcal{F}$.

Proof. It is established in Theorem 6 that $\text{dist}(m_k, \mathcal{G}_i m_k) = 0$. Hence, one can assume that

$$\lim_{k \to \infty} f(\text{dist}(m_k, \mathcal{F})) \leq \lim_{k \to \infty} \text{dist}(m_k, \mathcal{G}_i m_k) = 0.$$

Thus, it is implied that $\lim_{k \to \infty} f(\text{dist}(m_k, \mathcal{F})) = 0$. Because f is an increasing self-function defined on $[0, \infty)$ with $f(0) = 0$, we know that $\lim_{k \to \infty} \text{dist}(m_k, \mathcal{F}) = 0$. The conclusion of the proof follows from Theorem 8. □

7. Numerical Example

In this section, we provide examples of mappings which satisfy condition (E) but do not satisfy condition (C). We carry out numerical experiment to show the efficiency and applicability of new method (6) with some existing iterative methods.

Example 2. Let $\mathcal{Q} = \mathbb{R}$ with the distance metric $d(m, w) = |m - w|$ and $\mathcal{J} = [0, \infty)$. Let $\mathcal{G}_1, \mathcal{G}_2 : \mathcal{J} \to \mathcal{P}(\mathcal{J})$ be defined by

$$\mathcal{G}_1 m = \begin{cases} [0, \frac{3m}{4}], & \text{if } m \in [\frac{1}{5}, \infty), \\ \{0\}, & \text{if } m \in [0, \frac{1}{5}); \end{cases}$$

and

$$\mathcal{G}_2 m = \begin{cases} [0, \frac{m}{2}], & \text{if } m \in (2, \infty], \\ \{0\}, & \text{if } m \in [0, 2], \end{cases}$$

for all $m \in \mathcal{J}$.

Clearly, $\mathcal{F} = \mathcal{F}(\mathcal{G}_1) \cap \mathcal{F}(\mathcal{G}_2) = \{0\}$. Because $\mathcal{G}_1$ and $\mathcal{G}_2$ are not continuous at $\frac{1}{5}$ and 2, respectively, so $\mathcal{G}_1$ and $\mathcal{G}_2$ are not nonexpansive mappings. Next, we show that $\mathcal{G}_1$ and $\mathcal{G}_2$ do not satisfy condition (C). For $\mathcal{G}_1$, let $m = \frac{1}{15}$ and $w = \frac{1}{5}$. Then,

$$\frac{1}{2}\text{dist}(m, \mathcal{G}_1 m) = \frac{1}{2}\text{dist}\left(\frac{1}{15}, \mathcal{G}_1 \frac{1}{15}\right) = \frac{1}{30} < \frac{2}{15} = d(m, w).$$

However,

$$\mathcal{H}(\mathcal{G}_1 m, \mathcal{G}_1 w) = \mathcal{H}(\mathcal{G}_1 \frac{1}{15}, \mathcal{G}_1 \frac{1}{5}) = \mathcal{H}(\{0\}, [0, \frac{3}{20}]) = \frac{3}{20} > \frac{2}{15} = d(m, w). \quad (61)$$

Thus, $\mathcal{G}_1$ does not satisfy condition (C).
Similarly, for $m = \frac{3}{2}$ and $w = \frac{5}{2}$, we can show that $\mathcal{G}_2$ does not satisfy condition (C).
Finally, we show that $\mathcal{G}_1$ and $\mathcal{G}_2$ are multivalued mappings satisfying condition (E). First, we consider $\mathcal{G}_1$ and the following possible cases:

Case 1: If $m, w \in [\frac{1}{5}, \infty)$, then

$$\text{dist}(m, \mathcal{G}_1 m) = \text{dist}\left(m, \left[0, \frac{3m}{4}\right]\right) = \left|m - \frac{3m}{4}\right| = \left|\frac{m}{4}\right|.$$

Therefore,

$$\begin{aligned}
dist(m, \mathcal{G}_1 w) &= dist\left(m, \left[0, \frac{3w}{4}\right]\right) \\
&= \left|m - \frac{3w}{4}\right| \\
&= \left|m - \frac{3m}{4} + \frac{3m}{4} - \frac{3w}{4}\right| \\
&\leq \left|m - \frac{3m}{4}\right| + \left|\frac{3m}{4} - \frac{3w}{4}\right| \\
&\leq 4\left|\frac{m}{4}\right| + \frac{3}{4}|m - w| \\
&\leq 4\left|\frac{m}{4}\right| + |m - w| \\
&= 4 dist(m, \mathcal{G}_1 m) + d(m, w).
\end{aligned}$$

Case 2: If $m, w \in [0, \frac{1}{5})$, then

$$dist(m, \mathcal{G}_1 m) = dist(m, \{0\}) = |m - 0| = |m|.$$

Therefore,

$$\begin{aligned}
dist(m, \mathcal{G}_1 w) &= dist(m, \{0\}) \\
&= |m| \\
&\leq 4|m| + |m - w| \\
&= 4 dist(m, \mathcal{G}_1 m) + d(m, w).
\end{aligned}$$

Case 3: If $m \in [\frac{1}{5}, \infty)$ and $w \in [0, \frac{1}{5})$, then

$$dist(m, \mathcal{G}_1 m) = dist\left(m, \left[0, \frac{3m}{4}\right]\right) = \left|m - \frac{3m}{4}\right| = \left|\frac{m}{4}\right|.$$

Therefore,

$$\begin{aligned}
dist(m, \mathcal{G}_1 w) &= dist(m, \{0\}) \\
&= |m| \\
&= 4\left|\frac{m}{4}\right| \\
&\leq 4\left|\frac{m}{4}\right| + |m - w| \\
&= 4 dist(m, \mathcal{G}_1 m) + d(m, w).
\end{aligned}$$

Case 4: If $m \in [0, \frac{1}{5})$ and $w \in [\frac{1}{5}, \infty)$, then

$$dist(m, \mathcal{G}_1 m) = dist(m, \{0\}) = |m - 0| = |m|.$$

Therefore,

$$\begin{aligned}
dist(m, \mathcal{G}_1 w) &= dist\left(m, \left[0, \frac{3w}{4}\right]\right) \\
&= \left|m - \frac{3w}{4}\right| \\
&= \left|m - \frac{3m}{4} + \frac{3m}{4} - \frac{3w}{4}\right| \\
&\leq \left|m - \frac{3m}{4}\right| + \left|\frac{3m}{4} - \frac{3w}{4}\right| \\
&= \left|\frac{m}{4}\right| + \frac{3}{4}|m - w| \\
&\leq |m| + |m - w| \\
&\leq 4|m| + |m - w| \\
&= 4 dist(m, \mathcal{G}_1 m) + d(m, w).
\end{aligned}$$

For all $m, w \in \mathcal{J}$, we seen that $\mathcal{G}_1$ satisfies (1) for some $\mu = 4$. Hence, $\mathcal{G}_1$ is a multivalued mapping satisfying condition (E).

Following the same approach above, we can show that $\mathcal{G}_2$ is a multivalued mapping satisfying condition (E) for some $\mu = 2$.

Now, for control parameters $\xi_k = \eta_k = \zeta_k = \frac{1}{2}$, for all $k \in \mathbb{N}$ and starting point $m_1 = 5$. Then by using MATLAB R2015a, we obtain the following Tables 3 and 4 and Figures 3 and 4.

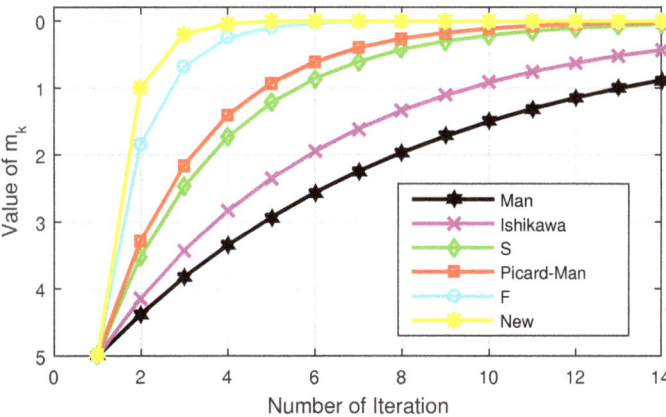

Figure 3. Graph corresponding to Table 3.

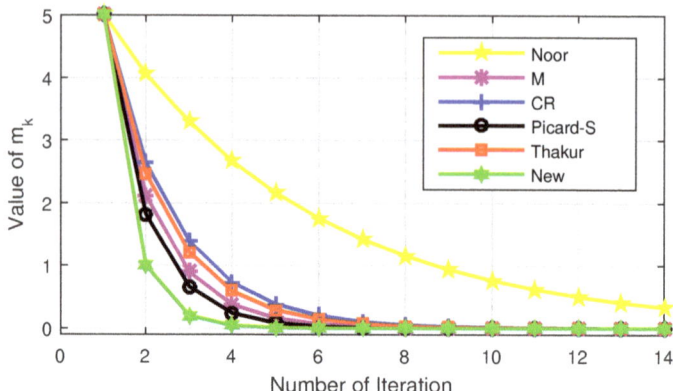

Figure 4. Graph corresponding to Table 4.

Table 3. Convergence behavior of various iterative algorithms.

m_k	Mann	Ishikawa	S	Picard-Mann	F	New
m_1	5.00000000	5.00000000	5.00000000	5.00000000	5.00000000	5.00000000
m_2	4.37500000	4.14062500	3.51562500	3.28125000	1.84570313	0.99609375
m_3	3.82812500	3.42895508	2.47192383	2.15332031	0.68132401	0.19844055
m_4	3.34960938	2.83960342	1.73807144	1.41311646	0.25150437	0.03953308
m_5	2.93090820	2.35154659	1.22208148	0.92735767	0.09284048	0.00787573
m_6	2.56454468	1.94737452	0.85927604	0.60857847	0.03427119	0.00156899
m_7	2.24397659	1.61266952	0.60417847	0.39937962	0.01265089	0.00031257
m_8	1.96347952	1.33549195	0.42481298	0.26209288	0.00466996	0.00006227
m_9	1.71804458	1.10595427	0.29869663	0.17199845	0.00172387	0.00001241
m_{10}	1.50328901	0.91586838	0.21002107	0.11287398	0.00063635	0.00000247
m_{11}	1.31537788	0.75845350	0.14767106	0.07407355	0.00023490	0.00000049
m_{12}	1.15095565	0.62809431	0.10383122	0.04861077	0.00008671	0.00000010
m_{13}	1.00708619	0.52014060	0.07300632	0.03190082	0.00003201	0.00000002
m_{14}	0.88120042	0.43074143	0.05133257	0.02093491	0.00001182	0.00000000

The reds show the point of convergence of various iterative methods.

Table 4. Convergence behavior of various iterative algorithms.

m_k	Noor	CR	Thakur	Picard-S	M	New
m_1	5.00000000	5.00000000	5.00000000	5.00000000	5.00000000	5.00000000
m_2	4.05273438	2.11914063	2.63671875	1.81640625	2.46093750	0.99609375
m_3	3.28493118	0.89815140	1.39045715	0.65986633	1.21124268	0.19844055
m_4	2.66259070	0.38066182	0.73324889	0.23971707	0.59615850	0.03953308
m_5	2.15815458	0.16133519	0.38667422	0.08708472	0.29342176	0.00787573
m_6	1.74928545	0.06837839	0.20391023	0.03163624	0.14441852	0.00156899
m_7	1.41787785	0.02898068	0.10753079	0.01149285	0.07108099	0.00031257
m_8	1.14925646	0.01228283	0.05670569	0.00417514	0.03498518	0.00006227
m_9	0.93152623	0.00520581	0.02990339	0.00151675	0.01721927	0.00001241
m_{10}	0.75504568	0.00220637	0.01576937	0.00055101	0.00847511	0.00000247
m_{11}	0.61199991	0.00093512	0.00831588	0.00020017	0.00417134	0.00000049
m_{12}	0.49605462	0.00039633	0.00438533	0.00007272	0.00205308	0.00000010
m_{13}	0.40207552	0.00016798	0.00231257	0.00002642	0.00101050	0.00000002
m_{14}	0.32590106	0.00007119	0.00121952	0.00000960	0.00049736	0.00000000

The reds show the point of convergence of various iterative methods.

From Tables 3 and 4 and Figures 3 and 4 above, it is very clear that our new iterative algorithm (6) converges faster to 0 than Mann [29], Ishikawa [30], Thakur [37], S [19], M [32], Noor [33], CR [38], Picard–Man [35], Picard-S [36], and F [22] iteration processes.

8. Conclusions

(i) In this work, we have introduced a new iterative algorithm (6) in hyperbolic spaces.

(ii) We have proven the strong convergence of the newly defined iterative algorithm (6) to the common fixed point of two multivalued almost contractive mappings.

(ii) We have also provided some examples of multivalued, almost contractive mappings. We show with the aid of the examples that our iterative algorithm (6) converges faster than many existing iterative algorithms.

(iii) We have introduced the concepts of weak w^2-stability and data dependence results involving two multivalued almost contractive mappings. These concepts are relatively new in the literature.

(iv) We have proved several strong and $\triangle$-convergence results of (6) for the common fixed point of multivalued mappings satisfying condition (E).

(v) We presented interesting examples of mappings which satisfy condition (E) but do not satisfy condition (C). We further performed numerical experiments to compare the efficiency and applicability of our iterative method with some leading iterative algorithms.

(vi) The results in this article extend and generalize the results in [24,39] and several others from the setting of Banach spaces to the setting hyperbolic spaces. Moreover, our results improve and generalize the results in [22,24,39] and several others from the setting of single-valued mappings to the setting of multivalued mappings. In addition, we improve and extend the results in [22,24,39] from the setting of fixed points of single mapping to the setting common fixed points of two mappings.

(vii) Our results give affirmative answers to the two interesting open questions raised by Ahmad et al. [21].

(viii) The main results derived in this article continue to be true in linear and CAT(0) spaces, because the hyperbolic space properly includes these spaces.

Author Contributions: Conceptualization, J.A.A.; Supervision, G.C.U. and O.K.N.; Writing—original draft, A.E.O.; Writing—review & editing, R.G. All authors have read and agreed to the published version of the manuscript.

Funding: This research received no external funding.

Data Availability Statement: The data used to support the findings of this study are included within the article.

Conflicts of Interest: The authors declare that they have no competing interests.

References

1. Kohlenbach, U. Some logical metatheorems with applications in functional analysis. *Trans. Am. Soc.* **2005**, *357*, 89–128. [CrossRef]
2. Goebel, K.; Kirk, W.A. Iteration processes for nonexpansive mappings Topological Methods in Nonlinear Functional Analysis. *Contemp. Math.* **1983**, *21*, 115–123.
3. Reich, S.; Shafrir, I. Nonexpansive iterations in hyperbolic spaces. *Nonlinear Anal.* **1990**, *15*, 537–558. [CrossRef]
4. Goebel, K.; Reich, S. *Uniform Convexity, Hyperbolic Geometry, and Nonexpansive Mappings*; Marcel Dekker: New York, NY, USA, 1984.
5. Imdad, M.; Dashputre, S. Fixed point approximation of Picard normal S-iteration process for generalized nonexpansive mappings in hyperbolic spaces. *Math. Sci.* **2016**, *10*, 131–138. [CrossRef]
6. Nadler, S.B. Multivalued contraction mappings. *Pacific J. Math.* **1969**, *30*, 475–488. [CrossRef]
7. Markin, J. Continuous dependence of fixed point sets. *Proc. Am. Math. Soc.* **1973**, *38*, 545–547. [CrossRef]
8. Berinde, V. Approximating fixed points of weak contractions using the Picard iteration. *Nonlinear Anal. Forum* **2004**, *9*, 43–53.
9. Berinde, M.; Berinde, V. On a general class of multivalued weakly Picard mappings. *J. Math. Anal.* **2007**, *326*, 772–782. [CrossRef]
10. Suzuki, T. Fixed point theorems and convergence theorems for some generalized nonexpansive mappings. *J. Math. Anal. Appl.* **2008**, *340*, 1088–1590. [CrossRef]

11. Eslamian, M.; Abkar, A. One-step iterative process for finite family of multivalued mappings. *Math. Comput. Model.* **2011**, *54*, 105–111. [CrossRef]
12. García-Falset, J.; Llorens-Fuster, E.; Suzuki, T. Fixed point theory for a class of generalized nonexpansive mappings. *J. Math. Anal. Appl.* **2011**, *375*, 185–195. [CrossRef]
13. Kim, J.K.; Pathak, R.P.; Dashputre, S.; Diwan, S.D.; Gupta, R. Convergence theorems for generalized nonexpansive multivalued mappings in hyperbolic spaces. *SpringerPlus* **2016**, *5*, 912. [CrossRef] [PubMed]
14. Abdeljawad, T.; Ullah, K.; Ahmad, J.; Mlaiki, N. Iterative approximation of endpoints for Multivalued Mappings in Banach spaces. *J. Funct. Spaces* **2020**, *2020*, 2179059. [CrossRef]
15. Chang, S.; Wanga, G.; Wanga, L.; Tang, Y.K.; Mab, Z.L. ∆-convergence theorems for multivalued nonexpansive. *Appl. Math. Comput.* **2014**, *249*, 535–540.
16. Karahan, I.; Jolaoso, L.O. A three steps iterative process for approximating the fixed points of multivalued generalized α–nonexpansive mappings in uniformly convex hyperbolic spaces. *Sigma J. Eng. Nat. Sci.* **2020**, *38*, 1031–1050.
17. Okeke, G.A.; Abbas, M.; de la Sen, M. Approximation of the mixed Point of multivalued quasi-nonexpansive mappings via a faster iterative process with applications. *Discret. Dyn. Nat. Soc.* **2020**, *2020*, 8634050. [CrossRef]
18. Shrama, N.; Mishra, L.N.; Mishra, V.N.; Almusawa, H. Endpoint Approximation of Standard Three-Step Multi-Valued Iteration Algorithm for Nonexpansive Mappings. *Appl. Math. Inf. Sci.* **2021**, *15*, 73–81.
19. Agarwal, R.P.; O'Regan, D.; Sahu, D.R. Iterative construction of fixed points of nearly asymptotically nonexpansive mappings. *J. Nonlinear Convex Anal.* **2007**, *8*, 61–79.
20. Chuadchawnay, P.; Farajzadehz, A.; Kaewcharoeny, A. On convergence theorems for two generalized nonexpansive multivalued mappings in hyperbolic spaces. *Thai J. Math.* **2019**, *17*, 445–461.
21. Ahmad, J.; Ullah, K.; Arshad, M. Convergence, weak w^2 stability, and data dependence results for the F iterative scheme in hyperbolic spaces. *Numer. Algorithms* **2022**. [CrossRef]
22. Ali, J.; Jubair, M.; Ali, F. Stability and convergence of F iterative scheme with an application to the fractional differential equation. *Eng. Comput.* **2020**, *38*, 693–702. [CrossRef]
23. Khan, A.R.; Fukhar-ud-din, H.; Ahmad, Khan, M.A. An implicit algorithm for two finite families of nonexpansive maps in hyperbolic spaces. *Fixed Point Theory Appl.* **2012**, *2012*, 54. [CrossRef]
24. Ofem, A.E.; Udofia, U.E.; Igbokwe, D.I. New iterative algorithm for solving constrained convex minimization problem and Split Feasibility Problem. *Eur. J. Math. Anal.* **2021**, *1*, 106–132. [CrossRef]
25. Leuștean, L. A quadratic rate of asymptotic regularity for CAT(0) space. *J. Math. Anal. Appl.* **2007**, *325*, 386–399. [CrossRef]
26. Soltuz, S.M.; Grosan, T. Data dependence for Ishikawa iteration when dealing with contractive like operators. *Fixed Point Theory Appl.* **2008**, *2008*, 242916. [CrossRef]
27. Cardinali, T.; Rubbioni, P. A generalization of the Caristi fixed point theorem in metric spaces. *Fixed Point Theory* **2010**, *11*, 3–10.
28. Timis, I. On the weak stability of Picard iteration for some contractive type mappings, Annals of the University of Craiova. *Math. Comput. Sci. Ser.* **2010**, *37*, 106–114.
29. Mann, W.R. Mean value methods in iteration. *Proc. Am. Math. Soc.* **1953**, *4*, 506–510. [CrossRef]
30. Ishikawa, S. Fixed points and iteration of a nonexpansive mapping in a Banach space. *Proc. Am. Math. Soc.* **1976**, *59*, 65–71. [CrossRef]
31. Abbas, M.; Nazir, T. A new faster iteration process applied to constrained minimization and feasibility problems. *Mat. Vesnik* **2014**, *66*, 223–234.
32. Ullah, K.; Arshad, M. Numerical Reckoning Fixed Points for Suzuki's Generalized Nonexpansive Mappings via New Iteration Process. *Filomat* **2018**, *32*, 187–196. [CrossRef]
33. Noor, M.A. New approximation schemes for general variational inequalities. *J. Math. Anal. Appl.* **2000**, *251*, 217–229. [CrossRef]
34. Phuengrattana, W.; Suantai, S. On the rate off convergence of Mann, Ishikawa, Noor and SP iterations for continuous functions on an arbitrary interval. *J. Comput. Appl. Math.* **2011**, *235*, 3006–3014. [CrossRef]
35. Khan, H.S. A Picard-Man hybrid iterative process. *Fixed Point Theory Appl.* **2013**, *2013*, 69. [CrossRef]
36. Güsoy, F. A Picard-S iterative Scheme for Approximating Fixed Point of Weak-Contraction Mappings. *Filomat* **2014**, *30*, 2829–2845. [CrossRef]
37. Thakur, B.S.; Thakur, D.; Postolache, M. A new iterative scheme for numerical reckoning of fixed points of Suzuki's generalized nonexpansive mappings. *Appl. Math. Comput.* **2016**, *275*, 147–155. [CrossRef]
38. Chugh, R.; Kumar, V.; Kumar, S. Strong convergence of a new three step iterative scheme in Banach spaces. *Am. J. Comput. Math.* **2012**, *2*, 345–357. [CrossRef]
39. Ofem, A.E.; Udofia, U.E.; Igbokwe, D.I. A robust iterative approach for solving nonlinear Volterra Delay integro-differential equations. *Ural. Math. J.* **2021**, *7*, 59–85. [CrossRef]

Article

Generalized Contractions and Fixed Point Results in Spaces with Altering Metrics

Adrian Nicolae Branga [†] and Ion Marian Olaru [*,†]

Department of Mathematics and Informatics, Lucian Blaga University of Sibiu, I. Rațiu Street, No. 5-7, 550012 Sibiu, Romania
* Correspondence: marian.olaru@ulbsibiu.ro
† These authors contributed equally to this work.

Abstract: In this paper, we have provided some fixed point results for self-mappings fulfilling generalized contractive conditions on altered metric spaces. In addition, some applications of the main results to continuous data dependence of the fixed points of operators defined on these spaces were shown.

Keywords: generalized contractions; fixed point theorems; spaces with altering metrics; data dependence

MSC: 47H10; 47H09; 54E50

1. Introduction

The fixed point theorems for an operator $T : X \to X$ related to altering distances between points in complete metric space were originally achieved by Delbosco [1], Skof [2], M.S. Khan, M. Swaleh and S. Sessa [3] by using some suitable distance control function $\mu : \mathbb{R}_+ \to \mathbb{R}_+$, where $\mathbb{R}_+$ is the real interval $[0, \infty)$, and contractive conditions of type

$$\mu(d(T(x), T(y))) \leq a \cdot \mu(d(x,y)) + b \cdot \mu(d(x, T(x))) + c \cdot \mu(d(y, T(y))), 0 \leq a+b+c < 1,$$

or more general

$$\mu(d(T(x), T(y))) \leq$$
$$a(d(x,y)) \cdot \mu((d(x,y)) + b(d(x,y)) \cdot \{\mu(d(x, T(x))) + \mu(d(y, T(y)))\} +$$
$$c(d(x,y)) \cdot \min\{\mu(x, T(y)), \mu(y, T(x))\},$$

for all $x, y \in X$, $x \neq y$ and $a, b, c : \mathbb{R}_+^* \to [0,1)$ being decreasing functions in order that $a(t) + 2 \cdot b(t) + c(t) < 1$ for every $t > 0$. Also in [4], the authors considered a contractive condition of type

$$\mu(d(T(x), T(y))) \leq \alpha(d(x,y)) \cdot \mu(d(x,y)), \forall x,y \in X,$$

where $\alpha : \mathbb{R}_+ \to [0,1)$ is the order that $\limsup_{s \to t} \alpha(s) < 1$. Further Akkouchi et al. [5], Pant et al. [6–8] and Sastry et al. [9] have obtained common fixed point results by altering the distance between the points of a metric space. Moreover, the fixed point results by altering distance between the points was extended to the setup of generalized metric spaces (fuzzy metrics spaces Masmali et al. [10], orthogonal complete metric Gungor [11], partially ordered metric spaces Gupta et al. [12]) or to cyclic operators, see Khaleel et al. [13]. Recently, Branga and Olaru [14] extended the above results by altering the distance between two points and considering a contractive condition of type

$$\mu(d(T(x), T(y))) \leq \eta(\mu(d(x,y))), \tag{1}$$

for all $x, y \in X$, $x \neq y$ and $\eta : [0, \infty) \to [0, \infty)$ is a monotone increasing, right continuous and satisfies $\eta(t) < t$ for each $t > 0$. A survey work on some fixed point theorems by altering distances between points on a metric space can be found on Jha et al. [15]. Some recent applications of fixed point theory may be found on Rezapour et al. [16], Zareen et al. [17] and Turab et al. [18]. Next, our aim is to extend the results from [14] by considering a contractive condition of type (1), η being a right upper semi-continuous function.

2. Preliminaries

Next, we recall the definitions of the upper semi-continuous and right upper semi-continuous functions.

Definition 1 ([19]). *Let us consider A a subset of $\mathbb{R}$, $a \in A$ a point and $f : A \to \mathbb{R}$ a function. The following can be affirmed:*

(1) *f is upper semicontinuous at a if for every $\varepsilon > 0$ there is $\delta(\varepsilon) > 0$ in order that*

$$f(x) < f(a) + \varepsilon \text{ for all } x \in (a - \delta(\varepsilon), a + \delta(\varepsilon)) \cap A;$$

(2) *f is upper semicontinuous if it is upper semicontinuous at every point $a \in A$;*
(3) *f is right upper semicontinuous at a if for each $\varepsilon > 0$ there is $\delta(\varepsilon) > 0$ in order that*

$$f(x) < f(a) + \varepsilon \text{ for all } x \in (a, a + \delta(\varepsilon)) \cap A;$$

(4) *f is right upper semicontinuous if it is right upper semicontinuous at every point $a \in A$.*

Remark 1. *Let us consider A a subset of $\mathbb{R}$, $a \in A$ a point and $f : A \to \mathbb{R}$ a function. The following can be remarked:*

(1) *if f is right-continuous at a, then f is right upper semi-continuous at a;*
(2) *if f is right upper semi-continuous at a and f is monotonically increasing, then f is right-continuous at a;*
(3) *if f is upper semi-continuous at a, then f is right upper semi-continuous at a.*

The following results will be used in order to proof Lemma 2:

Theorem 1 ([19]). *Let A be a subset of $\mathbb{R}$, $a \in A'$, (the set of accumulation points of A) and $f : A \to \mathbb{R}$ a function. Then:*

(1) *f is upper semi-continuous at a if and only if*

$$\limsup_{x \to a} f(x) \leq f(a);$$

(2) *f is right upper semi-continuous at a if and only if*

$$\limsup_{x \searrow a} f(x) \leq f(a).$$

Theorem 2 ([19]). *Let us consider A a subset of $\mathbb{R}$, $a \in A$ a point and $f : A \to \mathbb{R}$ a function. Then:*

(1) *f is upper semi-continuous at a if and only if, for each sequence $(a_n)_{n \in \mathbb{N}} \subseteq A$ satisfying $a_n \to a$ as $n \to \infty$, we have*

$$\limsup_{n \to \infty} f(a_n) \leq f(a);$$

(2) *f is right upper semicontinuous at a if and only if, for every sequence $(a_n)_{n \in \mathbb{N}} \subseteq A$ satisfying $a_n \to a$ as $n \to \infty$, $a_n \geq a$ for all $n \in \mathbb{N}$, we have*

$$\limsup_{n \to \infty} f(a_n) \leq f(a).$$

Theorem 3 ([19]). *If A is a subset of $\mathbb{R}$ and $f : A \to \mathbb{R}$ a function, then f is upper semi-continuous if and only if the superlevel set $U_y(f) := \{x \in A \mid f(x) \geq y\}$ is closed in A for every $y \in \mathbb{R}$.*

Theorem 4 ([19]). *Let $(a_n)_{n\in\mathbb{N}} \subseteq \mathbb{R}$ be a sequence and $a \in \mathbb{R}$. Then,*

$$\limsup_{n\to\infty} a_n \leq a,$$

if and only if there is a number $n_0 \in \mathbb{N}$ in order that

$$a_n \leq a \text{ for all } n \geq n_0.$$

Boyd and Wong [20] extend the contraction principle (the Picard–Banach theorem) in complete metric spaces.

Theorem 5 ([20]). *Let $\eta : \mathbb{R}_+ \to \mathbb{R}_+$ be a function fulfilling the statements: η is right upper semicontinuous and $\eta(t) < t$ for all $t > 0$. If (X,d) is a complete metric space and $T : X \to X$ is an operator in order that*

$$d(T(x),T(y)) \leq \eta(d(x,y)), \forall x,y \in X,$$

then T has a unique fixed point $x^* \in X$ and the sequence $T^m(x_0) \to x^*$ as $m \to \infty$, for any arbitrary point $x_0 \in X$.

The following result will represent a generalization of the above Boyd's result and it will be used in order to prove Lemma 3 and Theorem 8.

Definition 2 ([21]). *A function $\eta : \mathbb{R}_+^k \to \mathbb{R}_+$, $k \geq 1$ is a comparison function if:*
(i) *η is increasing with respect to each variable, i.e., the mapping $t_i \to \eta(t_1, \cdots, t_i, \cdots, t_k)$ is increasing for every $i \in \{1, \ldots, k\}$;*
(ii) *the iterates sequence $\mu^n(t) \to 0$ as $n \to \infty$, for every $t > 0$, where $\mu : \mathbb{R}_+ \to \mathbb{R}_+$ is defined by $\mu(t) := \eta(t, t, \cdots, t)$.*

Theorem 6 ([21]). *Let us consider (X,d) a complete metric space, $\eta : \mathbb{R}_+^5 \to \mathbb{R}_+$ a comparison function and $T : X \to X$ be an operator in order that*

$$d(T(x),T(y)) \leq \eta(d(x,y),d(x,Tx),d(y,Ty),d(x,Ty),d(y,Tx)), \forall x,y \in X,$$

T has a unique fixed point $x^* \in X$ and the sequence $T^m(x_0) \to x^*$ as $m \to \infty$, for any arbitrary point $x_0 \in X$.

3. Results

Definition 3 ([3]). *A function $\gamma : \mathbb{R}_+ \to \mathbb{R}_+$ belongs to the class Γ, if:*
(i) *γ is continuous;*
(ii) *γ is monotonically increasing;*
(iii) *$\gamma(t) = 0$ if and only if $t = 0$.*

Let us consider (X,d) a metric space. When the metric d is changed by a function $\gamma \in \Gamma$, it can be seen that, in the majority of cases, the application $\gamma \circ d$ does not keep the metric properties.

Example 1. *Let us consider $d : \mathbb{R} \times \mathbb{R} \to \mathbb{R}_+$, $d(x,y) = |x - y|$ and $\gamma : \mathbb{R}_+ \to \mathbb{R}_+$, $\gamma(t) = t^4$. The following can be affirmed:*
(1) *$\gamma \in \Gamma$;*
(2) *$\gamma \circ d$ is not a metric on X.*

Proof.

(1) It is obvious that γ verifies the conditions from Definition 3.
(2) By taking $x = 2$, $y = 3$ and $z = 2.1$, we observe that the triangle inequality is not verified for $\gamma \circ d$, and consequently it is not a metric on $\mathbb{R}$.

□

Lemma 1. *Let $\eta : \mathbb{R}_+ \to \mathbb{R}_+$ be a function, under the following hypothesis:*

(1) *is right upper semicontinuous;*
(2) *$\eta(t) < t$ for all $t > 0$.*

Then:
$$\liminf_{s \searrow t}(s - \eta(s)) > 0 \text{ for every } t > 0.$$

Proof. By using the hypothesis (2), it follows that $\liminf_{s \searrow t}(s - \eta(s)) \geq 0$ for every $t > 0$. Suppose that there exists $t_0 > 0$ such that $\liminf_{s \searrow t_0}(s - \eta(s)) = 0$. Taking into consideration the properties of the limit inferior and limit superior of a function, the fact that η is right upper semi-continuous, applying Theorem 1 (2) and the hypothesis (2), we obtain

$$t_0 = \liminf_{s \searrow t_0} \eta(s) \leq \limsup_{s \searrow t_0} \eta(s) \leq \eta(t_0) < t_0,$$

which is a contradiction. Consequently, $\liminf_{s \searrow t}(s - \eta(s)) > 0$ for every $t > 0$. □

Lemma 2. *Let be $\gamma \in \Gamma$, $\mu : \mathbb{R}_+ \to \mathbb{R}_+$ defined by:*

$$\mu(t) = \sup\{s \in \mathbb{R}_+ \mid \gamma(s) \leq \eta(\gamma(t))\}, \qquad (2)$$

and $\eta : \mathbb{R}_+ \to \mathbb{R}_+$ a function, under the following hypothesis:

(1) *$\eta(0) = 0$;*
(2) *η is right upper semicontinuous;*
(3) *$\eta(t) < t$ for all $t > 0$.*

Then:

(i) *μ is well defined;*
(ii) *$\mu(0) = 0$;*
(iii) *$\mu(t) \leq t$ for all $t \in \mathbb{R}_+$;*
(iv) *$\gamma(\mu(t)) \leq \eta(\gamma(t))$ for all $t \in \mathbb{R}_+$;*
(v) *$\mu(t) < t$ for all $t > 0$;*
(vi) *$\eta \circ \gamma$ is right upper semi-continuous;*
(vii) *μ is right upper semi-continuous.*

Proof. (i) Let us consider $t \in \mathbb{R}_+$ an arbitrary chosen number. We construct the set

$$A_t := \{s \in \mathbb{R}_+ \mid \gamma(s) \leq \eta(\gamma(t))\}. \qquad (3)$$

As $\gamma(0) = 0$ (in accordance with Definition 3 (iii)) and $\eta(\gamma(t)) \geq 0$ ($\eta, \gamma : \mathbb{R}_+ \to \mathbb{R}_+$), we obtain $\gamma(0) \leq \eta(\gamma(t))$, therefore $0 \in A_t$, so A_t is a non-empty set. The next cases can be differentiated:

1. $t = 0$:
   As $\gamma(0) = 0$ (in accordance with Definition 3 (iii)) and $\eta(0) = 0$ (by the hypothesis (1)) we obtain $\eta(\gamma(0)) = 0$, therefore $A_0 = \{s \in \mathbb{R}_+ \mid \gamma(s) \leq 0\}$. Taking into account Definition 3 (iii), it is obtained that $A_0 = \{0\}$. It results in $\mu(0) = \sup A_0 = \sup\{0\} = 0$.
2. $t > 0$:
   Select $s \in A_t$ is an arbitrary chosen element. One has $s \in \mathbb{R}_+$ and $\gamma(s) \leq \eta(\gamma(t))$. On

the opposite side, as $t > 0$, considering Definition 3 (iii), we obtain $\gamma(t) > 0$. Applying hypothesis (3), we obtain $\eta(\gamma(t)) < \gamma(t)$. It results that $\gamma(s) < \gamma(t)$. Taking into account that γ is monotonically increasing (using Definition 3 (ii)), it is found that $s < t$. Hence, $s \in [0, t)$. Considering that we have arbitrary selected $s \in A_t$, it follows that $A_t \subseteq [0, t)$. As a result, the set A_t is bounded from above by t. We conclude that, there is $\sup A_t \leq t$. Therefore, $\mu(t) := \sup A_t \leq t$ is well defined and we get $\mu(t) \leq t$.

(ii), (iii) follows from (i).

(iv) Let us consider $t \in \mathbb{R}_+$ an arbitrary selected element. In accordance with (i), the set A_t is bounded from above by t and $\mu(t) := \sup A_t$. It results that, there is a sequence $(s_n)_{n \in \mathbb{N}} \subseteq A_t$ in order that $s_n \to \mu(t)$ as $n \to \infty$ and $s_n \leq \mu(t)$ for all $n \in \mathbb{N}$. Considering that $s_n \in A_t$ for all $n \in \mathbb{N}$, it is concluded that

$$\gamma(s_n) \leq \eta(\gamma(t)) \text{ for all } n \in \mathbb{N}.$$

On the opposite side, as γ is continuous (using Definition 3 (i)), we obtain $\gamma(s_n) \to \gamma(\mu(t))$ as $n \to \infty$. Hence, from the previous inequality, we conclude that $\gamma(\mu(t)) \leq \eta(\gamma(t))$.

Specifically, $\mu(t) \in A_t$ and $A_t \subseteq [0, \mu(t)]$. Select $s \in [0, \mu(t)]$. We obtain $s \leq \mu(t)$, and taking into account that γ is monotonically increasing (in accordance with Definition 3 (ii)), it follows that $\gamma(s) \leq \gamma(\mu(t))$. Hence, $\gamma(s) \leq \eta(\gamma(t))$, i.e., $s \in A_t$. As a result, $A_t = [0, \mu(t)]$.

(v) From (iii), we obtain $\mu(t) \leq t$ for all $t \in \mathbb{R}_+$. Assume that there is $t > 0$ in order that $\mu(t) = t$. Applying (iv) we obtain $\gamma(t) \leq \eta(\gamma(t))$. On the other side, $t > 0$ implies $\gamma(t) > 0$ (in accordance with to Definition 3 (iii)) and applying hypothesis (3) we obtain $\eta(\gamma(t)) < \gamma(t)$. It results that $\gamma(t) < \gamma(t)$, which contradicts the initial assumption. Therefore, $\mu(t) < t$ for all $t > 0$.

(vi) As $\eta, \gamma : \mathbb{R}_+ \to \mathbb{R}_+$ we deduce $\eta \circ \gamma : \mathbb{R}_+ \to \mathbb{R}_+$. Let $t \in \mathbb{R}_+$ be an arbitrary point. We consider an arbitrary sequence $(t_n)_{n \in \mathbb{N}} \subseteq \mathbb{R}_+$ satisfying $t_n \to t$ as $n \to \infty$, $t_n \geq t$ for all $n \in \mathbb{N}$. Since γ is continuous (in accordance with Definition 3 (i)), we obtain $\gamma(t_n) \to \gamma(t)$ as $n \to \infty$. Because γ is monotonically increasing (by Definition 3 (ii)), we find that $\gamma(t_n) \geq \gamma(t)$ for all $n \in \mathbb{N}$. Therefore, the sequence $(\gamma(t_n))_{n \in \mathbb{N}} \subseteq \mathbb{R}_+$ has the following properties: $\gamma(t_n) \to \gamma(t)$ as $n \to \infty$, $\gamma(t_n) \geq \gamma(t)$ for all $n \in \mathbb{N}$. On the other hand, η is right upper semi-continuous, hence it is right upper semi-continuous at $\gamma(t) \in \mathbb{R}_+$. Applying Theorem 2 (2), it follows that $\limsup_{n \to \infty} \eta(\gamma(t_n)) \leq \eta(\gamma(t))$, i.e.,

$$\limsup_{n \to \infty} (\eta \circ \gamma)(t_n) \leq (\eta \circ \gamma)(t). \tag{4}$$

Since the sequence $(t_n)_{n \in \mathbb{N}} \subseteq \mathbb{R}_+$ satisfying $t_n \to t$ as $n \to \infty$, $t_n \geq t$ for all $n \in \mathbb{N}$, was chosen arbitrarily, from the inequality (4), by using Theorem 2 (2), it results that $\eta \circ \gamma$ is right upper semi-continuous at $t \in \mathbb{R}_+$. Because the point $t \in \mathbb{R}_+$ was arbitrarily selected, we deduce that $\eta \circ \gamma$ is right upper semi-continuous.

(vii) Let $t \in \mathbb{R}_+$ be an arbitrary point. We consider an arbitrary sequence $(t_n)_{n \in \mathbb{N}} \subseteq \mathbb{R}_+$ satisfying $t_n \to t$ as $n \to \infty$, $t_n \geq t$ for all $n \in \mathbb{N}$. Since γ is continuous (in accordance with Definition 3 (i)), we obtain $\gamma(t_n) \to \gamma(t)$ as $n \to \infty$. Because γ is monotonically increasing (by Definition 3 (ii)), we find that $\gamma(t_n) \geq \gamma(t)$ for all $n \in \mathbb{N}$. Therefore, the sequence $(\gamma(t_n))_{n \in \mathbb{N}} \subseteq \mathbb{R}_+$ has the following properties: $\gamma(t_n) \to \gamma(t)$ as $n \to \infty$, $\gamma(t_n) \geq \gamma(t)$ for all $n \in \mathbb{N}$. On the other hand, η is right upper semi-continuous, hence it is right upper semi-continuous at $\gamma(t) \in \mathbb{R}_+$. Applying Theorem 2 (2), it follows that

$$\limsup_{n \to \infty} \eta(\gamma(t_n)) \leq \eta(\gamma(t)). \tag{5}$$

Taking into account Theorem 4, from the relation (5) we deduce that there exists a number $n_0 \in \mathbb{N}$ such that

$$\eta(\gamma(t_n)) \leq \eta(\gamma(t)) \text{ for all } n \geq n_0. \tag{6}$$

From the relation (6) we obtain

$$\{s \in \mathbb{R}_+ \mid \gamma(s) \leq \eta(\gamma(t_n))\} \subseteq \{s \in \mathbb{R}_+ \mid \gamma(s) \leq \eta(\gamma(t))\} \text{ for all } n \geq n_0,$$

hence

$$\sup\{s \in \mathbb{R}_+ \mid \gamma(s) \leq \eta(\gamma(t_n))\} \leq \sup\{s \in \mathbb{R}_+ \mid \gamma(s) \leq \eta(\gamma(t))\} \text{ for all } n \geq n_0,$$

and considering the definition of the function μ (the relation (2)) we find

$$\mu(t_n) \leq \mu(t) \text{ for all } n \geq n_0. \tag{7}$$

Using Theorem 4, the inequality (7) implies

$$\limsup_{n \to \infty} \mu(t_n) \leq \mu(t). \tag{8}$$

Since the sequence $(t_n)_{n \in \mathbb{N}} \subseteq \mathbb{R}_+$ satisfying $t_n \to t$ as $n \to \infty$, $t_n \geq t$ for all $n \in \mathbb{N}$, was chosen arbitrarily, from the inequality (8), by using Theorem 2 (2), it results that μ is right upper semi-continuous at $t \in \mathbb{R}_+$. Because the point $t \in \mathbb{R}_+$ was arbitrarily selected, we deduce that μ is right upper semi-continuous. □

Lemma 3. *Let $\eta : \mathbb{R}_+^5 \to \mathbb{R}_+$ be a function under the following hypothesis:*
1. *$t \to \eta(t, t, t, t, t) \in \mathbb{R}_+$ is increasing and right upper semi-continuous;*
2. *$\eta(t_1, t_2, t_3, t_4, t_5) < \max\{t_1, t_2, t_3, t_4, t_5\}$, for all $(t_1, t_2, t_3, t_4, t_5) \in \mathbb{R}_+^5 \setminus \{(0,0,0,0,0)\}$;*
3. *η is increasing with respect to each variable*

and a function $\gamma \in \Gamma$. We define the functions $\mu : \mathbb{R}_+^5 \to \mathbb{R}_+$ and $\alpha : \mathbb{R}_+ \to \mathbb{R}_+$ by

$$\mu(t_1, t_2, t_3, t_4, t_5) = \sup\{s \in \mathbb{R}_+ \mid \gamma(s) \leq \eta(\gamma(t_1), \gamma(t_2), \gamma(t_3), \gamma(t_4), \gamma(t_5))\} \tag{9}$$

and

$$\alpha(t) := \mu(t, t, t, t, t). \tag{10}$$

Then, the following statements are true:
(i) *μ is well defined and increasing with respect to each variable;*
(ii) *α is well defined and increasing;*
(iii) *$\alpha(t) < t$ for all $t > 0$;*
(iv) *α is right upper semicontinuous;*
(v) *for every $t > 0$, the iterates sequence $\{\alpha^n(t)\}_{n \in \mathbb{N}}$ converges to zero as $n \to \infty$;*
(vi) *μ is a comparison function.*

Proof.
(i) For every $(t_1, t_2, t_3, t_4, t_5) \in \mathbb{R}_+^5$ we define the set

$$A_{(t_1, t_2, t_3, t_4, t_5)} := \{s \in \mathbb{R}_+ \mid \gamma(s) \leq \eta(\gamma(t_1), \gamma(t_2), \gamma(t_3), \gamma(t_4), \gamma(t_5))\}. \tag{11}$$

Since $\gamma(0) = 0$ and $\eta(\gamma(t_1), \gamma(t_2), \gamma(t_3), \gamma(t_4), \gamma(t_5)) \in \mathbb{R}_+$, we obtain that

$$\gamma(0) \leq \eta(\gamma(t_1), \gamma(t_2), \gamma(t_3), \gamma(t_4), \gamma(t_5)),$$

hence $0 \in A_{(t_1, t_2, t_3, t_4, t_5)}$ and thus $A_{(t_1, t_2, t_3, t_4, t_5)}$ is a non-empty set. On the other hand the hypothesis (1) leads us to the fact that α is increasing on $\mathbb{R}_+$ and taking into account that $\alpha(\mathbb{R}_+) \subseteq \mathbb{R}_+$ one has $\alpha(0) = \mu(0,0,0,0,0) = 0$. Further, let us consider $(t_1, t_2, t_3, t_4, t_5) \in \mathbb{R}_+^5$. Then, for every $s \in A_{(t_1, t_2, t_3, t_4, t_5)}$, we have

$$\gamma(s) \leq \eta(\gamma(t_1), \gamma(t_2), \gamma(t_3), \gamma(t_4), \gamma(t_5)) \leq \max\{\gamma(t_1), \gamma(t_2), \gamma(t_3), \gamma(t_4), \gamma(t_5)\}.$$

Therefore, there exists $i_0 \in \{1,2,3,4,5\}$ such that $s \leq t_{i_0} \leq \max\{t_1, t_2, t_3, t_4, t_5\}$. Thus,
$$A_{(t_1,t_2,t_3,t_4,t_5)} \subseteq [0, \max\{t_1, t_2, t_3, t_4, t_5\})$$
and consequently
$$\mu(t_1, t_2, t_3, t_4, t_5) \leq \max\{t_1, t_2, t_3, t_4, t_5\}.$$
From here, we find that $\alpha(t) \leq t$ for each $t \geq 0$. Finally, by using the hypothesis (3) and definition of $A_{(t_1,t_2,t_3,t_4,t_5)}$, we find that μ is increasing with respect to each variable.

(ii) It follows from (i).

(iii) Let us assume that there is $t_0 > 0$ in order that
$$t_0 = \alpha(t_0) = \mu(t_0, t_0, t_0, t_0, t_0) = \sup A_{(t_0,t_0,t_0,t_0,t_0)}.$$
Then, there exists a sequence $\{s_n\}_{n \in \mathbb{N}} \subseteq A_{(t_0,t_0,t_0,t_0,t_0)}$ such that $s_n \nearrow \alpha(t_0)$ as $n \to \infty$. Therefore, for all $n \in \mathbb{N}$, we have that $\gamma(s_n) \leq \eta(\gamma(t_0), \gamma(t_0), \gamma(t_0), \gamma(t_0), \gamma(t_0))$ and taking into consideration that γ is continuous, we find that
$$\gamma(t_0) = \gamma(\alpha(t_0)) \leq \eta(\gamma(t_0), \gamma(t_0), \gamma(t_0), \gamma(t_0), \gamma(t_0)) < \gamma(t_0),$$
which is a contradiction.

(iv) Let us consider $t \in \mathbb{R}_+$ and $\{t_n\}_{n \in \mathbb{N}} \subseteq \mathbb{R}_+$ such that $t_n \searrow t$ as $n \to \infty$. Then $\gamma(t_n) \searrow \gamma(t)$ as $n \to \infty$ and by considering the hypothesis (1) we find that
$$\limsup_{n \to \infty} \eta(\gamma(t_n), \gamma(t_n), \gamma(t_n), \gamma(t_n), \gamma(t_n)) \leq \eta(\gamma(t), \gamma(t), \gamma(t), \gamma(t), \gamma(t)).$$
From here, by using Theorem 4, we deduce that there exists a number $n_0 \in \mathbb{N}$ such that
$$\eta(\gamma(t_n), \gamma(t_n), \gamma(t_n), \gamma(t_n), \gamma(t_n)) \leq \eta(\gamma(t), \gamma(t), \gamma(t), \gamma(t), \gamma(t))$$
for all $n \geq n_0$. Hence,
$$A_{(t_n,t_n,t_n,t_n,t_n)} \subseteq A_{(t,t,t,t,t)},$$
which implies that
$$\alpha(t_n) = \mu(t_n, t_n, t_n, t_n, t_n) \leq \mu(t, t, t, t, t) = \alpha(t),$$
for all $n \geq n_0$. By passing to the limit as $n \to \infty$ one has that
$$\limsup_{n \to \infty} \alpha(t_n) \leq \alpha(t),$$
i.e., that α is right upper semi-continuous on $\mathbb{R}_+$.

(v) From (ii) and (iii), we obtain
$$0 \leq \alpha^{n+1}(t) \leq \alpha^n(t) \leq \alpha(t),$$
for all $t > 0$. Then, there is $l \geq 0$ in order that $\alpha^n(t) \searrow l$ as $n \to \infty$. If $l > 0$, then from (iii) and (iv), we find that $l = \alpha(l) < l$, which is a contradiction. Thus, $l = 0$.

(vi) By taking into consideration (i) and (v), we find that the function μ fulfills the Definition 2 i.e., it is a comparison function. □

Example 2. Let us consider $\eta : \mathbb{R}_+ \to \mathbb{R}_+$ defined:
$$\eta(t) = \begin{cases} \frac{t}{t+1}, & t \in [0, 1] \\ \frac{t}{2 \cdot t+1}, & t \in (1, \infty). \end{cases}$$
Then,

(i) η verifies the condition of Lemma 2;
(ii) η is not right continuous at $t = 1$;
(iii) for every $\alpha \in (0,1)$ there exists $t_0 > 0$ such that $\alpha \cdot t_0 < \eta(t_0)$.

Proof.
(i) It is obvious that $\eta(0) = 0$ and $\eta(t) < t$ for each $t > 0$. On the other hand, we observe that for every $\varepsilon > 0$ we have $\eta(t) \leq \eta(1) + \varepsilon$ for each $t \in (1, \infty)$. Thus, η is right upper semicontinuous.
(ii) Since $\lim_{t \searrow 1} \eta(t) = \frac{1}{3} \neq \frac{1}{2} = \eta(1)$, it follows that η is not right continuous at $t = 1$.
(iii) Let us consider $\alpha \in (0,1)$. We distinguish the following cases:
Case 1: $\alpha \geq \frac{1}{2}$. Then, there exists $0 < t_0 < \frac{1-\alpha}{\alpha} \leq 1$ such that $\alpha \cdot t_0 < \eta(t_0)$.
Case 2: $\alpha < \frac{1}{3}$. Then, there exists $1 < t_0 < \frac{1-\alpha}{2 \cdot \alpha}$ such that $\alpha \cdot t_0 < \eta(t_0)$.
Case 3: $\frac{1}{3} \leq \alpha < \frac{1}{2}$. Then, there exists $1 < t_0$ such that $\alpha \cdot t_0 < \eta(t_0)$.
□

We aim to analyze the existence and uniqueness of fixed points for operators described on spaces endowed with such altering metrics. In the following part, we set up some fixed point results on spaces with altering metrics.

Theorem 7. *Let $\gamma \in \Gamma$ and $\eta : \mathbb{R}_+ \to \mathbb{R}_+$ be such that:*
(1) $\eta(0) = 0$;
(2) η is right upper semi-continuous;
(3) $\eta(t) < t$ for all $t > 0$.

If (X,d) is a complete metric space and $T : X \to X$ is an operator such that:

$$\gamma(d(T(x), T(y))) \leq \eta(\gamma(d(x,y))), \; \forall x, y \in X, \tag{12}$$

then the following statements are true:
(i) $\mu(0) = 0$, μ is right upper semi-continuous and $\mu(t) < t$ for all $t > 0$, where the function $\mu : \mathbb{R}_+ \to \mathbb{R}_+$ is defined by the relation (2);
(ii) *T verifies the inequality*

$$d(T(x), T(y)) \leq \mu(d(x,y)), \; \forall x, y \in X. \tag{13}$$

(iii) *T has a unique fixed point $x^* \in X$ and the sequence $T^m(x_0) \to x^*$ as $m \to \infty$, for any arbitrary point $x_0 \in X$.*

Proof.
(i) We notice that the functions η, γ satisfy the hypotheses of Lemma 2. It results that, we can take into consideration the function $\mu : \mathbb{R}_+ \to \mathbb{R}_+$ defined by the relation (2), which has the properties: $\mu(0) = 0$ (by Lemma 2 (ii)), μ is right upper semicontinuous (in accordance with Lemma 2 (vii)) and $\mu(t) < t$ for all $t > 0$ (by Lemma 2 (v)).
(ii) Let $x, y \in X$ be arbitrary elements. Considering that the operator $T : X \to X$ fulfills the inequality (12), we obtain

$$d(T(x), T(y)) \in \{s \in \mathbb{R}_+ \mid \gamma(s) \leq \eta(\gamma(d(x,y)))\},$$

hence,

$$d(T(x), T(y)) \leq \sup\{s \in \mathbb{R}_+ \mid \gamma(s) \leq \eta(\gamma(d(x,y)))\} = \mu(d(x,y)).$$

As the elements $x, y \in X$ are chosen arbitrarily, from the previous relation we deduce that T verifies the inequality (13).
(iii) $\mu : \mathbb{R}_+ \to \mathbb{R}_+$ is right upper semi-continuous (by (i)), $\mu(t) < t$ for all $t > 0$ (from (i)), (X, d) is a complete metric space (in accordance with the hypothesis) and $T : X \to X$

is an operator verifying the inequality (13) (by (ii)). Applying Theorem 5, we find that T has a unique fixed point $x^* \in X$ and the sequence $T^m(x_0) \to x^*$ as $m \to \infty$, for any arbitrary point $x_0 \in X$. □

Theorem 8. *Let us consider $\eta : \mathbb{R}_+^5 \to \mathbb{R}_+$, $\gamma \in \Gamma$ under hypothesis of Lemma 3, (X, d) a complete metric space and $T : X \to X$ an operator such that:*

$$\gamma(d(T(x), T(y))) \leq \eta(\gamma(d(x,y)), \gamma(d(x, T(x))), \gamma(d(y, T(y))), \gamma(d(x, T(y))), \gamma(d(y, T(x))))$$,

$\forall x, y \in X$. Then:

(i) *T verifies the inequality*

$$d(T(x), T(y)) \leq \mu(d(x,y), d(x, T(x)), d(y, T(y)), d(x, T(y)), d(y, T(x))), \forall x, y \in X,$$

where the function $\mu : \mathbb{R}_+ \to \mathbb{R}_+$ is defined by the relation (9) from Lemma 3.

(ii) *T has a unique fixed point $x^* \in X$ and the sequence $T^m(x_0) \to x^*$ as $m \to \infty$, for any arbitrary point $x_0 \in X$.*

Proof.

(i) Let $x, y \in X$ be arbitrary elements. Then, for all $x, y \in X$ we have that

$$d(T(x), T(y)) \in$$

$$\{s \in \mathbb{R}_+ \mid \gamma(s) \leq \eta(\gamma(d(x,y)), \gamma(d(x, T(x))), \gamma(d(y, T(y))), \gamma(d(x, T(y))), \gamma(d(y, T(x))))\},$$

hence,

$$d(T(x), T(y)) \leq$$

$$\sup\{s \in \mathbb{R}_+ \mid \gamma(s) \leq \eta(\gamma(d(x,y)), \gamma(d(x, T(x))), \gamma(d(y, T(y))), \gamma(d(x, T(y))), \gamma(d(y, T(x))))\}$$

$$= \mu(d(x,y), d(x, T(x)), d(y, T(y)), d(x, T(y)), d(y, T(x))).$$

(ii) From Lemma 3 (vi), we have that μ defined by Equation (9) is a comparison function. Now, the conclusion follows by taking into account (i) and by applying Theorem 6 to operator T. □

Corollary 1. *Let (X, d) be a complete metric space $\gamma \in \Gamma$, $a, b, c \in \mathbb{R}_+$, $a + b + c < 1$ and $T : X \to X$ be an operator such that:*

$$\gamma(d(T(x), T(y))) \leq a \cdot \gamma(d(x,y)) + b \cdot \gamma(d(x, T(x))) + c \cdot \gamma(d(y, T(y))),$$

for all $x, y \in X$. Then, T has a unique fixed point $x^* \in X$ and the sequence $T^m(x_0) \to x^*$ as $m \to \infty$, for any arbitrary point $x_0 \in X$.

Proof. Let us consider $\eta : \mathbb{R}_+^5 \to \mathbb{R}_+$ defined by

$$\eta(t_1, t_2, t_3, t_4, t_5) = a \cdot t_1 + b \cdot t_2 + c \cdot t_3.$$

We remark that η fulfills the conditions from Theorem 8 and the conclusion follows from it. □

Corollary 2. *Let (X, d) be a complete metric space, $\gamma \in \Gamma$, $a, b, c : \mathbb{R}_+ \setminus \{0\} \to \mathbb{R}_+$ and $T : X \to X$ be an operator such that:*

(1) *a, b, c are increasing;*
(2) *$a(t) + 2 \cdot b(t) + c(t) < 1$ for every $t > 0$;*
(3) *the function $t \to a(t) + 2 \cdot b(t) + c(t) \in \mathbb{R}_+$ is right upper semi-continuous;*

(4) for all $x, y \in X$, $x \neq y$ we have:

$$\gamma(d(T(x), T(y))) \leq$$
$$a(d(x,y)) \cdot \gamma((d(x,y)) + b(d(x,y)) \cdot \{\gamma(d(x, T(x))) + \gamma(d(y, T(y)))\} +$$
$$c(d(x,y)) \cdot \min\{\gamma(d(x, T(y))), \gamma(d(y, T(x)))\}.$$

Then, T has a unique fixed point $x^* \in X$ and the sequence $T^m(x_0) \to x^*$ as $m \to \infty$, for any arbitrary point $x_0 \in X$.

Proof. Let us consider $\eta : \mathbb{R}_+^5 \to \mathbb{R}_+$ described by:

$$\eta(t_1, t_2, t_3, t_4, t_5) = a(t_1) \cdot t_1 + b(t_1) \cdot (t_2 + t_3) + c(t_1) \cdot \min\{t_4, t_5\}.$$

We remark that η fulfills the conditions from Theorem 8 and the conclusion follows from it. □

Further, Theorem 7 will be applied to continuous data dependence of the fixed points of Picard operators defined on spaces with altering metrics.

Let us consider a function $\mu : \mathbb{R}_+ \to \mathbb{R}_+$ satisfying the conditions: $\mu(0) = 0$, μ is right upper semi-continuous and $\mu(t) < t$ for all $t > 0$. According with [21], if

$$s - \mu(s) \to \infty \text{ as } s \to \infty, \tag{14}$$

we can define the function

$$\theta_\mu : \mathbb{R}_+ \to \mathbb{R}_+, \; \theta_\mu(t) = \sup\{s \in \mathbb{R}_+ \mid s - \mu(s) \leq t\}. \tag{15}$$

We notice that θ_μ is monotonically increasing and $\theta_\mu(t) \to 0$ as $t \to 0$. The function θ_μ appears when we analyze the data dependence of the fixed points.

Theorem 9. *Let $\gamma \in \Gamma$ and $\eta : \mathbb{R}_+ \to \mathbb{R}_+$ under the following hypothesis:*
(1) $\eta(0) = 0$;
(2) η is right upper semi-continuous;
(3) $\eta(t) < t$ for all $t > 0$.
If (X, d) is a complete metric space and $T : X \to X$ is an operator such that:

$$\gamma(d(T(x), T(y))) \leq \eta(\gamma(d(x,y))), \; \forall x, y \in X, \tag{16}$$

then the statements are true:
(i) *T has a unique fixed point $x^* \in X$;*
(ii) *$d(x, x^*) \leq \theta_\mu(d(x, T(x)))$, $\forall x \in X$;*
(iii) *if $\{y_n\}_{n \in \mathbb{N}}$ is a sequence in X such that $d(y_n, T(y_n)) \to 0$ as $n \to \infty$ then $y_n \to x^*$ as $n \to \infty$, i.e., T has the Ostrowski property;*
(iv) *if the function $\mu : \mathbb{R}_+ \to \mathbb{R}_+$ described by the relation (2) satisfies the hypothesis (14) and $U : X \to X$ is an operator verifying the conditions:*
   (a) *F_U, the fixed point set of operator U is not empty,*
   (b) *there is $\eta > 0$ in order that $d(U(x), T(x)) \leq \eta$, $\forall x \in X$,*
then $d(y^*, x^*) \leq \theta_\mu(\eta)$, $\forall y^* \in F_U$.

Proof. We notice that the hypotheses of Theorem 7 are satisfied.
(i) Applying Theorem 7 (iii), we obtain that T has a unique fixed point $x^* \in X$.
(ii) By using Theorem 7 (ii), we obtain that T verifies the inequality

$$d(T(x), T(y)) \leq \mu(d(x,y)), \; \forall x, y \in X.$$

Let us consider $x \in X$ an arbitrary selected element. Taking into account the properties of the metric d and the previous inequality we obtain

$$d(x, x^*) \leq d(x, T(x)) + d(T(x), x^*)$$
$$= d(x, T(x)) + d(T(x), T(x^*)) \leq d(x, T(x)) + \mu(d(x, x^*)),$$

hence,

$$d(x, x^*) - \mu(d(x, x^*)) \leq d(x, T(x)),$$

thus,

$$d(x, x^*) \in \{s \in \mathbb{R}_+ \mid s - \mu(s) \leq d(x, T(x))\}.$$

Considering the definition of the function θ_μ (by relation (15)), from the previous relation we deduce

$$d(x, x^*) \leq \sup\{s \in \mathbb{R}_+ \mid s - \mu(s) \leq d(x, T(x))\} = \theta_\mu(d(x, T(x))).$$

(iii) Let us consider $\{y_n\}_{n \in \mathbb{N}}$ a sequence in X such that $d(y_n, f(y_n)) \to 0$ as $n \to \infty$. Taking into account (ii) one has $d(y_n, x^*) \leq \theta_\mu(d(y_n, f(y_n))) \to 0$ as $n \to \infty$ and thus $y_n \to x^*$ as $n \to \infty$.

(iv) Let us consider $y^* \in F_U$ an arbitrary-selected fixed point of the operator U. From (ii), using the condition (b) and the fact that θ_μ is monotonically increasing, it results that

$$d(y^*, x^*) \leq \theta_\mu(d(y^*, T(y^*))) = \theta_\mu(d(U(y^*), T(y^*))) \leq \theta_\mu(\eta).$$

□

The following examples represent applications of our main results (Theorems 7 and 8) to the existence and uniqueness of fixed point for certain operators.

Example 3. *Let us consider $\gamma, \eta : \mathbb{R}_+ \to \mathbb{R}_+$ defined as in Example 1, respectively, Example 2 and the integral equation*

$$x(t) = \int_0^t K(t, s, x(s))ds + g(t), \ t \in [0, 1], \quad (17)$$

under the following conditions:

(H_0) $K \in C([0,1] \times [0,1] \times \mathbb{R}, \mathbb{R})$, $g \in C([0,1], \mathbb{R})$;
(H_1) $|K(t, s, u) - K(t, s, v)|^4 \leq \eta(|u-v|^4)$ for all $t, s \in [0, 1]$ and $u, v \in \mathbb{R}$.

Then, the Equation (17) has a unique solution in $C([0, 1], \mathbb{R})$ (the class of continuous functions $x : [0, 1] \to \mathbb{R}$).

Proof. Let us consider $C([0, 1], \mathbb{R})$ endowed with $\|x\|_\infty = \sup\limits_{t \in [0,1]} |x(t)|$, and let

$$T : C([0, 1], \mathbb{R}) \to C([0, 1], \mathbb{R}),$$

defined by

$$Tx(t) = \int_0^t K(t, s, x(s))ds + g(t).$$

Then, for each $x, y \in C([0, 1], \mathbb{R})$ and $t \in [0, 1]$, we have

$$\gamma(|Tx(t) - Ty(t)|) = |Tx(t) - Ty(t)|^4 \leq$$

$$\left(\int_0^t |K(t,s.x(s)) - K(t,s,y(s))|ds\right)^4 \leq \int_0^t |K(t,s.x(s)) - K(t,s,y(s))|^4 ds \leq$$

$$\int_0^t \eta(|x(s)-y(s)|^4)ds \leq \eta(\|x-y\|_\infty^4) = \eta(\gamma(\|x-y\|_\infty)).$$

Since γ is increasing, we find that $\gamma(\|Tx - Ty\|_\infty) \leq \eta(\gamma(\|x-y\|_\infty))$ for each $x,y \in C([0,1], \mathbb{R})$ The conclusion now follows from Theorem 7 applied to operator T. □

Example 4. *Let us consider*
(a) $X = \{1, 2, 3, 4\}$ *and* $d : X \times X \to \mathbb{R}_+$ *described by:*

$$d(1,1) = d(2,2) = d(3,3) = d(4,4) = 0,$$

$$d(1,2) = d(2,1) = \frac{2}{6}, \; d(1,3) = d(3,1) = \frac{1}{6}, \; d(1,4) = d(4,1) = \frac{4}{6},$$

$$d(2,3) = d(3,2) = \frac{2}{6}, \; d(2,4) = d(4,2) = 1, \; d(3,4) = d(4,3) = \frac{\sqrt{2}}{2};$$

(b) $T : X \to X$ *described by:*

$$T(1) = T(3) = T(4) = 1, \; T(2) = 4.$$

Then, T has a unique fixed point.

Proof. It results from Corollary 1 applied for $\gamma : \mathbb{R}_+ \to \mathbb{R}_+$, $\gamma(t) = t^2$ and $\eta : \mathbb{R}_+^5 \to \mathbb{R}_+$, $\eta(t_1, t_2, t_3, t_4, t_5) = \frac{1}{36} \cdot t_1 + \frac{1}{2} \cdot t_2 + \frac{4}{9} \cdot t_3$. □

4. Conclusions

In this paper, we have extended the results from [14] by considering for an operator $T : X \to X$ a general contractive condition. First, we proved that for a given control function $\gamma : \mathbb{R}_+ \to \mathbb{R}_+$ and a contractive condition of type

$$\gamma(d(T(x), T(y))) \leq \eta(\gamma(d(x,y))), \forall x,y \in X,$$

we can build a function $\mu : \mathbb{R}_+ \to \mathbb{R}_+$ such that

$$d(T(x), T(y)) \leq \mu(d(x,y)), \forall x,y \in X.$$

Further, we built Example 2, where we gave an example of function $\eta : \mathbb{R}_+ \to \mathbb{R}_+$, which satisfies Lemma 2, but does not satisfy the setup from [14]. Next, we provided an existence and uniqueness result and a data dependence result for fixed point of operator T and we showed additionally that it has the Ostrowski property. The paper is completed by Example 3 as an application of Theorem 7 to an integral equation. Next, we considered a more general contractive condition of type

$$\gamma(d(T(x), T(y))) \leq \eta(\gamma(d(x,y)), \gamma(d(x, T(x))), \gamma(d(y, T(y))), \gamma(d(x, T(y))), \gamma(d(y, T(x)))),$$

$\forall x,y \in X$. Corollary 1 showed us that Theorem 1 from [3] is obtained as a particular case of Theorem 8, and additionally we obtained in Corollary 2 a similar result as in Theorem 2 from [3], but imposing different condition to the functions a,b,c. Moreover, for $\gamma(t) = t$ in Theorem 7 we get Theorem 5. As future research direction we would like to point the following ones:

- To extend the main results to common fixed point theory;

- To generalize the above results to the setup of general metric spaces, e.g., fuzzy, orthogonal or partially ordered metric spaces.

Author Contributions: Conceptualization, I.M.O. and A.N.B.; methodology, I.M.O. and A.N.B.; formal analysis, I.M.O. and A.N.B.; writing—original draft preparation, I.M.O. and A.N.B.; writing—review and editing, I.M.O. and A.N.B.; funding acquisition, I.M.O. and A.N.B. All authors have read and agreed to the published version of the manuscript.

Funding: Project financed by Lucian Blaga University of Sibiu through the research grant LBUS-IRG-2022-08.

Data Availability Statement: Not applicable.

Acknowledgments: The authors thank the anonymous reviewers for their valuable comments and suggestions which helped us to improve the content of this paper.

Conflicts of Interest: The authors declare no conflict of interest.

References

1. Delbosco, D. Un'estensione di un teorema sul punto fisso di S. Reich. *Rend. Sem. Mat. Univers. Politean. Torino* **1977**, *35*, 233–238.
2. Skof, F. Teorema di punti fisso per applicazioni negli spazi metrici. *Atti. Accad. Aci. Torino* **1977**, *111*, 323–329.
3. Khan, M.S.; Swalesh, M.; Sessa, S. Fixed point theorems by altering distances between the points. *Bull. Aust. Math. Soc.* **1984**, *30*, 323–326. [CrossRef]
4. Morales, J.R.; Rojas, E. Some fixed point theorems by altering distance functions. *Palest. J. Math.* **2012**, *1*, 110–116.
5. Akkouchi, M. Common fixed point theorems by altering the distances between the points in bounded complete metric spaces. *Demonstr. Math.* **2000**, *33*, 843–850. [CrossRef]
6. Pant, R.P.; Jha, K.; Lohani, A.B. A note on common fixed points by altering distances. *Tamkang J. Math.* **2003**, *34*, 59–62. [CrossRef]
7. Pant, R.P.; Jha, K.; Pande, V.P. Common fixed point for by altering distances between points. *Bull. Cal. Math. Soc.* **2003**, *95*, 421–428. [CrossRef]
8. Pant, R.P.; Jha, K.; Padaliya, S. On common fixed point by altering distances between the points. *Tamkang J. Math.* **2003**, *34*, 239–243. [CrossRef]
9. Sastry, K.P.R.; Naidu, S.V.R.; Babu, G.V.R.; Naidu, G.A. Generalization of common fixed point theorems for weakly commuting maps by altering distances. *Tamkang J. Math.* **2000**, *31*, 243–250. [CrossRef]
10. Masmali, I.; Dalal, S.; Rehman, N. Fixed Point Results by Altering Distances in Fuzzy Metric Spaces. *Adv. Pure Math.* **2015**, *5*, 377–382. [CrossRef]
11. Gungor, N.B. Some Fixed Point Theorems on Orthogonal Metric Spaces via Extensions of Orthogonal Contractions. *Commun. Fac. Sci. Univ. Ank. Ser. A1 Math. Stat.* **2022**, *71*, 481–489. [CrossRef]
12. Gupta, V.; Jungck, G.; Mani, N. Some novel fixed point theorems in partially ordered metric spaces. *AIMS Math.* **2020**, *5*, 4444–4452. [CrossRef]
13. Al-Khaleel, M.; Al-Sharif, S. Cyclical Nonlinear Contractive Mappings Fixed Point Theorems with Application to Integral Equations. *TWMS J. App. Eng. Math.* **2022**, *12*, 224–234.
14. Branga, A.N.; Olaru, I.M. Some Fixed Point Results in Spaces with Perturbed Metrics. *Carpathian J. Math.* **2022**, *38*, 641–654. [CrossRef]
15. Jha, K.; Pant, R.P.; Thapa, P. Some fixed points results by altering distances between points. *Kathmandu Univ. J. Sci. Eng. Technol.* **2010**, *6*, 123–134. [CrossRef]
16. Rezapour, S.; Deressa, C.T.; Hussain, A.; Etemad, S.; George, R.; Ahmad, B. A Theoretical Analysis of a Fractional Multi-Dimensional System of Boundary Value Problems on the Methylpropane Graph via Fixed Point Technique. *Mathematics* **2022**, *10*, 568. [CrossRef]
17. Khan, Z.A.; Ahmad, I.; Shah, K. Applications of Fixed Point Theory to Investigate a System of Fractional Order Differential Equations. *J. Funct. Spaces* **2021**, *2021*, 1399764. [CrossRef]
18. Turab, A.; Mlaiki, N.; Fatima, N.; Mitrović, Z.D.; Ali, W. Analysis of a Class of Stochastic Animal Behavior Models under Specific Choice Preferences. *Mathematics* **2022**, *10*, 1975. [CrossRef]
19. Royden, H.L.; Fitzpatrick, P.M. *Real Analysis*; China Machine Press: Beijing, China, 2009.
20. Boyd, D.W.; Wong, J.S.W. On nonlinear contractions. *Proc. Am. Math. Soc.* **1969**, *20*, 458–464. [CrossRef]
21. Rus, I.A. *Generalized Contractions and Applications*; Cluj University Press: Cluj-Napoca, Romania, 2001.

Article

Study of Fractional Differential Equations Emerging in the Theory of Chemical Graphs: A Robust Approach

Ali Turab [1] and Norhayati Rosli [2,*]

[1] Centre of Excellence for Artificial Intelligence & Data Science, Universiti Malaysia Pahang, Lebuhraya Tun Razak, Gambang, Kuantan 26300, Pahang, Malaysia
[2] Centre for Mathematical Sciences, Universiti Malaysia Pahang, Lebuhraya Tun Razak, Gambang, Kuantan 26300, Pahang, Malaysia
* Correspondence: norhayati@ump.edu.my

Abstract: The study of the interconnections between chemical systems is known as chemical graph theory. Through the use of star graphs, a limited group of researchers has examined the space of possible solutions for boundary-value problems. They recognized that for their strategy to function, they needed a core node related to other nodes but not to itself; as a result, they opted to use star graphs. In this sense, the graphs of neopentane will be helpful in extending the scope of our technique. It has the CAS number 463-82-1 and the chemical formula C_5H_{12}, and it is a component of a petrochemical precursor. In order to determine whether or not the suggested boundary-value problems on these graphs have any known solutions, we use the theorems developed by Schaefer and Krasnoselskii on fixed points. In addition, we illustrate our preliminary results with the help of an example that we present.

Keywords: fractional calculus; chemical graph theory; neopentane graph; fixed points

MSC: 26A33; 47H10; 05C90

1. Introduction

Mathematical applications have proliferated in the twenty-first century. When quantum chemistry emerged in the 1920s, it left a trail of several mathematical specialties chemists felt compelled to understand. These included calculus and various branches of linear algebra, including matrix and group theories. Group theory is often used in fields such as crystallography and molecular structure analysis since it has gained widespread acceptance among chemists. However, graph theory is being used in a number of fields including categorizing, systematization, enumeration, and construction of chemical interest systems.

We have reached a stage where we believe that it is appropriate to say that, due to the applications of mathematics that have been developed in the chemical world, mathematics plays an essential role in contemporary chemistry. We believe that the era of the 1990s represents a precious time to present excessive applications of the varied directions of mathematics to chemistry. In order to distinguish the subject that is concerned with the unique and challenging application of mathematics to chemistry, the phrase "mathematical chemistry" was first used in the early 1980s. As is customary in this field, we can broadly define chemistry to cover the classic areas of inorganic, organic, and physical chemistry and its hybrid descendants, including chemical physics and biochemistry.

The contemporary landscape of chemical theory is primarily built around fundamentally graph-theoretical premises. Today, all of the main fields of chemistry employ chemical graphs for various reasons. The history of the first implicit use of the graph theory is of significant relevance given the current extensive use of the chemical graph. The second part of the eighteenth century saw the invention of chemical diagrams. It will be essential to discuss the dominant viewpoints in nineteenth-century chemistry to comprehend their necessity at the time and the conditions of their entrance into the chemical literature.

The Scottish scientist William Cullen designed the first chemical graphs that were easily identifiable as such. To illustrate the alleged forces that exist between pairs of molecules undergoing different chemical reactions, Cullen began using so-called "affinity diagrams" in his lectures in 1758. Sadly, none of these diagrams were ever published and they were instead just used to illustrate his chemistry lecture notes (see [1]). Similar images to Cullen's were subsequently posted by Black, who claimed erroneously to have originated them (see [2]); by the end of the eighteenth century, similar diagrams were prevalent in British chemistry textbooks. Figure 1 displays copies of two Cullen-attributed surviving schematics.

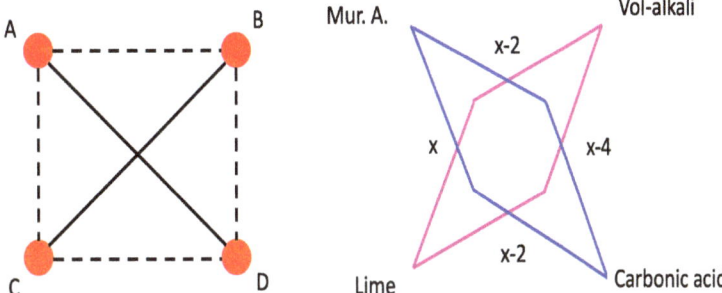

Figure 1. Examples of the earliest chemical graphs Cullen and Black developed to depict chemical interactions in 1758.

The goal of using graph theory in chemical graph theory is to characterize molecules in order to investigate their many different physical properties. A set Θ of vertices (or nodes) and a set Ξ of unordered pairings of various components of Θ that create the edges make up the components of a graph denoted by the equation $\mathbb{G} = (\Theta, \Xi)$. In chemistry, the atoms that make up a molecule are represented by the vertices of the structure, while the edges show the chemical bonds.

On the other hand, recently, there has been significant theoretical and practical progress in the area of differential equations (see, [3–9]). In the context of special functions, publications on fractional calculus focus mainly on the solution of differential equations (for detail, see [10–17]). Recently, many new articles on nonlinear fractional differential equations and their solutions employing approaches such as the Leray–Schauder theorem, stability analysis, variational iteration methods, and fixed-point theory methods have been publicly released (see [18–24] and references therein).

Lumer was the first to apply the principles of differential equation theory to graphs (for details, see [25]). He studied extended evolution equations by altering stated operators on implications spaces. In 1989, Zavgorodnij explored differential equations using a geometric net (see [26]), with the recommended solutions to boundary value problems placed at the inner vertices of the system. However, in [27], the authors used the double-sweep technique, which they discovered to be more effective on graphs, to obtain numerical solutions for differential equations.

Although only a tiny amount of work has been dedicated to the topic, using fixed point theory approaches (see [28,29]), it has been proven that solutions exist for boundary value issues involving star graphs (see Figure 2). One can see the most up-to-date research in this area in which the authors use different types of graphs (i.e., ethane [30,31], glucose [32], methylpropane [33], hexasilinane [34], cyclohexane [35], octane [36], etc.) and defined the differential equations on their edges.

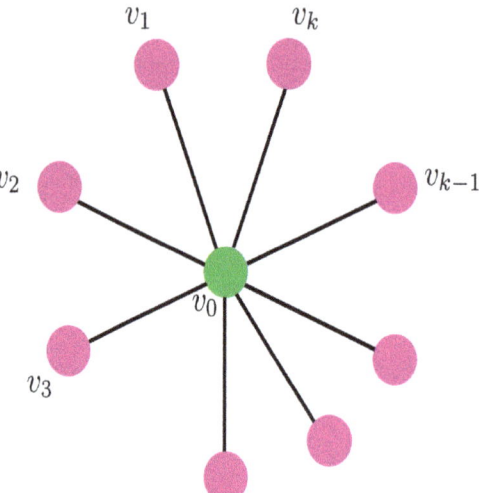

Figure 2. An illustration of the star graph.

Neopentane graphs, which are more pliable than star graphs, were used here to broaden this problem by utilizing the notion of neopentane graphs (see Figure 3).

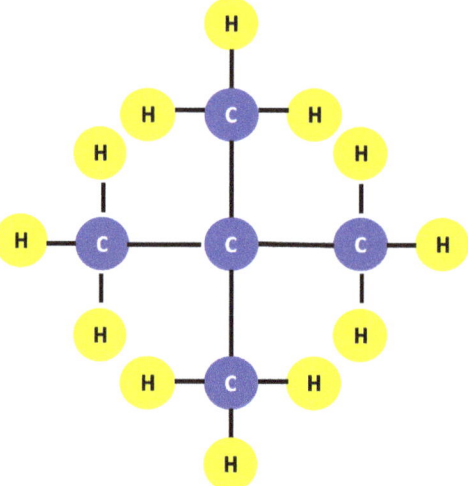

Figure 3. An illustration of a neopentane molecule C_5H_{12} framework.

Furthermore, the methods used in [28,29] are insufficient since, as compared to the star graph, neopentane graphs have several junction points. As a robust approach, we use an alternative method in which we assign integer values (0 or 1) to the vertices and edge lengths $|\tilde{b}_\tau| = 1$ of the last graph (see Figure 4).

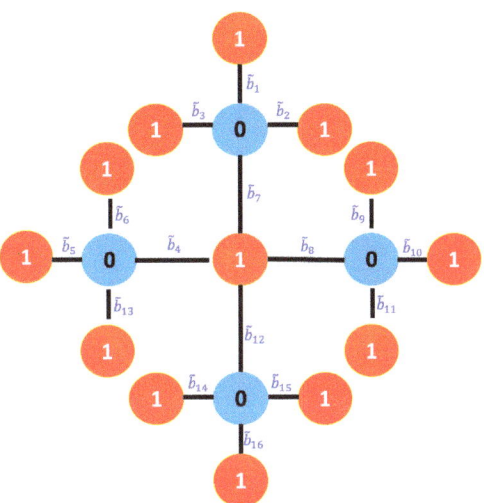

Figure 4. Neopentane compound graph with vertices 0 or 1.

By utilizing the above idea, here, we consider the following system, which is stated for each $\tau = 1, 2, \ldots, 25$ by

$$\begin{cases} \mathfrak{D}^r z_\tau(s) = \mathcal{W}_\tau(s, z_\tau(s), \mathfrak{D}^q z_\tau(s), z'_\tau(s)) & (s \in [0,1]), \\ z_\tau(0) = \mathfrak{D}^{r-1} z_\tau(1), \quad \ell_1 z'_\tau(0) + \ell_2 z'_\tau(1) = \ell_3 \int_0^a \mathfrak{D}^{r-1} z_\tau(\theta) d\theta, \end{cases} \quad (1)$$

where $z_\tau : [0,1] \to \infty$ is an unknown function, $\ell_k (k = 1, 2, 3) \in \mathbb{R}$ with $\ell_k \neq 0$, $a \in (0,1)$, $\mathfrak{D}^r$ and $\mathfrak{D}^q$ are the Caputo fractional derivative of orders $1 < r \leq 2$ and $q \in (0,1)$, respectively. Moreover, $\mathcal{W}_\tau : [0,1] \times \mathbb{R} \times \mathbb{R} \times \mathbb{R} \to \mathbb{R}$ is a given continuously differentiable function, where $\tau = 16$ is the neopentane graph's vertex count with $|\tilde{b}_\tau| = 1$.

We want to apply relevant fixed point theorems to establish the existence of workable solutions to the Problem (1) at hand. Finally, we show how our findings fit into the larger body of literature by providing a concrete example.

2. Preliminaries

We shall need the following results in the next sections.

Definition 1 ([37])**.** *Let $\hbar > 0$. The fractional derivative of Caputo for $\mathcal{W} \in C^{\chi}[0, +\infty)$ can be defined as*

$$\mathfrak{D}^{\hbar} \mathcal{W}(s) = \frac{1}{\Gamma(\chi - \hbar)} \int_0^s (s - \theta)^{\chi - \hbar - 1} \mathcal{W}^{(\chi)}(\theta) d\theta \quad (\chi - 1 < \hbar < \chi),$$

where $\chi = [\hbar] + 1$ and $\Gamma(\cdot)$ is a gamma function.

For $\hbar > 0$, the general solution of $\mathfrak{D}^{\hbar} \mathcal{W}(\nu) = 0$ is given as

$$\mathcal{W}(\nu) = \varrho_0 + \varrho_1 \nu + \varrho_2 \nu^2 + \ldots + \varrho_{n-1} \nu^{n-1}.$$

Additionally,

$$\mathbb{I}^{\hbar} \mathfrak{D}^{\hbar} \mathcal{W}(\nu) = z(\nu) + \varrho_0 + \varrho_1 \nu + \varrho_2 \nu^2 + \ldots + \varrho_{n-1} \nu^{n-1},$$

where $\varrho_k \in \mathbb{R}, k = 0, 1, \ldots, n-1$ $(n - 1 < \hbar < n)$.

Now, we will show the proof of the following lemma, which will be used in the latter portion of the study.

Lemma 1. *Suppose that $\phi \in C([0,1], \mathbb{R})$. Then, $z^\star : [0,1] \to \mathbb{R}$ is a solution of the subsequent system*

$$\begin{cases} \mathfrak{D}^r z(s) = \phi(s) \ (s \in [0,1]), \\ z(0) = \mathfrak{D}^{r-1} z(1), \ \ell_1 z'(0) + \ell_2 z'(1) = \ell_3 \int_0^a \mathfrak{D}^{r-1} z(\theta) d\theta, \end{cases} \quad (2)$$

iff $z^\star$ is a solution for the equation stated below

$$\begin{aligned} z(s) &= \int_0^s \frac{(s-\theta)^{r-1}}{\Gamma(r)} \phi(\theta) d\theta + \int_0^1 \phi(\theta) d\theta \\ &+ \left(\frac{1}{\Gamma(3-r)} + s \right) \left[\frac{\ell_3}{A_0} \int_0^a \int_0^\theta \phi(\zeta) d\zeta d\theta - \frac{\ell_2}{A_0} \int_0^1 \frac{(1-\theta)^{r-2}}{\Gamma(r-1)} \phi(\theta) d\theta \right], \end{aligned} \quad (3)$$

where

$$A_0 = \left[\ell_1 + \ell_2 - \frac{a^{3-r}}{\Gamma(4-r)} \right].$$

Proof. Assume that $z^\star : [0,1] \to \mathbb{R}$ is a solution of (2). Thus, there are constants $d_0, d_1 \in \mathbb{R}$ such that

$$z^\star(s) = \int_0^s \frac{(s-\theta)^{r-1}}{\Gamma(r)} \phi(\theta) d\theta + d_0 + d_1 s. \quad (4)$$

We use the boundary conditions from (2) to achieve this goal. Therefore,

$$\begin{aligned} d_1 &= \frac{1}{A_0} \left[\ell_3 \int_0^a \int_0^\theta \phi(\zeta) d\zeta d\theta - \ell_2 \int_0^1 \frac{(1-\theta)^{r-2}}{\Gamma(r-1)} \phi(\theta) d\theta \right], \\ d_0 &= \int_0^1 \phi(\theta) d\theta + \frac{1}{A_0 \Gamma(3-r)} \left[\ell_3 \int_0^a \int_0^\theta \phi(\zeta) d\zeta d\theta - \ell_2 \int_0^1 \frac{(1-\theta)^{r-2}}{\Gamma(r-1)} \phi(\theta) d\theta \right]. \end{aligned}$$

A solution (3) is obtained by substituting the values of d_0, d_1 into (4). If $z^\star$ is a solution of (3), then it follows that it is also a solution of (2). □

The Schaefer and Krasnoselskii fixed point theorems are now provided.

Theorem 1 ([38]). *Let $\mathcal{Y}$ be a Banach space. If $\mathcal{A}$ is completely continuous, then either $\mathcal{A}$ has at least one fixed point or $\{z \in \mathcal{Y} : z = b\mathcal{A}z \text{ for some } 0 < b < 1\}$ is unbounded.*

Theorem 2 ([38]). *Let $\mathcal{V}$ be a nonempty, bounded, closed, and convex subset of Banach space $\mathcal{Y}$ and the operators $\mathcal{A}_1, \mathcal{A}_2 : \mathcal{V} \to \mathcal{Y}$ with $\mathcal{A}_1 k + \mathcal{A}_2 k' \in \mathcal{V}, \forall k, k' \in \mathcal{V}, \mathcal{A}_1$ is compact and continuous and $\mathcal{A}_2$ is a contraction map. Then, $\mathcal{A}_1 + \mathcal{A}_2$ has a fixed point.*

3. Main Results

Define $\tilde{\mathcal{Y}} = \{z : [0,1] \to \mathbb{R} : z, \mathfrak{D}^q z, z' \in C([0,1], \mathbb{R})\}$ as a Banach space with

$$\|z\|_{\tilde{\mathcal{Y}}} = \sup_{s \in [0,1]} |z(s)| + \sup_{s \in [0,1]} |\mathfrak{D}^q z(s)| + \sup_{s \in [0,1]} |z'(s)|.$$

Hence, it can be clearly seen that $\mathcal{Y} = \tilde{\mathcal{Y}}_{16}$ is a Banach space with

$$\|z = (z_1, z_2, \ldots, z_{16})\|_{\mathcal{Y}} = \sum_{\tau=1}^{16} \|z_\tau\|_{\tilde{\mathcal{Y}}}.$$

As addressing Lemma 1, for each $(z_1, z_2, \ldots, z_{16}) \in \mathcal{Y}$, we introduce $\mathcal{A}: \mathcal{Y} \to \mathcal{Y}$ by

$$\mathcal{A}(z_1, z_2, \ldots, z_{16}) := (\mathcal{A}_1(z_1, z_2, \ldots, z_{16}), \mathcal{A}_2(z_1, z_2, \ldots, z_{16}), \ldots, \mathcal{A}_{16}(z_1, z_2, \ldots, z_{16})), \quad (5)$$

for each $\tau = 1, 2, \ldots, 16$ and $(z_1, z_2, \ldots, z_{16}) \in \mathcal{Y}$, we define $\mathcal{A}_\tau : \mathcal{Y} \to \tilde{\mathcal{Y}}$ by

$$\begin{aligned}
\mathcal{A}_\tau(z_1, z_2, \ldots, z_{16})(s) &= \int_0^s \frac{(s-\theta)^{r-1}}{\Gamma(r)} \mathcal{W}_\tau(\theta, z_\tau(\theta), \mathfrak{D}^q z_\tau(\theta), z'_\tau(\theta)) d\theta \\
&+ \int_0^1 \mathcal{W}_\tau(\theta, z_\tau(\theta), \mathfrak{D}^q z_\tau(\theta), z'_\tau(\theta)) d\theta + \left(\frac{1}{\Gamma(3-r)} + s\right) \times \\
&\quad \left[\frac{\ell_3}{A_0} \int_0^a \int_0^\theta \mathcal{W}_\tau(\zeta, z_\tau(\zeta), \mathfrak{D}^q z_\tau(\zeta), z'_\tau(\zeta)) d\zeta d\theta \right. \\
&\quad \left. - \frac{\ell_2}{A_0} \int_0^1 \frac{(1-\theta)^{r-2}}{\Gamma(r-1)} \mathcal{W}_\tau(\theta, z_\tau(\theta), \mathfrak{D}^q z_\tau(\theta), z'_\tau(\theta)) d\theta\right],
\end{aligned} \quad (6)$$

for all $s \in [0, 1]$.

For the purpose of clarity, we will be performing all computations using the following notation:

$$A_0 = \left[\ell_1 + \ell_2 - \frac{a^{3-r}}{\Gamma(4-r)}\right] \neq 0 \quad (7)$$

$$A_1 = \left[|\ell_1| + |\ell_2| + \frac{1}{\Gamma(4-r)}\right] \neq 0 \quad (8)$$

$$\mathcal{Y}_0^* = \frac{1}{\Gamma(r+1)} + 1 + \frac{1}{A_1}\left(\frac{1}{\Gamma(3-r)} + 1\right)\left(\frac{|\ell_3|}{2} + \frac{|\ell_2|}{\Gamma(r)}\right) \quad (9)$$

$$\mathcal{Y}_1^* = \frac{1}{\Gamma(r-q+1)} + \left(\frac{1}{A_1 \Gamma(2-q)}\right)\left(\frac{|\ell_3|}{2} + \frac{|\ell_2|}{\Gamma(r)}\right) \quad (10)$$

$$\mathcal{Y}_2^* = \frac{1}{\Gamma(r)} + \frac{1}{A_1}\left(\frac{|\ell_3|}{2} + \frac{|\ell_2|}{\Gamma(r)}\right) \quad (11)$$

$$\mathcal{V}_0^* = 1 + \frac{1}{A_1}\left(\frac{1}{\Gamma(3-r)} + 1\right)\left(\frac{|\ell_3|}{2} + \frac{|\ell_2|}{\Gamma(r)}\right) \quad (12)$$

$$\mathcal{V}_1^* = \frac{1}{A_1 \Gamma(2-q)}\left(\frac{|\ell_3|}{2} + \frac{|\ell_2|}{\Gamma(r)}\right) \quad (13)$$

$$\mathcal{V}_2^* = \frac{1}{A_1}\left(\frac{|\ell_3|}{2} + \frac{|\ell_2|}{\Gamma(r)}\right). \quad (14)$$

Now, we will discuss the most important findings from this section.

Theorem 3. *Consider the proposed Problem (1). Assume that $\mathcal{W}_1, \mathcal{W}_2, \ldots, \mathcal{W}_{16} : [0, 1] \times \mathbb{R} \times \mathbb{R} \times \mathbb{R} \to \mathbb{R}$ are continuous functions and there is $Y_\tau > 0$, $\forall \tau = 1, 2, \ldots, 16$ with $|\mathcal{W}_\tau(s, z, \tilde{z}, \tilde{\tilde{z}})| \leq Y_\tau$, $\forall z, \tilde{z}, \tilde{\tilde{z}} \in \mathbb{R}$ and $s \in [0, 1]$. Then, there exists a solution to Problem (1).*

Proof. The existence of the fixed points of $\mathcal{A}$ specified by (5) is a foregone conclusion if and only if (1) has a solution, as implied by (6). Here, the complete continuity of operator $\mathcal{A}'$ is established first.

As $\mathcal{W}_1, \mathcal{W}_2, \ldots, \mathcal{W}_{16}$ are continuous, so $\mathcal{A} : \mathcal{Y} \to \mathcal{Y}$ is also continuous. Consider a bounded set $\mathcal{O} \in \mathcal{Y}$ and $z = (z_1, z_2, \ldots, z_{16}) \in \mathcal{Y}$, so, for each $s \in [0, 1]$, we have

$$|(\mathcal{A}_\tau z)(s)| \leq \int_0^s \frac{(s-\theta)^{r-1}}{\Gamma(r)} |\mathcal{W}_\tau(\theta, z_\tau(\theta), \mathfrak{D}^q z_\tau(\theta), z'_\tau(\theta))| d\theta$$

$$+ \int_0^1 |\mathcal{W}_\tau(\theta, z_\tau(\theta), \mathfrak{D}^q z_\tau(\theta), z'_\tau(\theta))| d\theta$$

$$+ \frac{1}{|A_0|} \left(\frac{1}{\Gamma(3-r)} + s \right) \times \left[|\ell_3| \int_0^a \int_0^\theta |\mathcal{W}_\tau(\zeta, z_\tau(\zeta), \mathfrak{D}^q z_\tau(\zeta), z'_\tau(\zeta))| d\zeta d\theta \right.$$

$$+ |\ell_2| \int_0^1 \frac{(1-\theta)^{r-2}}{\Gamma(r-1)} |\mathcal{W}_\tau(\theta, z_\tau(\theta), \mathfrak{D}^q z_\tau(\theta), z'_\tau(\theta))| d\theta \Bigg]$$

$$\leq \mathrm{Y}_\tau \mathcal{Y}_0^*,$$

where $\mathcal{Y}_0^*$ is given in (9). Additionally,

$$|(\mathfrak{D}^q \mathcal{A}_\tau z)(s)| \leq \int_0^s \frac{(s-\theta)^{r-q-1}}{\Gamma(r-q)} |\mathcal{W}_\tau(\theta, z_\tau(\theta), \mathfrak{D}^q z_\tau(\theta), z'_\tau(\theta))| d\theta$$

$$+ \left(\frac{s^{1-q}}{|A_0|\Gamma(2-q)} \right) \times \left[|\ell_3| \int_0^a \int_0^\theta |\mathcal{W}_\tau(\zeta, z_\tau(\zeta), \mathfrak{D}^q z_\tau(\zeta), z'_\tau(\zeta))| d\zeta d\theta \right.$$

$$+ |\ell_2| \int_0^1 \frac{(1-\theta)^{r-2}}{\Gamma(r-1)} |\mathcal{W}_\tau(\theta, z_\tau(\theta), \mathfrak{D}^q z_\tau(\theta), z'_\tau(\theta))| d\theta \Bigg]$$

$$\leq \mathrm{Y}_\tau \mathcal{Y}_1^*$$

and

$$|(\mathcal{A}'_\tau z)(s)| \leq \int_0^s \frac{(s-\theta)^{r-2}}{\Gamma(r-1)} |\mathcal{W}_\tau(\theta, z_\tau(\theta), \mathfrak{D}^q z_\tau(\theta), z'_\tau(\theta))| d\theta$$

$$+ \left(\frac{1}{|A_0|} \right) \times \left[|\ell_3| \int_0^a \int_0^\theta |\mathcal{W}_\tau(\zeta, z_\tau(\zeta), \mathfrak{D}^q z_\tau(\zeta), z'_\tau(\zeta))| d\zeta d\theta \right.$$

$$+ |\ell_2| \int_0^1 \frac{(1-\theta)^{r-2}}{\Gamma(r-1)} |\mathcal{W}_\tau(\theta, z_\tau(\theta), \mathfrak{D}^q z_\tau(\theta), z'_\tau(\theta))| d\theta \Bigg]$$

$$\leq \mathrm{Y}_\tau \mathcal{Y}_2^*,$$

for all $s \in [0, 1]$, where $\mathcal{Y}_1^*, \mathcal{Y}_2^*$ are given in (10) and (11), respectively. Therefore,

$$\|(\mathcal{A}_\tau z)(s)\|_{\tilde{y}} \leq \mathrm{Y}_\tau (\mathcal{Y}_0^* + \mathcal{Y}_1^* + \mathcal{Y}_2^*).$$

Hence,

$$\|(\mathcal{A} z)(s)\|_\mathcal{Y} = \sum_{\tau=1}^{16} \|(\mathcal{A}_\tau z)(s)\|_{\tilde{y}}$$

$$\leq \sum_{\tau=1}^{16} \mathrm{Y}_\tau (\mathcal{Y}_0^* + \mathcal{Y}_1^* + \mathcal{Y}_2^*)$$

$$< \infty.$$

This proves that there exists a uniform bound on $\mathcal{A}$.

The next step is to demonstrate the equicontinuity of $\mathcal{A}$. For this purpose, let $z = (z_1, z_2, \ldots, z_{16}) \in \mathcal{O}$ and $s_1, s_2 \in [0,1]$ with $s_1 < s_2$. Then, we have

$$|(\mathcal{A}_\tau z)(s_2) - (\mathcal{A}_\tau z)(s_1)| \leq \int_0^{s_1} \frac{(s_2-\theta)^{r-1} - (s_1-\theta)^{r-1}}{\Gamma(r)} \times$$
$$|\mathcal{W}_\tau(\theta, z_\tau(\theta), \mathfrak{D}^q z_\tau(\theta), z'_\tau(\theta))| d\theta$$
$$+ \int_{s_1}^{s_2} \frac{(s_2-\theta)^{r-1}}{\Gamma(r)} |\mathcal{W}_\tau(\theta, z_\tau(\theta), \mathfrak{D}^q z_\tau(\theta), z'_\tau(\theta))| d\theta$$
$$+ \left(\frac{s_2 - s_1}{|A_0|}\right) \times \Bigg[|\ell_3|$$
$$\int_0^a \int_0^\theta |\mathcal{W}_\tau(\zeta, z_\tau(\zeta), \mathfrak{D}^q z_\tau(\zeta), z'_\tau(\zeta))| d\zeta d\theta$$
$$+ |\ell_2| \int_0^1 \frac{(1-\theta)^{r-2}}{\Gamma(r-1)} |\mathcal{W}_\tau(\theta, z_\tau(\theta), \mathfrak{D}^q z_\tau(\theta), z'_\tau(\theta))| d\theta \Bigg].$$

It is clear that if $s_1 \to s_2$ then, independently, the RHS of the above expression converges to zero. Moreover,

$$\lim_{s_1 \to s_2} |(\mathfrak{D}^q \mathcal{A}_\tau z)(s_2) - (\mathfrak{D}^q \mathcal{A}_\tau z)(s_1)| = 0, \quad \lim_{s_1 \to s_2} |(\mathcal{A}'_\tau z)(s_2) - (\mathcal{A}'_\tau z)(s_1)| = 0.$$

For this reason, $\|(\mathcal{A}z)(s_2) - (\mathcal{A}z)(s_1)\|_\mathcal{Y} \to 0$ as $s_1 \to s_2$. This shows that $\mathcal{A}$ is an equicontinuous on $\mathcal{Y} = \mathcal{Y}_1 \times \mathcal{Y}_2 \times \ldots \times \mathcal{Y}_{16}$. For this reason, we know that the operator is completely continuous because of the Arzela–Ascoli theorem.

Further, we define

$$\Theta := \{(z_1, z_2, \ldots, z_{16}) \in \mathcal{Y} : (z_1, z_2, \ldots, z_{16}) = b\mathcal{A}(z_1, z_2, \ldots, z_{16}), \ b \in (0,1)\}$$

of $\mathcal{Y}$. We will demonstrate the boundedness property of Θ here. To this end, let $(z_1, z_2, \ldots, z_{16}) \in \Theta$. Then, we can write

$$(z_1, z_2, \ldots, z_{16}) = b\mathcal{A}(z_1, z_2, \ldots, z_{16}),$$

and so

$$z_\tau(s) = b\mathcal{A}_\tau(z_1, z_2, \ldots, z_{16}), \ \forall s \in [0,1], \text{ and } \tau = 1, 2, \ldots, 16.$$

Thus,

$$|z_\tau(s)| \leq b\Bigg[\int_0^s \frac{(s-\theta)^{r-1}}{\Gamma(r)} |\mathcal{W}_\tau(\theta, z_\tau(\theta), \mathfrak{D}^q z_\tau(\theta), z'_\tau(\theta))| d\theta$$
$$+ \int_0^1 |\mathcal{W}_\tau(\theta, z_\tau(\theta), \mathfrak{D}^q z_\tau(\theta), z'_\tau(\theta))| d\theta$$
$$+ \frac{1}{|A_0|}\left(\frac{1}{\Gamma(3-r)} + s\right) \times \Bigg\{|\ell_3| \int_0^a \int_0^\theta |\mathcal{W}_\tau(\zeta, z_\tau(\zeta), \mathfrak{D}^q z_\tau(\zeta), z'_\tau(\zeta))| d\zeta d\theta$$
$$+ |\ell_2| \int_0^1 \frac{(1-\theta)^{r-2}}{\Gamma(r-1)} |\mathcal{W}_\tau(\theta, z_\tau(\theta), \mathfrak{D}^q z_\tau(\theta), z'_\tau(\theta))| d\theta \Bigg\}\Bigg]$$
$$\leq bY_\tau \mathcal{Y}_0^*,$$

and by similar computations, we obtain

$$|\mathfrak{D}^q z_\tau(s)| \leq bY_\tau \mathcal{Y}_1^*,$$
$$|z'_\tau(s)| \leq bY_\tau \mathcal{Y}_2^*,$$

where $\mathcal{Y}_0^* - \mathcal{Y}_2^*$ are given in (9)–(11). Hence,

$$\|z\|_\mathcal{Y} = \sum_{\tau=1}^{16} \|z_\tau\|_{\hat{\mathcal{Y}}}$$
$$\leq b \sum_{\tau=1}^{16} Y_\tau(\mathcal{Y}_0^* + \mathcal{Y}_1^* + \mathcal{Y}_2^*)$$
$$< \infty.$$

It demonstrates that Θ is bounded. We now know that the operator $\mathcal{A}$ has a fixed point in $\mathcal{Y}$ by applying Theorem 1 and Lemma 1. This demonstrates that the problem described in (1) has a solution. □

We will now consider the solution to the Problem (1) under a variety of assumptions

Theorem 4. *Consider the proposed Problem (1). Suppose that $\mathcal{W}_1, \mathcal{W}_2, \ldots, \mathcal{W}_{16} : [0,1] \times \mathbb{R} \times \mathbb{R} \times \mathbb{R} \to \mathbb{R}$ are continuous functions and there are bounded continuous functions $\mathcal{G}_1, \mathcal{G}_2, \ldots, \mathcal{G}_{16} : [0,1] \to \mathbb{R}$, $\mathcal{F}_1, \mathcal{F}_2, \ldots, \mathcal{F}_{16} : [0,1] \to [0,\infty)$ and nondecreasing continuous functions $\mathcal{M}_1, \mathcal{M}_2, \ldots, \mathcal{M}_{16} : [0,1] \to [0,\infty)$ with the properties*

$$|\mathcal{W}_\tau(s,z,\tilde{z},\tilde{\tilde{z}})| \leq \mathcal{F}_\tau(s)\mathcal{M}_\tau(|z| + |\tilde{z}| + |\tilde{\tilde{z}}|)$$

and

$$|\mathcal{W}_\tau(s,z_1,z_2,z_3) - \mathcal{W}_\tau(s,\tilde{z}_1,\tilde{z}_2,\tilde{z}_3)| \leq \mathcal{G}_\tau(s)(|z_1 - \tilde{z}_1| + |z_2 - \tilde{z}_2| + |z_3 - \tilde{z}_3|)$$

$\forall s \in [0,1], z_1, z_2, z_3, \tilde{z}_1, \tilde{z}_2, \tilde{z}_3 \in \mathbb{R}$ and $\tau = 1, 2, \ldots, 16$. If

$$\Lambda := (\mathcal{V}_0^* + \mathcal{V}_1^* + \mathcal{V}_2^*) \sum_{\tau=1}^{16} \|\mathcal{G}_\tau\| < 1,$$

then (1) has a solution, where $\|\mathcal{G}_\tau\| = \sup_{s \in [0,1]} |\mathcal{G}_\tau(s)|$ and the constants $\mathcal{V}_0^* - \mathcal{V}_2^*$ are defined in (12)–(14), respectively.

Proof. Let $\|\mathcal{F}_\tau\| = \sup_{s \in [0,1]} |\mathcal{F}_\tau(s)|$ and for appropriate constants ε_τ, we have

$$\varepsilon_\tau \geq \sum_{\tau=1}^{16} \mathcal{M}_\tau\left(\|z_\tau\|_{\mathcal{Y}_\tau}\right) \|\mathcal{F}_\tau\| \{\mathcal{Y}_0^* + \mathcal{Y}_1^* + \mathcal{Y}_2^*\}, \tag{15}$$

where $\mathcal{Y}_0^* - \mathcal{Y}_2^*$ are defined in (9)–(11). Here, we introduce a set

$$\mathcal{O}_{\varepsilon_\tau} := \{z = (z_1, z_2, \ldots, z_{16}) \in \mathcal{Y} : \|z\|_\mathcal{Y} \leq \varepsilon_\tau\},$$

where ε_τ can be seen in (15). Here, $\mathcal{O}_{\varepsilon_\tau}$ is obviously a closed, bounded, nonempty, and convex subset of $\mathcal{Y} = \mathcal{Y}_1 \times \mathcal{Y}_2 \times \ldots \times \mathcal{Y}_{16}$. Now, we define $\mathcal{A}_1$ and $\mathcal{A}_2$ on $\mathcal{O}_{\varepsilon_\tau}$ by

$$\mathcal{A}_1(z_1, z_2, \ldots, z_{16})(s) := \left(\mathcal{A}_1^{(1)}(z_1, z_2, \ldots, z_{16})(s), \ldots, \mathcal{A}_1^{(16)}(z_1, z_2, \ldots, z_{16})(s)\right),$$

$$\mathcal{A}_2(z_1, z_2, \ldots, z_{16})(s) := \left(\mathcal{A}_2^{(1)}(z_1, z_2, \ldots, z_{16})(s), \ldots, \mathcal{A}_2^{(16)}(z_1, z_2, \ldots, z_{16})(s)\right),$$

where

$$\left(\mathcal{A}_1^{(\tau)} z\right)(s) = \int_0^s \frac{(s-\theta)^{r-1}}{\Gamma(r)} \mathcal{W}_\tau(\theta, z_\tau(\theta), \mathfrak{D}^q z_\tau(\theta), z_\tau'(\theta)) d\theta \tag{16}$$

and

$$\left(\mathcal{A}_2^{(\tau)}z\right)(s) = \int_0^1 \mathcal{W}_\tau(\theta, z_\tau(\theta), \mathfrak{D}^q z_\tau(\theta), z'_\tau(\theta))d\theta$$
$$+ \frac{1}{A_0}\left(\frac{1}{\Gamma(3-r)} + s\right)\left[\ell_3 \int_0^a \int_0^\theta \mathcal{W}_\tau(\zeta, z_\tau(\zeta), \mathfrak{D}^q z_\tau(\zeta), z'_\tau(\zeta))d\zeta d\theta\right.$$
$$\left. - \ell_2 \int_0^1 \frac{(1-\theta)^{r-2}}{\Gamma(r-1)}\mathcal{W}_\tau(\theta, z_\tau(\theta), \mathfrak{D}^q z_\tau(\theta), z'_\tau(\theta))d\theta\right] \quad (17)$$

for all $s \in [0,1]$ and $z = (z_1, z_2, \ldots, z_{16}) \in \mathcal{O}_{\varepsilon_\tau}$.

Let $\tilde{\mathcal{M}}_\tau = \sup_{z_\tau \in \mathcal{Y}_\tau} \mathcal{M}_\tau\left(\|z_\tau\|_{\mathcal{Y}_\tau}\right)$. Now, for every $\tilde{z} = (\tilde{z}_1, \tilde{z}_2, \ldots, \tilde{z}_{16})$, $z = (z_1, z_2, \ldots, z_{16}) \in \mathcal{O}_{\varepsilon_\tau}$, we have

$$\left|\left(\mathcal{A}_1^{(\tau)}\tilde{z} + \mathcal{A}_2^{(\tau)}z\right)(s)\right| \leq \int_0^s \frac{(s-\theta)^{r-1}}{\Gamma(r)}|\mathcal{W}_\tau(\theta, \tilde{z}_\tau(\theta), \mathfrak{D}^q \tilde{z}_\tau(\theta), \tilde{z}'_\tau(\theta))|d\theta$$
$$+ \int_0^1 |\mathcal{W}_\tau(\theta, z_\tau(\theta), \mathfrak{D}^q z_\tau(\theta), z'_\tau(\theta))|d\theta$$
$$+ \frac{1}{|A_0|}\left(\frac{1}{\Gamma(3-r)} + s\right) \times [|\ell_3|$$
$$\int_0^a \int_0^\theta |\mathcal{W}_\tau(\zeta, z_\tau(\zeta), \mathfrak{D}^q z_\tau(\zeta), z'_\tau(\zeta))|d\zeta d\theta$$
$$+ |\ell_2|\int_0^1 \frac{(1-\theta)^{r-2}}{\Gamma(r-1)}|\mathcal{W}_\tau(\theta, z_\tau(\theta), \mathfrak{D}^q z_\tau(\theta), z'_\tau(\theta))|d\theta\right]$$
$$\leq \int_0^s \frac{(s-\theta)^{r-1}}{\Gamma(r)}\mathcal{F}_\tau(\theta)\mathcal{M}_\tau\left(|\tilde{z}_\tau(\theta)| + |\mathfrak{D}^q \tilde{z}_\tau(\theta)| + |\tilde{z}'_\tau(\theta)|\right)d\theta$$
$$+ \int_0^1 \mathcal{F}_\tau(\theta)\mathcal{M}_\tau\left(|z_\tau(\theta)| + |\mathfrak{D}^q z_\tau(\theta)| + |z'_\tau(\theta)|\right)d\theta$$
$$+ \frac{1}{|A_0|}\left(\frac{1}{\Gamma(3-r)} + s\right) \times$$
$$\left[|\ell_3|\int_0^a \int_0^\theta \mathcal{F}_\tau(\zeta)\mathcal{M}_\tau\left(|z_\tau(\zeta)| + |\mathfrak{D}^q z_\tau(\zeta)| + |z'_\tau(\zeta)|\right)d\zeta d\theta\right.$$
$$+ |\ell_2|\int_0^1 \frac{(1-\theta)^{r-2}}{\Gamma(r-1)} \times$$
$$\left.\mathcal{F}_\tau(\theta)\mathcal{M}_\tau\left(|z_\tau(\theta)| + |\mathfrak{D}^q z_\tau(\theta)| + |z'_\tau(\theta)|\right)d\theta\right]$$
$$\leq \|\mathcal{F}_\tau\|\tilde{\mathcal{M}}_\tau \mathcal{Y}_0^*.$$

By using similar computations, we obtain

$$\left|\left(\mathfrak{D}^q \mathcal{A}_1^{(\tau)}\tilde{z}\right)(s) + \left(\mathfrak{D}^q \mathcal{A}_2^{(\tau)}z\right)(s)\right| \leq \|\mathcal{F}_\tau\|\tilde{\mathcal{M}}_\tau \mathcal{Y}_1^*,$$

and

$$\left|\left(\mathcal{A}_1^{(\tau)}\tilde{z}\right)'(s) + \left(\mathcal{A}_2^{(\tau)}z\right)'(s)\right| \leq \|\mathcal{F}_\tau\|\tilde{\mathcal{M}}_\tau \mathcal{Y}_2^*.$$

This yields that

$$\|\mathcal{A}_1\tilde{z}+\mathcal{A}_2 z\|_{\mathcal{Y}} = \sum_{\tau=1}^{16}\left\|\mathcal{A}_1^{(\tau)}\tilde{z}+\mathcal{A}_2^{(k)}z\right\|_{\tilde{\mathcal{Y}}}$$
$$\leq \|\mathcal{F}_\tau\|\tilde{\mathcal{M}}_\tau(\mathcal{Y}_0^* + \mathcal{Y}_1^* + \mathcal{Y}_2^*)$$
$$\leq \varepsilon_\tau,$$

and so $\mathcal{A}_1\tilde{z}+\mathcal{A}_2 z \in \mathcal{O}_{\varepsilon_\tau}$. Furthermore, the continuity of $\mathcal{W}_\tau$ refers $\mathcal{A}_1$'s continuity.

We will now prove that there exists a uniform bound on the expression $\mathcal{A}_1$. To this end, we have

$$\left|\left(\mathcal{A}_1^{(\tau)}z\right)(s)\right| \leq \int_0^s \frac{(s-\theta)^{r-1}}{\Gamma(r)}|\mathcal{W}_\tau(\theta, z_\tau(\theta), \mathfrak{D}^q z_\tau(\theta), z'_\tau(\theta))|d\theta$$
$$\leq \frac{1}{\Gamma(r+1)}\|\mathcal{F}_\tau\|\mathcal{M}_\tau(|z_\tau(\theta)| + |\mathfrak{D}^q z_\tau(\theta)| + |z'_\tau(\theta)|).$$

for all $z \in \mathcal{O}_{\varepsilon_\tau}$. Additionally,

$$\left|\left(\mathfrak{D}^q\mathcal{A}_1^{(\tau)}z\right)(s)\right| \leq \int_0^s \frac{(s-\theta)^{r-q-1}}{\Gamma(r-q)}|\mathcal{W}_\tau(\theta, z_\tau(\theta), \mathfrak{D}^q z_\tau(\theta), z'_\tau(\theta))|d\theta$$
$$\leq \frac{1}{\Gamma(r-q+1)}\|\mathcal{F}_\tau\|\mathcal{M}_\tau(|z_\tau(\theta)| + |\mathfrak{D}^q z_\tau(\theta)| + |z'_\tau(\theta)|),$$

and

$$\left|\left(\mathcal{A}_1^{(\tau)}z\right)'(s)\right| \leq \frac{1}{\Gamma(r)}\|\mathcal{F}_\tau\|\mathcal{M}_\tau(|z_\tau(\theta)| + |\mathfrak{D}^q z_\tau(\theta)| + |z'_\tau(\theta)|),$$

for all $z \in \mathcal{O}_{\varepsilon_\tau}$. Thus,

$$\|\mathcal{A}_1 z\|_{\mathcal{Y}} = \sum_{\tau=1}^{16}\left\|\mathcal{A}_1^{(\tau)}z\right\|_{\tilde{\mathcal{Y}}}$$
$$\leq \left\{\frac{r+1}{\Gamma(r+1)} + \frac{1}{\Gamma(r-q+1)}\right\}\sum_{\tau=1}^{16}\|\mathcal{F}_\tau\|\mathcal{M}_\tau\left(\|z_\tau\|_{\mathcal{Y}_\tau}\right),$$

which demonstrates the uniformly boundedness property of the operator $\mathcal{A}_1$ on $\mathcal{O}_{\varepsilon_\tau}$.

Here, it remains for us to show the compactness of the operator $\mathcal{A}_1$ on $\mathcal{O}_{\varepsilon_\tau}$. To this end, let $s_1, s_2 \in [0,1]$ with $s_1 < s_2$. Then, we have

$$\left|\left(\mathcal{A}_1^{(\tau)}z\right)(s_2) - \left(\mathcal{A}_1^{(\tau)}z\right)(s_1)\right| \leq \left|\int_0^{s_2}\frac{(s_2-\theta)^{r-1}}{\Gamma(r)}\mathcal{W}_\tau(\theta, z_\tau(\theta), \mathfrak{D}^q z_\tau(\theta), z'_\tau(\theta))d\theta\right.$$
$$\left.- \int_0^{s_1}\frac{(s_1-\theta)^{r-1}}{\Gamma(r)}\mathcal{W}_\tau(\theta, z_\tau(\theta), \mathfrak{D}^q z_\tau(\theta), z'_\tau(\theta))d\theta\right|$$

$$
\begin{aligned}
&\leq \left| \int_0^{s_1} \frac{(s_2-\theta)^{r-1}-(s_1-\theta)^{r-1}}{\Gamma(r)} \times \right.\\
&\qquad \mathcal{W}_\tau(\theta, z_\tau(\theta), \mathfrak{D}^q z_\tau(\theta), z'_\tau(\theta)) d\theta \bigg|\\
&\quad + \left| \int_{s_1}^{s_2} \frac{(s_2-\theta)^{r-1}}{\Gamma(r)} \mathcal{W}_\tau(\theta, z_\tau(\theta), \mathfrak{D}^q z_\tau(\theta), z'_\tau(\theta)) d\theta \right|\\
&\leq \int_0^{s_1} \frac{(s_2-\theta)^{r-1}-(s_1-\theta)^{r-1}}{\Gamma(r)} \times\\
&\qquad |\mathcal{W}_\tau(\theta, z_\tau(\theta), \mathfrak{D}^q z_\tau(\theta), z'_\tau(\theta))| d\theta\\
&\quad + \int_{s_1}^{s_2} \frac{(s_2-\theta)^{r-1}}{\Gamma(r)} |\mathcal{W}_\tau(\theta, z_\tau(\theta), \mathfrak{D}^q z_\tau(\theta), z'_\tau(\theta))| d\theta\\
&\leq \left\{ \frac{s_2^r - s_1^r - (s_2-s_1)^r}{\Gamma(r+1)} + \frac{(s_2-s_1)^r}{\Gamma(r+1)} \right\} \times\\
&\qquad \|\mathcal{F}_\tau\| \mathcal{M}_\tau \left(\|z_\tau\|_{\mathcal{Y}_\tau} \right).
\end{aligned}
$$

Hence, $\left|\left(\mathcal{A}_1^{(\tau)} z\right)(s_2) - \left(\mathcal{A}_1^{(\tau)} z\right)(s_1)\right| \to 0$ as $s_1 \to s_2$. Additionally, we have

$$\lim_{s_1 \to s_2} \left| \left(\mathfrak{D}^q \mathcal{A}_1^{(\tau)} z\right)(s_2) - \left(\mathfrak{D}^q \mathcal{A}_1^{(\tau)} z\right)(s_1) \right| = 0,$$

$$\lim_{s_1 \to s_2} \left| \left(\mathcal{A}_1^{(\tau)} z\right)'(s_2) - \left(\mathcal{A}_1^{(\tau)} z\right)'(s_1) \right| = 0.$$

Hence, $\|(\mathcal{A}_1 z)(s_2) - (\mathcal{A}_1 z)(s_1)\|_{\mathcal{Y}}$ tends to zero as $s_1 \to s_2$. As a result, the operator $\mathcal{A}_1$ defined on $\mathcal{O}_{\varepsilon_\tau}$ is relatively compact since it is equicontinuous. By utilizing the results proven by Arzela–Ascoli, we claim that the operator $\mathcal{A}_1$ is compact on $\mathcal{O}_{\varepsilon_\tau}$.

In end, it still needs to be shown that $\mathcal{A}_2$ is a contraction mapping. As evidence, we let $\tilde{z}, z \in \mathcal{O}_{\varepsilon_\tau}$,

$$
\begin{aligned}
\left|\left(\mathcal{A}_2^{(\tau)} \tilde{z}\right)(s) - \left(\mathcal{A}_2^{(\tau)} z\right)(s)\right| &\leq \int_0^1 \mathcal{G}_\tau(\theta)(|\tilde{z}_\tau(\theta) - z_\tau(\theta)| + |\mathfrak{D}^q \tilde{z}_\tau(\theta) - \mathfrak{D}^q z_\tau(\theta)|\\
&\quad + |\tilde{z}'_\tau(\theta) - z'_\tau(\theta)|) d\theta\\
&\quad + \frac{1}{|A_0|} \left(\frac{1}{\Gamma(3-r)} + s \right) [|\ell_3| \times\\
&\qquad \int_0^a \int_0^\theta \mathcal{G}_\tau(\zeta)(|\tilde{z}_\tau(\zeta) - z_\tau(\zeta)|\\
&\qquad + |\mathfrak{D}^q \tilde{z}_\tau(\zeta) - \mathfrak{D}^q z_\tau(\zeta)| + |\tilde{z}'_\tau(\zeta) - z'_\tau(\zeta)|) d\zeta d\theta\\
&\quad + |\ell_2| \int_0^1 \frac{(1-\theta)^{r-2}}{\Gamma(r-1)} \mathcal{G}_\tau(\theta)(|\tilde{z}_\tau(\theta) - z_\tau(\theta)|\\
&\qquad + |\mathfrak{D}^q \tilde{z}_\tau(\theta) - \mathfrak{D}^q z_\tau(\theta)| + |\tilde{z}'_\tau(\theta) - z'_\tau(\theta)|) d\theta \bigg]\\
&\leq \|\mathcal{G}_\tau\| \mathcal{V}_0^* \|\tilde{z}_\tau - z_\tau\|_{\mathcal{Y}_\tau}
\end{aligned}
$$

for each $\tau = 1, 2, \ldots, 16$, where $\mathcal{V}_0^*$ is given in (12). According to the same kind of calculations, we also have

$$\sup_{s \in [0,1]} \left| \left(\mathfrak{D}^q \mathcal{A}_2^{(\tau)} \tilde{z}\right)(s) - \left(\mathfrak{D}^q \mathcal{A}_2^{(\tau)} z\right)(s) \right| \leq \|\mathcal{G}_\tau\| \mathcal{V}_1^* \|\tilde{z}_\tau - z_\tau\|_{\mathcal{Y}_\tau}.$$

$$\sup_{s \in [0,1]} \left| \left(\mathcal{A}_2^{(\tau)} \tilde{z}\right)'(s) - \left(\mathcal{A}_2^{(\tau)} z\right)'(s) \right| \leq \|\mathcal{G}_\tau\| \mathcal{V}_2^* \|\tilde{z}_\tau - z_\tau\|_{\mathcal{Y}_\tau},$$

where $\mathcal{V}_1^*$ and $\mathcal{V}_2^*$ are given in (13) and (14), respectively. Thus, we have

$$\|\mathcal{A}_2\tilde{z} - \mathcal{A}_2 z\|_{\mathcal{Y}} = \sum_{\tau=1}^{16}\left\|\mathcal{A}_2^{(\tau)}\tilde{z} - \mathcal{A}_2^{(\tau)}z\right\|_{\hat{\mathcal{Y}}}$$

$$\leq (\mathcal{V}_0^* + \mathcal{V}_1^* + \mathcal{V}_2^*)\sum_{\tau=1}^{16}\|\mathcal{G}_\tau\|\|\tilde{z}_\tau - z_\tau\|_{\mathcal{Y}_\tau},$$

and so

$$\|\mathcal{A}_2\tilde{z} - \mathcal{A}_2 z\|_{\mathcal{Y}} \leq \Lambda\|\tilde{z} - z\|_{\mathcal{Y}}.$$

As $\Lambda < 1$, which means that $\mathcal{A}_2$ is a contraction on $\mathcal{O}_{\varepsilon_\tau}$. In this demonstration, we use Theorem 2, to show that there exists a fixed point of $\mathcal{A}$ such that the problem has a solution (1). □

4. An Example

The following illustration demonstrates the relevance of our findings.

Example 1. *Consider the problem stated below:*

$$\begin{cases} \mathfrak{D}^{1.5}z_1(s) = \dfrac{36e^s[z_1(s)]^2}{40,000(1+[z_1(s)]^2)} + 0.0009e^s\sin\left(\mathfrak{D}^{0.08}z_1(s)\right) + \dfrac{180e^s\arctan z_1'(s)}{200,000}, \\[2mm] \mathfrak{D}^{1.5}z_2(s) = \dfrac{s(\arctan z_2(s))}{25,000} + 0.00004s\left(\sin\left(\mathfrak{D}^{0.08}z_2(s)\right)\right) + \dfrac{4s[z_2'(s)]^2}{100,000\left(1+[z_2'(s)]^2\right)}, \\[2mm] \mathfrak{D}^{1.5}z_3(s) = 0.0001s\left(\sinh^{-1}z_3(s)\right) + \dfrac{60s\left[\mathfrak{D}^{0.08}z_3(s)\right]^2}{600,000+600,000[\mathfrak{D}^{0.08}z_3(s)]^2} + \dfrac{3s(\arctan z_3'(s))}{30,000}, \end{cases} \quad (18)$$

associated with the following boundary conditions:

$$\begin{cases} z_1(0) = \mathfrak{D}^{0.5}z_1(1) \\[1mm] \dfrac{13}{17}z_1'(0) + \dfrac{6}{29}z_1'(1) = \dfrac{15}{43}\int_0^1 \mathfrak{D}^{0.5}z_1(\theta)d\theta \\[2mm] z_2(0) = \mathfrak{D}^{0.5}z_2(1) \\[1mm] \dfrac{13}{17}z_2'(0) + \dfrac{6}{29}z_2'(1) = \dfrac{15}{43}\int_0^1 \mathfrak{D}^{0.5}z_2(\theta)d\theta \\[2mm] z_3(0) = \mathfrak{D}^{0.5}z_3(1) \\[1mm] \dfrac{13}{17}z_3'(0) + \dfrac{6}{29}z_3'(1) = \dfrac{15}{43}\int_0^1 \mathfrak{D}^{0.5}z_3(\theta)d\theta \end{cases} \quad (19)$$

where $r = 1.5, q = 0.08, \ell_1 = \frac{13}{17}, \ell_2 = \frac{6}{29}, \ell_3 = \frac{15}{43}$ and $\mathfrak{D}^r, \mathfrak{D}^q$ serve as the Caputo derivative of order r and q, respectively. Let $\mathcal{W}_1, \mathcal{W}_2, \mathcal{W}_3 : [0,1] \times \mathbb{R} \times \mathbb{R} \times \mathbb{R} \to \mathbb{R}$ be continuous functions given by

$$\begin{cases} \mathcal{W}_1(s, z, \tilde{z}, \bar{z}) = \dfrac{36e^s[z]^2}{40,000(1+[z]^2)} + 0.0009e^s\left(\sin(\mathfrak{D}^{0.08}\tilde{z})\right) + \dfrac{180e^s(\arctan \bar{z})}{200,000}, \\[2mm] \mathcal{W}_2(s, z, \tilde{z}, \bar{z}) = \dfrac{s(\arctan z)}{25,000} + 0.00004s\left(\sin\left(\mathfrak{D}^{0.08}\tilde{z}\right)\right) + \dfrac{4s[\bar{z}]^2}{100,000\left(1+[\bar{z}]^2\right)}, \\[2mm] \mathcal{W}_3(s, z, \tilde{z}, \bar{z}) = 0.0001s\left(\sinh^{-1}z\right) + \dfrac{60s\left[\mathfrak{D}^{0.08}\tilde{z}\right]^2}{600,000+600,000[\mathfrak{D}^{0.08}\tilde{z}]^2} + \dfrac{3s(\arctan \bar{z})}{30,000}, \end{cases}$$

for all $z, \tilde{z}, \tilde{\tilde{z}} \in \mathbb{R}$, $s \in [0,1]$, and $\mathcal{W}_4, \mathcal{W}_5, \ldots, \mathcal{W}_{16} : [0,1] \times \mathbb{R} \times \mathbb{R} \times \mathbb{R} \to \mathbb{R}$ are zero functions. Let $z_1, z_2, \tilde{z}_1, \tilde{z}_2, \tilde{\tilde{z}}_1, \tilde{\tilde{z}}_2 \in \mathbb{R}$ and $s \in [0,1]$. Then, we have

$$|\mathcal{W}_1(s, z_1, \tilde{z}_1, \tilde{\tilde{z}}_1) - \mathcal{W}_1(s, z_2, \tilde{z}_2, \tilde{\tilde{z}}_2)| \leq \frac{9e^s}{10{,}000}\left(|z_1 - z_2| + |\tilde{z}_1 - \tilde{z}_2| + |\tilde{\tilde{z}}_1 - \tilde{\tilde{z}}_2|\right),$$

$$|\mathcal{W}_2(s, z_1, \tilde{z}_1, \tilde{\tilde{z}}_1) - \mathcal{W}_2(s, z_2, \tilde{z}_2, \tilde{\tilde{z}}_2)| \leq \frac{s}{25{,}000}\left(|z_1 - z_2| + |\tilde{z}_1 - \tilde{z}_2| + |\tilde{\tilde{z}}_1 - \tilde{\tilde{z}}_2|\right),$$

$$|\mathcal{W}_3(s, z_1, \tilde{z}_1, \tilde{\tilde{z}}_1) - \mathcal{W}_3(s, z_2, \tilde{z}_2, \tilde{\tilde{z}}_2)| \leq \frac{s}{10{,}000}\left(|z_1 - z_2| + |\tilde{z}_1 - \tilde{z}_2| + |\tilde{\tilde{z}}_1 - \tilde{\tilde{z}}_2|\right).$$

Here, $\mathcal{G}_1(s) = \frac{9e^s}{10{,}000}$, $\mathcal{G}_2(s) = \frac{s}{25{,}000}$, $\mathcal{G}_3(s) = \frac{s}{10{,}000}$, and $\mathcal{G}_4(s) = \mathcal{G}_5(s) = \ldots = \mathcal{G}_{16}(s) = 0$, where $\|\mathcal{G}_1\| = \frac{9}{10{,}000}$, $\|\mathcal{G}_2\| = \frac{1}{25{,}000}$, $\|\mathcal{G}_3\| = \frac{1}{10{,}000}$, and $\|\mathcal{G}_4\| = \|\mathcal{G}_5\| = \ldots = \|\mathcal{G}_{16}\| = 0$. Let $\mathcal{M}_1, \mathcal{M}_2, \ldots, \mathcal{M}_{16} : [0, \infty) \to \mathbb{R}$ be identity functions. Thus, we obtain

$$|\mathcal{W}_1(s, z, \tilde{z}, \tilde{\tilde{z}})| \leq \frac{9e^s}{10{,}000}(|z| + |\tilde{z}| + |\tilde{\tilde{z}}|),$$

$$|\mathcal{W}_2(s, z, \tilde{z}, \tilde{\tilde{z}})| \leq \frac{s}{25{,}000}(|z| + |\tilde{z}| + |\tilde{\tilde{z}}|),$$

$$|\mathcal{W}_3(s, z, \tilde{z}, \tilde{\tilde{z}})| \leq \frac{s}{10{,}000}(|z| + |\tilde{z}| + |\tilde{\tilde{z}}|),$$

for all $z, \tilde{z}, \tilde{\tilde{z}}$ and $s \in [0,1]$, where the continuous function $\mathcal{F}_1, \mathcal{F}_2, \ldots, \mathcal{F}_{16} : [0,1] \to \mathbb{R}$ are defined by

$$\mathcal{F}_1(s) = \frac{9e^s}{10{,}000}, \quad \mathcal{F}_2(s) = \frac{s}{25{,}000}, \quad \mathcal{F}_3(s) = \frac{s}{10{,}000}, \quad \mathcal{F}_4(s) = \mathcal{F}_5(s) = \ldots = \mathcal{F}_{16}(s) = 0.$$

Additionally,

$$\mathcal{V}_0^* \simeq 1.3773, \quad \mathcal{V}_1^* \simeq 0.1779 \text{ and } \mathcal{V}_2^* \simeq 0.1773,$$

and so

$$\mathcal{V}_0^* + \mathcal{V}_1^* + \mathcal{V}_2^* \simeq 1.7325.$$

Furthermore,

$$\Lambda := (\mathcal{V}_0^* + \mathcal{V}_1^* + \mathcal{V}_2^*)(\|\mathcal{G}_1\| + \|\mathcal{G}_2\| + \|\mathcal{G}_3\| + \|\mathcal{G}_4\|) \simeq 0.0018 < 1.$$

According to Theorem 4, there exists a solution to Problems (18) and (19).

5. Discussion and Conclusions

The scope of the study on chemical graph theory encompasses all aspects of the applications of graph theory to the field of chemistry. The word "chemical" is used to distinguish chemical graph theory from traditional graph theory, where rigorous mathematical proofs are often preferred to the intuitive grasp of key ideas and theorems. However, graph theory is used to represent the structural features of chemical substances. The tremendous growth of this discipline over the last several decades has resulted in the development of a plethora of cutting-edge concepts and methods for conducting this kind of study.

Using the idea of star graphs, several scholars have studied the solutions of fractional differential equations. They chose to utilize star graphs since their method required a central node connected to nearby vertices through interconnections, but there are no edges between the nodes.

The purpose of this study was to extend the technique's applicability by introducing the concept of a neopentane graph, a fundamental molecule in chemistry with the formula C_5H_{12}. In this manner, we explored a network in which the vertices were either labeled with 0 or 1, and the structure of the chemical molecule neopentane was shown to have an effect on this network. To study whether or not there were solutions to the offered boundary value problems within the context of the Caputo fractional derivative, we used the fixed point theorems developed by Schaefer and Krasnoselskii. In conclusion, an example was given to illustrate the significance of the findings obtained from this research line.

Our method can be used for various graphs, such as digraphs, which are necessary for protein networks in biomedical engineering. The following open problems are presented for the consideration of readers interested in this topic:

- Is there another approach that leads to the same conclusion as we proposed?
- Can this concept be applied to graphs with a circular ring structure?
- We also present the suggested fractional differential Equation (1)'s stability as an unsolved problem.

Author Contributions: Conceptualization, A.T. and N.R.; methodology, A.T.; validation, A.T. and N.R.; formal analysis, A.T. and N.R.; writing—original draft preparation, A.T. and N.R. All authors have read and agreed to the published version of the manuscript.

Funding: The authors would like to thank the Ministry of Higher Education for providing financial support under Fundamental research grant No. FRGS/1/2019/STG06/UMP/02/2 (University reference RDU1901139).

Data Availability Statement: Not applicable.

Acknowledgments: The authors would like to thank the Ministry of Higher Education for providing financial support under Fundamental research grant No. FRGS/1/2019/STG06/UMP/02/2 (University reference RDU1901139). The authors would also like to thank the anonymous referees for their insightful comments, which enhanced the paper's readability and quality.

Conflicts of Interest: The authors declare no conflict of interest.

References

1. Thackray, A. *Atoms and Powers*; Harvard University Press: Cambridge, MA, USA, 1970.
2. Bonchev, B. *Chemical Graph Theory: Introduction and Fundamentals*; CRC Press: Boca Raton, FL, USA, 1991.
3. Oldham, K.B.; Spanier, J. *The Fractional Calculus*; Academic Press: New York, NY, USA, 1974.
4. Debnath, P.; Srivastava, H.M.; Kumam, P.; Hazarika, B. *Fixed Point Theory and Fractional Calculus–Recent Advances and Applications*; Springer: Singapore, 2022.
5. Lakshmikantham, V.; Leela, S.; Devi, J.V. *Theory of Fractional Dynamic Systems*; Cambridge Academic: Cambridge, UK, 2009.
6. Podlubny, I. *Fractional Differential Equations*; Academic Press: New York, NY, USA, 1999.
7. Miller, K.S.; Ross, B. *An Introduction to the Fractional Calculus and Fractional Differential Equation*; John Wiley: New York, NY, USA, 1993.
8. Turab, A.; Sintunavarat, W. A unique solution of the iterative boundary value problem for a second-order differential equation approached by fixed point results. *Alex. Eng. J.* **2021**, *60*, 5797–5802. [CrossRef]
9. Sintunavarat, W.; Turab, A. Mathematical analysis of an extended SEIR model of COVID–19 using the ABC-fractional operator. *Math. Comput. Simul.* **2022**, *198*, 65–84. [CrossRef] [PubMed]
10. Abdeljawad, A.; Agarwal, R.P.; Karapinar, E.; Kumari, P.S. Solutions of the nonlinear integral equation and fractional differential equation using the technique of a fixed point with a numerical experiment in extended b-metric space. *Symmetry* **2019**, *11*, 686. [CrossRef]
11. Adiguzel, R.S.; Aksoy, U.; Karapinar, E.; Erhan, I.M. On the solution of a boundary value problem associated with a fractional differential equation. *Math. Meth. Appl Sci.* **2020**, 1–12. [CrossRef]
12. Sabatier, J.; Agarwal, O.P.; Machado, J.A.T. *Advances in Fractional Calculus, Theoretical Developments and Applications in Physics and Engineering*; Springer: Berlin, Germany, 2007.
13. Agarwal, R.P.; Lakshmikantham, V.; Nieto, J.J. On the concept of solution for fractional differential equations with uncertainty. *Nonlinear Anal. Theory* **2010**, *72*, 2859–2862. [CrossRef]
14. Machado, J.A.T.; Kiryakova, V.; Mainardi, F. Recent history of fractional calculus. *Commun. Nonlinear Sci.* **2011**, *16*, 1140–1153. [CrossRef]
15. Baleanu, D.; Diethelm, K.; Scalas, E.; Trujillo, J.J. *Fractional Calculus Models and Numerical Methods, Series on Complexity. Nonlinearity and Chaos*; World Scientific: London, UK, 2012.
16. Qiu, T.; Bai, Z. Existence of positive solution for singular fractional equations. *Electr. J. Differ. Equ.* **2008**, *146*, 1–9.
17. Debnath, P.; Konwar, N.; Radenovic, S. *Metric Fixed Point Theory: Applications in Science, Engineering and Behavioural Sciences*; Springer: Berlin/Heidelberg, Germany, 2021.

8. Afshari, H.; Kalantari, S.; Karapinar, E. Solution of fractional differential equations via coupled fixed point. *Electron. J. Differ. Equ.* **2015**, *286*, 1–12.
9. Alqahtani, B.; Aydi, H.; Karapinar, E.; Rakocevic, V. A solution for Volterra fractional integral equations by hybrid contractions. *Mathematics* **2019**, *7*, 694. [CrossRef]
10. Karapinar, E.; Fulga, A.; Rashid, M.; Shahid, L.; Aydi, H. Large contractions on quasi-metric spaces with an application to nonlinear fractional differential equations. *Mathematics* **2019**, *7*, 444. [CrossRef]
11. Zhang, S. Existence of positive solutions for some class of nonlinear fractional equation. *J. Math. Anal. Appl.* **2003**, *278*, 136–148. [CrossRef]
12. Hashim, I.; Abdulaziz, O.; Momani, S. Homotopy analysis method for fractional IVPs. *Commun. Nonlinear Sci.* **2009**, *14*, 674–684. [CrossRef]
13. Al-Mdallal, M.; Syam, M.I.; Anwar, M.N. A collocation-shooting method for solving fractional boundary value problems. *Commun. Nonlinear Sci.* **2010**, *15*, 3814–3822. [CrossRef]
14. Zhang, S. The existence of a positive solution for nonlinear fractional differential equation. *J. Math. Anal. Appl.* **2000**, *252*, 804–812. [CrossRef]
15. Lumer, G. Connecting of local operators and evolution equations on a network. *Lect. Notes Math.* **1985**, *787*, 219–234.
16. Zavgorodnii, M.G.; Pokornyi, Y.V. On the spectrum of second-order boundary value problems on spatial networks. *Usp. Mat. Nauk.* **1989**, *44*, 220–221.
17. Gordeziani, D.G.; Kupreishvli, M.; Meladze, H.V.; Davitashvili, T.D. On the solution of boundary value problem for differential equations given in graphs. *Appl. Math. Lett.* **2008**, *13*, 80–91.
18. Mehandiratta, V.; Mehra, M.; Leugering, G. Existence and uniqueness results for a nonlinear Caputo fractional boundary value problem on a star graph. *J. Math. Anal. Appl.* **2019**, *477*, 1243–1264. [CrossRef]
19. Graef, J.R.; Kong, L.J.; Wang, M. Existence and uniqueness of solutions for a fractional boundary value problem on a graph. *Fract. Calc. Appl. Anal.* **2014**, *17*, 499–510. [CrossRef]
20. Etemad, S.; Rezapour, S. On the existence of solutions for fractional boundary value problems on the ethane graph. *Adv. Differ. Equ.* **2020**, *276*, 2020. [CrossRef]
21. Turab, A.; Sintunavarat, W. The novel existence results of solutions for a nonlinear fractional boundary value problem on the ethane graph. *Alex. Eng. J.* **2021**, *60*, 5365–5374. [CrossRef]
22. Baleanu, D.; Etemad, S.; Mohammadi, H.; Rezapour, S. A novel modeling of boundary value problems on the glucose graph. *Comm. Nonlinear Sci. Num. Simul.* **2021**, *100*, 105844. [CrossRef]
23. Rezapour, S.; Deressa, C.T.; Hussain, A.; Etemad, S.; George, R.; Ahmad, B. A theoretical analysis of a fractional multi-dimensional system of boundary value problems on the methylpropane graph via fixed point technique. *Mathematics* **2022**, *10*, 568. [CrossRef]
24. Turab, A.; Mitrovic, Z.D.; Savic, A. Existence of solutions for a class of nonlinear boundary value problems on the hexasilinane graph. *Adv. Differ. Equ.* **2021**, *494*, 2021. [CrossRef]
25. Ali, W.; Turab, A.; Nieto, J.J. On the novel existence results of solutions for a class of fractional boundary value problems on the cyclohexane graph. *J. Inequal. Appl.* **2022**, *5*, 2022. [CrossRef]
26. Sintunavarat, W.; Turab, A. A unified fixed point approach to study the existence of solutions for a class of fractional boundary value problems arising in a chemical graph theory. *PLoS ONE* **2022**, *17*, e0270148. [CrossRef]
27. Caputo, M.; Fabrizio, M. A new definition of fractional derivative without singular kernel. *Prog. Fract. Differ. Appl.* **2015**, *1*, 1–13.
28. Smart, D.R. *Fixed Point Theorems*; Cambridge University Press: Cambridge, UK, 1990.

Article

A Relaxed Inertial Tseng's Extragradient Method for Solving Split Variational Inequalities with Multiple Output Sets

Timilehin Opeyemi Alakoya * and Oluwatosin Temitope Mewomo

School of Mathematics, Statistics and Computer Science, University of KwaZulu-Natal, Durban 4041, South Africa
* Correspondence: timimaths@gmail.com or alakoyat1@ukzn.ac.za

Abstract: Recently, the split inverse problem has received great research attention due to its several applications in diverse fields. In this paper, we study a new class of split inverse problems called the split variational inequality problem with multiple output sets. We propose a new Tseng extragradient method, which uses self-adaptive step sizes for approximating the solution to the problem when the cost operators are pseudomonotone and non-Lipschitz in the framework of Hilbert spaces. We point out that while the cost operators are non-Lipschitz, our proposed method does not involve any linesearch procedure for its implementation. Instead, we employ a more efficient self-adaptive step size technique with known parameters. In addition, we employ the relaxation method and the inertial technique to improve the convergence properties of the algorithm. Moreover, under some mild conditions on the control parameters and without the knowledge of the operators' norm, we prove that the sequence generated by our proposed method converges strongly to a minimum-norm solution to the problem. Finally, we apply our result to study certain classes of optimization problems, and we present several numerical experiments to demonstrate the applicability of our proposed method. Several of the existing results in the literature in this direction could be viewed as special cases of our results in this study.

Keywords: split inverse problems; non-Lipschitz operators; pseudomonotone operators; Tseng's extragradient method; relaxation and inertial techniques

MSC: 65K15; 47J25; 65J15; 90C33

1. Introduction

Let H be a real Hilbert space endowed with inner product $\langle \cdot, \cdot \rangle$ and induced norm $||\cdot||$. Let C be a nonempty, closed and convex subset of H, and let $A : H \to H$ be an operator. Recall that the variational inequality problem (VIP) is formulated as finding an element $p \in C$ such that

$$\langle x - p, Ap \rangle \geq 0, \quad \forall x \in C. \tag{1}$$

The solution set of the VIP (1) is denoted by $VI(C, A)$. Fichera [1] and Stampacchia [2] were the first to introduce and initiate a study independently on variational inequality theory. The variational inequality model is known to provide a general and useful framework for solving several problems in engineering, optimal control, data sciences, mathematical programming, economics, etc. (see [3–8] and the references therein). In recent times, the VIP has received great research attention owing to its several applications in diverse fields, such as economics, operations research, optimization theory, structural analysis, sciences and engineering (see [9–14] and the references therein). Several methods have been proposed and analyzed by authors for solving the VIP (see [15–19] and references therein).

One of the well-known and highly efficient methods is the Tseng extragradient method [20] (which is also known as the forward–backward–forward algorithm). The method is a two-step projection iterative method, which only requires single computation of the projection onto the feasible set per iteration. Several authors have modified and improved on the Tseng extragradient method to approximate the solution of the VIP (1) (for instance, see [19,21–23] and the references therein).

Another active area of research interest in recent years is the *split inverse problem* (SIP). The SIP finds applications in various fields, such as in medical image reconstruction, intensity-modulated radiation therapy, signal processing, phase retrieval, data compression, etc. (for instance, see [24–27]). The SIP model is presented as follows:

$$\text{Find } \hat{x} \in H_1 \text{ that solves IP}_1 \tag{2}$$

such that

$$\hat{y} := T\hat{x} \in H_2 \quad \text{solves IP}_2, \tag{3}$$

where H_1 and H_2 are real Hilbert spaces, IP$_1$ denotes an inverse problem formulated in H_1, and IP$_2$ denotes an inverse problem formulated in H_2, and $T : H_1 \to H_2$ is a bounded linear operator.

The first instance of the SIP, called the *split feasibility problem* (SFP), was introduced in 1994 by Censor and Elfving [26] for modeling inverse problems that arise from medical image reconstruction. The SFP has numerous areas of applications, for instance, in signal processing, biomedical engineering, control theory, approximation theory, geophysics, communications, etc. [25,27,28]. The SFP is formulated as follows:

$$\text{Find } \hat{x} \in C \text{ such that } \hat{y} = T\hat{x} \in Q, \tag{4}$$

where C and Q are nonempty, closed and convex subsets of Hilbert spaces H_1 and H_2, respectively, and $T : H_1 \to H_2$ is a bounded linear operator.

A well-known method for solving the SFP is the CQ method proposed by Byrne [29]. The CQ method has been improved and extended by several researchers. Moreover, many authors have proposed and analyzed several other iterative methods for approximating the solution of SFP (4) both in the framework of Hilbert and Banach spaces (for instance, see [25,27,28,30,31]).

Censor et al. [32] introduced an important generalization of the SFP called the *split variational inequality problem* (SVIP). The SVIP is defined as follows:

$$\text{Find } \hat{x} \in C \text{ that solves } \langle A_1 \hat{x}, x - \hat{x} \rangle \geq 0, \quad \forall x \in C \tag{5}$$

such that

$$\hat{y} = T\hat{x} \in H_2 \text{ solves } \langle A_2 \hat{y}, y - \hat{y} \rangle \geq 0, \quad \forall y \in Q, \tag{6}$$

where $A_1 : H_1 \to H_1$, $A_2 : H_2 \to H_2$ are single-valued operators. Many authors have proposed and analyzed several iterative techniques for solving the SVIP (e.g., see [33–36]).

Very recently, Reich and Tuyen [37] introduced and studied a new split inverse problem called the *split feasibility problem with multiple output sets* (SFPMOS) in the framework of Hilbert spaces. Let C and Q_i be nonempty, closed and convex subsets of Hilbert spaces H and $H_i, i = 1, 2, \ldots, N$, respectively. Let $T_i : H \to H_i, i = 1, 2, \ldots, N$ be bounded linear operators. The SFPMOS is formulated as follows: find an element $u^\dagger \in H$ such that

$$u^\dagger \in \Gamma := C \cap (\cap_{i=1}^N T_i^{-1}(Q_i)) \neq \emptyset. \tag{7}$$

Reich and Tuyen [38] proposed and analyzed two iterative methods for solving the SFPMOS (7) in the framework of Hilbert spaces. The proposed algorithms are presented as follows:

$$x_{n+1} = P_C\left[x_n - \gamma_n \sum_{i=1}^N T_i^*(I - P_{Q_i})T_i x_n\right], \tag{8}$$

and
$$x_{n+1} = \alpha_n f(x_n) + (1 - \alpha_n) P_C \left[x_n - \gamma_n \sum_{i=1}^{N} T_i^*(I - P_{Q_i}) T_i x_n \right], \quad (9)$$

where $f : C \to C$ is a strict contraction, $\{\gamma_n\} \subset (0, +\infty)$ and $\{\alpha_n\} \subset (0, 1)$. The authors obtained weak and strong convergence results for Algorithm (8) and Algorithm (9), respectively.

Motivated by the importance and several applications of the split inverse problems, in this paper, we examine a new class of split inverse problems called the split variational inequality problem with multiple output sets. Let $H, H_i, i = 1, 2, \ldots, N$, be real Hilbert spaces and let C, C_i be nonempty, closed and convex subsets of real Hilbert spaces H and $H_i, i = 1, 2, \ldots, N$, respectively. Let $T_i : H \to H_i, i = 1, 2, \ldots, N$, be bounded linear operators and let $A : H \to H, A_i : H_i \to H_i, i = 1, 2, \ldots, N$, be mappings. The *split variational inequality problem with multiple output sets* (SVIPMOS) is formulated as finding a point $x^* \in C$ such that

$$x^* \in \Omega := VI(C, A) \cap (\cap_{i=1}^{N} T_i^{-1} VI(C_i, A_i)) \neq \emptyset. \quad (10)$$

Observe that the SVIPMOS (10) is a more general problem than the SFPMOS (7).

In recent times, developing algorithms with high rates of convergence for solving optimization problems has become of great interest to researchers. There are two important techniques that are generally employed by researchers to improve the rate of convergence of iterative methods. These techniques include the *inertial technique* and the *relaxation technique*. The inertial technique first introduced by Polyak [39] originates from an implicit time discretization method (the heavy ball method) of second-order dynamical systems. The main feature of the inertial-algorithm is that the method uses the previous two iterates to generate the next iterate. We note that this small change can significantly improve the speed of convergence of an iterative method (for instance, see [21,23,40–45]). The relaxation method is another well-known technique employed by authors to improve the rate of convergence of iterative methods (see, e.g., [46–48]). The influence of these two techniques on the convergence properties of iterative methods was investigated in [46].

In this study, we introduce and analyze the convergence of a relaxed inertial Tseng extragradient method for solving the SVIPMOS (10) in the framework of Hilbert spaces when the cost operators are pseudomonotone and non-Lipschitz. Our proposed algorithm has the following key features:

- The proposed method does not require the Lipschitz continuity condition often imposed by the cost operator in the literature when solving variational inequality problems. In addition, while the cost operators are non-Lipschitz, the design of our algorithm does not involve any linesearch procedure, which could be time-consuming and too expensive to implement.
- Our proposed method does not require knowledge of the operators' norm for its implementation. Rather, we employ a very efficient self-adaptive step size technique with known parameters. Moreover, some of the control parameters are relaxed to enlarge the range of values of the step sizes of the algorithm.
- Our algorithm combines the relaxation method and the inertial techniques to improve its convergence properties.
- The sequence generated by our proposed method converges strongly to a minimum-norm solution to the SVIPMOS (10). Finding the minimum-norm solution to a problem is very important and useful in several practical problems.

Finally, we apply our result to study certain classes of optimization problems, and we carry out several numerical experiments to illustrate the applicability of our proposed method.

This paper is organized as follows: In Section 2, we present some definitions and lemmas needed to analyze the convergence of the proposed algorithm, while in Section 3, we present the proposed method. In Section 4, we discuss the convergence of the proposed method, and in Section 5, we apply our result to study certain classes of optimization problems. In Section 6, we present several numerical experiments with graphical illustrations. Finally, in Section 7, we give a concluding remark.

2. Preliminaries

Definition 1 ([21,22]). *An operator $A : H \to H$ is said to be*
(i) *α-strongly monotone, if there exists $\alpha > 0$ such that*

$$\langle x - y, Ax - Ay \rangle \geq \alpha \|x - y\|^2, \quad \forall\, x, y \in H;$$

(ii) *monotone, if*

$$\langle x - y, Ax - Ay \rangle \geq 0, \quad \forall\, x, y \in H;$$

(iii) *pseudomonotone, if*

$$\langle Ay, x - y \rangle \geq 0 \implies \langle Ax, x - y \rangle \geq 0,\ \forall x, y \in H,$$

(iv) *L-Lipschitz continuous, if there exists a constant $L > 0$ such that*

$$\|Ax - Ay\| \leq L\|x - y\|, \quad \forall\, x, y \in H;$$

(v) *uniformly continuous, if for every $\epsilon > 0$, there exists $\delta = \delta(\epsilon) > 0$, such that*

$$\|Ax - Ay\| < \epsilon \quad \text{whenever} \quad \|x - y\| < \delta, \quad \forall x, y \in H;$$

(vi) *sequentially weakly continuous, if for each sequence $\{x_n\}$, we have $x_n \rightharpoonup x \in H$ implies that $Ax_n \rightharpoonup Ax \in H$.*

Remark 1. *It is known that the following implications hold: $(i) \implies (ii) \implies (iii)$ but the converses are not generally true. We also note that uniform continuity is a weaker notion than Lipschitz continuity.*

It is well-known that if D is a convex subset of H, then $A : D \to H$ is uniformly continuous if and only if, for every $\epsilon > 0$, there exists a constant $K < +\infty$ such that

$$\|Ax - Ay\| \leq K\|x - y\| + \epsilon \quad \forall x, y \in D. \tag{11}$$

Lemma 1 ([49]). *Suppose $\{a_n\}$ is a sequence of nonnegative real numbers, $\{\alpha_n\}$ is a sequence in $(0, 1)$ with $\sum_{n=1}^{\infty} \alpha_n = +\infty$ and $\{b_n\}$ is a sequence of real numbers. Assume that*

$$a_{n+1} \leq (1 - \alpha_n)a_n + \alpha_n b_n \quad \text{for all } n \geq 1.$$

If $\limsup_{k \to \infty} b_{n_k} \leq 0$ for every subsequence $\{a_{n_k}\}$ of $\{a_n\}$ satisfying $\liminf_{k \to \infty}(a_{n_k+1} - a_{n_k}) \geq 0$, then $\lim_{n \to \infty} a_n = 0$.

Lemma 2 ([50]). *Suppose $\{\lambda_n\}$ and $\{\theta_n\}$ are two nonnegative real sequences such that*

$$\lambda_{n+1} \leq \lambda_n + \phi_n, \quad \forall n \geq 1.$$

If $\sum_{n=1}^{\infty} \phi_n < +\infty$, then $\lim_{n \to \infty} \lambda_n$ exists.

Lemma 3 ([51]). *Let H be a real Hilbert space. Then, the following results hold for all $x, y \in H$ and $\delta \in (0, 1)$:*
(i) $\|x + y\|^2 \leq \|x\|^2 + 2\langle y, x + y \rangle;$
(ii) $\|x + y\|^2 = \|x\|^2 + 2\langle x, y \rangle + \|y\|^2;$

(iii) $\|\delta x + (1-\delta)y\|^2 = \delta\|x\|^2 + (1-\delta)\|y\|^2 - \delta(1-\delta)\|x-y\|^2$.

Lemma 4 ([52]). *Consider the VIP (1) with C being a nonempty, closed, convex subset of a real Hilbert space H and $A : C \to H$ being pseudomonotone and continuous. Then p is a solution of VIP (1) if and only if*

$$\langle Ax, x - p \rangle \geq 0, \qquad \forall x \in C$$

3. Main Results

In this section, we present our proposed iterative method for solving the SVIPMOS (10). We establish our convergence result for the proposed method under the following conditions:

Let C, C_i be nonempty, closed and convex subsets of real Hilbert spaces $H, H_i, i = 1, 2, \ldots, N$, respectively, and let $T_i : H \to H_i, i = 1, 2, \ldots, N$ be bounded linear operators with adjoints T_i^*. Let $A : H \to H, A_i : H_i \to H_i, i = 1, 2, \ldots, N$, be uniformly continuous pseudomonotone operators satisfying the following property:

whenever $\{T_i x_n\} \subset C_i, T_i x_n \rightharpoonup T_i z$, then $\|A_i T_i z\| \leq \liminf_{n\to\infty} \|A_i T_i x_n\|$, $i = 0, 1, 2 \ldots, N, C_0 = C, A_0 = A, T_0 = I^H$. (12)

Moreover, we assume that the solution set $\Omega \neq \emptyset$ and the control parameters satisfy the following conditions:

Assumption B:

(A1) $\{\alpha_n\} \subset (0,1)$, $\lim_{n\to\infty} \alpha_n = 0$, $\sum_{n=1}^{\infty} \alpha_n = +\infty$, $\lim_{n\to\infty} \frac{\epsilon_n}{\alpha_n} = 0$, $\{\xi_n\} \subset [a,b] \subset (0,1), \theta > 0$;

(A2) $0 < c_i < c_i' < 1, 0 < \phi_i < \phi_i' < 1$, $\lim_{n\to\infty} c_{n,i} = \lim_{n\to\infty} \phi_{n,i} = 0, \lambda_{1,i} > 0, \forall i = 0, 1, 2, \ldots, N$;

(A3) $\{\rho_{n,i}\} \subset \mathbb{R}_+, \sum_{n=1}^{\infty} \rho_{n,i} < +\infty, 0 < a_i \leq \delta_{n,i} \leq b_i < 1, \sum_{i=0}^{N} \delta_{n,i} = 1$ for each $n \geq 1$.

Now, the Algorithm 1 is presented as follows:

Algorithm 1. A Relaxed Inertial Tseng's Extragradient Method for Solving SVIPMOS (10).

Step 0. Select initial points $x_0, x_1 \in H$. Let $C_0 = C, T_0 = I^H, A_0 = A$ and set $n = 1$.

Step 1. Given the $(n-1)$th and nth iterates, choose θ_n such that $0 \leq \theta_n \leq \hat{\theta}_n$ with $\hat{\theta}_n$ defined by

$$\hat{\theta}_n = \begin{cases} \min\left\{\theta, \frac{\epsilon_n}{\|x_n - x_{n-1}\|}\right\}, & \text{if } x_n \neq x_{n-1}, \\ \theta, & \text{otherwise.} \end{cases} \quad (13)$$

Step 2. Compute

$$w_n = (1 - \alpha_n)(x_n + \theta_n(x_n - x_{n-1})).$$

Step 3. Compute

$$y_{n,i} = P_{C_i}(T_i w_n - \lambda_{n,i} A_i T_i w_n).$$

Step 4. Compute

$$u_{n,i} = y_{n,i} - \lambda_{n,i}(A_i y_{n,i} - A_i T_i w_n),$$

$$\lambda_{n+1,i} = \begin{cases} \min\left\{\frac{(c_{n,i}+c_i)\|T_i w_n - y_{n,i}\|}{\|A_i T_i w_n - A_i y_{n,i}\|}, \lambda_{n,i} + \rho_{n,i}\right\}, & \text{if } A_i T_i w_n - A_i y_{n,i} \neq 0, \\ \lambda_{n,i} + \rho_{n,i}, & \text{otherwise.} \end{cases}$$

Step 5. Compute

$$v_n = \sum_{i=0}^{N} \delta_{n,i}(w_n + \eta_{n,i} T_i^*(u_{n,i} - T_i w_n)),$$

where

$$\eta_{n,i} = \begin{cases} \frac{(\phi_{n,i}+\phi_i)\|T_i w_n - u_{n,i}\|^2}{\|T_i^*(T_i w_n - u_{n,i})\|^2}, & \text{if } \|T_i^*(T_i w_n - u_{n,i})\| \neq 0, \\ 0, & \text{otherwise.} \end{cases} \quad (14)$$

Step 6. Compute

$$x_{n+1} = \xi_n w_n + (1 - \xi_n) v_n.$$

Set $n := n+1$ and return to **Step 1**.

Remark 2. *Observe that by conditions (C1) and (C2) together with (13), we have that*

$$\lim_{n\to\infty} \theta_n \|x_n - x_{n-1}\| = 0 \quad \text{and} \quad \lim_{n\to\infty} \frac{\theta_n}{\alpha_n}\|x_n - x_{n-1}\| = 0.$$

Remark 3. *We also note that while the cost operators $A_i, i = 0, 1, 2, \ldots, N$ are non-Lipschitz, our method does not require any linesearch procedure, which could be computationally very expensive to implement. Rather, we employ self-adaptive step size techniques that only require simple computations of known parameters per iteration. Moreover, some of the parameters are relaxed to accommodate larger intervals for the step sizes.*

Remark 4. *We remark that condition (12) is a weaker assumption than the sequentially weakly continuity condition. We present the following example satisfying condition (12), which also illustrates that the condition is a weaker assumption than the sequentially weakly continuity condition.*
Let $A : \ell_2(\mathbb{R}) \to \ell_2(\mathbb{R})$ be an operator defined by

$$Ax = x\|x\|, \quad \forall x \in \ell_2(\mathbb{R}).$$

Suppose $\{z_n\} \subset \ell_2(\mathbb{R})$ such that $z_n \rightharpoonup z$. Then, by the weakly lower semi-continuity of the norm we obtain

$$\|z\| \leq \liminf_{n\to+\infty} \|z_n\|.$$

Thus, we have

$$\|Az\| = \|z\|^2 \leq (\liminf_{n\to+\infty} \|z_n\|)^2 \leq \liminf_{n\to+\infty} \|z_n\|^2 = \liminf_{n\to+\infty} \|Az_n\|.$$

Therefore, A satisfies condition (12).
On the other hand, to establish that A is not sequentially weakly continuous, choose $z_n = e_n + e_1$, where $\{e_n\}$ is a standard basis of $\ell_2(\mathbb{R})$, that is, $e_n = (0, 0, \ldots, 1, \ldots)$ with 1 at the n-th position. It is clear that $z_n \rightharpoonup e_1$ and $Az_n = A(e_n + e_1) = (e_n + e_1)\|e_n + e_1\| \rightharpoonup \sqrt{2}e_1$, but $Ae_1 = e_1\|e_1\| = e_1$. Consequently, A is not sequentially weakly continuous. Therefore, condition (12) is strictly weaker than the sequentially weakly continuity condition.

4. Convergence Analysis

First, we prove some lemmas needed for our strong convergence theorem.

Lemma 5. *Let $\{\lambda_{n,i}\}$ be the sequence generated by Algorithm 1 such that Assumption B holds. Then $\{\lambda_{n,i}\}$ is well-defined for each $i = 0, 1, 2, \ldots, N$ and $\lim_{n\to\infty} \lambda_{n,i} = \lambda_{1,i} \in [\min\{\frac{c_i}{M_i}, \lambda_{1,i}\}, \lambda_{1,i} + \Phi_i]$, where $\Phi_i = \sum_{n=1}^{\infty} \rho_{n,i}$.*

Proof. Observe that since A_i is uniformly continuous for each $i = 0, 1, 2, \ldots, N$, it follows from (11) that for any given $\epsilon_i > 0$, there exists $K_i < +\infty$ such that $\|A_i T_i w_n - A_i y_{n,i}\| \leq K_i \|T_i w_n - y_{n,i}\| + \epsilon_i$. Thus, for the case $A_i T_i w_n - A_i y_{n,i} \neq 0$ for all $n \geq 1$, we obtain

$$\frac{(c_{n,i} + c_i)\|T_i w_n - y_{n,i}\|}{\|A_i T_i w_n - A_i y_{n,i}\|} \geq \frac{(c_{n,i} + c_i)\|T_i w_n - y_{n,i}\|}{K_i \|T_i w_n - y_{n,i}\| + \epsilon_i} = \frac{(c_{n,i} + c_i)\|T_i w_n - y_{n,i}\|}{(K_i + \zeta_i)\|T_i w_n - y_{n,i}\|} = \frac{(c_{n,i} + c_i)}{M_i} \geq \frac{c_i}{M_i},$$

where $\epsilon_i = \zeta_i \|T_i w_n - y_{n,i}\|$ for some $\zeta_i \in (0, 1)$ and $M_i = K_i + \zeta_i$. Therefore, by the definition of $\lambda_{n+1,i}$, the sequence $\{\lambda_{n,i}\}$ has lower bound $\min\{\frac{c_i}{M_i}, \lambda_{1,i}\}$ and has upper bound $\lambda_{1,i} + \Phi_i$. By Lemma 2, the limit $\lim_{n\to\infty} \lambda_{n,i}$ exists and is denoted by $\lambda_i = \lim_{n\to\infty} \lambda_{n,i}$. Clearly, $\lambda_i \in [\min\{\frac{c_i}{M_i}, \lambda_{1,i}\}, \lambda_{1,i} + \Phi_i]$ for each $i = 0, 1, 2 \ldots, N$. □

Lemma 6. *If $\|T_i^*(T_i w_n - u_{n,i})\| \neq 0$, then the sequence $\{\eta_{n,i}\}$ defined by (14) has a positive lower bounded for each $i = 0, 1, 2, \ldots, N$.*

Proof. If $\|T_i^*(T_iw_n - u_{n,i})\| \neq 0$, it follows that for each $i = 0, 1, 2, \ldots, N$

$$\eta_{n,i} = \frac{(\phi_{n,i} + \phi_i)\|T_iw_n - u_{n,i}\|^2}{\|T_i^*(T_iw_n - u_{n,i})\|^2}.$$

Since T_i is a bounded linear operator and $\lim_{n \to \infty} \phi_{n,i} = 0$ for each $i = 0, 1, 2, \ldots, N$, we have

$$\frac{(\phi_{n,i} + \phi_i)\|T_iw_n - u_{n,i}\|^2}{\|T_i^*(T_iw_n - u_{n,i})\|^2} \geq \frac{(\phi_{n,i} + \phi_i)\|T_iw_n - u_{n,i}\|^2}{\|T_i\|^2\|T_iw_n - u_{n,i}\|^2} \geq \frac{\phi_i}{\|T_i\|^2},$$

which implies that $\frac{\phi_i}{\|T_i\|^2}$ is a lower bound of $\{\eta_{n,i}\}$ for each $i = 0, 1, 2, \ldots, N$. □

Lemma 7. *Suppose Assumption B of Algorithm 1 holds. Then, there exists a positive integer N such that*

$$\phi_i + \phi_{n,i} \in (0,1), \quad \text{and} \quad \frac{\lambda_{n,i}(c_{n,i} + c_i)}{\lambda_{n+1,i}} \in (0,1), \quad \forall n \geq N.$$

Proof. Since $0 < \phi_i < \phi_i' < 1$ and $\lim_{n \to \infty} \phi_{n,i} = 0$ for each $i = 0, 1, 2, \ldots, N$, there exists a positive integer $N_{1,i}$ such that

$$0 < \phi_i + \phi_{n,i} \leq \phi_i' < 1, \quad \forall n \geq N_{1,i}.$$

Similarly, since $0 < c_i < c_i' < 1$, $\lim_{n \to \infty} c_{n,i} = 0$ and $\lim_{n \to \infty} \lambda_{n,i} = \lambda_i$ for each $i = 0, 1, 2, \ldots, N$, we have

$$\lim_{n \to \infty} \left(1 - \frac{\lambda_{n,i}(c_{n,i} + c_i)}{\lambda_{n+1,i}}\right) = 1 - c_i > 1 - c_i' > 0.$$

Thus, for each $i = 0, 1, 2, \ldots, N$, there exists a positive integer $N_{2,i}$ such that

$$1 - \frac{\lambda_{n,i}(c_{n,i} + c_i)}{\lambda_{n+1,i}} > 0, \quad \forall n \geq N_{2,i}.$$

Now, setting $N = \max\{N_{1,i}, N_{2,i} : i = 0, 1, 2, \ldots, N\}$, we have the required result. □

Lemma 8. *Let $\{x_n\}$ be a sequence generated by Algorithm 1 under Assumption B. Then the following inequality holds for all $p \in \Omega$:*

$$\|u_{n,i} - T_ip\|^2 \leq \|T_iw_n - T_ip\|^2 - \left(1 - \frac{\lambda_{n,i}^2}{\lambda_{n+1,i}^2}(c_{n,i} + c_i)^2\right)\|T_iw_n - y_{n,i}\|^2.$$

Proof. From the definition of $\lambda_{n+1,i}$, we have

$$\|A_iT_iw_n - A_iy_{n,i}\| \leq \frac{(c_{n,i} + c_i)}{\lambda_{n+1,i}}\|T_iw_n - y_{n,i}\|, \quad \forall n \in \mathbb{N}, \ i = 0, 1, \ldots, N. \tag{15}$$

Observe that (15) holds both for $A_iT_iw_n - A_iy_{n,i} = 0$ and $A_iT_iw_n - A_iy_{n,i} \neq 0$. Let $p \in \Omega$. Then, it follows that $T_ip \in VI(C_i, A_i)$, $i = 0, 1, 2, \ldots, N$. Using the definition of $u_{n,i}$ and applying Lemma 3, we have

$$\begin{aligned}
\|u_{n,i} - T_i p\|^2 &= \|y_{n,i} - \lambda_{n,i}(A_i y_{n,i} - A_i T_i w_n) - T_i p\|^2 \\
&= \|y_{n,i} - T_i p\|^2 + \lambda_{n,i}^2 \|A_i y_{n,i} - A_i T_i w_n\|^2 - 2\lambda_{n,i}\langle y_{n,i} - T_i p, A_i y_{n,i} - A_i T_i w_n\rangle \\
&= \|T_i w_n - T_i p\|^2 + \|y_{n,i} - T_i w_n\|^2 + 2\langle y_{n,i} - T_i w_n, T_i w_n - T_i p\rangle + \lambda_{n,i}^2\|A_i y_{n,i} - A_i T_i w_n\|^2 \\
&\quad - 2\lambda_{n,i}\langle y_{n,i} - T_i p, A_i y_{n,i} - A_i T_i w_n\rangle \\
&= \|T_i w_n - T_i p\|^2 + \|y_{n,i} - T_i w_n\|^2 - 2\langle y_{n,i} - T_i w_n, y_{n,i} - T_i w_n\rangle + 2\langle y_{n,i} - T_i w_n, y_{n,i} - T_i p\rangle \\
&\quad + \lambda_{n,i}^2\|A_i y_{n,i} - A_i T_i w_n\|^2 - 2\lambda_{n,i}\langle y_{n,i} - T_i p, A_i y_{n,i} - A_i T_i w_n\rangle \\
&= \|T_i w_n - T_i p\|^2 - \|y_{n,i} - T_i w_n\|^2 + 2\langle y_{n,i} - T_i w_n, y_{n,i} - T_i p\rangle + \lambda_{n,i}^2\|A_i y_{n,i} - A_i T_i w_n\|^2 \\
&\quad - 2\lambda_{n,i}\langle y_{n,i} - T_i p, A_i y_{n,i} - A_i T_i w_n\rangle.
\end{aligned} \tag{16}$$

Since $y_{n,i} = P_{C_i}(T_i w_n - \lambda_{n,i} A_i T_i w_n)$ and $T_i p \in VI(C_i, A_i)$, $i = 0, 1, 2, \ldots, N$, by the property of the projection map we have

$$\langle y_{n,i} - T_i w_n + \lambda_{n,i} A_i T_i w_n, y_{n,i} - T_i p\rangle \leq 0,$$

which is equivalent to

$$\langle y_{n,i} - T_i w_n, y_{n,i} - T_i p\rangle \leq -\lambda_{n,i}\langle A_i T_i w_n, y_{n,i} - T_i p\rangle. \tag{17}$$

Furthermore, since $y_{n,i} \in C_i$, $i = 0, 1, 2, \ldots, N$, we have

$$\langle A_i T_i p, y_{n,i} - T_i p\rangle \geq 0,$$

By the pseudomonotonicity of A_i, it follows that $\langle A_i y_{n,i}, y_{n,i} - T_i p\rangle \geq 0$. Since $\lambda_{n,i} > 0$, $i = 0, 1, 2, \ldots, N$, we obtain

$$\lambda_{n,i}\langle A_i y_{n,i}, y_{n,i} - T_i p\rangle \geq 0. \tag{18}$$

Next, by applying (15), (17) and (18) in (16), we obtain

$$\begin{aligned}
\|u_{n,i} - T_i p\|^2 &\leq \|T_i w_n - T_i p\|^2 - \|y_{n,i} - T_i w_n\|^2 - 2\lambda_{n,i}\langle A_i T_i w_n, y_{n,i} - T_i p\rangle + (c_{n,i} + c_i)^2 \frac{\lambda_{n,i}^2}{\lambda_{n+1,i}^2}\|T_i w_n - y_{n,i}\|^2 \\
&\quad - 2\lambda_{n,i}\langle y_{n,i} - T_i p, A_i y_{n,i} - A_i T_i w_n\rangle \\
&= \|T_i w_n - T_i p\|^2 - \left(1 - \frac{\lambda_{n,i}^2}{\lambda_{n+1,i}^2}(c_{n,i} + c_i)^2\right)\|T_i w_n - y_{n,i}\|^2 - 2\lambda_{n,i}\langle y_{n,i} - T_i p, A_i y_{n,i}\rangle \\
&\leq \|T_i w_n - T_i p\|^2 - \left(1 - \frac{\lambda_{n,i}^2}{\lambda_{n+1,i}^2}(c_{n,i} + c_i)^2\right)\|T_i w_n - y_{n,i}\|^2,
\end{aligned} \tag{19}$$

which is the required inequality. □

Lemma 9. *Suppose $\{x_n\}$ is a sequence generated by Algorithm 1 such that Assumption B holds. Then $\{x_n\}$ is bounded.*

Proof. Let $p \in \Omega$. By the definition of w_n and applying the triangular inequality, we have

$$\begin{aligned}
\|w_n - p\| &= \|(1 - \alpha_n)(x_n + \theta_n(x_n - x_{n-1})) - p\| \\
&= \|(1 - \alpha_n)(x_n - p) + (1 - \alpha_n)\theta_n(x_n - x_{n-1}) - \alpha_n p\| \\
&\leq (1 - \alpha_n)\|x_n - p\| + (1 - \alpha_n)\theta_n\|x_n - x_{n-1}\| + \alpha_n\|p\| \\
&= (1 - \alpha_n)\|x_n - p\| + \alpha_n\left[(1 - \alpha_n)\frac{\theta_n}{\alpha_n}\|x_n - x_{n-1}\| + \|p\|\right].
\end{aligned}$$

By Remark (2), we obtain

$$\lim_{n\to\infty}\left[(1-\alpha_n)\frac{\theta_n}{\alpha_n}\|x_n - x_{n-1}\| + \|p\|\right] = \|p\|.$$

Thus, there exists $M_1 > 0$ such that $(1-\alpha_n)\frac{\theta_n}{\alpha_n}\|x_n - x_{n-1}\| + \|p\| \leq M_1$ for all $n \in \mathbb{N}$. It follows that

$$\|w_n - p\| \leq (1-\alpha_n)\|x_n - p\| + \alpha_n M_1. \tag{20}$$

By Lemma 7, there exists a positive integer N such that $1 - \frac{\lambda_{n_k,i}}{\lambda_{n_k+1,i}}(c_{n_k,i} + c_i) > 0$, $\forall n \geq N$, $i = 0,1,2,\ldots,N$. Consequently, it follows from (19) that for all $n \geq N$ and $i = 0,1,2,\ldots,N$

$$\leq \|u_{n,i} - T_i p\|^2 \leq \|T_i w_n - T_i p\|^2. \tag{21}$$

Next, since the function $\|\cdot\|^2$ is convex, we have

$$\|v_n - p\|^2 = \|\sum_{i=0}^{N}\delta_{n,i}(w_n + \eta_{n,i}T_i^*(u_{n,i} - T_i w_n)) - p\|^2$$

$$\leq \sum_{i=0}^{N}\delta_{n,i}\|w_n + \eta_{n,i}T_i^*(u_{n,i} - T_i w_n) - p\|^2. \tag{22}$$

By Lemma 7, there exists a positive integer N such that $0 < \phi_{n,i} + \phi_i < 1$, $i = 0,1,2,\ldots,N$ for all $n \geq N$. From (22) and by applying Lemma 3 and (21), we obtain

$$\|w_n + \eta_{n,i}T_i^*(u_{n,i} - T_i w_n) - p\|^2 = \|w_n - p\|^2 + \eta_{n,i}^2\|T_i^*(u_{n,i} - T_i w_n)\|^2 + 2\eta_{n,i}\langle w_n - p, T_i^*(u_{n,i} - T_i w_n)\rangle$$

$$= \|w_n - p\|^2 + \eta_{n,i}^2\|T_i^*(u_{n,i} - T_i w_n)\|^2 + 2\eta_{n,i}\langle T_i w_n - T_i p, u_{n,i} - T_i w_n\rangle$$

$$= \|w_n - p\|^2 + \eta_{n,i}^2\|T_i^*(u_{n,i} - T_i w_n)\|^2 + \eta_{n,i}[\|u_{n,i} - T_i p\|^2 - \|T_i w_n - T_i p\|^2$$

$$- \|u_{n,i} - T_i w_n\|^2]$$

$$\leq \|w_n - p\|^2 + \eta_{n,i}^2\|T_i^*(u_{n,i} - T_i w_n)\|^2 - \eta_{n,i}\|u_{n,i} - T_i w_n\|^2$$

$$= \|w_n - p\|^2 - \eta_{n,i}[\|u_{n,i} - T_i w_n\|^2 - \eta_{n,i}\|T_i^*(u_{n,i} - T_i w_n)\|^2]. \tag{23}$$

If $\|T_i^*(u_{n,i} - T_i w_n)\| \neq 0$, then by the definition of $\eta_{n,i}$, we have

$$\|u_{n,i} - T_i w_n\|^2 - \eta_{n,i}\|T_i^*(u_{n,i} - T_i w_n)\|^2 = [1 - (\phi_{n,i} + \phi_i)]\|T_i w_n - u_{n,i}\|^2 \geq 0. \tag{24}$$

Now, applying (24) in (23) and substituting in (22), we have

$$\|v_n - p\|^2 \leq \|w_n - p\|^2 - \sum_{i=0}^{N}\delta_{n,i}\eta_{n,i}[1 - (\phi_{n,i} + \phi_i)]\|T_i w_n - u_{n,i}\|^2$$

$$\leq \|w_n - p\|^2. \tag{25}$$

Observe that if $\|T_i^*(u_{n,i} - T_i w_n)\| = 0$, (25) still holds from (23).

Next, using the definition of x_{n+1}, and applying (20) and (25), we have

$$\begin{aligned}\|x_{n+1} - p\| &= \|\xi_n w_n + (1-\xi_n)v_n - p\| \\ &\leq \xi_n \|w_n - p\| + (1-\xi_n)\|v_n - p\| \\ &\leq \xi_n \|w_n - p\| + (1-\xi_n)\|w_n - p\| \\ &= \|w_n - p\| \\ &\leq (1-\alpha_n)\|x_n - p\| + \alpha_n M_1 \\ &\leq \max\{\|x_n - p\|, M_1\} \\ &\vdots \\ &\leq \max\{\|x_N - p\|, M_1\},\end{aligned}$$

which implies that $\{x_n\}$ is bounded. Hence, $\{w_n\}$, $\{y_{n,i}\}$, $\{u_{n,i}\}$ and $\{v_n\}$ are all bounded. □

Lemma 10. *Let $\{w_n\}$ and $\{v_n\}$ be two sequences generated by Algorithm 1 with subsequences $\{w_{n_k}\}$ and $\{v_{n_k}\}$, respectively, such that $\lim_{k\to\infty}\|w_{n_k} - v_{n_k}\| = 0$. Suppose $w_{n_k} \rightharpoonup z \in H$, then $z \in \Omega$.*

Proof. From (25), we have

$$\|v_{n_k} - p\|^2 \leq \|w_{n_k} - p\|^2 - \sum_{i=0}^{N} \delta_{n_k,i}\eta_{n_k,i}[1 - (\phi_{n_k,i} + \phi_i)]\|T_i w_{n_k} - u_{n_k,i}\|^2. \tag{26}$$

From the last inequality, we obtain

$$\sum_{i=0}^{N} \delta_{n_k,i}\eta_{n_k,i}[1 - (\phi_{n_k,i} + \phi_i)]\|T_i w_{n_k} - u_{n_k,i}\|^2 \leq \|w_{n_k} - p\|^2 - \|v_{n_k} - p\|^2$$

$$\leq \|w_{n_k} - v_{n_k}\|^2 + 2\|w_{n_k} - v_{n_k}\|\|v_{n_k} - p\| \tag{27}$$

Since by the hypothesis of the lemma $\lim_{k\to\infty}\|w_{n_k} - v_{n_k}\| = 0$, it follows from (27) that

$$\sum_{i=0}^{N} \delta_{n_k,i}\eta_{n_k,i}[1 - (\phi_{n_k,i} + \phi_i)]\|T_i w_{n_k} - u_{n_k,i}\|^2 \to 0, \quad k \to \infty,$$

which implies that

$$\delta_{n_k,i}\eta_{n_k,i}[1 - (\phi_{n_k,i} + \phi_i)]\|T_i w_{n_k} - u_{n_k,i}\|^2 \to 0, \quad k \to \infty, \ \forall i = 0,1,2,\ldots,N.$$

By the definition of $\eta_{n,i}$, we have

$$\delta_{n_k,i}(\phi_{n_k,i} + \phi_i)[1 - (\phi_{n_k,i} + \phi_i)]\frac{\|T_i w_{n_k} - u_{n_k,i}\|^4}{\|T_i^*(T_i w_{n_k} - u_{n_k,i})\|^2} \to 0, \quad k \to \infty, \ \forall i = 0,1,2,\ldots,N.$$

From this, we obtain

$$\frac{\|T_i w_{n_k} - u_{n_k,i}\|^2}{\|T_i^*(T_i w_{n_k} - u_{n_k,i})\|} \to 0, \quad k \to \infty, \ \forall i = 0,1,2,\ldots,N,$$

Since $\{\|T_i^*(T_i w_{n_k} - u_{n_k,i})\|\}$ is bounded, it follows that

$$\|T_i w_{n_k} - u_{n_k,i}\| \to 0, \quad k \to \infty, \ \forall i = 0,1,2,\ldots,N. \tag{28}$$

Hence, we have

$$\|T_i^*(T_iw_{n_k} - u_{n_k,i})\| \leq \|T_i^*\|\|(T_iw_{n_k} - u_{n_k,i})\| = \|T_i\|\|(T_iw_{n_k} - u_{n_k,i})\| \to 0, \quad k \to \infty, \ \forall i = 0, 1, 2, \ldots, N. \tag{29}$$

From (19), we obtain

$$\left(1 - \frac{\lambda_{n_k,i}^2}{\lambda_{n_k+1,i}^2}(c_{n_k,i} + c_i)^2\right)\|T_iw_{n_k} - y_{n_k,i}\|^2 \leq \|T_iw_{n_k} - T_ip\|^2 - \|u_{n_k,i} - T_ip\|^2$$

$$\leq \|T_iw_{n_k} - u_{n_k,i}\|(\|T_iw_{n_k} - T_ip\| + \|u_{n_k,i} - T_ip\|). \tag{30}$$

By applying (28), it follows from (30) that

$$\left(1 - \frac{\lambda_{n_k,i}^2}{\lambda_{n_k+1,i}^2}(c_{n_k,i} + c_i)^2\right)\|T_iw_{n_k} - y_{n_k,i}\|^2 \to 0, \quad k \to \infty, \ i = 0, 1, \ldots, N.$$

Consequently, we have

$$\|T_iw_{n_k} - y_{n_k,i}\| \to 0, \quad k \to \infty, \ i = 0, 1, \ldots, N. \tag{31}$$

Since $y_{n,i} = P_{C_i}(T_iw_n - \lambda_{n,i}A_iT_iw_n)$, by the property of the projection map, we obtain

$$\langle T_iw_{n_k} - \lambda_{n_k,i}A_iT_iw_{n_k} - y_{n_k,i}, T_ix - y_{n_k,i}\rangle \leq 0, \quad \forall T_ix \in C_i, \ i = 0, 1, 2, \ldots, N,$$

which implies that

$$\frac{1}{\lambda_{n_k,i}}\langle T_iw_{n_k} - y_{n_k,i}, T_ix - y_{n_k,i}\rangle \leq \langle A_iT_iw_{n_k}, T_ix - y_{n_k,i}\rangle, \quad \forall T_ix \in C_i, \ i = 0, 1, 2, \ldots, N.$$

From the last inequality, it follows that

$$\frac{1}{\lambda_{n_k,i}}\langle T_iw_{n_k} - y_{n_k,i}, T_ix - y_{n_k,i}\rangle + \langle A_iT_iw_{n_k}, y_{n_k,i} - T_iw_{n_k}\rangle \leq \langle A_iT_iw_{n_k}, T_ix - T_iw_{n_k}\rangle, \ \forall T_ix \in C_i, \ i = 0, 1, 2, \ldots, N. \tag{32}$$

By applying (31) and the fact that $\lim_{k \to \infty} \lambda_{n_k,i} = \lambda_i > 0$, from (32) we obtain

$$\liminf_{k \to \infty}\langle A_iT_iw_{n_k}, T_ix - T_iw_{n_k}\rangle \geq 0, \quad \forall T_ix \in C_i, \ i = 0, 1, 2, \ldots, N. \tag{33}$$

Observe that

$$\langle A_iy_{n_k,i}, T_ix - y_{n_k,i}\rangle = \langle A_iy_{n_k,i} - A_iT_iw_{n_k}, T_ix - T_iw_{n_k}\rangle + \langle A_iT_iw_{n_k}, T_ix - T_iw_{n_k}\rangle + \langle A_iy_{n_k,i}, T_iw_{n_k} - y_{n_k,i}\rangle. \tag{34}$$

By the continuity of A_i, from (31) we obtain

$$\|A_iT_iw_{n_k} - A_iy_{n_k,i}\| \to 0, \quad k \to \infty, \ \forall i = 0, 1, 2, \ldots, N. \tag{35}$$

Using (31) and (35), it follows from (33) and (34) that

$$\liminf_{k \to \infty}\langle A_iy_{n_k,i}, T_ix - y_{n_k,i}\rangle \geq 0, \quad \forall T_ix \in C_i, \ i = 0, 1, 2, \ldots, N. \tag{36}$$

Next, let $\{\vartheta_{k,i}\}$ be a decreasing sequence of positive numbers such that $\vartheta_{k,i} \to 0$ as $k \to \infty$, $i = 0, 1, 2, \ldots, N$. For each k, let N_k denote the smallest positive integer such that

$$\langle A_iy_{n_j,i}, T_ix - y_{n_j,i}\rangle + \vartheta_{k,i} \geq 0, \quad \forall j \geq N_k, \ T_ix \in C_i, \ i = 0, 1, 2, \ldots, N, \tag{37}$$

where the existence of N_k follows from (36). Since $\{\vartheta_{k,i}\}$ is decreasing, then $\{N_k\}$ is increasing. Moreover, since $\{y_{N_k,i}\} \subset C_i$ for each k, we can suppose $A_iy_{N_k,i} \neq 0$ (otherwise, $y_{N_k,i} \in VI(C_i, A_i)$, $i = 0, 1, 2 \ldots, N$) and let

$$z_{N_k,i} = \frac{A_i y_{N_k,i}}{\|A_i y_{N_k,i}\|^2}$$

Then, $\langle A_i y_{N_k,i}, z_{N_k,i} \rangle = 1$ for each k, $i = 0, 1, 2, \ldots, N$. From (37), we have

$$\langle A_i y_{N_k,i}, T_i x + \vartheta_{k,i} z_{N_k,i} - y_{N_k,i} \rangle \geq 0, \quad \forall T_i x \in C_i, i = 0, 1, 2, \ldots, N.$$

It follows from the pseudomonotonicity of A_i that

$$\langle A_i(T_i x + \vartheta_{k,i} z_{N_k,i}), T_i x + \vartheta_{k,i} z_{N_k,i} - y_{N_k,i} \rangle \geq 0, \quad \forall T_i x \in C_i, i = 0, 1, 2, \ldots, N,$$

which is equivalent to

$$\langle A_i T_i x, T_i x - y_{N_k,i} \rangle \geq \langle A_i T_i x - A_i(T_i x + \vartheta_{k,i} z_{N_k,i}), T_i x + \vartheta_{k,i} z_{N_k,i} - y_{N_k,i} \rangle - \vartheta_{k,i} \langle A_i T_i x, z_{N_k,i} \rangle, \forall T_i x \in C_i, i = 0, 1, \ldots, N. \quad (38)$$

In order to complete the proof, we need to establish that $\lim_{k \to \infty} \vartheta_{k,i} z_{N_k,i} = 0$. Since $w_{n_k} \rightharpoonup z$ and T_i is a bounded linear operator for each $i = 0, 1, 2, \ldots, N$, we have $T_i w_{n_k} \rightharpoonup T_i z$, $\forall i = 0, 1, 2, \ldots, N$. Thus, from (31), we obtain $y_{n_k,i} \rightharpoonup T_i z$, $\forall i = 0, 1, 2, \ldots, N$. Since $\{y_{n_k,i}\} \subset C_i$, $i = 0, 1, 2, \ldots, N$, we have $T_i z \in C_i$. If $A_i T_i z = 0$, $\forall i = 0, 1, 2, \ldots, N$, then $T_i z \in VI(C_i, A_i)$ $\forall i = 0, 1, 2, \ldots, N$, which implies that $z \in \Omega$. On the contrary, we suppose $A_i T_i z \neq 0$, $\forall i = 0, 1, 2, \ldots, N$. Since A_i satisfies condition (12), we have for all $i = 0, 1, 2, \ldots, N$

$$0 < \|A_i T_i z\| \leq \liminf_{k \to \infty} \|A_i y_{n_k,i}\|.$$

Applying the facts that $\{y_{N_k,i}\} \subset \{y_{n_k,i}\}$ and $\vartheta_{k,i} \to 0$ as $k \to \infty$, $i = 0, 1, 2, \ldots, N$, we have

$$0 \leq \limsup_{k \to \infty} \|\vartheta_{k,i} z_{N_k,i}\| = \limsup_{k \to \infty} \left(\frac{\vartheta_{k,i}}{\|A_i y_{n_k,i}\|} \right) \leq \frac{\limsup_{k \to \infty} \vartheta_{k,i}}{\liminf_{k \to \infty} \|A_i y_{n_k,i}\|} = 0,$$

which implies that $\limsup_{k \to \infty} \vartheta_{k,i} z_{N_k,i} = 0$. Applying the facts that A_i is continuous, $\{y_{N_k,i}\}$ and $\{z_{N_k,i}\}$ are bounded and $\lim_{k \to \infty} \vartheta_{k,i} z_{N_k,i} = 0$, from (38) we get

$$\liminf_{k \to \infty} \langle A_i T_i x, T_i x - y_{N_k,i} \rangle \geq 0, \quad \forall T_i x \in C_i, i = 0, 1, 2, \ldots, N.$$

From the last inequality, we have

$$\langle A_i T_i x, T_i x - T_i z \rangle = \lim_{k \to \infty} \langle A_i T_i x, T_i x - y_{N_k,i} \rangle = \liminf_{k \to \infty} \langle A_i T_i x, T_i x - y_{N_k,i} \rangle \geq 0, \forall T_i x \in C_i, i = 0, 1, 2, \ldots, N.$$

By Lemma 4, we obtain

$$T_i z \in VI(C_i, A_i), \quad i = 0, 1, 2, \ldots, N,$$

which implies that

$$z \in T_i^{-1}(VI(C_i, A_i)), \quad i = 0, 1, 2, \ldots, N,$$

Consequently, we have $z \in \bigcap_{i=0}^{N} T_i^{-1}(VI(C_i, A_i))$, which implies that $z \in \Omega$ as desired. □

Lemma 11. *Suppose $\{x_n\}$ is a sequence generated by Algorithm 1 under Assumption B. Then, the following inequality holds for all $p \in \Omega$:*

$$\|x_{n+1} - p\|^2 \leq (1 - \alpha_n)\|x_n - p\|^2 + \alpha_n d_n - (1 - \xi_n) \sum_{i=0}^{N} \delta_{n,i} \eta_{n,i} [1 - (\phi_{n,i} + \phi_i)] \|T_i w_n - u_{n,i}\|^2 - \xi_n (1 - \xi_n) \|w_n - v_n\|^2.$$

Proof. Let $p \in \Omega$. By applying Lemma 3 together with the definition of w_n, we obtain

$$\begin{aligned}
\|w_n - p\|^2 &= \|(1-\alpha_n)(x_n - p) + (1-\alpha_n)\theta_n(x_n - x_{n-1}) - \alpha_n p\|^2 \\
&\leq \|(1-\alpha_n)(x_n - p) + (1-\alpha_n)\theta_n(x_n - x_{n-1})\|^2 + 2\alpha_n \langle -p, w_n - p \rangle \\
&\leq (1-\alpha_n)^2 \|x_n - p\|^2 + 2(1-\alpha_n)\theta_n \|x_n - p\| \|x_n - x_{n-1}\| + (1-\alpha_n)^2 \theta_n^2 \|x_n - x_{n-1}\|^2 \\
&\quad + 2\alpha_n \langle -p, w_n - x_{n+1} \rangle + 2\alpha_n \langle -p, x_{n+1} - p \rangle \\
&\leq (1-\alpha_n)\|x_n - p\|^2 + 2\theta_n \|x_n - p\| \|x_n - x_{n-1}\| + \theta_n^2 \|x_n - x_{n-1}\|^2 + 2\alpha_n \|p\| \|w_n - x_{n+1}\| \\
&\quad + 2\alpha_n \langle p, p - x_{n+1} \rangle.
\end{aligned} \quad (39)$$

Now, using the definition of x_{n+1}, (25), (39) and applying Lemma 3, we obtain

$$\begin{aligned}
\|x_{n+1} - p\|^2 &= \|\xi_n w_n + (1-\xi_n)v_n - p\|^2 \\
&= \xi_n \|w_n - p\|^2 + (1-\xi_n)\|v_n - p\|^2 - \xi_n(1-\xi_n)\|w_n - v_n\|^2 \\
&\leq \xi_n \|w_n - p\|^2 + (1-\xi_n)\left[\|w_n - p\|^2 - \sum_{i=0}^{N} \delta_{n,i}\eta_{n,i}[1-(\phi_{n,i} + \phi_i)]\|T_i w_n - u_{n,i}\|^2\right] \\
&\quad - \xi_n(1-\xi_n)\|w_n - v_n\|^2 \\
&= \|w_n - p\|^2 - (1-\xi_n)\sum_{i=0}^{N} \delta_{n,i}\eta_{n,i}[1-(\phi_{n,i} + \phi_i)]\|T_i w_n - u_{n,i}\|^2 - \xi_n(1-\xi_n)\|w_n - v_n\|^2 \\
&\leq (1-\alpha_n)\|x_n - p\|^2 + 2\theta_n \|x_n - p\| \|x_n - x_{n-1}\| + \theta_n^2 \|x_n - x_{n-1}\|^2 + 2\alpha_n \|p\| \|w_n - x_{n+1}\| \\
&\quad + 2\alpha_n \langle p, p - x_{n+1} \rangle - (1-\xi_n)\sum_{i=0}^{N} \delta_{n,i}\eta_{n,i}[1-(\phi_{n,i}+\phi_i)]\|T_i w_n - u_{n,i}\|^2 - \xi_n(1-\xi_n)\|w_n - v_n\|^2 \\
&= (1-\alpha_n)\|x_n - p\|^2 + \alpha_n\left[2\|x_n - p\|\frac{\theta_n}{\alpha_n}\|x_n - x_{n-1}\| + \theta_n \|x_n - x_{n-1}\|\frac{\theta_n}{\alpha_n}\|x_n - x_{n-1}\| \right. \\
&\quad \left. + 2\|p\|\|w_n - x_{n+1}\| + 2\langle p, p - x_{n+1}\rangle\right] - (1-\xi_n)\sum_{i=0}^{N}\delta_{n,i}\eta_{n,i}[1-(\phi_{n,i}+\phi_i)]\|T_i w_n - u_{n,i}\|^2 \\
&\quad - \xi_n(1-\xi_n)\|w_n - v_n\|^2 \\
&= (1-\alpha_n)\|x_n - p\|^2 + \alpha_n d_n - (1-\xi_n)\sum_{i=0}^{N}\delta_{n,i}\eta_{n,i}[1-(\phi_{n,i}+\phi_i)]\|T_i w_n - u_{n,i}\|^2 - \xi_n(1-\xi_n)\|w_n - v_n\|^2,
\end{aligned}$$

where $d_n = 2\|x_n - p\|\frac{\theta_n}{\alpha_n}\|x_n - x_{n-1}\| + \theta_n \|x_n - x_{n-1}\|\frac{\theta_n}{\alpha_n}\|x_n - x_{n-1}\| + 2\|p\|\|w_n - x_{n+1}\| + 2\langle p, p - x_{n+1}\rangle$, which is the required inequality. □

Theorem 1. *Let $\{x_n\}$ be a sequence generated by Algorithm 1 under Assumption B. Then, $\{x_n\}$ converges strongly to $\hat{x} \in \Omega$, where $\|\hat{x}\| = \min\{\|p\| : p \in \Omega\}$.*

Proof. Let $\|\hat{x}\| = \min\{\|p\| : p \in \Omega\}$, that is, $\hat{x} = P_\Omega(0)$. Then, from Lemma 11, we obtain

$$\|x_{n+1} - \hat{x}\|^2 \leq (1-\alpha_n)\|x_n - \hat{x}\|^2 + \alpha_n \hat{d}_n, \quad (40)$$

where $\hat{d}_n = 2\|x_n - \hat{x}\|\frac{\theta_n}{\alpha_n}\|x_n - x_{n-1}\| + \theta_n \|x_n - x_{n-1}\|\frac{\theta_n}{\alpha_n}\|x_n - x_{n-1}\| + 2\|\hat{x}\|\|w_n - x_{n+1}\| + 2\langle \hat{x}, \hat{x} - x_{n+1}\rangle$.

Next, we claim that the sequence $\{\|x_n - \hat{x}\|\}$ converges to zero. To do this, in view of Lemma 1 it suffices to show that $\limsup_{k\to\infty} \hat{d}_{n_k} \leq 0$ for every subsequence $\{\|x_{n_k} - \hat{x}\|\}$ of $\{\|x_n - \hat{x}\|\}$ satisfying

$$\liminf_{k\to\infty}(\|x_{n_k+1} - \hat{x}\| - \|x_{n_k} - \hat{x}\|) \geq 0. \quad (41)$$

Suppose that $\{\|x_{n_k} - \hat{x}\|\}$ is a subsequence of $\{\|x_n - \hat{x}\|\}$ such that (41) holds. Again, from Lemma 11, we obtain

$$(1-\xi_{n_k})\sum_{i=0}^{N}\delta_{n_k,i}\eta_{n_k,i}[1-(\phi_{n_k,i}+\phi_i)]\|T_iw_{n_k}-u_{n_k,i}\|^2 + \xi_{n_k}(1-\xi_{n_k})\|w_{n_k}-v_{n_k}\|^2$$
$$\leq (1-\alpha_{n_k})\|x_{n_k}-\hat{x}\|^2 - \|x_{n_k+1}-\hat{x}\|^2 + \alpha_{n_k}\hat{d}_{n_k}.$$

By (41), Remark 2 and the fact that $\lim_{k\to\infty}\alpha_{n_k}=0$, we obtain

$$(1-\xi_{n_k})\sum_{i=0}^{N}\delta_{n_k,i}\eta_{n_k,i}[1-(\phi_{n_k,i}+\phi_i)]\|T_iw_{n_k}-u_{n_k,i}\|^2 + \xi_{n_k}(1-\xi_{n_k})\|w_{n_k}-v_{n_k}\|^2 \to 0, \quad k\to\infty.$$

Consequently, we obtain

$$\lim_{k\to\infty}\|w_{n_k}-v_{n_k}\|=0; \quad \lim_{k\to\infty}\|T_iw_{n_k}-u_{n_k,i}\|=0, \quad \forall i=0,1,2,\ldots,N. \tag{42}$$

From the definition of w_n and by Remark 2, we have

$$\|w_{n_k}-x_{n_k}\| = \|(1-\alpha_{n_k})(x_{n_k}+\theta_{n_k}(x_{n_k}-x_{n_k-1}))-x_{n_k}\|$$
$$= \|(1-\alpha_{n_k})(x_{n_k}-x_{n_k}) + (1-\alpha_{n_k})\theta_{n_k}(x_{n_k}-x_{n_k-1}) - \alpha_{n_k}x_{n_k}\|$$
$$\leq (1-\alpha_{n_k})\|x_{n_k}-x_{n_k}\| + (1-\alpha_{n_k})\theta_{n_k}\|x_{n_k}-x_{n_k-1}\| + \alpha_{n_k}\|x_{n_k}\| \to 0, \quad k\to\infty. \tag{43}$$

Using (42) and (43), we obtain

$$\|v_{n_k}-x_{n_k}\| \to 0, \quad k\to\infty. \tag{44}$$

From the definition of x_{n+1} and by applying (43) and (44), we obtain

$$\|x_{n_k+1}-x_{n_k}\| = \|\xi_{n_k}w_{n_k} + (1-\xi_{n_k})v_{n_k} - x_{n_k}\|$$
$$\leq \xi_{n_k}\|w_{n_k}-x_{n_k}\| + (1-\xi_{n_k})\|v_{n_k}-x_{n_k}\| \to 0, \quad k\to\infty. \tag{45}$$

Next, by combining (43) and (45), we obtain

$$\|w_{n_k}-x_{n_k+1}\| \to 0, \quad k\to\infty. \tag{46}$$

Since $\{x_n\}$ is bounded, $w_\omega(x_n) \neq \emptyset$. We choose an element $x^* \in w_\omega(x_n)$ arbitrarily. Then, there exists a subsequence $\{x_{n_k}\}$ of $\{x_n\}$ such that $x_{n_k} \rightharpoonup x^*$. From (42), it follows that $w_{n_k} \rightharpoonup x^*$. Now, by invoking Lemma 10 and applying (42), we obtain $x^* \in \Omega$. Since $x^* \in w_\omega(x_n)$ was selected arbitrarily, it follows that $w_\omega(x_n) \subset \Omega$.

Next, by the boundedness of $\{x_{n_k}\}$, there exists a subsequence $\{x_{n_{k_j}}\}$ of $\{x_{n_k}\}$ such that $x_{n_{k_j}} \rightharpoonup q$ and

$$\limsup_{k\to\infty}\langle \hat{x}, \hat{x}-x_{n_k}\rangle = \lim_{j\to\infty}\langle \hat{x}, \hat{x}-x_{n_{k_j}}\rangle.$$

Since $\hat{x} = P_\Omega(0)$, it follows from the property of the metric projection map that

$$\limsup_{k\to\infty}\langle \hat{x}, \hat{x}-x_{n_k}\rangle = \lim_{j\to\infty}\langle \hat{x}, \hat{x}-x_{n_{k_j}}\rangle = \langle \hat{x}, \hat{x}-q\rangle \leq 0, \tag{47}$$

Thus, from (45) and (47), we obtain

$$\limsup_{k\to\infty}\langle \hat{x}, \hat{x}-x_{n_k+1}\rangle \leq 0. \tag{48}$$

Next, by Remark 2, (46) and (48) we have $\limsup_{k\to\infty} \hat{a}_{n_k} \leq 0$. Therefore, by invoking Lemma 1, it follows from (40) that $\{\|x_n - \hat{x}\|\}$ converges to zero as required. □

5. Applications

In this section, we apply our result to study related optimization problems.

5.1. Generalized Split Variational Inequality Problem

First, we apply our result to study and approximate the solution of the generalized split variational inequality problem (see [37]). Let D_i be nonempty, closed and convex subsets of real Hilbert spaces $H_i, i = 1, 2, \ldots, N$, and let $S_i : H_i \to H_{i+1}, i = 1, 2, \ldots, N-1$, be bounded linear operators, such that $S_i \neq 0$. Let $B_i : H_i \to H_i, i = 1, 2, \ldots, N$, be single-valued operators. The *generalized split variational inequality problem* (GSVIP) is formulated as finding a point $x^* \in D_1$ such that

$$x^* \in \Gamma := VI(D_1, B_1) \cap S_1^{-1}(VI(D_2, B_2)) \cap \ldots S_1^{-1}(S_2^{-1} \ldots (S_{N-1}^{-1}(VI(D_N, B_N)))) \neq \emptyset; \quad (49)$$

that is, $x^* \in D_1$ such that

$$x^* \in VI(D_1, B_1), S_1 x^* \in VI(D_2, B_2), \ldots, S_{N-1}(S_{N-2} \ldots S_1 x^*) \in VI(D_N, B_N).$$

We note that by setting $C = D_1, C_i = D_{i+1}, A = B_1, A_i = B_{i+1}, 1 \leq i \leq N-1, T_1 = S_1, T_2 = S_2 S_1, \ldots,$ and $T_{N-1} = S_{N-1} S_{N-2} \ldots S_1$, then the SVIPMOS (10) becomes the GSVIP (49). Consequently, we obtain the following strong convergence theorem for finding the solution of GSVIP (49) in Hilbert spaces when the cost operators are pseudomonotone and uniformly continuous.

Theorem 2. *Let D_i be nonempty, closed and convex subsets of real Hilbert spaces $H_i, i = 1, 2, \ldots, N$, and suppose $S_i : H_i \to H_{i+1}, i = 1, 2, \ldots, N-1$, are bounded linear operators with adjoints S_i^* such that $S_i \neq 0$. Let $B_i : H_i \to H_i, 1, 2, \ldots, N$ be uniformly continuous pseudomonotone operators that satisfy condition (12), and suppose Assumption B of Theorem 1 holds and the solution set $\Gamma \neq \emptyset$. Then, the sequence $\{x_n\}$ generated by the following Algorithm 2 converges in norm to $\hat{x} \in \Gamma$, where $\|\hat{x}\| = \min\{\|p\| : p \in \Gamma\}$.*

Algorithm 2. A Relaxed Inertial Tseng's Extragradient Method for Solving GSVIP (49).

Step 0. Select initial points $x_0, x_1 \in H_1$. Let $S_0 = I^{H_1}$, $\hat{S}_{i-1} = S_{i-1}S_{i-2}\ldots S_0$, $\hat{S}^*_{i-1} = S_0^* S_1^* \ldots S_{i-1}^*$, $i = 1, 2, \ldots, N$ and set $n = 1$.

Step 1. Given the $(n-1)$th and nth iterates, choose θ_n such that $0 \le \theta_n \le \hat{\theta}_n$ with $\hat{\theta}_n$ defined by

$$\hat{\theta}_n = \begin{cases} \min\left\{\theta, \frac{\epsilon_n}{\|x_n - x_{n-1}\|}\right\}, & \text{if } x_n \ne x_{n-1}, \\ \theta, & \text{otherwise.} \end{cases}$$

Step 2. Compute
$$w_n = (1 - \alpha_n)(x_n + \theta_n(x_n - x_{n-1})).$$

Step 3. Compute
$$y_{n,i} = P_{D_i}(\hat{S}_{i-1}w_n - \lambda_{n,i}B_i\hat{S}_{i-1}w_n).$$

Step 4. Compute
$$u_{n,i} = y_{n,i} - \lambda_{n,i}(B_i y_{n,i} - B_i \hat{S}_{i-1}w_n),$$

$$\lambda_{n+1,i} = \begin{cases} \min\left\{\frac{(c_{n,i}+c_i)\|\hat{S}_{i-1}w_n - y_{n,i}\|}{\|B_i\hat{S}_{i-1}w_n - B_i y_{n,i}\|}, \lambda_{n,i} + \rho_{n,i}\right\}, & \text{if } B_i\hat{S}_{i-1}w_n - B_i y_{n,i} \ne 0, \\ \lambda_{n,i} + \rho_{n,i}, & \text{otherwise.} \end{cases}$$

Step 5. Compute
$$v_n = \sum_{i=1}^{N} \delta_{n,i}\left(w_n + \eta_{n,i}\hat{S}^*_{i-1}(u_{n,i} - \hat{S}_{i-1}w_n)\right),$$

where
$$\eta_{n,i} = \begin{cases} \frac{(\phi_{n,i}+\phi_i)\|\hat{S}_{i-1}w_n - u_{n,i}\|^2}{\|\hat{S}^*_{i-1}(\hat{S}_{i-1}w_n - u_{n,i})\|^2}, & \text{if } \|\hat{S}^*_{i-1}(\hat{S}_{i-1}w_n - u_{n,i})\| \ne 0, \\ 0, & \text{otherwise.} \end{cases}$$

Step 6. Compute
$$x_{n+1} = \xi_n w_n + (1 - \xi_n)v_n.$$

Set $n := n + 1$ and return to **Step 1**.

5.2. Split Convex Minimization Problem with Multiple Output Sets

Let C be a nonempty, closed and convex subset of a real Hilbert space H. The convex minimization problem is defined as finding a point $x^* \in C$, such that

$$g(x^*) = \min_{x \in C} g(x), \tag{50}$$

where g is a real-valued convex function. The solution set of Problem (50) is denoted by arg min g.

Let C, C_i be nonempty, closed and convex subsets of real Hilbert spaces $H, H_i, i = 1, 2, \ldots, N$, respectively, and let $T_i : H \to H_i, i = 1, 2, \ldots, N$, be bounded linear operators with adjoints T_i^*. Let $g : H \to \mathbb{R}, g_i : H_i \to \mathbb{R}$ be convex and differentiable functions. In this subsection, we apply our result to find the solution of the following *split convex minimization problem with multiple output sets* (SCMPMOS): Find $x^* \in C$ such that

$$x^* \in \Psi := \arg\min g \cap \left(\cap_{i=1}^{N} T_i^{-1}(\arg\min g_i)\right) \ne \emptyset. \tag{51}$$

The following lemma is required to establish our next result.

Lemma 12 ([53]). *Suppose C is a nonempty, closed and convex subset of a real Banach space E, and let g be a convex function of E into $\mathbb{R}$. If g is Fréchet differentiable, then x is a solution of Problem (50) if and only if $x \in VI(C, \nabla g)$, where ∇g is the gradient of g.*

Applying Theorem 1 and Lemma 12, we obtain the following strong convergence theorem for finding the solution of the SCMPMOS (51) in the framework of Hilbert spaces.

Theorem 3. *Let C, C_i be nonempty, closed and convex subsets of real Hilbert spaces $H, H_i, i = 1, 2, \ldots, N$, respectively, and suppose $T_i : H \to H_i, i = 1, 2, \ldots, N$, are bounded linear operators with adjoints T_i^*. Let $g : H \to \mathbb{R}, g_i : H_i \to \mathbb{R}$ be fréchet differentiable convex functions such that $\nabla g, \nabla g_i$ are uniformly continuous. Suppose that Assumption B of Theorem 1 holds and the solution set $\Psi \neq \emptyset$. Then, the sequence $\{x_n\}$ generated by the following Algorithm 3 converges strongly to $\hat{x} \in \Psi$, where $\|\hat{x}\| = \min\{\|p\| : p \in \Psi\}$.*

Algorithm 3. A Relaxed Inertial Tseng's Extragradient Method for Solving SCMPMOS (51).

Step 0. Select initial points $x_0, x_1 \in H$. Let $C_0 = C$, $T_0 = I^H$, $\nabla g_0 = \nabla g$ and set $n = 1$.
Step 1. Given the $(n-1)$th and nth iterates, choose θ_n such that $0 \leq \theta_n \leq \hat{\theta}_n$ with $\hat{\theta}_n$ defined by

$$\hat{\theta}_n = \begin{cases} \min\left\{\theta, \frac{\epsilon_n}{\|x_n - x_{n-1}\|}\right\}, & \text{if } x_n \neq x_{n-1}, \\ \theta, & \text{otherwise.} \end{cases}$$

Step 2. Compute
$$w_n = (1 - \alpha_n)(x_n + \theta_n(x_n - x_{n-1})).$$

Step 3. Compute
$$y_{n,i} = P_{C_i}(T_i w_n - \lambda_{n,i} \nabla g_i T_i w_n).$$

Step 4. Compute
$$u_{n,i} = y_{n,i} - \lambda_{n,i}(\nabla g_i y_{n,i} - \nabla g_i T_i w_n),$$

$$\lambda_{n+1,i} = \begin{cases} \min\left\{\frac{(c_{n,i}+c_i)\|T_i w_n - y_{n,i}\|}{\|\nabla g_i T_i w_n - \nabla g_i y_{n,i}\|}, \lambda_{n,i} + \rho_{n,i}\right\}, & \text{if } \nabla g_i T_i w_n - \nabla g_i y_{n,i} \neq 0, \\ \lambda_{n,i} + \rho_{n,i}, & \text{otherwise.} \end{cases}$$

Step 5. Compute
$$v_n = \sum_{i=0}^{N} \delta_{n,i}(w_n + \eta_{n,i} T_i^*(u_{n,i} - T_i w_n)),$$

where

$$\eta_{n,i} = \begin{cases} \frac{(\phi_{n,i}+\phi_i)\|T_i w_n - u_{n,i}\|^2}{\|T_i^*(T_i w_n - u_{n,i})\|^2}, & \text{if } \|T_i^*(T_i w_n - u_{n,i})\| \neq 0, \\ 0, & \text{otherwise.} \end{cases}$$

Step 6. Compute
$$x_{n+1} = \xi_n w_n + (1 - \xi_n) v_n.$$

Set $n := n + 1$ and return to **Step 1**.

Proof. We know that since g_i, $i = 0, 1, 2, \ldots, N$ are convex, then ∇g_i are monotone [53] and, hence, pseudomonotone. Therefore, the required result follows by applying Lemma 12 and taking $A_i = \nabla g_i$ in Theorem 1. □

6. Numerical Experiments

Here, we carry out some numerical experiments to demonstrate the applicability of our proposed method (Proposed Algorithm 1). For simplicity, in all the experiments, we consider the case when $N = 5$. All numerical computations were carried out using Matlab version R2021(b).

In all the computations, we choose $\alpha_n = \frac{1}{3n+2}$, $\epsilon_n = \frac{5}{(3n+2)^3}$, $\xi_n = \frac{n+1}{2n+1}$, $\theta = 1.50$, $\lambda_{1,i} = i + 1.25$, $c_i = 0.10$, $\phi_i = 0.20$, $\rho_{n,i} = \frac{50}{n^2}$, $\delta_{n,i} = \frac{1}{6}$.

Now, we consider the following numerical examples both in finite and infinite dimensional Hilbert spaces for the proposed algorithm.

Example 1. For each $i = 0, 1, \ldots, 5$, we define the feasible set $C_i = \mathbb{R}^m$, $T_i x = \frac{3x}{i+3}$ and $A_i(x) = Mx$, where M is a square $m \times m$ matrix given by

$$a_{j,k} = \begin{cases} -1, & \text{if } k = m+1-j \text{ and } k > j, \\ 1, & \text{if } k = m+1-j \text{ and } k \leq j, \\ 0, & \text{otherwise.} \end{cases}$$

We note that M is a Hankel-type matrix with a nonzero reverse diagonal.

Example 2. Let $H_i = \mathbb{R}^2$ and $C_i = [-2-i, 2+i]^2$, $i = 0, 1, \ldots, 5$. We define $T_i x = \frac{2x}{i+2}$, and the cost operator $A_i : \mathbb{R}^2 \to \mathbb{R}^2$ is defined by

$$A_i(x, y) = (i+1)(-xe^y, y), \quad (i = 0, 1, \ldots, 5).$$

Finally, we consider the last example in infinite dimensional Hilbert spaces.

Example 3. Let $H_i = \ell_2 := \{x = (x_1, x_2, \ldots, x_i, \ldots) : \sum_{j=1}^{\infty} |x_j|^2 < +\infty\}$, $i = 0, 1, \ldots, 5$. Let $r_i, R_i \in \mathbb{R}^+$ be such that $\frac{R_i}{k_i+1} < \frac{r_i}{k_i} < r_i < R_i$ for some $k_i > 1$. The feasible sets are defined as follows for each $i = 0, 1, \ldots, 5$:

$$C_i = \{x \in H_i : \|x\| \leq r_i\}.$$

The cost operators $A_i : H_i \to H_i$ are defined by

$$A_i(x) = (R_i - \|x\|)x.$$

Then A_i are pseudomonotone and uniformly continuous. We choose $R_i = 1.4 + i$, $r_i = 0.8 + i$, $k_i = 1.2 + i$, and we define $T_i x = \frac{4x}{i+4}$.

We test Examples 1–3 under the following experiments:

Experiment 1. In this experiment, we check the behavior of our method by fixing the other parameters and varying $c_{n,i}$ in Example 1. We do this to check the effects of this parameter and the sensitivity of our method on it.

We consider $c_{n,i} \in \{0, \frac{20}{n^{0.1}}, \frac{40}{n^{0.01}}, \frac{60}{n^{0.001}}, \frac{80}{n^{0.0001}}\}$ with $m = 20$, $m = 40$, $m = 60$ and $m = 80$. Using $\|x_{n+1} - x_n\| < 10^{-3}$ as the stopping criterion, we plot the graphs of $\|x_{n+1} - x_n\|$ against the number of iterations for each m. The numerical results are reported in Figures 1–4 and Table 1.

Table 1. Numerical results for Experiment 1.

	$m = 20$		$m = 40$		$m = 60$		$m = 80$	
Proposed Algorithm 1	Iter.	CPU Time	Iter.	CPU Time	Iter.	CPU Time	Iter.	CPU Time
$c_{n,i} = 0$	128	0.0889	156	0.1235	174	0.2028	189	0.2412
$c_{n,i} = \frac{20}{n^{0.1}}$	128	0.0652	156	0.1241	174	0.2664	189	0.2930
$c_{n,i} = \frac{40}{n^{0.01}}$	128	0.0719	156	0.1495	174	0.3013	189	0.3220
$c_{n,i} = \frac{60}{n^{0.001}}$	128	0.0695	156	0.1549	174	0.2959	189	0.3342
$c_{n,i} = \frac{80}{n^{0.0001}}$	128	0.0701	156	0.1678	174	0.2877	189	0.3129

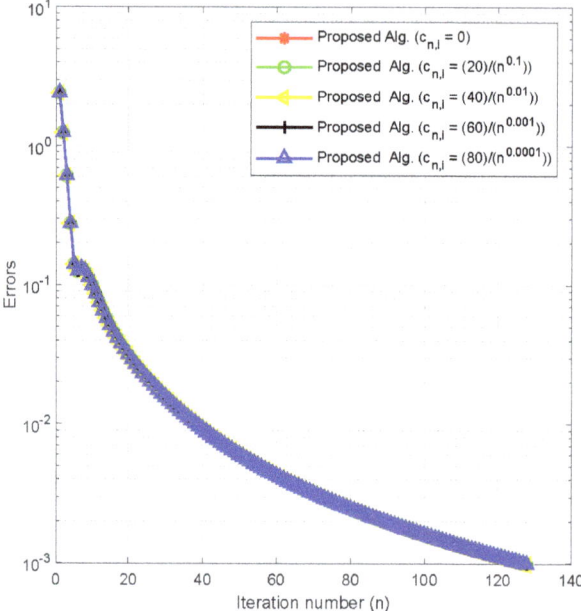

Figure 1. Experiment 1 : $m = 20$.

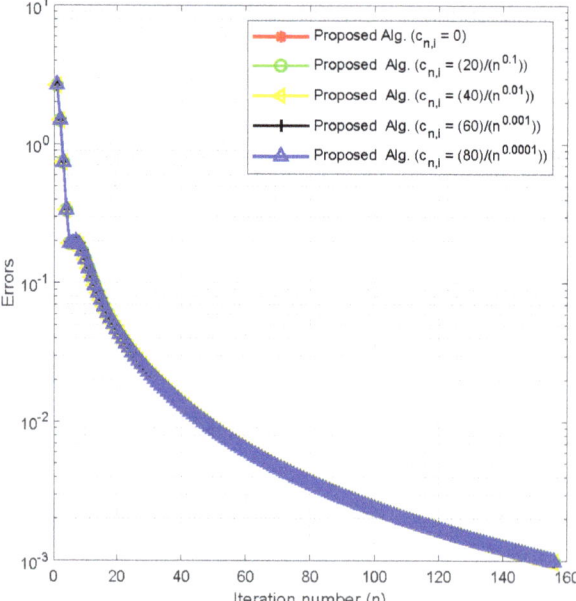

Figure 2. Experiment 1: $m = 40$.

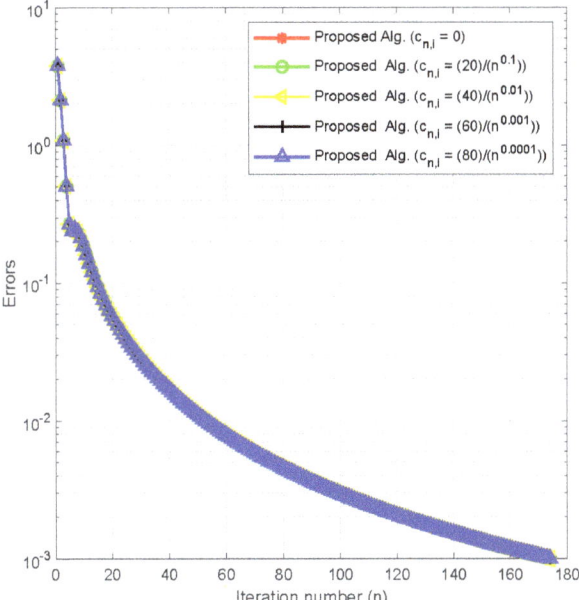

Figure 3. Experiment 1: $m = 60$.

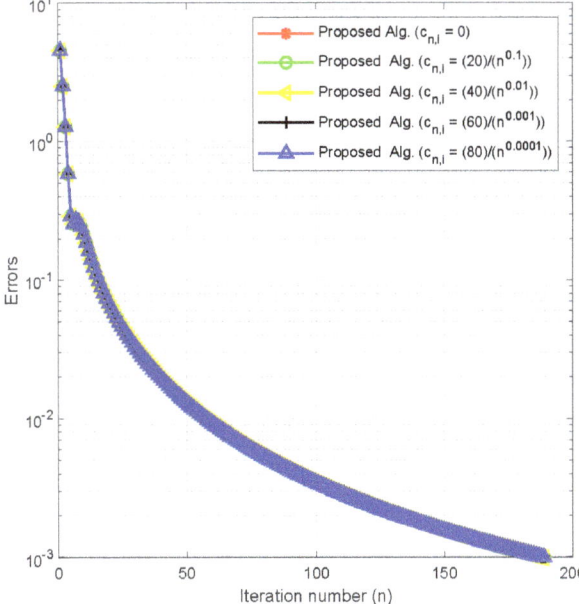

Figure 4. Experiment 1: $m = 80$.

Experiment 2. *In this experiment, we check the behavior of our method by fixing the other parameters and varying $c_{n,i}$ in Example 2. We do this to check the effects of this parameter and the sensitivity of our method to it.*

We consider $c_{n,i} \in \{0, \frac{20}{n^{0.1}}, \frac{40}{n^{0.01}}, \frac{60}{n^{0.001}}, \frac{80}{n^{0.0001}}\}$ with the following two cases of initial values x_0 and x_1:

Case I: $x_0 = (2,1)$; $x_1 = (0,3)$;
Case II: $x_0 = (3,2)$; $x_1 = (1,1)$.

Using $\|x_{n+1} - x_n\| < 10^{-3}$ as the stopping criterion, we plot the graphs of $\|x_{n+1} - x_n\|$ against the number of iterations in each case. The numerical results are reported in Figures 5 and 6 and Table 2.

Table 2. Numerical results for Experiment 2.

	Proposed Algorithm 1	**Case I** Iter.	**Case I** CPU Time	**Case II** Iter.	**Case II** CPU Time
	$c_{n,i} = 0$	248	0.0916	248	4.0980
	$c_{n,i} = \frac{20}{n^{0.1}}$	248	0.0778	248	0.0816
	$c_{n,i} = \frac{40}{n^{0.01}}$	248	0.0852	248	0.0818
	$c_{n,i} = \frac{60}{n^{0.001}}$	248	0.0875	248	0.0753
	$c_{n,i} = \frac{80}{n^{0.0001}}$	248	0.0817	248	0.0811

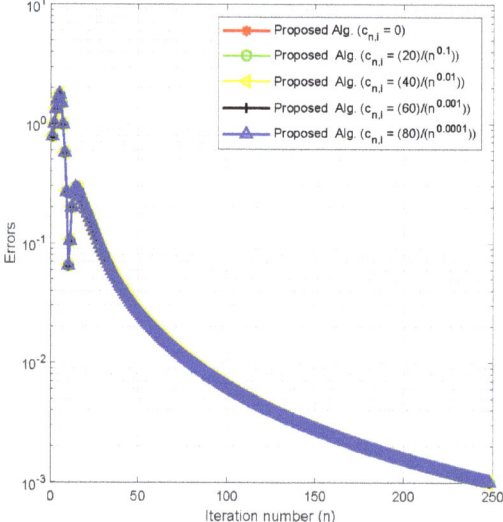

Figure 5. Experiment 2: Case 1.

Finally, we test Example 3 under the following experiment:

Experiment 3. *In this experiment, we check the behavior of our method by fixing the other parameters and varying $c_{n,i}$ in Example 3. We do this to check the effects of these parameters and the sensitivity of our method to it.*

We consider $c_{n,i} \in \{0, \frac{20}{n^{0.1}}, \frac{40}{n^{0.01}}, \frac{60}{n^{0.001}}, \frac{80}{n^{0.0001}}\}$ with the following two cases of initial values x_0 and x_1:

Case I: $x_0 = (\frac{1}{10}, \frac{1}{100}, \frac{1}{1000}, \cdots)$; $x_1 = (\frac{1}{2}, \frac{1}{4}, \frac{1}{8}, \cdots)$;
Case II: $x_0 = (\frac{3}{10}, \frac{3}{100}, \frac{3}{100}, \cdots)$; $x_1 = (\frac{1}{3}, \frac{1}{9}, \frac{1}{27}, \cdots)$.

Using $\|x_{n+1} - x_n\| < 10^{-4}$ as the stopping criterion, we plot the graphs of $\|x_{n+1} - x_n\|$ against the number of iterations in each case. The numerical results are reported in Figures 7 and 8 and Table 3.

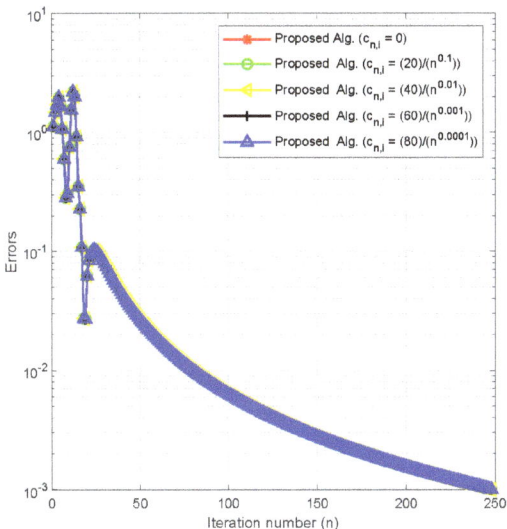

Figure 6. Experiment 2: Case 2.

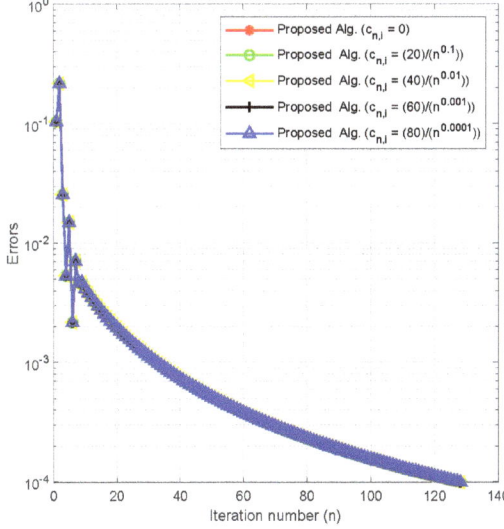

Figure 7. Experiment 3: Case 1.

Table 3. Numerical results for Experiment 3.

		Case I		Case II	
Proposed Algorithm 1	**Iter.**	**CPU Time**	**Iter.**	**CPU Time**	
$c_{n,i} = 0$	128	0.0682	128	0.0620	
$c_{n,i} = \frac{20}{n^{0.1}}$	128	0.0434	128	0.0422	
$c_{n,i} = \frac{40}{n^{0.01}}$	128	0.0446	128	0.0474	
$c_{n,i} = \frac{60}{n^{0.001}}$	128	0.0423	128	0.0414	
$c_{n,i} = \frac{80}{n^{0.0001}}$	128	0.0416	128	0.0424	

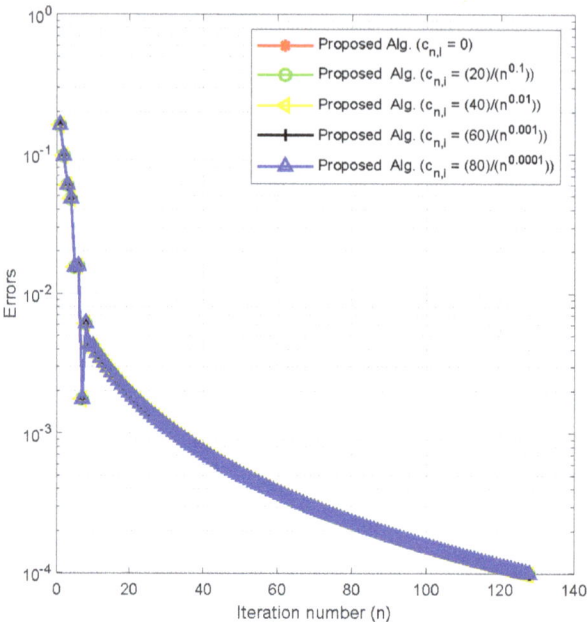

Figure 8. Experiment 3: Case 2.

Remark 5. *By using different initial values, cases of m and varying the key parameter in Experiments 1–3, we obtained the numerical results displayed in Tables 1–3 and Figures 1–8. In Figures 1–4, we considered different initial values and cases of m with varying values of the key parameter $c_{n,i}$ for Experiment 1 in $\mathbb{R}^m$. As observed from the figures, these varying choices do not have a significant effect on the behavior of the algorithm. Similarly, Figures 5 and 6 show that the behavior of our algorithm is consistent under varying initial starting points and different values of the key parameter $c_{n,i}$ for Experiment 2 in $\mathbb{R}^2$. Likewise, Figures 7 and 8 reveal that the behavior of the algorithm is not affected by varying starting points and values of $c_{n,i}$ for Experiment 3 in ℓ_2. From these results, we can conclude that our method is well-behaved since the choice of the key parameter and initial starting points do not affect the number of iterations or the CPU time in all the experiments.*

7. Conclusions

In this article, we studied a new class of split inverse problems called the split variational inequality problem with multiple output sets. We introduced a relaxed inertial Tseng extragradient method with self-adaptive step sizes for finding the solution to the problem when the cost operators are pseudomonotone and non-Lipschitz in the framework of Hilbert spaces. Moreover, we proved a strong convergence theorem for the proposed method under some mild conditions. Finally, we applied our result to study and approximate the solutions of certain classes of optimization problems, and we presented several numerical experiments to demonstrate the applicability of our proposed algorithm. The results of this study open up several opportunities for future research. As part of our future research, we would like to extend the results in this paper to a more general space, such as the reflexive Banach space. Furthermore, we would consider extending the results to a larger class of operators, such as the classes of quasimonotone and non-monotone operators. Moreover, in our future research, we would be interested in investigating the stochastic variant of our results in this study.

Author Contributions: Conceptualization, T.O.A.; Methodology, T.O.A.; Validation, O.T.M.; Formal analysis, T.O.A.; Investigation, T.O.A.; Resources, O.T.M.; Writing—original draft, T.O.A.; Writing —review & editing, O.T.M.; Visualization, O.T.M.; Supervision, O.T.M.; Project administration, O.T.M.; Funding acquisition, O.T.M. All authors have read and agreed to the published version of the manuscript.

Funding: The research of the first author is wholly supported by the University of KwaZulu-Natal, Durban, South Africa, Postdoctoral Fellowship. He is grateful for the funding and financial support. The second author is supported by the National Research Foundation (NRF) of South Africa Incentive Funding for Rated Researchers (Grant Number 119903). Opinions expressed and conclusions arrived at are those of the authors and are not necessarily to be attributed to the NRF.

Acknowledgments: The authors thank the Reviewers and the Editor for the time spent in carefully going through the manuscript, and pointing out typos and areas of corrections, including constructive comments and suggestions, which have all helped to improve on the quality of the manuscript.

Conflicts of Interest: The authors declare that they have no competing interest.

References

1. Fichera, G. Sul problema elastostatico di Signorini con ambigue condizioni al contorno. *Atti Accad. Naz. Lincei VIII. Ser. Rend. Cl. Sci. Fis. Mat. Nat.* **1963**, *34*, 138–142.
2. Stampacchia, G. Formes bilineaires coercitives sur les ensembles convexes. *C. R. Acad. Sci. Paris* **1964**, *258*, 4413–4416.
3. Alakoya, T.O.; Uzor, V.A.; Mewomo, O.T. A new projection and contraction method for solving split monotone variational inclusion, pseudomonotone variational inequality, and common fixed point problems. *Comput. Appl. Math.* **2022**, *42*, 1–33. [CrossRef]
4. Ansari, Q.H.; Islam, M.; Yao, J.C. Nonsmooth variational inequalities on Hadamard manifolds. *Appl. Anal.* **2020**, *99*, 340–358. [CrossRef]
5. Cubiotti, P.; Yao, J.C. On the Cauchy problem for a class of differential inclusions with applications. *Appl. Anal.* **2020**, *99*, 2543–2554. [CrossRef]
6. Eskandari, Z.; Avazzadeh, Z.; Ghaziani, K.R.; Li, B. Dynamics and bifurcations of a discrete-time Lotka–Volterra model using nonstandard finite difference discretization method. *Math. Meth. Appl. Sci.* **2022**, 1–16. [CrossRef]
7. Li, B.; Liang, H.; He, Q. Multiple and generic bifurcation analysis of a discrete Hindmarsh-Rose model, Chaos. *Solitons Fractals* **2021**, *146*, 110856. [CrossRef]
8. Vuong, P.T.; Shehu, Y. Convergence of an extragradient-type method for variational inequality with applications to optimal control problems. *Numer. Algorithms* **2019**, *81*, 269–291. [CrossRef]
9. Aubin, J.; Ekeland, I. *Applied Nonlinear Analysis*; Wiley: New York, NY, USA, 1984.
10. Baiocchi, C.; Capelo, A. *Variational and Quasivariational Inequalities*; Applications to Free Boundary Problems; Wiley: New York, NY, USA, 1984.
11. Gibali, A.; Reich, S.; Zalas, R. Outer approximation methods for solving variational inequalities in Hilbert space. *Optimization* **2017**, *66*, 417–437. [CrossRef]
12. Kinderlehrer, D.; Stampacchia, G. An introduction to variational inequalities and their applications. In *Classics in Applied Mathematics*; Society for Industrial and Applied Mathematics: Philadelphia, PA, USA, 2000.
13. Li, B.; Liang, H.; Shi, L.; He, Q. Complex dynamics of Kopel model with nonsymmetric response between oligopolists. *Solitons Fractals* **2022**, *156*, 111860. [CrossRef]
14. Ogwo, G.N.; Alakoya, T.O.; Mewomo, O.T. Iterative algorithm with self-adaptive step size for approximating the common solution of variational inequality and fixed point problems. *Optimization* **2021**. [CrossRef]
15. Alakoya, T.O.; Jolaoso, L.O.; Mewomo, O.T. Modified inertial subgradient extragradient method with self adaptive stepsize for solving monotone variational inequality and fixed point problems. *Optimization* **2021**, *70*, 545–574. [CrossRef]
16. Ceng, L.C.; Coroian, I.; Qin, X.; Yao, J.C. A general viscosity implicit iterative algorithm for split variational inclusions with hierarchical variational inequality constraints. *Fixed Point Theory* **2019**, *20*, 469–482. [CrossRef]
17. Hai, T.N. Continuous-time ergodic algorithm for solving monotone variational inequalities, *J. Nonlinear Var. Anal.* **2021**, *5*, 391–401.
18. Khan, S.H.; Alakoya, T.O.; Mewomo, O.T. Relaxed projection methods with self-adaptive step size for solving variational inequality and fixed point problems for an infinite family of multivalued relatively nonexpansive mappings in Banach spaces *Math. Comput. Appl.* **2020**, *25*, 54. [CrossRef]
19. Mewomo, O.T.; Alakoya, T.O.; Yao, J.-C.; Akinyemi, L. Strong convergent inertial Tseng's extragradient method for solving non-Lipschitz quasimonotone variational Inequalities in Banach spaces. *J. Nonlinear Var. Anal.* **2023**, *7*, 145–172.
20. Tseng, P. A modified forward-backward splitting method for maximal monotone mappings. *SIAM J. Control Optim.* **2000**, *38*, 431–446. [CrossRef]

21. Alakoya, T.O.; Mewomo, O.T.; Shehu, Y. Strong convergence results for quasimonotone variational inequalities. *Math. Methods Oper. Res.* **2022**, *2022*, 47. [CrossRef]
22. Godwin, E.C.; Alakoya, T.O.; Mewomo, O.T.; Yao, J.-C. Relaxed inertial Tseng extragradient method for variational inequality and fixed point problems. *Appl. Anal.* **2022**. [CrossRef]
23. Uzor, V.A.; Alakoya, T.O.; Mewomo, O.T. Strong convergence of a self-adaptive inertial Tseng's extragradient method for pseudomonotone variational inequalities and fixed point problems. *Open Math.* **2022**, *20*, 234–257. [CrossRef]
24. Alakoya, T.O.; Uzor, V.A.; Mewomo, O.T.; Yao, J.-C. On System of Monotone Variational Inclusion Problems with Fixed-Point Constraint. *J. Inequal. Appl.* **2022**, *2022*, 47. [CrossRef]
25. Censor, Y.; Borteld, T.; Martin, B.; Trofimov, A. A unified approach for inversion problems in intensity-modulated radiation therapy. *Phys. Med. Biol.* **2006**, *51*, 2353–2365. [CrossRef] [PubMed]
26. Censor, Y.; Elfving, T. A multiprojection algorithm using Bregman projections in a product space. *Numer. Algorithms* **1994**, *8*, 221–239. [CrossRef]
27. López, G.; Martín-Márquez, V.; Xu, H.K. Iterative algorithms for the multiple-sets split feasibility problem. In *Biomedical Mathematics: Promising Directions in Imaging, Therapy Planning and Inverse Problems*, Medical Physics Publishing, Madison; Medical Physics Publishing: Madison, WI, USA, 2010; pp. 243–279.
28. Moudafi, A.; Thakur, B.S. Solving proximal split feasibility problems without prior knowledge of operator norms. *Optim. Lett.* **2014**, *8*, 2099–2110. [CrossRef]
29. Byrne, C. Iterative oblique projection onto convex sets and the split feasibility problem. *Inverse Probl.* **2002**, *18*, 441–453. [CrossRef]
30. Censor, Y.; Motova, A.; Segal, A. Perturbed projections and subgradient projections for the multiple-sets split feasibility problem. *J. Math. Anal. Appl.* **2007**, *327*, 1244–1256. [CrossRef]
31. Godwin, E.C.; Izuchukwu, C.; Mewomo, O.T. Image restoration using a modified relaxed inertial method for generalized split feasibility problems. *Math. Methods Appl. Sci.* **2022**. [CrossRef]
32. Censor, Y.; Gibali, A.; Reich, S. Algorithms for the split variational inequality problem. *Numer. Algorithms* **2012**, *59*, 301–323. [CrossRef]
33. He, H.; Ling, C.; Xu, H.K. A relaxed projection method for split variational inequalities. *J. Optim. Theory Appl.* **2015**, *166*, 213–233. [CrossRef]
34. Kim, J.K.; Salahuddin, S.; Lim, W.H. General nonconvex split variational inequality problems. *Korean J. Math.* **2017**, *25*, 469–481.
35. Ogwo, G.N.; Izuchukwu, C.; Mewomo, O.T. Inertial methods for finding minimum-norm solutions of the split variational inequality problem beyond monotonicity. *Numer. Algorithms* **2022**, *88*, 1419–1456. [CrossRef]
36. Tian, M.; Jiang, B.-N. Weak convergence theorem for a class of split variational inequality problems and applications in Hilbert space. *J. Ineq. Appl.* **2017**, *2017*, 123. [CrossRef]
37. Reich, S.; Tuyen, T.M. Iterative methods for solving the generalized split common null point problem in Hilbert spaces. *Optimization* **2020**, *69*, 1013–1038. [CrossRef]
38. Reich, S.; Tuyen, T.M. The split feasibility problem with multiple output sets in Hilbert spaces. *Optim. Lett.* **2020**, *14*, 2335–2353. [CrossRef]
39. Polyak, B.T. Some methods of speeding up the convergence of iteration methods. *Politehn. Univ. Bucharest Sci. Bull. Ser. A Appl. Math. Phys.* **1964**, *4*, 1–17. [CrossRef]
40. Chang, S.-S.; Yao, J.-C.; Wang, L.; Liu, M.; Zhao, L. On the inertial forward-backward splitting technique for solving a system of inclusion problems in Hilbert spaces. *Optimization* **2021**, *70*, 2511–2525. [CrossRef]
41. Ogwo, G.N.; Alakoya, T.O.; Mewomo, O.T. Inertial Iterative Method With Self-Adaptive Step Size for Finite Family of Split Monotone Variational Inclusion and Fixed Point Problems in Banach Spaces. *Demonstr. Math.* **2022**, *55*, 193–216. [CrossRef]
42. Uzor, V.A.; Alakoya, T.O.; Mewomo, O.T. On Split Monotone Variational Inclusion Problem with Multiple Output Sets with fixed point constraints. *Comput. Methods Appl. Math.* **2022**. [CrossRef]
43. Wang, Z.-B.; Long, X.; Lei, Z.-Y.; Chen, Z.-Y. New self-adaptive methods with double inertial steps for solving splitting monotone variational inclusion problems with applications. *Commun. Nonlinear Sci. Numer. Simul.* **2022**, *114*, 106656. [CrossRef]
44. Yao, Y.; Iyiola, O.S.; Shehu, Y. Subgradient extragradient method with double inertial steps for variational inequalities. *J. Sci. Comput.* **2022**, *90*, 71. [CrossRef]
45. Godwin, E.C.; Alakoya, T.O.; Mewomo, O.T.; Yao, J.-C. Approximation of solutions of split minimization problem with multiple output sets and common fixed point problem in real Banach spaces. *J. Nonlinear Var. Anal.* **2022**, *6*, 333–358.
46. Iutzeler, F.; Hendrickx, J.M. A generic online acceleration scheme for optimization algorithms via relaxation and inertia. *Optim. Methods Softw.* **2019**, *34*, 383–405. [CrossRef]
47. Alvarez, F. Weak convergence of a relaxed-inertial hybrid projection-proximal point algorithm for maximal monotone operators in Hilbert Space. *SIAM J. Optim.* **2004**, *14*, 773–782. [CrossRef]
48. Attouch, H.; Cabot, A. Convergence of a relaxed inertial forward-backward algorithm for structured monotone inclusions. *Optimization* **2019**, *80*, 547–598. [CrossRef]
49. Saejung, S.; Yotkaew, P. Approximation of zeros of inverse strongly monotone operators in Banach spaces. *Nonlinear Anal.* **2012**, *75*, 742–750. [CrossRef]

50. Tan, K.K.; Xu, H.K. Approximating fixed points of nonexpansive mappings by the Ishikawa iteration process. *J. Math. Anal. Appl.* **1993**, *178*, 301–308. [CrossRef]
51. Chuang, C.S. Strong convergence theorems for the split variational inclusion problem in Hilbert spaces. *Fixed Point Theory Appl.* **2013**, *350*. [CrossRef]
52. Cottle, R.W.; Yao, J.C. Pseudomonotone complementary problems in Hilbert space. *J. Optim. Theory Appl.* **1992**, *75*, 281–295. [CrossRef]
53. Tian, M.; Jiang, B.-N. Inertial Haugazeau's hybrid subgradient extragradient algorithm for variational inequality problems in Banach spaces. *Optimization* **2021**, *70*, 987–1007. [CrossRef]

Disclaimer/Publisher's Note: The statements, opinions and data contained in all publications are solely those of the individual author(s) and contributor(s) and not of MDPI and/or the editor(s). MDPI and/or the editor(s) disclaim responsibility for any injury to people or property resulting from any ideas, methods, instructions or products referred to in the content.

Article

New Fixed Point Results in Orthogonal B-Metric Spaces with Related Applications

Arul Joseph Gnanaprakasam [1], Gunaseelan Mani [2], Ozgur Ege [3], Ahmad Aloqaily [4,5] and Nabil Mlaiki [4,*]

[1] Department of Mathematics, College of Engineering and Technology, SRM Institute of Science and Technology, Kattankulathur 603203, India
[2] Department of Mathematics, Saveetha School of Engineering, Saveetha Institute of Medical and Technical Sciences, Chennai 602105, India
[3] Department of Mathematics, Ege University, Bornova, Izmir 35100, Turkey
[4] Department of Mathematics and Sciences, Prince Sultan University, Riyadh 11586, Saudi Arabia
[5] School of Computer, Data and Mathematical Sciences, Western Sydney University, Sydney 2150, Australia
* Correspondence: nmlaiki@psu.edu.sa or nmlaiki2012@gmail.com

Abstract: In this article, we present the concept of orthogonal α-almost Istrătescu contraction of types **D** and **D**∗ and prove some fixed point theorems on orthogonal b-metric spaces. We also provide an illustrative example to support our theorems. As an application, we establish the existence and uniqueness of the solution of the fractional differential equation and the solution of the integral equation using Elzaki transform.

Keywords: fixed point; orthogonal b-metric space; orthogonal α-almost Istrătescu contractions; Elzaki transform convolution

MSC: 47H10; 54H25

Citation: Gnanaprakasam, A.J.; Mani, G.; Ege, O.; Aloqaily, A.; Mlaiki, N. New Fixed Point Results in Orthogonal B-Metric Spaces with Related Applications. *Mathematics* **2023**, *11*, 677. https://doi.org/10.3390/math11030677

Academic Editor: Timilehin Opeyemi Alakoya

Received: 12 January 2023
Revised: 25 January 2023
Accepted: 27 January 2023
Published: 28 January 2023

Copyright: © 2023 by the authors. Licensee MDPI, Basel, Switzerland. This article is an open access article distributed under the terms and conditions of the Creative Commons Attribution (CC BY) license (https://creativecommons.org/licenses/by/4.0/).

1. Introduction

Around a century ago, the first fixed-point result was introduced. Banach [1] initially abstracted the successive approximation method for resolving differential equations, and he later defined it as a concept of contraction mapping. This Banach principle was not only succinctly stated, but it was also demonstrated by showing how to obtain the desired fixed point. The fixed point theory is extremely applicable to many qualitative sciences and is also particularly fascinating to researchers because of the simplicity with which equations in many research areas can be converted into fixed point problems. Banach's fixed point result has been improved, expanded, and generalized by numerous authors in numerous ways [2–6]. Istrătescu [7,8] provided one of the most significant ideas of convex contraction and proved some fixed point results. Another interesting extension of the fixed point theory called "almost contraction map" was introduced by Berinde [9]. In contrast, the concept of metric was developed in a number of ways, and these contraction principles have been extended to these new contexts. The idea of the b-metric was initiated by Bakhtin [10] in 1989. Czerwik [11] gave an axiom that was weaker than the triangular inequality and formally defined a b-metric space with a view of generalizing "the Banach contraction mapping theorem". Furthermore, Hussain et al. [12] improved the b-metric due to the modified triangle condition without a continuous function. Latif et al. [13] established some new results on the existence of fixed points for generalized multi-valued contractive mappings with respect to the w_b-distance in metric space. In 2022, Haghi and Bakhshi [14] proved some coupled fixed point results by using a without mixed monotone property. Yao et al. [15] presented a Tseng-type self-adaptive algorithm for solving a variational inequality and a fixed point problem involving pseudo-monotone and pseudo-contractive operators in Hilbert spaces.

Recently, the idea of orthogonality was introduced by Gordji et al. [16] and proved fixed point theorems in the setting of orthogonal complete metric spaces. In 2022, Aiman et al. [17] introduced the concept of an orthogonal L contraction map and proved some fixed point theorems. Furthermore, many researchers improved and generalized the concept of orthogonal metric spaces (see [18–24]). By motivating all the above the literature work, here we present the new notion of orthogonal α-almost Istrătescu contraction of type **D** and **D*** and prove some fixed point theorems in the setting of orthogonal complete b-metric spaces. As an application, we apply our main result to the Reiman–Liouville fractional differential equation and the solution of the second kind Volterra integral equation using Elzaki transform to strengthen and validate our main results.

2. Preliminaries

The concept of an "almost contraction map" was introduced by Berinde [9], as follows:

Definition 1. *[9] Let $(W, \mathcal{X})$ be a metric space. A mapping $\chi \colon W \to W$ is called an almost contraction if there exist a constant $\sigma \in (0,1)$ and some $\mathscr{P} \geq 0$ s.t*

$$\mathcal{X}(\chi\varrho, \chi\iota) \leq \sigma \mathcal{X}(\varrho, \iota) + \mathscr{P}\mathcal{X}(\iota, \chi\varrho), \ \forall \ \varrho, \iota \in W.$$

Bakhtin [10] introduced the notion of b-metric space as below:

Definition 2. *[10] Let W be a nonempty set and $\mathfrak{g} \geq 1$. Suppose that the map $\mathcal{X} \colon W \times W \to [0, \infty)$ satisfies the following axioms:*

(i) $\mathcal{X}(\varrho, \iota) = 0$ iff $\varrho = \iota$, $\forall \varrho, \iota \in W$;
(ii) $\mathcal{X}(\varrho, \iota) = \mathcal{X}(\iota, \varrho)$, $\forall \varrho, \iota \in W$;
(iii) $\mathcal{X}(\varrho, \iota) \leq \mathfrak{g}[\mathcal{X}(\varrho, \mathfrak{c}) + \mathcal{X}(\mathfrak{c}, \iota)]$, $\forall \varrho, \iota, \mathfrak{c} \in W$.

Then, $\mathcal{X}$ is called b-metric and $(W, \mathcal{X})$ is said to be a b-metric space.

In 2017, Miculescu et al. [25] explained the Cauchy criterion in the context of b-metric spaces.

Lemma 1. *[25] Every sequence $\{\varrho_j\}$ of elements from a b-metric space $(W, \mathcal{X})$ of constant $\mathfrak{g}$ having property that there $\exists \mathfrak{p} \in [0,1)$ s.t*

$$\mathcal{X}(\varrho_j, \varrho_{j+1}) \leq \mathfrak{p}\mathcal{X}(\varrho_j, \varrho_{j-1}), \tag{1}$$

for every $j \in \mathbb{N}$ is Cauchy.

Popescu [26] demonstrated the concept of an α-orbital admissible as below:

Definition 3. *[26] Let $\chi \colon W \to W$ be a map and $\alpha \colon W \times W \to [0, \infty)$ be a function. Then, χ is said to be α-orbital admissible if*

$$\alpha(\varrho, \chi\varrho) \geq 1 \implies \alpha(\chi\varrho, \chi^2\varrho) \geq 1, \ \forall \varrho \in W.$$

Now, we recall some concepts of orthogonality, which will be needed in the sequel.

Definition 4. *[16] Let W be a non-void set and $\perp \subseteq W \times W$ be a binary relation. If $\perp$ fulfilled the following axiom:*

$$\exists \varrho_0 : \forall \iota, \ \iota \perp \varrho_0 \ (or) \ \forall \iota, \ \varrho_0 \perp \iota,$$

then $(W, \perp)$ is called an orthogonal set.

Gordji et al. [16] presented the definition of an orthogonal sequence in 2017 as follows:

Definition 5. *[16] Let $(\mathcal{W}, \perp)$ be a orthogonal set. A sequence $\{\varrho_j\}_{j \in \mathbb{N}}$ is called an orthogonal sequence if*

$$(\forall j, \varrho_j \perp \varrho_{j+1}) \text{ or } (\forall j, \varrho_{j+1} \perp \varrho_j).$$

Now, we initiated the new concepts of orthogonal b-metric space, convergent and Cauchy sequence as follows:

Definition 6. *A triplet $(\mathcal{W}, \perp, \mathcal{X})$ is called an orthogonal b-metric space if $(\mathcal{W}, \perp)$ is an orthogonal set and $(\mathcal{W}, \mathcal{X})$ is a b-metric space and $\mathfrak{g} \geq 1$.*

Definition 7. *Let $(\mathcal{W}, \perp, \mathcal{X})$ be an orthogonal b-metric space and a map $\chi : \mathcal{W} \to \mathcal{W}$*
1. *$\{\iota_j\}$ is an orthogonal sequence in $\mathcal{W}$ that converges at a point ι if*

$$\lim_{j \to \infty} (\chi(\iota_j, \iota)) = 0.$$

2. *$\{\iota_j\}, \{\iota_m\}$ are two orthogonal sequences in $\mathcal{W}$ that are said to be an orthogonal Cauchy sequence if*

$$\lim_{j,m \to \infty} (\chi(\iota_j, \iota_m)) < \infty.$$

Gordji et al. [27] introduced the concept of orthogonal continuous as below:

Definition 8. *[27] Let $(\mathcal{W}, \perp, \mathcal{X})$ be a orthogonal b-metric space. Then, $\chi : \mathcal{W} \to \mathcal{W}$ is said to be orthogonal continuous at $\iota \in \mathcal{W}$ if, for each orthogonal sequence $\{\iota_j\}_{j \in \mathbb{N}}$ in $\mathcal{W}$ with $\iota_j \to \iota$. We have $\chi(\iota_j) \to \chi(\iota)$. Additionally, χ is said to be orthogonal continuous on $\mathcal{W}$ if χ is orthogonal continuous in each $\iota \in \mathcal{W}$.*

Definition 9. *Let $(\mathcal{W}, \perp, \mathcal{X})$ be an orthogonal b-metric space. Then, $\chi^2 : \mathcal{W} \to \mathcal{W}$ is said to be orthogonal continuous at $\iota \in \mathcal{W}$ if, for each orthogonal sequence $\{\iota_j\}_{j \in \mathbb{N}}$ in $\mathcal{W}$ with $\iota_j \to \iota$. We have $\chi^2(\iota_j) \to \chi^2(\iota)$. Additionally, χ^2 is said to be orthogonal continuous on $\mathcal{W}$ if χ^2 is orthogonal continuous in each $\iota \in \mathcal{W}$.*

The concept of orthogonal complete in metric spaces is defined by Gordji et al. [16] as follows.

Definition 10. *[16] Let $(\mathcal{W}, \perp, \mathcal{X})$ be an orthogonal metric space. Then, $\mathcal{W}$ is said to be orthogonal-complete if every orthogonal Cauchy sequence is convergent.*

Definition 11. *[16] Let $(\mathcal{W}, \perp)$ be an orthogonal set. A function $\chi : \mathcal{W} \to \mathcal{W}$ is called orthogonal-preserving if $\chi \varrho \perp \chi \iota$ whenever $\varrho \perp \iota$.*

Ramezani [28] introduced the notion of orthogonal α-admissible as follows:

Definition 12. *[28] Let $\chi : \mathcal{W} \to \mathcal{W}$ be a map and $\alpha : \mathcal{W} \times \mathcal{W} \to [0, \infty)$ be a function. Then, χ is said to be orthogonal-α-admissible if $\forall \ \varrho, \iota \in \mathcal{W}$ with $\varrho \perp \iota$*

$$\alpha(\varrho, \iota) \geq 1 \implies \alpha(\chi \varrho, \chi \iota) \geq 1.$$

Inspired by the α-almost Istrătescu contraction of types defined by Karapinar et al. [29], we implement a new orthogonally α-almost Istrătescu contraction type mapping and present some fixed point results in an orthogonal **CbMS** (complete b-metric space) for this contraction map.

3. Main Results

First, we introduce the concept of an orthogonally α-almost Istrătescu contraction of type **D**.

Definition 13. *Let $(\mathcal{W}, \perp, \mathcal{X})$ be an orthogonal **CbMS** and $\alpha : \mathcal{W} \times \mathcal{W} \to [0, \infty)$ be a function. A map $\chi : \mathcal{W} \to \mathcal{W}$ is called an orthogonally α-almost Istrătescu contraction of type **D** if there exist $\mathfrak{r} \in [0,1)$, $\beta \geq 0$ s.t for any $\varrho, \iota \in \mathcal{W}$ with $\varrho \perp \iota$*

$$\alpha(\varrho, \iota)\mathcal{X}(\chi^2\varrho, \chi^2\iota) \leq \mathfrak{r}\mathbf{D}(\varrho, \iota) + \beta N(\varrho, \iota), \tag{2}$$

where

$$\mathbf{D}(\varrho, \iota) = \mathcal{X}(\chi\varrho, \chi\iota) + |\mathcal{X}(\chi\varrho, \chi^2\varrho) - \mathcal{X}(\chi\iota, \chi^2\iota)|, \tag{3}$$

and

$$N(\varrho, \iota) = \min\{\mathcal{X}(\varrho, \chi\varrho), \mathcal{X}(\iota, \chi\iota), \mathcal{X}(\varrho, \chi\iota), \mathcal{X}(\iota, \chi\varrho)\mathcal{X}(\chi\varrho, \chi^2\iota), \mathcal{X}(\chi\iota, \chi^2\varrho)\}. \tag{4}$$

Definition 14. *Let $(\mathcal{W}, \perp, \mathcal{X})$ be an orthogonal **CbMS**. A map $\chi : \mathcal{W} \to \mathcal{W}$ is called an orthogonally α-almost Istrătescu contraction of type **D** if there exist $\mathfrak{r} \in [0,1)$, $\beta \geq 0$ s.t for any $\varrho, \iota \in \mathcal{W}$ with $\varrho \perp \iota$*

$$\mathcal{X}(\chi^2\varrho, \chi^2\iota) \leq \mathfrak{r}\mathbf{D}(\varrho, \iota) + \beta . N(\varrho, \iota), \tag{5}$$

where $\mathbf{D}(\varrho, \iota)$ and $N(\varrho, \iota)$ are defined by inequality (3) and (4), respectively.

Definition 15. *Let $(\mathcal{W}, \perp, \mathcal{X})$ be an orthogonal **CbMS** and $\alpha : \mathcal{W} \times \mathcal{W} \to [0, \infty)$ be a function. A map $\chi : \mathcal{W} \to \mathcal{W}$ is called an orthogonally α-almost Istrătescu contraction of type **D*** if there exist $\mathfrak{r} \in [0,1)$, $\beta \geq 0$ s.t for any $\varrho, \iota \in \mathcal{W}$ with $\varrho \perp \iota$*

$$\alpha(\varrho, \iota)\mathcal{X}(\chi^2\varrho, \chi^2\iota) \leq \mathfrak{r}\mathbf{D}^*(\varrho, \iota) + \beta . N(\varrho, \iota), \tag{6}$$

where

$$\mathbf{D}^*(\varrho, \iota) = |\mathcal{X}(\varrho, \chi\varrho) - \mathcal{X}(\chi\iota, \chi^2\iota)| + \mathcal{X}(\varrho, \iota) + |\mathcal{X}(\iota, \chi\iota) - \mathcal{X}(\chi\varrho, \chi^2\varrho)|, \tag{7}$$

and

$$N(\varrho, \iota) = \min\{\mathcal{X}(\varrho, \chi\varrho), \mathcal{X}(\iota, \chi\iota), \mathcal{X}(\varrho, \chi\iota), \mathcal{X}(\iota, \chi\varrho)\mathcal{X}(\chi\varrho, \chi^2\iota), \mathcal{X}(\chi\iota, \chi^2\varrho)\}. \tag{8}$$

Theorem 1. *Let $(\mathcal{W}, \perp, \mathcal{X})$ be an orthogonal **CbMS**, $\chi : \mathcal{W} \to \mathcal{W}$ be an orthogonally α-almost Istrătescu contraction of type **D** and $\alpha: \mathcal{W} \times \mathcal{W} \to [0, \infty)$, s.t the following conditions hold:*
(i) *χ is orthogonal preserving;*
(ii) *for any $\pi \in \mathcal{W}$, $\alpha(\kappa, \pi) \geq 1$ with $\kappa \perp \pi$, where $\kappa \in Fix_\chi(\mathcal{W})$;*
(iii) *χ is orthogonal continuous;*
(iv) *χ^2 is orthogonal continuous with $\chi\kappa \perp \kappa$ and $\alpha(\chi\kappa, \kappa) \geq 1$, for any $\kappa \in \mathcal{W}$.*
If χ is orthogonal $\alpha - OA$ and there exists $\varrho_0 \in \mathcal{W}$ s.t $\varrho_0 \perp \chi\varrho_0$ and $\alpha(\varrho_0, \chi\varrho_0) \geq 1$, then χ has a unique fixed point.

Proof. By the definition of orthogonality, we find that $\varrho_0 \perp \chi\varrho_0$ or $\chi\varrho_0 \perp \varrho_0$. Let

$$\varrho_j = \varrho_{j-1} = ... = \chi^j\varrho_0,$$

for all $j \in \mathbb{N}$. If $\varrho_j = \varrho_{j+1}$ for some $j^* \in \mathbb{N} \cup \{0\}$, then j_{j^*} is a fixed point of χ and so the proof is completed. Thus, we assume that $\varrho_j \neq \varrho_{j+1}$ for all $j \in \mathbb{N} \cup \{0\}$.

So, we have $\mathcal{X}(\chi\varrho_j, \chi\varrho_{j+1}) > 0$. Since χ is orthogonal-preserving, we obtain

$$\varrho_j \perp \varrho_{j+1} \text{ or } \varrho_{j+1} \perp \varrho_j, \quad \forall j \in \mathbb{N},$$

which implies that $\{\varrho_j\}$ is an orthogonal sequence. Since χ is an orthogonally α-almost Istrătescu contraction of type **D**, we have $\alpha(\chi\varrho_0, \chi^2\varrho_0) \geq 1$, and continuing this process, we obtain

$$\alpha(\chi^j\varrho_0, \chi^{j+1}\varrho_0) \geq 1, \text{ for } j \in \mathbb{N}. \tag{9}$$

Replacing ϱ by ϱ_0 and ι by $\chi\varrho_0$ in (2), we have

$$\mathcal{X}(\chi^2\varrho_0, \chi^3\varrho_0) \leq \alpha(\varrho_0, \chi\varrho_0)\mathcal{X}(\chi^2\varrho_0, \chi^2(\chi\varrho_0))$$
$$\leq \mathfrak{r}\mathbf{D}(\varrho_0, \chi\varrho_0) + \beta N(\varrho_0, \chi\varrho_0)$$
$$= \mathfrak{r}(\mathcal{X}(\chi\varrho_0, \chi(\chi\varrho_0)) + |\mathcal{X}(\chi\varrho_0, \chi^2\varrho_0) - \mathcal{X}(\chi(\chi\varrho_0), \chi^2(\chi\varrho_0))|)$$
$$+ \beta \min\{\mathcal{X}(\varrho_0, \chi\varrho_0), \mathcal{X}(\chi\varrho_0, \chi(\chi\varrho_0)), \mathcal{X}(\varrho_0, \chi(\chi\varrho_0)), \mathcal{X}(\chi\varrho_0, \chi\varrho_0)$$
$$\mathcal{X}(\chi\varrho_0, \chi^2(\chi\varrho_0)), \mathcal{X}(\chi(\chi\varrho_0), \chi^2\varrho_0)\}$$
$$\leq \mathfrak{r}(\mathcal{X}(\chi\varrho_0, \chi^2(\varrho_0)) + |\mathcal{X}(\chi\varrho_0, \chi^2\varrho_0) - \mathcal{X}(\chi^2\varrho_0, \chi^3\varrho_0)|) \tag{10}$$
$$+ \beta \min\{\mathcal{X}(\varrho_0, \chi\varrho_0), \mathcal{X}(\chi\varrho_0, \chi^2\varrho_0), \mathcal{X}(\varrho_0, \chi^2\varrho_0), \mathcal{X}(\chi\varrho_0, \chi\varrho_0)$$
$$\mathcal{X}(\chi\varrho_0, \chi^3\varrho_0), \mathcal{X}(\chi^2\varrho_0, \chi^2\varrho_0)\}$$
$$= \mathfrak{r}(\mathcal{X}(\chi\varrho_0, \chi^2(\varrho_0)) + |\mathcal{X}(\chi\varrho_0, \chi^2\varrho_0) - \mathcal{X}(\chi^2\varrho_0, \chi^3\varrho_0)|).$$

If $\mathcal{X}(\chi\varrho_0, \chi^2\varrho_0) \leq \mathcal{X}(\chi^2\varrho_0, \chi^3\varrho_0)$, then we have

$$\mathcal{X}(\chi^2\varrho_0, \chi^3\varrho_0) \leq \mathfrak{r}(\mathcal{X}(\chi\varrho_0, \chi^2(\varrho_0)) + \mathcal{X}(\chi^2\varrho_0, \chi^3\varrho_0) - \mathcal{X}(\chi\varrho_0, \chi^2\varrho_0))$$
$$= \mathfrak{r}\mathcal{X}(\chi\varrho_0, \chi^2(\varrho_0)) < \mathcal{X}(\chi^2\varrho_0, \chi^3\varrho_0),$$

this is a contradiction. Thus, $\mathcal{X}(\chi\varrho_0, \chi^2\varrho_0) > \mathcal{X}(\chi^2\varrho_0, \chi^3\varrho_0)$ and the inequality (10) becomes

$$\mathcal{X}(\chi^2\varrho_0, \chi^3\varrho_0) \leq \mathfrak{r}(\mathcal{X}(\chi\varrho_0, \chi^2(\varrho_0)) + \mathcal{X}(\chi^2\varrho_0, \chi^2\varrho_0) - \mathcal{X}(\chi^2\varrho_0, \chi^3\varrho_0))$$
$$= \mathfrak{r}(2\mathcal{X}(\chi\varrho_0, \chi^2(\varrho_0)) - \mathcal{X}(\chi^2\varrho_0, \chi^3\varrho_0)) \iff$$
$$\mathcal{X}(\chi^2\varrho_0, \chi^3\varrho_0) \leq \frac{2\mathfrak{r}}{1+\mathfrak{r}}\mathcal{X}(\chi\varrho_0, \chi^2(\varrho_0)). \tag{11}$$

For $\varrho = \varrho_0, \iota = \chi\varrho_0$, taking Equation (9) into account,

$$\mathcal{X}(\chi^3\varrho_0, \chi^4\varrho_0) \leq \alpha(\chi\varrho_0, \chi^2\varrho_0)\mathcal{X}(\chi^2(\chi\varrho_0), \chi^2(\chi^2\varrho_0)) \leq \mathfrak{r}\mathbf{D}(\chi\varrho_0, \chi^2\varrho_0) + \beta N(\chi\varrho_0, \chi^2\varrho_0)$$
$$= \mathfrak{r}(\mathcal{X}(\chi(\chi\varrho_0), \chi(\chi^2\varrho_0)) + |\mathcal{X}(\chi(\chi\varrho_0), \chi^2(\chi\varrho_0)) - \mathcal{X}(\chi(\chi^2\varrho_0), \chi^2(\chi^2\varrho_0))|)$$
$$+ \mathscr{P}\min\{\mathcal{X}(\chi\varrho_0, \chi(\chi\varrho_0)), \mathcal{X}(\chi^2\varrho_0, \chi^3\varrho_0), \mathcal{X}(\chi\varrho_0, \chi^3\varrho_0), \mathcal{X}(\chi\varrho_0, \chi\varrho_0)$$
$$\mathcal{X}(\chi^2\varrho_0, \chi^4\varrho_0), \mathcal{X}(\chi^3\varrho_0, \chi^3\varrho_0)\}$$
$$= \mathfrak{r}(\mathcal{X}(\chi^2\varrho_0, \chi^3\varrho_0) + |\mathcal{X}(\chi^2\varrho_0, \chi^3\varrho_0) - \mathcal{X}(\chi^3\varrho_0, \chi^4\varrho_0)|)$$
$$+ \beta \min\{\mathcal{X}(\varrho_0, \chi^2\varrho_0), \mathcal{X}(\chi^2\varrho_0, \chi^3\varrho_0), \mathcal{X}(\chi\varrho_0, \chi^3\varrho_0), \mathcal{X}(\chi\varrho_0, \chi\varrho_0)$$
$$\mathcal{X}(\chi^2\varrho_0, \chi^4\varrho_0), \mathcal{X}(\chi^3\varrho_0, \chi^3\varrho_0)\}$$
$$= \mathfrak{r}(\mathcal{X}(\chi^2\varrho_0, \chi^3(\varrho_0)) + |\mathcal{X}(\chi^2\varrho_0, \chi^3\varrho_0) - \mathcal{X}(\chi^3\varrho_0, \chi^4\varrho_0)|).$$

Since for the case $\mathcal{X}(\chi^2\varrho_0, \chi^3\varrho_0) \leq \mathcal{X}(\chi^3\varrho_0, \chi^4\varrho_0)$, we get

$$\mathcal{X}(\chi^3\varrho_0, \chi^4\varrho_0) \leq \mathfrak{r}(\mathcal{X}(\chi^2\varrho_0, \chi^3(\varrho_0)) + \mathcal{X}(\chi^3\varrho_0, \chi^4\varrho_0) - \mathcal{X}(\chi^2\varrho_0, \chi^3\varrho_0))$$
$$\leq \mathfrak{r}\mathcal{X}(\chi^3\varrho_0, \chi^4(\varrho_0)),$$

which is a contradiction. Thus, $\mathcal{X}(\chi^2\varrho_0, \chi^3\varrho_0) > \mathcal{X}(\chi^3\varrho_0, \chi^4\varrho_0)$ and

$$\mathcal{X}(\chi^3\varrho_0, \chi^4\varrho_0) \leq \mathfrak{r}(\mathcal{X}(\chi^2\varrho_0, \chi^3(\varrho_0)) + \mathcal{X}(\chi^2\varrho_0, \chi^3\varrho_0) - \mathcal{X}(\chi^3\varrho_0, \chi^4\varrho_0))$$
$$= \mathfrak{r}(2\mathcal{X}(\chi^2\varrho_0, \chi^3(\varrho_0)) - \mathcal{X}(\chi^3\varrho_0, \chi^4\varrho_0)), \quad \Longleftrightarrow$$
$$\mathcal{X}(\chi^3\varrho_0, \chi^4\varrho_0) \leq \frac{2\mathfrak{r}}{1+\mathfrak{r}} \mathcal{X}(\chi^2\varrho_0, \chi^3(\varrho_0)). \qquad (12)$$

By proceeding in this way,

$$\mathcal{X}(\chi^J\varrho_0, \chi^{J+1}\varrho_0) \leq \left(\frac{2\mathfrak{r}}{1+\mathfrak{r}}\right)\mathcal{X}(\chi^{J-1}\varrho_0, \chi^J(\varrho_0))$$
$$\leq \left(\frac{2\mathfrak{r}}{1+\mathfrak{r}}\right)^{J-1} \mathcal{X}(\chi\varrho_0, \chi^2(\varrho_0)) \to 0, \qquad (13)$$

as $J \to \infty$, because $J = \frac{2\mathfrak{r}}{1+\mathfrak{r}} < 1$.

Instead, considering the orthogonal sequence $\{\varrho_J\}_{J\in\mathbb{N}}$ defined as

$$\varrho_1 = \chi\varrho_0, \varrho_2 = \chi^2\varrho_0, \ldots \varrho_J = \chi^J\varrho_0,$$

where $\varrho_0 \in \mathcal{W}$, from Equation (13), we have

$$\mathcal{X}(\varrho_J, \varrho_{J+1}) \leq J.\mathcal{X}(\varrho_{J-1}, \varrho_J),$$

for $J \in \mathbb{N}$. Therefore, from Lemma 1, we obtain $\{\varrho_J\}_{J\in\mathbb{N}}$ from an orthogonal Cauchy sequence on orthogonal **CbMS**. Therefore, the orthogonal sequence is convergent. Then, $\exists \kappa \in \mathcal{W}$ s.t

$$\lim_{J\to\infty} \mathcal{X}(\varrho_J, \kappa) = 0. \qquad (14)$$

When the map χ is orthogonal continuous, it follows that

$$\lim_{J\to\infty} \mathcal{X}(\varrho_J, \chi\kappa) = \lim_{J\to\infty} \mathcal{X}(\varrho_{J-1}, \chi\kappa) = 0,$$

and thus, we decide $\chi\kappa = \kappa$, that is κ forms a fixed point of χ.
Keeping the continuity of χ^2, we obtain

$$\lim_{J\to\infty} \mathcal{X}(\varrho_J, \chi^2\kappa) = \lim_{J\to\infty} \mathcal{X}(\chi^2\varrho_{J-2}, \chi^2\kappa) = 0.$$

Since each orthogonal sequence in $(\mathcal{W}, \perp, \mathcal{X})$ has a unique limit, we obtain $\chi^2\kappa = \kappa$, that is, κ forms a fixed point of χ^2. In order to illustrate that κ also forms a fixed point of χ, we apply the method of reductio ad absurdum. We diminish the consequence and presume that $\chi\kappa \neq \kappa$. Therefore, from Equation (2), we obtain

$$0 < \mathcal{X}(\chi\kappa, \kappa) = \mathcal{X}(\chi^2(\chi\kappa), \chi^2\kappa) \leq \alpha(q\kappa, \kappa), \mathcal{X}(\chi^2(q\kappa), \chi^2\kappa) \leq \mathfrak{r}D(\chi\kappa, \kappa) + \beta N(\chi\kappa, \kappa)$$
$$= \mathfrak{r}(\mathcal{X}(\chi\kappa, \chi^2\kappa) + |\mathcal{X}(\chi\kappa, \chi^2\kappa) - \mathcal{X}(\chi^2\kappa, \chi^3\kappa)|)$$
$$+ \beta \min\{\mathcal{X}(\kappa, \chi\kappa), \mathcal{X}(\chi\kappa, \chi^2\kappa), \mathcal{X}(\kappa, \chi^2\kappa), \mathcal{X}(\chi\kappa, \chi\kappa), \mathcal{X}(\chi\kappa, \chi^3\kappa), \mathcal{X}(\chi^2\kappa, \chi^2\kappa)\}$$
$$= \mathfrak{r}(\mathcal{X}(\chi\kappa, \kappa) + |\mathcal{X}(\chi\kappa, \kappa) - \mathcal{X}(\kappa, \chi\kappa)|)$$
$$= \mathfrak{r}(\mathcal{X}(\chi\kappa, \kappa)) < \mathcal{X}(\chi\kappa, \kappa).$$

Hence, $\chi\kappa = \kappa$.

To prove the uniqueness of the fixed point, let $\pi \in \mathcal{W}$ be another fixed point of χ. Then, we have $\chi^j \pi = \pi$, $\forall j \in \mathbb{N}$. Given our choice of κ in the first part of the proof, we obtain

$$\kappa \perp \pi \text{ or } \pi \perp \kappa.$$

Since χ is orthogonal-preserving, we obtain

$$\chi^j \kappa \perp \chi^j \pi$$

or

$$\chi^j \pi \perp \chi^j \kappa, \quad \forall j \in \mathbb{N}.$$

On the other hand, χ is an orthogonal α-almost Istrătescu contraction. Then, we obtain

$$\begin{aligned}
\mathcal{X}(\kappa, \pi) &= \mathcal{X}(\chi^2\kappa, \chi^2\pi) \leq \alpha(\kappa, \iota) \mathcal{X}(\chi^2\kappa, \chi^2\pi) \leq \mathfrak{r}.\mathbf{D}(\kappa, \pi) + \beta.N(\kappa, \pi) \\
&\leq \mathfrak{r}(\mathcal{X}(\chi\kappa, \chi\pi) + |\mathcal{X}(\chi\kappa, \chi^2\kappa) - \mathcal{X}(\chi\pi, \chi^2\pi)|) \\
&\quad + \beta \min\{\mathcal{X}(\kappa, \chi\kappa), \mathcal{X}(\pi, \chi\pi), \mathcal{X}(\kappa, \chi\pi), \mathcal{X}(\pi, \chi\kappa), \mathcal{X}(\chi\kappa, \chi^2\pi), \mathcal{X}(\chi\pi, \chi^2\kappa)\} \\
&= \mathfrak{r}(\mathcal{X}(\kappa, \pi) + |\mathcal{X}(\kappa, \kappa) - \mathcal{X}(\pi, \pi)|) + \beta \min\{\mathcal{X}(\kappa, \kappa), \mathcal{X}(\pi, \pi), \mathcal{X}(\kappa, \pi), \mathcal{X}(\pi, \kappa)\} \\
&= \mathfrak{r}(\mathcal{X}(\kappa, \pi)) < \mathcal{X}(\kappa, \pi),
\end{aligned}$$

which is a contradiction. Therefore, χ has a unique fixed point. □

Example 1. Let $\mathcal{W} = [0, \infty)$ and the function $\mathcal{X} : \mathcal{W} \times \mathcal{W} \to [0, \infty)$ with $\mathcal{X}(\varrho, \iota) = (\varrho - \iota)^2$, for all $\varrho, \iota \in \mathcal{W}$. $\mathcal{W}$ be the Euclidean metric. Define $\varrho \perp \iota$ if $\varrho\iota \leq (\varrho \vee \iota)$ where $\varrho \vee \iota = \varrho$ or $\varrho \vee \iota = \iota$. Define a map $\chi : \mathcal{W} \to \mathcal{W}$ by

$$\chi\varrho = \begin{cases} \varrho^2, & \text{if } \varrho \in [0, 1) \\ 1, & \text{if } \varrho \in [1, 2) \\ \dfrac{6\varrho^2 + 3\varrho + 1}{4\varrho^2 + 4\varrho + 6}, & \text{if } \varrho \in [2, \infty). \end{cases}$$

We can see that χ is discontinuous at $\varrho = 2$, but χ^2 is orthogonal continuous and χ^2 is orthogonal preserving on $\mathcal{W}$, since

$$\chi^2\varrho = \begin{cases} \varrho^4, & \text{if } \varrho \in [0, 1) \\ 1, & \text{if } \varrho \in [1, \infty). \end{cases}$$

Let the map $\alpha : \mathcal{W} \times \mathcal{W} \to [0, \infty)$ with $\varrho \perp \iota$ be given by

$$\alpha(\varrho, \iota) = \begin{cases} 3, & \text{if } \varrho, \iota \in [1, \infty) \\ 0, & \text{if otherwise.} \end{cases}$$

It is clear that χ is an orthogonally α-almost Istrătescu contraction of type **D**. In fact, based on the definition of the function α, the only case we find interesting is $\varrho, \iota \in [1, \infty)$; we obtain for $\mathfrak{r} \in [0, 1)$

$$0 = 3\mathcal{X}(1, 1) = \alpha(\varrho, \iota)\mathcal{X}(\chi^2\varrho, \chi^2\iota) \leq \mathfrak{r}\mathbf{D}(\varrho, \iota) + \beta N(\varrho, \iota).$$

We can conclude that for any $\varrho, \iota \in \mathcal{W}$, all the conditions of Theorem 1 are satisfied, and $Fix_\chi \mathcal{W} = \{0, 1\}$.

Corollary 1. Suppose that a self-map χ, on orthogonal **CbMS** $(\mathcal{W}, \perp, \mathcal{X})$ fulfills

$$\mathcal{X}(\chi^2\varrho, \chi^2\iota) \leq \mathfrak{r}\mathbf{D}(\varrho, \iota), \tag{15}$$

for all $\varrho, \iota \in \mathcal{W}$. If either χ or χ^2 is orthogonal continuous. Then, χ has a unique fixed point.

Proof. It is sufficient to set $\alpha(\varrho, \iota) = 1$ and put $\beta = 0$ in Theorem 1. □

Theorem 2. *Let* $(\mathcal{W}, \perp, \mathcal{X})$ *be an orthogonal CbMS and* $\chi : \mathcal{W} \to \mathcal{W}$ *be an orthogonally α-almost Istrătescu contraction of type* $\mathbf{D}^*$ *with* $\beta \geq 0$, $\alpha \colon \mathsf{W} \times \mathsf{W} \to [0, \infty)$ *s.t the following conditions hold:*

(i) χ *is orthogonal preserving;*
(ii) *for any* $\pi \in \mathcal{W}$, $\alpha(\kappa, \pi) \geq 1$ *with* $\kappa \perp \pi$, *where* $\kappa \in Fix_\chi(\mathcal{W})$;
(iii) χ *is orthogonal continuous;*
(iv) χ^2 *is orthogonal continuous with* $\mathsf{q}\kappa \perp \kappa$ *and* $\alpha(\mathsf{q}\kappa, \kappa) \geq 1$ *for any* $\kappa \in Fix_{\chi^2}(\mathcal{W})$.

If χ is orthogonal $\alpha - OA$ and $\exists \varrho_0 \in \mathcal{W}$ s.t $\varrho_0 \perp \chi\varrho_0$ and $\alpha(\varrho_0, \chi\varrho_0) \geq 1$, then it has a unique fixed point in χ.

Proof. Let $\varrho_0 \in \mathcal{W}$ and we assume the orthogonal sequence $\{\varrho_j\}$ follows from Theorem 1. Then, for each $j \in \mathbb{N}$, we obtain

$$\mathbf{D}^*(\varrho_{j-1}, \varrho_j) = |\mathcal{X}(\varrho_{j-1}, \chi\varrho_{j-1}) - \mathcal{X}(\chi\varrho_j, \chi^2\varrho_j)| + \mathcal{X}(\varrho_{j-1}, \varrho_j) + |\mathcal{X}(\varrho_j, \chi\varrho_j) - \mathcal{X}(\chi\varrho_{j-1}, \chi^2\varrho_{j-1})|$$
$$= |\mathcal{X}(\varrho_{j-1}, \varrho_j) - \mathcal{X}(\varrho_{j+1}, \varrho_{j+2})| + \mathcal{X}(\varrho_{j-1}, \varrho_j) + |\mathcal{X}(\varrho_j, \varrho_{j+1}) - \mathcal{X}(\varrho_j, \varrho_{j+1})|$$
$$= |\mathcal{X}(\varrho_{j-1}, \varrho_j) - \mathcal{X}(\varrho_{j+1}, \varrho_{j+2})| + \mathcal{X}(\varrho_{j-1}, \varrho_j),$$

and

$$N(\varrho_{j-1}, \varrho_j) = \min\{\mathcal{X}(\varrho_{j-1}, \chi\varrho_{j-1}), \mathcal{X}(\varrho_j, \chi\varrho_j), \mathcal{X}(\varrho_{j-1}, \chi\varrho_j), \mathcal{X}(\varrho_j, \chi\varrho_{j-1})$$
$$\mathcal{X}(\chi\varrho_{j-1}, \chi^2\varrho_j), \mathcal{X}(\chi\varrho_j, \chi^2\varrho_{j-1})\}$$
$$= \min\{\mathcal{X}(\varrho_{j-1}, \varrho_j), \mathcal{X}(\varrho_j, \varrho_{j+1}), \mathcal{X}(\varrho_{j-1}, \varrho_{j+1}), \mathcal{X}(\varrho_j, \varrho_j)$$
$$\mathcal{X}(\varrho_j, \varrho_{j+2}), \mathcal{X}(\varrho_{j+1}, \varrho_{j+1})\} = 0.$$

Taking Equation (9), by Equation (6), we obtain

$$\mathcal{X}(\varrho_{j+1}, \varrho_{j+2}) = \mathcal{X}(\chi^2\varrho_{j-1}, \chi^2\varrho_j) \leq \alpha(\varrho_{j-1}, \varrho_j)\mathcal{X}(\chi^2\varrho_{j-1}, \chi^2\varrho_j)$$
$$\leq \mathfrak{r}\mathbf{D}^*(\varrho_{j-1}, \varrho_j) + \beta.N(\varrho_{j-1}, \varrho_j)$$
$$= \mathfrak{r}.(\mathcal{X}(\varrho_{j-1}, \varrho_j) + |\mathcal{X}(\varrho_{j-1}, \varrho_j) - \mathcal{X}(\varrho_{j+1}, \varrho_{j+2})|). \quad (16)$$

If we suppose that $\mathcal{X}(\varrho_{j-1}, \varrho_j) \leq \mathcal{X}(\varrho_{j+1}, \varrho_{j+2})$, by Equation (16), we obtain

$$\mathcal{X}(\varrho_{j+1}, \varrho_{j+2}) \leq \mathfrak{r}(\mathcal{X}(\varrho_{j+1}, \varrho_{j+2})) < \mathcal{X}(\varrho_{j+1}, \varrho_{j+2}),$$

this is a contradiction. If $\mathcal{X}(\varrho_{j-1}, \varrho_j) > \mathcal{X}(\varrho_{j+1}, \varrho_{j+2})$, then

$$\mathcal{X}(\varrho_{j+1}, \varrho_{j+2}) \leq \mathfrak{r}(2\mathcal{X}(\varrho_{j-1}, \varrho_j)) - \mathcal{X}(\varrho_{j+1}, \varrho_{j+2}),$$

which turns into

$$\mathcal{X}(\varrho_{j+1}, \varrho_{j+2}) \leq \frac{2\mathfrak{r}}{\mathfrak{r}+1}(2\mathcal{X}(\varrho_{j-1}, \varrho_j)), \quad \text{for } j \in \mathbb{N}. \quad (17)$$

Denoting by $\mathfrak{p} = \dfrac{2\mathfrak{r}}{\mathfrak{r}+1} < 1$, $\xi = \max\{\mathcal{X}(\varrho_0, \varrho_1), \mathcal{X}(\varrho_1, \varrho_2)\}$, respectively, and continuing in the process, we have

$$\mathcal{X}(\varrho_{J+1}, \varrho_{J+2}) \leq \mathfrak{p}\mathcal{X}(\varrho_{J-1}, \varrho_J)$$
$$\leq \mathfrak{p}\mathcal{X}(\varrho_{J-3}, \varrho_{J-2})$$
$$\cdot$$
$$\cdot$$
$$\leq \mathfrak{p}^{[\frac{J}{2}]} \max\{\mathcal{X}(\varrho_0, \varrho_1), \mathcal{X}(\varrho_1, \varrho_2)\}$$
$$= \mathfrak{p}^{[\frac{J}{2}]}\xi.$$

Therefore,

$$\mathcal{X}(\varrho_{J+1}, \varrho_{J+2}) \leq \mathfrak{p}^{[\frac{J}{2}]}\xi \quad \text{for} \quad J \in \mathbb{N} \tag{18}$$

and

$$\lim_{J \to \infty} \mathcal{X}(\varrho_J, \varrho_{J+1}) = 0. \tag{19}$$

From Lemma 1, the orthogonal sequence $\{\varrho_J\}$ is an orthogonal Cauchy sequence in orthogonal **CbMS**, so there exists κ s.t

$$\lim_{J \to \infty} \mathcal{X}(\varrho_J, \kappa) = 0.$$

If we consider that (i) holds, we obtain $\chi\kappa = \kappa$.

Instead, if we use hypotheses (ii), we have $\chi^2\kappa = \kappa$ and $\alpha(\chi\kappa, \kappa) \geq 1$. We apply the method of reductio ad absurdum and suppose that $\chi\kappa \neq \kappa$, so by Equation (6), we have

$$\mathcal{X}(\chi\kappa, \kappa) = \mathcal{X}(\chi^2(\chi\kappa), \chi^2\kappa) \leq \alpha(\chi\kappa, \kappa)\mathcal{X}(\chi^2(\chi\kappa), \chi^2\kappa) \leq \mathfrak{r}\mathbf{D}^*(\chi\kappa, \kappa) + \beta N(\chi\kappa, \kappa)$$
$$= \mathfrak{r}(\mathcal{X}(\chi\kappa, \kappa) + |\mathcal{X}(\chi\kappa, \chi^2\kappa) - \mathcal{X}(\chi\kappa, \chi^2\kappa)| + |\mathcal{X}(\kappa, \chi\kappa) - \mathcal{X}(\chi^2\kappa, \chi^3\kappa)|)$$
$$= \mathfrak{r}\mathcal{X}(\chi\kappa, \kappa) < \mathcal{X}(\chi\kappa, \kappa),$$

which is a contradiction. Therefore, $\chi\kappa = \kappa$.

Now, we prove the unique fixed point, let $\pi \in \mathcal{W}$ be another fixed point of χ. Then, we have $\chi^J\pi = \pi$, $\forall J \in \mathbb{N}$. Given our choice of κ in the proof of the first part, we obtain

$$\kappa \perp \pi \quad \text{or} \quad \pi \perp \kappa.$$

Since χ is orthogonal-preserving, we obtain

$$\chi^J \kappa \perp \chi^J \pi$$
or
$$\chi^J \pi \perp \chi^J \kappa, \quad \forall J \in \mathbb{N}.$$

On the other hand, χ is an orthogonal α-almost Istrătescu contraction. Then, we obtain

$$\mathcal{X}(\kappa, \pi) = \mathcal{X}(\chi^2\kappa, \chi^2\pi)$$
$$\leq \alpha(\kappa, \pi)\mathcal{X}(\chi^2\kappa, \chi^2\pi)$$
$$\leq \mathfrak{r}\mathbf{D}^*(\kappa, \pi) + \beta N(\kappa, \pi)$$
$$= \mathfrak{r}\mathcal{X}(\kappa, \pi) < \mathcal{X}(\kappa, \pi).$$

This is a contradiction, so that $\mathcal{X}(\kappa, \pi) = 0$ then χ has a unique fixed point. $\square$

Example 2. Let $(\mathcal{W}, \perp, \mathcal{X})$ be an orthogonal **CbMS**, where $\mathcal{W} = [0, \infty)$ and the mapping $\mathcal{X} : \mathcal{W} \times \mathcal{W} \to [0, \infty)$ is defined as $\mathcal{X}(\varrho, \iota) = (\varrho - \iota)^2$, for every $\varrho, \iota \in \mathcal{W}$. Consider the binary relation $\perp$ on $\mathcal{W}$ by $\varrho \perp \iota$ if $\varrho\iota \leq (\varrho \vee \iota)$ where $\varrho \vee \iota = \varrho$ or $\varrho \vee \iota = \iota$.

Let $\chi : \mathcal{W} \to \mathcal{W}$ be an orthogonal continuous map, defined by

$$\chi\varrho = \begin{cases} -\dfrac{\varrho}{2}, & \text{if } \varrho \in [-1, 0) \\ 2\varrho, & \text{if } \varrho \geq 0. \end{cases}$$

Then,

$$\chi^2\varrho = \begin{cases} -\varrho, & \text{if } \varrho \in [-1, 0) \\ 4\varrho, & \text{if } \varrho \geq 0. \end{cases}$$

In addition, let the map $\alpha : \mathcal{W} \times \mathcal{W} \to [0, \infty)$,

$$\alpha(\varrho, \iota) = \begin{cases} 1, & \text{if } \varrho, \iota \in [-1, 0) \\ 0, & \text{otherwise.} \end{cases}$$

Of course, χ is orthogonal $\alpha - OA$ and $\alpha(0, \chi 0) = \alpha(\chi 0, 0) = \alpha(0, 0) = 1$. If $\varrho, \iota \in [-1, 0]$, then we obtain $\mathcal{X}(\chi^2\varrho, \chi^2\iota) = (\varrho - \iota)^2$ and

$$\mathbf{D}^*(\varrho, \iota) = \mathcal{X}(\varrho, \iota) + |\mathcal{X}(\varrho, \chi\varrho) - \mathcal{X}(\chi\iota, \chi^2\iota)| + |\mathcal{X}(\iota, \chi\iota - \mathcal{X}(\chi\varrho, \chi^2\varrho))|$$

$$= (\varrho - \iota)^2 + |(\varrho + \dfrac{\varrho}{2})^2 - (\iota - \dfrac{\iota}{2})^2| + |(\iota + \dfrac{\iota}{2})^2 - (\varrho - \dfrac{\varrho}{2})^2|$$

$$= (\varrho - \iota)^2 + |(\dfrac{3\varrho}{2})^2 - (\dfrac{\iota}{2})^2| + |(\dfrac{3\iota}{2})^2 - (\dfrac{\varrho}{2})^2|$$

$$= (\varrho - \iota)^2 + \left|\dfrac{9\varrho^2 - \iota^2}{4}\right| + \left|\dfrac{9\iota^2 - \varrho^2}{4}\right|.$$

Thus, we can find $\mathfrak{r} \in [0, 1)$ s.t

$$\alpha(\varrho, \iota)\mathcal{X}(\chi^2\varrho, \chi^2\iota) = (\varrho - \iota)^2$$

$$\leq \mathfrak{r}\left((\varrho - \iota)^2 + \left|\dfrac{9\varrho^2 - \iota^2}{4}\right| + \left|\dfrac{9\iota^2 - \varrho^2}{4}\right|\right)$$

$$= \mathfrak{r}\mathbf{D}^*(\varrho, \iota).$$

Otherwise, we obtain $\alpha(\varrho, \iota) = 0$.

Clearly, χ is orthogonal continuous. Consequently, from Theorem 2, the map χ has a fixed point.

4. Applications

4.1. Fractional Differential Equations

For a function $\mathfrak{s} \in \mathcal{C}[0, 1]$, the Riemann–Liouville fractional derivative of order $\delta > 0, \jmath - 1 \leq \delta \leq \jmath \in \mathbb{N}$ is given by

$$\dfrac{1}{\Gamma(\jmath - \delta)} \dfrac{d^\jmath}{d\xi^\jmath} \int_0^\xi \dfrac{\mathfrak{s}(\pi)d\pi}{(\xi - \pi)^{\delta - \jmath + 1}} = \mathcal{D}^\delta \mathfrak{s}(\xi),$$

Γ is the Euler gamma function, given that the right-hand side is defined point-wise on $[0,1]$, where $[\delta]$ is the integer component of δ, Γ. Consider the fractional differential equation as follows:

$$\begin{aligned} {}^\pi\mathcal{D}^\sigma \mathfrak{s}(\xi) + \mathcal{X}(\xi, \mathfrak{s}(\xi)) &= 0, \quad 0 \leq \xi \leq 1, \quad 0 \leq \sigma \leq 1; \\ \mathfrak{s}(0) = \mathfrak{s}(1) &= 0, \end{aligned} \quad (20)$$

where $\mathcal{X}: [0,1] \times \mathbb{R} \to \mathbb{R}$ is a continuous function and ${}^\pi\mathcal{D}^\sigma$ represents the Caputo fractional derivative of order σ and is defined by

$$ {}^\pi\mathcal{D}^\sigma = \frac{1}{\Gamma(\jmath - \sigma)} \int_0^\xi \frac{\mathfrak{s}^\jmath(\pi) d\pi}{(\xi - \pi)^{\sigma - \jmath + 1}}, $$

where $\jmath - 1 \leq \sigma \leq \jmath \in \mathbb{N}, \sigma \in \mathbb{R}$. Let $\mathcal{P}, \mathcal{S} = (\mathcal{C}[0,1], [0,\infty))$ be the set of all the continuous functions defined on $[0,1]$ with $[0,\infty)$. Consider $\varphi : \mathcal{P} \times \mathcal{S} \to \mathbb{R}^+$ to be defined by

$$ \varphi(\mathfrak{s}, \mathfrak{s}') = \sup_{\xi \in [0,1]} |\mathfrak{s}(\xi) - \mathfrak{s}'(\xi)|^2 $$

and $\Omega(\mathfrak{s}, \mathfrak{s}') = 3$ for all $(\mathfrak{s}, \mathfrak{s}') \in \mathcal{P} \times \mathcal{S}$. Then, $(\mathcal{P}, \mathcal{S}, \varphi)$ is a complete bipolar controlled metric space.

Theorem 3. *Assume the nonlinear fractional differential equation (20). Suppose that the following conditions are satisfied:*

1. $\exists \xi \in [0,1], \chi \in (0,1)$ and $(\mathfrak{s}, \mathfrak{s}') \in \mathcal{P} \times \mathcal{S}$ s.t

$$ |\mathcal{X}(\xi, \mathfrak{s}) - \mathcal{X}(\xi, \mathfrak{s}')| \leq \sqrt{\chi} |\mathfrak{s}(\xi) - \mathfrak{s}'(\xi)|; $$

2.
$$ \sup_{\xi \in [0,1]} \int_0^1 |\mathcal{G}(\xi, \pi)|^2 d\pi \leq 1. $$

Then, the Equation (20) has a unique solution in $\mathcal{P} \cup \mathcal{S}$.

Proof. The given fractional differential equation (20) is equivalent to the succeeding integral equation with the orthogonal set $(\mathcal{W}, \perp)$,

$$ \mathfrak{s}(\xi) = \int_0^1 \mathcal{G}(\xi, \pi) \mathcal{X}(\mathfrak{q}, \mathfrak{s}(\pi)) d\pi, \ \forall\, \xi, \pi \in \mathcal{W}. $$

Take the orthogonal function $\mathcal{G}(\xi, \pi)$ with $\xi \perp \pi$,

$$ \mathcal{G}(\xi, \pi) = \begin{cases} \frac{[\xi(1-\pi)]^{\sigma-1} - (\xi - \pi)^{\sigma-1}}{\Gamma(\sigma)}, & 0 \leq \pi \leq \xi \leq 1, \\ \frac{[\xi(1-\pi)]^{\sigma-1}}{\Gamma(\sigma)}, & 0 \leq \xi \leq \pi \leq 1. \end{cases} $$

Define the covariant mapping $\mathcal{T}: \mathcal{P} \cup \mathcal{S} \to \mathcal{P} \cup \mathcal{S}$ and $\mathcal{T}$ is orthogonal preserving. For each $\xi, \pi \in \mathcal{W}$ with $\xi \perp \pi$ as defined by

$$ \mathcal{T}\mathfrak{s}(\xi) = \int_0^1 \mathcal{G}(\xi, \pi) \mathcal{X}(\mathfrak{q}, \mathfrak{s}(\pi)) d\pi. $$

It is easy to note that if $\mathfrak{s}^* \in \mathcal{T}$ is a fixed point then $\mathfrak{s}^*$ is a solution of the problem (20). Let $\mathfrak{s}, \mathfrak{s}\prime \in \mathcal{P} \times \mathcal{S}$ with $\mathfrak{s} \perp \mathfrak{s}'$. Now,

$$|\mathcal{T}\mathfrak{s}(\xi) - \mathcal{T}\mathfrak{s}'(\xi)|^2 = \left| \int_0^1 \mathcal{G}(\xi, \pi) \mathcal{X}(\mathfrak{q}, \mathfrak{s}(\pi)) d\pi - \int_0^1 \mathcal{G}(\xi, \pi) \mathcal{X}(\mathfrak{q}, \mathfrak{s}'(\pi)) d\pi \right|^2$$

$$\leq \int_0^1 |\mathcal{G}(\xi, \pi)|^2 d\pi \cdot \int_0^1 \left| \mathcal{X}(\mathfrak{q}, \mathfrak{s}(\pi)) - \mathcal{X}(\mathfrak{q}, \mathfrak{s}'(\pi)) \right|^2 d\pi$$

$$\leq \chi |\mathfrak{s}(\xi) - \mathfrak{s}'(\xi)|^2.$$

Taking the supremum on both sides, we obtain

$$\varphi(\mathcal{T}\mathfrak{s}, \mathcal{T}\mathfrak{s}') \leq \chi \varphi(\mathfrak{s}, \mathfrak{s}').$$

Hence, all the hypotheses of Theorem 1 are verified, and consequently, the fractional differential Equation (20) has a unique solution. □

Example 3. *The linear fractional differential equation is as follows:*

$$^\pi \mathcal{D}^\sigma \mathfrak{s}(\xi) + \mathfrak{s}(\xi) = \frac{2}{\Gamma(3-\sigma)} \xi^{2-\sigma} + \xi^3, \tag{21}$$

where $^\pi \mathcal{D}^\sigma$ represents the Caputo fractional derivative of order σ with the initial condition: $\mathfrak{s}(0) = 0$, $\mathfrak{s}'(\mathfrak{o}) = 0$.

The exact solution of Equation (21) with $\sigma = 1.9$:

$$\mathfrak{s}(\xi) = \xi^2.$$

Clearly, $\mathfrak{s}(\xi)$ is an orthogonal continuous function on $[0, 1]$. In virtue of Equation (20), we can write Equation (21) in the homotopy form;

$$\mathcal{D}^\sigma \mathfrak{s}(\xi) + \mathfrak{ps}(\xi) - \frac{2}{\Gamma(3-\sigma)} \xi^{2-\sigma} - \xi^3 = 0, \tag{22}$$

the solution of Equation (21) is:

$$\mathfrak{s}(\xi) = \mathfrak{s}_0(\xi) + \mathfrak{ps}_1(\xi) + \mathfrak{p}^2 \mathfrak{s}_2(\xi) + \cdots. \tag{23}$$

Substituting Equation (23) into (22) and collecting terms with the power of $\mathfrak{p}$, we obtain

$$\begin{cases} \mathfrak{p}^0 : & \mathcal{D}^\sigma \mathfrak{s}_0(\xi) = 0 \\ \mathfrak{p}^1 : & \mathcal{D}^\sigma \mathfrak{s}_1(\xi) = -\mathfrak{s}_0(\xi) + \mathfrak{X}(\xi) \\ \mathfrak{p}^2 : & \mathcal{D}^\sigma \mathfrak{s}_2(\xi) = -\mathfrak{s}_1(\xi) \\ \mathfrak{p}^3 : & \mathcal{D}^\sigma \mathfrak{s}_3(\xi) = -\mathfrak{s}_2(\xi) \\ & \vdots \end{cases} \tag{24}$$

Applying Ω^σ and the inverse operation of $\mathcal{D}^\sigma$, on both sides of Equation (24) and fractional integral operation (Ω^σ) of order $\sigma > 0$, we have

$$\mathfrak{s}_0(\zeta) = \sum_{i=0}^{1} \mathfrak{s}^i(0) \frac{\zeta^i}{i!}$$

$$= \mathfrak{s}(0) \frac{\zeta^0}{0!} + \mathfrak{s}'(0) \frac{\zeta^1}{1!}$$

$$\mathfrak{s}_1(\zeta) = -\Omega^\sigma \left[\mathfrak{s}_0(\zeta) + \Omega^\sigma [\mathfrak{X}(\zeta)] \right]$$

$$= \zeta^2 + \frac{\Gamma(4)}{\Gamma(4+\sigma)} \zeta^{3+\sigma},$$

$$\mathfrak{s}_2(\zeta) = -\Omega^\sigma \left[\mathfrak{s}_1(\zeta) \right]$$

$$= \frac{2}{\Gamma(3+\sigma)} \zeta^{2+\sigma} - \frac{6}{\Gamma(3+2\sigma)} \zeta^{3+2\sigma},$$

$$\mathfrak{s}_3(\zeta) = -\Omega^\sigma \left[\mathfrak{s}_2(\zeta) \right]$$

$$= \frac{2}{\Gamma(3+2\sigma)} \zeta^{2+2\sigma} - \frac{6}{\Gamma(3+3\sigma)} \zeta^{3+3\sigma}.$$

Hence, the solution of Equation (21) is

$$\mathfrak{s}(\zeta) = \mathfrak{s}_0(\zeta) + \mathfrak{s}_1(\zeta) + \mathfrak{s}_2(\zeta) + \cdots \tag{25}$$

$$\mathfrak{s}(\zeta) = \zeta^2 + \frac{\Gamma(4)}{\Gamma(4+\sigma)} \zeta^{(3+\sigma)} - \frac{2}{\Gamma(3+\sigma)} \zeta^{(2+\sigma)} - \frac{6}{\Gamma(4+2\sigma)} \zeta^{(3+2\sigma)} + \cdots, \tag{26}$$

when $\sigma = 1.9$

$$\mathfrak{s}(\zeta) = \zeta^2 + \frac{6}{\Gamma(5.9)} \zeta^{(4.9)} - \frac{2}{\Gamma(4.9)} \zeta^{(3.9)} - \frac{6}{\Gamma(7.8)} \zeta^{(6.8)} + \cdots$$

$$= \zeta^2 - \text{small terms}$$

$$\approx \zeta^2.$$

Table 1 displays the numerical and exact results using the matrix approach method with $\sigma = 1.9$ and $\mathcal{N} = 51$.

Table 1. The numerical and exact solution using the matrix approach method.

ζ	$\mathfrak{s}(\zeta)$	$\mathfrak{s}_j(\zeta)$	$|\mathfrak{s}(\zeta) - \mathfrak{s}_j(\zeta)|$
0.00000	0.00000	0.00000	0.00000
0.10000	0.01000	0.00862	0.00138
0.20000	0.04000	0.03769	0.00231
0.30000	0.09000	0.08654	0.00346
0.40000	0.16000	0.15474	0.00526
0.50000	0.25000	0.24193	0.00807
0.60000	0.36000	0.34786	0.01214
0.70000	0.49000	0.47244	0.01756
0.80000	0.64000	0.61581	0.02419
0.90000	0.81000	0.77841	0.03159
1.00000	1.00000	0.96098	0.03902

Figure 1 compares both the numerical and exact solutions for the fractional differential Equation (21). Moreover, Figure 2 shows the absolute error between the numerical and exact solutions.

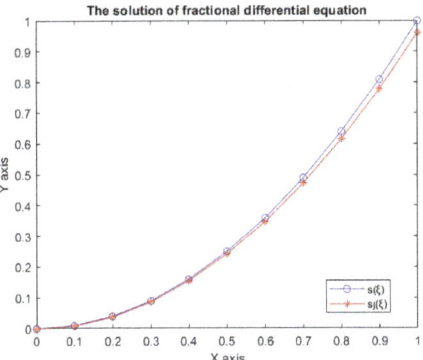

Figure 1. The convergence between an approximate and exact solution with an interval difference of 0.1 for Example 3.

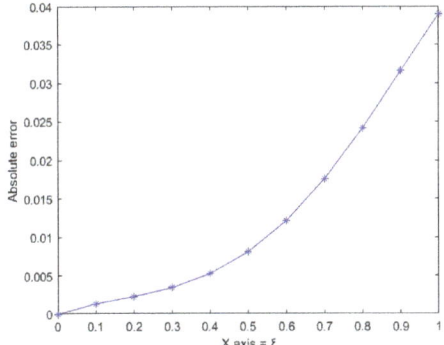

Figure 2. The absolute error with an interval difference of 0.1 for Example 3.

The exact and absolute solution is an equal value of 0 in this case. Therefore, the unique solution to this problem is 0. Hence the unique fixed point at 0.

4.2. Application of Elzaki transformation

We prove the convolution of the Elzaki transform by a different method with Elzaki.

$$E(\mathfrak{X} \star \mathfrak{g}) = \frac{1}{\mathfrak{a}} E(\mathfrak{X}) E(\mathfrak{g})$$

for $E(\mathfrak{X})$ is the Elzaki transform of $\mathfrak{X}$. In general, we can find the solution by using the Elzaki transform as follows:

Theorem 4. *Let us consider the Volterra integral equation of the second kind as follows:*

$$\iota(\ell) = \varrho(\ell) + \int_a^\ell K(\ell - t)\iota(t)dt. \qquad (27)$$

It can be expressed as

$$\iota(\ell) = E^{-1}(\mathscr{T}(\mathfrak{a})) = E^{-1}\left(\frac{\mathfrak{a}\mathcal{X}}{\mathfrak{a} - K}\right),$$

where K is the kernel and $E[\iota(\ell)] = \mathscr{T}(\mathfrak{a})$.

Proof. Let $E[\iota(\ell)] = \mathcal{T}(\mathfrak{a})$, $E(\mathfrak{r}) = \mathcal{L}$ and $E(\mathfrak{q}) = \mathcal{T}$. If $\mathfrak{X}(\iota(\ell)) = \mathfrak{r}(\ell)$ is given, define the orthogonal relation $\perp$ on $\mathcal{W}$ by

$$\mathfrak{r} \perp \mathfrak{q} \text{ or } \mathfrak{q} \perp \mathfrak{r}.$$

let us take both sides on the Elzaki transform; we have

$$\mathcal{T}(\mathfrak{a}) = \frac{1}{\mathfrak{a}} E(\mathfrak{r}) E(\mathfrak{q}) = \frac{1}{\mathfrak{a}} \mathcal{L} \mathcal{T},$$

for $\mathcal{T}$ is the transfer function. If we take the inverse Elzaki transform, we obtain

$$\iota = \mathcal{T}^{-1}(\mathfrak{a}) = \mathfrak{r} \star \mathfrak{q} = \mathcal{T}^{-1}\left(\frac{1}{\mathfrak{a}} \mathcal{L} \mathcal{T}\right), \forall \mathfrak{r} \perp \mathfrak{q},$$

for $\star$ is the standard notation of convolution.

Let us take the Elzaki transform on Equation (27). Then we obtain

$$\mathcal{T}(\mathfrak{a}) = \mathcal{X} = E(\iota \star \mathfrak{r}) = \mathcal{X} + \frac{1}{\mathfrak{a}} \mathcal{T}(\mathfrak{a}) K, \forall \iota \perp \mathfrak{r},$$

for $\mathcal{X} = E(\varrho)$ and for $K = E(\mathfrak{r})$ is orthogonal continuous. Organizing the equality, we obtain

$$\mathcal{T}(\mathfrak{a}) = \frac{\mathfrak{a} \mathcal{X}}{\mathfrak{a} - K},$$

for the kernel. Therefore, we obtain

$$\iota(\ell) = E^{-1}(\mathcal{T}(\mathfrak{a})) = E^{-1}\left(\frac{\mathfrak{a} \mathcal{X}}{\mathfrak{a} - K}\right).$$

□

Example 4. *Let us consider the Volterra integral equation*

$$\iota(\ell) - \int_0^\ell t\iota(\ell - t) dt = 1. \tag{28}$$

Solution. Writing

$$\iota - \ell \star \iota = 1,$$

for $\iota \perp \ell$, we obtain

$$\mathcal{T}(\mathfrak{a}) - \frac{1}{\mathfrak{a}} E(\ell) \mathcal{T}(\mathfrak{a}) = E(1),$$

for $E[\iota(\ell)] = \mathcal{T}(\mathfrak{a})$. From the table of the Elzaki transform Table A1 in Appendix A, we obtain

$$\mathcal{T}(\mathfrak{a}) - \frac{1}{\mathfrak{a}} \mathfrak{a}^3 \mathcal{T}(\mathfrak{a}) = \mathfrak{a}^2.$$

Arranging the inequality, we obtain

$$\mathcal{T}(\mathfrak{a}) = \frac{\mathfrak{a}^2}{1 - \mathfrak{a}^2}.$$

Taking the inverse Elzaki transform, we obtain

$$\iota(\ell) = \cos(h\ell),$$

for h is a hyperbolic function.

It is a well-known fact that the first order ODE

$$\frac{d\iota}{d\varrho} = \mathfrak{X}(\varrho, \iota), \ \forall \varrho \perp \iota,$$

with the condition $\iota(a) = \iota_0$ is rewritten to

$$\phi(\varrho) = \iota_0 + \int_a^\varrho \mathfrak{X}(\ell, \phi(\ell)) d\ell,$$

where $\mathfrak{X}$ is orthogonal continuous and contains the point (a, ι_0). Similarly, an initial value problem

$$\iota'' + A(\ell)\iota' + B(\ell)\iota = 0$$

with the condition $\iota(a) = \iota_0, \iota'(a) = \iota_1$ is rewritten to the Volterra integral equation of the second kind

$$\iota(\ell) = \mathfrak{X}(\ell) + \int_a^\ell K(\ell, t)\iota(t) dt, \qquad (29)$$

where $K(\ell, t) = -A(t) + (t - \ell)(B(t) - A'(t))$. Additionally, the above $\mathfrak{X}(\ell)$ is orthogonal continuous on $[a, b]$ and the kernel K is orthogonal continuous on the triangular region R in the ℓt-plane given by $a \leq t \leq \ell, a \leq \ell \leq b$. Then we know that (29) has a unique solution ι on $[a, b]$.

Example 5. *Solve the Volterra integral equation*

$$\iota(\ell) = \int_0^\ell \iota(t) \sin(\ell - t) dt = \ell.$$

Solution. *The given equation can be written by*

$$\iota - \iota \star \sin \ell = \ell,$$

for $\ell \perp t$, $\ell \in [0, 1]$. Let us write $E[\iota(\ell)] = \mathcal{T}(\mathfrak{a})$ and apply the convolution theorem. Then, we obtain

$$\mathcal{T}(\mathfrak{a}) - \frac{1}{\mathfrak{a}}\mathcal{T}(\mathfrak{a})\frac{\mathfrak{a}^3}{1 + \mathfrak{a}^2} = \mathfrak{a}^3.$$

We obtain

$$\mathcal{T}(\mathfrak{a}) = \mathfrak{a}^3(1 + \mathfrak{a}^2)$$
$$= \mathfrak{a}^3 + \mathfrak{a}^5$$

As we scan a table of Elzaki transformations Table A1, we obtain

$$\iota(\ell) = \ell + \frac{\ell^3}{6}.$$

It is clear that $\iota(\ell)$ is orthogonal continuous on $[0, 1]$. Its shown in Figure 3 as follow:

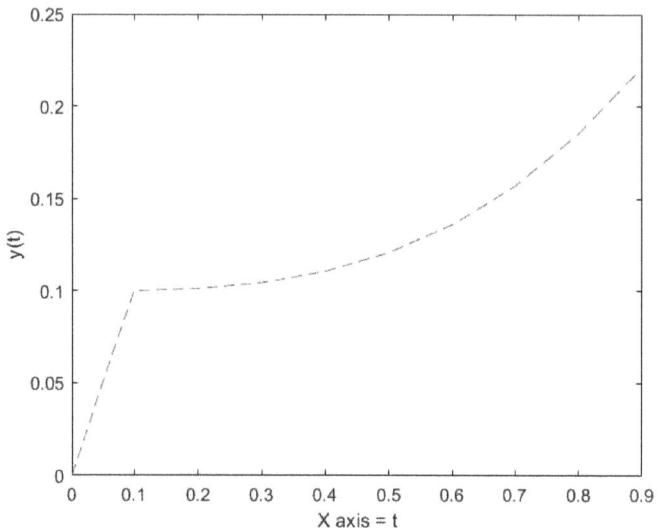

Figure 3. Graph of $\iota(\ell)$ with an interval difference of 0.1 for Example 5.

5. Conclusions

In this paper, we proved some fixed point theorems for an orthogonal Istrăţescu type contraction of maps in an orthogonal **CbMS**. Furthermore, we presented examples that elaborated on the usability of our results. Meanwhile, we provided applications to the existence of a solution for a fractional differential equation and second kind Volterra integral equation through an Elzaki transform by using our main results.

Author Contributions: Writing—original draft, A.J.G., G.M., O.E., A.A. and N.M. All authors have read and agreed to the published version of the manuscript.

Funding: This research received no external funding.

Data Availability Statement: Not applicable.

Acknowledgments: The authors A. ALoqaily and N. Mlaiki would like to thank Prince Sultan University for paying the publication fees for this work through TAS LAB.

Conflicts of Interest: The authors declare no conflict of interest.

Appendix A

Table A1. Elzaki transform of some functions.

t	$\chi(\mathfrak{a})$
1	$\mathfrak{a}^2$
t	$\mathfrak{a}^3$
$\dfrac{t^3}{6}$	$\mathfrak{a}^5$
t^j	$j!\mathfrak{a}^{j+2}$
e^{bt}	$\dfrac{\mathfrak{a}^2}{1-b\mathfrak{a}}$
$\sin(bt)$	$\dfrac{b\mathfrak{a}^3}{1+b^2\mathfrak{a}^2}$

References

1. Banach, S. Sur les operations dans les ensembles abstraits et leurs applications aux equations integrales. *Fundam. Math.* **1992**, *3*, 133–181. [CrossRef]
2. Shatanawi, W. On w-compatible mappings and common coupled coincidence point in cone metric spaces. *Appl. Math. Lett.* **2012**, *25*, 925–931. [CrossRef]
3. Shatanawi, W.; Rajic, R.V.; Radenovic, S.; Al-Rawashhdeh, A. Mizoguchi-Takahashi-type theorems in tvs-cone metric spaces. *Fixed Point Theory Appl.* **2012**, *11*, 106. [CrossRef]
4. Al-Rawashdeh, A.; Hassen, A.; Abdelbasset, F.; Sehmim, S.; Shatanawi, W. On common fixed points for $\alpha - F$-contractions and applications. *J. Nonlinear Sci. Appl.* **2016**, *9*, 3445–3458. [CrossRef]
5. Shatanawi, W.; Mustafa, Z.; Tahat, N. Some coincidence point theorems for nonlinear contraction in ordered metric spaces. *Fixed Point Theory Appl.* **2011**, *2011*, 68. [CrossRef]
6. Shatanawi, W. Some fixed point results for a generalized Ψ-weak contraction mappings in orbitally metric spaces. *Chaos Solitons Fractals* **2012**, *45*, 520–526. [CrossRef]
7. Istrătescu, V. Some fixed point theorems for convex contraction mappings and mappings with convex diminishing diameters (I). *Ann. Mat. Pura Appl.* **1982**, *130*, 89–104.
8. Istrătescu, V. Some fixed point theorems for convex contraction mappings and mappings with convex diminishing diameters (II). *Ann. Mat. Pura Appl.* **1983**, *134*, 327–362.
9. Berinde, V. Approximating fixed points of weak contractions using the Picard iteration. *Nonlinear Anal. Forum* **2004**, *9*, 43–53.
10. Bakhtin, I.A. The contraction mapping principle in quasimetric spaces. *J. Funct. Anal.* **1989**, *30*, 26–37.
11. Czerwik, S. Nonlinear set-valued contraction mappings in b-metric spaces. *Atti Del Semin. Mat. Fis. Dell'Universita Modena* **1998**, *46*, 263–276.
12. Hussain, N.; Doric, D.; Kadelburg, Z.; Radenovi´c, S. Suzuki-type fixed point results in metric type spaces. *J. Inequalities Appl.* **2014**, *2014*, 229. [CrossRef]
13. Latif, A.; Al Subaie, R.F.; Alansari, M.O. Fixed points of generalized multi-valued contractive mappings in metric type spaces. *J. Nonlinear Var. Anal.* **2022**, *6*, 123–138.
14. Haghi, R.H.; Bakhshi, N. Some coupled fixed point results without mixed monotone property. *J. Adv. Math. Stud.* **2022**, *15*, 456–463.
15. Yao, Y.; Shahzad, N.; Yao, J.C. Convergence of Tseng-type self-adaptive al-gorithms for variational inequalities and fixed point problems. *Carpathian J. Math.* **2021**, *37*, 541–550. [CrossRef]
16. Gordji, M.E.; Habibi, H. Fixed point theory in generalized orthogonal metric space. *J. Linear Topol. Algebra* **2017**, *6*, 251–260.
17. Aiman, M.; Arul Joseph, G.; Absar, U.H.; Senthil Kumar, P.; Gunaseelan, M.; Imran, A.B. Solving an Integral Equation via Orthogonal Brianciari Metric Spaces. *J. Funct. Spaces* **2022**, *2022*, 7251823.
18. Gnanaprakasam, A.J.; Mani, G.; Lee, J.R.; Park, C. Solving a nonlinear integral equation via orthogonal metric space. *AIMS Math.* **2022**, *7*, 1198–1210. [CrossRef]
19. Mani, G.; Gnanaprakasam, A.J.; Kausar, N.; Munir, M. Orthogonal F-Contraction mapping on O-Complete Metric Space with Applications. *Int. J. Fuzzy Log. Intell. Syst.* **2021**, *21*, 243–250. [CrossRef]
20. Arul Joseph, G.; Gunaseelan, M.; Vahid, P.; Hassen, A. Solving a Nonlinear Fredholm Integral Equation via an Orthogonal Metric. *Adv. Math. Phys.* **2021**, *2021*, 8.
21. Prakasam, S.K.; Gnanaprakasam, A.J.; Kausar, N.; Mani, G.; Munir, M. Solution of Integral Equation via Orthogonally Modified F-Contraction Mappings on O-Complete Metric-Like Space. *Int. J. Fuzzy Log. Intell. Syst.* **2022**, *22*, 287–295. [CrossRef]
22. Senthil Kumar, P.; Arul Joseph, G.; Ege, O.; Gunaseelan, M.; Haque, S.; Mlaiki, N. Fixed point for an $\mathbb{O}g\mathfrak{F}$-c in $\mathbb{O}$-complete b-metric-like spaces. *AIMS Math.* **2022**, *8*, 1022–1039.
23. Gnanaprakasam, A.J.; Nallaselli, G.; Haq, A.U.; Mani, G.; Baloch, I.A.; Nonlaopon, K. Common Fixed-Points Technique for the Existence of a Solution to Fractional Integro-Differential Equations via Orthogonal Brianciari Metric Spaces. *Symmetry* **2022**, *14*, 1859. [CrossRef]
24. Mani, G.; Prakasam, S.K.; Gnanaprakasam, A.J.; Ramaswamy, R.; Abdelnaby, O.A.A.; Khan, K.H.; Radenović, S. Common Fixed Point Theorems on Orthogonal Branciari Metric Spaces with an Application. *Symmetry* **2022**, *14*, 2420. [CrossRef]
25. Miculescu, R.; Mihail, A. New fixed point theorems for set-valued contractions in b-metric spaces. *J. Fixed Point Theory Appl.* **2017**, *19*, 2153–2163. [CrossRef]
26. Popescu, O. Some new fixed point theorems for a α Geraghty-contraction type maps in metric spaces. *Fixed Point Theory Appl.* **2014**, *2014*, 190. [CrossRef]
27. Gordji, M.E.; Ramezani, M.; De La Sen, M.; Cho, Y.J. On orthogonal sets and Banach fixed point theorem. *Fixed Point Theory* **2017**, *18*, 569–578. [CrossRef]
28. Ramezani, M. Orthogonal metric space and convex contractions. *Int. J. Nonlinear Anal. Appl.* **2015**, *6*, 127–132.
29. Karapinar, E.; Fulga, A.; Petrusel, A. On Istrătescu Type contraction in b-Metric Space. *Mathematics* **2020**, *8*, 388. [CrossRef]

Disclaimer/Publisher's Note: The statements, opinions and data contained in all publications are solely those of the individual author(s) and contributor(s) and not of MDPI and/or the editor(s). MDPI and/or the editor(s) disclaim responsibility for any injury to people or property resulting from any ideas, methods, instructions or products referred to in the content.

Article

On Cyclic Contractive Mappings of Kannan and Chatterjea Type in Generalized Metric Spaces

Mohammad Al-Khaleel [1,2,*], Sharifa Al-Sharif [2] and Rami AlAhmad [2,3]

1. Department of Mathematics, Khalifa University, Abu Dhabi 127788, United Arab Emirates
2. Department of Mathematics, Yarmouk University, Irbid 21163, Jordan
3. Department of Mathematics and Natural Sciences, Higher Colleges of Technology, Ras AlKhaimah 4793, United Arab Emirates
* Correspondence: mohammad.alkhaleel@ku.ac.ae

Abstract: Novel cyclic contractions of the Kannan and Chatterjea type are presented in this study. With the aid of these brand-new contractions, new results for the existence and uniqueness of fixed points in the setting of complete generalized metric space have been established. Importantly, the results are generalizations and extensions of fixed point theorems by Chatterjea and Kannan and their cyclical expansions that are found in the literature. Additionally, several of the existing results on fixed points in generalized metric space will be generalized by the results presented in this work. Interestingly, the findings have a variety of applications in engineering and sciences. Examples have been given at the end to show the reliability of the demonstrated results.

Keywords: fixed point; Kannan contraction; Chatterjea contraction; $\mathcal{G}$-metric; nonlinear cyclic mapping

MSC: 54H25; 46T99; 47H10

1. Introduction

Over the years, a large number of researchers have attempted to generalize the usual metric space concept, e.g., the studies in [1–3]. However, many of these generalizations were refuted by other studies, e.g., [4–7], due to the fundamental flaws they contained. A solid generalization known as $\mathcal{G}$-metric space was introduced in 2006 [8], in an appropriate structure, which corrected all of the shortcomings of earlier generalizations. The so-called $\mathcal{G}$-metric space, as introduced in [8], is given below.

Definition 1 ([8]). *Let $\mathcal{A}$ be a nonempty set and let the mapping $\mathcal{G} : \mathcal{A} \times \mathcal{A} \times \mathcal{A} \to \mathbb{R}^+$ satisfy*

- $\mathcal{G}(\zeta_1, \zeta_2, \zeta_3) = 0$ if $\zeta_1 = \zeta_2 = \zeta_3$,
- $0 < \mathcal{G}(\zeta_1, \zeta_1, \zeta_2)$ whenever $\zeta_1 \neq \zeta_2$, for all $\zeta_1, \zeta_2 \in \mathcal{A}$,
- $\mathcal{G}(\zeta_1, \zeta_1, \zeta_2) \leq \mathcal{G}(\zeta_1, \zeta_2, \zeta_3)$ whenever $\zeta_2 \neq \zeta_3$, for all $\zeta_1, \zeta_2, \zeta_3 \in \mathcal{A}$,
- $\mathcal{G}(\zeta_1, \zeta_2, \zeta_3) = \mathcal{G}(\zeta_1, \zeta_3, \zeta_2) = \mathcal{G}(\zeta_2, \zeta_1, \zeta_3) = \ldots$,
- $\mathcal{G}(\zeta_1, \zeta_2, \zeta_3) \leq \mathcal{G}(\zeta_1, \zeta, \zeta) + \mathcal{G}(\zeta, \zeta_2, \zeta_3)$, for all $\zeta_1, \zeta_2, \zeta_3, \zeta \in \mathcal{A}$.

Then, the mapping $\mathcal{G}$ is called a generalized metric and is denoted by the $\mathcal{G}$-metric on $\mathcal{A}$. In addition, $(\mathcal{A}, \mathcal{G})$ is called a generalized metric space and is denoted by $\mathcal{G}$-metric space.

In what follows, examples of the presented $\mathcal{G}$-metric space are given.

Example 1 ([8]). *Let $(\mathcal{A}, h)$ be any metric space and let the mappings $\mathcal{G}_r : \mathcal{A} \times \mathcal{A} \times \mathcal{A} \to \mathbb{R}^+$ and $\mathcal{G}_t : \mathcal{A} \times \mathcal{A} \times \mathcal{A} \to \mathbb{R}^+$ be defined as*

$$\mathcal{G}_r(\zeta_1, \zeta_2, \zeta_3) = h(\zeta_1, \zeta_2) + h(\zeta_2, \zeta_3) + h(\zeta_1, \zeta_3),$$
$$\mathcal{G}_t(\zeta_1, \zeta_2, \zeta_3) = \max\{h(\zeta_1, \zeta_2), h(\zeta_2, \zeta_3), h(\zeta_1, \zeta_3)\}, \forall \zeta_1, \zeta_2, \zeta_3 \in \mathcal{A}.$$

Citation: Al-Khaleel, M.; Al-Sharif, S.; AlAhmad, R. On Cyclic Contractive Mappings of Kannan and Chatterjea Type in Generalized Metric Spaces. *Mathematics* **2023**, *11*, 890. https://doi.org/10.3390/math11040890

Academic Editor: Timilehin Opeyemi Alakoya

Received: 21 December 2022
Revised: 19 January 2023
Accepted: 26 January 2023
Published: 9 February 2023

Copyright: © 2023 by the authors. Licensee MDPI, Basel, Switzerland. This article is an open access article distributed under the terms and conditions of the Creative Commons Attribution (CC BY) license (https://creativecommons.org/licenses/by/4.0/).

Then, $(\mathcal{A}, \mathcal{G}_r)$ and $(\mathcal{A}, \mathcal{G}_t)$ are generalized metric spaces.

Definition 2 ([8]). *Let $(\mathcal{A}, \mathcal{G})$ be a generalized metric space and let $\{a_n\}$ be a sequence of points in $\mathcal{A}$. Then,*

- *If $\lim_{n,m \to \infty} \mathcal{G}(a, a_n, a_m) = 0$, i.e., for any $\epsilon > 0$, $\exists$ an integer $N \in \mathbb{N}$ such that $\mathcal{G}(a, a_n, a_m) < \epsilon$, for all $n, m \geq N$, then the point $a \in \mathcal{A}$ is called the limit of the sequence $\{a_n\}$, and $\{a_n\}$ is said to be $\mathcal{G}$-convergent to a;*
- *If $\lim_{n,m,k \to \infty} \mathcal{G}(a_n, a_m, a_k) = 0$, i.e., for any given $\epsilon > 0$, $\exists$ an integer $N \in \mathbb{N}$ such that $\mathcal{G}(a_n, a_m, a_k) < \epsilon$, for all $n, m, k \geq N$, then the sequence $\{a_n\}$ is called $\mathcal{G}$-Cauchy;*
- *The space $(\mathcal{A}, \mathcal{G})$ is said to be a complete $\mathcal{G}$-metric space if every $\mathcal{G}$-Cauchy sequence $\{a_n\}$ in $\mathcal{A}$ is $\mathcal{G}$-convergent in $\mathcal{A}$.*

Proposition 1 ([8]). *Let $(\mathcal{A}, \mathcal{G})$ be a generalized metric, $\mathcal{G}$-metric, space. Then, the sequence $\{a_m\}$ is $\mathcal{G}$-convergent to a if and only if $\lim_{m \to \infty} \mathcal{G}(a_m, a_m, a) = 0$ if and only if $\lim_{m \to \infty} \mathcal{G}(a_m, a, a) = 0$ if and only if $\lim_{m,n \to \infty} \mathcal{G}(a_m, a_n, a) = 0$.*

Proposition 2 ([8]). *Let $(\mathcal{A}, \mathcal{G})$ be a generalized metric, $\mathcal{G}$-metric, space. Then, the sequence $\{a_m\}$ is $\mathcal{G}$-Cauchy in $\mathcal{A}$ if and only if $\lim_{m,n \to \infty} \mathcal{G}(a_m, a_n, a_n) = 0$.*

Recalling that a point a^* is called a fixed point for a function f whenever $f(a^*) = a^*$, impressively, several theorems on the existence and uniqueness of fixed points and other conclusions were obtained in the aforementioned generalization of the usual metric space; for instance, one can refer to the studies in [9–12] and references therein.

Interestingly, throughout the past years, there have also been various attempts to expand and generalize Banach's contraction mapping principle [13], which is a fundamental concept that is applied to many problems in science and engineering. It needs to be affirmed that one of the key findings in analysis is the fixed point theorem of Banach, which is very well-known and has been applied in numerous mathematical areas. Kannan [14] successfully extended the Banach contraction principle as described below.

Definition 3 ([14]). *A mapping $\mathcal{K} : \mathcal{A} \to \mathcal{A}$, where $(\mathcal{A}, h)$ is a usual metric space, is called Kannan contraction if $\exists v \in \left[0, \frac{1}{2}\right)$ such that $\forall \zeta_1, \zeta_2 \in \mathcal{A}$, the inequality*

$$h(\mathcal{K}\zeta_1, \mathcal{K}\zeta_2) \leq v[h(\zeta_1, \mathcal{K}\zeta_1) + h(\zeta_2, \mathcal{K}\zeta_2)],$$

holds.

Kannan was able to prove that if $\mathcal{K}$ is a Kannan contraction mapping, then it has a unique fixed point provided $\mathcal{A}$ is complete. Another extension of Banach contraction was introduced by Chatterjea [15] and is given below.

Definition 4 ([15]). *A mapping $\mathcal{K} : \mathcal{A} \to \mathcal{A}$, where $(\mathcal{A}, h)$ is a usual metric space, is called a Chatterjea contraction if $\exists v \in \left[0, \frac{1}{2}\right)$ such that $\forall \zeta_1, \zeta_2 \in \mathcal{A}$, the inequality*

$$h(\mathcal{K}\zeta_1, \mathcal{K}\zeta_2) \leq v[h(\zeta_1, \mathcal{K}\zeta_2) + h(\zeta_2, \mathcal{K}\zeta_1)],$$

holds.

Similar to Kannan, Chatterjea [15], using his new definition, managed to prove that Chatterjea contraction mapping has a unique fixed point provided $\mathcal{A}$ is complete. Interestingly, Zamfirescu [16] in 1972 presented a fixed point result that combines the contractions of Chatterjea, Kannan, and Banach, which is stated below.

Theorem 1 ([16]). *Let $(\mathcal{A}, h)$ be a complete metric space and let $\mathcal{K} : \mathcal{A} \to \mathcal{A}$ be a mapping for which $\exists$ scalars $v_1, v_2,$ and v_3 that satisfy $0 \leq v_1 < 1$, $0 \leq v_2, v_3 < \frac{1}{2}$, such that for any $\zeta_1, \zeta_2 \in \mathcal{A}$ at least one of the following is satisfied.*

- $h(\mathcal{K}\zeta_1, \mathcal{K}\zeta_2) \leq v_1 h(\zeta_1, \zeta_2)$;
- $h(\mathcal{K}\zeta_1, \mathcal{K}\zeta_2) \leq v_2[h(\zeta_1, \mathcal{K}\zeta_1) + h(\zeta_2, \mathcal{K}\zeta_2)]$;
- $h(\mathcal{K}\zeta_1, \mathcal{K}\zeta_2) \leq v_3[h(\zeta_1, \mathcal{K}\zeta_2) + h(\zeta_2, \mathcal{K}\zeta_1)]$.

Then, $\mathcal{K}$ has a unique fixed point a^*. Moreover, the Picard iteration, $\{a_n\}_{n=0}^{\infty}$, which is given by $a_{n+1} = \mathcal{K}a_n$, $n = 0, 1, 2, \ldots$ converges to a^* for any $a_0 \in \mathcal{A}$.

By taking into consideration non-empty closed subsets $\{B_j\}_{j=1}^{q}$ of a complete metric space and a cyclical operator $\mathcal{K} : \bigcup_{j=1}^{q} B_j \to \bigcup_{j=1}^{q} B_j$, i.e., satisfies $\mathcal{K}(B_j) \subseteq B_{j+1} \forall j \in \{1, 2, \ldots, q\}$, the cyclical extensions for the above fixed point results were discovered later by researchers. With the use of fixed point structure arguments, Rus gave a cyclical extension for Kannan's result in his work [17], while Petric gave cyclical extensions for Zamfirescu and Chatterjea results in [18].

Khan et al. [19] addressed the idea of a control function in light of altering distances that led to a new class of fixed point problems. Numerous publications on metric fixed point theory have employed altering distances, for instance, see [20–24] and references therein.

Here, in this work, we consider the generalization of the usual metric space that was introduced in [8] and present new extensions and generalizations of Banach, Kannan, and Chatterjea contractions and their cyclical expansions. In addition, some of the fixed point theorems that are found in the literature in the setting of $\mathcal{G}$-metric spaces are generalized here in this study. The presented results are obtained with the help of the continuous function $\Theta : [0, \infty)^3 \to [0, \infty)$ that satisfies $\Theta(\zeta_1, \zeta_2, \zeta_3) = 0$ if and only if $\zeta_1 = \zeta_2 = \zeta_3 = 0$, and the altering distance function Π that is defined in the sequel. In the end, examples have been given to show the reliability of the demonstrated results, and we conclude with a section of conclusions.

Definition 5. *Let $\Pi : [0, \infty) \to [0, \infty)$ be a function that is continuous, non-decreasing, and satisfies $\Pi(s) = 0$ if and only if $s = 0$. Then, Π shall be called an altering distance function.*

2. Main New Results in $\mathcal{G}$-Metric Spaces

We start this section by presenting what shall be called a $\mathcal{G}$-$(\Pi - \Theta)$-cyclic Kannan contraction and a $\mathcal{G}$-$(\Pi - \Theta)$-cyclic Chatterjea contraction. Then, we give our main work and results.

Definition 6. *Let $\mathcal{K} : \bigcup_{j=1}^{q} B_j \to \bigcup_{j=1}^{q} B_j$ be a cyclical operator, where $\{B_i\}_{j=1}^{q}$ are non-empty closed subsets of a $\mathcal{G}$-metric space $(\mathcal{A}, \mathcal{G})$. Then $\mathcal{K}$ is called a $\mathcal{G}$-$(\Pi - \Theta)$-cyclic Kannan contraction if $\exists$ scalars α, γ with $0 \leq \beta < 1$ and $0 < \alpha + \beta < 1$, such that for any $\zeta_1 \in B_j, \zeta_2, \zeta_3 \in B_{j+1}, j = 1, 2, \ldots, q$, we have*

$$\Pi(\mathcal{G}(\mathcal{K}\zeta_1, \mathcal{K}\zeta_2, \mathcal{K}\zeta_3)) \leq \Pi(\alpha \mathcal{G}(\zeta_1, \mathcal{K}\zeta_1, \mathcal{K}\zeta_1) + \beta(\mathcal{G}(\zeta_2, \mathcal{K}\zeta_2, \mathcal{K}\zeta_2) + \mathcal{G}(\zeta_3, \mathcal{K}\zeta_3, \mathcal{K}\zeta_3)))$$
$$- \Theta(\mathcal{G}(\zeta_1, \mathcal{K}\zeta_1, \mathcal{K}\zeta_1), \mathcal{G}(\zeta_2, \mathcal{K}\zeta_2, \mathcal{K}\zeta_2), \mathcal{G}(\zeta_3, \mathcal{K}\zeta_3, \mathcal{K}\zeta_3)),$$

where Π and Θ are the two functions given earlier.

Definition 7. *Consider the same assumptions given in Definition 6. Then, $\mathcal{K}$ is called a $\mathcal{G}$-$(\Pi - \Theta)$-cyclic Chatterjea contraction if $\exists$ scalars α, β with $0 \leq \alpha \leq \frac{1}{2}$ and $0 < \alpha + \beta < 1$, such that for any $a \in B_j, b, c \in B_{j+1}, j = 1, 2, \ldots, q$, we have*

$$\Pi(\mathcal{G}(\mathcal{K}a, \mathcal{K}b, \mathcal{K}c)) \leq \Pi(\alpha \mathcal{G}(a, \mathcal{K}b, \mathcal{K}c) + \beta \mathcal{G}(b, c, \mathcal{K}a))$$
$$- \Theta(\mathcal{G}(a, \mathcal{K}b, \mathcal{K}c), \mathcal{G}(b, c, \mathcal{K}a), \mathcal{G}(c, b, \mathcal{K}a)),$$

where again, Π and Θ are the two functions given earlier.

Theorem 2. *Let $\{B_i\}_{j=1}^q$ be non-empty closed subsets of a complete $\mathcal{G}$-metric space $(\mathcal{A}, \mathcal{G})$ and $\mathcal{K} : \bigcup_{j=1}^q B_j \to \bigcup_{j=1}^q B_j$ be a cyclical operator. Assume $\mathcal{K}$ satisfies at least one of the following statements:*

S1. *$\exists$ real numbers α, γ with $0 \leq \gamma < 1$ and $0 < \alpha + \gamma < 1$, such that for any $a \in B_j, b \in B_{j+1}, j = 1, 2, \ldots, q$, we have*

$$\Pi(\mathcal{G}(\mathcal{K}a, \mathcal{K}b, \mathcal{K}b)) \leq \Pi(\alpha \mathcal{G}(a, \mathcal{K}a, \mathcal{K}a) + \gamma \mathcal{G}(b, \mathcal{K}b, \mathcal{K}b))$$
$$- \Theta(\mathcal{G}(a, \mathcal{K}a, \mathcal{K}a), \mathcal{G}(b, \mathcal{K}b, \mathcal{K}b), \mathcal{G}(b, \mathcal{K}b, \mathcal{K}b)).$$

S2. *$\exists$ real numbers α, δ with $0 \leq \alpha \leq \frac{1}{2}$ and $0 < \alpha + \delta < 1$, such that for any $a \in B_j, b \in B_{j+1}, j = 1, 2, \ldots, q$, we have*

$$\Pi(\mathcal{G}(\mathcal{K}a, \mathcal{K}b, \mathcal{K}b)) \leq \Pi(\alpha \mathcal{G}(a, \mathcal{K}b, \mathcal{K}b) + \delta \mathcal{G}(b, b, \mathcal{K}a))$$
$$- \Theta(\mathcal{G}(a, \mathcal{K}b, \mathcal{K}b), \mathcal{G}(b, b, \mathcal{K}a), \mathcal{G}(b, b, \mathcal{K}b)).$$

Then, $\mathcal{K}$ has a unique fixed point $a^* \in \bigcap_{j=1}^q B_j$.

Proof. Consider the recursive sequence $a_{n+1} = \mathcal{K}a_n, n \geq 0$ with an arbitrary initial starting value $a_0 \in \bigcup_{j=1}^q B_j$. If $\exists$ a value $n_0 \in \mathbb{N}$ such that $a_{n_0+1} = a_{n_0}$, then the existence of the fixed point is achieved. Hence, we assume $a_{n+1} \neq a_n$, for all the values $n = 0, 1, \ldots$. Due to this assumption, one shall be sure that $\exists j_n \in \{1, \ldots, q\}$ such that $a_{n-1} \in B_{j_n}$ and $a_n \in B_{j_{n+1}}$. Now, let first $\mathcal{K}$ satisfy the first statement, i.e., S1. Then, we have

$$\begin{aligned}
\Pi(\mathcal{G}(a_n, a_{n+1}, a_{n+1})) &= \Pi(\mathcal{G}(\mathcal{K}a_{n-1}, \mathcal{K}a_n, \mathcal{K}a_n)) \\
&\leq \Pi(\alpha \mathcal{G}(a_{n-1}, \mathcal{K}a_{n-1}, \mathcal{K}a_{n-1}) + \gamma \mathcal{G}(a_n, \mathcal{K}a_n, \mathcal{K}a_n)) \\
&\quad - \Theta(\mathcal{G}(a_{n-1}, \mathcal{K}a_{n-1}, \mathcal{K}a_{n-1}), \mathcal{G}(a_n, \mathcal{K}a_n, \mathcal{K}a_n), \mathcal{G}(a_n, \mathcal{K}a_n, \mathcal{K}a_n)) \\
&= \Pi(\alpha \mathcal{G}(a_{n-1}, a_n, a_n) + \gamma \mathcal{G}(a_n, a_{n+1}, a_{n+1})) \\
&\quad - \Theta(\mathcal{G}(a_{n-1}, a_n, a_n), \mathcal{G}(a_n, a_{n+1}, a_{n+1}), \mathcal{G}(a_n, a_{n+1}, a_{n+1})) \\
&\leq \Pi(\alpha \mathcal{G}(a_{n-1}, a_n, a_n) + \gamma \mathcal{G}(a_n, a_{n+1}, a_{n+1})).
\end{aligned}$$

Due to the fact that Π is non-decreasing, one gets

$$\mathcal{G}(a_n, a_{n+1}, a_{n+1}) \leq \alpha \mathcal{G}(a_{n-1}, a_n, a_n) + \gamma \mathcal{G}(a_n, a_{n+1}, a_{n+1}),$$

which leads to

$$\mathcal{G}(a_n, a_{n+1}, a_{n+1}) \leq \frac{\alpha}{1-\gamma} \mathcal{G}(a_{n-1}, a_n, a_n), \forall n. \tag{1}$$

Since $0 < \alpha + \gamma < 1$, one gets $\mathcal{G}(a_n, a_{n+1}, a_{n+1})$ is a non-increasing sequence of non-negative real numbers. Therefore, $\exists l \geq 0$ such that

$$\lim_{n \to \infty} \mathcal{G}(a_n, a_{n+1}, a_{n+1}) = l.$$

Exploiting the continuity of the functions Π and Θ, one gets

$$\begin{aligned}\Pi(l) &\leq \Pi((\alpha+\gamma)l) - \Theta(l,l,l) \\ &\leq \Pi(r) - \Theta(l,l,l),\end{aligned}$$

which leads to $\Theta(l,l,l) = 0$, and as a result, $l = 0$.

In the same way, if $\mathcal{K}$ satisfies the second statement, i.e., S2, then we get

$$\begin{aligned}\Pi(\mathcal{G}(a_n, a_{n+1}, a_{n+1})) &= \Pi(\mathcal{G}(\mathcal{K}a_{n-1}, \mathcal{K}a_n, \mathcal{K}a_n)) \\ &\leq \Pi(\alpha \mathcal{G}(a_{n-1}, \mathcal{K}a_n, \mathcal{K}a_n) + \gamma \mathcal{G}(a_n, a_n, \mathcal{K}a_{n-1})) \\ &\quad -\Theta(\mathcal{G}(a_{n-1}, \mathcal{K}a_n, \mathcal{K}a_n), \mathcal{G}(a_n, a_n, \mathcal{K}a_{n-1}), \mathcal{G}(a_n, a_n, \mathcal{K}a_{n-1})) \\ &= \Pi(\alpha \mathcal{G}(a_{n-1}, a_{n+1}, a_{n+1}) + \gamma \mathcal{G}(a_n, a_n, a_n)) \\ &\quad -\Theta(\mathcal{G}(a_{n-1}, a_{n+1}, a_{n+1}), \mathcal{G}(a_n, a_n, a_n), \mathcal{G}(a_n, a_n, a_n)) \\ &\leq \Pi(\alpha G(a_{n-1}, a_{n+1}, a_{n+1})).\end{aligned}$$

Now, as Π is non-decreasing, one gets

$$\mathcal{G}(a_n, a_{n+1}, a_{n+1}) \leq \alpha \mathcal{G}(a_{n-1}, a_{n+1}, a_{n+1}). \tag{2}$$

Using the rectangular inequality implies

$$\begin{aligned}\mathcal{G}(a_n, a_{n+1}, a_{n+1}) &\leq \alpha \mathcal{G}(a_{n-1}, a_{n+1}, a_{n+1}) \\ &\leq \alpha[\mathcal{G}(a_{n-1}, a_n, a_n) + \mathcal{G}(a_n, a_{n+1}, a_{n+1})],\end{aligned}$$

which leads to

$$\mathcal{G}(a_n, a_{n+1}, a_{n+1}) \leq \frac{\alpha}{1-\alpha} \mathcal{G}(a_{n-1}, a_n, a_n). \tag{3}$$

Due to the fact that $0 \leq \alpha \leq \frac{1}{2}$, we have $\{\mathcal{G}(a_n, a_{n+1}, a_{n+1})\}$ is a non-increasing sequence of non-negative real numbers. Therefore, $\exists\, l \geq 0$ such that

$$\lim_{n\to\infty} \mathcal{G}(a_n, a_{n+1}, a_{n+1}) = l.$$

For the case $\alpha = 0$, one clearly gets, $l = 0$, and, for $0 < \alpha < \frac{1}{2}$, one gets $\frac{\alpha}{1-\alpha} < 1$, and hence by induction, one gets

$$\mathcal{G}(a_n, a_{n+1}, a_{n+1}) \leq \left(\frac{\alpha}{1-\alpha}\right)^n \mathcal{G}(a_0, a_1, a_1),$$

and therefore, $l = 0$.

Lastly, for $\alpha = \frac{1}{2}$, from (2), one gets

$$\mathcal{G}(a_{n-1}, a_{n+1}, a_{n+1}) \geq 2\mathcal{G}(a_n, a_{n+1}, a_{n+1}),$$

and therefore,

$$\lim_{n\to\infty} \mathcal{G}(a_{n-1}, a_{n+1}, a_{n+1}) \geq 2l;$$

however,

$$\mathcal{G}(a_{n-1}, a_{n+1}, a_{n+1}) \leq \mathcal{G}(a_{n-1}, a_n, a_n) + \mathcal{G}(a_n, a_{n+1}, a_{n+1}),$$

which leads, as $n \to \infty$, to

$$\lim_{n\to\infty} \mathcal{G}(a_{n-1}, a_{n+1}, a_{n+1}) \leq 2l.$$

Hence, $\lim\limits_{n\to\infty} \mathcal{G}(a_{n-1}, a_{n+1}, a_{n+1}) = 2l$.

Now, with the use of the continuity of the functions Π and Θ, and as $\alpha = \frac{1}{2}$, one gets

$$\begin{aligned}\Pi(l) &\leq \Pi\left(\frac{1}{2}\cdot 2l\right) - \Theta(2l, 0, 0) \\ &= \Pi(l) - \Theta(2l, 0, 0),\end{aligned}$$

which leads to $\Theta(2l, 0, 0) = 0$, and therefore, $l = 0$.

Next, we show that for every $\epsilon > 0$, $\exists\, n \in \mathbb{N}$ such that if $r, s \geq n$ with $r - s \equiv 1(m)$, then $\mathcal{G}(a_r, a_s, a_s) < \epsilon$ which is needed in order to prove that $\{a_n\}$ is indeed a $\mathcal{G}$-Cauchy sequence in $\mathcal{A}$.

We use the proof by contradiction, and hence we assume that $\exists\, \epsilon > 0$ such that for any $n \in \mathbb{N}$, we can find $r_n > s_n \geq n$ with $r_n - s_n \equiv 1(m)$ that satisfy $\mathcal{G}(a_{r_n}, a_{s_n}, a_{s_n}) \geq \epsilon$. Taking $n > 2m$, one then can choose r_n corresponding to $s_n \geq n$ in such a way that it is the smallest integer with $r_n > s_n$ satisfying $r_n - s_n \equiv 1(m)$ and $\mathcal{G}(a_{r_n}, a_{s_n}, a_{s_n}) \geq \epsilon$. Hence, $\mathcal{G}(a_{s_n}, a_{s_n}, a_{r_n - m}) < \epsilon$.

Applying the rectangular inequality, one gets

$$\begin{aligned}\epsilon \leq \mathcal{G}(a_{r_n}, a_{s_n}, a_{s_n}) &\leq \mathcal{G}(a_{r_n-1}, a_{s_n}, a_{s_n}) + \mathcal{G}(a_{r_n-1}, a_{r_n-1}, a_{r_n}) \\ &\leq \mathcal{G}(a_{r_n-2}, a_{s_n}, a_{s_n}) + \mathcal{G}(a_{r_n-2}, a_{r_n-2}, a_{r_n-1}) + \mathcal{G}(a_{r_n-1}, a_{r_n-1}, a_{r_n}) \\ &\vdots \\ &\leq \mathcal{G}(a_{s_n}, a_{s_n}, a_{r_n-m}) + \sum_{j=1}^{m} \mathcal{G}\left(a_{r_n-j}, a_{r_n-j}, a_{r_n-j+1}\right) \\ &< \epsilon + \sum_{j=1}^{m} \mathcal{G}\left(a_{r_n-j}, a_{r_n-j}, a_{r_n-j+1}\right).\end{aligned}$$

Taking the limit as n goes to infinity, and considering

$$\lim_{n\to\infty} \mathcal{G}(a_n, a_{n+1}, a_{n+1}) = 0,$$

lead to

$$\epsilon \leq \lim_{n\to\infty} \mathcal{G}(a_{r_n}, a_{s_n}, a_{s_n}) < \epsilon + 0 = \epsilon,$$

and hence, $\lim\limits_{n\to\infty} \mathcal{G}(a_{r_n}, a_{s_n}, a_{s_n}) = \epsilon$.

Using the rectangle inequality implies

$$\begin{aligned}\mathcal{G}(a_{s_n}, a_{s_n}, a_{r_n}) &\leq \mathcal{G}(a_{r_n}, a_{r_n+1}, a_{r_n+1}) + \mathcal{G}(a_{r_n+1}, a_{s_n}, a_{s_n}) \\ &\leq \mathcal{G}(a_{r_n}, a_{r_n+1}, a_{r_n+1}) + \mathcal{G}(a_{r_n+1}, a_{s_n+1}, a_{s_n+1}) + \mathcal{G}(a_{s_n+1}, a_{s_n}, a_{s_n}) \\ &\leq \mathcal{G}(a_{r_n}, a_{r_n+1}, a_{r_n+1}) + \mathcal{G}(a_{r_n+1}, a_{s_n+1}, a_{s_n+1}) + \mathcal{G}(a_{s_n}, a_{s_n+1}, a_{s_n+1}) \\ &\quad + \mathcal{G}(a_{s_n+1}, a_{s_n+1}, a_{s_n}).\end{aligned}$$

Additionally,

$$\begin{aligned}\mathcal{G}(a_{r_n+1}, a_{s_n+1}, a_{s_n+1}) &\leq \mathcal{G}(a_{r_n+1}, a_{s_n}, a_{s_n}) + \mathcal{G}(a_{s_n}, a_{s_n+1}, a_{s_n+1}) \\ &\leq \mathcal{G}(a_{r_n+1}, a_{r_n}, a_{r_n}) + \mathcal{G}(a_{r_n}, a_{s_n}, a_{r_n}) + \mathcal{G}(a_{s_n}, a_{s_n+1}, a_{s_n+1}) \\ &\leq \mathcal{G}(a_{r_n}, a_{r_n+1}, a_{r_n+1}) + \mathcal{G}(a_{r_n+1}, a_{r_n+1}, a_{r_n}) + \mathcal{G}(a_{r_n}, a_{s_n}, a_{s_n}) \\ &\quad + \mathcal{G}(a_{s_n}, a_{s_n+1}, a_{s_n+1}).\end{aligned}$$

Letting n go to infinity and considering $\lim\limits_{n\to\infty} \mathcal{G}(a_n, a_{n+1}, a_{n+1}) = 0$ implies $\epsilon \leq \lim\limits_{n\to\infty} \mathcal{G}(a_{r_n+1}, a_{s_n+1}, a_{s_n+1}) \leq \epsilon$, which leads to $\lim\limits_{n\to\infty} \mathcal{G}(a_{r_n+1}, a_{s_n+1}, a_{s_n+1}) = \epsilon$.

Now, let $\mathcal{K}$ satisfy the first statement. Then, since a_{r_n} and a_{s_n} are in distinct consecutively labeled sets B_j and B_{j+1}, for a particular $1 \leq j \leq m$, one gets

$$\begin{aligned}\Pi(\mathcal{G}(a_{s_{n+1}}, a_{s_{n+1}}, a_{r_{n+1}})) &= \Pi(\mathcal{G}(\mathcal{K}a_{s_n}, \mathcal{K}a_{s_n}, \mathcal{K}a_{r_n}))\\ &\leq \Pi(\alpha\mathcal{G}(a_{s_n}, \mathcal{K}a_{s_n}, \mathcal{K}a_{s_n}) + \gamma\mathcal{G}(a_{r_n}, \mathcal{K}a_{r_n}, \mathcal{K}a_{r_n}))\\ &- \Theta(\mathcal{G}(a_{r_n}, \mathcal{K}a_{r_n}, \mathcal{K}a_{r_n}), \mathcal{G}(a_{s_n}, \mathcal{K}a_{s_n}, \mathcal{K}a_{s_n}), \mathcal{G}(a_{s_n}, \mathcal{K}a_{s_n}, \mathcal{K}a_{s_n})).\end{aligned}$$

Taking the limit as n goes to infinity in the last inequality, one obtains

$$\Pi(\epsilon) \leq \Pi(0) - \Theta(0,0,0) = 0.$$

Hence, $\epsilon = 0$ which leads to a contradiction.

Similarly, if $\mathcal{K}$ satisfies the second statement, then one gets

$$\begin{aligned}\Pi(\mathcal{G}(a_{s_{n+1}}, a_{s_{n+1}}, a_{r_{n+1}})) &= \Pi(\mathcal{G}(\mathcal{K}a_{s_n}, \mathcal{K}a_{s_n}, \mathcal{K}a_{r_n}))\\ &\leq \Pi(\alpha\mathcal{G}(a_{r_n}, \mathcal{K}a_{s_n}, \mathcal{K}a_{s_n}) + \gamma\mathcal{G}(a_{s_n}, a_{s_n}, \mathcal{K}a_{r_n}))\\ &- \Theta(\mathcal{G}(a_{r_n}, \mathcal{K}a_{s_n}, \mathcal{K}a_{s_n}), \mathcal{G}(a_{s_n}, a_{s_n}, \mathcal{K}a_{r_n}), \mathcal{G}(a_{s_n}, a_{s_n}, \mathcal{K}a_{r_n})).\end{aligned}$$

Again, taking the limit as n goes to infinity in the last inequality, one gets

$$\Pi(\epsilon) \leq \Pi((\alpha + \gamma)\epsilon) - \Theta(\epsilon, \epsilon, \epsilon).$$

Since $0 < \alpha + \gamma < 1$, we get $\Theta(\epsilon, \epsilon, \epsilon) = 0$, and therefore, $\epsilon = 0$, which is again a contradiction.

As a consequence, one can find for $\epsilon > 0$, an integer $n_0 \in \mathbb{N}$ such that if $r, s > n_0$ with $r - s = 1(m)$, then $\mathcal{G}(a_r, a_s, a_s) < \epsilon$.

Using the fact that $\lim_{n \to \infty} \mathcal{G}(a_n, a_{n+1}, a_{n+1}) = 0$, one can find an integer $n_1 \in \mathbb{N}$ such that

$$\mathcal{G}(a_n, a_{n+1}, a_{n+1}) \leq \frac{\epsilon}{m}, \text{ for } n > n_1.$$

In addition, for some integers $p, q > \max\{n_0, n_1\}$ and $q > p$, $\exists \ell \in \{1, 2, \ldots, m\}$ such that $q - p = \ell(m)$. Hence, $q - p + i = 1(m)$ for $i = m - \ell + 1$. Therefore, one gets

$$\mathcal{G}(a_p, a_p, a_q) \leq \mathcal{G}(a_p, a_p, a_{q+i}) + \mathcal{G}(a_{q+i}, a_{q+i}, a_{q+i-1}) + \ldots + \mathcal{G}(a_{q+1}, a_{q+1}, a_q),$$

which leads to

$$\mathcal{G}(a_p, a_p, a_q) \leq \epsilon + \frac{\epsilon}{m} \sum_{i=1}^{m} 1 = 2\epsilon.$$

Hence, $\{a_n\}$ is a $\mathcal{G}$-Cauchy sequence in $\bigcup_{j=1}^{q} B_j$, and consequently converges to some $a^* \in \bigcup_{j=1}^{q} B_j$. However, in view of the cyclical condition, the sequence $\{a_n\}$ has an infinite number of terms in each B_j, for $j = 1, 2, \ldots, q$. Therefore, $a^* \in \bigcap_{j=1}^{q} B_j$.

In order to show that a^* is a fixed point of $\mathcal{K}$, we assume $a^* \in B_j$, and $\mathcal{K}a^* \in B_{j+1}$, and we consider a sub-sequence a_{n_ℓ} of $\{a_n\}$ where $a_{n_\ell} \in B_{j-1}$. Now, if $\mathcal{K}$ satisfies the first statement, then

$$\begin{aligned}\Pi(\mathcal{G}(a_{n_{\ell+1}}, \mathcal{K}a^*, \mathcal{K}a^*)) &= \Pi(\mathcal{G}(\mathcal{K}a_{n_\ell}, \mathcal{K}a^*, \mathcal{K}a^*))\\ &\leq \Pi(\alpha\mathcal{G}(a_{n_\ell}, \mathcal{K}a_{n_\ell}, \mathcal{K}a_{n_\ell}) + \gamma\mathcal{G}(a^*, \mathcal{K}a^*, \mathcal{K}a^*))\\ &- \Theta(\mathcal{G}(a_{n_\ell}, \mathcal{K}a_{n_\ell}, \mathcal{K}a_{n_\ell}), \mathcal{G}(a^*, \mathcal{K}a^*, \mathcal{K}a^*), \mathcal{G}(a^*, \mathcal{K}a^*, \mathcal{K}a^*))\\ &\leq \Pi(\alpha\mathcal{G}(a_{n_\ell}, \mathcal{K}a_{n_\ell}, \mathcal{K}a_{n_\ell}) + \gamma\mathcal{G}(a^*, \mathcal{K}a^*, \mathcal{K}a^*)).\end{aligned}$$

Taking the limit as ℓ goes to infinity, one gets

$$\Pi(\mathcal{G}(a^*, \mathcal{K}a^*, \mathcal{K}a^*)) \leq \Pi(\alpha \mathcal{G}(a^*, a^*, a^*) + \gamma \mathcal{G}(a^*, \mathcal{K}a^*, \mathcal{K}a^*)).$$

Knowing that the function Π is non-decreasing, one gets

$$\mathcal{G}(a^*, \mathcal{K}a^*, \mathcal{K}a^*) \leq \gamma \mathcal{G}(a^*, \mathcal{K}a^*, \mathcal{K}a^*).$$

Now, using $0 \leq \gamma < 1$, one gets $\mathcal{G}(a^*, \mathcal{K}a^*, \mathcal{K}a^*) = 0$, and therefore, $a^* = \mathcal{K}a^*$. In a similar way, if $\mathcal{K}$ satisfies the second statement, then

$$\begin{aligned}
\Pi(\mathcal{G}(a_{n_{\ell+1}}, \mathcal{K}a^*, \mathcal{K}a^*)) &= \Pi(\mathcal{G}(\mathcal{K}a_{n_\ell}, \mathcal{K}a^*, \mathcal{K}a^*)) \\
&\leq \Pi(\alpha \mathcal{G}(a_{n_\ell}, \mathcal{K}a^*, \mathcal{K}a^*) + \gamma \mathcal{G}(a^*, a^*, \mathcal{K}a_{n_\ell})) \\
&\quad - \Theta(\mathcal{G}(a_{n_\ell}, \mathcal{K}a^*, \mathcal{K}a^*), \mathcal{G}(a^*, a^*, \mathcal{K}a_{n_\ell}), \mathcal{G}(a^*, a^*, \mathcal{K}a_{n_\ell})) \\
&\leq \Pi(\alpha \mathcal{G}(a_{n_\ell}, \mathcal{K}a^*, \mathcal{K}a^*) + \gamma \mathcal{G}(a^*, a^*, \mathcal{K}a_{n_\ell})).
\end{aligned}$$

Taking again the limit as ℓ goes to infinity, one gets

$$\Pi(\mathcal{G}(a^*, \mathcal{K}a^*, \mathcal{K}a^*)) \leq \Pi(\alpha \mathcal{G}(a^*, \mathcal{K}a^*, \mathcal{K}a^*) + \gamma \mathcal{G}(a^*, a^*, a^*)).$$

Again, exploiting that the function Π is non-decreasing, one obtains

$$\mathcal{G}(a^*, \mathcal{K}a^*, \mathcal{K}a^*) \leq \alpha \mathcal{G}(a^*, \mathcal{K}a^*, \mathcal{K}a^*).$$

Now, since $0 \leq \alpha \leq \frac{1}{2}$, one gets $\mathcal{G}(a^*, \mathcal{K}a^*, \mathcal{K}a^*) = 0$, and therefore, $a^* = \mathcal{K}a^*$. □

Theorem 3. *Let $\{B_j\}_{j=1}^q$ be non-empty closed subsets of a complete $\mathcal{G}$-metric space $(\mathcal{A}, \mathcal{G})$ and $\mathcal{K} : \bigcup_{j=1}^q B_j \to \bigcup_{j=1}^q B_j$ be a cyclical operator. Further, assume $\mathcal{K}$ is either a $\mathcal{G}$-$(\Pi - \Theta)$-cyclic Kannan contraction, Definition 6, or a $\mathcal{G}$-$(\Pi - \Theta)$-cyclic Chatterjea contraction, Definition 7. Then, $\mathcal{K}$ has a unique fixed point $a^* \in \bigcap_{j=1}^q B_j$.*

Proof. Taking $\zeta_3 = \zeta_2$ in Definition 6 and $c = b$ in Definition 7, the proof follows directly from the proof of Theorem 2 with $\gamma = 2\beta$ for the first statement and $\delta = \beta$ for the second statement. □

3. Applications and Examples

In this section, applications of the results are given in order to show the reliability of the demonstrated results.

Example 2. *Consider the complete $\mathcal{G}$-metric space, $(\mathcal{A}, \mathcal{G})$ and the mapping $\mathcal{K} : \mathcal{A} \to \mathcal{A}$ that is a cyclical operator, where $\mathcal{A} = \bigcup_{j=1}^n B_j$ and $\{B_j\}_{j=1}^n$ are non-empty closed subsets of $(\mathcal{A}, \mathcal{G})$. If, for any $\zeta_1 \in B_j, \zeta_2 \in B_{j+1}, j = 1, 2, \ldots, n$, with $B_{n+1} = B_1$, at least one of the following holds:*

$$\int_0^{\mathcal{G}(\mathcal{K}\zeta_1, \mathcal{K}\zeta_2, \mathcal{K}\zeta_2)} \omega(u)\, du \leq \int_0^{\alpha \mathcal{G}(\zeta_1, \mathcal{K}\zeta_1, \mathcal{K}\zeta_1) + \gamma \mathcal{G}(\zeta_2, \mathcal{K}\zeta_2, \mathcal{K}\zeta_2)} \omega(u)\, du,$$

or

$$\int_0^{\mathcal{G}(\mathcal{K}\zeta_1, \mathcal{K}\zeta_2, \mathcal{K}\zeta_2)} \omega(u)\, du \leq \int_0^{\alpha \mathcal{G}(\zeta_1, \mathcal{K}\zeta_2, \mathcal{K}\zeta_2) + \gamma \mathcal{G}(\mathcal{K}\zeta_1, \zeta_2, \zeta_2)} \omega(u)\, du,$$

where $\omega : [0, \infty) \to [0, \infty)$ is a Lebesgue integrable mapping that satisfies $\int_0^u \omega(\tau)\, d\tau > 0$, for $u > 0$, then $\mathcal{K}$ has a unique fixed point $a^* \in \bigcap_{j=1}^n B_j$.

This is a straightforward conclusion that one can easily obtain. To that end, let $\Pi : [0, \infty) \to [0, \infty)$ be defined as $\Pi(u) = \int_0^u \omega(\tau) \, d\tau > 0$. Then, Π is an altering distance function, and by choosing $\Theta(\zeta_1, \zeta_2, \zeta_3) = 0$, one gets the result.

Example 3. Let $\mathcal{G}(\zeta_1, \zeta_2, \zeta_3) = |\zeta_1 - \zeta_2| + |\zeta_2 - \zeta_3| + |\zeta_1 - \zeta_3|$ and $\mathcal{A} = [-1, 1] \subseteq \mathbb{R}$. Moreover, consider the mapping $\mathcal{K} : [-1, 0] \cup [0, 1] \to [-1, 0] \cup [0, 1]$ which is defined by

$$\mathcal{K}(t) = \begin{cases} -\frac{1}{3} t e^{-\frac{1}{|t|}}, & t \in [-1, 0), \\ 0, & t = 0, \\ -\frac{1}{2} t e^{-\frac{1}{|t|}}, & t \in (0, 1]. \end{cases}$$

By taking $\Theta(s, t, u) = 0$, $\Pi(s) = s$, and $a \in [0, 1]$, $b \in [-1, 0]$, one obtains

$$\begin{aligned}
\mathcal{G}(\mathcal{K}\zeta_1, \mathcal{K}\zeta_2, \mathcal{K}\zeta_2) &= |\mathcal{K}\zeta_1 - \mathcal{K}\zeta_2| + |\mathcal{K}\zeta_1 - \mathcal{K}\zeta_2| + |\mathcal{K}\zeta_2 - \mathcal{K}\zeta_2| \\
&= |\mathcal{K}\zeta_1 - \mathcal{K}\zeta_2| + |\mathcal{K}\zeta_1 - \mathcal{K}\zeta_2| \\
&= \left| -\frac{1}{2}\zeta_1 e^{-\frac{1}{|\zeta_1|}} + \frac{1}{3}\zeta_2 e^{-\frac{1}{|\zeta_2|}} \right| + \left| -\frac{1}{2}\zeta_1 e^{-\frac{1}{|\zeta_1|}} + \frac{1}{3}\zeta_2 e^{-\frac{1}{|\zeta_2|}} \right| \\
&\leq \frac{1}{2}|\zeta_1| + \frac{1}{3}|\zeta_2| + \frac{1}{2}|\zeta_1| + \frac{1}{3}|\zeta_2| \\
&\leq \frac{1}{2}\left| \zeta_1 + \frac{1}{2}\zeta_1 e^{-\frac{1}{|\zeta_1|}} \right| + \frac{1}{3}\left| \zeta_2 + \frac{1}{3}\zeta_2 e^{-\frac{1}{|\zeta_2|}} \right| + \frac{1}{2}\left| \zeta_1 + \frac{1}{2}\zeta_1 e^{-\frac{1}{|\zeta_1|}} \right| \\
&\quad + \frac{1}{3}\left| \zeta_2 + \frac{1}{3}\zeta_2 e^{-\frac{1}{|\zeta_2|}} \right| \\
&= \frac{1}{2}|\mathcal{K}\zeta_1 - \zeta_1| + \frac{1}{3}|\mathcal{K}\zeta_2 - \zeta_2| + \frac{1}{2}|\mathcal{K}\zeta_1 - \zeta_1| + \frac{1}{3}|\mathcal{K}\zeta_2 - \zeta_2| \\
&= \frac{1}{2}(|\mathcal{K}\zeta_1 - \zeta_1| + |\mathcal{K}\zeta_1 - \zeta_1|) + \frac{1}{3}(|\mathcal{K}\zeta_2 - \zeta_2| + |\mathcal{K}\zeta_2 - \zeta_2|) \\
&= \frac{1}{2}\mathcal{G}(\zeta_1, \mathcal{K}\zeta_1, \mathcal{K}\zeta_1) + \frac{1}{3}\mathcal{G}(\zeta_2, \mathcal{K}\zeta_2, \mathcal{K}\zeta_2),
\end{aligned}$$

and hence, $\mathcal{K}$ has a unique fixed point in the intersection of $[-1, 0]$ and $[0, 1]$ which is a^* equals zero.

4. Conclusions

New results on the existence and uniqueness of fixed points in the context of complete generalized metric space have been proved using the novel cyclic contractions of Kannan and Chatterjea type that have been introduced in this study. Importantly, the findings are expansions and generalizations of existing fixed point theorems by Kannan and Chatterjea and their cyclical extensions. Moreover, the results given in this paper will also extend number of previous results on fixed points in generalized metric spaces.

Author Contributions: Conceptualization, M.A.-K. and S.A.-S.; formal analysis, M.A.-K., S.A.-S. and R.A.; writing—original draft, M.A.-K.; writing—review and editing, M.A.-K., S.A.-S. and R.A.; project administration, M.A.-K.; funding acquisition, M.A.-K. All authors have read and agreed to the published version of the manuscript.

Funding: This research received no external funding.

Data Availability Statement: Not applicable.

Acknowledgments: The authors extend their appreciation to the Mathematics Department at Khalifa University for supporting this work.

Conflicts of Interest: The authors declare no conflict of interest.

References

1. Gahler, S. 2-metrische raume and ihre topologische struktur. *Math. Nachrichten* **1963**, *26*, 115–148. [CrossRef]
2. Gahler, S. Zur geometric 2-metrische raume. *Rev. Roum. Math. Pures Appl.* **1966**, *11*, 665–667.
3. Dhage, B.C. Generalized metric space and mappings with fixed point. *Bull. Calc. Math. Soc.* **1992**, *84*, 329–336.
4. Ha, K.S.; Cho, Y.J.; White, A. Strictly convex and strictly 2-convex 2-normed spaces. *Math. Jpn.* **1988**, *33*, 375–384.
5. Mustafa, Z.; Sims, B. Some remarks concerning D-metric spaces. In Proceedings of the International Conference on Fixed Point Theory and Applications, Valencia, Spain, 13–19 July 2003; Yokohama Publishers: Silverwater, NSW, Australia, 2004; pp. 189–198.
6. Naidu, S.; Rao, K.; Rao, N.S. On the concepts of balls in a D-metric space. *Int. J. Math. Math. Sci.* **2005**, *1*, 133–141. [CrossRef]
7. Naidu, S.; Rao, K.; Rao, N.S. On convergent sequences and fixed point theorems in a D-metric space. *Int. J. Math. Math. Sci.* **2005**, *12*, 1969–1988. [CrossRef]
8. Mustafa, Z.; Sims, B. A new approach to generalized metric spaces. *J. Nonlinear Convex Anal.* **2006**, *7*, 289–297.
9. Khandaqji, M.; Al-Sharif, S.; Al-Khaleel, M. Property P and some fixed point results on (ψ, Φ)-weakly contractive G-metric spaces. *Int. Math. Math. Sci.* **2012**, *2012*, 675094. [CrossRef]
10. Asadi, M.; Karapınar, E.; Salimi, P. A new approach to G-metric and related fixed point theorems. *J. Inequalities Appl.* **2013**, *454*, 4. [CrossRef]
11. Al-Khaleel, M.; Alahmari, A.; Al-Sharif, S. Coincidence and common fixed points for a sequence of mappings in G-metric spaces. *Int. J. Math. Anal.* **2015**, *9*, 1769–1783. [CrossRef]
12. Al-Sharif, S.; Alahmari, A.; Al-Khaleel, M.; Salim, A. New results on fixed points for an infinite sequence of mappings in G-metric space. *Ital. J. Pure Appl. Math.* **2017**, *2017*, 517–540. [CrossRef]
13. Banach, S. Surles operations dans les ensembles et leur application aux equation sitegrales. *Fund. Math.* **1922**, *3*, 133–181.
14. Kannan, R. Some results on fixed points. *Bull. Calcutta Math. Soc.* **1968**, *10*, 71–76. [CrossRef]
15. Chatterjea, S. Fixed point theorems. *C. R. Acad. Bulgare Sci.* **1972**, *25*, 727–730.
16. Zamfirescu, T. Fixed point theorems in metric spaces. *Arch. Math.* **1972**, *23*, 292–298. [CrossRef]
17. Rus, I. Cyclic representations and fixed points. *Ann. Tiberiu Popoviciu Semin. Funct. Equ. Approx. Convexity* **2005**, *3*, 171–178. [CrossRef]
18. Petric, M. Some results concerning cyclical contractive mappings. *Gen. Math.* **2010**, *18*, 213–226.
19. Khan, M.; Swaleh, M.; Sessa, S. Fixed point theorem by altering distances between points. *Bull. Austral. Math. Soc.* **1984**, *30*, 1–9.
20. Sastry, K.R.; Babu, G. Some fixed point theorems by altering distances between the points. *Indian J. Pure Appl. Math.* **1999**, *30*, 641–647. [CrossRef]
21. Sastry, K.; Naidu, S.; Babu, G.R.; Naidu, G.A. Generalization of common fixed point theorems for weakly commuting map by altering distances. *Tamkang J. Math.* **2000**, *31*, 243–250.
22. Naidu, S. Some fixed point theorems in metric spaces by altering distances. *Czechoslov. Math. J.* **2003**, *53*, 205–212. [CrossRef]
23. Al-Khaleel, M.; Al-Sharif, S. On cyclic (ϕ-ψ)-Kannan and (ϕ-ψ)-Chatterjea contractions in metric spaces. *Ann. Univ. Craiova Math. Comput. Sci. Ser.* **2019**, *46*, 320–327. [CrossRef]
24. Al-Khaleel, M.; Al-Sharif, S., Cyclical Nonlinear Contractive Mappings Fixed Point Theorems with Application to Integral Equations. *TWMS J. App. Eng. Math.* **2022**, *12*, 224–234.

Disclaimer/Publisher's Note: The statements, opinions and data contained in all publications are solely those of the individual author(s) and contributor(s) and not of MDPI and/or the editor(s). MDPI and/or the editor(s) disclaim responsibility for any injury to people or property resulting from any ideas, methods, instructions or products referred to in the content.

Article

New Versions of Some Results on Fixed Points in *b*-Metric Spaces

Zoran D. Mitrović [1], Abasalt Bodaghi [2], Ahmad Aloqaily [3,4], Nabil Mlaiki [3] and Reny George [5,*]

[1] Faculty of Electrical Engineering, University of Banja Luka, Patre 5, 78000 Banja Luka, Bosnia and Herzegovina
[2] Department of Mathematics, Garmsar Branch, Islamic Azad University, Garmsar, Iran
[3] Department of Mathematics and Sciences, Prince Sultan University, Riyadh 11586, Saudi Arabia
[4] School of Computer, Data and Mathematical Sciences, Western Sydney University, Sydney 2150, Australia
[5] Department of Mathematics, College of Science and Humanities in Al-Kharj, Prince Sattam Bin Abdulaziz University, Al-Kharj 11942, Saudi Arabia
* Correspondence: r.kunnelchacko@psau.edu.sa

Abstract: The main and the most important objective of this paper is to nominate some new versions of several well-known results about fixed-point theorems such as Caristi's theorem, Pant et al.'s theorem and Karapınar et al.'s theorem in the case of *b*-metric spaces. We use a new technique provided by Miculescu and Mihail in order to prove our theorems. Some illustrative applications and examples are given to strengthen our new findings and the main results.

Keywords: iterative methods; fixed point; *b*-metric; Caristi theorem; orbitally continuous; *k*-continuous

MSC: 47H10; 54H25

Citation: Mitrović, Z.D.; Bodaghi, A.; Aloqaily, A.; Mlaiki, N.; George, R. New Versions of Some Results on Fixed Points in *b*-Metric Spaces. *Mathematics* 2023, 11, 1118. https://doi.org/10.3390/math11051118

Academic Editor: Timilehin Opeyemi Alakoya

Received: 29 January 2023
Revised: 11 February 2023
Accepted: 15 February 2023
Published: 23 February 2023

Copyright: © 2023 by the authors. Licensee MDPI, Basel, Switzerland. This article is an open access article distributed under the terms and conditions of the Creative Commons Attribution (CC BY) license (https://creativecommons.org/licenses/by/4.0/).

1. Introduction and Preliminaries

Banach's theorem for fixed point theory is known to be a very useful tool in nonlinear analysis. The Banach result has been generalized in various ways and many applications have been presented. In the past thirty years, a lot of results have been obtained on fixed points of different classes of mappings defined on generalized metric spaces, for example, see [1–27] and references therein. Note that iterative methods and contraction mapping plays a key role in metric fixed-point theory. In addition, fractals can be generated via contraction mappings (Hutchinson's iterated function system) [28]. Some of the topics include *b*-metric space and the corresponding results about fixed point. Bakhtin [3] and Czerwik [6] introduced the notion about *b*-metric space and proved the number of fixed-point theorems in both single-valued and multi-valued mappings upon *b*-metric spaces.

Throughout this manuscript, we use the terms fixed point (FP), metric space (MS), *b*-metric space (bMS), and complete *b*-metric space ($CbMS$).

First, we look back on some background definitions, notations, and results in the bMS setting.

Definition 1. *Suppose $s \geq 1$ and Y is a nonempty set. A function $\mathcal{D}: Y \times Y \longrightarrow [0, +\infty)$ denotes a b-metric if $x, \eta, z \in Y$ are valid:*

(1) $\mathcal{D}(x, \eta) = 0$ *if and only if* $x = \eta$;
(2) $\mathcal{D}(x, \eta) = \mathcal{D}(\eta, x)$;
(3) $\mathcal{D}(x, z) \leq s[\mathcal{D}(x, \eta) + \mathcal{D}(\eta, z)]$.

A triplet $(Y, \mathcal{D}, s)$ is a bMS.

For bMS, the examples are the spaces $l^p(\mathbb{R})$ and $L^p[0, 1]$, $p \in (0, 1)$.
Recall that the convergence in bMS is defined as in metric spaces as follows.

Definition 2. *Suppose $(Y, \mathcal{D}, s)$ is a bMS, $x \in Y$ and $\{x_n\}$ is a sequence in Y.*
(a) $\{x_n\}$ is convergent in $(Y, \mathcal{D}, s)$ and converges to x, if for each $\varepsilon > 0$ there exists $n_\varepsilon \in \mathbb{N}$ where $\mathcal{D}(x_n, x) < \varepsilon$ for all $n > n_\varepsilon$, we denote this as $\lim_{n \to \infty} x_n = x$ or $x_n \to x$ where $n \to \infty$.
(b) $\{x_n\}$ is the Cauchy sequence in $(Y, \mathcal{D}, s)$, if for each $\varepsilon > 0$ there exists $n_\varepsilon \in \mathbb{N}$ such that $\mathcal{D}(x_n, x_m) < \varepsilon$ for all $n, m > n_\varepsilon$.
(c) $(Y, \mathcal{D}, s)$ is a CbMS if every Cauchy sequence in Y converges to some $x \in Y$.

Next, the lemma for Miculescu and Mihail is a crucial result for achieving our aims.

Lemma 1 (([19], Lemma 2.6)). *Suppose $(Y, \mathcal{D}, s)$ is a bMS and $\{x_n\}$ is a sequence in Y. If there exists $\alpha > \log_2 s$ where the series $\sum_{n=1}^{+\infty} n^\alpha \mathcal{D}(x_n, x_{n+1})$ converges, then the sequence $\{x_n\}$ is Cauchy.*

Remark 1. *If $\alpha \geq \log_2 s$, then Lemma 1 is not valid. Let $Y = \mathbb{R}, \mathcal{D}(x, \mathfrak{y}) = (x - \mathfrak{y})^2, x_n = \sum_{k=2}^{n} \frac{1}{k \ln k}, n = 2, 3, \cdots$. Then, $s = 2$ and*

$$\sum_{n=2}^{+\infty} n \mathcal{D}(x_n, x_{n+1}) = \sum_{n=2}^{+\infty} \frac{n}{(n+1)^2 \ln^2(n+1)}$$
$$\leq \sum_{n=2}^{+\infty} \frac{1}{(n+1) \ln^2(n+1)}.$$

Therefore, $\sum_{n=2}^{+\infty} n \mathcal{D}(x_n, x_{n+1})$ converges but this sequence $\{x_n\}$ is not Cauchy (using the integral criterion for series convergence, we see that $\sum_{k=2}^{+\infty} \frac{1}{k \ln^p k}$ converges for $p > 1$ and diverges for $p \leq 1$).

The next two results are the consequences of Lemma 1.

Lemma 2 (([18], Lemma 2.2)). *Suppose $(Y, \mathcal{D}, s)$ is a bMS and $\{x_n\}$ is a sequence in Y. If there exists $k \in (0, 1)$ such that*

$$\mathcal{D}(x_{n+1}, x_{n+2}) \leq k \mathcal{D}(x_n, x_{n+1}), \tag{1}$$

for all $n \in \mathbb{N}$, this leads to the sequence $\{x_n\}$ being Cauchy.

Lemma 3 (([19], Corollary 2.8)). *Suppose $(Y, \mathcal{D}, s)$ is a bMS and $\{x_n\}$ is a sequence in Y. If there exists $h > 1$ where the series*

$$\sum_{n=1}^{+\infty} h^n \mathcal{D}(x_n, x_{n+1}) \tag{2}$$

converges, then the sequence $\{x_n\}$ is Cauchy.

Remark 2. *Note that if condition (2) is replaced by*

$$\sum_{n=1}^{+\infty} h^{(s-1)n} \mathcal{D}(x_n, x_{n+1}), \tag{3}$$

then in this case, we get the appropriate condition for MS as well.

In [4], Caristi presented the next theorem.

Theorem 1 ([4]). *Suppose* $(Y, \mathcal{D})$ *is a CMS,* $\mathcal{T} : Y \longrightarrow Y$ *is a mapping such that*

$$\mathcal{D}(x, \mathcal{T}x) \leq \varphi(x) - \varphi(\mathcal{T}x), \qquad (4)$$

for all $x \in Y$, *where* $\varphi : Y \longrightarrow [0, +\infty)$ *is a lower semicontinuous mapping. This leads to* $\mathcal{T}$ *having FP.*

Dung and Hang [8] showed that Caristi's theorem does not fully extend to bMS. It is a negative answer to the latter Kirk-Shahzad's question ([17], Remark 12.6). One year later, Miculescu and Mihail [19] obtained the version of Caristi's theorem in bMS. One of the aims of the current work is to improve the mentioned result ([19], Theorem 3.1). Khojasteh et al. [16] gave a light version of Caristi's theorem as follows.

Theorem 2. ([16], Corollary 2.1) *Let* $(Y, \mathcal{D})$ *be a CMS. Assume that* $\mathcal{T} : Y \longrightarrow Y$ *and* $\psi : Y \times Y \to [0, +\infty)$ *are mappings such that* $x \mapsto \psi(x, \eta)$ *is lower semicontinuous for each* $\eta \in Y$. *If*

$$\mathcal{D}(x, \eta) \leq \psi(x, \eta) - \psi(\mathcal{T}x, \mathcal{T}\eta), \qquad (5)$$

for all $x, \eta \in Y$, *then* $\mathcal{T}$ *has a unique FP.*

The second objective of this paper is to present an alternative of the above theorem in bMS (Theorem 5).

Remark 3. *Note that in [16], The partial answers were given by Khojasteh et al. to Reich, Mizoguchi and Takahashi's and Amini-Harandi's conjectures by using a light version of Caristi's FP theorem. In addition, they have shown that some known FP theorems can be obtained from the previously mentioned theorem.*

Definition 3. *Let* $(Y, \mathcal{D})$ *be an MS and* $\mathcal{T} : Y \longrightarrow Y$ *be a mapping.*
(i) (See [7]) *The set* $O(x, \mathcal{T}) = \{\mathcal{T}^n x : n = 0, 1, 2, \ldots\}$ *is called the orbit of* $\mathcal{T}$ *at* x. *A map* $\mathcal{T}$ *is said to be orbitally continuous if* $u \in Y$ *and such that* $u = \lim_{i \to +\infty} \mathcal{T}^{n_i} x$ *for some* $x \in Y$, *then* $\mathcal{T} u = \lim_{i \to +\infty} \mathcal{T} \mathcal{T}^{n_i} x$, *where* $\{n_i\}$ *is a subsequence of the sequence* $\{n\}$;
(ii) (See [27]) *A mapping* $\mathcal{T}$ *is called weakly orbitally continuous if the set* $\{\eta \in Y : \lim_{i \to +\infty} \mathcal{T}^{n_i} \eta = u \text{ implies } \lim_{i \to +\infty} \mathcal{T} \mathcal{T}^{n_i} \eta = \mathcal{T} u\}$ *is nonempty, whenever the set* $\{x \in Y : \lim_{i \to +\infty} \mathcal{T}^{n_i} x = u\}$ *is nonempty;*
(iii) (See [26]) *A mapping* $\mathcal{T}$ *is called k-continuous,* $k = 1, 2, 3, \ldots$ *if* $\lim_{n \to +\infty} \mathcal{T}^k x = \mathcal{T} u$ *whenever* $\{x_n\}$ *is a sequence in* Y *such that* $\lim_{n \to +\infty} \mathcal{T}^{k-1} x_n = u$.

Here, we recall the next theorem of Pant et al. [25].

Theorem 3. ([25], Theorem 2.1) *Let* $(Y, \mathcal{D})$ *be the CMS and the mappings* $\mathcal{T} : Y \longrightarrow Y$, $\varphi : Y \to [0, +\infty)$. *If*

$$\mathcal{D}(\mathcal{T}x, \mathcal{T}\eta) \leq \varphi(x) - \varphi(\mathcal{T}x) + \varphi(\eta) - \varphi(\mathcal{T}\eta). \qquad (6)$$

for all $x, \eta \in Y$, *then* $\mathcal{T}$ *has a unique fixed point, under one of the following conditions:*
(i) $\mathcal{T}$ *is weakly orbitally continuous;*
(ii) $\mathcal{T}$ *is orbitally continuous;*
(iii) $\mathcal{T}$ *is k-continuous.*

Remark 4. *Note that from condition* (6), *we obtain*

$$\varphi(\mathcal{T}x) \leq \varphi(x). \qquad (7)$$

for all $x \in Y$.

The third goal of this paper is to bring a new version of Theorem 3 in bMS.

Remark 5. Pant et al. [25] have shown that Theorem 3 contains results of Banach, Kannan, Chatterjea, Ćirić and Suzuki on fixed points as particular cases. In addition, Theorem 3 is independent of the result of Caristi on fixed point. Note that, Theorem 3 is a new solution to the Rhoades problem about discontinuity at the FP.

The main and the most important objective of this paper is to nominate some new versions of several well-known results about FP such as Caristi's theorem, Pant et al.'s theorem and Karapınar et al.'s theorem in the case of bMS. We use a new technique given by Miculescu and Mihail in [19] in order to prove our theorems. Some illustrative applications and examples are given to strengthen our new findings and the main results.

2. Main Results

In this part, we indicate the various known fixed-point theorems in b-metric space settings.

2.1. A New Version of the Theorem by Caristi

In this subsection, we afford a new version of Caristi's theorem in bMS. The terms orbit, orbitally continuous, weakly orbitally continuous and k-continuous in bMS are introduced analogously to metric space, see Definition 3.

Lemma 4. Let $(Y, \mathcal{D}, s)$ be a $bCMS$ and $\mathcal{T} : Y \longrightarrow Y$ be weakly orbitally continuous mapping. If there exist $u \in Y$ and $x_0 \in Y$ such that $u = \lim_{n \to +\infty} \mathcal{T}^n x_0$, then $u = \mathcal{T}u$.

Proof. Let $u = \lim_{n \to +\infty} \mathcal{T}^n x_0$. Then, $u = \lim_{n \to +\infty} \mathcal{T}\mathcal{T}^n x_0$. The weak orbital continuity of $\mathcal{T}$ leads to $\lim_{n \to +\infty} \mathcal{T}^n x_0 = u = \lim_{n \to +\infty} \mathcal{T}\mathcal{T}^n x_0 = \mathcal{T}u$. So, $u = \mathcal{T}u$. □

Theorem 4. Let $(Y, \mathcal{D}, s)$ be a $bCMS$ and $\mathcal{T} : Y \longrightarrow Y$ be weakly orbitally continuous mapping such that
$$\mathcal{D}(x, \mathcal{T}x) \leq \varphi(x) - h^{s-1}\varphi(\mathcal{T}^r x), \tag{8}$$
for all $x \in Y$, where $r \in \mathbb{N}$ and $h > 1$ and $\varphi : Y \to [0, +\infty)$. Then, $\mathcal{T}$ has at least an FP.

Proof. Let $x_0 \in$ and $x_n = \mathcal{T}^n x_0, n \in \mathbb{N}$. Put $\lambda = h^{\frac{s-1}{r}}$. From (8), we have
$$\begin{aligned}
\mathcal{D}(x_0, x_1) &\leq \varphi(x_0) - \lambda^r \varphi(x_r) \\
\lambda \mathcal{D}(x_1, x_2) &\leq \lambda \varphi(x_1) - \lambda^{r+1} \varphi(x_{r+1}) \\
&\vdots \\
\lambda^r \mathcal{D}(x_r, x_{r+1}) &\leq \lambda^r \varphi(x_r) - \lambda^{2r} \varphi(x_{2r}) \\
&\vdots \\
\lambda^n \mathcal{D}(x_n, x_{n+1}) &\leq \lambda^n \varphi(x_n) - \lambda^{n+r} \varphi(x_{n+r}).
\end{aligned}$$

The previous inequalities necessitate that
$$\begin{aligned}
\sum_{k=0}^{n} \lambda^k \mathcal{D}(x_k, x_{k+1}) &\leq \varphi(x_0) + \lambda \varphi(x_1) + \cdots + \lambda^{r-1} \varphi(x_{r-1}) \\
&\quad - (\lambda^{r+1} \varphi(x_{r+1}) + \lambda^{r+2} \varphi(x_{r+2}) + \cdots + \lambda^{r+n} \varphi(x_{r+n}) \\
&\leq \varphi(x_0) + \lambda \varphi(x_1) + \cdots + \lambda^{r-1} \varphi(x_{r-1}).
\end{aligned}$$

We now conclude from Lemma 3 that $\{T^n x_0\}$ is Cauchy. Since Y is complete, this means there is $u \in Y$ where $u = \lim_{n \to +\infty} T^n x_0$. Therefore, we find that u is an *FP* of the mapping T by Lemma 4. □

Remark 6. *One should remember that by putting $r = 1$ in Theorem 4, we obtain Theorem 3.1. from [19]. Moreover, by setting $r = 1$ and $s = 1$, we reach the classical Caristi theorem in MS (refer also to [27], Theorem 2.10).*

Example 1. *Let $Y = [0,1]$ and the functions $T : Y \longrightarrow Y$, $\varphi : Y \longrightarrow [0, +\infty)$ and $\mathcal{D} : Y \times Y \longrightarrow [0, +\infty)$ defined by $Tx = x^2$, $\varphi(x) = \sqrt{x}$, $\mathcal{D}(x, \mathfrak{y}) = |x - \mathfrak{y}|$. Then, $(Y, \mathcal{D})$ is a metric space and we have*

$$\mathcal{D}(x, Tx) = |x - x^2| = (\sqrt{x} - x)(\sqrt{x} + x) \geq 2x(\sqrt{x} - x) > \sqrt{x} - x = \varphi(x) - \varphi(Tx),$$

for all $x \in (\frac{1}{2}, 1]$. Therefore, condition (4) is not fulfilled and we cannot apply Theorem 1. On the other hand, by putting $r = 2, s = 1$ in Theorem 4, we arrive at

$$\varphi(x) - \varphi(T^2 x) = \sqrt{x} - x^2 \geq x - x^2 = \mathcal{D}(x, Tx).$$

2.2. *Light Version of Caristi's Theorem*

Another version from Caristi's theorem in *bMS*, namely, the *light version of Caristi's theorem*, is the goal of this subsection.

Theorem 5. *Let $(Y, \mathcal{D}, s)$ be a CbMS and $T : Y \longrightarrow Y$, $\psi : Y \times Y \to [0, +\infty)$ be mappings and T weakly orbitally continuous mapping. If*

$$\mathcal{D}(x, \mathfrak{y}) \leq \psi(x, \mathfrak{y}) - h^{s-1} \psi(T^r x, T^r \mathfrak{y}), \qquad (9)$$

for every $x, \mathfrak{y} \in Y$, where $r \in \mathbb{N}$ and $h > 1$, then T has a unique FP.

Proof. Suppose $\mathfrak{y} = Tx$ and $\varphi(x) = \psi(x, Tx)$, for all $x \in Y$. It follows from Theorem 4 that T has a *FP* $u \in Y$. If $Tv = v$ where $v \in Y$, then from (9), we attain

$$\mathcal{D}(u, v) \leq \psi(u, v) - h^{s-1} \psi(u, v) \leq 0,$$

which shows that $u = v$. □

Example 2. *Let $Y = \mathbb{R}$, $\mathcal{D} : Y \times Y \longrightarrow [0, +\infty)$ be a b-metric on Y, defined by $\mathcal{D}(x, \mathfrak{y}) = |x - \mathfrak{y}|^2$. $T : Y \longrightarrow Y$ is a weakly orbitally continuous contraction defined by $Tx = \frac{x}{2}$ and $\psi : Y \times Y \longrightarrow [0, +\infty)$ defined by $\psi(x, \mathfrak{y}) = 2|x - \mathfrak{y}|^2$. Then $(Y, \mathcal{D})$ is a CbMS when $s = 2$. Next, let us consider $h = 2$ and $r \in \mathbb{N}$. Then, we have*

$$\psi(x, \mathfrak{y}) - h^{s-1} \psi(T^r x, T^r \mathfrak{y}) = |x - \mathfrak{y}|^2 (2 - \frac{1}{2^{2(r-1)}}) \geq \mathcal{D}(x, \mathfrak{y}).$$

Therefore, the conditions of Theorem 5 are fulfilled.

Remark 7. *Note that for the case $s = 1$ and $r = 1$ from Theorem 5, we obtain the results from Khojasteh et al. [16].*

2.3. *On the Result of Pant et al. [25]*

In this part, we will introduce the next theorem, as a version of Theorem 3 from [25]. We will not state the proof because it has the same proof as Theorem 4.

Theorem 6. Let $(Y, \mathcal{D}, s)$ be a CbMS. Let $\mathcal{T}: Y \longrightarrow Y$ and $\psi: Y \times Y \longrightarrow [0, +\infty)$ be mappings. If
$$\mathcal{D}(\mathcal{T}x, \mathcal{T}\mathfrak{y}) \leq \psi(x, \mathfrak{y}) - h^{s-1}\psi(\mathcal{T}x, \mathcal{T}\mathfrak{y}). \tag{10}$$
for all $x, \mathfrak{y} \in Y$, where $h > 1$, this implies $\mathcal{T}$ has a unique FP, under one of the following conditions:
(i) $\mathcal{T}$ is weakly orbitally continuous;
(ii) $\mathcal{T}$ is orbitally continuous;
(iii) $\mathcal{T}$ is k-continuous.

Here, we present a concrete example for the above Theorem, and we show that the conditions for Theorem 6 are satisfied.

Example 3. Let $Y = [0, 1]$ and $\mathcal{D}: Y \times Y \longrightarrow [0, +\infty)$ be a b-metric on Y, defined by $\mathcal{D}(x, \mathfrak{y}) = |x - \mathfrak{y}|^2$, $\mathcal{T}: Y \longrightarrow Y$ is a contraction, defined by $\mathcal{T}x = \frac{x}{3}$, $\psi: Y \times Y \longrightarrow [0, +\infty)$ is a function defined by $\psi(x, \mathfrak{y}) = \frac{(x+\mathfrak{y})^2}{2}$. Obviously, $(\mathcal{X}, \mathcal{D}, 2)$ is a complete b-metric space. Let $h = 2$. We obtain
$$(\mathcal{T}x, \mathcal{T}\mathfrak{y}) = |\mathcal{T}x - \mathcal{T}\mathfrak{y}|^2 = \frac{|x - \mathfrak{y}|^2}{9}.$$

On the other side,
$$\psi(x, \mathfrak{y}) - h^{s-1}\psi(\mathcal{T}x, \mathcal{T}\mathfrak{y}) = \frac{7(x + \mathfrak{y})^2}{18}.$$

When
$$\frac{|x - \mathfrak{y}|^2}{9} \leq \frac{7(x + \mathfrak{y})^2}{18},$$
for all $x, \mathfrak{y} \in [0, 1]$, we deduce that the conditions for Theorem 6 are met.

From Theorem 6, we realize following corollary.

Corollary 1. Let $(Y, \mathcal{D}, s)$ be a complete b-metric space and $\mathcal{T}: Y \longrightarrow Y$, and let $\varphi_i: Y \longrightarrow [0, +\infty)$, $i = 1, 2$ be mappings such that $\mathcal{T}$ is weakly orbitally continuous. If
$$\mathcal{D}(\mathcal{T}x, \mathcal{T}\mathfrak{y}) \leq \varphi_1(x) - h^{s-1}\varphi_1(\mathcal{T}x) + \varphi_2(\mathfrak{y}) - h^{s-1}\varphi_2(\mathcal{T}\mathfrak{y}). \tag{11}$$
for each $x, \mathfrak{y} \in Y$, such that $h > 1$, then $\mathcal{T}$ has a unique FP.

Proof. Putting $\psi(x, \mathfrak{y}) = \varphi_1(x) + \varphi_2(\mathfrak{y}), x, \mathfrak{y} \in Y$ in Theorem 6, we obtain the proof. □

Remark 8. If $\varphi_1 = \varphi_2$ and $s = 1$ from Corollary 1, we obtain Theorem 3.

2.4. On the Result of Karapınar et al. [15]

We first modify Theorem 1 given by Karapınar et al. [15] in the bMS setting as follows.

Theorem 7. Let $(Y, \mathcal{D}, s)$ be a complete bMS, $\mathcal{T}, \mathcal{I}: Y \longrightarrow Y$, and let $\psi: Y \times Y \longrightarrow \mathbb{R}$ be mappings such that:
(a) $\inf_{x,y \in X} \psi(x, y) > -\infty$;
(b) $\mathcal{T}(\mathcal{I}x) = \mathcal{I}(\mathcal{T}x)$, for all $x \in Y$;
(c) the range of $\mathcal{I}$ contains the range of $\mathcal{T}$;
(d) $\mathcal{I}$ is continuous;
(e)
$$\mathcal{D}(\mathcal{I}x, \mathcal{T}x) > 0 \text{ implies } d(\mathcal{T}x, \mathcal{T}\mathfrak{y}) \leq (\psi(\mathcal{I}x, \mathcal{I}\mathfrak{y}) - \psi(\mathcal{T}x, \mathcal{T}\mathfrak{y}))\mathcal{D}(\mathcal{I}x, \mathcal{I}\mathfrak{y}), \tag{12}$$
for all $x, \mathfrak{y} \in Y$.

Then, $\mathcal{T}$ and $\mathcal{I}$ have a coincidence point, which means there exists $u \in Y$ where $\mathcal{T}u = \mathcal{I}u$.

Proof. Let $x_0 \in Y$. Since $\mathcal{T}x_0 \in \mathcal{I}(Y)$, there is an $x_1 \in Y$ such that $\mathcal{I}x_1 = \mathcal{T}x_0$. Similarly, for any given $x_n \in Y$, there is $x_{n+1} \in Y$ such that $\mathcal{I}x_{n+1} = \mathcal{T}x_n$. If $\mathcal{D}(\mathcal{I}x_n, \mathcal{T}x_n) = 0$ for some $n \in \mathbb{N}$, then x_n is a coincidence point. Suppose that

$$\mathcal{D}(\mathcal{I}x_n, \mathcal{T}x_n) > 0, \tag{13}$$

for each $n \in \mathbb{N}$. From (12), we obtain

$$\begin{aligned}\mathcal{D}(\mathcal{T}x_{n+1}, \mathcal{T}x_n) &\leq (\psi(\mathcal{I}x_{n+1}, \mathcal{I}x_n) - \psi(\mathcal{T}x_{n+1}, \mathcal{T}x_n))\mathcal{D}(\mathcal{I}x_{n+1}, \mathcal{I}x_n) \\ &= (\psi(\mathcal{I}x_{n+1}, \mathcal{I}x_n) - \psi(\mathcal{I}x_{n+2}, \mathcal{I}x_{n+1}))\mathcal{D}(\mathcal{I}x_{n+1}, \mathcal{I}x_n).\end{aligned}$$

Hence,

$$\mathcal{D}(\mathcal{I}x_{n+2}, \mathcal{I}x_{n+1}) \leq (\psi(\mathcal{I}x_{n+1}, \mathcal{I}x_n) - \psi(\mathcal{I}x_{n+2}, \mathcal{I}x_{n+1}))\mathcal{D}(\mathcal{I}x_{n+1}, \mathcal{I}x_n), \tag{14}$$

for all $n \in \mathbb{N}$. Recalling condition (13), from (14) we have

$$\frac{\mathcal{D}(\mathcal{I}x_{n+2}, \mathcal{I}x_{n+1})}{\mathcal{D}(\mathcal{I}x_{n+1}, \mathcal{I}x_n)} \leq \psi(\mathcal{I}x_{n+1}, \mathcal{I}x_n) - \psi(\mathcal{I}x_{n+2}, \mathcal{I}x_{n+1}), \tag{15}$$

for each $n \in \mathbb{N}$. From inequality (15) and condition (a), we obtain

$$\sum_{j=1}^{n} \frac{\mathcal{D}(\mathcal{I}x_{j+2}, \mathcal{I}x_{j+1})}{\mathcal{D}(\mathcal{I}x_{j+1}, \mathcal{I}x_j)} < +\infty. \tag{16}$$

Therefore, the series $\sum_{j=1}^{+\infty} \frac{\mathcal{D}(\mathcal{I}x_{j+2}, \mathcal{I}x_{j+1})}{\mathcal{D}(\mathcal{I}x_{j+1}, \mathcal{I}x_j)}$ converges and

$$\lim_{j \to +\infty} \frac{\mathcal{D}(\mathcal{I}x_{j+2}, \mathcal{I}x_{j+1})}{\mathcal{D}(\mathcal{I}x_{j+1}, \mathcal{I}x_j)} = 0. \tag{17}$$

From (17), we conclude that for $k \in (0,1)$, there exists $n_0 \in \mathbb{N}$ where

$$\mathcal{D}(\mathcal{I}x_{j+2}, \mathcal{I}x_{j+1}) \leq k\mathcal{D}(\mathcal{I}x_{j+1}, \mathcal{I}x_j), \tag{18}$$

for all $j \geq n_0$. Now, by applying Lemma 2, the sequence $\mathcal{I}x_n$ is Cauchy. Let

$$u = \lim_{n \to +\infty} \mathcal{I}x_n = \lim_{n \to +\infty} \mathcal{T}x_{n-1}. \tag{19}$$

While $\mathcal{I}$ is continuous, (12) leads to both $\mathcal{I}$ and $\mathcal{T}$ being continuous. On the other hand, $\mathcal{T}$ and $\mathcal{I}$ commute and thus

$$\mathcal{I}u = \mathcal{I}(\lim_{n \to +\infty} \mathcal{T}x_n) = \lim_{n \to +\infty} \mathcal{I}\mathcal{T}x_n = \lim_{n \to +\infty} \mathcal{T}\mathcal{I}x_n = \mathcal{T}(\lim_{n \to +\infty} \mathcal{I}x_n) = \mathcal{T}u. \tag{20}$$

As a result, u is a coincidence point for $\mathcal{T}$ and $\mathcal{I}$. □

Corollary 2. Suppose $(Y, \mathcal{D}, s)$ is a CbMS. Let $T : Y \longrightarrow Y$ and $\varphi : Y \times Y \longrightarrow \mathbb{R}$ be mappings where $\inf_{x \in Y} \varphi(x) > -\infty$. If

$$d(x, Tx) > 0 \text{ reveals } d(Tx, Ty) \leq (\varphi(x) - \varphi(Tx))d(x,y), \tag{21}$$

this means that T has an FP.

Proof. Put $Ix = x$ and $\psi(x,y) = \varphi(x)$ by Theorem 7. □

Remark 9. *Note that Corollary 2 improves Theorem 1 from [15] to the class of bMS.*

3. Conclusions

The importance of the results obtained here is reflected in the fact that we have improved some known results in the fixed-point theory and demonstrated this validated by the examples presented. On the other hand, the results obtained in metric spaces were obtained in the broad class of spaces in b-metric spaces. A natural question is whether these results can be obtained for some wider classes of spaces such as rectangular b-metric spaces [10], $b_v(s)$-metric spaces [20], orthogonal b-metric-like spaces [29] and modular spaces [30].

Author Contributions: Conceptualization, Z.D.M., A.B., A.A., N.M. and R.G.; formal analysis, Z.D.M., A.B. and A.A.; writing—original draft preparation, Z.D.M., A.B., A.A., N.M. and R.G.; writing—review and editing, Z.D.M., A.B., A.A., N.M. and R.G.; funding acquisition, R.G. All authors have read and agreed to the published version of the manuscript.

Funding: This research received no external funding.

Institutional Review Board Statement: Not applicable.

Informed Consent Statement: Not applicable.

Data Availability Statement: Not applicable.

Acknowledgments: This study is supported via funding from Prince Sattam bin Abdulaziz University project number (PSAU/2023/R/1444). The authors would like to thank the reviewers for their valuable remarks and recommendations.

Conflicts of Interest: The authors declare no conflict of interest.

References

1. Aleksić, S.; Mitrović, Z.D.; Radenović, S. A fixed point theorem of Jungck in $b_v(s)$-metric spaces. *Period. Math. Hung.* **2018**, *77*, 224–231. [CrossRef]
2. Aleksić, S.; Mitrović, Z.D.; Radenović, S. Picard sequences in b-metric spaces. *Fixed Point Theory* **2020**, *21*, 35–46. [CrossRef]
3. Bakhtin, I.A. The contraction mapping principle in almost metric space. (Russ.) *Funct. Anal. Unianowsk Gos. Ped. Inst.* **1989**, *30*, 26–37.
4. Caristi, J. Fixed point theorems for mappings satisfying inwardness conditions. *Trans. Am. Math. Soc.* **1976**, *215*, 241–251. [CrossRef]
5. Carić, B.; Došenović, T.; George, R.; Mitrović, Z.D.; Radenović, S. On Jungck-Branciari-Wardowski type fixed point results. *Mathematics* **2021**, *9*, 161. [CrossRef]
6. Czerwik, S. Contraction mappings in b-metric spaces. *Acta Math. Inform. Univ. Ostrav.* **1993**, *1*, 5–11.
7. Ćirić, Lj, B. Generalised contractions and fixed point theorems. *Publ. Inst. Math.* **1971**, *12*, 19–26.
8. Dung, N.V.; Hang, V.T.L. On relaxations of contraction constants and Caristi's theorem in b-metric spaces. *J. Fixed Point Theory Appl.* **2016**, *18*, 267–284. [CrossRef]
9. Fisher, B. Four mappings with a common fixed point. *Kuwait J. Sci.* **1981**, *8*, 131–139.
10. George, R.; Radenović, S.; Reshma, K.P.; Shukla, S. Rectangular b-metric space and contraction principles. *J. Nonlinear Sci. Appl.* **2015**, *8*, 1005–1013. [CrossRef]
11. Hussain, N.; Mitrović, Z.D.; Radenović, S. A common fixed point theorem of Fisher in b-metric spaces. *Rev. R. Acad. Cienc. Exactas Fís. Nat. Ser. A Mat. RACSAM* **2019**, *113*, 949–956. [CrossRef]
12. Jovanović, M.; Kadelburg, Z.; Radenović, S. Common Fixed Point Results in Metric-Type Spaces. *Fixed Point Theory Appl.* **2010**, *2010*, 978121. [CrossRef]
13. Jungck, G. Commuting mappings and fixed points. *Am. Math. Mon.* **1976**, *83*, 261–263. [CrossRef]
14. Jungck, G. Compatible mappings and common fixed points. *Int. J. Math. Math. Sci.* **1986**, *9*, 771–779. [CrossRef]
15. Karapınar, E.; Khojasteh, F.; Mitrović, Z.D. A proposal for revisiting Banach and Caristi type theorems in b-metric spaces. *Mathematics* **2019**, *7*, 308. [CrossRef]
16. Khojasteh, F.; Karapınar, E.; Khandani, H. Some applications of Caristi's fixed point theorem in metric spaces. *Fixed Point Theory Appl.* **2016**, *2016*, 16. [CrossRef]
17. Kirk, W.; Shahzad, N. *Fixed Point Theory in Distance Spaces*; Springer: Cham, Switzerland, 2014. [CrossRef]
18. Miculescu, R.; Mihail, A. New fixed point theorems for set-valued contractions in b-metric spaces. *J. Fixed Point Theory Appl.* **2017**, *19*, 2153–2163. [CrossRef]

19. Miculescu, R.; Mihail, A. Caristi-Kirk type and Boyd-Wong-Browder-Matkowski-Rus type fixed point results in b-metric spaces. *Filomat* **2017**, *31*, 4331–4340. [CrossRef]
20. Mitrović, Z.D.; Radenović, S.; Reich, S.; Zaslavski, A. Iterating nonlinear contractive mappings in Banach spaces. *Carpathian J. Math.* **2020**, *36*, 286–293. [CrossRef]
21. Mitrović, Z.D.; Radenović, S. The Banach and Reich contractions in $b_v(s)$-metric spaces. *J. Fixed Point Theory Appl.* **2017**, *19*, 3087–3095. [CrossRef]
22. Mitrović, Z.D.; Radenović, S. A common fixed point theorem of Jungck in rectangular b-metric spaces. *Acta Math. Hungar.* **2017**, *153*, 401–407. [CrossRef]
23. Mitrović, Z.D. A note on a Banach's fixed point theorem in b-rectangular metric space and b-metric space. *Math. Slovaca* **2018**, *68*, 1113–1116. [CrossRef]
24. Mitrović, Z.D.; Hussain, N. On results of Hardy-Rogers and Reich in cone b-metric space over Banach algebra and applications. *U.P.B. Sci. Bull. Ser. A* **2019**, *81*, 147–154.
25. Pant, R.P.; Rakočević, V.; Gopal, D.; Pant, A.; Ram, M. A General Fixed Point Theorem. *Filomat* **2021**, *35*, 4061–4072. [CrossRef]
26. Pant, A.; Pant, R.P. Fixed points and continuity of contractive maps. *Filomat* **2017**, *31*, 3501–3506. [CrossRef]
27. Pant, A.; Pant, R.P.; Joshi, M.C. Caristi type and Meir-Keeler type fixed point theorems. *Filomat* **2019**, *33*, 3711–3721. [CrossRef]
28. Hutchinson, J. Fractals and Self-Similarity. *Indiana Univ. Math. J.* **1981**, *30*, 713–747. [CrossRef]
29. Gardašević-Filipović, M.; Kukić, K.; Gardašević, D.; Mitrović, Z.D. Some best proximity point results in the orthogonal 0-complete b-metric like spaces. *J. Contemp. Math. Anal. Armen. Acad.* **2023**, *58*, 1–14. in press.
30. Nakano, H. Modular semi-ordered spaces. *Tokyo Math. Book Series*; Maruzen. I: Tokyo, Japan, 1950; Volume 1, p. 288.

Disclaimer/Publisher's Note: The statements, opinions and data contained in all publications are solely those of the individual author(s) and contributor(s) and not of MDPI and/or the editor(s). MDPI and/or the editor(s) disclaim responsibility for any injury to people or property resulting from any ideas, methods, instructions or products referred to in the content.

($\alpha - \psi$) Meir–Keeler Contractions in Bipolar Metric Spaces

Manoj Kumar [1], Pankaj Kumar [1], Rajagopalan Ramaswamy [2,*], Ola A. Ashour Abdelnaby [2,3], Amr Elsonbaty [4] and Stojan Radenović [5]

1. Department of Mathematics, Baba Mastnath University, Asthal Bohar, Rohtak 124021, Haryana, India
2. Department of Mathematics, College of Science and Humanities in Alkharj, Prince Sattam Bin Abdulaziz University, Alkharj 11942, Saudi Arabia
3. Department of Mathematics, Cairo University, Cairo 12613, Egypt
4. Mathematics and Engineering Physics Department, Mansoura University, Mansoura 35516, Egypt
5. Faculty of Mechanical Engineering, University of Belgrade, Kraljice Marije 16, 11120 Belgrade, Serbia
* Correspondence: r.gopalan@psau.edu.sa

Abstract: In this paper, we introduce the new notion of contravariant ($\alpha - \psi$) Meir–Keeler contractive mappings by defining α-orbital admissible mappings and covariant Meir–Keeler contraction in bipolar metric spaces. We prove fixed point theorems for these contractions and also provide some corollaries of main results. An example is also be given in support of our main result. In the end, we also solve an integral equation using our result.

Keywords: fixed point; ($\alpha - \psi$) Meir–Keeler contractive mappings; covariant and contravariant mappings; bipolar metric space

MSC: 47H9; 47H10; 30G35; 46N99; 54H25

1. Introduction

Fixed point theory is the major branch of non-linear analysis. It has number of applications in other branch of sciences, economics, etc. In 1922, Banach [1] gave a contraction principle to obtain a fixed point theorem in complete metric space. Some other researchers tried to generalize the concept of metric space; see [2–4]. Due to the various applications of the Banach contraction principle, the contraction mapping theorem has been generalized by many researchers in the setting of various topological spaces using different contractive conditions; see [5–14]. In 2012, Samet et al. [15] introduced the new contraction by defining the α-admissible mappings and established fixed point results thereon. In 2013, Kumam et al. [16] extended and generalized the α-admissible mapping of [15], introduced ($\alpha - \psi$) Meir–Keeler contractive mappings and proved some fixed point theorems in complete metric space. In 2014, Popescu [17] introduced α-orbital admissible mapping to get fixed point theorems.

Recently, in 2016, Mutlu et al. [18] introduced the new type of metric space called bipolar metric space. Since then, researchers have established several fixed point theorems using various contractive conditions in the setting of bipolar metric spaces; see [19–24].

Inspired by this, in the present work, we introduce ($\alpha - \psi$) Meir–Keeler contractive mappings and establish fixed point theorems in the setting of bipolar metric spaces. The rest of the paper is organized as follows. In Section 2, we review some preliminary definitions and monographs that are required for our main result. In Section 3, we present our main results and establish a fixed point result using ($\alpha - \psi$) Meir–Keeler contractive mappings in the setting of bipolar metric space. We supplement the derived results with suitable non-trivial examples. In Section 4, we apply the derived fixed point result to find an analytical solution to the integral equation. Finally, we conclude the paper with some open problems for future work.

2. Preliminaries

To prove our main results, we need some basic definitions from the literature as follows:

Definition 1 ([18]). *Let X and Y be two non-empty sets and $d : X \times Y \to [0, \infty)$ be a map satisfying the following conditions:*
1. $d(x, y) = 0$ if and only if $x = y$ for all $(x, y) \in X \times Y$;
2. $d(x, y) = d(y, x)$ for all $x, y \in X \cap Y$;
3. $d(x_1, y_2) \leq d(x_1, y_1) + d(x_2, y_1) + d(x_2, y_2)$;
   for all $x_1, x_2 \in X$ and $y_1, y_2 \in Y$.

Then, d is called bipolar metric and (X, Y, d) is called bipolar metric space.

If $X \cap Y = \phi$, then the space is called disjoint; otherwise, it is called joint. The set X is called the left pole and the set Y is called the right pole of (X, Y, d). The elements of X, Y and $X \cap Y$ are called left, right and central elements, respectively.

Definition 2 ([18]). *Let (X, Y, d) be a bipolar metric space. Then, any sequence $\{x_n\} \subseteq X$ is called a left sequence and is said to be convergent to the right element; for example, y if $d(x_n, y) \to 0$ as $n \to \infty$. Similarly, a right sequence $\{y_n\} \subseteq Y$ is said to be convergent to a left element; for example, x if $d(x, y_n) \to 0$ as $n \to \infty$.*

Definition 3 ([18]). *Let (X, Y, d) be a bipolar metric space.*
1. *A sequence $\{x_n, y_n\}$ on $X \times Y$ is called a bisequence on (X, Y, d).*
2. *If both the sequences $\{x_n\}$ and $\{y_n\}$ converge, then the bisequence $\{x_n, y_n\}$ is said to be convergent. If both sequences $\{x_n\}$ and $\{y_n\}$ converge to the same point $u \in X \cap Y$, then the bisequence $\{x_n, y_n\}$ is called biconvergent.*
3. *A bisequence $\{x_n, y_n\}$ on (X, Y, d) is said to be a Cauchy bisequence if for each $\epsilon > 0$ there exists a positive integer $N \in \mathbb{N}$ such that $d(x_n, y_m) < \epsilon$ for all $n, m \geq N$.*
4. *A bipolar metric space is said to be complete if every Cauchy bisequence is convergent in this space.*

Definition 4 ([18]). *Let (X_1, Y_1, d_1) and (X_2, Y_2, d_2) be two bipolar metric spaces and $T : X_1 \cup Y_1 \to X_2 \cup Y_2$ be a function:*
1. *If $TX_1 \subseteq X_2$ and $TY_1 \subseteq Y_2$, then T is called covariant mapping and is denoted by $T : (X_1, Y_1, d_1) \rightrightarrows (X_2, Y_2, d_2)$.*
2. *If $TX_1 \subseteq Y_2$ and $TY_1 \subseteq X_2$, then T is called contravariant mapping and is denoted by $T : (X_1, Y_1, d_1) \rightleftarrows (X_2, Y_2, d_2)$.*

Definition 5 ([18]). *Let (X_1, Y_1, d_1) and (X_2, Y_2, d_2) be two bipolar metric spaces.*
1. *A map $T : (X_1, Y_1, d_1) \rightrightarrows (X_2, Y_2, d_2)$ is called left continuous at a point $x_0 \in X$ if for every $\epsilon > 0$ there exists a $\delta > 0$ such that $d_2(Tx_0, Ty) < \epsilon$ whenever $d_1(x_0, y) < \delta$.*
2. *A map $T : (X_1, Y_1, d_1) \rightrightarrows (X_2, Y_2, d_2)$ is called right continuous at a point $y_0 \in Y$ if for every $\epsilon > 0$ there exists a $\delta > 0$ such that $d_2(Tx, Ty_0) < \epsilon$ whenever $d_1(x, y_0) < \delta$.*
3. *A map $T : (X_1, Y_1, d_1) \rightrightarrows (X_2, Y_2, d_2)$ is called continuous if it is left continuous at each $x_0 \in X$ and right continuous at each $y_0 \in Y$.*
4. *A map $T : (X_1, Y_1, d_1) \rightleftarrows (X_2, Y_2, d_2)$ is called continuous if and only if it is continuous as a covariant map $T : (X_1, Y_1, d_1) \rightrightarrows (X_2, Y_2, d_2)$.*

Definition 6 ([20]). *Let $T : (X, Y) \rightrightarrows (X, Y)$ and $\alpha : X \times Y \to [0, \infty)$. Then, T is called α-admissible if*

$$\alpha(x, y) \geq 1 \text{ implies } \alpha(Tx, Ty) \geq 1, \tag{1}$$

for all $(x, y) \in X \times Y$.

Definition 7 ([20]). *Let $T : (X,Y) \rightleftarrows (X,Y)$ and $\alpha : X \times Y \to [0, \infty)$. Then, T is called α-admissible if*

$$\alpha(x,y) \geq 1 \text{ implies } \alpha(Ty, Tx) \geq 1, \tag{2}$$

for all $(x,y) \in X \times Y$.

Definition 8 ([15]). *Let Ψ be the family of functions $\psi : [0, \infty) \to [0, \infty)$ satisfying the following conditions:*

1. *ψ is non-decreasing.*
2. *$\sum_{n=1}^{+\infty} \psi^n < \infty$ for all $t > 0$, where ψ^n is the nth iterate of ψ.*

These functions are known as (c)-comparison functions. It can be easily verified that $\psi(t) < t$ for any $t > 0$.

3. Results

Here, we introduce $(\alpha - \psi)$ Meir–Keeler contractions and α-orbital admissible mappings and prove fixed point theorems for these contractions in bipolar metric spaces.

Definition 9. *Let $T : (X,Y) \rightleftarrows (X,Y)$ and $\alpha : X \times Y \to \mathbb{R}$. Then, T is called an α-orbital admissible mapping if*

$$\alpha(x, Tx) \geq 1 \Rightarrow \alpha(T^2 x, Tx) \geq 1, \tag{3}$$

and

$$\alpha(Ty, y) \geq 1 \Rightarrow \alpha(Ty, T^2 y) \geq 1, \tag{4}$$

For all $(x,y) \in X \times Y$.

Definition 10. *Let (X,Y,d) be a bipolar metric space and $\psi \in \Psi$. Suppose $T : (X,Y) \rightleftarrows (X,Y)$ is an contravariant mapping and if for every $\epsilon > 0$ there exists $\delta > 0$ such that*

$$\epsilon \leq \psi(d(x,y)) < \epsilon + \delta \Rightarrow \alpha(x, Tx)\alpha(Ty, y)\psi(d(Ty, Tx)) < \epsilon, \tag{5}$$

for all $(x,y) \in X \times Y$ and $\alpha : X \times Y \to \mathbb{R}$.
Then, T is said to be contravariant $(\alpha - \psi)$ Meir–Keeler contractive mapping.

Remark 1. *From (5), we get $\alpha(x, Tx)\alpha(Ty, y)\psi(d(Ty, Tx)) < \psi(d(x,y))$, when $x \neq y$. If $x = y$ then $\alpha(x, Tx)\alpha(Ty, y)\psi(d(Ty, Tx)) \leq \psi(d(x,y))$.*

Now, we present our first theorem.

Theorem 1. *Let (X,Y,d) be a complete bipolar metric space. Suppose that $T : (X,Y) \rightleftarrows (X,Y)$ is a contravariant $(\alpha - \psi)$ Meir–Keeler contractive mapping. If the following conditions hold,*

1. *T is α-orbital admissible,*
2. *There exists $x_0 \in X$ such that $\alpha(x_0, Tx_0) \geq 1$,*
3. *T is continuous,*

then T has a fixed point.

Proof. Let $x_0 \in X$ such that $\alpha(x_0, Tx_0) \geq 1$. Construct the sequences $\{x_n\}$ and $\{y_n\}$ by taking $y_n = Tx_n$ and $x_{n+1} = Ty_n$ for all $n \in \mathbb{N}$. Clearly, $\{x_n, y_n\}$ is a bisequence.
Since T is α-admissible, we obtain

$$\begin{aligned}
\alpha(x_0, y_0) &= \alpha(x_0, Tx_0) \geq 1 \Rightarrow \alpha(T^2 x_0, Tx_0) = \alpha(x_1, y_0) \geq 1, \\
\alpha(x_1, y_0) &= \alpha(Ty_0, y_0) \geq 1 \Rightarrow \alpha(Ty_0, T^2 y_0) = \alpha(x_1, y_1) \geq 1, \\
\alpha(x_1, y_1) &= \alpha(x_1, Tx_1) \geq 1 \Rightarrow \alpha(T2x_1, Tx_1) = \alpha(x_2, y_1) \geq 1, \\
\alpha(x_2, y_1) &= \alpha(Ty_1, y_1) \Rightarrow \alpha(Ty_1, T^2 y_1) = \alpha(x_2, y_2) \geq 1.
\end{aligned}$$

By continuing this process, we get

$$\alpha(x_n, y_n) \geq 1 \text{ and } \alpha(x_{n+1}, y_n) \geq 1 \text{ for all } n \in \mathbb{N}. \tag{6}$$

Using Remark 1 and (6), we get

$$\begin{aligned}
\psi(d(x_n, y_n)) &= \psi(d(Ty_{n-1}, Tx_n)) \leq \alpha(x_n, y_n)\alpha(x_n, y_{n-1})\psi(d(Ty_{n-1}, Tx_n)), \\
&= \alpha(x_n, Tx_n)\alpha(Ty_{n-1}, y_{n-1})\psi(d(Ty_{n-1}, Tx_n)), \\
&< \psi(d(x_n, y_{n-1})).
\end{aligned} \tag{7}$$

Using again Remark 1 and (6), we get

$$\begin{aligned}
\psi(d(x_{n+1}, y_n)) &= \psi(d(Ty_n, Tx_n)) \leq \alpha(x_n, y_n)\alpha(x_{n+1}, y_n), \\
&= \alpha(x_n, Tx_n)\alpha(d(Ty_n, y_n))\psi(d(x_n, y_n)), \\
&< \psi(d(x_n, y_n)).
\end{aligned} \tag{8}$$

From (7) and (8), using mathematical induction, we have

$$\psi(d(x_n, y_n)) < \psi(d(x_{n-1}, y_{n-1})) \forall n \in \mathbb{N} \tag{9}$$

and

$$\psi(d(x_{n+1}, y_n)) < \psi(d(x_n, y_{n-1})) \forall n \in \mathbb{N}. \tag{10}$$

From (9) and (10), it is clear that $\{\psi(d(x_n, y_n))\}$ and $\{\psi(d(x_{n+1}, y_n))\}$ are monotonically decreasing sequences of positive reals and hence convergent. Let $\{\psi(d(x_n, y_n))\} \to s_1$ and $\{\psi(d(x_{n+1}, y_n))\} \to s_2$ as $n \to \infty$, where $s_1, s_2 \geq 0$.

Now, we prove that $s_1 = 0$ and $s_2 = 0$.

Firstly, suppose if possible that $s_1 > 0$.

Clearly, $\psi(d(x_n, y_n)) \geq s_1 > 0$ for all $n \in \mathbb{N}$.

Let $\epsilon = s_1$. Then, by hypothesis, there exist $\delta > 0$ and $n_0 \in \mathbb{N}$ such that

$$\epsilon \leq \psi(d(x_{n_0}, y_{n_0})) < \epsilon + \delta. \tag{11}$$

From (5), we have

$$\begin{aligned}
\psi(d(x_{n_0+1}, y_{n_0+1})) &\leq \alpha(x_{n_0+1}, y_{n_0+1})\alpha(x_{n_0+1}, y_{n_0})\psi(d(x_{n_0+1}, y_{n_0+1})), \\
&= \alpha(x_{n_0+1}, Tx_{n_0+1})\alpha(Ty_{n_0}, y_{n_0})\psi(d(Ty_{n_0}, Tx_{n_0+1})) < \epsilon = s_1,
\end{aligned}$$

a contradiction.

So, $s_1 = 0$.

Similarly, one can prove easily that $s_2 = 0$.

Hence, $\psi(d(x_n, y_n)) \to 0$ and $\psi(d(x_{n+1}, y_n)) \to 0$ as $n \to \infty$. By using the definition of continuity of ψ at $t = 0$, we can say that

$$d(x_n, y_n) \to 0 \text{ and } d(x_{n+1}, y_n) \to 0 \text{ as } n \to \infty. \tag{12}$$

For a given $\epsilon > 0$, by the hypothesis, there exists $\delta > 0$ such that (5) holds. Without loss of generality, let us assume that $\delta < \epsilon$.

Since $\psi(d(x_n, y_n)) \to 0$ and $\psi(d(x_{n+1}, y_n)) \to 0$, there exist $N_1, N_2 \in \mathbb{N}$ such that

$$\psi(d(x_{n-1}, y_{n-1})) < \frac{\delta}{3} \text{ for all } n \geq N_1, \tag{13}$$

$$\psi(d(x_n, y_{n-1})) < \frac{\delta}{3} \text{ for all } n \geq N_2. \tag{14}$$

Now, we shall prove that
$$\psi(d(x_{n+l}, y_n)) < \epsilon \tag{15}$$
and
$$\psi(d(x_n, y_{n+l})) < \epsilon, \text{ for all } n \geq N. \tag{16}$$
where $N = \max\{N_1, N_2\}$.

Firstly, using mathematical induction, we prove (15), that is $\psi(d(x_{n+l}, y_n)) < \epsilon$. From (14), clearly the inequality holds for $l = 1$.

Suppose that the result is true for some $l = k$, that is
$$\psi(d(x_{n+k}, y_n)) < \epsilon, \text{ for all } n \geq N. \tag{17}$$

Now, by using the definition of bipolar metric space, (13), (14) and (17), we get
$$\begin{aligned}
\psi(d(x_{n+k}, y_{n-1})) &\leq \psi(d(x_{n+k}, y_n) + d(x_n, y_n) + d(x_n, y_{n-1})) \\
&\leq \psi(d(x_{n+k}, y_n)) + \psi(d(x_n, y_n)) + \psi(d(x_n, y_{n-1})) \\
&< \frac{\delta}{3} + \frac{\delta}{3} + \epsilon = \frac{2\delta}{3} + \epsilon < \epsilon + \delta.
\end{aligned} \tag{18}$$

If $\psi(d(x_{n+k}, y_{n-1})) \geq \epsilon$, then by (5), we have
$$\begin{aligned}
\psi(d(x_{n+k+1}, y_n)) &\leq \alpha(x_n, y_n)\alpha(x_{n+k+1}, y_{n+k})\psi(d(x_{n+k+1}, y_n)), \\
&= \alpha(x_n, Tx_n)\alpha(Ty_{n+k}, y_{n+k})\psi(d(Ty_{n+k}, Tx_n)), \\
&< \epsilon.
\end{aligned}$$

Hence, (15) holds.

If $\psi(d(x_{n+k}, y_{n-1})) \leq \epsilon$, then by Remark 1, we have
$$\begin{aligned}
\psi(d(x_{n+k+1}, y_n)) &\leq \alpha(x_n, y_n)\alpha(x_{n+k+1}, y_{n+k})\psi(d(x_{n+k+1}, y_n)), \\
&= \alpha(x_n, Tx_n)\alpha(Ty_{n+k}, y_{n+k})\psi(d(Ty_{n+k}, x_n)), \\
&< \psi(d(x_n, y_{n+k})) < \epsilon.
\end{aligned}$$

So, (15) holds for $l = k + 1$.

Hence,
$$d(x_n, y_m) < \epsilon \text{ for all } n > m \geq N. \tag{19}$$

Again, using mathematical induction, we prove (16).

Using the definition of bipolar metric space, (13) and (14), we get
$$\begin{aligned}
\psi(d(x_n, y_{n+1})) &\leq \psi(d(x_n, y_n) + d(x_{n+1}, y_n) + d(x_{n+1}, y_{n+1})) \\
&\leq \psi(d(x_{n+1}, y_{n+1})) + \psi(d(x_{n+1}, y_n)) + \psi(d(x_n, y_n)) \\
&\leq \frac{\delta}{3} + \frac{\delta}{3} + \frac{\delta}{3} = \delta < \epsilon.
\end{aligned}$$

So, (16) holds for $l = 1$.

Now, let us suppose that the result is true for some $l = k$, that is,
$$\psi(d(x_n, y_{n+k})) < \epsilon \text{ for all } n \geq N. \tag{20}$$

Now, by using the definition of bipolar metric space, (13), (14) and (20), we get
$$\begin{aligned}
\psi(d(x_{n-1}, y_{n+k})) &\leq \psi(d(x_{n-1}, y_{n-1}) + d(x_n, y_{n-1}) + d(x_n, y_{n+k})), \\
&\leq \psi(d(x_{n-1}, y_{n-1})) + \psi(d(x_n, y_{n-1})) + \psi(d(x_n, y_{n+k})) \\
&< \frac{\delta}{3} + \frac{\delta}{3} + \epsilon = \frac{2\delta}{3} + \epsilon < \epsilon + \delta.
\end{aligned} \tag{21}$$

If $\psi(d(x_{n-1}, y_{n+k})) \geq \epsilon$, then by (5), we have

$$\psi(d(x_n, y_{n+k+1})) \leq \alpha(x_{n+k}, y_{n+k})\alpha(x_{n+1}, y_n)\psi(d(x_n, y_{n+k+1})),$$
$$= \alpha(x_{n+k}, Tx_{n+k})\alpha(Ty_n, y_n)\psi(d(Tx_{n+k}, Ty_n)),$$
$$< \epsilon.$$

Hence, (16) holds.
If $\psi(d(x_{n-1}, y_{n+k})) < \epsilon$, then by Remark 1, we have

$$\psi(d(x_n, y_{n+k+1})) \leq \alpha(x_{n+k}, y_{n+k})\alpha(x_{n+1}, y_n)\psi(d(x_n, y_{n+k+1})),$$
$$= \alpha(x_{n+k}, Tx_{n+k})\alpha(Ty_n, y_n)\psi(d(Tx_{n+k}, y_n)),$$
$$< \psi(d(x_{n+k}, y_n)) < \epsilon.$$

So, (16) holds for $l = k+1$.
Hence,
$$d(x_n, y_m) < \epsilon \ for \ all \ m > n \geq N. \tag{22}$$

From (19) and (22), we can say that $\{x_n, y_n\}$ is a Cauchy bisequence. Since (X, Y, d) is a complete bipolar metric space, then $\{x_n, y_n\}$ biconverges. That is, there exists $u \in X \cap Y$ such that $\{x_n\} \to u$ and $\{y_n\} \to u$ as $n \to \infty$. As T is a continuous map, one has

$$(x_n) \to u \ implies \ that \ y_n = Tx_n \to Tu.$$

Combining $y_n = Tx_n \to Tu$ with $(y_n) \to u$, we get $Tu = u$. □

In the next theorem, we omit continuity and give a new condition to get the fixed point.

Theorem 2. *Let (X, Y, d) be a complete bipolar metric space. Suppose that $T : (X, Y) \rightleftarrows (X, Y)$ is a contravariant $(\alpha - \psi)$ Meir–Keeler contractive mapping. If the following conditions hold,*

1. *T is α-orbital admissible,*
2. *There exists $x_0 \in X$ such that $\alpha(x_0, Tx_0) \geq 1$,*
3. *If $\{x_n, y_n\}$ is a bisequence such that $\alpha(x_n, y_n) \geq 1$ for all n and $y_n \to u \in X \cap Y$ as $n \to \infty$, then $\alpha(Tu, u) \geq 1$,*

then T has a fixed point.

Proof. From the proof of Theorem 1, we conclude that $\{x_n, y_n\}$ is a Cauchy bisequence. Since (X, Y, d) is a complete bipolar metric space, then $\{x_n, y_n\}$ is biconvergent. Hence, there exist $u \in X \cap Y$ such that $x_n \to u$, $y_n \to u$.
From condition (3), we get $\alpha(Tu, u) \geq 1$.
By applying the definition of bipolar metric space, ψ, Remark 1, (6) and the above inequality, we get

$$\psi(d(Tu, u)) \leq \psi(d(Tu, Tx_n) + d(Ty_n, Tx_n) + d(Ty_n, u)),$$
$$\leq \psi(d(Tu, Tx_n)) + \psi(d(Ty_n, Tx_n)) + \psi(d(Ty_n, u)),$$
$$\leq \alpha(x_n, y_n)\alpha(Tu, u)\psi(d(Tu, Tx_n)),$$
$$+ \alpha(x_n, Tx_n)\alpha(Ty_n, y_n)\psi(d(Ty_n, Tx_n)),$$
$$+ \alpha(x_n, Tx_n)\alpha(Ty_n, y_n)\psi(d(Ty_n, Tx_n)) + \psi(d(Ty_n, u)),$$
$$\leq \psi(d(x_n, u)) + \psi(d(x_n, y_n)) + \psi(d(u, y_n)).$$

Letting $n \to \infty$ in the above inequality and using (22), we get

$$\psi(d(Tu, u)) \leq 0.$$

That is, $d(Tu, u) = 0$.

Hence, $Tu = u$. □

Now, we introduce generalized $(\alpha - \psi)$ Meir–Keeler contractive mappings and prove fixed point theorem for these mappings.

Definition 11. *Let (X, Y, d) be a bipolar metric space and $\psi \in \Psi$. Suppose $T : (X, Y) \rightleftarrows (X, Y)$ be an contravariant mapping and that for every $\epsilon > 0$ there exists $\delta > 0$ such that*

$$\epsilon \leq \psi(M(x,y)) < \epsilon + \delta \Rightarrow \alpha(x, Tx)\alpha(Ty, y)\psi(d(Ty, Tx)) < \epsilon, \tag{23}$$

where $M(x,y) = \max\{d(x,y), d(x, Tx), d(Ty, y), \frac{d(x, Tx) + d(Ty, y)}{2}\}$; for all $(x, y) \in X \times Y$. Then, T is said to be a generalized contravariant $(\alpha - \psi)$ Meir–Keeler contractive mapping.

Remark 2. *From (23), we get $\alpha(x, Tx)\alpha(Ty, y)\psi(d(Ty, Tx)) < \psi(M(x,y))$, when $x \neq y$. If $x = y$ then $\alpha(x, y)\psi(d(Ty, Tx)) \leq \psi(M(x,y))$.*

Theorem 3. *Let (X, Y, d) be a complete bipolar metric space. Suppose that $T : (X, Y) \rightleftarrows (X, Y)$ is a generalized contravariant $(\alpha - \psi)$ Meir–Keeler contractive mapping. If the following conditions hold,*

1. *T is α-orbital admissible,*
2. *There exists $x_0 \in X$ such that $\alpha(x_0, Tx_0) \geq 1$,*
3. *T is orbital continuous,*

then T has a fixed point.

Proof. Let $x_0 \in X$ such that $\alpha(x_0, Tx_0) \geq 1$. Construct sequences $\{x_n\}$ and $\{y_n\}$ by taking $y_n = Tx_n$ and $x_{n+1} = Ty_n$ for all $n \in \mathbb{N}$. Clearly $\{x_n, y_n\}$ is a bisequence.

Since T is α-orbital admissible, from Theorem 1, we get

$$\alpha(x_n, y_n) \geq 1 \text{ and } \alpha(x_{n+1}, y_n) \geq 1 \text{ for all } n \in \mathbb{N}. \tag{24}$$

Using Remark 2 and (24), we get

$$\begin{aligned}
\psi(d(x_n, y_n)) &= \psi(d(Ty_{n-1}, Tx_n)) \leq \alpha(x_n, Tx_n)\alpha(Ty_{n-1}, y_{n-1})\psi(d(Ty_{n-1}, Tx_n)), \\
&< \psi(M(x_n, y_{n-1})), \\
&= \psi(\max\{d(x_n, y_{n-1}), d(x_n, Tx_n), d(Ty_{n-1}, y_{n-1}), \frac{d(x_n, Tx_n) + d(Ty_{n-1}, y_{n-1})}{2}\}), \\
&= \psi(\max\{d(x_n, y_{n-1}), d(x_n, y_n), d(x_n, y_{n-1}), \frac{d(x_n, y_n) + d(x_n, y_{n-1})}{2}\}), \\
&\leq \psi(\max\{d(x_n, y_n), d(x_n, y_{n-1})\}).
\end{aligned}$$

Now, since ψ is a non-decreasing function, one has $d(x_n, y_n) \leq \max\{d(x_n, y_n), d(x_n, y_{n-1})\}$.

If possible, suppose that $d(x_n, y_n) > d(x_n, y_{n-1})$, then $d(x_n, y_n) < d(x_n, y_n)$, a contradiction.

Hence,

$$d(x_n, y_n) \leq d(x_n, y_{n-1}), \text{ for all } n \in \mathbb{N}. \tag{25}$$

Similarly, by using Remark 2 and (24), one can easily obtain

$$d(x_{n+1}, y_n) \leq d(x_n, y_n), \text{ for all } n \in \mathbb{N}. \tag{26}$$

From (25) and (26), it is clear that $\{d(x_n, y_n)\}$ and $\{d(x_{n+1}, y_n)\}$ are monotonically decreasing sequences of positive reals and hence convergent. Let $\{d(x_n, y_n)\} \to s_1$ and $\{d(x_{n+1}, y_n)\} \to s_2$ as $n \to \infty$, where $s_1, s_2 \geq 0$. This implies that

$$\lim\{psid(x_n, y_n)\} = \lim\{\psi(M(x_n, y_n))\} = \psi(s_1) \text{ as } n \to \infty. \tag{27}$$

and
$$\lim\{\psi(d(x_{n+1},y_n))\} = \lim\{\psi(M(x_{n+1},y_n))\} = \psi(s_2) \text{ as } n \to \infty. \tag{28}$$

Now, we prove that $s_1 = 0$ and $s_2 = 0$.
Firstly, suppose that $s_1 > 0$.
Clearly, $d(x_n, y_n) \geq s_1 > 0$ for all $n \in \mathbb{N}$.
Let $\epsilon = s_1$. Then, by hypothesis, there exists $\delta > 0$ and $n_0 \in \mathbb{N}$ such that

$$\psi(\epsilon) \leq \psi(M(x_{n_0}, y_{n_0})) < \psi(\epsilon) + \delta. \tag{29}$$

From (23), we have

$$\psi(d(x_{n_0+1}, y_{n_0+1})) \leq \alpha(x_{n_0+1}, y_{n_0+1})\alpha(x_{n_0+1}, y_{n_0})\psi(d(x_{n_0+1}, y_{n_0+1})),$$
$$= \alpha(Ty_{n_0}, y_{n_0})\alpha(x_{n_0+1}, Tx_{n_0+1})\psi(d(Ty_{n_0}, Tx_{n_0+1})) < \psi(\epsilon).$$

Using non-decreasing nature of ψ, we get

$$d(x_{n_0+1}, y_{n_0+1}) < \epsilon = s_1. \tag{30}$$

a contradiction. So, $s_1 = 0$.
Similarly, one can prove easily that $s_2 = 0$.
Now, we prove that $\{x_n, y_n\}$ is a Cauchy bisequence; that is, $\lim_{n,m \to \infty} d(x_n, y_m) = 0$
Indeed, if we suppose that $\{x_n, y_n\}$ is not a Cauchy bisequence, then there exists $\epsilon > 0$ and subsequences $\{n(i)\}$ and $\{n(i+1)\}$ of natural numbers such that

$$d(x_{n(i)}, y_{n(i+1)}) > 2\epsilon, \tag{31}$$

for all $i \in \mathbb{N}$. For this $\epsilon > 0$ there exists $\delta > 0$ such that $\epsilon \leq \psi(M(x,y)) < \epsilon + \delta$ implies that $\alpha(x, Tx)\alpha(Ty, y)\psi(d(Ty, Tx)) < \epsilon$.
Set $r = \min\{\epsilon, \delta\}$. Since $d(x_n, y_n)$ and $d(x_{n+1}, y_n) \to 0$ as $n \to \infty$, there exists $n_1, n_2 \in \mathbb{N}$ such that

$$d(x_n, y_n) < \frac{r}{8} \text{ for all } n \geq n_1, \text{ and} \tag{32}$$

$$d(x_{n+1}, y_n) < \frac{r}{8} \text{ for all } n \geq n_2. \tag{33}$$

Choose $N = \max\{n_1, n_2\}$. Then, the above inequalities still hold for all $n \geq N$.
Let $n(i) > N$. We get $n(i) \leq n(i+1) - 1$. If $d(x_{n(i)}, y_{n(i+1)-1}) \leq \epsilon + \frac{r}{2}$; then, using the definition of bipolar metric space, (32) and (33), we have

$$d(x_{n(i)}, y_{n(i+1)}) \leq d(x_{n(i)}, y_{n(i+1)-1}) + d(x_{n(i+1)}, y_{n(i+1)-1}) + d(x_{n(i+1)}, y_{n(i+1)}),$$
$$< \epsilon + \frac{r}{2} + \frac{r}{8} + \frac{r}{8},$$
$$= \epsilon + \frac{3}{4}r < 2\epsilon,$$

a contradiction. So, there exists k such that $n(i) \leq k \leq n(i+1)$ and $d(x_{n(i)}, y_k) > \epsilon + \frac{r}{2}$.
Now if $d(x_{n(i)+1}, y_{n(i)}) \geq \epsilon + \frac{r}{2}$, then by (35), $d(x_{n(i)+1}, y_{n(i)}) \geq \epsilon + \frac{r}{2} > r + \frac{r}{2} > \frac{r}{8}$, a contradiction.
So, there exist values of k such that $n(i) \leq k \leq n(i+1)$ such that $d(x_{n(i)}, y_k) < \epsilon + \frac{r}{2}$. Choose the smallest integer k with $k \geq n(i)$ such that $d(x_{n(i)}, y_k) \geq \epsilon + \frac{r}{2}$. Thus, $d(x_{n(i)}, y_{k-1}) < \epsilon + \frac{r}{2}$.
Using the definition of bipolar metric space and (33), we get

$$d(x_{n(i)}, y_k) \leq d(x_{n(i)}, y_{k-1}) + d(x_k, y_{k-1}) + d(x_k, y_k)$$
$$\leq \epsilon + \frac{r}{2} + \frac{r}{8} + \frac{r}{8} = \epsilon + \frac{3}{4}r.$$

Now, we can choose a natural number k satisfying $n(i) \leq l \leq n(i+1)$ such that

$$\epsilon + \frac{r}{2} \leq d(x_{n(i)}, y_k) < \epsilon + \frac{3}{4}r. \tag{34}$$

Therefore,

$$d(x_{n(i)}, y_k) \leq \epsilon + \frac{3}{4}r < \epsilon + r, \tag{35}$$

$$d(x_{n(i)}, y_{n(i)}) \leq \frac{r}{8} < \epsilon + r, \tag{36}$$

$$d(x_{k+1}, y_k) \leq \frac{r}{8} < \epsilon + r. \tag{37}$$

Now, (35)–(37) imply that $\epsilon \leq M(x_{n(i)}, y_k) < \epsilon + r \leq \epsilon + \delta$ and so $\psi(\epsilon) \leq \psi(M(x_{n(i)}, y_k)) < \psi(\epsilon + r) \leq \psi(\epsilon + \delta) \leq \psi(\epsilon) + \psi(\delta)$.

Since T is a generalized $(\alpha - \psi)$ Meir–Keeler contractive mapping,

$$\psi(d(x_{k+1}, y_{n(i)})) \leq \alpha(x_{n(i)}, Tx_{n(i)}) \alpha(Ty_k, y_k) \psi(d(Ty_k, Tx_{n(i)})) < \psi(\epsilon).$$

This implies that

$$d(x_{k+1}, y_{n(i)}) < \epsilon. \tag{38}$$

Using the definition of bipolar metric space, we get

$$d(x_{n(i)}, y_k) \leq d(x_{n(i)}, y_{n(i)}) + d(x_{k+1}, y_{n(i)}) + d(x_{k+1}, y_k),$$

which implies that

$$d(x_{n(i)}, y_k) - d(x_{n(i)}, y_{n(i)}) - d(x_{k+1}, y_k) \leq d(x_{k+1}, y_{n(i)})$$
$$\epsilon + \frac{r}{2} - \frac{r}{8} - \frac{r}{8} < d(x_{k+1}, y_{n(i)}).$$

This shows that

$$\epsilon < d(x_{k+1}, y_{n(i)}). \tag{39}$$

This contradicts (38).

So, $\{x_n, y_n\}$ is a Cauchy bisequence. Since (X, Y, d) is a complete bipolar metric space, then $\{x_n, y_n\}$ biconverges. That is, there exists $u \in X \cap Y$ such that $\{x_n\} \to u$ and $\{y_n\} \to u$ as $n \to \infty$. As T is an orbital continuous map,

$$\{x_n\} \to u \text{ implies that } y_n = Tx_n \to Tu.$$

Combining $y_n = Tx_n \to Tu$ with $y_n \to u$, we have $Tu = u$. □

In the next theorem, we add a condition to get a unique fixed point.

Theorem 4. *If in Theorems 1–3 we add the following hypothesis (H), then we get the unique fixed point.*
(H) *If $Tx = x$ then $\alpha(x, Tx) \geq 1$.*

Proof. If possible, let us suppose that T has two distinct fixed points u and v. Then, from the hypothesis (H),
$\alpha(u, Tu), \alpha(v, Tv) \geq 1$.
 Now, by Remark 1,

$$d(u, v) = d(Tu, Tv) \leq \alpha(u, Tu)\alpha(v, Tv)d(Tu, Tv) < d(u, v)$$

which is a contradiction and so $u = v$. In a similar way, one can prove Theorems 2 and 3. □

Definition 12. Let (X, Y, d) be a bipolar metric space. Suppose $T : (X, Y) \rightrightarrows (X, Y)$ be a covariant mapping and for every $\epsilon > 0$ there exists $\delta > 0$ such that

$$\epsilon \leq d(x, y) < \epsilon + \delta \Rightarrow d(Tx, Ty) < \epsilon, \tag{40}$$

for all $(x, y) \in X \times Y$.
Then, T is said to be a covariant Meir–Keeler contractive mapping.

Remark 3. From (40), we get $d(Tx, Ty) < d(x, y)$, whenever $x \neq y$. If $x = y$ then $d(Tx, Ty) \leq d(x, y)$.

Theorem 5. Let (X, Y, d) be a complete bipolar metric space. Suppose that $T : (X, Y) \rightrightarrows (X, Y)$ is a covariant Meir–Keeler contractive mapping. Then, T has a unique fixed point.

Proof. Using Remark 3 and (40), we get

$$d(x_n, y_n) = d(Tx_{n-1}, Ty_{n-1}) \leq d(x_{n-1}, y_{n-1}) \tag{41}$$

Again, using Remark 3 and (40), we get

$$d(x_n, y_n) = d(Tx_{n-1}, Ty_{n-1}) \leq d(x_{n-1}, y_{n-1}) \tag{42}$$

From (41) and (42), it is clear that $\{d(x_n, y_n)\}$ and $\{d(x_n, y_{n+1})\}$ are monotonically decreasing sequences of positive reals and hence convergent. Let $\{d(x_n, y_n)\} \to s_1$ and $\{d(x_n, y_{n+1})\} \to s_2$ as $n \to \infty$, where $s_1, s_2 \geq 0$.
Now, we prove that $s_1 = 0$ and $s_2 = 0$.
Firstly, suppose, if possible that $s_1 > 0$.
Clearly, $d(x_n, y_n) \geq s_1 > 0$ for all $n \in \mathbb{N}$.
Let $\epsilon = s_1$. Then, by hypothesis, there exists $\delta > 0$ and $n_0 \in \mathbb{N}$ such that

$$\epsilon \leq d(x_{n_0}, y_{n_0}) < \epsilon + \delta. \tag{43}$$

From (40), we have

$$\begin{aligned} d(x_{n_0+1}, y_{n_0+1}) &\leq d(x_{n_0+1}, y_{n_0+1}), \\ &= d(Tx_{n_0}, Ty_{n_0}) < \epsilon = s_1. \end{aligned}$$

a contradiction. So $s_1 = 0$.
Similarly, one can prove easily that $s_2 = 0$.
Hence,

$$d(x_n, y_n) \to 0 \text{ and } d(x_n, y_{n+1}) \to 0 \text{ as } n \to \infty. \tag{44}$$

For given $\epsilon > 0$, by the hypothesis, there exists $\delta > 0$ such that (40) holds. Without loss of generality, let us assume that $\delta < \epsilon$.
Since $d(x_n, y_n) \to 0$ and $d(x_n, y_{n+1}) \to 0$, then there exists $N_1, N_2 \in \mathbb{N}$ such that

$$d(x_{n-1}, y_{n-1}) < \frac{\delta}{3} \text{ for all } n \geq N_1, \tag{45}$$

$$d(x_{n-1}, y_n) < \frac{\delta}{3} \text{ for all } n \geq N_2. \tag{46}$$

Now, we shall prove that

$$d(x_n, y_{n+l}) < \epsilon \tag{47}$$

and

$$d(x_{n+l}, y_n) < \epsilon, \text{ for all } n \geq N. \tag{48}$$

where $N = \max\{N_1, N_2\}$.

Firstly, using mathematical induction, we prove (47), that is $d(x_n, y_{n+l}) < \epsilon$.
From (44), the inequality clearly holds for $l = 1$.
Suppose that it is true for some $l = k$, that is

$$d(x_n, y_{n+k}) < \epsilon, \text{ for all } n \geq N. \tag{49}$$

Now, by using the definition of bipolar metric space, (45), (46) and (49), we get

$$\begin{aligned} d(x_{n-1}, y_{n+k}) &\leq d(x_{n-1}, y_n) + d(x_n, y_n) + d(x_n, y_{n+k}) \\ &\leq d(x_{n-1}, y_n) + d(x_n, y_n) + d(x_n, y_{n+k}) \\ &< \frac{\delta}{3} + \frac{\delta}{3} + \epsilon = \frac{2\delta}{3} + \epsilon < \epsilon + \delta. \end{aligned} \tag{50}$$

If $d(x_{n-1}, y_{n+k}) \geq \epsilon$, then by (40), we have

$$d(x_n, y_{n+k+1}) < \epsilon.$$

Hence, (47) holds.
If $d(x_{n+k}, y_{n-1}) \leq \epsilon$, then by Remark 3, we have

$$d(x_{n+k+1}, y_n) < d(x_{n+k}, y_{n-1}) < \epsilon$$

So, Equation (47) holds for $l = k + 1$.
Hence,

$$d(x_n, y_m) < \epsilon \text{ for all } n > m \geq N. \tag{51}$$

Similarly, one can prove Equation (48), from which we conclude that

$$d(x_n, y_m) < \epsilon \text{ for all } m > n \geq N. \tag{52}$$

From (51) and (52), we can say that $\{x_n, y_n\}$ is a Cauchy bisequence. Since (X, Y, d) is a complete bipolar metric space, then $\{x_n, y_n\}$ biconverges. That is, there exists $u \in X \cap Y$ such that $\{x_n\} \to u$ and $\{y_n\} \to u$ as $n \to \infty$. Since, T is continuous,

$$\{x_n\} \to u \text{ implies that } x_{n+1} = Tx_n \to Tu,$$

We get $Tu = u$.

Uniqueness: If possible, suppose that u and v are two different fixed points of T. Then, by Remark 3,

$$d(u, v) = d(Tu, Tv) < d(u, v),$$

which holds only when $u = v$. □

Example 1. Let $X = (-\infty, 0]$, $Y = [0, \infty)$ and $d : (-\infty, 0] \times [0, \infty) \to [0, \infty)$ as $d(x, y) = |x - y|$. Then, (X, Y, d) is a complete bipolar metric space. Define $T : (-\infty, 0] \cup [0, \infty) \rightleftarrows (-\infty, 0] \cup [0, \infty)$ by $Tx = \frac{-x}{3}$, for all $x \in (-\infty, 0] \cup [0, \infty)$, and $\psi(t) = \frac{t}{2}$, $\alpha(x, y) = 1$ for all $(x, y) \in X \times Y$. $T((-\infty, 0]) \subset [0, \infty)$ and $T([0, \infty)) \subset (-\infty, 0]$. It is clear that T is a continuous contravariant mapping.

As $x \in (-\infty, 0]$, there exists $a \in [0, \infty)$ such that $x = -a$. Now,

$$\psi(d(x, y)) = \psi(|x - y|) = \psi(|-a - y|) = \psi(a + y) = \frac{a + y}{2},$$

$$\psi(d(Ty, Tx)) = \psi(d(\frac{-y}{3}, \frac{-x}{3})) = \psi(|\frac{-y}{3} + (\frac{-x}{3})|) = \frac{a + y}{6}.$$

Clearly, by taking $\delta = 2\epsilon$, (5) is satisfied. So, all the conditions of Theorem 1 hold and T has a fixed point. Clearly, 0 is the fixed point of T.

4. Consequences

The following are the consequences of our main results.

Corollary 1. *Let (X, Y, d) be a bipolar metric space and $\psi \in \Psi$. Suppose $T : (X, Y) \rightleftarrows (X, Y)$ be a contravariant mapping and if for every $\epsilon > 0$ there exists $\delta > 0$ such that*

$$\epsilon \leq \psi(d(x,y)) < \epsilon + \delta \Rightarrow \psi(d(Ty, Tx)) < \frac{\epsilon}{L}. \tag{53}$$

where $\psi \in \Psi$ and $L \geq 1$. Then, T has a fixed point.

Proof. Taking $\alpha(x, y) = \sqrt{L}$ in Theorem 1, one can obtain the proof. □

Corollary 2. *Let (X, Y, d) be a bipolar metric space and $\psi \in \Psi$. Suppose $T : (X, Y) \rightleftarrows (X, Y)$ be a contravariant mapping and if for every $\epsilon > 0$ there exists $\delta > 0$ such that*

$$\epsilon \leq M(d(x,y)) < \epsilon + \delta \Rightarrow \psi(d(Ty, Tx)) < \frac{\epsilon}{L}. \tag{54}$$

where $\psi \in \Psi$ and $L \geq 1$. Then, T has a fixed point.

Proof. Taking $\alpha(x, y) = \sqrt{L}$ in Theorem 3, one can obtain the proof. □

5. Application

Theorem 6. *Let us consider the following integral equation*

$$\mathfrak{w}(\beta) = \mathfrak{m}(\beta) + \lambda_1 \int \mathfrak{P}_1(\beta, \xi, \mathfrak{w}(\xi)) d\xi + \lambda_2 \int \mathfrak{P}_2(\beta, \xi, \mathfrak{w}(\xi)) d\xi \tag{55}$$

$\beta \in F_1 \cup F_2$, $F_1 \cup F_2$ is a Lebesgue measurable set with finite measure and λ_1, λ_2 are constants.
Suppose that $\mathfrak{P}_1 : F_1^2 \cup F_2^2 \times [0, \infty) \to [0, \infty)$ and $\mathfrak{P}_2 : F_1^2 \cup F_2^2 \times [0, \infty) \to [0, \infty)$.
There is a continuous function $\zeta : F_1^2 \cup F_2^2 \to [0, \infty)$ and $k \in (0, 1)$ such that for all $(\beta, \xi) \in F_1^2 \cup F_2^2$ and $\mathfrak{m}(\beta) \in L^\infty(F_1) \cup L^\infty(F_2)$

$$|\lambda_i(\mathfrak{P}_i(\beta, \xi, \mathfrak{w}(\xi))) - \lambda_i(\mathfrak{P}_i(\beta, \xi, \mathfrak{y}(\xi)))| \leq \frac{k}{4} \zeta(\beta, \xi) |\mathfrak{w}(\xi) - \mathfrak{y}(\xi)|$$

for all $i = 1, 2$ and $||\int \zeta(\beta, \xi) d\xi|| \leq 1$ that is $\sup_{\beta \in F_1 \cup F_2} \int |\zeta(\beta, \xi) d\xi| \leq 1$.
Then, (55) has a unique solution in $L^\infty(F_1) \cup L^\infty(F_2)$.

Proof. Let $X = L^\infty(F_1)$ and $Y = L^\infty(F_2)$ be two normed linear spaces, where F_1 and F_2 are two Lebesgue measurable sets with $m(F_1 \cup F_2) < \infty$.

Consider $d : X \times Y \to [0, \infty)$ as $d(x, y) = ||x - y||_\infty$. (X, Y, d) is a complete bipolar metric space. Define a covariant mapping as $T(\mathfrak{w}(\beta)) = \mathfrak{m}(\beta) + \lambda_1 \int \mathfrak{P}_1(\beta, \xi, \mathfrak{w}(\xi)) d\xi + \lambda_2 \int \mathfrak{P}_2(\beta, \xi, \mathfrak{w}(\xi)) d\xi$.

Now, for any $\epsilon > 0$, there exists $\delta > 0$ such that $\epsilon \leq d(\mathfrak{w}(\xi), \mathfrak{y}(\xi)) < \epsilon + \delta$.

$$\begin{aligned}
d(T\mathfrak{w}(\xi), T\mathfrak{y}(\xi)) &= ||T\mathfrak{w}(\xi) - T\mathfrak{y}(\xi)|| \\
&= ||\mathfrak{m}(\xi) + \lambda_1 \int \mathfrak{P}_1(\beta, \xi, \mathfrak{w}(\xi))d\xi + \lambda_2 \int \mathfrak{P}_2(\beta, \xi, \mathfrak{w}(\xi))d\xi \\
&\quad - \mathfrak{m}(\xi) - \lambda_1 \int \mathfrak{P}_1(\beta, \xi, \mathfrak{y}(\xi))d\xi - \lambda_2 \int \mathfrak{P}_2(\beta, \xi, \mathfrak{y}(\xi))d\xi|| \\
&\leq \frac{1}{2}\zeta(\beta, \xi)|\mathfrak{w}(\xi) - \mathfrak{y}(\xi)| \\
&\leq \frac{1}{2}d(\mathfrak{w}(\xi), \mathfrak{y}(\xi)) \\
&< \frac{1}{2}(\epsilon + \delta) \\
&< \epsilon.
\end{aligned}$$

Hence, all the conditions of Theorem 5 are satisfied. So, T has a unique fixed point, and (55) has a unique solution. □

Example 2. *Consider the following integral equation:*

$$\mathfrak{w}(\beta) = 0.01\beta + 0.2 \int_0^\beta \left(\frac{\xi}{4} - 0.2\beta\right) \mathfrak{w}(\beta) \, d\xi + \sin(0.1)\left(\int_0^\beta \left(-\beta + \frac{\xi}{3} + 1\right) \mathfrak{w}(\beta) \, d\xi\right).$$

It can be verified that the solution of the above integral equation is given by

$$\mathfrak{w}(\beta) = \frac{0.01\beta}{0.0982\beta^2 - 0.0998\beta + 1}.$$

This solution is depicted in Figure 1.

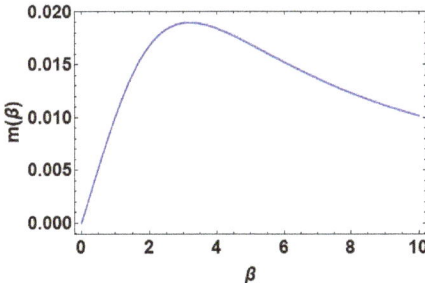

Figure 1. Solution of the integral equation in the example of Section 5.

6. Conclusions

In this paper, we have introduced a new notion of α-orbital admissible mappings, and using this we have defined $(\alpha - \psi)$ Meir–Keeler Contractive mappings and established fixed point results. Our results have generalized some proven results in the past. The derived results have been supported with non-trivial examples. The results have been applied to find analytical solutions of integral equation. It is an open problem to extend/generalize our results in the setting of other topological spaces such as bipolar controlled metric space, neutrosophic metric spaces, etc.

Author Contributions: Investigation: M.K., P.K. and R.R.; Methodology: R.R. and M.K.; Project administration: R.R. and S.R.; Software: A.E., O.A.A.A. and P.K.; Supervision: R.R. and S.R.; Writing—original draft: M.K., R.R. and A.E.; Writing—review and editing: R.R., M.K., P.K., O.A.A.A., A.E. and S.R. All authors have read and agreed to the published version of the manuscript.

Funding: This study is supported via funding from Prince sattam bin Abdulaziz University project number (PSAU/2023/R/1444).

Data Availability Statement: Not applicable.

Acknowledgments: This study is supported via funding from Prince sattam bin Abdulaziz University project number (PSAU/2023/R/1444). The authors convey sincere thanks to anonymous reviewers for their valuable comments, which helped in bringing the manuscript to its present form.

Conflicts of Interest: The authors declare no conflict of interest.

References

1. Banach, S. Sur les operations dans les ensembles abstraits et leur application aux equations integrals. *Fundam. Math.* **1922**, *3*, 133–181. [CrossRef]
2. Bakhtin, I.A. The contraction mapping principle in quasimetric spaces. *Funct. Anal.* **1989**, *30*, 26–37.
3. Matthews, S.G. Partial metric topology. *Ann. N. Y. Acad. Sci.* **1994**, *728*, 183–197. [CrossRef]
4. Mustafa, Z.; Sims, B. A new approach to generalized metric spaces. *J. Nonlinear Convex Anal.* **2006**, *7*, 289–297.
5. Chatterjea, S.K. Fixed point theorems. *C.R. Acad. Bulgare Sci.* **1972**, *25*, 727–730. [CrossRef]
6. Hardy, G.C.; Rogers, T. A generalization of fixed point theorem of S.Riech. *Can. Math. Bull.* **1973**, *16*, 201–206. [CrossRef]
7. Jaggi, D.S. Some unique fixed point theorems. *Indian J. Pure Appl. Math.* **1977**, *8*, 223–230.
8. Karapinar, E. A note on common fixed point theorems in partial metric spaces. *Miskolc Math. Notes* **2011**, *12*, 185–191. [CrossRef]
9. Karapinar, E.; Erhan, I.M. Fixed point theorems for operators on partial metric spaces. *Appl. Math. Lett.* **2011**, *24*, 1894–1899. [CrossRef]
10. Karapinar, E. Fixed point theorems for cyclic weak ϕ-contraction. *Appl. Math. Lett.* **2011**, *24*, 822–825. [CrossRef]
11. Karapinar, E. Fixed point theorems in cone Banach spaces. *Fixed Point Theory Appl.* **2009**, *2009*, 609281. [CrossRef]
12. Karapinar, E. Some non unique fixed point theorems of Ciric type on cone metric spaces. In *Abstract and Applied Analysis*; Hindawi: London, UK, 2010; p. 123094.
13. Karapinar, E. Weak ϕ-contractions on partial metric spaces. *J. Comput. Anal. Appl.* **2012**, *14*, 206–210.
14. Kirk, W.A.; Srinavasan, P.S.; Veeramani, P. Fixed points for mappings satisfying cyclical contractive conditions. *Fixed Point Appl.* **2003**, *4*, 79–89.
15. Samet, B.; Vetro, C.; Vetro, P. Fixed ppoint theorems for $(\alpha - \psi)$ contractive types mappings. *Nonlinear Anal.* **2012**, *75*, 2154–2165. [CrossRef]
16. Karapinar, E.; Kumam, P.; Salimi, P. On α-ψ-Meir-Keeler contractive mappings. *Fixed Point Theory Appl.* **2013**, *2013*, 94. [CrossRef]
17. Popescu, O. Some new fixed point theorems for α-Geraghty contraction type maps in metric spaces. *Fixed Point Theory Appl.* **2014**, *2014*, 190. [CrossRef]
18. Mutlu, A.; Gurdal, U. Bipolar metric spaces and some fixed point theorems. *J. Nonlinear Sci. Appl.* **2016**, *9*, 5362–5373. [CrossRef]
19. Murthy, P.P.; Mitrovic, Z.; Dhuri, C.P.; Radenovic, S. The common fixed point theorems in bipolar metric space. *Gulf J. Math.* **2022**, *12*, 31–38. [CrossRef]
20. Mutlu, A.; Gurdal, U.; Ozkan, K. Fixed point results for $\alpha - \psi$-contractive mappings in bipolar metric space. *J. Inequalities Spec. Funct.* **2020**, *11*, 64–75.
21. Mutlu, A.; Gurdal, U.; Ozkan, K. Fixed point theorems for multivalued mappings on bipolar metric spaces. *Fixed Point Theory* **2020**, *21*, 271–280. [CrossRef]
22. Ramaswamy, R.; Mani, G.; Gnanaprakasam, A.J.; Abdelnaby, O.A.A.; Stojiljković, V.; Radojevic, S.; Radenovic, S. Fixed Points on Covariant and Contravariant Maps with an Application. *Mathematics* **2022**, *10*, 4385. [CrossRef]
23. Mani, G.; Ramaswamy, R.; Gnanaprakasam, A.J.; Stojiljkovic, V.; Fadail, Z.M.; Radenović, S. Application of fixed point results in the setting of F-contraction and simulation function in the setting of bipolar metric space. *AIMS Math.* **2023**, *8*, 3269–3285. [CrossRef]
24. Murthy, P.P.; Dhuri, C.P.; Kumar, S.; Ramaswamy, R.; Alaskar, M.A.S.; Radenovic, S. Common Fixed Point for Meir-Keeler Type Contraction in Bipolar Metric Space. *Fractal Fract.* **2022**, *6*, 649. [CrossRef]

Disclaimer/Publisher's Note: The statements, opinions and data contained in all publications are solely those of the individual author(s) and contributor(s) and not of MDPI and/or the editor(s). MDPI and/or the editor(s) disclaim responsibility for any injury to people or property resulting from any ideas, methods, instructions or products referred to in the content.

Article

The Study of Bicomplex-Valued Controlled Metric Spaces with Applications to Fractional Differential Equations

Gunaseelan Mani [1], Salma Haque [2], Arul Joseph Gnanaprakasam [3], Ozgur Ege [4] and Nabil Mlaiki [2,*]

[1] Department of Mathematics, Saveetha School of Engineering, Saveetha Institute of Medical and Technical Sciences, Chennai 602105, Tamil Nadu, India; mathsguna@yahoo.com
[2] Department of Mathematics and Sciences, Prince Sultan University, Riyadh 11586, Saudi Arabia; shaque@psu.edu.sa
[3] Department of Mathematics, Faculty of Engineering and Technology, SRM Institute of Science and Technology, SRM Nagar, Kattankulathur 603203, Tamil Nadu, India; aruljoseph.alex@gmail.com
[4] Department of Mathematics, Ege University, Bornova, 35100 Izmir, Turkey; ozgur.ege@ege.edu.tr
* Correspondence: nmlaiki2012@gmail.com

Abstract: In this paper, we introduce the concept of bicomplex-valued controlled metric spaces and prove fixed point theorems. Our results mainly focus on generalizing and expanding some recently established results. Finally, we explain an application of our main result to a certain type of fractional differential equation.

Keywords: controlled-type metric spaces; bicomplex-valued controlled metric spaces; integral equation; fixed point

MSC: 47H09; 47H10; 30G35; 46N99; 54H25

Citation: Mani, G.; Haque, S.; Gnanaprakasam, A.J.; Ege, O.; Mlaiki, N. The Study of Bicomplex-Valued Controlled Metric Spaces with Applications to Fractional Differential Equations. *Mathematics* 2023, 11, 2742. https://doi.org/10.3390/math11122742

Academic Editor: Timilehin Opeyemi Alakoya

Received: 8 May 2023
Revised: 12 June 2023
Accepted: 13 June 2023
Published: 16 June 2023

Copyright: © 2023 by the authors. Licensee MDPI, Basel, Switzerland. This article is an open access article distributed under the terms and conditions of the Creative Commons Attribution (CC BY) license (https://creativecommons.org/licenses/by/4.0/).

1. Introduction

Fixed point theory is an important branch of non-linear analysis. After the celebrated Banach contraction principle [1], a number of authors have been working in this area of research. Fixed point theorems (FPTs) are important instruments for proving the existence and uniqueness of solutions to variational inequalities. Metric FPTs expanded after the well-known Banach contraction theorem was established. From this point forward, there have been numerous results related to maps fulfilling various contractive conditions and many types of metric spaces (see, for example, [2–9]).

The authors of [10,11] presented a novel extension of the b-metric space known as controlled metric spaces (CMSs) and demonstrated the FPTs on the CMSs, providing an example by employing a control function $\aleph(x,y)$ in the triangle inequality.

Serge [12] made a pioneering attempt at developing special algebra. He conceptualized commutative generalizations of complex numbers as briefly bicomplex numbers (BCN), briefly tricomplex numbers (tcn), etc., as elements of an infinite set of algebra. Subsequently, many researchers contributed in this area, (see, for example, [13–19]).

In 2021, the authors of [20] proved a common fixed point for a pair of contractive-type maps in bicomplex-valued metric spaces. Later, several authors discussed their results using this concept, see [21–24]. Guechi [25] introduced the concept of optimal control of ϕ-Hilfer fractional equations and proved the fixed point results. For details, see [26–28] and the references therein.

In this paper, we introduce the notion of bicomplex-valued CMSs (BVCMSs) and prove FPT under Banach, Kannan and Fisher contractions on BVCMSs. Then, we give an application to solve a fractional differential equation (FDE) and show that this extension is different from bicomplex-valued metric spaces in terms of Beg, Kumar Datta and Pal [20].

2. Preliminaries

We use standard notations throughout this paper: The real, complex, and bicomplex number sets are represented by $\mathbb{C}_0$, $\mathbb{C}_1$ and $\mathbb{C}_2$, respectively. The following complex numbers were described by Segre [12].

$$z = \vartheta_1 + \vartheta_2 i_1,$$

where $\vartheta_1, \vartheta_2 \in \mathbb{C}_0$, $i_1^2 = -1$. We represent $\mathbb{C}_1$ as:

$$\mathbb{C}_1 = \{z : z = \vartheta_1 + \vartheta_2 i_1, \vartheta_1, \vartheta_2 \in \mathbb{C}_0\}.$$

Let $z \in \mathbb{C}_1$, then $|z| = (\vartheta_1^2 + \vartheta_2^2)^{\frac{1}{2}}$. Every element in $\mathbb{C}_1$ with a positive real-valued norm function $\|.\| : \mathbb{C}_1 \to \mathbb{C}_0^+$ is defined by

$$\|z\| = (\vartheta_1^2 + \vartheta_2^2)^{\frac{1}{2}}.$$

Segre [12] described the bicomplex number (BCN) as:

$$f = \vartheta_1 + \vartheta_2 i_1 + \vartheta_3 i_2 + \vartheta_4 i_1 i_2,$$

where $\vartheta_1, \vartheta_2, \vartheta_3, \vartheta_4 \in \mathbb{C}_0$, and the independent units i_1, i_2 satisfy $i_1^2 = i_2^2 = -1$ and $i_1 i_2 = i_2 i_1$. We represent the BCN set $\mathbb{C}_2$ as:

$$\mathbb{C}_2 = \{f : f = \vartheta_1 + \vartheta_2 i_1 + \vartheta_3 i_2 + \vartheta_4 i_1 i_2, \vartheta_1, \vartheta_2, \vartheta_3, \vartheta_4 \in \mathbb{C}_0\},$$

that is,

$$\mathbb{C}_2 = \{f : f = z_1 + i_2 z_2, z_1, z_2 \in \mathbb{C}_1\},$$

where $z_1 = \vartheta_1 + \vartheta_2 i_1 \in \mathbb{C}_1$ and $z_2 = \vartheta_3 + \vartheta_4 i_1 \in \mathbb{C}_1$. If $f = z_1 + i_2 z_2$ and $\nu = w_1 + i_2 w_2$ are any two BCNs, then their sum is

$$f \pm \nu = (z_1 + i_2 z_2) \pm (w_1 + i_2 w_2)$$
$$= z_1 \pm w_1 + i_2 (z_2 \pm w_2), \text{ and the product is}$$
$$f.\nu = (z_1 + i_2 z_2)(w_1 + i_2 w_2)$$
$$= (z_1 w_1 - z_2 w_2) + i_2 (z_1 w_2 + z_2 w_1).$$

There are four idempotent elements in $\mathbb{C}_2$. They are $0, 1, e_1 = \frac{1+i_1 i_2}{2}, e_2 = \frac{1-i_1 i_2}{2}$ of which e_1 and e_2 are non-trivial, such that $e_1 + e_2 = 1$ and $e_1 e_2 = 0$. Every BCN $z_1 + i_2 z_2$ can be uniquely expressed as a combination of e_1 and e_2, namely,

$$f = z_1 + i_2 z_2 = (z_1 - i_1 z_2) e_1 + (z_1 + i_1 z_2) e_2.$$

This representation of f is known as the idempotent representation of a BCN, and the complex coefficients $f_1 = (z_1 - i_1 z_2)$ and $f_2 = (z_1 + i_1 z_2)$ are known as the idempotent components of the BCN f.

Each element in $\mathbb{C}_2$ with a positive real-valued norm function $\|.\| : \mathbb{C}_2 \to \mathbb{C}_0^+$ is defined by

$$\|f\| = \|z_1 + i_2 z_2\| = \{\|z_1\|^2 + \|z_2\|^2\}^{\frac{1}{2}}$$
$$= \left[\frac{|z_1 - i_1 z_2|^2 + |z_1 + i_1 z_2|^2}{2}\right]^{\frac{1}{2}}$$
$$= (\vartheta_1^2 + \vartheta_2^2 + \vartheta_3^2 + \vartheta_4^2)^{\frac{1}{2}},$$

where $f = \vartheta_1 + \vartheta_2 i_1 + \vartheta_3 i_2 + \vartheta_4 i_1 i_2 = z_1 + i_2 z_2 \in \mathbb{C}_2$.

The linear space $\mathbb{C}_2$ with respect to a defined norm is a normed linear space, and $\mathbb{C}_2$ is complete. Therefore, $\mathbb{C}_2$ is a Banach space. If $f, v \in \mathbb{C}_2$, then $\|fv\| \leq \sqrt{2}\|f\|\|v\|$ holds instead of $\|fv\| \leq \|f\|\|v\|$, and therefore $\mathbb{C}_2$ is not a Banach algebra. For any two BCN $f, v \in \mathbb{C}_2$, then

1. $f \preceq_{i_2} v \iff \|f\| \leq \|v\|$;
2. $\|f + v\| \leq \|f\| + \|v\|$;
3. $\|\vartheta f\| = |\vartheta|\|f\|$, where ϑ is in $\mathbb{C}_0$;
4. $\|fv\| \leq \sqrt{2}\|f\|\|v\|$, and $\|fv\| = \sqrt{2}\|f\|\|v\|$ holds when only one of f or v is degenerated;
5. $\|f^{-1}\| = \|f\|^{-1}$, if f is degenerated with $f \succ 0$;
6. $\left\|\frac{f}{v}\right\| = \frac{\|f\|}{\|v\|}$, if v is a degenerated BCN.

The relation $\preceq_{i_2}$ (partial order) is defined on $\mathbb{C}_2$ as given below. Let $\mathbb{C}_2$ be a set of BCNs and $f = z_1 + i_2 z_2$ and $v = \omega_1 + i_2 \omega_2 \in \mathbb{C}_2$. Then, $f \preceq_{i_2} v$ if and only if $z_1 \preceq_{i_2} \omega_1$ and $z_2 \preceq_{i_2} \omega_2$, i.e., $f \preceq_{i_2} v$, if one of the following conditions is fulfilled:

1. $z_1 = \omega_1, z_2 = \omega_2$;
2. $z_1 \prec_{i_2} \omega_1, z_2 = \omega_2$;
3. $z_1 = \omega_1, z_2 \prec_{i_2} \omega_2$;
4. $z_1 \prec_{i_2} \omega_1, z_2 \prec_{i_2} \omega_2$.

Clearly, we can write $f \precnsim_{i_2} v$ iff $f \preceq_{i_2} v$ and $f \neq v$, i.e., if 2, 3 or 4 are satisfied, and we will write $f \prec_{i_2} v$ if only 4 is satisfied.

Definition 1 ([10]). *Let $\zeta \neq \emptyset$ and $\varphi \colon \zeta \times \zeta \to [1, \infty)$. The functional $\pounds_{cm} \colon \zeta \times \zeta \to [0, \infty)$ is called the briefly controlled-type metric CMT if*

(CMT_1) $\pounds_{cm}(\aleph, i) = 0 \iff \aleph = i$,
(CMT_2) $\pounds_{cm}(\aleph, i) = \pounds_{cm}(i, \aleph)$,
(CMT_3) $\pounds_{cm}(\aleph, \flat) \leq \varphi(\aleph, i)\pounds_{cm}(\aleph, i) + \varphi(i, \flat)\pounds_{cm}(i, \flat)$,

for all $\aleph, i, \flat \in \zeta$. Then, the doublet $(\zeta, \pounds_{cm})$ is called a CMT space.

Several researchers have proven FPTs using this notion (see [3,4,6,11]).

Definition 2. *Let $\zeta \neq \emptyset$ and consider $\varphi \colon \zeta \times \zeta \to [1, \infty)$. The functional $\pounds_{bvcms} \colon \zeta \times \zeta \to \mathbb{C}_2$ is said to be a BVCMS if*

$(BCCMS_1)$ $0 \preceq_{i_2} \pounds_{bvcms}(\aleph, i)$ also $\pounds_{bvcms}(\aleph, i) = 0 \iff \aleph = i$,
$(BCCMS_2)$ $\pounds_{bvcms}(\aleph, i) = \pounds_{bvcms}(i, \aleph)$,
$(BCCMS_3)$ $\pounds_{bvcms}(\aleph, \flat) \preceq_{i_2} \varphi(\aleph, i)\pounds_{bvcms}(\aleph, i) + \varphi(i, \flat)\pounds_{bvcms}(i, \flat)$,

for all $\aleph, i, \flat \in \zeta$, Then, the pair $(\zeta, \pounds_{bvcms})$ is known as a BVCMS.

Example 1. *Let $\zeta = [0, \infty)$ and $\varphi \colon \zeta \times \zeta \to [1, \infty)$ be defined as*

$$\varphi(\aleph, i) = \begin{cases} 1, & \text{if } \aleph, i \in [0, 1], \\ 1 + \aleph + i, & \text{otherwise.} \end{cases}$$

and $\pounds_{bvcms} \colon \zeta \times \zeta \to [0, \infty)$ be defined as follows

$$\pounds_{bvcms}(\aleph, i) := \begin{cases} 0, & \aleph = i \\ i_2, & \aleph \neq i \end{cases}$$

Then $(\zeta, \pounds_{bvcms})$ is a bvcms.

Remark 1. *If we take $\varphi(\aleph, i) = t \geq 1$, for all $\aleph, i \in \zeta$, then $(\zeta, \pounds_{bvcms})$ is a bicomplex-valued b-metric space, that is, every bicomplex-valued b-metric space is a BVCMS.*

Example 2. Let $\zeta = \mathcal{V} \cup \mathcal{W}$ with $\mathcal{V} = \{(\frac{1}{v})|v \in \mathbb{N}\}$, $\mathcal{W}$ is the set of all positive integers and $\varphi: \zeta \times \zeta \to [1, \infty)$ is defined for all $\aleph, i \in \zeta$ as

$$\varphi(\aleph, i) = 5\mathfrak{p}$$

where $\mathfrak{p} > 0$ and $\mathcal{L}_{bvcms}: \zeta \times \zeta \to \mathbb{C}_2$ defined as follows

$$\mathcal{L}_{bvcms}(\aleph, i) := \begin{cases} 0, & iff \ \aleph = i \\ 2\mathfrak{p} i_2, & if \ \aleph, i \in \mathcal{V} \\ \frac{\mathfrak{p} i_2}{2}, & otherwise \end{cases}$$

where $\mathfrak{p} > 0$.

Now, the conditions $(BCCMS_1)$ and $(BCCMS_2)$ hold. Furthermore, $(BCCMS_3)$ holds under the following cases.

Case 1. If $\aleph = i$ and $i = \flat$;
Case 2. If $\aleph = i \neq \flat$ or if $\aleph \neq i = \flat$ or if $\aleph = \flat \neq i$ or if $\aleph \neq i \neq \flat$;

    SubCase 1. If $\aleph \in \mathcal{V}$ and $i, \flat \in \mathcal{W}$;
    SubCase 2. If $i \in \mathcal{V}$ and $\aleph, \flat \in \mathcal{W}$;
    SubCase 3. If $\flat \in \mathcal{V}$ and $\aleph, i \in \mathcal{W}$;
    SubCase 4. If $\aleph, i \in \mathcal{V}$ and $\flat \in \mathcal{W}$;
    SubCase 5. If $\aleph, \flat \in \mathcal{V}$ and $i \in \mathcal{W}$;
    SubCase 6. If $i, \flat \in \mathcal{V}$ and $\aleph \in \mathcal{W}$;
    SubCase 7. If $\aleph, i, \flat \in \mathcal{V}$;
    SubCase 8. If $\aleph, i, \flat \in \mathcal{W}$.

Then $(\zeta, \mathcal{L}_{bvcms})$ is a BVCMS.

Remark 2. If $\varphi(\aleph, i) = \varphi(i, \flat)$ (as in the above example) for all $\aleph, i, \flat \in \zeta$, then $(\zeta, \mathcal{L}_{bvcms})$ is a bicomplex-valued extended b-metric space. We can conclude that every bicomplex-valued extended b-metric space is a BVCMS. However, the converse may not true in general.

Example 3. Let $\zeta = \{1, 2, 3\}$ and $\mathcal{L}_{bvcms}: \zeta \times \zeta \to \mathbb{C}_2$ be defined as

$$\mathcal{L}_{bvcms}(1,1) = \mathcal{L}_{bvcms}(2,2) = \mathcal{L}_{bvcms}(3,3) = 0,$$

$$\mathcal{L}_{bvcms}(2,1) = \mathcal{L}_{bvcms}(1,2) = 4 + 4i_2,$$
$$\mathcal{L}_{bvcms}(3,2) = \mathcal{L}_{bvcms}(2,3) = 1 + 2i_2,$$
$$\mathcal{L}_{bvcms}(3,1) = \mathcal{L}_{bvcms}(1,3) = 1 - i_2,$$

and $\varphi: \zeta \times \zeta \to [1, \infty)$ be defined as

$$\varphi(1,1) = \varphi(2,2) = \varphi(3,3) = 3,$$

$$\varphi(1,2) = \varphi(2,1) = 2,$$
$$\varphi(2,3) = \varphi(3,2) = 4,$$
$$\varphi(1,3) = \varphi(3,1) = 1.$$

Clearly, the conditions $(BCCMS_1)$ and $(BCCMS_2)$ hold. Now,
Case 1. If $\aleph = \flat$ the condition $(BCCMS_3)$ holds.

Case 2. If $\aleph = 1$ and $\flat = 3$ (same as $\flat = 1$ and $\aleph = 3$) and $\mathfrak{i} = 2$

$$\begin{aligned}
\pounds_{bvcms}(\aleph, \flat) = |\pounds_{bvcms}(1,3)| = |1 - i_2| &\precsim_{i_2} |12 + 16i_2| \\
&= |2(4 + 4i_2) + 4(1 + 2i_2)| \\
&\precsim_{i_2} 2|(4 + 4i_2)| + 4|(1 + 2i_2)| \\
&= \varphi(1,2)\pounds_{bvcms}(1,2) + \varphi(2,3)\pounds_{bvcms}(2,3) \\
&= \varphi(\aleph, \mathfrak{i})\pounds_{bvcms}(\aleph, \mathfrak{i}) + \varphi(\mathfrak{i}, \flat)\pounds_{bvcms}(\mathfrak{i}, \flat).
\end{aligned}$$

Case 3. If $\aleph = 1$ and $\flat = 2$ (same as $\flat = 1$ and $\aleph = 2$) and $\mathfrak{i} = 3$

$$\begin{aligned}
\pounds_{bvcms}(\aleph, \flat) = |\pounds_{bvcms}(1,2)| = |4 + 4i_2| &\precsim_{i_2} |5 + 7i_2| \\
&= |1(1 - i_2) + 4(1 + 2i_2)| \\
&\precsim_{i_2} 1|(1 - i_2)| + 4|(1 + 2i_2)| \\
&= \varphi(1,3)\pounds_{bvcms}(1,3) + \varphi(3,2)\pounds_{bvcms}(3,2) \\
&= \varphi(\aleph, \mathfrak{i})\pounds_{bvcms}(\aleph, \mathfrak{i}) + \varphi(\mathfrak{i}, \flat)\pounds_{bvcms}(\mathfrak{i}, \flat).
\end{aligned}$$

Case 4. If $\aleph = 2$ and $\flat = 3$ (same as $\flat = 3$ and $\aleph = 2$) and $\mathfrak{i} = 1$

$$\begin{aligned}
\pounds_{bvcms}(\aleph, \flat) = |\pounds_{bvcms}(2,3)| = |1 + 2i_2| &\precsim_{i_2} |9 + 7i_2| \\
&= |2(4 + 4i_2) + 1(1 - i_2)| \\
&\precsim_{i_2} 2|(4 + 4i_2)| + 1|(1 - i_2)| \\
&= \varphi(2,1)\pounds_{bvcms}(2,1) + \varphi(1,3)\pounds_{bvcms}(1,3) \\
&= \varphi(\aleph, \mathfrak{i})\pounds_{bvcms}(\aleph, \mathfrak{i}) + \varphi(\mathfrak{i}, \flat)\pounds_{bvcms}(\mathfrak{i}, \flat).
\end{aligned}$$

Then, $(\zeta, \pounds_{bvcms})$ is a BVCMS.

Definition 3. Let $(\zeta, \pounds_{bvcms})$ be a BVCMS with a sequence $\{\aleph_v\}$ in ζ and $\aleph \in \zeta$. Then,

(i) A sequence $\{\aleph_v\}$ in ζ is convergent to $\aleph \in \zeta$ if $\forall \, 0 \prec_{i_2} \alpha \in \mathbb{C}_2$, $\exists$ a natural number N so that $\pounds_{bvcms}(\aleph_v, \aleph) \prec_{i_2} \alpha$ for each $v \geq N$. Then, $\lim_{v \to \infty} \aleph_v = \aleph$ or $\aleph_v \to \aleph$ as $v \to \infty$.

(ii) If, for each $0 \prec_{i_2} \alpha$ where $\alpha \in \mathbb{C}_2$, $\exists$ a natural number N so that $\pounds_{bvcms}(\aleph_v, \aleph_{v+\varsigma}) \prec_{i_2} \alpha$ for each $\varsigma \in \mathbb{N}$ and $v > N$. Then, $\{\aleph_v\}$ is called a Cauchy sequence in $(\zeta, \pounds_{\alpha \varepsilon \alpha})$.

(iii) BVCMS $(\zeta, \pounds_{bvcms})$ is termed complete if every Cauchy sequence is convergent.

Lemma 1. Let $(\zeta, \pounds_{bvcms})$ be a BVCMS. Then a sequence $\{\aleph_v\}$ in ζ is a Cauchy sequence, such that $\aleph_\varsigma \neq \aleph_v$, with $\varsigma \neq v$. Then, $\{\aleph_v\}$ converges to one point at most.

Proof. Let $\aleph^*$ and $\mathfrak{i}^*$ be two limits of the sequence $\{\aleph_v\} \in \zeta$ and $\lim_{v \to \infty} \pounds_{bvcms}(\aleph_v, \aleph^*) = 0 = \pounds_{bvcms}(\aleph_v, \mathfrak{i}^*)$. Since $\{\aleph_v\}$ is a Cauchy sequence, from (BCCMS3), for $\aleph_\varsigma \neq \aleph_v$, whenever $\varsigma \neq v$, we can write

$$\begin{aligned}
\|\pounds_{bvcms}(\aleph^*, \mathfrak{i}^*)\| &\precsim_{i_2} [\varphi(\aleph^*, \aleph_v)\|\pounds_{bvcms}(\aleph^*, \aleph_v)\| \\
&+ \varphi(\aleph_v, \mathfrak{i}^*)\|\pounds_{bvcms}(\aleph_v, \mathfrak{i}^*)\|] \to 0 \quad \text{as} \quad v \to \infty.
\end{aligned}$$

We obtain $\|\pounds_{bvcms}(\aleph^*, \mathfrak{i}^*)\| = 0$, i.e., $\aleph^* = \mathfrak{i}^*$. Thus, $\{\aleph_v\}$ converges to one point at most. $\square$

Lemma 2. For a given BVCMS $(\zeta, \pounds_{bvcms})$, the tricomplex-valued controlled metric map $\pounds_{bvcms} : \zeta \times \zeta \to \mathbb{C}_2$ is continuous with respect to "$\precsim_{i_2}$".

Proof. Let $\mathfrak{s}, \mathfrak{q} \in \mathbb{C}_2$, such that $\mathfrak{s} \succ \mathfrak{q}$, then we show that the set $\pounds_{bvcms}^{-1}(\mathfrak{q}, \mathfrak{s})$ given by

$$\pounds_{bvcms}^{-1}(\mathfrak{q}, \mathfrak{s}) := \{(\aleph, \mathfrak{i}) \in \zeta \times \zeta \mid \mathfrak{q} \prec_{i_2} \pounds_{bvcms}(\aleph, \mathfrak{i}) \prec_{i_2} \mathfrak{s}\},$$

is open in the product topology on $\zeta \times \zeta$. Then, let $(\aleph, i) \in \pounds_{bvcms}^{-1}(q, s)$. We choose $\epsilon = \frac{1}{200} \min(\pounds_{bvcms}(\aleph, i) - q, s - \pounds_{bvcms}(\aleph, i))$. Then, for $(\varphi, \lambda) \in \beta(\aleph, \epsilon) \times \beta(i, \epsilon)$ we obtain

$$\pounds_{bvcms}(\varphi, \lambda) \precsim_{i_2} \pounds_{bvcms}(\lambda, \aleph) + \pounds_{bvcms}(\aleph, i) + \pounds_{bvcms}(i, \lambda)$$
$$\prec_{i_2} 2\epsilon + \pounds_{bvcms}(\aleph, i) \prec_{i_2} s$$

and

$$q \precsim_{i_2} \pounds_{bvcms}(\aleph, i) - 2\epsilon \prec_{i_2} \pounds_{bvcms}(\varphi, \lambda) + \pounds_{bvcms}(\aleph, \lambda) - \epsilon + \pounds_{bvcms}(i, \lambda) - \epsilon$$
$$\prec_{i_2} \pounds_{bvcms}(\varphi, \lambda).$$

Then, $(\aleph, i) \in \beta(\varkappa, \epsilon) \times \beta(i, \epsilon) \subseteq \pounds_{bvcms}^{-1}(q, s)$. □

Defining Fix $\eta := \{\aleph^* \in \zeta | \aleph^* = \eta(\aleph^*)\}$ will be the set of fixed points.

In this paper, we introduce the notion of BVCMS and FPT in the context of BVCMSs.

3. Main Results

Now, we prove the Banach-type contraction principle.

Theorem 1. *Let $(\zeta, \pounds_{bvcms})$ be a complete BVCMS and $\eta: \zeta \to \zeta$ a continuous map, such that*

$$\pounds_{bvcms}(\eta \aleph, \eta i) \precsim_{i_2} \mathfrak{a} \pounds_{bvcms}(\aleph, i), \tag{1}$$

for all $\aleph, i \in \zeta$, where $0 < \mathfrak{a} < 1$. For $\aleph_0 \in \zeta$, we denote $\aleph_v = \eta^v \aleph_0$. Suppose that

$$\max_{\varsigma \geq 1} \lim_{q \to \infty} \frac{\varphi(\aleph_{q+1}, \aleph_{q+2})}{\varphi(\aleph_q, \aleph_{q+1})} \varphi(\aleph_{q+1}, \aleph_\varsigma) < \frac{1}{\mathfrak{a}}, \tag{2}$$

Moreover, for every $\aleph \in \zeta$ the limits

$$\lim_{v \to \infty} \varphi(\aleph_v, \aleph) \quad \text{and} \quad \lim_{v \to \infty} \varphi(\aleph, \aleph_v) \quad \text{exists and are finite.} \tag{3}$$

Then η has a unique fixed point (UFP).

Proof. Let $\{\aleph_v = \eta^v \aleph_0\}$. By (1), we obtain

$$\pounds_{bvcms}(\aleph_v, \aleph_{v+1}) \precsim_{i_2} \mathfrak{a} \pounds_{bvcms}(\aleph_{v-1}, \aleph_v)$$
$$\precsim_{i_2}$$
$$\cdots$$
$$\precsim_{i_2} \mathfrak{a}^v \pounds_{bvcms}(\aleph_0, \aleph_1), \quad \forall v \geq 0.$$

For all $v < \varsigma$, where $v, \varsigma \in \mathbb{N}$, we have

$$\pounds_{bvcms}(\aleph_v, \aleph_\varsigma) \precsim_{i_2} \varphi(\aleph_v, \aleph_{v+1}) \pounds_{bvcms}(\aleph_v, \aleph_{v+1}) + \varphi(\aleph_{v+1}, \aleph_\varsigma) \pounds_{bvcms}(\aleph_{v+1}, \aleph_\varsigma)$$
$$\precsim_{i_2} \varphi(\aleph_v, \aleph_{v+1}) \pounds_{bvcms}(\aleph_v, \aleph_{v+1})$$
$$+ \varphi(\aleph_{v+1}, \aleph_\varsigma) \varphi(\aleph_{v+1}, \aleph_{v+2}) \pounds_{bvcms}(\aleph_{v+1}, \aleph_{v+2})$$
$$+ \varphi(\aleph_{v+1}, \aleph_\varsigma) \varphi(\aleph_{v+2}, \aleph_\varsigma) \pounds_{bvcms}(\aleph_{v+2}, \aleph_\varsigma)$$

$$\mathcal{L}_{bvcms}(\aleph_v, \aleph_\varsigma) \precsim_{i_2} \varphi(\aleph_v, \aleph_{v+1})\mathcal{L}_{bvcms}(\aleph_v, \aleph_{v+1})$$
$$+ \varphi(\aleph_{v+1}, \aleph_\varsigma \varphi(\aleph_{v+1}, \aleph_{v+2})\mathcal{L}_{bvcms}(\aleph_{v+1}, \aleph_{v+2})$$
$$+ \varphi(\aleph_{v+1}, \aleph_\varsigma \varphi(\aleph_{v+2}, \aleph_\varsigma \varphi(\aleph_{v+2}, \aleph_{v+3}))\mathcal{L}_{bvcms}(\aleph_{v+2}, \aleph_\varsigma)$$
$$+ \varphi(\aleph_{v+1}, \aleph_\varsigma \varphi(\aleph_{v+2}, \aleph_\varsigma \varphi(\aleph_{v+3}, \aleph_\varsigma)\mathcal{L}_{bvcms}(\aleph_{v+2}, \aleph_\varsigma)$$
$$\precsim_{i_2} \cdots \precsim_{i_2} \varphi(\aleph_v, \aleph_{v+1})\mathcal{L}_{bvcms}(\aleph_v, \aleph_{v+1})$$
$$+ \sum_{\iota=v+1}^{\varsigma-2} \prod_{j=v+1}^{\iota} \varphi(\aleph_j, \aleph_\varsigma \varphi(\aleph_\iota, \aleph_{\iota+1})\mathcal{L}_{bvcms}(\aleph_\iota, \aleph_{\iota+1})$$
$$+ \prod_{p=v+1}^{\varsigma-1} \varphi(\aleph_p, \aleph_\varsigma)\mathcal{L}_{bvcms}(\aleph_{\varsigma-1}, \aleph_\varsigma)$$
$$\precsim_{i_2} \varphi(\aleph_v, \aleph_{v+1})\mathfrak{a}^v \mathcal{L}_{bvcms}(\aleph_0, \aleph_1)$$
$$+ \sum_{\iota=v+1}^{\varsigma-2} \prod_{j=v+1}^{\iota} \varphi(\aleph_j, \aleph_\varsigma \varphi(\aleph_\iota, \aleph_{\iota+1})\mathfrak{a}^\iota \mathcal{L}_{bvcms}(\aleph_0, \aleph_1)$$
$$+ \prod_{p=v+1}^{\varsigma-1} \varphi(\aleph_p, \aleph_\varsigma)\mathfrak{a}^{\varsigma-1} \mathcal{L}_{bvcms}(\aleph_0, \aleph_1)$$
$$\precsim_{i_2} \varphi(\aleph_v, \aleph_{v+1})\mathfrak{a}^v \mathcal{L}_{bvcms}(\aleph_0, \aleph_1)$$
$$+ \sum_{\iota=v+1}^{\varsigma-2} \prod_{j=v+1}^{\iota} \varphi(\aleph_j, \aleph_\varsigma \varphi(\aleph_\iota, \aleph_{\iota+1})\mathfrak{a}^\iota \mathcal{L}_{bvcms}(\aleph_0, \aleph_1)$$
$$+ \prod_{p=v+1}^{\varsigma-1} \varphi(\aleph_p, \aleph_\varsigma)\mathfrak{a}^{\varsigma-1} \varphi(\aleph_{\varsigma-1}, \aleph_\varsigma)\mathcal{L}_{bvcms}(\aleph_0, \aleph_1)$$
$$= \varphi(\aleph_v, \aleph_{v+1})\mathfrak{a}^v \mathcal{L}_{bvcms}(\aleph_0, \aleph_1)$$
$$+ \sum_{\iota=v+1}^{\varsigma-1} \prod_{j=v+1}^{\iota} \varphi(\aleph_j, \aleph_\varsigma \varphi(\aleph_\iota, \aleph_{\iota+1})\mathfrak{a}^\iota \mathcal{L}_{bvcms}(\aleph_0, \aleph_1)$$
$$\precsim_{i_2} \varphi(\aleph_v, \aleph_{v+1})\mathfrak{a}^v \mathcal{L}_{bvcms}(\aleph_0, \aleph_1)$$
$$+ \sum_{\iota=v+1}^{\varsigma-1} \prod_{j=v+1}^{\iota} \varphi(\aleph_j, \aleph_\varsigma \varphi(\aleph_\iota, \aleph_{\iota+1})\mathfrak{a}^\iota \mathcal{L}_{bvcms}(\aleph_0, \aleph_1)$$

Furthermore, using $\varphi(\aleph, i) \geq 1$. Let

$$S_\flat = \sum_{\iota=0}^{\flat} \prod_{j=0}^{\iota} \varphi(\aleph_j, \aleph_\varsigma \varphi(\aleph_\iota, \aleph_{\iota+1}))\mathfrak{a}^\iota.$$

Hence, we have

$$\mathcal{L}_{bvcms}(\aleph_v, \aleph_\varsigma) \precsim_{i_2} \mathcal{L}_{bvcms}(\aleph_0, \aleph_1)[\mathfrak{a}^v \varphi(\aleph_v, \aleph_{v+1}) + (S_{\varsigma-1}, S_v)]. \tag{4}$$

Applying the ratio test and (2), we obtain $\lim_{\varsigma, v \to \infty} S_v$ exists and the sequence $\{S_v\}$ is a real Cauchy sequence. Letting $\varsigma, v \to \infty$, we have

$$\lim_{\varsigma, v \to \infty} \mathcal{L}_{bvcms}(\aleph_v, \aleph_\varsigma) = 0. \tag{5}$$

Then, $\{\aleph_v\}$ is a Cauchy sequence in a BVCMSs $(\zeta, \mathcal{L}_{bvcms})$; then $\{\aleph_v\}$ converges to $\aleph^* \in \zeta$. By the definition of continuity, we obtain

$$\aleph^* = \lim_{v \to \infty} \aleph_{v+1} = \lim_{v \to \infty} \eta \aleph_v = \eta(\lim_{v \to \infty} \aleph_v) = \eta \aleph^*.$$

Let $\aleph^*, i^* \in$ fix η. Then,
$$\mathcal{L}_{bvcms}(\aleph^*, i^*) = \mathcal{L}_{bvcms}(\eta \aleph^*, \eta i^*) \precsim_{i_2} \varphi \mathcal{L}_{bvcms}(\aleph^*, i^*).$$

Therefore, $\mathcal{L}_{bvcms}(\aleph^*, i^*) = 0$; so $\aleph^* = i^*$. Hence, η has a UFP. □

Theorem 2. *Let $(\zeta, \mathcal{L}_{bvcms})$ be a complete BVCMS and $\eta: \zeta \to \zeta$ a map, such that*
$$\mathcal{L}_{bvcms}(\eta \aleph, \eta i) \precsim_{i_2} \varphi \mathcal{L}_{bvcms}(\aleph, i), \tag{6}$$
for all $\aleph, i \in \zeta$, where $0 < \mathfrak{a} < 1$. For $\aleph_0 \in \zeta$ we denote $\aleph_v = \eta^v \aleph_0$. Suppose that
$$\max_{\varsigma \geq 1} \lim_{l \to \infty} \frac{\varphi(\aleph_{l+1}, \aleph_{l+2})}{\varphi(\aleph_l, \aleph_{l+1})} \varphi(\aleph_{l+1}, \aleph_\varsigma) < \frac{1}{\mathfrak{a}}. \tag{7}$$

In addition, for each $\aleph \in \zeta$,
$$\lim_{v \to \infty} \varphi(\aleph_v, \aleph) \quad \text{and} \quad \lim_{v \to \infty} \varphi(\aleph, \aleph_v) \quad \text{exists and it is finite.} \tag{8}$$

Then, η has a UFP.

Proof. Using the proof of Theorem 1 and Lemma 2, we obtain a Cauchy sequence $\{\aleph_v\}$ in a complete BVCMS $(\zeta, \mathcal{L}_{bvcms})$. Then, the sequence $\{\aleph_v\}$ converges to $\aleph^* \in \zeta$. Therefore,

$$\mathcal{L}_{bvcms}(\aleph^*, \aleph_{v+1}) \precsim_{i_2} \varphi(\aleph^*, \aleph_v) \mathcal{L}_{bvcms}(\aleph^*, \aleph_v) + \varphi(\aleph_v, \aleph_{v+1}) \mathcal{L}_{bvcms}(\aleph^*, \aleph_{v+1}).$$

Using (7), (8) and (18), we obtain
$$\lim_{v \to \infty} \mathcal{L}_{bvcms}(\aleph^*, \aleph_{v+1}) = 0. \tag{9}$$

Using the triangular inequality and (6),
$$\mathcal{L}_{bvcms}(\aleph^*, \eta \aleph^*) \precsim_{i_2} \varphi(\aleph^*, \aleph_{v+1}) \mathcal{L}_{bvcms}(\aleph^*, \aleph_{v+1}) + \varphi(\aleph_{v+1}, \eta \aleph^*) \mathcal{L}_{bvcms}(\aleph_{v+1}, \eta \aleph^*)$$
$$\precsim_{i_2} \varphi(\aleph^*, \aleph_{v+1}) \mathcal{L}_{bvcms}(\aleph^*, \aleph_{v+1}) + \mathfrak{a} \varphi(\aleph_{v+1}, \eta \aleph^*) \mathcal{L}_{bvcms}(\aleph_{v+1}, \eta \aleph^*)$$

Taking the limit $v \to \infty$ from (8) and (19), we find that $\mathcal{L}_{bvcms}(\aleph^*, \eta \aleph^*) = 0$. By Lemma 1, the sequence $\{\aleph_v\}$ uniquely converges at $\aleph^* \in \zeta$. □

Example 4. *Let $\zeta = \{0, 1, 2\}$ and $\mathcal{L}_{bvcms}: \zeta \times \zeta \to \mathbb{C}_2$ be a symmetrical metric given by*
$$\mathcal{L}_{bvcms}(\aleph, \aleph) = 0, \quad \text{for each} \quad \aleph \in \zeta$$
and
$$\mathcal{L}_{bvcms}(0, 1) = 1 + i_2, \mathcal{L}_{bvcms}(1, 2) = 1 + i_2, \mathcal{L}_{bvcms}(0, 2) = 4 + 4i_2.$$

Define $\varphi: \zeta \times \zeta \to [1, \infty)$ by
$$\varphi(2,2) = \frac{6}{5}, \varphi(0,0) = 2, \varphi(1,1) = \frac{4}{3},$$
$$\varphi(0,2) = \frac{4}{3}, \varphi(0,1) = \frac{3}{2}, \varphi(1,2) = \frac{5}{4}.$$

Hence, it is a BVCMS.
Consider a map $\eta: \zeta \to \zeta$ is defined by $\eta(0) = 0, \eta(1) = 0, \eta(2) = 0$.
Letting $\mathfrak{a} = \frac{2}{5}$. Then,

Case 1. If $\aleph = i = 0, \aleph = i = 1, \aleph = i = 2$, then the results is obvious.

Case 2. *If* $\aleph = 0, i = 1$, *we obtain*

$$\pounds_{bvcms}(\eta\aleph, \eta i) = \pounds_{bvcms}(\eta 0, \eta 1) = \pounds_{bvcms}(2,2) = 0$$
$$\precsim_{i_2} \frac{2}{5}(1 + i_2)$$
$$= \mathfrak{a}(\pounds_{bvcms}(0,1)) = \mathfrak{a}(\pounds_{bvcms}(\aleph, i)).$$

Case 3. *If* $\aleph = 0, i = 2$, *we have*

$$\pounds_{bvcms}(\eta\aleph, \eta i) = \pounds_{bvcms}(\eta 0, \eta 1) = \pounds_{bvcms}(2,2) = 0$$
$$\precsim_{i_2} \frac{2}{5}(4 + 4i_2) = \mathfrak{a}(\pounds_{bvcms}(0,2))$$
$$= \mathfrak{a}(\pounds_{bvcms}(\aleph, i)).$$

Case 4. *If* $\aleph = 1, i = 2$, *we have*

$$\pounds_{bvcms}(\eta\aleph, \eta i) = \pounds_{bvcms}(\eta 1, \eta 2) = \pounds_{bvcms}(2,2) = 0$$
$$\precsim_{i_2} \frac{2}{5}(1 + i_2)$$
$$= \mathfrak{a}(\pounds_{bvcms}(1,2)) = \mathfrak{a}(\pounds_{bvcms}(\aleph, i)).$$

Therefore, all axioms of Theorem 2 are fulfilled. Hence, η has a UFP, which is $\aleph^* = 0$.

Next, we show a Kannan-type contraction map.

Theorem 3. *Let $(\zeta, \pounds_{bvcms})$ be a complete BVCMS and $\eta: \zeta \to \zeta$ a continuous map, such that*

$$\pounds_{bvcms}(\eta\aleph, \eta i) \precsim_{i_2} \eta(\pounds_{bvcms}(\aleph, \eta\aleph) + (\pounds_{bvcms}(i, \eta i)), \qquad (10)$$

for all $\aleph, i \in \zeta$, where $0 \le \eta < \frac{1}{2}$. For $\aleph_0 \in \zeta$ we denote $\aleph_v = \eta^v \aleph_0$. Suppose that

$$\max_{\varsigma \ge 1} \lim_{\iota \to \infty} \frac{\varphi(\aleph_{\iota+1}, \aleph_{\iota+2})}{\varphi(\aleph_\iota, \aleph_{\iota+1})} \varphi(\aleph_{\iota+1}, \aleph_\varsigma) < \frac{1}{\mathfrak{a}}, \quad \text{where} \quad \mathfrak{a} = \frac{\eta}{1 - \eta}. \qquad (11)$$

Moreover, for each $\aleph \in \zeta$,

$$\lim_{v \to \infty} \varphi(\aleph_v, \aleph) \quad \text{and} \quad \lim_{v \to \infty} \varphi(\aleph, \aleph_v), \qquad (12)$$

exists and is finite. Then, η has a UFP.

Proof. For $\aleph_0 \in \zeta$, consider a sequence $\{\aleph_v = \eta^v \aleph_0\}$. If $\exists \aleph_0 \in \mathbb{N}$ for which $\aleph_{v_0+1} = \aleph_{v_0}$, then $\eta \aleph_{v_0} = \aleph_{v_0}$. Thus, there is nothing to prove. Now we assume that $\aleph_{v+1} \ne \aleph_v$ for all $v \in \mathbb{N}$. By using (1) we obtain

$$\pounds_{bvcms}(\aleph_v, \aleph_{v+1}) = \pounds_{bvcms}(\eta\aleph_{v-1}, \eta\aleph_v)$$
$$\precsim_{i_2} \eta(\pounds_{bvcms}(\aleph_{v-1}, \eta\aleph_{v-1}) + \pounds_{bvcms}(\aleph_v, \eta\aleph_v))$$
$$= \eta(\pounds_{bvcms}(\aleph_{v-1}, \aleph_v) + \pounds_{bvcms}(\aleph_v, \aleph_{v+1})), \text{ which implies}$$
$$\pounds_{bvcms}(\aleph_v, \aleph_{v+1}) \precsim_{i_2} \left(\frac{\eta}{1 - \eta}\right) \pounds_{bvcms}(\aleph_{v-1}, \aleph_v)$$
$$= \mathfrak{a}\pounds_{bvcms}(\aleph_{v-1}, \aleph_v).$$

In the same way

$$\mathcal{L}_{bvcms}(\aleph_{v-1}, \aleph_v) = \mathcal{L}_{bvcms}(\eta \aleph_{v-2}, \eta \aleph_{v-1})$$
$$\precsim_{i_2} \eta(\mathcal{L}_{bvcms}(\aleph_{v-2}, \eta \aleph_{v-2}) + \mathcal{L}_{bvcms}(\aleph_{v-1}, \eta \aleph_{v-1}))$$
$$= \eta(\mathcal{L}_{bvcms}(\aleph_{v-2}, \aleph_{v-1}) + \mathcal{L}_{bvcms}(\aleph_{v-1}, \aleph_v)), \text{ which implies}$$
$$\mathcal{L}_{bvcms}(\aleph_{v-1}, \aleph_v) \precsim_{i_2} \left(\frac{\eta}{1-\eta}\right) \mathcal{L}_{bvcms}(\aleph_{v-2}, \aleph_{v-1})$$
$$= \mathfrak{a} \mathcal{L}_{bvcms}(\aleph_{v-2}, \aleph_{v-1}).$$

Continuing in the same way, we have

$$\mathcal{L}_{bvcms}(\aleph_v, \aleph_{v+1}) \precsim_{i_2} \mathfrak{a} \mathcal{L}_{bvcms}(\aleph_{v-1}, \aleph_v) \precsim_{i_2} \mathfrak{a}^2 \mathcal{L}_{bvcms}(\aleph_{v-2}, \aleph_{v-1})$$
$$\precsim_{i_2} \cdots \precsim_{i_2} \mathfrak{a}^v \mathcal{L}_{bvcms}(\aleph_0, \aleph_1).$$

Thus, $\mathcal{L}_{bvcms}(\aleph_v, \aleph_{v+1}) \precsim_{i_2} \mathfrak{a}^v \mathcal{L}_{bvcms}(\aleph_0, \aleph_1)$ for all $v \geq 0$. For all $v < \varsigma$, where v and ς are natural numbers, we have

$$\mathcal{L}_{bvcms}(\aleph_v, \aleph_\varsigma) \precsim_{i_2} \varphi(\aleph_v, \aleph_{v+1}) \mathcal{L}_{bvcms}(\aleph_v, \aleph_{v+1}) + \varphi(\aleph_{v+1}, \aleph_\varsigma) \mathcal{L}_{bvcms}(\aleph_{v+1}, \aleph_\varsigma)$$
$$\precsim_{i_2} \varphi(\aleph_v, \aleph_{v+1}) \mathcal{L}_{bvcms}(\aleph_v, \aleph_{v+1})$$
$$+ \varphi(\aleph_{v+1}, \aleph_\varsigma) \varphi(\aleph_{v+1}, \aleph_{v+2}) \mathcal{L}_{bvcms}(\aleph_{v+1}, \aleph_{v+2})$$
$$+ \varphi(\aleph_{v+1}, \aleph_\varsigma) \varphi(\aleph_{v+2}, \aleph_\varsigma) \mathcal{L}_{bvcms}(\aleph_{v+2}, \aleph_\varsigma)$$
$$\precsim_{i_2} \varphi(\aleph_v, \aleph_{v+1}) \mathcal{L}_{bvcms}(\aleph_v, \aleph_{v+1})$$
$$+ \varphi(\aleph_{v+1}, \aleph_\varsigma) \varphi(\aleph_{v+1}, \aleph_{v+2}) \mathcal{L}_{bvcms}(\aleph_{v+1}, \aleph_{v+2})$$
$$+ \varphi(\aleph_{v+1}, \aleph_\varsigma) \varphi(\aleph_{v+2}, \aleph_\varsigma) \varphi(\aleph_{v+2}, \aleph_{v+3}) \mathcal{L}_{bvcms}(\aleph_{v+2}, \aleph_{v+3})$$
$$+ \varphi(\aleph_{v+1}, \aleph_\varsigma) \varphi(\aleph_{v+2}, \aleph_\varsigma) \varphi(\aleph_{v+3}, \aleph_\varsigma) \mathcal{L}_{bvcms}(\aleph_{v+3}, \aleph_\varsigma)$$

$$\vdots$$

$$\precsim_{i_2} \varphi(\aleph_v, \aleph_{v+1}) \mathcal{L}_{bvcms}(\aleph_v, \aleph_{v+1}) \sum_{\iota=v+1}^{\varsigma-2} \prod_{j=v+1}^{\iota} \varphi(\aleph_j, \aleph_\varsigma) \varphi(\aleph_\iota, \aleph_{\iota+1}) \mathcal{L}_{bvcms}(\aleph_\iota, \aleph_{\iota+1})$$
$$+ \prod_{p=v+1}^{\varsigma-1} \varphi(\aleph_p, \aleph_\varsigma) \mathcal{L}_{bvcms}(\aleph_{\varsigma-1}, \aleph_\varsigma)$$
$$\precsim_{i_2} \varphi(\aleph_v, \aleph_{v+1}) \mathfrak{a}^v \mathcal{L}_{bvcms}(\aleph_0, \aleph_1)$$
$$+ \sum_{\iota=v+1}^{\varsigma-2} \prod_{j=v+1}^{\iota} \varphi(\aleph_j, \aleph_\varsigma) \varphi(\aleph_\iota, \aleph_{\iota+1}) \mathfrak{a}^\iota \mathcal{L}_{bvcms}(\aleph_\iota, \aleph_{\iota+1})$$
$$+ \prod_{p=v+1}^{\varsigma-1} \varphi(\aleph_p, \aleph_\varsigma) \mathfrak{a}^{\varsigma-1} \mathcal{L}_{bvcms}(\aleph_0, \aleph_1)$$
$$\precsim_{i_2} \varphi(\aleph_v, \aleph_{v+1}) \mathfrak{a}^v \mathcal{L}_{bvcms}(\aleph_0, \aleph_1)$$
$$+ \sum_{\iota=v+1}^{\varsigma-2} \prod_{j=v+1}^{\iota} \varphi(\aleph_j, \aleph_\varsigma) \varphi(\aleph_\iota, \aleph_{\iota+1}) \mathfrak{a}^\iota \mathcal{L}_{bvcms}(\aleph_\iota, \aleph_{\iota+1})$$
$$+ \prod_{p=v+1}^{\varsigma-1} \varphi(\aleph_p, \aleph_\varsigma) \varphi(\aleph_{\varsigma-1}, \aleph_\varsigma) \mathcal{L}_{bvcms}(\aleph_0, \aleph_1)$$

$$\mathcal{L}_{bvcms}(\aleph_v, \aleph_\varsigma) = \varphi(\aleph_v, \aleph_{v+1})\mathfrak{a}^v \mathcal{L}_{bvcms}(\aleph_0, \aleph_1)$$
$$+ \sum_{\iota=v+1}^{\varsigma-1} \prod_{j=v+1}^{\iota} \varphi(\aleph_j, \aleph_\varsigma) \varphi(\aleph_\iota, \aleph_{\iota+1})\mathfrak{a}^\iota \mathcal{L}_{bvcms}(\aleph_\iota, \aleph_{\iota+1})$$
$$\precsim_{i_2} \varphi(\aleph_v, \aleph_{v+1})\mathfrak{a}^v \mathcal{L}_{bvcms}(\aleph_0, \aleph_1)$$
$$+ \sum_{\iota=v+1}^{\varsigma-1} \prod_{j=v+1}^{\iota} \aleph(\aleph_j, \aleph_\varsigma) \varphi(\aleph_\iota, \aleph_{\iota+1})\mathfrak{a}^\iota \mathcal{L}_{bvcms}(\aleph_\iota, \aleph_{\iota+1}).$$

Furthermore, using $\varphi(\aleph, i) \geq 1$. Let

$$\mathcal{S}_\flat = \sum_{\iota=0}^{\flat} \prod_{j=0}^{\iota} \varphi(\aleph_j, \aleph_\varsigma) \varphi(\aleph_\iota, \aleph_{\iota+1})\mathfrak{a}^\iota.$$

Hence, we have

$$\mathcal{L}_{bvcms}(\aleph_v, \aleph_\varsigma) \precsim_{i_2} \mathcal{L}_{bvcms}(\aleph_0, \aleph_1)[\mathfrak{a}^v \varphi(\aleph_v, \aleph_{v+1}) + (\mathcal{S}_{\varsigma-1}, \mathcal{S}_v)]. \tag{13}$$

By applying the ratio test, we obtain $\lim_{\varsigma,v \to \infty} \mathcal{S}_v$ exists and so the sequence $\{\mathcal{S}_v\}$ is a Cauchy sequence. Letting $\varsigma, v \to \infty$, we have

$$\lim_{\varsigma,v \to \infty} \mathcal{L}_{bvcms}(\aleph_v, \aleph_\varsigma) = 0.$$

Then $\{\aleph_v\}$ is a Cauchy sequence in a complete BVCMS $(\zeta, \mathcal{L}_{bvcms})$. This means the sequence $\{\aleph_v\}$ converges to some $\aleph^* \in \zeta$. By the definition of continuity, we obtain

$$\aleph^* = \lim_{v \to \infty} \aleph_{v+1} = \lim_{v \to \infty} \eta \aleph_v = \eta(\lim_{v \to \infty} \aleph_v) = \eta \aleph^*.$$

Let $\aleph^*, i^* \in \text{fix } \eta$. Then,

$$\mathcal{L}_{bvcms}(\aleph^*, i^*) = \mathcal{L}_{bvcms}(\eta \aleph^*, \eta i^*)$$
$$\precsim_{i_2} \eta[\mathcal{L}_{bvcms}(\aleph^*, \eta \aleph^*) + \mathcal{L}_{bvcms}(i^*, \eta i^*)]$$
$$\precsim_{i_2} \eta[\mathcal{L}_{bvcms}(\aleph^*, \aleph^*) + \mathcal{L}_{bvcms}(i^*, i^*)] = 0.$$

Therefore, $\mathcal{L}_{bvcms}(\aleph^*, i^*) = 0$, then $\aleph^* = i^*$. Hence, η has a UFP. □

Theorem 4. *Let $(\zeta, \mathcal{L}_{bvcms})$ be a complete BVCMS and $\eta : \zeta \to \zeta$ a map, such that*

$$\mathcal{L}_{bvcms}(\eta \aleph, \eta i) \precsim_{i_2} \eta(\mathcal{L}_{bvcms}(\aleph, \eta \aleph) + \mathcal{L}_{bvcms}(i, \eta i)) \tag{14}$$

for all $\aleph, i \in \zeta$ where $0 \leq \eta < \frac{1}{2}$. For $\aleph_0 \in \zeta$ we denote $\aleph_v = \eta^v \aleph_0$. Suppose that

$$\max_{\varsigma \geq 1} \lim_{\iota \to \infty} \frac{\varphi(\aleph_{\iota+1}, \aleph_{\iota+2})}{\varphi(\aleph_\iota, \aleph_{\iota+1})} \varphi(\aleph_{\iota+1}, \aleph_\varsigma) < \frac{1}{\mathfrak{a}}, \quad \text{where} \quad \mathfrak{a} = \frac{\eta}{1-\eta}. \tag{15}$$

Moreover, for each $\aleph \in \zeta$,

$$\lim_{v \to \infty} \varphi(\aleph_v, \aleph) \quad \text{and} \quad \lim_{v \to \infty} \varphi(\aleph, \aleph_v), \tag{16}$$

exists and is finite. Then η has a UFP.

Proof. By proving Theorem 3 and using Lemma 2, we show a Cauchy sequence $\{\aleph_v\}$ in a complete BVCMS $(\zeta, \mathcal{L}_{bvcms})$. Then the sequence $\{\aleph_v\}$ converges to a $\aleph^* \in \zeta$. Then,

$$\mathcal{L}_{bvcms}(\aleph^*, \aleph_{v+1}) \precsim_{i_2} \varphi(\aleph^*, \aleph_v)\mathcal{L}_{bvcms}(\aleph^*, \aleph_v) + \varphi(\aleph_v, \aleph_{v+1})\mathcal{L}_{bvcms}(\aleph_v, \aleph_{v+1})$$

Using (2), (3) and (18), we deduce

$$\lim_{v\to\infty} \aleph_{bvcms}(\aleph^*, \aleph_{v+1}) = 0.$$

Using the triangular inequality and (1), we obtain

$$\begin{aligned}\pounds_{bvcms}(\aleph^*, \eta\aleph^*) &\precsim_{i_2} \varphi(\aleph^*, \aleph_{v+1})\pounds_{bvcms}(\aleph^*, \aleph_{v+1}) \\ &+ \varphi(\aleph_{v+1}, \eta\aleph^*)\pounds_{bvcms}(\aleph_{v+1}, \eta\aleph^*) \\ &\precsim_{i_2} \varphi(\aleph^*, \aleph_{v+1})\pounds_{bvcms}(\aleph^*, \aleph_{v+1}) \\ &+ \varphi(\aleph_{v+1}, \eta\aleph^*)[\eta(\pounds_{bvcms}(\aleph_v, \aleph_{v+1}) + \pounds_{bvcms}(\aleph^*, \eta\aleph^*))].\end{aligned}$$

As $v \to \infty$ from (3) and (19), we conclude that $\pounds_{bvcms}(\aleph^*, \eta\aleph^*) = 0$. From Lemma 1, the sequence $\{\aleph_v\}$ uniquely converges at $\aleph^* \in \zeta$. □

Example 5. *Let $\zeta = \{0, 1, 2\}$ and $\pounds_{bvcms}: \zeta \times \zeta \to \mathbb{C}_2$ be a symmetrical metric as follows*

$$\pounds_{bvcms}(\aleph, \aleph) = 0 \quad \text{for each} \quad \aleph \in \zeta$$

and

$$\pounds_{bvcms}(0, 1) = 1 + i_2, \pounds_{bvcms}(1, 2) = 1 + i_2, \pounds_{bvcms}(0, 2) = 4 + 4i_2.$$

Define $\varphi: \zeta \times \zeta \to [1, \infty)$ by

$$\varphi(2, 2) = \frac{9}{5}, \varphi(0, 0) = 5, \varphi(1, 1) = \frac{7}{3},$$
$$\varphi(1, 2) = 2, \varphi(0, 1) = 3, \varphi(0, 2) = \frac{7}{3}.$$

A self-map η on ζ can be defined by $\eta(0) = \eta(1) = \eta(2) = 2$.
Taking $\eta = \frac{2}{5}$; then,

Case 1. *If $\aleph = i = 0, \aleph = i = 1, \aleph = i = 2$, then the result is obvious.*
Case 2. *If $\aleph = 0, i = 1$, we obtain*

$$\begin{aligned}\pounds_{bvcms}(\eta\aleph, \eta i) &= \pounds_{bvcms}(\eta 0, \eta 1) = \pounds_{bvcms}(2, 2) = 0 \precsim_{i_2} \frac{10}{5}(1 + i_2) \\ &= \frac{2}{5}(4 + 4i_2 + (1 + i_2)) = \eta(\pounds_{bvcms}(0, 2) + \pounds_{bvcms}(1, 2)) \\ &= \eta(\pounds_{bvcms}(\aleph, \eta\aleph) + \pounds_{bvcms}(i, \eta i)).\end{aligned}$$

Case 3. *If $\aleph = 0, i = 2$, we have*

$$\begin{aligned}\pounds_{bvcms}(\eta\aleph, \eta i) &= \pounds_{bvcms}(\eta 0, \eta 2) = \pounds_{bvcms}(2, 2) = 0 \precsim_{i_2} \frac{8}{5}(1 + i_2) \\ &= \frac{2}{5}(4 + 4i_2 + 0) = \eta(\pounds_{bvcms}(0, 2) + \pounds_{bvcms}(2, 2)) \\ &= \eta(\pounds_{bvcms}(\aleph, \eta\aleph) + \pounds_{bvcms}(i, \eta i)).\end{aligned}$$

Case 4. *If $\aleph = 1, i = 2$, we have*

$$\begin{aligned}\pounds_{bvcms}(\eta\aleph, \eta i) &= \pounds_{bvcms}(\eta 1, \eta 2) = \pounds_{bvcms}(2, 2) = 0 \precsim_{i_2} \frac{2}{5}(1 + i_2) \\ &= \frac{2}{5}((1 + i_2) + 0) = \eta(\pounds_{bvcms}(1, 2) + \pounds_{bvcms}(2, 2)) \\ &= \eta(\pounds_{bvcms}(\aleph, \eta\aleph) + \pounds_{bvcms}(i, \eta i)).\end{aligned}$$

Then, all hypothesis of Theorem 4 are fulfilled. Hence, $\mathcal{T}$ has a UFP, which is $\aleph^* = 2$.

Finally, we show that FPT in a Fisher-type contraction map.

Theorem 5. *Let $(\zeta, \pounds_{bvcms})$ be a complete BVCMS and $\eta: \zeta \to \zeta$ a continuous map, such that*

$$\pounds_{bvcms}(\eta\aleph, \eta i) \precsim_{i_2} \omega \pounds_{bvcms}(\aleph, i) + f\frac{\pounds_{bvcms}(\aleph, \eta\aleph)\pounds_{bvcms}(i, \eta i)}{1 + \pounds_{bvcms}(\aleph, i)}, \tag{17}$$

for all $\aleph, i \in \zeta$, where $\omega, f \in [0,1)$, such that $\nu = \frac{\omega}{1-f} < 1$. For $\aleph_0 \in \zeta$ we denote $\aleph_v = \eta^v \aleph_0$. Suppose that

$$\max_{\varsigma \geq 1} \lim_{i_2 \to \infty} \frac{\varphi(\aleph_{i_2+1}, \aleph_{i_2+2})}{\varphi(\aleph_{i_2}, \aleph_{i_2+1})} \varphi(\aleph_{i_2+1}, \aleph_\varsigma) < \frac{1}{\nu}, \qquad (18)$$

Moreover, suppose that for every $\varkappa \in \zeta$ we have

$$\lim_{v \to \infty} \varphi(\aleph_v, \aleph) \quad \text{and} \quad \lim_{v \to \infty} \varphi(\aleph, \aleph_v), \qquad (19)$$

exist and are finite. Then η has a UFP.

Proof. For $\aleph_0 \in \zeta$. Let $\aleph_v = \eta^v \aleph_0$. If $\exists \aleph_0 \in \mathbb{N}$ for which $\aleph_{v_0+1} = \aleph_{v_0}$, then $\eta \aleph_{v_0} = \aleph_{v_0}$. Thus, there is nothing to prove. Now we assume that $\aleph_{v+1} \neq \aleph_v$ for all $v \in \mathbb{N}$. By using (1), we obtain

$$\mathcal{L}_{bvcms}(\aleph_v, \aleph_{v+1}) = \mathcal{L}_{bvcms}(\eta \aleph_{v-1}, \eta \aleph_v)$$
$$\precsim_{i_2} \omega \mathcal{L}_{bvcms}(\aleph_{v-1}, \aleph_v) + f \frac{\mathcal{L}_{bvcms}(\aleph_{v-1}, \eta \aleph_v) \mathcal{L}_{bvcms}(\aleph_v, \eta \aleph_v)}{1 + \mathcal{L}_{bvcms}(\aleph_{v-1}, \aleph_v)}$$
$$= \omega \mathcal{L}_{bvcms}(\aleph_{v-1}, \aleph_v) + f \frac{\mathcal{L}_{bvcms}(\aleph_{v-1}, \aleph_v) \mathcal{L}_{bvcms}(\varkappa_v, \aleph_v)}{1 + \mathcal{L}_{bvcms}(\aleph_{v-1}, \aleph_v)}$$
$$\precsim_{i_2} \mathcal{L}_{bvcms}(\varkappa_{v-1}, \aleph_v) + f \mathcal{L}_{bvcms}(\aleph_v, \aleph_{v+1})$$

which implies

$$\mathcal{L}_{bvcms}(\aleph_v, \aleph_{v+1}) \precsim_{i_2} \left(\frac{\omega}{1-f}\right) \mathcal{L}_{bvcms}(\aleph_{v-1}, \aleph_v)$$
$$= \nu \mathcal{L}_{bvcms}(\aleph_{v-1}, \aleph_v)$$

In the same way

$$\mathcal{L}_{bvcms}(\aleph_{v-1}, \aleph_v) = \mathcal{L}_{bvcms}(\eta \aleph_{v-2}, \eta \aleph_{v-1})$$
$$\precsim_{i_2} \omega \mathcal{L}_{bvcms}(\aleph_{v-2}, \aleph_{v-1}) + f \frac{\mathcal{L}_{bvcms}(\aleph_{v-2}, \eta \aleph_{v-2}) \mathcal{L}_{bvcms}(\aleph_{v-1}, \eta \aleph_{v-1})}{1 + \mathcal{L}_{bvcms}(\aleph_{v-2}, \aleph_{v-1})}$$
$$= \omega \mathcal{L}_{bvcms}(\aleph_{v-2}, \aleph_{v-1}) + f \frac{\mathcal{L}_{bvcms}(\aleph_{v-2}, \aleph_{v-1}) \mathcal{L}_{bvcms}(\aleph_{v-1}, \aleph_v)}{1 + \mathcal{L}_{bvcms}(\aleph_{v-2}, \aleph_{v-1})}$$
$$\precsim_{i_2} \omega \mathcal{L}_{bvcms}(\aleph_{v-2}, \aleph_{v-1}) + f \mathcal{L}_{bvcms}(\aleph_{v-1}, \aleph_v)$$

which implies

$$\mathcal{L}_{bvcms}(\aleph_{v-1}, \aleph_v) \precsim_{i_2} \left(\frac{\omega}{1-f}\right) \mathcal{L}_{bvcms}(\aleph_{v-2}, \aleph_{v-1})$$
$$= \nu(\aleph_{v-2}, \aleph_{v-1})$$

Continuing in the same way, we have

$$\mathcal{L}_{bvcms}(\aleph_v, \aleph_{v+1}) \precsim_{i_2} \nu \mathcal{L}_{bvcms}(\aleph_{v-1}, \aleph_v)$$
$$\precsim_{i_2} \nu^2 \mathcal{L}_{bvcms}(\aleph_{v-2}, \aleph_{v-1})$$
$$\vdots$$
$$\precsim_{i_2} \nu^v \mathcal{L}_{bvcms}(\aleph_0, \aleph_1). \qquad (20)$$

Thus, $\mathcal{L}_{bvcms}(\aleph_v, \aleph_{v+1}) \precsim_{i_2} \nu^v \mathcal{L}_{bvcms}(\aleph_0, \aleph_1)$ for all $v \geq 0$. For all $v < \varsigma$, where v and ς are natural numbers, giving

$$\pounds_{bvcms}(\aleph_v, \aleph_\varsigma) \precsim_{i_2} \varphi(\aleph_v, \aleph_{v+1})\pounds_{bvcms}(\aleph_v, \aleph_{v+1}) + \varphi(\aleph_{v+1}, \aleph_\varsigma)\pounds_{bvcms}(\aleph_{v+1}, \aleph_\varsigma)$$

$$\precsim_{i_2} \varphi(\aleph_v, \aleph_{v+1})\pounds_{bvcms}(\aleph_v, \aleph_{v+1})$$
$$+ \varphi(\aleph_{v+1}, \aleph_\varsigma)\varphi(\aleph_{v+1}, \aleph_{v+2})\pounds_{bvcms}(\aleph_{v+1}, \aleph_{v+2})$$
$$+ \varphi(\aleph_{v+1}, \aleph_\varsigma)\varphi(\aleph_{v+2}, \aleph_\varsigma)\pounds_{bvcms}(\aleph_{v+2}, \aleph_\varsigma)$$

$$\precsim_{i_2} \varphi(\aleph_v, \aleph_{v+1})\pounds_{bvcms}(\aleph_v, \aleph_{v+1})$$
$$+ \varphi(\aleph_{v+1}, \aleph_\varsigma)\varphi(\aleph_{v+1}, \aleph_{v+2})\pounds_{bvcms}(\aleph_{v+1}, \aleph_{v+2})$$
$$+ \varphi(\aleph_{v+1}, \aleph_\varsigma)\varphi(\aleph_{v+2}, \aleph_\varsigma)\varphi(\aleph_{v+2}, \aleph_{v+3})\pounds_{bvcms}(\aleph_{v+2}, \aleph_{v+3})$$
$$+ \varphi(\aleph_{v+1}, \aleph_\varsigma)\varphi(\aleph_{v+2}, \aleph_\varsigma)\varphi(\aleph_{v+3}, \aleph_\varsigma)\pounds_{bvcms}(\aleph_{v+3}, \aleph_\varsigma)$$

$$\precsim_{i_2} \cdots \precsim_{i_2} \varphi(\aleph_v, \aleph_{v+1})\pounds_{bvcms}(\aleph_v, \aleph_{v+1})$$
$$+ \sum_{\iota=v+1}^{\varsigma-2}\left(\prod_{j=v+1}^{\iota} \varphi(\aleph_j, \aleph_\varsigma)\right)\varphi(\aleph_\iota, \aleph_{\iota+1})\pounds_{bvcms}(\aleph_\iota, \aleph_{\iota+1})$$
$$+ \prod_{p=v+1}^{\varsigma-1} \varphi(\aleph_p, \aleph_\varsigma)\pounds_{bvcms}(\aleph_{\varsigma-1}, \aleph_\varsigma)$$

$$\precsim_{i_2} \varphi(\aleph_v, \aleph_{v+1})\mathfrak{a}^v\pounds_{bvcms}(\aleph_0, \aleph_1)$$
$$+ \sum_{\iota=v+1}^{\varsigma-2}\left(\prod_{j=v+1}^{\iota} \varphi(\aleph_j, \aleph_\varsigma)\right)\varphi(\aleph_\iota, \aleph_{\iota+1})\mathfrak{a}^\iota\pounds_{bvcms}(\aleph_0, \aleph_1)$$
$$+ \prod_{p=v+1}^{\varsigma-1} \varphi(\aleph_p, \aleph_\varsigma)\mathfrak{a}^{\varsigma-1}\pounds_{bvcms}(\aleph_0, \aleph_1)$$

$$\precsim_{i_2} \varphi(\aleph_v, \aleph_{v+1})\mathfrak{a}^v\pounds_{bvcms}(\aleph_0, \aleph_1)$$
$$+ \sum_{\iota=v+1}^{\varsigma-2}\left(\prod_{j=v+1}^{\iota} \varphi(\aleph_j, \aleph_\varsigma)\right)\varphi(\aleph_\iota, \aleph_{\iota+1})\mathfrak{a}^\iota\pounds_{bvcms}(\aleph_0, \aleph_1)$$
$$+ \left(\prod_{p=v+1}^{\varsigma-1} \varphi(\aleph_p, \aleph_\varsigma)\right)\mathfrak{a}^{\varsigma-1}\varphi(\aleph_{\varsigma-1}, \aleph_\varsigma)\pounds_{bvcms}(\aleph_0, \aleph_1)$$

$$= \varphi(\aleph_v, \aleph_{v+1})\mathfrak{a}^v\pounds_{bvcms}(\aleph_0, \aleph_1)$$
$$+ \sum_{\iota=v+1}^{\varsigma-1}\left(\prod_{j=v+1}^{\iota} \varphi(\aleph_j, \aleph_\varsigma)\right)\varphi(\aleph_\iota, \aleph_{\iota+1})\mathfrak{a}^\iota\pounds_{bvcms}(\aleph_0, \aleph_1)$$

$$\precsim_{i_2} \varphi(\aleph_v, \aleph_{v+1})\mathfrak{a}^v\pounds_{bvcms}(\aleph_0, \aleph_1)$$
$$+ \sum_{\iota=v+1}^{\varsigma-1}\left(\prod_{j=0}^{\iota} \varphi(\aleph_j, \aleph_\varsigma)\right)\varphi(\aleph_\iota, \aleph_{\iota+1})\mathfrak{a}^\iota\pounds_{bvcms}(\aleph_0, \aleph_1).$$

Furthermore, using $\varphi(\aleph, i) \geq 1$. Let

$$\mathcal{S}_\flat = \sum_{\iota=0}^{\flat}\left(\prod_{j=0}^{\iota} \varphi(\aleph_j, \aleph_\varsigma)\right)\varphi(\aleph_\iota, \aleph_{\iota+1})\mathfrak{a}^\iota.$$

Hence, we have

$$\pounds_{bvcms}(\aleph_v, \aleph_\varsigma) \precsim_{i_2} \pounds_{bvcms}(\aleph_0, \aleph_1)[v^v\varphi(\aleph_v, \aleph_{v+1}) + (\mathcal{S}_{\varsigma-1}, \mathcal{S}_v)]. \tag{21}$$

By using the ratio test, ensuring that $\lim_{\varsigma, v \to \infty} \mathcal{S}_v$ exists, the sequence $\{\mathcal{S}_v\}$ is a real Cauchy sequence. As $\varsigma, v \to \infty$, we conclude that

$$\lim_{\varsigma, v \to \infty} \pounds_{bvcms}(\aleph_v, \aleph_\varsigma) = 0,$$

Then, $\{\aleph_v\}$ is a Cauchy sequence in the complete BVCMS $(\zeta, \pounds_{bvcms})$. Therefore, the sequence $\{\aleph_v\}$ converges to $\aleph^* \in \zeta$.

By the definition of continuity, we obtain

$$\aleph^* = \lim_{v \to \infty} \aleph_{v+1} = \lim_{v \to \infty} \eta \aleph_v = \eta(\lim_{v \to \infty} \aleph_v) = \eta \aleph^*.$$

Let $\aleph^*, i^* \in$ fix η as two fixed points of η. Then,

$$\pounds_{bvcms}(\eta\aleph^*, \eta i^*) \precsim_{i_2} \omega \pounds_{bvcms}(\aleph^*, i^*) + f \frac{\pounds_{bvcms}(\aleph^*, \eta i^*) \pounds_{bvcms}(\aleph^*, \eta i^*)}{1 + \pounds_{bvcms}(\aleph^*, i^*)}$$

$$\precsim_{i_2} \omega \pounds_{bvcms}(\aleph^*, i^*) + f \frac{\pounds_{bvcms}(\aleph^*, \aleph^*) \pounds_{bvcms}(i^*, i^*)}{1 + \pounds_{bvcms}(\aleph^*, i^*)}$$

$$\precsim_{i_2} \omega \pounds_{bvcms}(\aleph^*, i^*).$$

Therefore, $\pounds_{bvcms}(\aleph^*, i^*) = 0$; then $\aleph^* = i^*$. Hence, η has a UFP. □

If we drop the continuous condition, we obtain

Theorem 6. *Let $(\zeta, \pounds_{bvcms})$ be a complete BVCMS and $\eta: \zeta \to \zeta$ a map, such that*

$$\pounds_{bvcms}(\eta\aleph, \eta i) \precsim_{i_2} \omega \pounds_{bvcms}(\aleph, i) + f \frac{\pounds_{bvcms}(\aleph, \eta\aleph) \pounds_{bvcms}(i, \eta i)}{1 + \pounds_{bvcms}(\aleph, i)}, \tag{22}$$

for all $\aleph, i \in \zeta$, where $\omega, f \in [0,1)$, such that $\nu = \frac{\omega}{1-f} < 1$. For $\aleph_0 \in \zeta$ we denote $\aleph_v = \eta^v \aleph_0$. Suppose that

$$\max_{\varsigma \geq 1} \lim_{i_2 \to \infty} \frac{\varphi(\aleph_{i_2+1}, \aleph_{i_2+2})}{\varphi(\aleph_{i_2}, \aleph_{i_2+1})} \varphi(\aleph_{i_2+1}, \aleph_\varsigma) < \frac{1}{\nu}, \tag{23}$$

In addition, assume that for every $\aleph \in \zeta$ we have

$$\lim_{v \to \infty} \varphi(\aleph_v, \aleph) \quad \text{and} \quad \lim_{v \to \infty} \varphi(\aleph, \aleph_v) \quad \text{exists.} \tag{24}$$

Therefore, it is finite. Then η has a UFP.

Proof. By proving Theorem 5 and using Lemma 2, we obtain a Cauchy sequence $\{\aleph_v\}$ which converges to $\aleph^* \in \zeta$. Then,

$$\pounds_{bvcms}(\aleph^*, \aleph_{v+1}) \precsim_{i_2} \varphi(\aleph^*, \aleph_v) \pounds_{bvcms}(\aleph^*, \aleph_v) + \varphi(\aleph_v, \aleph_{v+1}) \pounds_{bvcms}(\aleph_v, \aleph_{v+1}).$$

Using (2), (3) and (23), we deduce that

$$\lim_{v \to \infty} \pounds_{bvcms}(\aleph^*, \aleph_{v+1}) = 0.$$

Using the triangular inequality and (1),

$$\pounds_{bvcms}(\aleph^*, \eta\aleph^*) \precsim_{i_2} \varphi(\aleph^*, \aleph_{v+1}) \pounds_{bvcms}(\aleph^*, \aleph_{v+1}) + \varphi(\aleph_{v+1}, \eta^*) \pounds_{bvcms}(\aleph_{v+1}, \eta\aleph^*)$$

$$\precsim_{i_2} \varphi(\aleph^*, \aleph_{v+1}) \pounds_{bvcms}(\aleph^*, \aleph_{v+1}) + \varphi(\aleph_{v+1}, \eta^*)[\omega \pounds_{bvcms}(\aleph_v, \aleph^*)$$

$$+ f \frac{\pounds_{bvcms}(\aleph_v, \eta\aleph_v) \pounds_{bvcms}(\aleph^*, \eta\aleph^*)}{1 + \pounds_{bvcms}(\aleph_v, \aleph^*)}]$$

$$= \varphi(\aleph^*, \aleph_{v+1}) \pounds_{bvcms}(\aleph^*, \aleph_{v+1}) + \varphi(\aleph_{v+1}, \eta^*)[\omega \pounds_{bvcms}(\aleph_v, \aleph^*)$$

$$+ f \frac{\pounds_{bvcms}(\aleph_v, \eta\aleph_v) \pounds_{bvcms}(\aleph^*, \eta\aleph^*)}{1 + \pounds_{bvcms}(\aleph_v, \aleph^*)}].$$

As $v \to \infty$ in (3) and (24), we find that $\pounds_{bvcms}(\aleph^*, \eta\aleph^*) = 0$. From Lemma 1, the sequence $\{\aleph_v\}$ uniquely converge at $\aleph^* \in \zeta$. □

Example 6. *Let $\zeta = \{0,1,2\}$ and $\pounds_{bvcms} : \zeta \times \zeta \to \mathbb{C}$ be a symmetrical metric defined as*

$$\pounds_{bvcms}(\aleph, \aleph) = 0 \quad \text{for each} \quad \aleph \in \zeta$$

and

$$\pounds_{bvcms}(0,1) = 1 + i_2, \pounds_{bvcms}(1,2) = 1 + i_2, \pounds_{bvcms}(0,2) = 4 + 4i_2.$$

Defining $\varphi : \zeta \times \zeta \to [1, \infty)$ by

$$\varphi(2,2) = \frac{9}{5}, \varphi(0,0) = 5, \varphi(1,1) = \frac{7}{3},$$
$$\varphi(1,2) = 2, \varphi(0,1) = 3, \varphi(0,2) = \frac{7}{3}.$$

Clearly, $(\zeta, \pounds_{bvcms})$ is a BVCMS. A self-map η on ζ defined by $\eta(0) = \eta(1) = \eta(2) = 1$. If we assume that $\omega = f = \frac{1}{5}$, we obtain

Case 1. *If $\aleph = i = 0, \aleph = i = 1, \aleph = i = 2$ we have $\pounds_{bvcms}(\eta\aleph, \eta i) = 0$.*

Case 2. *If $\aleph = 0, i = 1$, we obtained $\pounds_{bvcms}(\eta\aleph, \eta i) = 0 \precsim_{i_2} \omega \pounds_{bvcms}(\aleph, i)$*
$+ f \frac{\pounds_{bvcms}(\aleph, \eta\aleph) \pounds_{bvcms}(i, \eta i)}{1 + \pounds_{bvcms}(\aleph, i)}$

Case 3. *If $\aleph = 0, i = 2$, we have $\pounds_{bvcms}(\eta\aleph, \eta i) = 0 \precsim_{i_2} \omega \pounds_{bvcms}(\aleph, i)$*
$+ f \frac{\pounds_{bvcms}(\aleph, \eta\aleph) \pounds_{bvcms}(i, \eta i)}{1 + \pounds_{bvcms}(\aleph, i)}$

Case 4. *If $\aleph = 1, i = 2$, we have $\pounds_{bvcms}(\eta\aleph, \eta i) = 0 \precsim_{i_2} \omega \pounds_{bvcms}(\aleph, i)$*
$+ f \frac{\pounds_{bvcms}(\aleph, \eta\aleph) \pounds_{bvcms}(i, \eta i)}{1 + \pounds_{bvcms}(\aleph, i)}$

Therefore, all axioms of Theorem 6 are fulfilled. Hence, η has a UFP, which is $\aleph^* = 1$.

Application

Now, we see some basic definitions from the fractional calculus.

Let $\varkappa \in C[0,1]$ be a function, the Rieman–Liouville fractional derivatives of order $\delta > 0$ are defined as:

$$\frac{1}{\Gamma(n - \delta)} \frac{d^n}{d\flat^n} \int_0^\flat \frac{\varkappa(c)dc}{(\flat - c)^{\delta - n + 1}} = \mathcal{D}^\delta \varkappa(\flat),$$

presenting that the right-hand side is point-wise on $[0,1]$, where Γ is the Euler Γ function and $[\delta]$ is the integer part of δ.

Consider the following FDE

$$^c\mathcal{D}^\xi \varkappa(\flat) + f(\flat, \varkappa(\flat)) = 0, \quad 1 \leq \flat \leq 0, \quad 2 \leq \xi > 1;$$
$$\varkappa(0) = \varkappa(1) = 0, \qquad (25)$$

where $^c\mathcal{D}^\xi$ represents the order of ξ as the Caputo fractional derivatives and $f : [0,1] \times \mathbb{R} \to \mathbb{R}$ as a continuous map defined by

$$^c\mathcal{D}^\xi = \frac{1}{\Gamma(n - \xi)} \int_0^\flat \frac{\varkappa^n(c)dc}{(\flat - c)^{\xi - n + 1}}.$$

The given FDE (25) is equivalent to

$$\varkappa(\flat) = \int_0^1 \Omega(\flat, c) f(\flat, \varkappa(c)) dc,$$

for all $\varkappa \in \zeta$ and $\flat \in [0,1]$, where

$$\Omega(\flat, c) = \begin{cases} \frac{[\flat(1-c)]^{\xi-1}-(\flat-c)^{\xi-1}}{\Gamma(\xi)}, & 0 \leq c \leq \flat \leq 1, \\ \frac{[\flat(1-c)]^{\xi-1}}{\Gamma(\xi)}, & 0 \leq \flat \leq c \leq 1. \end{cases}$$

Consider $\mathcal{C}([0,1], \mathbb{R}) = \zeta$ as the space of the continuous map described by $[0,1]$, and $\mathcal{L}_{bvcms} : \zeta \times \zeta \to \mathbb{C}_2$ a bicomplex-valued controlled metric, such that

$$\mathcal{L}_{bvcms}(\varkappa, \gamma) = \sup_{\flat \in [0,1]} |\varkappa(\flat) - \gamma(\flat)|^2 + i_2 \sup_{\flat \in [0,1]} |\varkappa(\flat) - \gamma(\flat)|^2,$$

for all $\varkappa, \gamma \in \zeta$. Let $\varphi_\flat : \zeta \times \zeta \to [1, \infty)$ be defined by

$$\varphi_\flat(\varkappa, \gamma) = 2,$$

for all $\varkappa, \gamma \in \zeta$. Then, $(\zeta, \mathcal{L}_{bvcms})$ is a complete BVCMS.

Theorem 7. *Consider the non-linear FDE (25). Suppose that the following assertions are satisfied:*

(i) *There exists* $\mathfrak{m} \in [0,1]$ *and* $\varkappa, \gamma \in \mathcal{C}([0,1], \mathbb{R})$*, such that*

$$|f(\flat, \varkappa) - f(\flat, \gamma)| \leq \sqrt{\mathfrak{m}}|\varkappa(\flat) - \gamma(\flat)|;$$

(ii)

$$\sup_{\flat \in [0,1]} \int_0^1 \Omega(\flat, c) dc < 1.$$

Then, FDE (25) has a unique solution in ζ.

Proof. Consider the map $\eta : \zeta \to \zeta$ defined by

$$\eta\varkappa(\flat) = \int_0^1 \Omega(\flat, c) f(\flat, \varkappa(c)) dc.$$

Now, for all $\varkappa, \gamma \in \zeta$, we deduce

$$|\eta\varkappa(\flat) - \eta\gamma(\flat)|^2 (1 + i_2) = \left|\int_0^1 \Omega(\flat, c) f(\flat, \varkappa(c)) dc - \int_0^1 \Omega(\flat, c) f(\flat, \gamma(c)) dc\right|^2 (1 + i_2)$$

$$\leq \left(\int_0^1 \Omega(\flat, c) |f(\flat, \varkappa(c)) - f(\flat, \gamma(c))| dc\right)^2 (1 + i_2)$$

$$\leq \left(\int_0^1 \Omega(\flat, c) dc\right)^2 \int_0^1 \mathfrak{m}|\varkappa(\flat) - \gamma(\flat)|^2 dc(1 + i_2).$$

Taking the supreme, we obtain

$$\mathcal{L}_{bvcms}(\eta\varkappa, \eta\gamma) \leq \mathfrak{m}\mathcal{L}_{bvcms}(\varkappa, \gamma).$$

Therefore, all conditions of Theorem 1 are fulfilled and the operator η has a UFP. □

4. Conclusions

In this paper we introduced the concept of BVCMS and FPTs for Banach-, Kannan- and Fisher-type contractions concepts. Furthermore, we presented examples that elaborated the usability of our results. Meanwhile, we provided an application for the existence of a solution to an FDE using one of our results. This concept can be applied for further investigations into studying BVCMSs for other structures in metric spaces.

Author Contributions: All authors contributed equally towards writing this article. All authors have read and agreed to the published version of the manuscript.

Funding: This research received no external funding.

Data Availability Statement: Not applicable.

Acknowledgments: The authors S.H. and N.M. would like to thank Prince Sultan University for paying the publication fees through the TAS research LAB.

Conflicts of Interest: The authors declare no conflict of interest.

References

1. Banach, S. Sur les opérations dans les ensembles abstraits et leur application aux équations intégrales. *Fund. Math.* **1922**, *3*, 133–181. [CrossRef]
2. Luna-Elizaarrarás, M.E.; Shapiro, M.; Struppa, D.C.; Vajiac, A. Bicomplex numbers and their elementary functions. *Cubo* **2012**, *14*, 61–80.
3. Aslam, M.S.; Bota, M.F.; Chowdhury, M.S.R.; Guran, L.; Saleem, N. Common fixed points technique for existence of a solution of Urysohn type integral equations system in complex valued b-metric spaces. *Mathematics* **2021**, *9*, 400. [CrossRef]
4. Lateef, D., Fisher type fixed point results in controlled metric spaces. *J. Math. Comput. Sci.* **2020**, *20*, 234–240. [CrossRef]
5. Shatanawi, W.; Mlaiki, N.; Rizk, D. Fredholm-type integral equation in controlled metric-like spaces. *Adv. Differ. Equ.* **2021**, *358*, 1–13. [CrossRef]
6. Lateef, D. Kannan fixed point theorem in C-metric spaces. *J. Math. Anal.* **2019**, *10*, 34–40.
7. Shatanawi, W.; Shatnawi, T.A. Some fixed point results based on contractions of new types for extended b−metric spaces. *AIMS Math.* **2023**, *8*, 10929–10946. [CrossRef]
8. Shatanawi, W.; Shatnawi, T.A. New fixed point results in controlled metric type spaces based on new contractive conditions. *AIMS Math.* **2023**, *8*, 9314–9330. [CrossRef]
9. Rezazgui, A.-Z.; Tallafha, A.A.; Shatanawi, W. Common fixed point results via $A_\vartheta - \alpha$−contractions with a pair and two pairs of self-mappings in the frame of an extended quasi b-metric space. *AIMS Math.* **2023**, *8*, 7225–7241. [CrossRef]
10. Mlaiki, N.; Aydi, H.; Souayah, N.; Abdeljawad, T. Controlled metric type spaces and related contraction principle. *Mathematics* **2018**, *6*, 1–6. [CrossRef]
11. Mlaiki, N.; Aydi, H.; Souayah, N.; Abdeljawad, T. An improvement of recent results in controlled metric type spaces. *Filomat* **2020**, *34*, 1853–1862. [CrossRef]
12. Segre, C. Le Rappresentazioni Reali delle Forme Complesse a Gli Enti Iperalgebrici. *Math. Ann.* **1892**, *40*, 413–467. [CrossRef]
13. Dragoni, G.S. Sulle funzioni olomorfe di una variabile bicomplessa. *Reale Accad. d'Italia Mem. Classes Sci. Nat. Fis. Mat.* **1934**, *5*, 597–665.
14. Spampinato, N. Estensione nel campo bicomplesso di due teoremi, del Levi-Civita e del Severi, per le funzioni olomorfe di due variablili bicomplesse I, II. *Reale Accad. Naz. Lincei.* **1935**, *22*, 38–43.
15. Spampinato, N. Sulla rappresentazione delle funzioni do variabile bicomplessa totalmente derivabili. *Ann. Mat. Pura Appl.* **1936**, *14*, 305–325. [CrossRef]
16. Price, G.B. *An Introduction to Multicomplex Spaces and Functions*; Marcel Dekker: New York, NY, USA, 1991.
17. Colombo, F.; Sabadini, I.; Struppa, D.C.; Vajiac, A.; Vajiac, M. Singularities of functions of one and several bicomplex variables. *Ark. Math.* **2010**, *49*, 277–294. [CrossRef]
18. Choi, J.; Datta, S.K.; Biswas, T.; Islam, N. Some fixed point theorems in connection with two weakly compatible mappings in bicomplex valued metric spaces. *Honam Math. J.* **2017**, *39*, 115–126. [CrossRef]
19. Jebril, I.H.; Datta, S.K.; Sarkar, R.; Biswas, N. Common fixed point theorems under rational contractions for a pair of mappings in bicomplex valued metric spaces. *J. Interdiscip. Math.* **2019**, *22*, 1071–1082. [CrossRef]
20. Beg, I.; Kumar, Datta, S.; Pal, D. Fixed point in bicomplex valued metric spaces. *Int. J. Nonlinear Anal. Appl.* **2021**, *12*, 717–727. ISSN:2008-6822.
21. Gu, Z.; Mani, G.; Gnanaprakasam, A.J.; Li, Y. Solving a Fredholm integral equation via coupled fixed point on bicomplex partial metric space. *AIMS Math.* **2022**, *7*, 15402–15416. [CrossRef]
22. Gu, Z.; Mani, G.; Gnanaprakasam, A.J.; Li, Y. Solving a System of Nonlinear Integral Equations via Common Fixed Point Theorems on Bicomplex Partial Metric Space. *Mathematics* **2021**, *9*, 1584. [CrossRef]
23. Dattaa, S.K.; Palb, D.; Sarkarc, R.; Mannad, A. On a Common Fixed Point Theorem in Bicomplex Valued b-metric Space. *Montes Taurus J. Pure Appl. Math.* **2021**, *3*, 358–366.
24. Samei, M.E. Convergence of an iterative scheme for multifunctions on fuzzy metric spaces. *Sahand Commun. Math. Anal.* **2019**, *15*, 91–106. [CrossRef]
25. Guechi, S.; Dhayal, R.; Debbouche, A.; Malik, M. Analysis and Optimal Control of ϕ-Hilfer Fractional Semilinear Equations Involving Nonlocal Impulsive Conditions. *Symmetry* **2021**, *13*, 2084. [CrossRef]

26. Karthikeyan, K.; Karthikeyan, P.; Chalishajar, D.N.; Raja, D.S.; Sundararajan, P. Analysis on ψ-Hilfer Fractional Impulsive Differential Equations. *Symmetry* **2021**, *13*, 1895. [CrossRef]
27. Hakkar, N.; Dhayal, R.; Debbouche, A.; Torres, D.F.M. Approximate Controllability of Delayed Fractional Stochastic Differential Systems with Mixed Noise and Impulsive Effects. *Fractal Fract.* **2023**, *7*, 104. [CrossRef]
28. Vijayakumar, V.; Nisar, K.S.; Chalishajar, D.; Shukla, A.; Malik, M.; Alsaadi, A.; Aldosary, S.F. A Note on Approximate Controllability of Fractional Semilinear Integrodifferential Control Systems via Resolvent Operators. *Fractal Fract.* **2022**, *6*, 73. [CrossRef]

Disclaimer/Publisher's Note: The statements, opinions and data contained in all publications are solely those of the individual author(s) and contributor(s) and not of MDPI and/or the editor(s). MDPI and/or the editor(s) disclaim responsibility for any injury to people or property resulting from any ideas, methods, instructions or products referred to in the content.

Article

Existence and Uniqueness of Non-Negative Solution to a Coupled Fractional q-Difference System with Mixed q-Derivative via Mixed Monotone Operator Method

Yuan Meng, Conghong He, Renhao Ma and Huihui Pang *

College of Science, China Agricultural University, Beijing 100083, China; mengyuan_mzy@163.com (Y.M.); hechch2022@163.com (C.H.); marenhao1997@163.com (R.M.)
* Correspondence: phh2000@163.com

Abstract: In this paper, we study a nonlinear Riemann-Liouville fractional a q-difference system with multi-strip and multi-point mixed boundary conditions under the Caputo fractional q-derivative, where the nonlinear terms contain two coupled unknown functions and their fractional derivatives. Using the fixed point theorem for mixed monotone operators, we constructe iteration functions for arbitrary initial value and acquire the existence and uniqueness of extremal solutions. Moreover, a related example is given to illustrate our research results.

Keywords: the coupled Riemann-Liouville fractional q-difference system; the Caputo fractional q-derivative boundary conditions; mixed monotone operator

MSC: 34B18; 26A33; 34B27

1. Introduction

Fractional calculus come into people's view in 1695 [1], extending the traditional integral calculus concept to the whole field of real numbers. It is originally of great significance in many areas [2]. As we all know, in the research process of these fields, equations need to be established to describe the specific change process. On the other hand, fractional calculus has the nice property of being able to accurately describe these processes with genetic and memory traits. Therefore, the fractional differential equation has gradually become the focus of people's research. At the same time, the existence analysis, uniqueness analysis, stability analysis of solutions in fractional differential equation become an important research direction. Many scholars have studied them in recent years, and readers can refer to the literature [3–13].

At the beginning of the twentieth century, the appearance of Quantum Mechanics promoted the generation and development of Quantum calculus (q-calculus). F. H. Jackson made the first complete study of q-calculus [14,15]. Later W. A. Al-Salam [16] and R. P. Agarwal [17] proposed the basic concepts and properties of fractional q-calculus. Q-calculus has been an important bridge between mathematics and physics since its birth. It plays an extremely important role in quantum physics, spectral analysis and dynamical systems [18–21]. In recent years, q-calculus has also been increasingly used in engineering [22,23]. With the application and development of fractional differential equation and the extensive research and application of q-calculus in mathematics, physics and other fields, the study of fractional q-difference equation has become a topic of widespread concern. Increased experts begin to pay attention to the theoretical research of fractional q-difference equation [24–32].

In 2019, the authors [27] studied the boundary value problem of the following mixed fractional q-difference by the Guo–Krasnoselskii's fixed point theorem and the Banach contraction mapping principle:

$$\begin{cases} D_q^\alpha u(t) + f(t, u(t)) = 0, & t \in [0,1], \\ u(0) = {}^c D_q^\beta u(0) = {}^c D_q^\beta u(1), \end{cases}$$

where $0 < \beta \leq 1, 2 < \alpha < 2+\beta$, D_q^α, ${}^c D_q^\beta$ are the Riemann–Liouville fractional q-derivative and Caputo fractional q-derivative of order α, β.

In [30], utilizing the monotone iterative approach, the authors are considered with the fractional q-difference system involing four-point boundary conditions:

$$\begin{cases} D_q^\alpha u(t) + f(t, v(t)) = 0, & t \in (0,1), \\ D_q^\beta v(t) + f(t, u(t)) = 0, & t \in (0,1), \\ u(0) = 0, \ u(1) = \gamma_1 u(\eta_1), \\ v(0) = 0, \ v(1) = \gamma_2 v(\eta_2), \end{cases}$$

where $1 < \beta \leq \alpha \leq 2, 0 < \eta_1, \eta_2 < 1, 0 < \gamma_1 \eta_1^{\alpha-1} < 1$ and $0 < \gamma_2 \eta_2^{\beta-1} < 1$.

In [9], in view of the method of mixed monotone operators, the conclusion of the existence and uniqueness of solutions for the following coupled system is drawn:

$$\begin{cases} D_{0+}^\alpha x(\tau) + f_1\left(\tau, x(\tau), D_{0+}^\eta x(\tau)\right) + g_1(\tau, y(\tau)) = 0, \\ D_{0+}^\beta y(\tau) + f_2\left(\tau, y(\tau), D_{0+}^\gamma y(\tau)\right) + g_2(\tau, x(\tau)) = 0, \\ \tau \in (0,1), \quad n-1 < \alpha, \beta < n, \\ x^{(i)}(0) = y^{(i)}(0) = 0, \quad i = 0, 1, 2, \ldots, n-2, \\ \left[D_{0+}^\zeta y(\tau)\right]_{\tau=1} = k_1(y(1)), \ \left[D_{0+}^\zeta x(\tau)\right]_{\tau=1} = k_2(x(1)), \end{cases}$$

where the integer number $n > 3$ and $1 \leq \gamma \leq \xi \leq n-2, 1 \leq \eta \leq \zeta \leq n-2$, f_1, f_2: $[0,1] \times \mathbb{R}^+ \times \mathbb{R}^+ \to \mathbb{R}^+, g_1, g_2$: $[0,1] \times \mathbb{R}^+ \to \mathbb{R}^+$ and k_1, k_2: $\mathbb{R}^+ \to \mathbb{R}^+$ are continuous functions, D_{0+}^α and D_{0+}^β represent the Riemann-Liouville derivatives.

There are many ways to deal with the boundary value problem, such as monotone iteration techniques, the Banach contraction mapping principle and so on. In these methods, the constraints are often stringent, one of which is that completely continuity of the operator must be proved and the proving process is often very complicated. However, The mixed monotone operators have relatively loose requirements and only need to prove some properties like the upper bound. Now, there has been some literature using it to prove the existence and uniqueness of solutions, see [9–13,31,32]. Therefore, this paper also intends to introduce this method to prove the corresponding conclusion.

Motivated by the above mentioned papers, we investigate the following coupled nonlinear fractional q-difference system:

$$\begin{cases} D_q^{\alpha_1} u(t) + f_1(t, u(t), v(t), D_q^{\gamma_1} u(t), D_q^{\gamma_2} v(t)) = 0, & t \in (0,1), \\ D_q^{\alpha_2} v(t) + f_2(t, u(t), v(t), D_q^{\gamma_1} u(t), D_q^{\gamma_2} v(t)) = 0, & t \in (0,1), \end{cases} \quad (1)$$

subject to the multi-strip and multi-point mixed boundary conditions:

$$\begin{cases} u(0) = 0, \ v(0) = 0, \\ {}^c D_q^{\alpha_1 - 1} u(1) = \sum_{i=1}^{m} \lambda_{1i} I_q^{\beta_{1i}} v(\xi_i) + \sum_{j=1}^{n} b_{1j} v(\eta_j), \\ {}^c D_q^{\alpha_2 - 1} v(1) = \sum_{i=1}^{m} \lambda_{2i} I_q^{\beta_{2i}} u(\xi_i) + \sum_{j=1}^{n} b_{2j} u(\eta_j), \end{cases} \quad (2)$$

where $^cD_q^\alpha, D_q^\alpha$ are the Caputo fractional q-derivative and Riemann-Liouville fractional q-derivative of order α respectively, and $I_q^{\beta_{ki}}$ is the Riemann-Liouville fractional q-integral of order β_{ki}, for $k = 1, 2$ and $i = 1, 2, \ldots, m$. $\alpha_1, \alpha_2 \in [1, 2]$, $\gamma_1, \gamma_2 \in [0, 1]$; $\lambda_{1i}, \lambda_{2i} \in [0, +\infty)$, $\beta_{1i}, \beta_{2i} \in (0, +\infty)$, $\xi_i \in [0, 1]$, for $i = 1, 2, \ldots, m$; $b_{1j}, b_{2j} \in [0, +\infty)$, $\eta_j \in [0, 1]$, for $j = 1, 2, \ldots, n$.

The system has the following four main characteristics: First, it is based on q-calculus, so it is closely connected with Physics and has practical research significance. Second, there are two types of derivatives (the Caputo and Riemann-Liouville fractional q-derivative) in the system, which is more in line with the complex conditions of the real world. Third, the unknown functions $u(t)$ and $v(t)$ in the system influence each other which can have better practical applications. Fourth, the nonlinear part, f_1 and f_2, contain two derivative operators $D_q^{\gamma_1}, D_q^{\gamma_2}$. Due to the complexity of the model, it is difficult to find the Green's function and its upper and lower bounds. After that, we choose the mixed monotone operator method to get the existence and uniqueness of non-negative solution to our system. Compared with the monotone iterative method for the requirements of fixed initial values, mixed monotone operators do not need to prove complete continuity, and there are no restrictions for initial values, that is, the arbitrarily initial value works. Therefore, the mixed monotone method is more widely applicable.

This article is arranged as the following aspects: In Section 2, some fundamental definitions and lemmas are introduced. Moreover, some crucial results and their proofs are discussed. In Section 3, we set out the main conclusion: the existence and uniqueness results of non-negative solutions. At last, an example is given to illustrate our result.

2. Preliminaries

For the reader's convenience, we list some important definitions of q-calculus. On the other hand, there are also basic notion and lemmas for the proof which will be used in the next section.

Let $(E, \|\cdot\|)$ be a Banach space, partially ordered by a cone $P \subset E$. In other words, $x \preceq y$ if and only if $y - x \in P$. We use θ to represent the zero element of E. We consider a cone P to be normal if there exists a constant $M > 0$ such that for all $x, y \in E$, $\theta \leqslant x \leqslant y$ implies $\|x\| \leqslant M\|y\|$; on this condition M is called the normality constant of P. Giving $h > \theta$, we denote by P_h the set $P_h = \{x \in E | \exists \lambda, \mu > 0 : \lambda h \leqslant x \leqslant \mu h\}$.

Definition 1 ([33,34]). *$A : P \times P \to P$ is said to be a mixed monotone operator of $A(x, y)$ is increasing in x and decreasing in y, i.e., for $x_i, y_i \in P(i = 1, 2)$, $x_1 \leqslant x_2, y_1 \geqslant y_2$ implies that $A(x_1, y_1) \leqslant A(x_2, y_2)$. Element $x \in P$ is called a fixed point of A if $A(x, x) = x$.*

Lemma 1 ([35]). *Let P a normal cone of a real Banach space E. Also, let $A : P \times P \to P$ be a mixed monotone operator. Assume that*

(A_1) *there exists $h \in P$ with $h \neq \theta$ such that $A(h, h) \in P_h$;*

(A_2) *for any $u, v \in P$ and $t \in (0, 1)$, there exists $\varphi(t) \in (0, 1]$ such that $A(tu, t^{-1}v) \geqslant \varphi(t)A(u, v)$.*

Then operator A has a unique fixed point x^* in P_h. Moreover, for any initial $x_0, y_0 \in P_h$, constructing successively the sequences

$$x_n = A(x_{n-1}, y_{n-1}), \quad y_n = A(y_{n-1}, x_{n-1}), \quad n = 1, 2, \cdots,$$

one has $\|x_n - x^*\| \to 0$ and $\|y_n - x^*\| \to 0$ as $n \to \infty$.

For $q \in (0, 1)$ and $a \in \mathbb{R}$, define

$$[a]_q = \frac{1 - q^a}{1 - q}.$$

The q-analogue of the power function is

$$(a-b)_q^{(0)} = 1,$$

$$(a-b)_q^{(k)} = \prod_{i=0}^{k-1}(a-bq^i), \quad k \in \mathbb{N}, a,b \in \mathbb{R}.$$

Generally, if $\alpha \in \mathbb{R}$, there is

$$(a-b)_q^{(\alpha)} = a^\alpha \prod_{i=0}^{\infty} \frac{a-bq^i}{a-bq^{i+\alpha}}.$$

It is clearly that $a^{(\alpha)} = a^\alpha$ for $b=0$ and $0^{(\alpha)} = 0$ for $\alpha \geq 0$.

The q-Gamma function is given by

$$\Gamma_q(x) = \frac{(1-q)^{(x-1)}}{(1-q)^{x-1}}, \quad x \in \mathbb{R}\setminus\{0,-1,-2,\ldots\},$$

then we have $\Gamma_q(x+1) = [x]_q \Gamma_q(x)$.

For $x, y > 0$, we have

$$B_q(x,y) = \int_0^1 t^{x-1}(1-qt)^{(y-1)} d_q t, \tag{3}$$

especially,

$$B_q(x,y) = \frac{\Gamma_q(x)\Gamma_q(y)}{\Gamma_q(x+y)}.$$

The q-derivative of a function f is defined by

$$(D_q f)(x) = \frac{f(qx) - f(x)}{(q-1)x},$$

$$(D_q f)(0) = \lim_{x \to 0}(D_q f)(x),$$

and the q-derivative of higher order by

$$(D_q^0 f)(x) = f(x),$$

$$(D_q^n f)(x) = D_q(D_q^{n-1} f)(x), \quad n \in \mathbb{N}.$$

The q-integral of a function f defined on the interval $[0,b]$ is given by

$$(I_q f)(x) = \int_0^x f(s) d_q s = x(1-q)\sum_{k=0}^{\infty} f(xq^k)q^k, \quad x \in [0,b].$$

If $a \in [0,b]$ and f is defined in the interval $[0,b]$, then its integral from a to b is defined by

$$\int_a^b f(s) d_q s = \int_0^b f(s) d_q s - \int_0^a f(s) d_q s,$$

and similarly the q-integral of higher order is given by

$$(I_q^0 f)(x) = f(x),$$

$$(I_q^n f)(x) = I_q(I_q^{n-1} f)(x), \quad n \in \mathbb{N}.$$

Definition 2 ([17]). *Let $\alpha \geq 0$ and f be a real function defined on a certain interval $[a,b]$. The Riemann-Liouville fractional q-integral of order α is defined by*

$$(I_q^0 f)(t) = f(t),$$

$$(I_q^\alpha f)(t) = \frac{1}{\Gamma_q(\alpha)} \int_0^t (t - qs)^{(\alpha-1)} f(s) d_q s, \quad \alpha > 0.$$

Definition 3 ([17]). *The fractional q-derivative of the Riemann-Liouville type of order $\alpha \geq 0$ of a continuous and differential function f on the interval $[a,b]$ is given by*

$$(D_q^0 f)(t) = f(t),$$

$$(D_q^\alpha f)(t) = (D_q^l I_q^{l-\alpha} f)(t), \quad \alpha > 0,$$

where l is the smallest integer greater than or equal to α.

Definition 4 ([17]). *Let $\alpha \geq 0$, and the Caputo fractional q-derivatives of f be defined by*

$$(^c D_q^\alpha f)(t) = (I_q^{l-\alpha} D_q^l f)(t),$$

where l is the smallest integer greater than or equal to α.

Lemma 2 ([36]). *Let $\alpha, \beta \geq 0$ and $f : [a,b] \to \mathbb{R}$ be a continuous function defined on $[a,b]$ and its derivative exist. Then the following formulas hold:*

$$(D_q^\alpha I_q^\alpha f)(t) = f(t),$$

$$(I_q^\alpha I_q^\beta f)(t) = (I_q^{\alpha+\beta} f)(t).$$

Lemma 3 ([36]). *Let $\alpha > 0$ and p be a positive integer. Then the following equality holds:*

$$(I_q^\alpha D_q^p f)(t) = (D_q^p I_q^\alpha f)(t) - \sum_{k=0}^{p-1} \frac{t^{\alpha-p+k}}{\Gamma_q(\alpha-p+k+1)} (D_q^k f)(0).$$

Lemma 4 ([36,37]). *Let $\alpha > 0$ and $n = [\alpha] + 1$. Then we have*

$$(I_q^\alpha \, ^c D_q^\alpha f)(t) = f(t) + c_0 + c_1 t + c_2 t^2 + \ldots + c_{n-1} t^{n-1},$$

where $c_0, c_1, \ldots, c_{n-1}$ are some constants.

For convenience, we denote

$$\begin{cases} l_1 = \dfrac{1}{\Gamma_q(\alpha_2)} \left[\displaystyle\sum_{i=1}^m \dfrac{\lambda_{1i}}{\Gamma_q(\beta_{1i})} \int_0^{\xi_i} (\xi_i - qs)^{(\beta_{1i}-1)} s^{\alpha_2-1} d_q s + \sum_{j=1}^n b_{1j} \eta_j^{\alpha_2-1} \right], \\ l_2 = \dfrac{1}{\Gamma_q(\alpha_1)} \left[\displaystyle\sum_{i=1}^m \dfrac{\lambda_{2i}}{\Gamma_q(\beta_{2i})} \int_0^{\xi_i} (\xi_i - qs)^{(\beta_{2i}-1)} s^{\alpha_1-1} d_q s + \sum_{j=1}^n b_{2j} \eta_j^{\alpha_1-1} \right]. \end{cases} \quad (4)$$

The following assumptions are introduced for analysis:

(F_1) $1 \leq \alpha_k \leq 2$, $\beta_{ki} > 0$, for $k = 1, 2$ and $i = 1, 2, \ldots, m$;
(F_2) $0 \leq \eta_j, \xi_i \leq 1$, $\lambda_{1i}, \lambda_{2i} \geq 0$, $b_{1j}, b_{2j} \geq 0$, for $i = 1, 2, \ldots, m$, $j = 1, 2, \ldots, n$;
(F_3) $1 - l_1 l_2 > 0$, where l_1, l_2 are defined by (4);
(F_4) $f_k : [0, 1] \times [0, +\infty)^4 \to [0, +\infty)$ is continuous ($k = 1, 2$).

A corresponding linear differential system with BVP (1) and (2) is considered, and the expression of the corresponding Green's functions are established.

Lemma 5. *Assume that* (F_1)–(F_3) *hold. For* $h_1, h_2 \in C(0,1)$, *the fractional differential system*

$$\begin{cases} D_q^{\alpha_1} u(t) + h_1(t) = 0, & t \in (0,1), \\ D_q^{\alpha_2} v(t) + h_2(t) = 0, & t \in (0,1), \end{cases} \tag{5}$$

with boundary conditions (2) has an integral representation

$$\begin{cases} u(t) = \int_0^1 K_1(t,qs) h_1(s) d_q s + \int_0^1 H_1(t,qs) h_2(s) d_q s, \\ v(t) = \int_0^1 K_2(t,qs) h_2(s) d_q s + \int_0^1 H_2(t,qs) h_1(s) d_q s, \end{cases} \tag{6}$$

where

$$K_1(t,qs) = g_1(t,qs) + \frac{l_1 t^{\alpha_1 - 1}}{\Gamma_q(\alpha_1)(1 - l_1 l_2)} \left[\sum_{i=1}^m \frac{\lambda_{2i}}{\Gamma_q(\beta_{2i})} \int_0^{\xi_i} (\xi_i - q\tau)^{(\beta_{2i} - 1)} g_1(\tau, qs) d\tau + \sum_{j=1}^n b_{2j} g_1(\eta_j, qs) \right],$$

$$H_1(t,qs) = \frac{t^{\alpha_1 - 1}}{\Gamma_q(\alpha_1)(1 - l_1 l_2)} \left[\sum_{i=1}^m \frac{\lambda_{1i}}{\Gamma_q(\beta_{1i})} \int_0^{\xi_i} (\xi_i - q\tau)^{(\beta_{1i} - 1)} g_2(\tau, qs) d_q \tau + \sum_{j=1}^n b_{1j} g_2(\eta_j, qs) \right], \tag{7}$$

$$K_2(t,qs) = g_2(t,qs) + \frac{l_2 t^{\alpha_2 - 1}}{\Gamma_q(\alpha_2)(1 - l_1 l_2)} \left[\sum_{i=1}^m \frac{\lambda_{1i}}{\Gamma_q(\beta_{1i})} \int_0^{\xi_i} (\xi_i - q\tau)^{(\beta_{1i} - 1)} g_2(\tau, qs) d\tau + \sum_{j=1}^n b_{1j} g_2(\eta_j, qs) \right],$$

$$H_2(t,qs) = \frac{t^{\alpha_2 - 1}}{\Gamma_q(\alpha_2)(1 - l_1 l_2)} \left[\sum_{i=1}^m \frac{\lambda_{2i}}{\Gamma_q(\beta_{2i})} \int_0^{\xi_i} (\xi_i - q\tau)^{(\beta_{2i} - 1)} g_1(\tau, qs) d_q \tau + \sum_{j=1}^n b_{2j} g_1(\eta_j, qs) \right], \tag{8}$$

and for k = 1, 2,

$$g_k(t,qs) = \frac{1}{\Gamma_q(\alpha_k)} \begin{cases} t^{\alpha_k - 1} - (t - qs)^{(\alpha_k - 1)}, & 0 \leq qs \leq t \leq 1, \\ t^{\alpha_k - 1}, & 0 \leq t \leq qs \leq 1. \end{cases} \tag{9}$$

Proof. According to Lemma 3, the Equation (5) can be reduced to the following equivalent integral equations:

$$\begin{cases} u(t) = -I_q^{\alpha_1} h_1(t) + c_{11} t^{\alpha_1 - 1} + c_{12} t^{\alpha_1 - 2}, \\ v(t) = -I_q^{\alpha_2} h_2(t) + c_{21} t^{\alpha_2 - 1} + c_{22} t^{\alpha_2 - 2}, \end{cases} \tag{10}$$

where $c_{11}, c_{12}, c_{21}, c_{22}$ are constants.

From $u(0) = v(0) = 0$, we obtain $c_{12} = c_{22} = 0$. By using Lemma 4, we get

$$\begin{cases} {}^c D_q^{\alpha_1 - 1} u(t) = -{}^c D_q^{\alpha_1 - 1} I_q^{\alpha_1} h_1(t) + c_{11} {}^c D_q^{\alpha_1 - 1} t^{\alpha_1 - 1} = -I_q h_1(t) + c_{11} [\alpha_1 - 1]_q I_q^{2 - \alpha_1} t^{\alpha_1 - 2}, \\ {}^c D_q^{\alpha_2 - 1} v(t) = -{}^c D_q^{\alpha_2 - 1} I_q^{\alpha_2} h_2(t) + c_{21} {}^c D_q^{\alpha_2 - 1} t^{\alpha_2 - 1} = -I_q h_2(t) + c_{21} [\alpha_2 - 1]_q I_q^{2 - \alpha_2} t^{\alpha_2 - 2}. \end{cases} \tag{11}$$

Then from (3) we get

$$\begin{cases} {}^c D_q^{\alpha_1 - 1} u(1) = -I_q h_1(1) + c_{11} [\alpha_1 - 1]_q I_q^{2 - \alpha_1} 1 = -\int_0^1 h_1(s) d_q s + c_{11} \Gamma_q(\alpha_1), \\ {}^c D_q^{\alpha_2 - 1} v(1) = -I_q h_2(1) + c_{21} [\alpha_2 - 1]_q I_q^{2 - \alpha_2} 1 = -\int_0^1 h_2(s) d_q s + c_{21} \Gamma_q(\alpha_2). \end{cases} \tag{12}$$

157

From the rest of the condition of (2), it can be obtained that

$$\begin{cases} c_{11} = \dfrac{1}{\Gamma_q(\alpha_1)}\left[\displaystyle\sum_{i=1}^{m}\lambda_{1i}I_q^{\beta_{1i}}v(\xi_i) + \sum_{j=1}^{n}b_{1j}v(\eta_j) + \int_0^1 h_1(s)d_qs\right], \\ c_{21} = \dfrac{1}{\Gamma_q(\alpha_2)}\left[\displaystyle\sum_{i=1}^{m}\lambda_{2i}I_q^{\beta_{2i}}u(\xi_i) + \sum_{j=1}^{n}b_{2j}u(\eta_j) + \int_0^1 h_2(s)d_qs\right]. \end{cases} \quad (13)$$

Further, we can reduce (10) to

$$\begin{cases} u(t) = \dfrac{t^{\alpha_1-1}}{\Gamma(\alpha_1)}\left[\displaystyle\sum_{i=1}^{m}\dfrac{\lambda_{1i}}{\Gamma_q(\beta_{1i})}\int_0^{\xi_i}(\xi_i-qs)^{(\beta_{1i}-1)}v(s)d_qs + \sum_{j=1}^{n}b_{1j}v(\eta_j)\right] + \int_0^1 g_1(t,qs)h_1(s)d_qs, \\ v(t) = \dfrac{t^{\alpha_2-1}}{\Gamma(\alpha_2)}\left[\displaystyle\sum_{i=1}^{m}\dfrac{\lambda_{2i}}{\Gamma_q(\beta_{2i})}\int_0^{\xi_i}(\xi_i-qs)^{(\beta_{2i}-1)}u(s)d_qs + \sum_{j=1}^{n}b_{2j}u(\eta_j)\right] + \int_0^1 g_2(t,qs)h_2(s)d_qs, \end{cases} \quad (14)$$

where $g_k(t,qs)(k=1,2)$ are introduced by (9). Then we can get

$$\sum_{i=1}^{m}\dfrac{\lambda_{1i}}{\Gamma_q(\beta_{1i})}\int_0^{\xi_i}(\xi_i-qs)^{(\beta_{1i}-1)}v(s)d_qs + \sum_{j=1}^{n}b_{1j}v(\eta_j)$$
$$= \dfrac{1}{\Gamma_q(\alpha_2)}\left[\sum_{i=1}^{m}\dfrac{\lambda_{1i}}{\Gamma_q(\beta_{1i})}\int_0^{\xi_i}(\xi_i-qs)^{(\beta_{1i}-1)}s^{\alpha_2-1}d_qs + \sum_{j=1}^{n}b_{1j}\eta_j^{\alpha_2-1}\right]$$
$$\cdot \left[\sum_{i=1}^{m}\dfrac{\lambda_{2i}}{\Gamma_q(\beta_{2i})}\int_0^{\xi_i}(\xi_i-qs)^{(\beta_{2i}-1)}u(s)d_qs + \sum_{j=1}^{n}b_{2j}u(\eta_j)\right] \quad (15)$$
$$+ \sum_{i=1}^{m}\dfrac{\lambda_{1i}}{\Gamma_q(\beta_{1i})}\int_0^{\xi_i}(\xi_i-q\tau)^{(\beta_{1i}-1)}\int_0^1 g_2(\tau,qs)h_2(s)d_qsd_q\tau + \sum_{j=1}^{n}b_{1j}\int_0^1 g_2(\eta_j,qs)h_2(s)d_qs.$$

Moreover, we have

$$\sum_{i=1}^{m}\dfrac{\lambda_{2i}}{\Gamma_q(\beta_{2i})}\int_0^{\xi_i}(\xi_i-qs)^{(\beta_{2i}-1)}u(s)d_qs + \sum_{j=1}^{n}b_{2j}u(\eta_j)$$
$$= \dfrac{1}{\Gamma_q(\alpha_1)}\left[\sum_{i=1}^{m}\dfrac{\lambda_{2i}}{\Gamma_q(\beta_{2i})}\int_0^{\xi_i}(\xi_i-qs)^{(\beta_{2i}-1)}s^{\alpha_1-1}d_qs + \sum_{j=1}^{n}b_{2j}\eta_j^{\alpha_1-1}\right]$$
$$\cdot \left[\sum_{i=1}^{m}\dfrac{\lambda_{1i}}{\Gamma_q(\beta_{1i})}\int_0^{\xi_i}(\xi_i-qs)^{(\beta_{1i}-1)}v(s)d_qs + \sum_{j=1}^{n}b_{1j}v(\eta_j)\right] \quad (16)$$
$$+ \sum_{i=1}^{m}\dfrac{\lambda_{2i}}{\Gamma_q(\beta_{2i})}\int_0^{\xi_i}(\xi_i-q\tau)^{(\beta_{2i}-1)}\int_0^1 g_1(\tau,qs)h_1(s)d_qsd_q\tau + \sum_{j=1}^{n}b_{2j}\int_0^1 g_1(\eta_j,qs)h_1(s)d_qs.$$

Combining (15) and (16), it can be seen that

$$\sum_{i=1}^{m} \frac{\lambda_{1i}}{\Gamma_q(\beta_{1i})} \int_0^{\xi_i} (\xi_i - qs)^{(\beta_{1i}-1)} v(s) d_q s + \sum_{j=1}^{n} b_{1j} v(\eta_j)$$

$$= \frac{1}{1-l_1 l_2} \left[l_1 \left(\sum_{i=1}^{m} \frac{\lambda_{2i}}{\Gamma_q(\beta_{2i})} \int_0^{\xi_i} (\xi_i - q\tau)^{(\beta_{2i}-1)} \int_0^1 g_1(\tau, qs) h_1(s) d_q s d_q \tau + \sum_{j=1}^{n} b_{2j} \int_0^1 g_1(\eta_j, qs) h_1(s) d_q s \right) \right.$$
$$\left. + \sum_{i=1}^{m} \frac{\lambda_{1i}}{\Gamma_q(\beta_{1i})} \int_0^{\xi_i} (\xi_i - q\tau)^{(\beta_{1i}-1)} \int_0^1 g_2(\tau, qs) h_2(s) d_q s d_q \tau + \sum_{j=1}^{n} b_{1j} \int_0^1 g_2(\eta_j, qs) h_2(s) d_q s \right],$$

$$\sum_{i=1}^{m} \frac{\lambda_{2i}}{\Gamma_q(\beta_{2i})} \int_0^{\xi_i} (\xi_i - qs)^{(\beta_{2i}-1)} u(s) d_q s + \sum_{j=1}^{n} b_{2j} u(\eta_j) \qquad (17)$$

$$= \frac{1}{1-l_1 l_2} \left[l_2 \left(\sum_{i=1}^{m} \frac{\lambda_{1i}}{\Gamma_q(\beta_{1i})} \int_0^{\xi_i} (\xi_i - q\tau)^{(\beta_{1i}-1)} \int_0^1 g_2(\tau, qs) h_2(s) d_q s d_q \tau + \sum_{j=1}^{n} b_{1j} \int_0^1 g_2(\eta_j, qs) h_2(s) d_q s \right) \right.$$
$$\left. + \sum_{i=1}^{m} \frac{\lambda_{2i}}{\Gamma_q(\beta_{2i})} \int_0^{\xi_i} (\xi_i - q\tau)^{(\beta_{2i}-1)} \int_0^1 g_1(\tau, qs) h_1(s) d_q s d_q \tau + \sum_{j=1}^{n} b_{2j} \int_0^1 g_1(\eta_j, qs) h_1(s) d_q s \right],$$

where l_k ($k = 1, 2$) is defined by (4). According to (14) and (17), we can get

$$u(t) = \int_0^1 g_1(t, qs) h_1(s) d_q s$$
$$+ \frac{t^{\alpha_1 - 1}}{\Gamma_q(\alpha_1)(1 - l_1 l_2)} \left[\int_0^1 l_1 \left(\sum_{i=1}^{m} \frac{\lambda_{2i}}{\Gamma_q(\beta_{2i})} \int_0^{\xi_i} (\xi_i - q\tau)^{(\beta_{2i}-1)} g_1(\tau, qs) d_q \tau + \sum_{j=1}^{n} b_{2j} g_1(\eta_j, qs) \right) h_1(s) d_q s \right.$$
$$\left. + \int_0^1 \left(\sum_{i=1}^{m} \frac{\lambda_{1i}}{\Gamma_q(\beta_{1i})} \int_0^{\xi_i} (\xi_i - q\tau)^{(\beta_{1i}-1)} g_2(\tau, qs) d_q \tau + \sum_{j=1}^{n} b_{1j} g_2(\eta_j, qs) \right) h_2(s) d_q s \right]$$
$$= \int_0^1 K_1(t, qs) h_1(s) d_q s + \int_0^1 H_1(t, qs) h_2(s) d_q s,$$

where $K_1(t, qs)$ and $H_1(t, qs)$ are introduced by (7). Similarly, we also have

$$v(t) = \int_0^1 g_2(t, qs) h_2(s) d_q s$$
$$+ \frac{t^{\alpha_2 - 1}}{\Gamma_q(\alpha_2)(1 - l_1 l_2)} \left[\int_0^1 l_2 \left(\sum_{i=1}^{m} \frac{\lambda_{1i}}{\Gamma_q(\beta_{1i})} \int_0^{\xi_i} (\xi_i - q\tau)^{(\beta_{1i}-1)} g_2(\tau, qs) d_q \tau + \sum_{j=1}^{n} b_{1j} g_2(\eta_j, qs) \right) h_2(s) d_q s \right.$$
$$\left. + \int_0^1 \left(\sum_{i=1}^{m} \frac{\lambda_{2i}}{\Gamma_q(\beta_{2i})} \int_0^{\xi_i} (\xi_i - q\tau)^{(\beta_{2i}-1)} g_1(\tau, qs) d_q \tau + \sum_{j=1}^{n} b_{2j} g_1(\eta_j, qs) \right) h_1(s) d_q s \right]$$
$$= \int_0^1 K_2(t, qs) h_2(s) d_q s + \int_0^1 H_2(t, qs) h_1(s) d_q s,$$

where $K_2(t, qs)$ and $H_2(t, qs)$ are also given by (8).
This completes the proof of the lemma. □

Let
$$K_{\tilde{i}1}(t,qs) = D_q^{\gamma_{\tilde{i}}} K_1(t,qs)$$
$$= D_q^{\gamma_{\tilde{i}}} g_1(t,qs) + \frac{l_1 t^{\alpha_1 - \gamma_{\tilde{i}} - 1}}{\Gamma_q(\alpha_1 - \gamma_{\tilde{i}})(1 - l_1 l_2)}$$
$$\cdot \left[\sum_{i=1}^{m} \frac{\lambda_{2i}}{\Gamma_q(\beta_{2i})} \int_0^{\xi_i} (\xi_i - q\tau)^{(\beta_{2i}-1)} g_1(\tau, qs) d\tau + \sum_{j=1}^{n} b_{2j} g_1(\eta_j, qs) \right],$$
$$H_{\tilde{i}1}(t,qs) = D_q^{\gamma_{\tilde{i}}} H_1(t,qs)$$
$$= \frac{t^{\alpha_1 - \gamma_{\tilde{i}} - 1}}{\Gamma_q(\alpha_1 - \gamma_{\tilde{i}})(1 - l_1 l_2)}$$
$$\cdot \left[\sum_{i=1}^{m} \frac{\lambda_{1i}}{\Gamma_q(\beta_{1i})} \int_0^{\xi_i} (\xi_i - q\tau)^{(\beta_{1i}-1)} g_2(\tau, qs) d_q\tau + \sum_{j=1}^{n} b_{1j} g_2(\eta_j, qs) \right], \tag{18}$$

$$K_{\tilde{i}2}(t,qs) = D_q^{\gamma_{\tilde{i}}} K_2(t,qs)$$
$$= D_q^{\gamma_{\tilde{i}}} g_2(t,qs) + \frac{l_2 t^{\alpha_2 - \gamma_{\tilde{i}} - 1}}{\Gamma_q(\alpha_2 - \gamma_{\tilde{i}})(1 - l_1 l_2)}$$
$$\cdot \left[\sum_{i=1}^{m} \frac{\lambda_{1i}}{\Gamma_q(\beta_{1i})} \int_0^{\xi_i} (\xi_i - q\tau)^{(\beta_{1i}-1)} g_2(\tau, qs) d\tau + \sum_{j=1}^{n} b_{1j} g_2(\eta_j, qs) \right],$$
$$H_{\tilde{i}2}(t,qs) = D_q^{\gamma_{\tilde{i}}} H_2(t,qs)$$
$$= \frac{t^{\alpha_2 - \gamma_{\tilde{i}} - 1}}{\Gamma_q(\alpha_2 - \gamma_{\tilde{i}})(1 - l_1 l_2)}$$
$$\cdot \left[\sum_{i=1}^{m} \frac{\lambda_{2i}}{\Gamma_q(\beta_{2i})} \int_0^{\xi_i} (\xi_i - q\tau)^{(\beta_{2i}-1)} g_1(\tau, qs) d_q\tau + \sum_{j=1}^{n} b_{2j} g_1(\eta_j, qs) \right], \tag{19}$$

$$D_q^{\gamma_{\tilde{i}}} g_k(t,qs) = \frac{1}{\Gamma_q(\alpha_k - \gamma_{\tilde{i}})} \begin{cases} t^{\alpha_k - \gamma_{\tilde{i}} - 1} - (t - qs)^{(\alpha_k - \gamma_{\tilde{i}} - 1)}, & 0 \leq qs \leq t \leq 1, \\ t^{\alpha_k - \gamma_{\tilde{i}} - 1}, & 0 \leq t \leq qs \leq 1, \end{cases} \tag{20}$$

where $\tilde{i} = 1, 2$ and $k = 1, 2$.

Lemma 6. *Assume that* (F_1) *holds. Then the functions* $g_k(t,qs)$ *defined by (9) and* $D_q^{\gamma_{\tilde{i}}} g_k(t,qs)$ *defined by (20) for* $\tilde{i} = 1, 2, k = 1, 2$ *have the following properties:*

(1) $0 \leq \dfrac{1}{\Gamma_q(\alpha_k)}[1 - (1 - qs)^{(\alpha_k - 1)}] t^{\alpha_k - 1} \leq g_k(t,qs) \leq \dfrac{1}{\Gamma_q(\alpha_k)} t^{\alpha_k - 1};$

(2) $0 \leq \dfrac{1}{\Gamma_q(\alpha_k - \gamma_{\tilde{i}})}[1 - (1 - qs)^{(\alpha_k - \gamma_{\tilde{i}} - 1)}] t^{\alpha_k - \gamma_{\tilde{i}} - 1} \leq D_q^{\gamma_{\tilde{i}}} g_k(t,qs) \leq \dfrac{1}{\Gamma_q(\alpha_k - \gamma_{\tilde{i}})} t^{\alpha_k - \gamma_{\tilde{i}} - 1},$

for $t, qs \in [0, 1]$.

Proof. (1) For $0 \leq qs \leq t \leq 1$, we can get

$$g_k(t, qs) = \frac{1}{\Gamma_q(\alpha_k)} \left[t^{\alpha_k-1} - (t - qs)^{(\alpha_k-1)} \right]$$

$$\geq \frac{1}{\Gamma_q(\alpha_k)} \left[t^{\alpha_k-1} - (t - qs \cdot t)^{(\alpha_k-1)} \right]$$

$$= \frac{1}{\Gamma_q(\alpha_k)} [1 - (1 - qs)^{(\alpha_k-1)}] t^{\alpha_k-1} \geq 0,$$

$$g_k(t, qs) = \frac{1}{\Gamma_q(\alpha_k)} \left[t^{\alpha_k-1} - (t - qs)^{(\alpha_k-1)} \right]$$

$$\leq \frac{1}{\Gamma_q(\alpha_k)} t^{\alpha_k-1}.$$

For $0 \leq t \leq qs \leq 1$, we have

$$g_k(t, qs) = \frac{1}{\Gamma_q(\alpha_k)} t^{\alpha_k-1}$$

$$\geq \frac{1}{\Gamma_q(\alpha_k)} t^{\alpha_k-1} - \frac{1}{\Gamma_q(\alpha_k)} t^{\alpha_k-1} \cdot (1 - qs)^{(\alpha_k-1)}$$

$$= \frac{1}{\Gamma_q(\alpha_k)} [1 - (1 - qs)^{(\alpha_k-1)}] t^{\alpha_k-1} \geq 0,$$

$$g_k(t, qs) = \frac{1}{\Gamma_q(\alpha_k)} t^{\alpha_k-1}.$$

(2) For $0 \leq qs \leq t \leq 1$, we have

$$D_q^{\gamma_i} g_k(t, qs) = \frac{1}{\Gamma_q(\alpha_k - \gamma_i)} \left[t^{\alpha_k - \gamma_i - 1} - (t - qs)^{(\alpha_k - \gamma_i - 1)} \right]$$

$$\geq \frac{1}{\Gamma_q(\alpha_k - \gamma_i)} \left[t^{\alpha_k - \gamma_i - 1} - (t - qs \cdot t)^{(\alpha_k - \gamma_i - 1)} \right]$$

$$= \frac{1}{\Gamma_q(\alpha_k - \gamma_i)} [1 - (1 - qs)^{(\alpha_k - \gamma_i - 1)}] t^{\alpha_k - \gamma_i - 1} \geq 0,$$

$$D_q^{\gamma_i} g_k(t, qs) = \frac{1}{\Gamma_q(\alpha_k - \gamma_i)} \left[t^{\alpha_k - \gamma_i - 1} - (t - qs)^{(\alpha_k - \gamma_i - 1)} \right]$$

$$\leq \frac{1}{\Gamma_q(\alpha_k - \gamma_i)} t^{\alpha_k - \gamma_i - 1}.$$

For $0 \leq t \leq qs \leq 1$, we have

$$D_q^{\gamma_i} g_k(t, qs) = \frac{1}{\Gamma_q(\alpha_k - \gamma_i)} t^{\alpha_k - \gamma_i - 1}$$

$$\geq \frac{1}{\Gamma_q(\alpha_k - \gamma_i)} t^{\alpha_k - \gamma_i - 1} - \frac{1}{\Gamma_q(\alpha_k - \gamma_i)} t^{\alpha_k - \gamma_i - 1} \cdot (1 - qs)^{(\alpha_k - \gamma_i - 1)}$$

$$= \frac{1}{\Gamma_q(\alpha_k - \gamma_i)} [1 - (1 - qs)^{(\alpha_k - \gamma_i - 1)}] t^{\alpha_k - \gamma_i - 1} \geq 0,$$

$$D_q^{\gamma_i} g_k(t, qs) = \frac{1}{\Gamma_q(\alpha_k - \gamma_i)} t^{\alpha_k - \gamma_i - 1}.$$

This completes the proof of the lemma. □

For computational convenience, we introduce the following notations:

$$\varrho_1 = \frac{1}{\Gamma_q(\alpha_1)}\left[1 + \frac{l_1}{\Gamma_q(\alpha_1)(1-l_1l_2)}\left(\sum_{i=1}^{m}\frac{\lambda_{2i}}{\Gamma_q(\beta_{2i})}\int_0^{\xi_i}(\xi_i-q\tau)^{(\beta_{2i}-1)}\tau^{\alpha_1-1}d_q\tau + \sum_{j=1}^{n}b_{2j}\eta_j^{\alpha_1-1}\right)\right], \tag{21}$$

$$\varrho_2 = \frac{1}{\Gamma_q(\alpha_2)}\left[1 + \frac{l_2}{\Gamma_q(\alpha_2)(1-l_1l_2)}\left(\sum_{i=1}^{m}\frac{\lambda_{1i}}{\Gamma_q(\beta_{1i})}\int_0^{\xi_i}(\xi_i-q\tau)^{(\beta_{1i}-1)}\tau^{\alpha_2-1}d_q\tau + \sum_{j=1}^{n}b_{1j}\eta_j^{\alpha_2-1}\right)\right], \tag{22}$$

$$\varrho_3 = 1 + \frac{l_1}{\Gamma_q(\alpha_1)(1-l_1l_2)}\left(\sum_{i=1}^{m}\frac{\lambda_{2i}}{\Gamma_q(\beta_{2i})}\int_0^{\xi_i}(\xi_i-q\tau)^{(\beta_{2i}-1)}\tau^{\alpha_1-1}d_q\tau + \sum_{j=1}^{n}b_{2j}\eta_j^{\alpha_1-1}\right), \tag{23}$$

$$\varrho_4 = 1 + \frac{l_2}{\Gamma_q(\alpha_2)(1-l_1l_2)}\left(\sum_{i=1}^{m}\frac{\lambda_{1i}}{\Gamma_q(\beta_{1i})}\int_0^{\xi_i}(\xi_i-q\tau)^{(\beta_{1i}-1)}\tau^{\alpha_2-1}d_q\tau + \sum_{j=1}^{n}b_{1j}\eta_j^{\alpha_2-1}\right), \tag{24}$$

$$\rho_1 = \frac{1}{\Gamma_q(\alpha_1)\Gamma_q(\alpha_2)(1-l_1l_2)}\left[\sum_{i=1}^{m}\frac{\lambda_{1i}}{\Gamma_q(\beta_{1i})}\int_0^{\xi_i}(\xi_i-q\tau)^{(\beta_{1i}-1)}\tau^{\alpha_2-1}d_q\tau + \sum_{j=1}^{n}b_{1j}\eta_j^{\alpha_2-1}\right], \tag{25}$$

$$\rho_2 = \frac{1}{\Gamma_q(\alpha_1)\Gamma_q(\alpha_2)(1-l_1l_2)}\left[\sum_{i=1}^{m}\frac{\lambda_{2i}}{\Gamma_q(\beta_{2i})}\int_0^{\xi_i}(\xi_i-q\tau)^{(\beta_{2i}-1)}\tau^{\alpha_1-1}d_q\tau + \sum_{j=1}^{n}b_{2j}\eta_j^{\alpha_1-1}\right], \tag{26}$$

$$\rho_3 = \frac{1}{\Gamma_q(\alpha_2)(1-l_1l_2)}\left[\sum_{i=1}^{m}\frac{\lambda_{1i}}{\Gamma_q(\beta_{1i})}\int_0^{\xi_i}(\xi_i-q\tau)^{(\beta_{1i}-1)}\tau^{\alpha_2-1}d_q\tau + \sum_{j=1}^{n}b_{1j}\eta_j^{\alpha_2-1}\right], \tag{27}$$

$$\rho_4 = \frac{1}{\Gamma_q(\alpha_1)(1-l_1l_2)}\left[\sum_{i=1}^{m}\frac{\lambda_{2i}}{\Gamma_q(\beta_{2i})}\int_0^{\xi_i}(\xi_i-q\tau)^{(\beta_{2i}-1)}\tau^{\alpha_1-1}d_q\tau + \sum_{j=1}^{n}b_{2j}\eta_j^{\alpha_1-1}\right]. \tag{28}$$

Lemma 7. *Assume that* (F_1)–(F_3) *hold. Then for* $(t,qs) \in [0,1]\times[0,1]$, *the functions* $K_{\tilde{j}}(t,qs)$, $H_{\tilde{j}}(t,qs)$, $K_{\tilde{i}\tilde{j}}(t,qs)$ *and* $H_{\tilde{i}\tilde{j}}(t,qs)$ *for* $\tilde{i}=1,2, \tilde{j}=1,2$ *defined by* (7), (8), (18) *and* (19) *satisfy the following results:*

(1) $0 \leq \varrho_1 t^{\alpha_1-1}\left[1-(1-qs)^{(\alpha_1-1)}\right] \leq K_1(t,qs) \leq \varrho_1 t^{\alpha_1-1}$,

$0 \leq \varrho_2 t^{\alpha_2-1}\left[1-(1-qs)^{(\alpha_2-1)}\right] \leq K_2(t,qs) \leq \varrho_2 t^{\alpha_2-1}$,

$0 \leq \dfrac{\varrho_3}{\Gamma_q(\alpha_1-\gamma_{\tilde{i}})} t^{\alpha_1-\gamma_{\tilde{i}}-1}\left[1-(1-qs)^{(\alpha_1-\gamma_{\tilde{i}}-1)}\right] \leq K_{\tilde{i}1}(t,qs) \leq \dfrac{\varrho_3}{\Gamma_q(\alpha_1-\gamma_{\tilde{i}})} t^{\alpha_1-\gamma_{\tilde{i}}-1}$,

$0 \leq \dfrac{\varrho_4}{\Gamma_q(\alpha_2-\gamma_{\tilde{i}})} t^{\alpha_2-\gamma_{\tilde{i}}-1}\left[1-(1-qs)^{(\alpha_2-\gamma_{\tilde{i}}-1)}\right] \leq K_{\tilde{i}2}(t,qs) \leq \dfrac{\varrho_4}{\Gamma_q(\alpha_2-\gamma_{\tilde{i}})} t^{\alpha_2-\gamma_{\tilde{i}}-1}$,

(2) $0 \leq \rho_1 t^{\alpha_1-1}\left[1-(1-qs)^{(\alpha_2-1)}\right] \leq H_1(t,qs) \leq \rho_1 t^{\alpha_1-1}$,

$0 \leq \rho_2 t^{\alpha_2-1}\left[1-(1-qs)^{(\alpha_1-1)}\right] \leq H_2(t,qs) \leq \rho_2 t^{\alpha_2-1}$,

$0 \leq \dfrac{\rho_3}{\Gamma_q(\alpha_1-\gamma_{\tilde{i}})} t^{\alpha_1-\gamma_{\tilde{i}}-1}\left[1-(1-qs)^{(\alpha_2-\gamma_{\tilde{i}}-1)}\right] \leq H_{\tilde{i}1}(t,qs) \leq \dfrac{\rho_3}{\Gamma_q(\alpha_1-\gamma_{\tilde{i}})} t^{\alpha_1-\gamma_{\tilde{i}}-1}$,

$0 \leq \dfrac{\rho_4}{\Gamma_q(\alpha_2-\gamma_{\tilde{i}})} t^{\alpha_2-\gamma_{\tilde{i}}-1}\left[1-(1-qs)^{(\alpha_1-\gamma_{\tilde{i}}-1)}\right] \leq H_{\tilde{i}2}(t,qs) \leq \dfrac{\rho_4}{\Gamma_q(\alpha_2-\gamma_{\tilde{i}})} t^{\alpha_2-\gamma_{\tilde{i}}-1}$.

Proof. (1) Accordance with (F_3), Lemma 6 and the definition of $K_1(t,qs)$, we have

$$K_1(t,qs) = g_1(t,qs) + \frac{l_1 t^{\alpha_1-1}}{\Gamma_q(\alpha_1)(1-l_1l_2)}\left[\sum_{i=1}^{m}\frac{\lambda_{2i}}{\Gamma_q(\beta_{2i})}\int_0^{\xi_i}(\xi_i-q\tau)^{(\beta_{2i}-1)}g_1(\tau,qs)d_q\tau + \sum_{j=1}^{n}b_{2j}g_1(\eta_j,qs)\right]$$

$$\geq \frac{t^{\alpha_1-1}}{\Gamma_q(\alpha_1)}[1-(1-qs)^{(\alpha_1-1)}] + \frac{l_1 t^{\alpha_1-1}}{\Gamma_q(\alpha_1)(1-l_1l_2)}$$

$$\cdot \left[\sum_{i=1}^{m}\frac{\lambda_{2i}}{\Gamma_q(\beta_{2i})}\int_0^{\xi_i}(\xi_i-q\tau)^{(\beta_{2i}-1)}\frac{\tau^{\alpha_1-1}}{\Gamma_q(\alpha_1)}[1-(1-qs)^{(\alpha_1-1)}]d_q\tau + \sum_{j=1}^{n}b_{2j}\frac{\eta_j^{\alpha_1-1}}{\Gamma_q(\alpha_1)}[1-(1-qs)^{(\alpha_1-1)}]\right]$$

$$= \frac{t^{\alpha_1-1}}{\Gamma_q(\alpha_1)}[1-(1-qs)^{(\alpha_1-1)}]$$

$$\cdot \left[1 + \frac{l_1}{\Gamma_q(\alpha_1)(1-l_1l_2)}\left(\sum_{i=1}^{m}\frac{\lambda_{2i}}{\Gamma_q(\beta_{2i})}\int_0^{\xi_i}(\xi_i-q\tau)^{(\beta_{2i}-1)}\tau^{\alpha_1-1}d_q\tau + \sum_{j=1}^{n}b_{2j}\eta_j^{\alpha_1-1}\right)\right]$$

$$= \varrho_1 t^{\alpha_1-1}\left[1-(1-qs)^{(\alpha_1-1)}\right] \geq 0,$$

$$K_1(t,qs) = g_1(t,qs) + \frac{l_1 t^{\alpha_1-1}}{\Gamma_q(\alpha_1)(1-l_1l_2)}\left[\sum_{i=1}^{m}\frac{\lambda_{2i}}{\Gamma_q(\beta_{2i})}\int_0^{\xi_i}(\xi_i-q\tau)^{(\beta_{2i}-1)}g_1(\tau,qs)d_q\tau + \sum_{j=1}^{n}b_{2j}g_1(\eta_j,qs)\right]$$

$$\leq \frac{t^{\alpha_1-1}}{\Gamma_q(\alpha_1)} + \frac{l_1 t^{\alpha_1-1}}{\Gamma_q(\alpha_1)(1-l_1l_2)}\left[\sum_{i=1}^{m}\frac{\lambda_{2i}}{\Gamma_q(\beta_{2i})\Gamma_q(\alpha_1)}\int_0^{\xi_i}(\xi_i-q\tau)^{(\beta_{2i}-1)}\tau^{\alpha_1-1}d_q\tau + \frac{1}{\Gamma_q(\alpha_1)}\sum_{j=1}^{n}b_{2j}\eta_j^{\alpha_1-1}\right]$$

$$= \frac{t^{\alpha_1-1}}{\Gamma_q(\alpha_1)}\left[1 + \frac{l_1}{\Gamma_q(\alpha_1)(1-l_1l_2)}\left(\sum_{i=1}^{m}\frac{\lambda_{2i}}{\Gamma_q(\beta_{2i})}\int_0^{\xi_i}(\xi_i-q\tau)^{(\beta_{2i}-1)}\tau^{\alpha_1-1}d_q\tau + \sum_{j=1}^{n}b_{2j}\eta_j^{\alpha_1-1}\right)\right]$$

$$= \varrho_1 t^{\alpha_1-1},$$

where ϱ_1 is defined by (21).

$$K_{\tilde{1}1}(t,qs) = D_q^{\gamma_{\tilde{i}}}g_1(t,qs) + \frac{l_1 t^{\alpha_1-\gamma_{\tilde{i}}-1}}{\Gamma_q(\alpha_1-\gamma_{\tilde{i}})(1-l_1l_2)}\left[\sum_{i=1}^{m}\frac{\lambda_{2i}}{\Gamma_q(\beta_{2i})}\int_0^{\xi_i}(\xi_i-q\tau)^{(\beta_{2i}-1)}g_1(\tau,qs)d_q\tau + \sum_{j=1}^{n}b_{2j}g_1(\eta_j,qs)\right]$$

$$\geq \frac{t^{\alpha_1-\gamma_{\tilde{i}}-1}}{\Gamma_q(\alpha_1-\gamma_{\tilde{i}})}[1-(1-qs)^{(\alpha_1-\gamma_{\tilde{i}}-1)}] + \frac{l_1 t^{\alpha_1-\gamma_{\tilde{i}}-1}}{\Gamma_q(\alpha_1-\gamma_{\tilde{i}})(1-l_1l_2)}$$

$$\cdot \left[\sum_{i=1}^{m}\frac{\lambda_{2i}}{\Gamma_q(\beta_{2i})}\int_0^{\xi_i}(\xi_i-q\tau)^{(\beta_{2i}-1)}\frac{\tau^{\alpha_1-1}}{\Gamma_q(\alpha_1)}[1-(1-qs)^{(\alpha_1-1)}]d_q\tau + \sum_{j=1}^{n}b_{2j}\frac{\eta_j^{\alpha_1-1}}{\Gamma_q(\alpha_1)}[1-(1-qs)^{(\alpha_1-1)}]\right]$$

$$\geq \frac{t^{\alpha_1-\gamma_{\tilde{i}}-1}}{\Gamma_q(\alpha_1-\gamma_{\tilde{i}})}[1-(1-qs)^{(\alpha_1-\gamma_{\tilde{i}}-1)}]$$

$$\cdot \left[1 + \frac{l_1}{\Gamma_q(\alpha_1-\gamma_1)(1-l_1l_2)}\left(\sum_{i=1}^{m}\frac{\lambda_{2i}}{\Gamma_q(\beta_{2i})}\int_0^{\xi_i}(\xi_i-q\tau)^{(\beta_{2i}-1)}\tau^{\alpha_1-1}d_q\tau + \sum_{j=1}^{n}b_{2j}\eta_j^{\alpha_1-1}\right)\right]$$

$$= \frac{\varrho_3}{\Gamma_q(\alpha_1-\gamma_{\tilde{i}})}t^{\alpha_1-\gamma_{\tilde{i}}-1}\left[1-(1-qs)^{(\alpha_1-\gamma_{\tilde{i}}-1)}\right] \geq 0,$$

$$K_{\tilde{i}1}(t,qs) = D_q^{\gamma_{\tilde{i}}} g_1(t,qs) + \frac{l_1 t^{\alpha_1-\gamma_{\tilde{i}}-1}}{\Gamma_q(\alpha_1-\gamma_{\tilde{i}})(1-l_1l_2)} \left[\sum_{i=1}^{m} \frac{\lambda_{2i}}{\Gamma_q(\beta_{2i})} \int_0^{\xi_i} (\xi_i-q\tau)^{(\beta_{2i}-1)} g_1(\tau,qs) d_q\tau + \sum_{j=1}^{n} b_{2j} g_1(\eta_j,qs) \right]$$

$$\leq \frac{t^{\alpha_1-\gamma_{\tilde{i}}-1}}{\Gamma_q(\alpha_1-\gamma_{\tilde{i}})} + \frac{l_1 t^{\alpha_1-\gamma_{\tilde{i}}-1}}{\Gamma_q(\alpha_1-\gamma_{\tilde{i}})(1-l_1l_2)}$$

$$\cdot \left[\sum_{i=1}^{m} \frac{\lambda_{2i}}{\Gamma_q(\beta_{2i})\Gamma_q(\alpha_1)} \int_0^{\xi_i} (\xi_i-q\tau)^{(\beta_{2i}-1)} \tau^{\alpha_1-1} d_q\tau + \frac{1}{\Gamma_q(\alpha_1)} \sum_{j=1}^{n} b_{2j} \eta_j^{\alpha_1-1} \right]$$

$$= \frac{t^{\alpha_1-\gamma_{\tilde{i}}-1}}{\Gamma_q(\alpha_1-\gamma_{\tilde{i}})} \left[1 + \frac{l_1}{\Gamma_q(\alpha_1-\gamma_{\tilde{i}})(1-l_1l_2)} \left(\sum_{i=1}^{m} \frac{\lambda_{2i}}{\Gamma_q(\beta_{2i})} \int_0^{\xi_i} (\xi_i-q\tau)^{(\beta_{2i}-1)} \tau^{\alpha_1-1} d_q\tau + \sum_{j=1}^{n} b_{2j} \eta_j^{\alpha_1-1} \right) \right]$$

$$= \frac{\varrho_3}{\Gamma_q(\alpha_1-\gamma_{\tilde{i}})} t^{\alpha_1-\gamma_{\tilde{i}}-1},$$

where $\tilde{i} = 1, 2$ and ϱ_3 is defined by (23). Similarly, we get

$$0 \leq \varrho_2 t^{\alpha_2-1} \left[1 - (1-qs)^{(\alpha_2-1)} \right] \leq K_2(t,qs) \leq \varrho_2 t^{\alpha_2-1},$$

$$0 \leq \frac{\varrho_4}{\Gamma_q(\alpha_2-\gamma_{\tilde{i}})} t^{\alpha_2-\gamma_{\tilde{i}}-1} \left[1 - (1-qs)^{(\alpha_2-\gamma_{\tilde{i}}-1)} \right] \leq K_{\tilde{i}2}(t,qs) \leq \frac{\varrho_4}{\Gamma_q(\alpha_2-\gamma_{\tilde{i}})} t^{\alpha_2-\gamma_{\tilde{i}}-1},$$

where ϱ_2 and ϱ_4 are defined by (22) and (24).

(2) According to (F3), Lemma 6 and the definition of $H_1(t,qs)$, we can obtain

$$H_1(t,qs) = \frac{t^{\alpha_1-1}}{\Gamma_q(\alpha_1)(1-l_1l_2)} \left[\sum_{i=1}^{m} \frac{\lambda_{1i}}{\Gamma_q(\beta_{1i})} \int_0^{\xi_i} (\xi_i-q\tau)^{(\beta_{1i}-1)} g_2(\tau,qs) d_q\tau + \sum_{j=1}^{n} b_{1j} g_2(\eta_j,qs) \right]$$

$$\geq \frac{t^{\alpha_1-1}}{\Gamma_q(\alpha_1)(1-l_1l_2)} \left[\sum_{i=1}^{m} \frac{\lambda_{1i}}{\Gamma_q(\beta_{1i})} \int_0^{\xi_i} (\xi_i-q\tau)^{(\beta_{1i}-1)} \frac{\tau^{\alpha_2-1}}{\Gamma_q(\alpha_2)} [1-(1-qs)^{(\alpha_2-1)}] d_q\tau \right.$$

$$\left. + \sum_{j=1}^{n} b_{1j} \frac{\eta_j^{\alpha_2-1}}{\Gamma_q(\alpha_2)} [1-(1-qs)^{(\alpha_2-1)}] \right]$$

$$= \frac{t^{\alpha_1-1}}{\Gamma_q(\alpha_1)\Gamma_q(\alpha_2)(1-l_1l_2)} [1-(1-qs)^{(\alpha_2-1)}] \left[\sum_{i=1}^{m} \frac{\lambda_{1i}}{\Gamma_q(\beta_{1i})} \int_0^{\xi_i} (\xi_i-q\tau)^{(\beta_{1i}-1)} \tau^{\alpha_2-1} d_q\tau + \sum_{j=1}^{n} b_{1j} \eta_j^{\alpha_2-1} \right]$$

$$= \rho_1 t^{\alpha_1-1} \left[1 - (1-qs)^{(\alpha_2-1)} \right] \geq 0,$$

$$H_1(t,qs) = \frac{t^{\alpha_1-1}}{\Gamma_q(\alpha_1)(1-l_1l_2)} \left[\sum_{i=1}^{m} \frac{\lambda_{1i}}{\Gamma_q(\beta_{1i})} \int_0^{\xi_i} (\xi_i-q\tau)^{(\beta_{1i}-1)} g_2(\tau,qs) d_q\tau + \sum_{j=1}^{n} b_{1j} g_2(\eta_j,qs) \right]$$

$$\leq \frac{t^{\alpha_1-1}}{\Gamma_q(\alpha_1)(1-l_1l_2)} \left[\sum_{i=1}^{m} \frac{\lambda_{1i}}{\Gamma_q(\beta_{1i})\Gamma_q(\alpha_2)} \int_0^{\xi_i} (\xi_i-q\tau)^{(\beta_{1i}-1)} \tau^{\alpha_2-1} d_q\tau + \frac{1}{\Gamma_q(\alpha_2)} \sum_{j=1}^{n} b_{1j} \eta_j^{\alpha_2-1} \right]$$

$$= \frac{t^{\alpha_1-1}}{\Gamma_q(\alpha_1)\Gamma_q(\alpha_2)(1-l_1l_2)} \left[\sum_{i=1}^{m} \frac{\lambda_{1i}}{\Gamma_q(\beta_{1i})} \int_0^{\xi_i} (\xi_i-q\tau)^{(\beta_{1i}-1)} \tau^{\alpha_2-1} d_q\tau + \sum_{j=1}^{n} b_{1j} \eta_j^{\alpha_2-1} \right]$$

$$= \rho_1 t^{\alpha_1-1},$$

where ρ_1 is defined by (27).

$$H_{\tilde{i}1}(t,qs) = \frac{t^{\alpha_1-\gamma_{\tilde{i}}-1}}{\Gamma_q(\alpha_1-\gamma_{\tilde{i}})(1-l_1 l_2)} \left[\sum_{i=1}^{m} \frac{\lambda_{1i}}{\Gamma_q(\beta_{1i})} \int_0^{\xi_i} (\xi_i - q\tau)^{(\beta_{1i}-1)} g_2(\tau,qs) d_q\tau + \sum_{j=1}^{n} b_{1j} g_2(\eta_j, qs) \right]$$

$$\geq \frac{t^{\alpha_1-\gamma_{\tilde{i}}-1}}{\Gamma_q(\alpha_1-\gamma_{\tilde{i}})(1-l_1 l_2)} \left[\sum_{i=1}^{m} \frac{\lambda_{1i}}{\Gamma_q(\beta_{1i})} \int_0^{\xi_i} (\xi_i - q\tau)^{(\beta_{1i}-1)} \frac{\tau^{\alpha_2-1}}{\Gamma_q(\alpha_2)} [1-(1-qs)^{(\alpha_2-1)}] d_q\tau \right.$$
$$\left. + \sum_{j=1}^{n} b_{1j} \frac{\eta_j^{\alpha_2-1}}{\Gamma_q(\alpha_2)} [1-(1-qs)^{(\alpha_2-1)}] \right]$$

$$\geq \frac{t^{\alpha_1-\gamma_{\tilde{i}}-1}}{\Gamma_q(\alpha_1-\gamma_{\tilde{i}})\Gamma_q(\alpha_2)(1-l_1 l_2)} [1-(1-qs)^{(\alpha_2-\gamma_{\tilde{i}}-1)}]$$
$$\cdot \left[\sum_{i=1}^{m} \frac{\lambda_{1i}}{\Gamma_q(\beta_{1i})} \int_0^{\xi_i} (\xi_i-q\tau)^{(\beta_{1i}-1)} \tau^{\alpha_2-1} d_q\tau + \sum_{j=1}^{n} b_{1j} \eta_j^{\alpha_2-1} \right]$$

$$= \frac{\rho_3}{\Gamma_q(\alpha_1-\gamma_{\tilde{i}})} t^{\alpha_1-\gamma_{\tilde{i}}-1} \left[1-(1-qs)^{(\alpha_2-\gamma_{\tilde{i}}-1)}\right] \geq 0,$$

$$H_{\tilde{i}1}(t,qs) = \frac{t^{\alpha_1-\gamma_{\tilde{i}}-1}}{\Gamma_q(\alpha_1-\gamma_{\tilde{i}})(1-l_1 l_2)} \left[\sum_{i=1}^{m} \frac{\lambda_{1i}}{\Gamma_q(\beta_{1i})} \int_0^{\xi_i} (\xi_i - q\tau)^{(\beta_{1i}-1)} g_2(\tau,qs) d_q\tau + \sum_{j=1}^{n} b_{1j} g_2(\eta_j, qs) \right]$$

$$\leq \frac{t^{\alpha_1-\gamma_{\tilde{i}}-1}}{\Gamma_q(\alpha_1-\gamma_{\tilde{i}})(1-l_1 l_2)} \left[\sum_{i=1}^{m} \frac{\lambda_{1i}}{\Gamma_q(\beta_{1i})\Gamma_q(\alpha_2)} \int_0^{\xi_i} (\xi_i-q\tau)^{(\beta_{1i}-1)} \tau^{\alpha_2-1} d_q\tau + \frac{1}{\Gamma_q(\alpha_2)} \sum_{j=1}^{n} b_{1j} \eta_j^{\alpha_2-1} \right]$$

$$= \frac{t^{\alpha_1-\gamma_{\tilde{i}}-1}}{\Gamma_q(\alpha_1-\gamma_{\tilde{i}})\Gamma_q(\alpha_2)(1-l_1 l_2)} \left[\sum_{i=1}^{m} \frac{\lambda_{1i}}{\Gamma_q(\beta_{1i})} \int_0^{\xi_i} (\xi_i-q\tau)^{(\beta_{1i}-1)} \tau^{\alpha_2-1} d_q\tau + \sum_{j=1}^{n} b_{1j} \eta_j^{\alpha_2-1} \right]$$

$$= \frac{\rho_3}{\Gamma_q(\alpha_1-\gamma_{\tilde{i}})} t^{\alpha_1-\gamma_{\tilde{i}}-1},$$

where $\tilde{i} = 1, 2$ and ρ_3 is defined by (27). Analogously, we get

$$0 \leq \rho_2 t^{\alpha_2-1} \left[1-(1-qs)^{(\alpha_1-1)}\right] \leq H_2(t,qs) \leq \rho_2 t^{\alpha_2-1},$$

$$0 \leq \frac{\rho_4}{\Gamma_q(\alpha_2-\gamma_{\tilde{i}})} t^{\alpha_2-\gamma_{\tilde{i}}-1} \left[1-(1-qs)^{(\alpha_1-\gamma_{\tilde{i}}-1)}\right] \leq H_{\tilde{i}2}(t,qs) \leq \frac{\rho_4}{\Gamma_q(\alpha_2-\gamma_{\tilde{i}})} t^{\alpha_2-\gamma_{\tilde{i}}-1},$$

where ρ_2 and ρ_4 are defined by (26) and (28).
This completes the proof of the lemma. □

Lemma 8 ([38]). $K_h = P_{h_1} \times P_{h_2}$, where $K = P \times P$ and $h(\tau) = (h_1(\tau), h_2(\tau))$.

3. Existence Results of Monotone Iterative Non-Negative Solutions

Let $E = \{x | x, D_q^{\gamma_1} x(t), D_q^{\gamma_2} x(t) \in C[0,1]\}$ endowed with the norm

$$\|x\| = \max\left\{ \max_{0 \leq t \leq 1} |x(t)|, \max_{0 \leq t \leq 1} |D_q^{\gamma_1} x(t)|, \max_{0 \leq t \leq 1} |D_q^{\gamma_2} x(t)| \right\}.$$

Let $\|(x,y)\| = \max\{\|x\|, \|y\|\}$ for $(x,y) \in E \times E$, then $(E \times E, \|(x,y)\|)$ is a Banach space. Define a cone $P = \{x \in E \mid x, D_q^{\gamma_1} x(t), D_q^{\gamma_2} x(t) \geq \theta\}$. Let $K = P \times P$, it is obvious that K is a normal cone equipped with the following partial order:

$$(x_1, y_1) \preceq (x_2, y_2) \Leftrightarrow \begin{cases} x_1 \leq x_2, & D_q^{\gamma_1} x_1 \leq D_q^{\gamma_1} x_2, \quad D_q^{\gamma_2} x_1 \leq D_q^{\gamma_2} x_2, \\ y_1 \leq y_2, & D_q^{\gamma_1} y_1 \leq D_q^{\gamma_1} y_2, \quad D_q^{\gamma_2} y_1 \leq D_q^{\gamma_2} y_2. \end{cases} \quad (29)$$

For all $(u,v) \in P \times P$, in view of Lemma 5, let $T : K \times K \to K$ be the operator defined by

$$T(u,v) = \begin{pmatrix} T_1(u,v) \\ T_2(u,v) \end{pmatrix},$$

where

$$T_1(u,v)(t) = \int_0^1 K_1(t,qs) f_1(s, u(s), v(s), D_q^{\gamma_1} u(s), D_q^{\gamma_2} v(s)) d_q s$$
$$+ \int_0^1 H_1(t,qs) f_2(s, u(s), v(s), D_q^{\gamma_1} u(s), D_q^{\gamma_2} v(s)) d_q s,$$

$$T_2(u,v)(t) = \int_0^1 K_2(t,qs) f_2(s, u(s), v(s), D_q^{\gamma_1} u(s), D_q^{\gamma_2} v(s)) d_q s$$
$$+ \int_0^1 H_2(t,qs) f_1(s, u(s), v(s), D_q^{\gamma_1} u(s), D_q^{\gamma_2} v(s)) d_q s.$$

Theorem 1. *Assume that*

(S_1) For $t \in [0,1]$, $f_j(t, x_1, y_1, x_2, y_2)$ is increasing in $x_i \in [0,\infty)$ $(i=1,2)$ and decreasing in $y_i \in [0,\infty)$ $(i=1,2)$ for $j=1,2$;

(S_2) $\forall\, r \in (0,1)$, $\exists\, \varphi_1(r), \varphi_2(r) \in (r,1]$ such that

$$f_i(t, rx_1, r^{-1}y_1, rx_2, r^{-1}y_2) \geqslant \varphi_i(r) f_i(t, x_1, y_1, x_2, y_2) \quad (i=1,2),$$
$$\varphi_0(r) = \min\{\varphi_1(r), \varphi_2(r)\}.$$

Then

(1) $T(h,h) \in K_h$, where $h(t) = (h_1(t), h_2(t)) = (t^{\alpha_1-1}, t^{\alpha_2-1}), 0 \leqslant t \leqslant 1$;
(2) $T(ru, r^{-1}v) \geqslant \varphi_0(r) T(u,v)$;
(3) BVP (1) and (2) has a unique non-negative solutions (u^*, v^*) in K_h. For any initial $(x_{01}, x_{02}), (y_{01}, y_{02}) \in K_h$, there are two iterative sequences $\{(x_{n1}, x_{n2})\}, \{(y_{n1}, y_{n2})\}$ satisfying that $(x_{n1}, x_{n2}) \to (u^*, v^*)$, $(y_{n1}, y_{n2}) \to (u^*, v^*)$, where

$$(x_{n1}, x_{n2}) = \left(T_1(x_{(n-1)1}, y_{(n-1)1}), T_2(x_{(n-1)2}, y_{(n-1)2})\right)$$

$$= \begin{pmatrix} \int_0^1 K_1(t,qs) f_1(s, x_{(n-1)1}(s), y_{(n-1)1}(s), D_q^{\gamma_1} x_{(n-1)1}(s), D_q^{\gamma_2} y_{(n-1)1}(s)) d_q s \\ + \int_0^1 H_1(t,qs) f_2(s, x_{(n-1)1}(s), y_{(n-1)1}(s), D_q^{\gamma_1} x_{(n-1)1}(s), D_q^{\gamma_2} y_{(n-1)1}(s)) d_q s, \\ \int_0^1 K_2(t,qs) f_2(s, x_{(n-1)1}(s), y_{(n-1)1}(s), D_q^{\gamma_1} x_{(n-1)1}(s), D_q^{\gamma_2} y_{(n-1)1}(s)) d_q s \\ + \int_0^1 H_2(t,qs) f_1(s, x_{(n-1)1}(s), y_{(n-1)1}(s), D_q^{\gamma_1} x_{(n-1)1}(s), D_q^{\gamma_2} y_{(n-1)1}(s)) d_q s \end{pmatrix},$$

$$(y_{n1}, y_{n2}) = \left(T_1(y_{(n-1)1}, x_{(n-1)1}), T_2(y_{(n-1)2}, x_{(n-1)2})\right)$$

$$= \begin{pmatrix} \int_0^1 K_1(t,qs) f_1(s, y_{(n-1)1}(s), x_{(n-1)1}(s), D_q^{\gamma_1} y_{(n-1)1}(s), D_q^{\gamma_2} x_{(n-1)1}(s)) d_q s \\ + \int_0^1 H_1(t,qs) f_2(s, y_{(n-1)1}(s), x_{(n-1)1}(s), D_q^{\gamma_1} y_{(n-1)1}(s), D_q^{\gamma_2} x_{(n-1)1}(s)) d_q s, \\ \int_0^1 K_2(t,qs) f_2(s, y_{(n-1)1}(s), x_{(n-1)1}(s), D_q^{\gamma_1} y_{(n-1)1}(s), D_q^{\gamma_2} x_{(n-1)1}(s)) d_q s \\ + \int_0^1 H_2(t,qs) f_1(s, y_{(n-1)1}(s), x_{(n-1)1}(s), D_q^{\gamma_1} y_{(n-1)1}(s), D_q^{\gamma_2} x_{(n-1)1}(s)) d_q s \end{pmatrix},$$

$n = 1, 2, \ldots$.

Proof. By Lemma 7 we have

$$K_{\bar{j}}(t,qs), K_{\bar{ij}}(t,qs), H_{\bar{j}}(t,qs), H_{\bar{ij}}(t,qs) \geqslant 0, \quad \bar{i}=1,2, \bar{j}=1,2. \tag{30}$$

Regarding (30) and (F4), we get $T_1, T_2 : P \times P \to P$, $T : K \times K \to K$. It is obvious that T is a mixed monotone operator, because for any $(u_1, v_1), (u_2, v_2) \in K$ with $(u_1, v_1) \preceq (u_2, v_2)$, considering (S1), we acquire

$$T(u_1, v_1) \preceq T(u_2, v_1) \text{ for fixed } v_1 \text{ and } T(u_1, v_1) \succeq T(u_1, v_2) \text{ for fixed } u_1.$$

From Lemma 8, we obtain $K_h = P_{h_1} \times P_{h_2}$, where $h(t) = (h_1(t), h_2(t)) = (t^{\alpha_1-1}, t^{\alpha_2-1})$.

(1) In view of $h(t) = (h_1(t), h_2(t)) = (t^{\alpha_1-1}, t^{\alpha_2-1})$, we get

$$h_1(t) = t^{\alpha_1-1} \geqslant 0, \quad h_2(t) = t^{\alpha_2-1} \geqslant 0,$$

$$D_q^{\gamma_1} h_1(t) = D_q^{\gamma_1} t^{\alpha_1-1} = \frac{\Gamma_q(\alpha_1)}{\Gamma_q(\alpha_1 - \gamma_1)} t^{\alpha_1-\gamma_1-1} \geqslant 0, \quad D_q^{\gamma_1} h_2(t) = D_q^{\gamma_1} t^{\alpha_2-1} = \frac{\Gamma_q(\alpha_2)}{\Gamma_q(\alpha_2 - \gamma_1)} t^{\alpha_2-\gamma_1-1} \geqslant 0,$$

$$D_q^{\gamma_2} h_1(t) = D_q^{\gamma_2} t^{\alpha_1-1} = \frac{\Gamma_q(\alpha_1)}{\Gamma_q(\alpha_1 - \gamma_2)} t^{\alpha_1-\gamma_2-1} \geqslant 0, \quad D_q^{\gamma_2} h_2(t) = D_q^{\gamma_2} t^{\alpha_2-1} = \frac{\Gamma_q(\alpha_2)}{\Gamma_q(\alpha_2 - \gamma_2)} t^{\alpha_2-\gamma_2-1} \geqslant 0. \tag{31}$$

Consequently, from (31), we can see that $h_1, h_2 \in P$ and $h \in K$. Indeed

$$T_1(h_1, h_1)(t) = \int_0^1 K_1(t, qs) f_1(s, h_1(s), h_1(s), D_q^{\gamma_1} h_1(s), D_q^{\gamma_2} h_1(s)) d_q s$$

$$+ \int_0^1 H_1(t, qs) f_2(s, h_1(s), h_1(s), D_q^{\gamma_1} h_1(s), D_q^{\gamma_2} h_1(s)) d_q s$$

$$= \int_0^1 K_1(t, qs) f_1\left(s, s^{\alpha_1-1}, s^{\alpha_1-1}, \frac{\Gamma_q(\alpha_1)}{\Gamma_q(\alpha_1-\gamma_1)} s^{\alpha_1-\gamma_1-1}, \frac{\Gamma_q(\alpha_1)}{\Gamma_q(\alpha_1-\gamma_2)} s^{\alpha_1-\gamma_2-1}\right) d_q s$$

$$+ \int_0^1 H_1(t, qs) f_2\left(s, s^{\alpha_1-1}, s^{\alpha_1-1}, \frac{\Gamma_q(\alpha_1)}{\Gamma_q(\alpha_1-\gamma_1)} s^{\alpha_1-\gamma_1-1}, \frac{\Gamma_q(\alpha_1)}{\Gamma_q(\alpha_1-\gamma_2)} s^{\alpha_1-\gamma_2-1}\right) d_q s$$

$$\geqslant \int_0^1 \varrho_1 t^{\alpha_1-1}[1-(1-qs)^{(\alpha_1-1)}] f_1\left(s, 0, 1, 0, \frac{\Gamma_q(\alpha_1)}{\Gamma_q(\alpha_1-\gamma_2)}\right) d_q s$$

$$+ \int_0^1 \rho_1 t^{\alpha_1-1}[1-(1-qs)^{(\alpha_2-1)}] f_2\left(s, 0, 1, 0, \frac{\Gamma_q(\alpha_1)}{\Gamma_q(\alpha_1-\gamma_2)}\right) d_q s,$$

$$T_1(h_1, h_1)(t) = \int_0^1 K_1(t, qs) f_1(s, h_1(s), h_1(s), D_q^{\gamma_1} h_1(s), D_q^{\gamma_2} h_1(s)) d_q s$$

$$+ \int_0^1 H_1(t, qs) f_2(s, h_1(s), h_1(s), D_q^{\gamma_1} h_1(s), D_q^{\gamma_2} h_1(s)) d_q s$$

$$= \int_0^1 K_1(t, qs) f_1\left(s, s^{\alpha_1-1}, s^{\alpha_1-1}, \frac{\Gamma_q(\alpha_1)}{\Gamma_q(\alpha_1-\gamma_1)} s^{\alpha_1-\gamma_1-1}, \frac{\Gamma_q(\alpha_1)}{\Gamma_q(\alpha_1-\gamma_2)} s^{\alpha_1-\gamma_2-1}\right) d_q s$$

$$+ \int_0^1 H_1(t, qs) f_2\left(s, s^{\alpha_1-1}, s^{\alpha_1-1}, \frac{\Gamma_q(\alpha_1)}{\Gamma_q(\alpha_1-\gamma_1)} s^{\alpha_1-\gamma_1-1}, \frac{\Gamma_q(\alpha_1)}{\Gamma_q(\alpha_1-\gamma_2)} s^{\alpha_1-\gamma_2-1}\right) d_q s$$

$$\leqslant \int_0^1 \varrho_1 t^{\alpha_1-1} f_1\left(s, 1, 0, \frac{\Gamma_q(\alpha_1)}{\Gamma_q(\alpha_1-\gamma_1)}, 0\right) d_q s + \int_0^1 \rho_1 t^{\alpha_1-1} f_2\left(s, 1, 0, \frac{\Gamma_q(\alpha_1)}{\Gamma_q(\alpha_1-\gamma_1)}, 0\right) d_q s,$$

$$D_q^{\gamma_i}T_1(h_1,h_1)(t) = \int_0^1 K_{\tilde{i}1}(t,qs)f_1(s,h_1(s),h_1(s),D_q^{\gamma_1}h_1(s),D_q^{\gamma_2}h_1(s))d_qs$$

$$+ \int_0^1 H_{\tilde{i}1}(t,qs)f_2(s,h_1(s),h_1(s),D_q^{\gamma_1}h_1(s),D_q^{\gamma_2}h_1(s))d_qs$$

$$= \int_0^1 K_{\tilde{i}1}(t,qs)f_1\left(s,s^{\alpha_1-1},s^{\alpha_1-1},\frac{\Gamma_q(\alpha_1)}{\Gamma_q(\alpha_1-\gamma_1)}s^{\alpha_1-\gamma_1-1},\frac{\Gamma_q(\alpha_1)}{\Gamma_q(\alpha_1-\gamma_2)}s^{\alpha_1-\gamma_2-1}\right)d_qs$$

$$+ \int_0^1 H_{\tilde{i}1}(t,qs)f_2\left(s,s^{\alpha_1-1},s^{\alpha_1-1},\frac{\Gamma_q(\alpha_1)}{\Gamma_q(\alpha_1-\gamma_1)}s^{\alpha_1-\gamma_1-1},\frac{\Gamma_q(\alpha_1)}{\Gamma_q(\alpha_1-\gamma_2)}s^{\alpha_1-\gamma_2-1}\right)d_qs$$

$$\geqslant \int_0^1 \frac{\varrho_3}{\Gamma_q(\alpha_1-\gamma_{\tilde{i}})}t^{\alpha_1-\gamma_{\tilde{i}}-1}[1-(1-qs)^{(\alpha_1-\gamma_{\tilde{i}}-1)}]f_1\left(s,0,1,0,\frac{\Gamma_q(\alpha_1)}{\Gamma_q(\alpha_1-\gamma_2)}\right)d_qs$$

$$+ \int_0^1 \frac{\rho_3}{\Gamma_q(\alpha_1-\gamma_{\tilde{i}})}t^{\alpha_1-\gamma_{\tilde{i}}-1}[1-(1-qs)^{(\alpha_2-\gamma_{\tilde{i}}-1)}]f_2\left(s,0,1,0,\frac{\Gamma_q(\alpha_1)}{\Gamma_q(\alpha_1-\gamma_2)}\right)d_qs,$$

$$D_q^{\gamma_i}T_1(h_1,h_1)(t) = \int_0^1 K_{\tilde{i}1}(t,qs)f_1(s,h_1(s),h_1(s),D_q^{\gamma_1}h_1(s),D_q^{\gamma_2}h_1(s))d_qs$$

$$+ \int_0^1 H_{\tilde{i}1}(t,qs)f_2(s,h_1(s),h_1(s),D_q^{\gamma_1}h_1(s),D_q^{\gamma_2}h_1(s))d_qs$$

$$= \int_0^1 K_{\tilde{i}1}(t,qs)f_1\left(s,s^{\alpha_1-1},s^{\alpha_1-1},\frac{\Gamma_q(\alpha_1)}{\Gamma_q(\alpha_1-\gamma_1)}s^{\alpha_1-\gamma_1-1},\frac{\Gamma_q(\alpha_1)}{\Gamma_q(\alpha_1-\gamma_2)}s^{\alpha_1-\gamma_2-1}\right)d_qs$$

$$+ \int_0^1 H_{\tilde{i}1}(t,qs)f_2\left(s,s^{\alpha_1-1},s^{\alpha_1-1},\frac{\Gamma_q(\alpha_1)}{\Gamma_q(\alpha_1-\gamma_1)}s^{\alpha_1-\gamma_1-1},\frac{\Gamma_q(\alpha_1)}{\Gamma_q(\alpha_1-\gamma_2)}s^{\alpha_1-\gamma_2-1}\right)d_qs$$

$$\leqslant \int_0^1 \frac{\varrho_3}{\Gamma_q(\alpha_1-\gamma_{\tilde{i}})}t^{\alpha_1-\gamma_{\tilde{i}}-1}f_1\left(s,1,0,\frac{\Gamma_q(\alpha_1)}{\Gamma_q(\alpha_1-\gamma_1)},0\right)d_qs$$

$$+ \int_0^1 \frac{\rho_3}{\Gamma_q(\alpha_1-\gamma_{\tilde{i}})}t^{\alpha_1-\gamma_{\tilde{i}}-1}f_2\left(s,1,0,\frac{\Gamma_q(\alpha_1)}{\Gamma_q(\alpha_1-\gamma_1)},0\right)d_qs.$$

Let

$$a_{11} = \int_0^1 \varrho_1[1-(1-qs)^{(\alpha_1-1)}]f_1\left(s,0,1,0,\frac{\Gamma_q(\alpha_1)}{\Gamma_q(\alpha_1-\gamma_2)}\right)d_qs$$

$$+ \int_0^1 \rho_1[1-(1-qs)^{(\alpha_2-1)}]f_2\left(s,0,1,0,\frac{\Gamma_q(\alpha_1)}{\Gamma_q(\alpha_1-\gamma_2)}\right)d_qs,$$

$$a_{12} = \int_0^1 \varrho_1 f_1\left(s,1,0,\frac{\Gamma_q(\alpha_1)}{\Gamma_q(\alpha_1-\gamma_1)},0\right)d_qs + \int_0^1 \rho_1 f_2\left(s,1,0,\frac{\Gamma_q(\alpha_1)}{\Gamma_q(\alpha_1-\gamma_1)},0\right)d_qs,$$

$$a'_{11} = \int_0^1 \frac{\varrho_3}{\Gamma_q(\alpha_1)}[1-(1-qs)^{(\alpha_1-\gamma-1)}]f_1\left(s,0,1,0,\frac{\Gamma_q(\alpha_1)}{\Gamma_q(\alpha_1-\gamma_2)}\right)d_qs$$

$$+ \int_0^1 \frac{\rho_3}{\Gamma_q(\alpha_1)}[1-(1-qs)^{(\alpha_2-\gamma-1)}]f_2\left(s,0,1,0,\frac{\Gamma_q(\alpha_1)}{\Gamma_q(\alpha_1-\gamma_2)}\right)d_qs,$$

$$a'_{12} = \int_0^1 \frac{\varrho_3}{\Gamma_q(\alpha_1)}f_1\left(s,1,0,\frac{\Gamma_q(\alpha_1)}{\Gamma_q(\alpha_1-\gamma_1)},0\right)d_qs + \int_0^1 \frac{\rho_3}{\Gamma_q(\alpha_1)}f_2\left(s,1,0,\frac{\Gamma_q(\alpha_1)}{\Gamma_q(\alpha_1-\gamma_1)},0\right)d_qs,$$

where $\gamma = \max\{\gamma_1,\gamma_2\}$. Then, we obtain

$$T_1(h_1,h_1)(t) \geqslant a_{11}t^{\alpha_1-1} = a_{11}h_1(t),$$
$$T_1(h_1,h_1)(t) \leqslant a_{12}t^{\alpha_1-1} = a_{12}h_1(t),$$
$$D_q^{\gamma_i}T_1(h_1,h_1)(t) \geqslant a'_{11}\frac{\Gamma_q(\alpha_1)}{\Gamma_q(\alpha_1-\gamma_{\tilde{i}})}t^{\alpha_1-\gamma_{\tilde{i}}-1} = a'_{11}D_q^{\gamma_i}h_1(t), \qquad (32)$$
$$D_q^{\gamma_i}T_1(h_1,h_1)(t) \leqslant a'_{12}\frac{\Gamma_q(\alpha_1)}{\Gamma_q(\alpha_1-\gamma_{\tilde{i}})}t^{\alpha_1-\gamma_{\tilde{i}}-1} = a'_{12}D_q^{\gamma_i}h_1(t).$$

Also, let

$$a_{21} = \int_0^1 \varrho_2[1-(1-qs)^{(\alpha_2-1)}]f_2\left(s,0,1,0,\frac{\Gamma_q(\alpha_2)}{\Gamma_q(\alpha_2-\gamma_2)}\right)d_qs$$
$$+ \int_0^1 \rho_2[1-(1-qs)^{(\alpha_1-1)}]f_1\left(s,0,1,0,\frac{\Gamma_q(\alpha_2)}{\Gamma_q(\alpha_2-\gamma_2)}\right)d_qs,$$

$$a_{22} = \int_0^1 \varrho_2 f_2\left(s,1,0,\frac{\Gamma_q(\alpha_2)}{\Gamma_q(\alpha_2-\gamma_1)},0\right)d_qs + \int_0^1 \rho_2 f_2\left(s,1,0,\frac{\Gamma_q(\alpha_2)}{\Gamma_q(\alpha_2-\gamma_1)},0\right)d_qs,$$

$$a'_{21} = \int_0^1 \frac{\varrho_4}{\Gamma_q(\alpha_2)}[1-(1-qs)^{(\alpha_2-\gamma-1)}]f_2\left(s,0,1,0,\frac{\Gamma_q(\alpha_2)}{\Gamma_q(\alpha_2-\gamma_2)}\right)d_qs$$
$$+ \int_0^1 \frac{\rho_4}{\Gamma_q(\alpha_2)}[1-(1-qs)^{(\alpha_1-\gamma-1)}]f_1\left(s,0,1,0,\frac{\Gamma_q(\alpha_2)}{\Gamma_q(\alpha_2-\gamma_2)}\right)d_qs,$$

$$a'_{22} = \int_0^1 \frac{\varrho_4}{\Gamma_q(\alpha_2)}f_2\left(s,1,0,\frac{\Gamma_q(\alpha_2)}{\Gamma_q(\alpha_2-\gamma_1)},0\right)d_qs + \int_0^1 \frac{\rho_4}{\Gamma_q(\alpha_2)}f_1\left(s,1,0,\frac{\Gamma_q(\alpha_2)}{\Gamma_q(\alpha_2-\gamma_1)},0\right)d_qs,$$

we have

$$T_2(h_2,h_2)(t) \geqslant a_{21}t^{\alpha_2-1} = a_{21}h_2(t),$$
$$T_2(h_2,h_2)(t) \leqslant a_{22}t^{\alpha_2-1} = a_{22}h_2(t),$$
$$D_q^{\gamma_i}T_2(h_2,h_2)(t) \geqslant a'_{21}\frac{\Gamma_q(\alpha_2)}{\Gamma_q(\alpha_2-\gamma_i)}t^{\alpha_2-\gamma_i-1} = a'_{21}D_q^{\gamma_i}h_2(t), \quad (33)$$
$$D_q^{\gamma_i}T_2(h_2,h_2)(t) \leqslant a'_{22}\frac{\Gamma_q(\alpha_2)}{\Gamma_q(\alpha_2-\gamma_i)}t^{\alpha_2-\gamma_i-1} = a'_{22}D_q^{\gamma_i}h_2(t).$$

As a result, according to (32) and (33), we can get $T_1(h_1,h_1) \in P_{h_1}, T_2(h_2,h_2) \in P_{h_2}$. Further, it can be see that $T(h,h) \in K_h$, which satisfies (A1) in Lemma 1.

(2) For $u,v \in P$ and $t \in (0,1)$, it can be obtain that

$$T_1(ru,r^{-1}v) = \int_0^1 K_1(t,qs)f_1(s,ru,r^{-1}v,D_q^{\gamma_1}ru,D_q^{\gamma_2}r^{-1}v)d_qs$$
$$+ \int_0^1 H_1(t,qs)f_2(s,ru,r^{-1}v,D_q^{\gamma_1}ru,D_q^{\gamma_2}r^{-1}v)d_qs$$
$$\geqslant \int_0^1 K_1(t,qs)\varphi_1(r)f_1(s,u,v,D_q^{\gamma_1}u,D_q^{\gamma_2}v)d_qs$$
$$+ \int_0^1 H_1(t,qs)\varphi_2(r)f_2(s,u,v,D_q^{\gamma_1}u,D_q^{\gamma_2}v)d_qs$$
$$\geqslant \varphi_0(r)T_1(u,v),$$

$$T_2(ru,r^{-1}v) = \int_0^1 K_2(t,qs)f_2(s,ru,r^{-1}v,D_q^{\gamma_1}ru,D_q^{\gamma_2}r^{-1}v)d_qs$$
$$+ \int_0^1 H_2(t,qs)f_1(s,ru,r^{-1}v,D_q^{\gamma_1}ru,D_q^{\gamma_2}r^{-1}v)d_qs$$
$$\geqslant \int_0^1 K_2(t,qs)\varphi_2(r)f_2(s,u,v,D_q^{\gamma_1}u,D_q^{\gamma_2}v)d_qs$$
$$+ \int_0^1 H_2(t,qs)\varphi_1(r)f_1(s,u,v,D_q^{\gamma_1}u,D_q^{\gamma_2}v)d_qs$$
$$\geqslant \varphi_0(r)T_2(u,v),$$

$$D_q^{\gamma_i} T_1(ru, r^{-1}v) = \int_0^1 K_{\tilde{i}1}(t, qs) f_1(s, ru, r^{-1}v, D_q^{\gamma_1} ru, D_q^{\gamma_2} r^{-1}v) d_q s$$

$$+ \int_0^1 H_{\tilde{i}1}(t, qs) f_2(s, ru, r^{-1}v, D_q^{\gamma_1} ru, D_q^{\gamma_2} r^{-1}v) d_q s$$

$$\geqslant \int_0^1 K_{\tilde{i}1}(t, qs) \varphi_1(r) f_1(s, u, v, D_q^{\gamma_1} u, D_q^{\gamma_2} v) d_q s$$

$$+ \int_0^1 H_{\tilde{i}1}(t, qs) \varphi_2(r) f_2(s, u, v, D_q^{\gamma_1} u, D_q^{\gamma_2} v) d_q s$$

$$\geqslant \varphi_0(r) D_q^{\gamma_i} T_1(u, v),$$

$$D_q^{\gamma_i} T_2(ru, r^{-1}v) = \int_0^1 K_{\tilde{i}2}(t, qs) f_2(s, ru, r^{-1}v, D_q^{\gamma_1} ru, D_q^{\gamma_2} r^{-1}v) d_q s$$

$$+ \int_0^1 H_{\tilde{i}2}(t, qs) f_1(s, ru, r^{-1}v, D_q^{\gamma_1} ru, D_q^{\gamma_2} r^{-1}v) d_q s$$

$$\geqslant \int_0^1 K_{\tilde{i}2}(t, qs) \varphi_2(r) f_2(s, u, v, D_q^{\gamma_1} u, D_q^{\gamma_2} v) d_q s$$

$$+ \int_0^1 H_{\tilde{i}2}(t, qs) \varphi_1(r) f_1(s, u, v, D_q^{\gamma_1} u, D_q^{\gamma_2} v) d_q s$$

$$\geqslant \varphi_0(r) D_q^{\gamma_i} T_2(u, v).$$

Thus, it is obvious that $T(ru, r^{-1}v) \geqslant \varphi_0(r) T(u, v)$, which satisfies (A2) in Lemma 1.

(3) From what has been discussed in (1) and (2), according to Lemma 1, we obtain that BVP (1) and (2) has a unique non-negative solutions (u^*, v^*) in K_h. For any initial (x_{01}, x_{02}), $(y_{01}, y_{02}) \in K_h$, there are two iterative sequences $\{(x_{n1}, x_{n2})\}, \{(y_{n1}, y_{n2})\}$ satisfying that $(x_{n1}, x_{n2}) \to (u^*, v^*), (y_{n1}, y_{n2}) \to (u^*, v^*)$.

This completes the proof of the theorem. $\square$

Remark 1. *Let (u, v) be the solution of the BVP (1) and (2). If $u \geq 0, v \geq 0$, then (u, v) be the non-negative solution of the BVP (1) and (2).*

Example 1. *For $t \in [0, 1]$, consider the following fractional differential system:*

$$\begin{cases} D_{0.5}^{\frac{6}{5}} u(t) + (u(t))^{\frac{1}{6}} + (v(t))^{-\frac{1}{4}} + \left(D_q^{\frac{1}{2}} u(t)\right)^{\frac{1}{2}} + t \left(D_q^{\frac{1}{2}} v(t)\right)^{-\frac{1}{3}} = 0, \\ D_{0.5}^{\frac{7}{5}} v(t) + \dfrac{u}{u+1} + \dfrac{1}{v+2} + D_q^{\frac{1}{2}} u(t) + \dfrac{1}{D_q^{\frac{1}{2}} v(t)} = 0, \end{cases} \quad (34)$$

with the coupled integral and discrete mixed boundary conditions:

$$\begin{cases} u(0) = v(0) = 0, \\ {}^c D_{0.5}^{0.2} u(1) = \sum_{i=1}^{2} \lambda_{1i} I_{0.5}^{\beta_{1i}} v(\xi_i) + \sum_{j=1}^{2} b_{1j} v(\eta_j), \\ {}^c D_{0.5}^{0.4} v(1) = \sum_{i=1}^{2} \lambda_{2i} I_{0.5}^{\beta_{2i}} u(\xi_i) + \sum_{j=1}^{2} b_{2j} u(\eta_j). \end{cases} \quad (35)$$

In this model, we set

$\lambda_{11} = 0.25, \quad \lambda_{21} = 0.2, \quad \beta_{11} = 1.5, \quad \beta_{21} = 1.4, \quad \xi_1 = 0.25, \quad b_{11} = 0.33, \quad b_{21} = 0.17, \quad \eta_1 = 0.33,$

$\lambda_{12} = 0.5, \quad \lambda_{22} = 0.1, \quad \beta_{12} = 2.5, \quad \beta_{22} = 2.4, \quad \xi_2 = 0.75, \quad b_{12} = 0.67, \quad b_{22} = 0.83, \quad \eta_2 = 0.67,$

$$f_1(t, x_1, y_1, x_2, y_2) = x_1^{\frac{1}{6}} + y_1^{-\frac{1}{4}} + x_2^{\frac{1}{2}} + ty_2^{-\frac{1}{3}},$$

$$f_2(t, x_1, y_1, x_2, y_2) = \frac{x_1}{x_1+1} + \frac{1}{y_1+2} + x_2 + \frac{1}{y_2}.$$

It is not difficult to find that $f_i(t, x_1, y_1, x_2, y_2), (i = 1, 2)$ are satisfy (S_1) in Theorem 1. Further, for $\forall r \in (0, 1)$, we have

$$\begin{aligned}
f_1(t, rx_1, r^{-1}y_1, rx_2, r^{-1}y_2) &= (rx_1)^{\frac{1}{6}} + (r^{-1}y_1)^{-\frac{1}{4}} + (rx_2)^{\frac{1}{2}} + t(r^{-1}y_2)^{-\frac{1}{3}} \\
&= r^{\frac{1}{6}}x_1^{\frac{1}{6}} + r^{\frac{1}{4}}y_1^{-\frac{1}{4}} + r^{\frac{1}{2}}x_2^{\frac{1}{2}} + r^{\frac{1}{3}}ty_2^{-\frac{1}{3}} \\
&\geq rx_1^{\frac{1}{6}} + ry_1^{-\frac{1}{4}} + rx_2^{\frac{1}{2}} + rty_2^{-\frac{1}{3}} \\
&= rf_1(t, x_1, y_1, x_2, y_2) \\
&= \varphi_1(r) f_1(t, x_1, y_1, x_2, y_2),
\end{aligned}$$

$$\begin{aligned}
f_2(t, rx_1, r^{-1}y_1, rx_2, r^{-1}y_2) &= \frac{rx_1}{rx_1+1} + \frac{1}{r^{-1}y_1+2} + rx_2 + \frac{1}{r^{-1}y_2} \\
&\geq \frac{rx_1}{x_1+1} + \frac{r}{y_1+2} + rx_2 + \frac{r}{y_2} \\
&= rf_2(t, x_1, y_1, x_2, y_2) \\
&= \varphi_2(r) f_2(t, x_1, y_1, x_2, y_2).
\end{aligned}$$

So $\varphi_0(r) = \min\{\varphi_1(r), \varphi_2(r)\} = \min\{r, r\} = r$, which satisfy (S_2) in Theorem 1. Then from Theorem 1, we can assert that BVP (34) and (35) has a unique non-negative solutions (u^*, v^*) in $K_h = P_{h_1} \times P_{h_2}$, where $(h_1, h_2) = (t^{\frac{1}{5}}, t^{\frac{2}{5}})$.

4. Conclusions

The Q derivative has important applications in many fields, such as quantum physics, spectral analysis and dynamical systems, which make it as a powerful tool for solving physics problems mathematically. In the model studied in this paper, the equations and boundary conditions are universal, but it can be seen from Theorem 1 that utilizing the fixed point theorem for mixed monotone operators, it can be acquired that the conclusion of the existence and uniqueness of the solution only by two easily attainable constraints on the nonlinear term. One of the conditions is mixed monotonicity, and the other is to restrict its properties similar to the upper bound using another function. Compared with the monotone iterative method in [30], we prove the existence and uniqueness of non-negative solutions for more complex systems using more looser conditions.

Author Contributions: Conceptualization, Y.M., C.H., R.M. and H.P.; methodology, Y.M., C.H., R.M. and H.P.; validation, Y.M., C.H., R.M. and H.P.; visualization, Y.M., C.H., R.M. and H.P.; writing—original draft, Y.M., C.H., R.M. and H.P.; writing—review and editing, Y.M., C.H., R.M. and H.P. All authors have read and agreed to the published version of the manuscript.

Funding: This research received no external funding.

Data Availability Statement: Not applicable.

Conflicts of Interest: The authors declare no conflict of interest.

References

1. Kilbas, A.A.; Srivastava, H.M.; Trujillo, J.J. *Theory and Applications of Fractional Differential Equations*; Elsevier: Amsterdam, The Netherlands; Boston, MA, USA, 2006.
2. Podlubny, I. *Fractional Differential Equations*; Academic Press: San Diego, CA, USA, 1999.
3. Khan, H.; Gómez-Aguilar, J.F.; Abdeljawad, T.; Khan, A. Existence results and stability criteria for ABC-fuzzy-Volterra integro-differential equation. *Fractals* **2020**, *28*, 2040048. [CrossRef]
4. Shah, A.; Khan, R.A.; Khan, A.; Khan, H.; Gómez-Aguilar, J.F. Investigation of a system of nonlinear fractional order hybrid differential equations under usual boundary conditions for existence of solution. *Math. Meth. Appl. Sci.* **2020**, *44*, 1628–1638. [CrossRef]

5. Matar, M.M.; Abbas, M.I.; Alzabut, J.; Kaabar, M.K.A.; Etemad, S.; Rezapour, S. Investigation of the p-Laplacian nonperiodic nonlinear boundary value problem via generalized Caputo fractional derivatives. *Adv. Differ. Equ.* **2021**, *1*, 68. [CrossRef]
6. Subramanian, M.; Manigandan, M.; Tunc, C.; Gopal, T.N.; Alzabut, N. On system of nonlinear coupled differential equations and inclusions involving Caputo-type sequential derivatives of fractional order. *J. Taibah Univ. Sci.* **2022**, *16*, 1–23. [CrossRef]
7. Zhao, X.; Liu, Y.; Pang, H. Iterative positive solutions to a coupled fractional differential system with the multistrip and multipoint mixed boundary conditions. *Adv. Differ. Equ.* **2019**, *1*, 389. [CrossRef]
8. Du, X.; Meng, Y.; Pang, H. Iterative positive solutions to a coupled Hadamard-type fractional differential system on infinite domain with the multistrip and multipoint mixed boundary conditions. *J. Funct. Spaces* **2020**, *2020*, 6508075. [CrossRef]
9. Afshari, H.; Sajjadmanesh, M.; Baleanu, D. Existence and uniqueness of positive solutions for a new class of coupled system via fractional derivatives. *Adv. Differ. Equ.* **2020**, *1*, 111. [CrossRef]
10. Song, S.; Zhang, L.; Zhou, B.; Zhang, N. Existence-uniqueness of positive solutions to nonlinear impulsive fractional differential systems and optimal control. *Bound. Value Probl.* **2020**, *1*, 162. [CrossRef]
11. Wang, T.; Hao, Z. Existence and Uniqueness of Positive Solutions for Singular Nonlinear Fractional Differential Equation via Mixed Monotone Operator Method. *J. Funct. Spaces* **2020**, *2020*, 2354927. [CrossRef]
12. Sang, Y.; He, L. Existence of an approximate solution for a class of fractional multi-point boundary value problems with the derivative term. *Bound. Value Probl.* **2021**, *1*, 20. [CrossRef]
13. Harjani, J.; López, B.; Sadarangani, K. Positive solutions for a fractional boundary value problem via a mixed monotone operator. *Fixed Point Theory* **2021**, *22*, 189–203. [CrossRef]
14. Jackson, F.H. On q-Functions and a certain Difference Operator. *Trans. R. Soc. Edinb.* **1909**, *46*, 253–281. [CrossRef]
15. Jackson, F.H. q-difference equations. *Am. J. Math.* **1910**, *32*, 305–314. [CrossRef]
16. Al-Salam, W.A. Some fractional q-integrals and q-derivatives. *Proc. Edinb. Math. Soc.* **1966**, *15*, 135–140. [CrossRef]
17. Agarwal, R.P. Certain fractional q-integrals and q-derivatives. *Math. Proc. Camb. Philos. Soc.* **1969**, *66*, 365–370. [CrossRef]
18. Bekker, M.B.; Bohner, M.J.; Herega, A.N.; Voulov, H. Spectral analysis of a q-difference operator. *J. Phys. A-Math. Theor.* **2010**, *43*, 1189–1195. [CrossRef]
19. Field, C.M.; Joshi, N.; Nijhoff, F. q-Difference equations of KdV type and "Chazy-type" second-degree difference equations. *J. Phys. A-Math. Theor.* **2008**, *41*, 2444–2454. [CrossRef]
20. Mabrouk, H. q-heat operator and q-Poisson's operator. *Fract. Calc. Appl. Anal.* **2006**, *9*, 265–286.
21. Nemri, A.; Fitouhi, A. Polynomial expansions for solution of wave equation in quantum calculus. *Infin. Dimens. Anal. Quantum Probab. Relat. Top.* **2011**, *14*, 345–359. [CrossRef]
22. Ernst, T. Some results for q-functions of many variables. *Rend. Semin. Mat. Univ. Padova* **2004**, *112*, 199–235.
23. Ernst, T. q-Bernoulli and q-Euler polynomials, An umbral approach. *Int. J. Differ. Equ.* **2006**, *1*, 31–80.
24. Rui, A. Nontrivial solutions for fractional q-difference boundary value problems. *Electron. J. Qual. Theory Differ. Equ.* **2010**, *70*, 1–10.
25. Yuan, Q.; Yang, W. Positive solutions of nonlinear boundary value problems for delayed fractional q-difference systems. *Adv. Differ. Equ.* **2014**, *2014*, 51. [CrossRef]
26. Jafari, H.; Haghbin, A.; Johnston, S.J.; Baleanu, D. A new algorithm for solving dynamic equations on a time scale. *J. Comput. Appl. Math.* **2017**, *312*, 167–173. [CrossRef]
27. Zhang, L.; Sun, S. Existence and uniqueness of solutions for mixed fractional q-difference boundary value problems. *Bound. Value Probl.* **2019**, *2019*, 100. [CrossRef]
28. Samei, M.E. Existence of solutions for a system of singular sum fractional q-differential equations via quantum calculus. *Adv. Differ. Equ.* **2020**, *1*, 23. [CrossRef]
29. Samei, M.E.; Ahmadi, A.; Hajiseyedazizi, S.N.; Mishra, S.K.; Ram, B. The existence of nonnegative solutions for a nonlinear fractional q-differential problem via a different numerical approach. *J. Inequalities Appl.* **2021**, *1*, 75. [CrossRef]
30. Bai, C.; Yang, D. The iterative positive solution for a system of fractional q-difference equations with four-point boundary conditions. *Discret. Dyn. Nat. Soc.* **2020**, 3970903. [CrossRef]
31. Guo, F.; Kang, S. Positive solutions for a class of fractional boundary value problem with q-derivatives. *Mediterr. J. Math.* **2019**, *16*, 113. [CrossRef]
32. Yang, C. Positive solutions for a three-point boundary value problem of fractional q-difference equations. *Symmetry* **2018**, *10*, 358. [CrossRef]
33. Lakshmikantham, D.G. Coupled fixed points of nonlinear operators with applications. *Nonlinear Anal.* **1987**, *11*, 623–632.
34. Guo, D.J. Fixed points of mixed monotone operators with applications. *Appl. Anal.* **1988**, *31*, 215–224. [CrossRef]
35. Zhai, C.; Zhang, L. New fixed point theorems for mixed monotone operators and local existence-uniqueness of positive solutions for nonlinear boundary value problems. *J. Math. Anal. Appl.* **2011**, *382*, 594–614. [CrossRef]
36. Annaby, M.H.; Mansour, Z.S. q-fractional calculus and equations. *Lect. Notes Math.* **2012**, *2056*, 1–318.

37. Kac, V.; Cheung, P. *Quantum Calculus*; Mathematics Subject Classification; Springer: Berlin/Heidelberg, Germany, 2002.
38. Yang, C.; Zhai, C.; Zhang, L. Local uniqueness of positive solutions for a coupled system of fractional differential equations with integral boundary conditions. *Adv. Differ. Equ.* **2017**, *2017*, 282. [CrossRef]

Disclaimer/Publisher's Note: The statements, opinions and data contained in all publications are solely those of the individual author(s) and contributor(s) and not of MDPI and/or the editor(s). MDPI and/or the editor(s) disclaim responsibility for any injury to people or property resulting from any ideas, methods, instructions or products referred to in the content.

Article

A Novel Two-Step Inertial Viscosity Algorithm for Bilevel Optimization Problems Applied to Image Recovery

Rattanakorn Wattanataweekul [1], Kobkoon Janngam [2] and Suthep Suantai [3,*]

[1] Department of Mathematics, Statistics and Computer, Faculty of Science, Ubon Ratchathani University, Ubon Ratchathani 34190, Thailand; rattanakorn.w@ubu.ac.th
[2] Graduate Ph.D. Degree Program in Mathematics, Department of Mathematics, Faculty of Science, Chiang Mai University, Chiang Mai 50200, Thailand; kobkoon_jan@cmu.ac.th
[3] Research Center in Optimization and Computational Intelligence for Big Data Prediction, Department of Mathematics, Faculty of Science, Chiang Mai University, Chiang Mai 50200, Thailand
* Correspondence: suthep.s@cmu.ac.th

Abstract: This paper introduces a novel two-step inertial algorithm for locating a common fixed point of a countable family of nonexpansive mappings. We establish strong convergence properties of the proposed method under mild conditions and employ it to solve convex bilevel optimization problems. The method is further applied to the image recovery problem. Our numerical experiments show that the proposed method achieves faster convergence than other related methods in the literature.

Keywords: convex bilevel optimization; forward–backward algorithms; image restoration problems; two-step inertial; viscosity approximation

MSC: 47H09; 90C25; 65K10

1. Introduction

Bilevel optimization has received significant attention in recent years, having arisen as a powerful tool for many machine learning applications such as hyperparameter optimization [1,2], signal processing [3,4], and reinforcement learning [5]. It is defined as a mathematical program in which an optimization problem contains another optimization problem as a constraint. In this paper, we consider the bilevel optimization problem in which the following minima are sought:

$$\min_{x \in S_*} \omega(x), \qquad (1)$$

where $\omega : \mathbb{R}^n \to \mathbb{R}$ is assumed to be strongly convex and differentiable, while S_* is a nonempty set of inner level optimizers satisfying

$$\min_{x \in \mathbb{R}^n} \{\psi_1(x) + \psi_2(x)\}, \qquad (2)$$

where $\psi_1 : \mathbb{R}^n \to \mathbb{R}$ is a differentiable and convex function such that $\nabla \psi_1$ is L-Lipschitz continuous and $\psi_2 : \mathbb{R}^n \to \mathbb{R} \cup \{\infty\}$ is a convex, proper, and lower semi-continuous function. We let Λ be the solution set of (1).

Observe that this bilevel optimization model contains the inner level minimization problem (2) as a constraint to the outer level optimization problem (1). It is a well-known form (1) that

$$x^* \in \Lambda \text{ if and only if } \langle \nabla \omega(x^*), x - x^* \rangle \geq 0 \text{ for all } x \in S_*.$$

Many researchers have proposed algorithms for solving problem (2); see [6–10]. The basic algorithm is the proximal forward–backward technique, or proximal gradient method, defined by the iterative equation

$$x_{n+1} = prox_{\alpha_n \psi_2}(I - \alpha_n \nabla \psi_1)(x_n), \quad n \in \mathbb{N}, \tag{3}$$

where $\alpha_n > 0$ is the step-size, $prox_{\psi_2}$ is the proximity operator of ψ_2, and $\nabla \psi_1$ is the gradient of ψ_1 [6,11]. Equation (3) is referred to in the literature as the forward–backward splitting algorithm (FBSA). The FBSA can be used to solve the inner level optimization problem if ψ_1 is L-Lipschitz continuous [7].

The proximal gradient method can also be viewed as a fixed-point algorithm, where the iterated mapping is given by

$$T := prog_{\alpha \psi_2}(I - \alpha \nabla \psi_1) \tag{4}$$

and is called the forward–backward mapping [12]. The forward–backward mapping, T, is nonexpansive if $0 < \alpha < 2/L$, where L is a Lipschitz constant of $\nabla \psi_1$ and, in that case, $Fix(T) = argmin\{\psi_1(x) + \psi_2(x)\}$. It is noted that implementation of the forward–backward operator can be simplified by first changing the inner level optimization problem into a zero-point problem of the sum of two monotone operators, and then, after analysis, translating back into the fixed-point problem. Exemplifying the fixed-point approach, Sabach et al. [13] proposed the bilevel gradient sequential averaging method (BiG-SAM) for solving problems (1) and (2). The iterative process can be defined as

$$\begin{cases} u_n = prox_{cg}(x_{n-1} - c\nabla f(x_{n-1})), \\ v_n = x_{n-1} - \lambda \nabla \omega(x_{n-1}), \\ x_{n+1} = \gamma_n v_n + (1 - \gamma_n) u_n, \quad n \geq 1 \end{cases} \tag{5}$$

where $c \in (0, \frac{2}{L_f})$, $\lambda \in (0, \frac{2}{L_\omega + \sigma})$, ω is strongly convex with parameter σ, and where L_f and L_ω are Lipschitz constants for the gradients of f and ω. The authors analyzed the convergence behavior of BiG-SAM using an existing fixed-point algorithm and discussed its rate of convergence.

In optimization problems like those presented above, mathematicians frequently employ a technique known as inertial-type extrapolation [14,15] to accelerate the convergence of the iterative equations. This approach involves utilizing a term $\theta_n(x_n - x_{n-1})$, where θ_n denotes an inertial parameter, to govern the momentum $x_n - x_{n-1}$. One such algorithm that has enjoyed immense popularity was developed by Nesterov [14]. He used an inertial or extrapolation technique to solve convex optimization problems of the form of (2), where $F := \psi_1 + \psi_2$ is a convex, smooth function. Nesterov's algorithm takes the following form:

$$\begin{cases} z_n = x_n + \theta_n(x_n - x_{n-1}), \\ x_{n+1} = z_n + c\nabla F(z_n), \quad n \in \mathbb{N}, \end{cases} \tag{6}$$

where the inertial parameter $\theta_n \in (0,1)$ for all n and $c > 0$ is the step size depending on the Lipschitz continuity modulus of ∇F. Nesterov proved that Equation (6) has a faster convergence rate than the general gradient algorithm by selecting $\{\theta_n\}$ such that $\sup_n \theta_n = 1$. Similarly, in 2009, Beck et al. [16] introduced the fast iterative shrinkage-thresholding algorithm (FISTA) for solving linear inverse problems. Their result combined the proximity algorithm with the inertial technique, again resulting in the algorithm's convergence rate being considerably accelerated.

In 2019, Shehu et al. [17] presented an inertial forward–backward algorithm, called the inertial bilevel gradient sequential averaging method (iBiG-SAM) for solving problems (1) and (2). Their method was subsequently improved by Sabach et al. [13], using the following iterative algorithm:

$$\begin{cases} s_n = x_n + \theta_n(x_n - x_{n-1}), \\ u_n = prox_{cg}(I - c\nabla f)(s_n), \\ v_n = s_n - \lambda \nabla \omega(s_n), \\ x_{n+1} = \gamma_n v_n + (1 - \gamma_n)u_n, \ n \geq 1. \end{cases} \quad (7)$$

The authors transformed the bilevel optimization problem into a fixed-point problem for a nonexpansive mapping in an infinite dimensional Hilbert space and then proved strong convergence.

As the above suggests, research on fixed-point problems for nonexpansive mappings has become crucial for developing optimization methods. The Mann iterative process is a well-known method for approximating fixed points of nonexpansive mappings on Hilbert spaces. However, Mann's process provides only weak convergence. Many authors have demonstrated fixed-point problems exhibiting strong convergence for nonexpansive mappings on Hilbert spaces using the viscosity approximation method, expressed by the equation

$$x_{n+1} = \beta_n S(x_n) + (1 - \beta_n) T x_n, \ n \geq 1, \quad (8)$$

where $\{\beta_n\} \in (0,1)$, S is a contraction on Hilbert spaces H and $x_1 \in H$; see [18,19].

In 2009, Takahashi [20] modified the viscosity approximation method, selecting a particular fixed point of the nonexpansive self-mapping of Moudafi [18]. The iterative process is given by

$$x_{n+1} = \beta_n S(x_n) + (1 - \beta_n) T_n x_n, \ n \geq 1, \quad (9)$$

where $\{\beta_n\} \in (0,1)$, S is a contraction of C into itself, $\{T_n\}$ is a countable family of nonexpansive of C into itself, C is subset of a Banach space, and $x_1 \in C$. Takahashi proved the strong convergence of (9) to a common fixed point of T_n.

Jailoka et al. [21] introduced a fast viscosity forward–backward algorithm (FVFBA) with the inertial technique for finding a common fixed point of a countable family of nonexpansive mappings. They proved a strong convergence result and applied it to solving a convex minimization problem of the sum of two convex functions. The iterative process can be formulated by

$$\begin{cases} u_n = x_n + \theta_n(x_n - x_{n-1}), \\ v_n = (1 - \alpha_n) T_n u_n + \alpha_n S(u_n), \\ x_{n+1} = (1 - \beta_n) T_n u_n + \beta_n T_n v_n, \ n \geq 1, \end{cases} \quad (10)$$

where $\{\alpha_n\}, \{\beta_n\} \in (0,1)$, S is a contraction on Hilbert spaces H and $x_1 \in H$.

Recently, Janngam et al. [22] presented an inertial viscosity modified SP algorithm (IVMSPA). The authors proved a strong convergence of their algorithm and applied it to solving the convex bilevel optimization problems (problems 1 and 2). Their algorithm was given by

$$\begin{cases} y_n = x_n + \theta_n(x_n - x_{n-1}), \\ z_n = (1 - \alpha_n)y_n + \alpha_n S(y_n), \\ w_n = (1 - \beta_n)z_n + \beta_n T_n z_n, \\ x_{n+1} = (1 - \gamma_n)w_n + \gamma_n T_n w_n, \ n \geq 1, \end{cases} \quad (11)$$

where $\{\alpha_n\}, \{\beta_n\}, \{\gamma_n\} \in (0,1)$, S is contraction mapping on Hilbert spaces H and $x_1 \in H$.

The above authors all employ a single inertial parameter to accelerate the convergence of their algorithms. However, it has been noted that the incorporation of two inertial parameters enhances motion modeling, improves stability and robustness, increases redundancy and fault tolerance, expands the range of applications, and offers flexibility and adaptability in algorithm design. In [23], it was illustrated through an example that the one-step inertial extrapolation, expressed as $w_n = x_n + \theta_n(x_n - x_{n-1})$ with $\theta_n \in [0,1)$, may not produce acceleration. Additionally, Ref. [24] mentioned that incorporating more than two points, such as x_n and x_{n-1}, in the inertial process could lead to acceleration. For instance, consider the following two-step inertial extrapolation:

$$y_n = x_n + \theta(x_n - x_{n-1}) + \delta(x_{n-1} - x_{n-2}) \tag{12}$$

where $\theta > 0$ and $\delta < 0$ can provide acceleration. The limitations of employing one-step inertial acceleration in the alternating direction method of multipliers (ADMM) were dissused in [25], which led to the proposal of adaptive acceleration as an alternative solution. In addition, Polyak [26] discussed the potential for multi-step inertial methods to enhance the speed of optimization techniques despite the absence of established convergence or rate results in [26]. Recent research conducted in [27] has further explored and examined various aspects of multi-step inertial methods.

Based on the information provided above, our aim in this paper is to solve the convex bilevel optimization problem by introducing a new accelerated viscosity algorithm with the two-point inertial technique, which we then apply to image recovery. The remainder of the paper is organized as follows. In Section 2, we recall some basic definitions and results that are crucial in the paper. The proposed algorithm and the analysis of its convergence are presented in Section 3. The performance of deblurring images using our algorithm is analyzed and illustrated in Section 4. Finally, we give conclusions and discuss directions for future work in Section 5.

2. Preliminaries

In this section, we present some preliminary material that will be needed for the main theorems.

Let C be a nonempty subset of a real Hilbert space H with norm $\|\cdot\|$, $\mathbb{R}$ denote the set of real numbers, $\mathbb{R}_+$ denote the non-negative real numbers, $\mathbb{R}_{>0}$ denote the positive real numbers, $\mathbb{N}$ denote the set of positive integers, and let I denote the identity mapping on H.

Definition 1. *The mapping $T : C \to C$ is said to be L-Lipschitz with $L \geq 0$, if*

$$\|Tu - Tv\| \leq L\|u - v\|$$

for all $u, v \in C$. Furthermore, if $L \in [0,1)$ then T is called a contraction mapping, and it is nonexpansive if $L = 1$.

When $\{x_n\}$ is a sequence in C, we denote the strong convergence of x_n to $x \in C$ by $x_n \to x$, and $Fix(T)$ will symbolize the set of all fixed points of T.

Let $T : C \to C$ be a nonexpansive mapping and $\{T_n\}$ be a family of nonexpansive mappings of C into itself such that $\emptyset \neq Fix(T) \subset \Gamma := \bigcap_{n=1}^{\infty} Fix(T_n)$. The sequence $\{T_n\}$ is said to satisfy the NST-condition (I) with T [28], if for each bounded sequence $\{x_n\} \subset C$,

$$\lim_{n \to \infty} \|x_n - T_n x_n\| = 0 \text{ implies } \lim_{n \to \infty} \|x_n - T x_n\| = 0.$$

The following condition is an essential condition for proving our convergence theorem.

Definition 2 ([29,30]). *A sequence $\{T_n\}$ with $\bigcap_{n=1}^{\infty} Fix(T_n) \neq \emptyset$ is said to satisfy the condition (Z) if for every bounded sequence $\{u_n\}$ in C such that*

$$\lim_{n \to \infty} \|u_n - T_n u_n\| = 0,$$

then, every weak cluster point of $\{u_n\}$ belongs to $\bigcap_{n=1}^{\infty} Fix(T_n)$.

Recall that for a nonempty closed convex subset C of H, the metric projection on C is a mapping $P_C : H \to C$, defined by

$$P_C x = argmin\{\|x - y\| : y \in C\}$$

for all $x \in H$. Note that $v = P_C x$ if and only if $\langle x - v, y - v \rangle \leq 0$ for all $y \in C$.

The definition and properties of a proximity operator are presented below.

Definition 3 ([31,32]). *Let $g : H \to \mathbb{R} \cup \{\infty\}$ be a function that is convex, proper, and lower semi-continuous. The function $prox_g$, known as the proximity operator of g, is defined as follows:*

$$prox_g(x) := \min_{y \in H} \left(g(y) + \frac{1}{2}\|x - y\|^2 \right).$$

Alternatively, it can be expressed as:

$$prox_g = (I + \partial g)^{-1},$$

where ∂g represents the subdifferential of g defined by:

$$\partial g(x) := \{v \in H : g(x) + \langle v, u - x \rangle \leq g(u) \text{ for all } u \in H\}$$

for any $x \in H$. Additionally, for $\rho > 0$, we know that $prox_{\rho g}$ is firmly nonexpansive and

$$Fix(prox_{\rho g}) = Argmin(g) := \{v \in H : g(v) \leq g(u) \text{ for all } u \in H\},$$

where $Fix(prox_{\rho g})$ is the set of fixed points of $prox_{\rho g}$.

The following lemmas will be used for proving the convergence of our proposed algorithm.

Lemma 1 ([33]). *Let $\mathfrak{g} : H \to \mathbb{R} \cup \{\infty\}$ be a convex, proper, and lower semi-continuous function and let $\mathfrak{f} : H \to \mathbb{R}$ be a differentiable and convex function such that $\nabla \mathfrak{f}$ is L-Lipschitz continuous. Let*

$$T_n := prox_{\rho_n \mathfrak{g}}(I - \rho_n \nabla \mathfrak{f}) \quad \text{and} \quad T := prox_{\rho \mathfrak{g}}(I - \rho \nabla \mathfrak{f}),$$

where $\rho_n, \rho \in (0, 2/L)$ with $\rho_n \to \rho$ as $n \to \infty$. Then $\{T_n\}$ satisfies the NST-condition (I) with T.

Lemma 2 ([34]). *Let $x_1, x_2 \in H$ and $t \in [0, 1]$. Then, the following properties are true:*
(i) $\|x_1 \pm x_2\|^2 = \|x_1\|^2 \pm 2\langle x_1, x_2 \rangle + \|x_2\|^2$;
(ii) $\|x_1 + x_2\|^2 \leq \|x_1\|^2 + 2\langle x_2, x_1 + x_2 \rangle$;
(iii) $\|tx_1 + (1-t)x_2\|^2 = t\|x_1\|^2 + (1-t)\|x_2\|^2 - t(1-t)\|x_1 - x_2\|^2$.

Lemma 3 ([35]). *Let $\{a_n\}, \{b_n\} \subset \mathbb{R}_+$ and $\{t_n\} \subset (0,1)$ such that $\sum_{n=1}^{\infty} t_n = \infty$. Assume that*

$$a_{n+1} \leq (1 - t_n)a_n + t_n b_n$$

for all $n \in \mathbb{N}$. If $\limsup_{i \to \infty} b_{n_i} \leq 0$ for every subsequence $\{a_{n_i}\}$ of $\{a_n\}$ satisfying

$$\liminf_{i \to \infty}(a_{n_i+1} - a_{n_i}) \geq 0,$$

then $\lim_{n\to\infty} a_n = 0$.

3. Main Results

Throughout this section, we let C be closed convex with $\emptyset \neq C \subset H$ and a mapping $F : C \to C$ be a k-contraction where $0 < k < 1$. Let $\{T_n\}$ is a family of nonexpansive mappings of C into itself satisfying the condition (Z) such that $\Gamma := \bigcap_{n=1}^{\infty} Fix(T_n) \neq \emptyset$.

For the first of our main results, we draw upon the ideas of Jailoka et al. [21] and Liang [24] and introduce a modified two-step inertial viscosity algorithm (MTIVA) for finding a common fixed point of a family of nonexpansive mappings $\{T_n\}$, as follows:

In Theorem 1, we show that Algorithm 1 converges strongly.

Algorithm 1 Modified Two-Step Inertial Viscosity Algorithm (MTIVA)

Initialization: Let $\{\beta_n\}, \{\gamma_n\} \subset [0,1], \{\tau_n\} \subset \mathbb{R}_+$ and let $\{\mu_n\}, \{\rho_n\} \subset \mathbb{R}_{>0}$ be bounded sequences. Take $x_{-1}, x_0, x_1 \in H$ arbitrarily. For $n \in \mathbb{N}$.
Step 1. Compute the inertial step:

$$\vartheta_n = \begin{cases} \min\left\{\mu_n, \frac{\tau_n}{\|x_n - x_{n-1}\|}\right\} & \text{if } x_n \neq x_{n-1}, \\ \mu_n & \text{otherwise,} \end{cases} \tag{13}$$

and

$$\delta_n = \begin{cases} \max\left\{-\rho_n, \frac{-\tau_n}{\|x_{n-1} - x_{n-2}\|}\right\} & \text{if } x_{n-1} \neq x_{n-2}, \\ -\rho_n & \text{otherwise,} \end{cases} \tag{14}$$

$$w_n = x_n + \vartheta_n(x_n - x_{n-1}) + \delta_n(x_{n-1} - x_{n-2}). \tag{15}$$

Step 2. Compute the viscosity step:

$$z_n = (1 - \gamma_n)T_n w_n + \gamma_n F(w_n). \tag{16}$$

Step 3. Compute x_{n+1}:

$$x_{n+1} = (1 - \beta_n)T_n w_n + \beta_n T_n z_n. \tag{17}$$

Theorem 1. *Let a sequence $\{x_n\}$ be generated by Algorithm 1. Suppose the conditions (C1–C3) hold for the sequences $\{\tau_n\}, \{\gamma_n\},$ and $\{\beta_n\}$. Then, $x_n \to \check{p} \in \Gamma$, where $\check{p} = P_\Gamma F(\check{p})$.*

(C1) $\lim_{n\to\infty} \frac{\tau_n}{\gamma_n} = 0$;
(C2) $0 < \epsilon_1 \leq \beta_n \leq \epsilon_2 < 1$ for some $\epsilon_1, \epsilon_2 \in \mathbb{R}$;
(C3) $0 < \gamma_n < 1$, $\lim_{n\to\infty} \gamma_n = 0$ and $\sum_{n=1}^{\infty} \gamma_n = \infty$.

Proof. Let $\check{p} = P_\Gamma F(\check{p})$. By the definition of z_n, we obtain

$$\begin{aligned}\|z_n - \check{p}\| &= \|(1-\gamma_n)T_n w_n + \gamma_n F(w_n) - \check{p}\| \\ &\leq (1-\gamma_n)\|T_n w_n - \check{p}\| + \gamma_n \|F(w_n) - F(\check{p})\| + \gamma_n \|F(\check{p}) - \check{p}\| \\ &\leq (1 - \gamma_n(1-k))\|w_n - \check{p}\| + \gamma_n \|F(\check{p}) - \check{p}\|.\end{aligned} \tag{18}$$

By the definition of w_n, we obtain

$$\begin{aligned}\|w_n - \check{p}\| &= \|x_n + \vartheta_n(x_n - x_{n-1}) + \delta_n(x_{n-1} - x_{n-2}) - \check{p}\| \\ &\leq \|x_n - \check{p}\| + \vartheta_n \|x_n - x_{n-1}\| + \delta_n \|x_{n-1} - x_{n-2}\|.\end{aligned} \tag{19}$$

Using (18) and (19), we obtain

$$\begin{aligned}
\|x_{n+1} - \breve{p}\| &\leq (1-\beta_n)\|T_n w_n - \breve{p}\| + \beta_n \|T_n z_n - \breve{p}\| \\
&\leq (1-\beta_n)\|w_n - \breve{p}\| + \beta_n \|z_n - \breve{p}\| \\
&\leq (1 - \gamma_n \beta_n (1-k))\|w_n - \breve{p}\| + \beta_n \gamma_n \|F(\breve{p}) - \breve{p}\| \\
&\leq (1 - \gamma_n \beta_n (1-k))(\|x_n - \breve{p}\| + \vartheta_n \|x_n - x_{n-1}\| + \delta_n \|x_{n-1} - x_{n-2}\|) \\
&\quad + \beta_n \gamma_n \|F(\breve{p}) - \breve{p}\| \\
&\leq (1 - \gamma_n \beta_n (1-k))\|x_n - \breve{p}\| + \beta_n \gamma_n \left(\frac{\vartheta_n}{\beta_n \gamma_n} \|x_n - x_{n-1}\| \right. \\
&\quad \left. + \frac{\delta_n}{\beta_n \gamma_n} \|x_{n-1} - x_{n-2}\| + \|F(\breve{p}) - \breve{p}\| \right).
\end{aligned}$$

By (13), (14) and (C1), we have $\frac{\vartheta_n}{\beta_n \gamma_n} \|x_n - x_{n-1}\| \to 0$ as $n \to \infty$ and $\frac{\delta_n}{\beta_n \gamma_n} \|x_{n-1} - x_{n-2}\| \to 0$ as $n \to \infty$, and then $M_1, M_2 > 0$ exist such that

$$\frac{\vartheta_n}{\beta_n \gamma_n} \|x_n - x_{n-1}\| \leq M_1 \quad \text{and} \quad \frac{\delta_n}{\beta_n \gamma_n} \|x_{n-1} - x_{n-2}\| \leq M_2$$

for all $n \geq 1$. Then,

$$\begin{aligned}
\|x_{n+1} - \breve{p}\| &\leq (1 - \gamma_n \beta_n (1-k))\|x_n - \breve{p}\| + \beta_n \gamma_n (1-k) \left(\frac{M_1 + M_2 + \|F(\breve{p}) - \breve{p}\|}{1-k} \right) \\
&\leq \max \left\{ \|x_n - \breve{p}\|, \frac{M + \|F(\breve{p}) - \breve{p}\|}{1-k} \right\},
\end{aligned}$$

where $M = M_1 + M_2 > 0$. Thus, by mathematical induction, we deduce that

$$\|x_n - \breve{p}\| \leq \max \left\{ \|x_1 - \breve{p}\|, \frac{M + \|F(\breve{p}) - \breve{p}\|}{1-k} \right\}$$

for all $n \geq 1$. Hence, the sequence $\{x_n\}$ is bounded and so are the sequences $\{F(w_n)\}$, $\{T_n w_n\}$, $\{z_n\}$. Now, by Lemma 2, we obtain

$$\begin{aligned}
\|z_n - \breve{p}\|^2 &= \|(1-\gamma_n)(T_n w_n - \breve{p}) + \gamma_n (F(w_n) - F(\breve{p})) + \gamma_n (F(\breve{p}) - \breve{p})\|^2 \\
&\leq \|\gamma_n (F(w_n) - F(\breve{p})) + (1-\gamma_n)(T_n w_n - \breve{p})\|^2 + 2\gamma_n \langle F(\breve{p}) - \breve{p}, z_n - \breve{p} \rangle \\
&\leq \gamma_n \|F(w_n) - F(\breve{p})\|^2 + (1-\gamma_n)\|T_n w_n - \breve{p}\|^2 + 2\gamma_n \langle F(\breve{p}) - \breve{p}, z_n - \breve{p} \rangle \\
&\leq (1 - \gamma_n (1-k))\|w_n - \breve{p}\|^2 + 2\gamma_n \langle F(\breve{p}) - \breve{p}, z_n - \breve{p} \rangle
\end{aligned} \quad (20)$$

and

$$\begin{aligned}
\|w_n - \breve{p}\|^2 &= \|x_n - \breve{p}\|^2 + 2\langle x_n - \breve{p}, \vartheta_n (x_n - x_{n-1}) + \delta_n (x_{n-1} - x_{n-2}) \rangle \\
&\quad + \|\vartheta_n (x_n - x_{n-1}) + \delta_n (x_{n-1} - x_{n-2})\|^2 \\
&\leq \|x_n - \breve{p}\|^2 + 2\vartheta_n \|x_n - \breve{p}\|\|x_{n-1} - x_n\| + 2|\delta_n|\|x_n - \breve{p}\|\|x_{n-1} - x_{n-2}\| \\
&\quad + \vartheta_n^2 \|x_{n-1} - x_n\|^2 + 2\vartheta_n |\delta_n| \|x_{n-1} - x_n\|\|x_{n-1} - x_{n-2}\| \\
&\quad + \delta_n^2 \|x_{n-1} - x_{n-2}\|^2.
\end{aligned} \quad (21)$$

Also, from Lemma 2 (iii), (20) and (21), we obtain

$$\begin{aligned}
\|x_{n+1} - \check{p}\|^2 &= (1-\beta_n)\|T_n w_n - \check{p}\|^2 + \beta_n \|T_n z_n - \check{p}\|^2 - \beta_n(1-\beta_n)\|T_n w_n - T_n z_n\|^2 \\
&\leq (1-\beta_n)\|w_n - \check{p}\|^2 + \beta_n \|z_n - \check{p}\|^2 - \beta_n(1-\beta_n)\|T_n w_n - T_n z_n\|^2 \\
&\leq (1-\beta_n \gamma_n(1-k))\|w_n - \check{p}\|^2 + 2\gamma_n \beta_n \langle F(\check{p}) - \check{p}, z_n - \check{p}\rangle \\
&\quad - \beta_n(1-\beta_n)\|T_n w_n - T_n z_n\|^2 \\
&\leq (1-\beta_n \gamma_n(1-k))\|x_n - \check{p}\|^2 + 2\vartheta_n \|x_n - \check{p}\|\|x_{n-1} - x_n\| \\
&\quad + 2|\delta_n|\|x_n - \check{p}\|\|x_{n-1} - x_{n-2}\| + \vartheta_n^2 \|x_{n-1} - x_n\|^2 \\
&\quad + 2\vartheta_n |\delta_n|\|x_{n-1} - x_n\|\|x_{n-1} - x_{n-2}\| + \delta_n^2 \|x_{n-1} - x_{n-2}\|^2 \\
&\quad + 2\gamma_n \beta_n \langle F(\check{p}) - \check{p}, z_n - \check{p}\rangle - \beta_n(1-\beta_n)\|T_n w_n - T_n z_n\|^2 \\
&= (1-\beta_n \gamma_n(1-k))\|x_n - \check{p}\|^2 - \beta_n(1-\beta_n)\|T_n w_n - T_n z_n\|^2 \\
&\quad + \beta_n \gamma_n(1-k) b_n,
\end{aligned} \quad (22)$$

where

$$b_n = \frac{1}{1-k}\left(\frac{2\vartheta_n}{\beta_n \gamma_n}\|x_n - \check{p}\|\|x_{n-1} - x_n\| + \frac{2|\delta_n|}{\beta_n \gamma_n}\|x_n - \check{p}\|\|x_{n-1} - x_{n-2}\| \right.$$

$$+ \frac{2\vartheta_n |\delta_n|}{\beta_n \gamma_n}\|x_{n-1} - x_n\|\|x_{n-1} - x_{n-2}\| + \frac{\delta_n^2}{\beta_n \gamma_n}\|x_{n-1} - x_{n-2}\|^2$$

$$\left. + 2\langle F(\check{p}) - \check{p}, z_n - \check{p}\rangle \right).$$

It follows that

$$\beta_n(1-\beta_n)\|T_n w_n - T_n z_n\|^2 \leq \|x_n - \check{p}\|^2 - \|x_{n+1} - \check{p}\|^2 + \beta_n \gamma_n(1-k)M', \quad (23)$$

where $M' = \sup\{b_n : n \in \mathbb{N}\}$.

Next, we shall show that the sequence $\{x_n\}$ converges strongly to $\check{p}$. Take $a_n := \|x_n - \check{p}\|^2$ and $t_n = \beta_n \gamma_n(1-k)$. From (22), we have

$$a_{n+1} \leq (1-t_n)a_n + t_n b_n$$

for all $n \in \mathbb{N}$. To apply Lemma 3, we have to show that $\limsup_{i \to \infty} b_{n_i} \leq 0$ whenever a subsequence $\{a_{n_i}\}$ of $\{a_n\}$ satisfies

$$\liminf_{i \to \infty}(a_{n_i+1} - a_{n_i}) \geq 0. \quad (24)$$

Suppose that $\{a_{n_i}\}$ is a subsequence of $\{a_n\}$ satisfying (24). It follows from (23) and (C3) that

$$\limsup_{i \to \infty} \beta_{n_i}(1-\beta_{n_i})\|T_{n_i} w_{n_i} - T_{n_i} z_{n_i}\|^2 \leq \limsup_{i \to \infty}(a_{n_i} - a_{n_i+1} + \beta_{n_i} \gamma_{n_i}(1-k)M')$$

$$\leq \limsup_{i \to \infty}(a_{n_i} - a_{n_i+1}) + (1-k)M' \lim_{i \to \infty} \beta_{n_i} \gamma_{n_i}$$

$$= -\liminf_{i \to \infty}(a_{n_i+1} - a_{n_i})$$

$$\leq 0.$$

The condition (C2) and above inequality lead to

$$\lim_{i \to \infty}\|T_{n_i} w_{n_i} - T_{n_i} z_{n_i}\| = 0. \quad (25)$$

Using (C2) and (C3), and since

$$\beta_{n_i}\|z_{n_i} - T_{n_i}w_{n_i}\| = \beta_{n_i}\gamma_{n_i}\|F(w_{n_i}) - T_{n_i}w_{n_i}\|,$$

we obtain

$$\lim_{i\to\infty}\|z_{n_i} - T_{n_i}w_{n_i}\| = 0. \tag{26}$$

From (25) and (26), we obtain

$$\|z_{n_i} - T_{n_i}z_{n_i}\| \leq \|z_{n_i} - T_{n_i}w_{n_i}\| + \|T_{n_i}w_{n_i} - T_{n_i}z_{n_i}\| \to 0 \tag{27}$$

as $i \to \infty$. In order to prove that $\limsup_{i\to\infty} b_{n_i} \leq 0$, it suffices to show that

$$\limsup_{i\to\infty}\langle F(\breve{p}) - \breve{p}, z_{n_i} - \breve{p}\rangle \leq 0. \tag{28}$$

Since $\{z_{n_i}\}$ is bounded, a subsequence $\{z_{n_{i_j}}\}$ of $\{z_{n_i}\}$ and $y \in H$ exists such that $\{z_{n_{i_j}}\} \rightharpoonup y$ as $j \to \infty$ and

$$\limsup_{i\to\infty}\langle F(\breve{p}) - \breve{p}, z_{n_i} - \breve{p}\rangle = \lim_{j\to\infty}\langle F(\breve{p}) - \breve{p}, z_{n_{i_j}} - \breve{p}\rangle$$
$$= \langle F(\breve{p}) - \breve{p}, y - \breve{p}\rangle.$$

Since $\{T_n\}$ satisfies the condition (Z) and (27), we obtain $y \in \Gamma$. From $\breve{p} = P_\Gamma F(\breve{p})$, we obtain

$$\langle F(\breve{p}) - \breve{p}, z - \breve{p}\rangle \leq 0$$

For all $z \in \Gamma$. In particular, we have

$$\langle F(\breve{p}) - \breve{p}, y - \breve{p}\rangle \leq 0.$$

Hence, we obtain (28). Thus, in view of Lemma 3, $\{x_n\}$ converges to $\breve{p}$, as required. □

In what follows, we impose the assumptions on the mappings ψ_1, ψ_2, and ω associated with the convex bilevel optimization problems (1) and (2).

(A1) $\psi_1 : H \to \mathbb{R}$ is a convex and differentiable function such that $\nabla \psi_1$ is Lipschitz continuous with constant $L_{\psi_1} > 0$ and $\psi_2 : H \to (-\infty, \infty]$ are proper lower semi-continuous and convex functions;

(A2) $\omega : \mathbb{R}^n \to \mathbb{R}$ is strongly convex with parameter σ such that $\nabla\omega$ is L_ω-Lipschitz continuous and $s \in (0, \frac{2}{L_\omega + \sigma})$.

With the above assumptions in place, we propose the following algorithm, called the two-step inertial forward–backward bilevel gradient method (TIFB-BiGM), for solving problems (1) and (2).

The proposition below is attributable to Sabach and Shtern [13] and is critical to our next result.

Proposition 1. *Suppose that $\omega : \mathbb{R}^n \to \mathbb{R}$ is strongly convex with $\sigma > 0$ and $\nabla\omega$ is Lipschitz continuous with constant L_ω. Hence, it follows that for all $s \in (0, \frac{2}{\sigma + L_\omega})$, the mapping $S_s = I - s\nabla\omega$ is a contraction such that*

$$\|x - s\nabla\omega(u) - (v - s\nabla\omega(v))\| \leq \sqrt{1 - \frac{2s\sigma L_\omega}{\sigma + L_\omega}}\|u - v\|$$

for all $u, v \in \mathbb{R}^n$.

Theorem 2. *The sequence $\{x_n\}$ generated by Algorithm 2 converges strongly to $\check{p} \in \Lambda$, where Λ is the set of all solutions of (1) and $\check{p} = P_{S_*}(I - s\nabla\omega)(\check{p})$, provided that all conditions as in Theorem 1 hold.*

Algorithm 2 Two-Step Inertial Forward–Backward Bilevel Gradient Method (TIFB-BiGM)

Initialization: Let $\{\beta_n\}, \{\gamma_n\} \subset [0,1], \{\tau_n\} \subset \mathbb{R}_+$, and let $\{\mu_n\}, \{\rho_n\} \subset \mathbb{R}_{>0}$ be bounded sequences. Take $x_{-1}, x_0, x_1 \in H$ arbitrarily.
Let $\{c_n\} \subset (0, \frac{2}{L_{\psi_1}})$ with $c_n \to c$ as $n \to \infty$, where $c \in (0, \frac{2}{L_{\psi_1}})$. For $n \in \mathbb{N}$.
Step 1. Compute the inertial step:

$$\vartheta_n = \begin{cases} \min\left\{\mu_n, \frac{\tau_n}{\|x_n - x_{n-1}\|}\right\} & \text{if } x_n \neq x_{n-1}, \\ \mu_n & \text{otherwise}, \end{cases} \tag{29}$$

and

$$\delta_n = \begin{cases} \max\left\{-\rho_n, \frac{-\tau_n}{\|x_{n-1} - x_{n-2}\|}\right\} & \text{if } x_{n-1} \neq x_{n-2}, \\ -\rho_n & \text{otherwise}, \end{cases} \tag{30}$$

$$w_n = x_n + \vartheta_n(x_n - x_{n-1}) + \delta_n(x_{n-1} - x_{n-2}). \tag{31}$$

Step 2. Compute:

$$z_n = (1 - \gamma_n)\text{prox}_{c_n\psi_2}(I - c_n\nabla\psi_1)w_n + \gamma_n(I - s\nabla\omega)(w_n), \tag{32}$$
$$x_{n+1} = (1 - \beta_n)\text{prox}_{c_n\psi_2}(I - c_n\nabla\psi_1)w_n + \beta_n\text{prox}_{c_n\psi_2}(I - c_n\nabla\psi_1)z_n. \tag{33}$$

Proof. Put $F = I - s\nabla\omega$ and $T_n = \text{prox}_{c_n\psi_2}(I - c_n\nabla\psi_1)$, where $c_n \in (0, \frac{2}{L_{\psi_1}})$. Then, by Proposition 1, F is a contraction mapping. We also know that T_n is nonexpansive. Using Theorem 1, we conclude that $x_n \to \check{p} \in \Gamma$, where $\check{p} = P_\Gamma F(\check{p})$. It is noted that, $\Gamma = \bigcap_{n=1}^{\infty} \text{Fix}(T_n) = S_*$. Then, for all $x \in S_*$, we have

$$0 \geq \langle F(\check{p}) - \check{p}, x - \check{p}\rangle = \langle \check{p} - s\nabla\omega(\check{p}) - \check{p}, x - \check{p}\rangle = \langle -s\nabla\omega(\check{p}), x - \check{p}\rangle.$$

Dividing above inequalities by $-s$, we obtain

$$\langle \nabla\omega(\check{p}), x - \check{p}\rangle \geq 0$$

for all $x \in S_*$. Hence, $\check{p} \in \Lambda$, so $x_n \to \check{p} \in \Lambda$. This completes the proof. □

4. Application to Image Recovery

Algorithm 2 will now be applied to the problem of image restoration. The algorithm's performance will be compared to that of several existing methods, such as IVMSPA, FVFBA, BiG-SAM, and iBiG-SAM. Image restoration, also known as image deblurring or image deconvolution, is the process of removing or minimizing degradations (blur) in an image. Efforts along these lines began in the 1950s, and applications have been found in a number of areas, including consumer photography, scientific exploration, and image/video decoding; see [36,37]. Mathematically, image restoration can be modeled with the equation

$$v = \mathcal{A}x + \check{b}, \tag{34}$$

where $v \in \mathbb{R}^m$ is the observed image, $\mathcal{A} \in \mathbb{R}^{m \times n}$ is the blurring matrix, $x \in \mathbb{R}^n$ is an original image, and $\check{b}$ is an additive noise. The objective is to recover the original image $\bar{x} \in \mathbb{R}^n$ that satisfies (34) by minimizing the value of $\check{b}$ using the least squares method as shown in

Equation (35). This method aims to minimize the squared difference between v and $\mathcal{A}x$ defined as follows:

$$\min_x \|v - \mathcal{A}x\|_2^2, \tag{35}$$

where $\|\cdot\|_2$ is the Euclidean norm. Many iterations, such as the Richardson iteration, see [38], can be used to estimate the solution of (35). The problem stated in Equation (35) is considered ill-posed because there are more unknown variables than observations, resulting in a norm result that is too large to be meaningful. This issue is discussed in references [39,40]. To address this problem, various regularization methods have been introduced to improve the least squares problem. One commonly used method is Tikhonov regularization, which was proposed by Tikhonov and involves minimizing a specific equation.

$$\min_x \left\{ \|v - \mathcal{A}x\|_2^2 + \zeta \|Lx\|_2 \right\}, \tag{36}$$

where ζ is a positive parameter known as a regularization parameter, $\|\cdot\|_1$ is the l_1-norm and $\|\cdot\|_2$ is the Euclidean norm, and $L \in \mathbb{R}^{m \times n}$ is called the Tikhonov matrix. L is set to be the identity in the standard form. A well-known model for solving problem (34) is the least absolute shrinkage and selection operator (LASSO) [41], which is defined by the expression

$$\min_x \left\{ \|v - \mathcal{A}x\|_2^2 + \zeta \|x\|_1 \right\}. \tag{37}$$

The restoration of RGB images presents a challenge for the model (36) due to the significant size of the matrix A, as well as its associated elements, which can make computing the multiplication Ax and $\|x\|_1$ quite expensive. To address this, researchers in this field commonly implement a 2-D fast Fourier transform to transform the images, resulting in a modified version of the model (36) that overcomes this issue.

$$\min_x \left\{ \|v - Ax\|_2^2 + \zeta \|Wx\|_1 \right\}. \tag{38}$$

The blurring operation A, commonly selected as $A = RW$, plays a crucial role in the problem (34). R represents the blurring matrix, while W denotes the two-dimensional fast Fourier transform. The observed image $v \in \mathbb{R}^{m \times n}$ is affected by both blurring and noise, with its dimensions being $m \times n$.

Now, let S_* be the set of all solutions of (38). Among the solutions in S_*, we would also like to select a solution $x^* \in S_*$ in such a way that x^* is a minimizer of

$$\min_{x^* \in S_*} \frac{1}{2} \|x^*\|^2. \tag{39}$$

We consider 2 RGB images (Wat Chedi Luang [42] and Matsue Castle) with the size of 256×256 as the original images (see Figure 1). The pictures we used in this experiment were created by the third author. In order to simulate blurring, we convolved the images using a Gaussian blur filter with a size of 9×9 and a standard deviation of $\sigma = 4$ with noise 10^{-4}.

Peak signal-to-noise ratio (PSNR) [43] and signal-to-noise ratio (SNR) [44] were used as the metrics for evaluating the performance of each algorithm. The PSNR and SNR at x_n are given by

$$PSNR(x_n) = 10 \log_{10} \left(\frac{MAX^2}{MSE} \right), \tag{40}$$

$$SNR(x_n) = 10 \log_{10} \left(\frac{\|x - \bar{x}\|_2}{\|x_n - \bar{x}\|_2} \right), \tag{41}$$

where MAX is the maximum pixel value (usually 255 in 8-bit grayscale images) and $MSE = \frac{1}{256^2}\|x_n - x\|_2^2$ is the mean squared error between the original and the distorted image. Both and SNR are expressed in decibels (dB) as a logarithmic measure of the signal-to-noise or signal-to-error ratio.

(a) (b)

Figure 1. Original images: (**a**) Wat Chedi Luang, (**b**) Matsue Castle.

In image restoration, both PSNR and SNR are commonly used as metrics to assess the performance of deblurring results. However, it is important to note that these metrics provide different types of information.

PSNR measures the quality of a deblurred image by comparing it to the original image and evaluating the amount of noise introduced during the restoration process. It calculates the ratio between the peak signal power (the maximum possible value for the pixel) and the mean squared error (MSE) between the original and deblurred images. Higher PSNR values indicate better restoration quality as they indicate a lower level of distortion or noise.

On the other hand, SNR measures the ratio between the signal power and the noise power in the deblurred image. It quantifies the preservation of the original signal after the restoration process. Higher SNR values indicate less noise in the deblurred image.

While both PSNR and SNR are useful metrics, they focus on different aspects of image restoration. PSNR primarily considers the visual quality and fidelity of the deblurred image compared to the original, while SNR focuses more on the amount of noise present in the deblurred image.

To comprehensively evaluate the performance of your deblurring algorithm, it is recommended to consider both PSNR and SNR. They provide complementary information about the restoration quality.

We now employ our proposed algorithm (TIFB-BiGM) in Theorem 2 to solve the convex bilevel optimization problems (38) and (39). In our experiments, the algorithm developed in this paper (TIFB-BiGM) as well as the others are discussed and applied to solve the convex bilevel optimization problems (38) and (39), where $\omega(x) = \frac{1}{2}\|x\|_2^2$, $\psi_1(x) = \|v - Ax\|^2$, $\psi_2(x) = \zeta\|Wx\|_1$ and $\zeta = 5 \times 10^{-5}$. The observed images are blurred images. We compute the Lipschitz constant L_{ψ_1} by using the maximum eigenvalues of the matrix $A^\top A$.

For the first experiment, the parameters of the TIFB-BiGM are chosen as follows: $\beta_n = \frac{0.99n}{n+1}$, $\gamma_n = \frac{1}{50n}$, $c_n = \frac{1}{L_{\psi_1}}$, $\tau_n = \frac{10^{14}}{n^2}$ and $s = 0.01$. Now, the experiments for recovering the "Wat Chedi Luang" image with size of 256×256 using TIFB-BiGM with different inertial parameters are shown in Tables 1 and 2. We also observe from Tables 1 and 2 that μ_n tends to 1 and ρ_n tends to 0

$$\mu_n = \frac{0.99n}{n + 0.001} \text{ and } \rho_n = \frac{1}{n^2}$$

gives the highest values of PSNR and SNR for our method.

Table 1. PSNR values for restoration of "Wat Chedi Luang" image by TIFB-BiGM after 300 iterations for different choices of parameters μ_n and ρ_n.

$\mu_n \rightarrow$ $\rho_n \downarrow$	0.1	0.3	0.5	0.9	$\frac{0.99n}{n+0.001}$	1
0.1	22.9755	23.2143	23.5185	24.6769	25.3398	25.4489
0.3	22.7791	22.9764	23.2154	23.9454	24.2129	24.2479
0.5	22.6116	22.7799	22.9773	23.5215	23.6923	23.7133
0.9	22.3362	22.4662	22.6129	22.9789	23.0805	23.0924
$\frac{1}{n^2}$	23.0847	23.3513	23.7038	25.4271	26.2116	24.9267

Table 2. SNR values for restoration of "Wat Chedi Luang" image by TIFB-BiGM after 300 iterations for different choices of parameters μ_n and ρ_n.

$\mu_n \rightarrow$ $\rho_n \downarrow$	0.1	0.3	0.5	0.9	$\frac{0.99n}{n+0.001}$	1
0.1	18.9503	19.1890	19.4932	20.6516	21.3144	21.4236
0.3	18.7539	18.9510	19.1901	19.9200	20.1876	20.2225
0.5	18.5864	18.7545	18.9519	19.4961	19.6670	19.6879
0.9	18.3110	18.4408	18.5875	18.9536	19.0551	19.0670
$\frac{1}{n^2}$	19.0595	18.3260	19.6784	21.4018	22.1913	20.9014

The parameter values for each algorithm were chosen for optimum performance, based on the published literature. The value for γ_n in Table 3 is the best choice for BiG-SAM considered in [13]. For iBiG-SAM, $\alpha = 3$ is the best choice over other values considered in [17], and the same authors found, based on their numerical experiments, $\mu_n = \frac{n}{n+1}$ to be the best choice for FVFBA.

Table 3. Parameters selection of TIFB-BiGM, IVMSPA, FVFBA, BiG-SAM, and iBiG-SAM.

Methods	Setting
TIFB-BiGM	$s = 0.01, c_n = \frac{1}{L_{\varphi_1}}, \beta_n = \frac{0.99n}{n+1}, \gamma_n = \frac{1}{50n},$ $\tau_n = \frac{10^{18}}{n^2}, \mu_n = \frac{0.99n}{n+0.001}, \rho_n = \frac{1}{n^2}$
IVMSPA	$s = 0.01, c_n = \frac{1}{L_f}, \alpha_n = \frac{1}{50n}, \beta_n = \gamma_n = 0.5,$ $\tau_n = \frac{10^{20}}{n}$ $\theta_n = \begin{cases} \min\left\{\frac{p_n-1}{p_{n+1}}, \frac{\alpha_n \tau_n}{\|x_n - x_{n-1}\|}\right\} & \text{if } x_n \neq x_{n-1} \\ \frac{p_n-1}{p_{n+1}} & \text{otherwise} \end{cases}$ where $p_1 = 1$ and $p_{n+1} = \frac{1+\sqrt{1+4p_n^2}}{2}$
FVFBA	$c_n = \frac{n}{n+1}, \beta_n = \frac{0.99n}{n+1}, \gamma_n = \frac{1}{50n}, \tau_n = \frac{10^{15}}{n^2}$ $\theta_n = \begin{cases} \min\left\{\frac{n}{n+1}, \frac{\tau_n}{\|x_n - x_{n-1}\|}\right\} & \text{if } x_n \neq x_{n-1} \\ \frac{n}{n+1} & \text{otherwise} \end{cases}$

Table 3. Cont.

Methods	Setting
BiG-SAM	$\lambda = 0.01, c = \frac{1}{L_{\varphi_1}}, \gamma_n = \frac{2(0.1)}{1-n\frac{2+cL_{\varphi_1}}{4}}$
iBiG-SAM	$\lambda = 0.01, c = \frac{1}{L_{\varphi_1}}, \gamma_n = \frac{2(0.1)}{1-n\frac{2+cL_{\varphi_1}}{4}}, \beta_n = \frac{\gamma_n}{n^{0.01}}$ $\theta_n = \begin{cases} \min\left\{\frac{n}{n+\alpha-1}, \frac{\beta_n}{\|x_n - x_{n-1}\|}\right\} & \text{if } x_n \neq x_{n-1}, \\ \frac{n}{n+\alpha-1} & \text{otherwise} \end{cases}$

The following experiments demonstrate Algorithm 2's efficiency for image restoration in comparison to IVMSPA, FVFBA, BiG-SAM, and iBiG-SAM using PSNR and SNR as measurements.

The efficiency of restoring images using various algorithms under different iterations are illustrated in Figures 2–7. The results indicate that TIFB-BiGM achieves higher PSNR and SNR values than IVMSPA, FVFBA, BiG-SAM, and iBiG-SAM. Therefore, our algorithm demonstrates superior convergence behavior compared to the aforementioned methods.

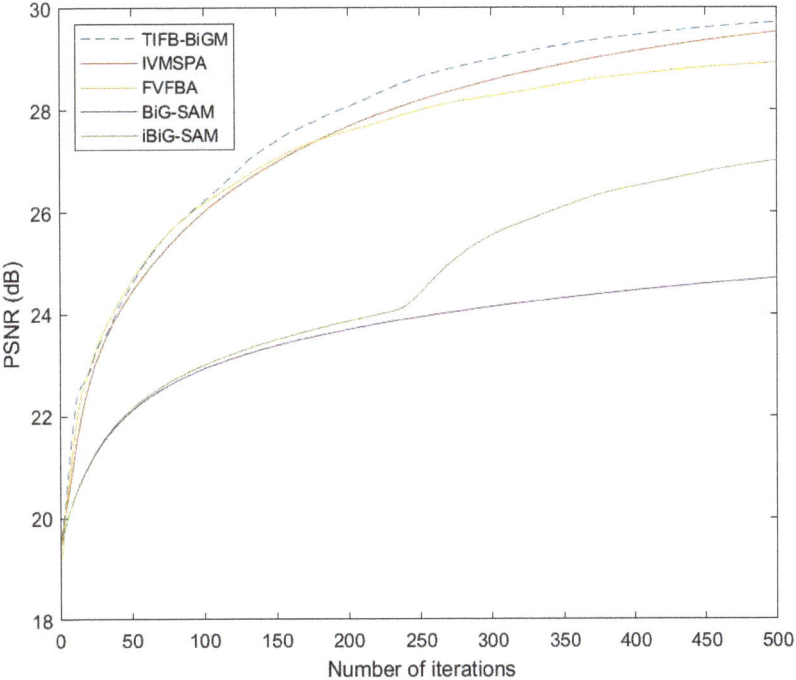

Figure 2. The graphs of PSNR of each algorithm for Wat Chedi Luang.

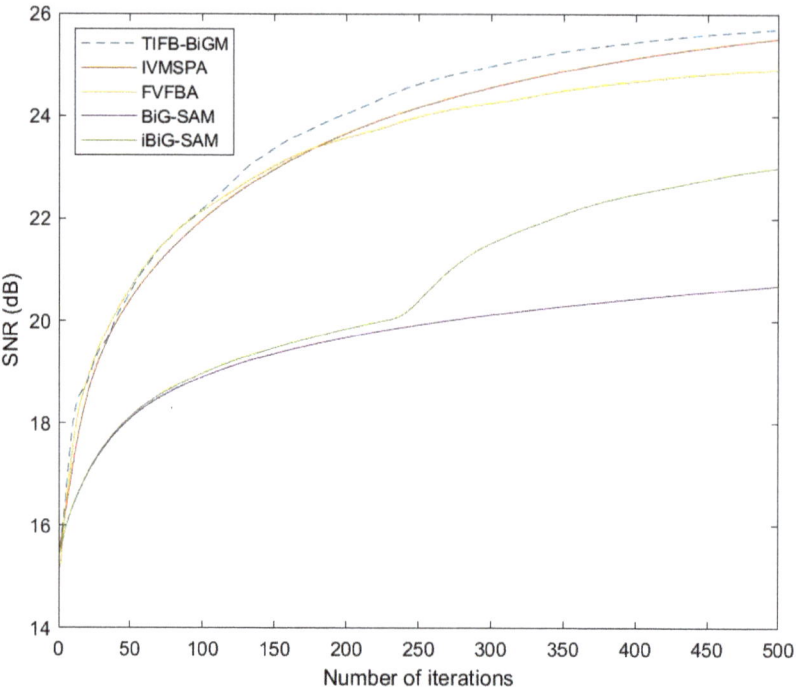

Figure 3. The graphs of SNR of each algorithm for Wat Chedi Luang.

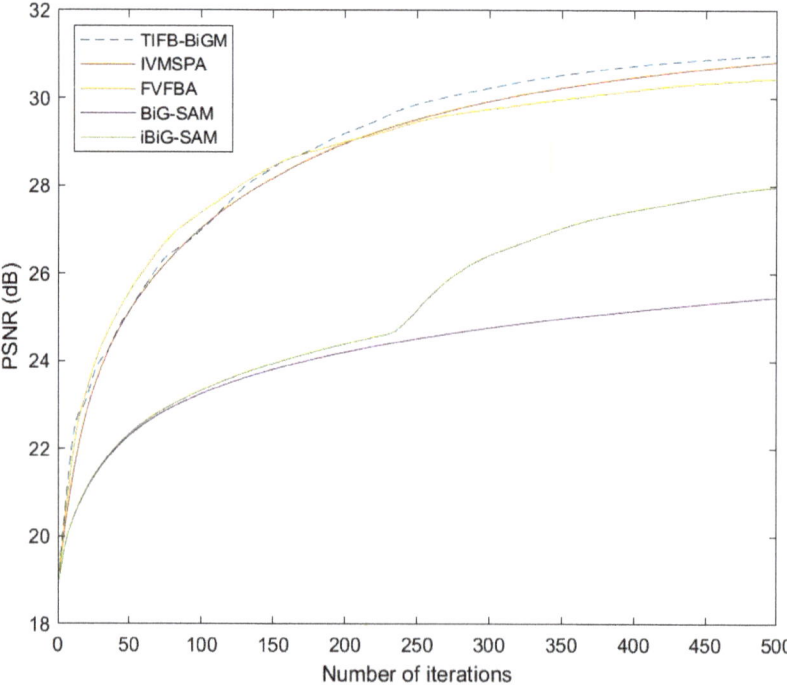

Figure 4. The graphs of PSNR of each algorithm for Matsue Castle.

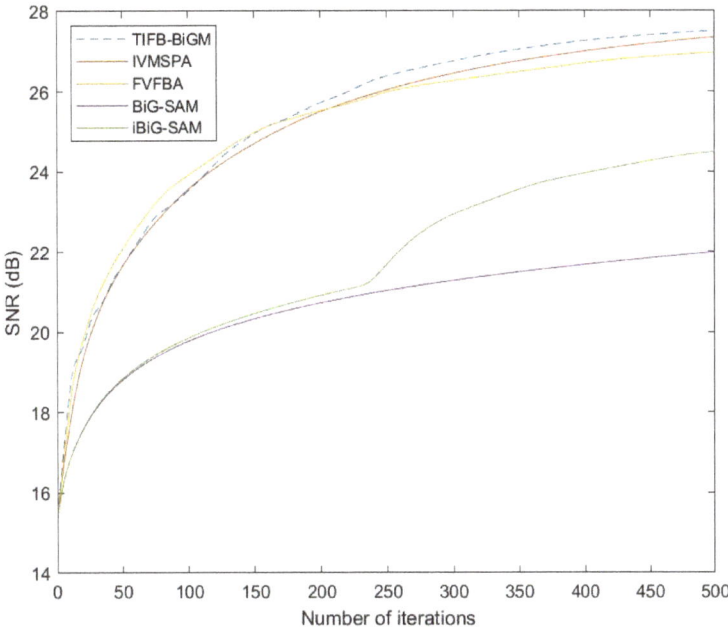

Figure 5. The graphs of SNR of each algorithm for Matsue Castle.

Figure 6. *Cont.*

(e)

(f)

Figure 6. Results for deblurring "Wat Chedi Luang" image using various algorithms at the 500th iteration. (**a**) Gaussian blurred image, (**b**) TIFB-BiGM (PSNR = 29.7216, SNR = 25.6962), (**c**) IVMSPA (PSNR = 29.5375, SNR = 25.5121), (**d**) FVFBA (PSNR = 28.9243, SNR = 24.8989), (**e**) BiG-SAM (PSNR = 24.7118, SNR = 20.6864), and (**f**) iBiG-SAM (PSNR = 27.0172, SNR = 22.9918).

Figure 7. *Cont.*

(e)   (f)

Figure 7. Results for deblurring "Matsue Castle" image using various algorithms at the 500th iteration. (**a**) Gaussian blurred image, (**b**) TIFB-BiGM (PSNR = 30.9830, SNR = 27.5075), (**c**) IVMSPA (PSNR = 30.8212, SNR = 27.3457), (**d**) FVFBA (PSNR = 30.43625, SNR = 26.9636), (**e**) BiG-SAM (PSNR = 25.4625, SNR = 21.9870), and (**f**) iBiG-SAM (PSNR = 27.9712, SNR = 24.4957).

5. Conclusions

In this paper, algorithmic solutions to a family of convex bilevel optimization problems are developed and applied to image processing. An interesting connection between minization problems and fixed-point methods is observed. We first present a modified two-step inertial viscosity algorithm (MTIVA) for finding a common fixed point of a family of nonexpansive operators in a Hilbert space and prove strong convergence under relatively mild conditions. This is the applied to the solution of a convex bilevel optimization problem by introducing a novel two-step inertial forward–backward bilevel gradient method (TIFB-BiGM). The main results are then employed in the solution of an image restoration problem. Through careful comparative analysis, we demonstrate that our algorithm outperforms several existing algorithms such as IVMSPA, FVFBA, BiG-SAM, and iBiG-SAM, in terms of image recovery efficiency, as verified through numerical experiments conducted under specific parameter settings.

There are several potential avenues for future research. Firstly, investigating the adaptability and performance of the proposed algorithm in different image processing tasks could provide valuable insights. Additionally, one might explore the algorithm's scalability to large-scale image datasets or investigate the incorporation of parallel computing techniques that could enhance the algorithm's computational efficiency. Moreover, conducting comparative studies with other state-of-the-art image restoration algorithms would provide a comprehensive evaluation of the algorithm's strengths and limitations. Finally, exploring the applicability of the proposed algorithm to other domains beyond image processing, such as computer vision or signal processing, would broaden its potential impact.

Author Contributions: Conceptualization, S.S.; formal analysis, R.W. and S.S.; investigation, R.W. and K.J.; methodology, R.W. and S.S.; software, K.J.; supervision, S.S.; validation, R.W. and S.S.; writing—original draft, R.W. and K.J.; and writing—review and editing, R.W. and S.S. All authors have read and agreed to the published version of the manuscript.

Funding: NSRF via the program Management Unit for Human Resources & Institutional Development, Research, and Innovation (grant number B05F640183).

Data Availability Statement: Not applicable.

Acknowledgments: This research has received funding support from the NSRF via the Program Management Unit for Human Resources and Institutional Development, Research, and Innovation (grant number B05F640183), and it was also partially supported by Chiang Mai University and Ubon Ratchathani University.

Conflicts of Interest: The authors declare no conflict of interest.

References

1. Franceschi, L.; Frasconi, P.; Salzo, S.; Grazzi, R.; Pontil, M. Bilevel programming for hyperparameter optimization and meta-learning. In Proceedings of the International Conference on Machine Learning (ICML), Stockholm, Sweden, 10–15 July 2018; pp. 1568–1577.
2. Shaban, A.; Cheng, C.-A.; Hatch, N.; Boots, B. Truncated back-propagation for bilevel optimization. In Proceedings of the International Conference on Artificial Intelligence and Statistics (AISTATS), Okinawa, Japan, 16–18 April 2019; pp. 1723–1732.
3. Kunapuli, G.; Bennett, K.P.; Hu, J.; Pang, J.-S. Classification model selection via bilevel programming. *Optim. Methods Softw.* **2008**, 23, 475–489. [CrossRef]
4. Flamary, R.; Rakotomamonjy, A.; Gasso, G. Learning constrained task similarities in graph regularized multitask learning. In *Regularization, Optimization, Kernels, and Support Vector Machines*; Chapman and Hall/CRC: Boca Raton, FL, USA, 2014; Volume 103, ISBN 978-0367658984.
5. Konda, V.R.; Tsitsiklis, J.N. Actor-critic algorithms. In Proceedings of the Advances in Neural Information Processing Systems (NeurIPS), Denver, CO, USA, 30 November-2 December 1999; pp. 1008–1014.
6. Bruck, R.E., Jr. On the weak convergence of an ergodic iteration for the solution of variational inequalities for monotone operators in Hilbert space. *J. Math. Anal. Appl.* **1977**, 61, 159–164. [CrossRef]
7. Lions, P.L.; Mercier, B. Splitting algorithms for the sum of two nonlinear operators. *SIAM J. Numer. Anal.* **1979**, 16, 964–979. [CrossRef]
8. Janngam, K.; Suantai, S. An inertial modified S-Algorithm for convex minimization problems with directed graphs and their applications in classification problems. *Mathematics* **2022**, 10, 4442. [CrossRef]
9. Cabot A. Proximal point algorithm controlled by a slowly vanishing term: Applications to hierarchial minimization. *SIAM J. Optim.* **2005**, 15, 555–572. [CrossRef]
10. Xu, H.K. Averaged mappings and the gradient-projection algorithm. *J. Optim. Theory Appl.* **2011**, 150, 360–378. [CrossRef]
11. Passty, G.B. Ergodic convergence to a zero of the sum of monotone operators in Hilbert space. *J. Math. Anal. Appl.* **1979**, 72, 383–390. [CrossRef]
12. Beck, A.; Sabach, S. A first order method for finding minimal norm-like solutions of convex optimization problems. *Math. Program.* **2014**, 147, 25–46. [CrossRef]
13. Sabach, S.; Shtern, S. A first order method for solving convex bilevel optimization problems. *SIAM J. Optim.* **2017**, 27, 640–660. [CrossRef]
14. Nesterov, Y.E. A method for solving the convex programming problem with convergence rate $O(1/k^2)$. *Sov. Math. Dokl.* **1983**, 27, 372–376.
15. Polyak, B.T. Some methods of speeding up the convergence of iteration methods. *USSR Comput. Math. Math. Phys.* **1964**, 4, 1–17. [CrossRef]
16. Beck, A.; Teboulle, M. A fast iterative shrinkage-thresholding algorithm for linear inverse problems. *SIAM J. Imaging Sci.* **2009**, 2, 183–202. [CrossRef]
17. Shehu, Y.; Vuong, P.T.; Zemkoho, A. An inertial extrapolation method for convex simple bilevel optimization. *Optim Methods Softw.* **2019**, 36, 1–19. [CrossRef]
18. Moudafi, A. Viscosity approximation method for fixed-points problems. *J. Math. Anal. Appl.* **2000**, 241, 46–55. [CrossRef]
19. Xu, H.K. Viscosity approximation methods for nonexpansive mappings. *J. Math. Anal. Appl.* **2004**, 298, 279–291. [CrossRef]
20. Takahashi, W. Viscosity approximation methods for countable families of nonexpansive mappings in Banach spaces. *Nonlinear Anal.* **2009**, 70, 719–734. [CrossRef]
21. Jailoka, P.; Suantai, S. and Hanjing, A. A fast viscosity forward–backward algorithm for convex minimization problems with an application in image recovery. *Carpathian J. Math.* **2021**, 37, 449–461. [CrossRef]
22. Janngam, K.; Suantai, S.; Cho, Y.J.; Kaewkhao, A.; Wattanataweekul, R. A Novel Inertial Viscosity Algorithm for Bilevel Optimization Problems Applied to Classification Problems. *Mathematics* **2023**, 11, 3241. [CrossRef]
23. Poon, C.; Liang, J. Geometry of First-order Methods and Adaptive Acceleration. *arXiv* **2020**, arXiv:2003.03910.
24. Liang, J. Convergence Rates of First-Order Operator Splitting Methods. Ph.D. Thesis, Normandie Universit'e, Normaundie, France, 2016.
25. Poon, C.; Liang, J. Trajectory of Alternating Direction Method of Multiplier and Adaptive Acceleration. In Proceedings of the Advances in Neural Information Processing Systems, Vancouver, BC, Canada, 8–14 December 2019.
26. Polyak, B.T. *Introduction to Optimization*; Optimization Software, Publication Division: New York, NY, USA, 1987.
27. Combettes, P.L.; Glaudin, L. Quasi-Nonexpansive Iterations on the Affine Hull of Orbits: From Mann's Mean Value Algorithm to Inertial Methods. *SIAM J. Optim.* **2017**, 27, 2356–2380. [CrossRef]
28. Nakajo, K.; Shimoji, K.; Takahashi, W. On strong convergence by the hybrid method for families of mappings in Hilbert spaces. *Nonlinear Anal.* **2009**, 71, 112–119. [CrossRef]
29. Aoyama, K.; Kimura, Y. Strong convergence theorems for strongly nonexpansive sequences. *Appl. Math. Comput.* **2011**, 217, 7537–7545. [CrossRef]

30. Aoyama, K.; Kohsaka, F.; Takahashi, W. Strong convergence theorems by shrinking and hybrid projection methods for relatively nonexpansive mappings in Banach spaces. *Nonlinear Anal. Convex Anal.* **2009**, *10*, 7–26.
31. Moreau, J.J. Fonctions convexes duales et points proximaux dans un espace hilbertien. *Comptes Rendus Acad. Sci. Paris Ser. A Math.* **1962**, *255*, 2897–2899.
32. Bauschke, H.H.; Combettes, P.L. *Convex Analysis and Monotone Operator Theory in Hilbert Spaces*; Springer: New York, NY, USA, 2011.
33. Bussaban, L.; Suantai, S.; Kaewkhao, A. A parallel inertial S-iteration forward–backward algorithm for regression and classification problems. *Carpathian J. Math.* **2020**, *36*, 35–44. [CrossRef]
34. Takahashi, W. *Introduction to Nonlinear and Convex Analysis*; Yokohama Publishers: Yokohama, Japan, 2009.
35. Saejung, S.; Yotkaew, P. Approximation of zeros of inverse strongly monotone operators in Banach spaces. *Nonlinear Anal.* **2012**, *75*, 724–750. [CrossRef]
36. Maurya, A.; Tiwari, R. A Novel Method of Image Restoration by using Different Types of Filtering Techniques. *Int. J. Eng. Sci. Innov. Technol.* **2014**, *3*, 124–129.
37. Suseela, G.; Basha, S.A.; Babu, K.P. Image Restoration Using Lucy Richardson Algorithm For X-Ray Images. *IJISET Int. J. Innov.Sci. Eng. Technol.* **2016**, *3*, 280–285.
38. Vogel, C.R. *Computational Methods for Inverse Problems*; SIAM: Philadelphia, PA, USA, 2002.
39. Eldén, L. Algorithms for the Regularization of Ill-Conditioned Least Squares Problems. *BIT Numer. Math.* **1977**, *17*, 134–145. [CrossRef]
40. Hansen, P.C.; Nagy, J.G.; O'Leary, D.P. *Deblurring Images: Matrices, Spectra, and Filtering (Fundamentals of Algorithms 3) (Fundamentals of Algorithms)*; SIAM: Philadelphia, PA, USA, 2006.
41. Tibshirani, R. Regression shrinkage and selection via the lasso. *J. R. Stat. Soc. B Methodol.* **1996**, *58*, 267–288. [CrossRef]
42. Yatakoat, P.; Suantai, S.; Hanjing, A. On Some Accelerated Optimization Algorithms Based on Fixed Point and Linesearch Techniques for Convex Minimization Problems with Applications. *Adv. Cont. Discr. Mod.* **2022**, *2022*, 43:1–43:13. [CrossRef]
43. Thung, K.; Raveendran, P. A survey of image quality measures. In Proceedings of the 2009 International Conference for Technical Postgraduates (TECHPOS), Kuala Lumpur, Malaysia, 14–15 December 2009; pp. 1–4.
44. Chen, D.Q.; Zhang, H.; Cheng, L.Z. A fast fixed-point algorithmfixed-point algorithmfixed-point algorithmfixed-point algorithm for total variation deblurring and segmentation. *J. Math. Imaging Vis.* **2012**, *43*, 167–179. [CrossRef]

Disclaimer/Publisher's Note: The statements, opinions and data contained in all publications are solely those of the individual author(s) and contributor(s) and not of MDPI and/or the editor(s). MDPI and/or the editor(s) disclaim responsibility for any injury to people or property resulting from any ideas, methods, instructions or products referred to in the content.

Article

Czerwik Vector-Valued Metric Space with an Equivalence Relation and Extended Forms of Perov Fixed-Point Theorem

Monairah Alansari [1], Yahya Almalki [2] and Muhammad Usman Ali [3,*]

[1] Department of Mathematics, King Abdulaziz University, P.O. Box 80203, Jeddah 21589, Saudi Arabia; malansari@kau.edu.sa
[2] Department of Mathematics, College of Sciences, King Khalid University, Abha 61413, Saudi Arabia; yalmalki@kku.edu.sa
[3] Department of Mathematics, COMSATS University Islamabad, Islamabad Campus, Islamabad 45550, Pakistan
* Correspondence: muh_usman_ali@yahoo.com or musman.ali@cuiatk.edu.pk

Abstract: In this article, we shall generalize the idea of vector-valued metric space and Perov fixed-point theorem. We shall introduce the notion of Czerwik vector-valued $\mathcal{R}$-metric space by involving an equivalence relation. A few basic concepts and properties related to Czerwik vector-valued $\mathcal{R}$-metric space shall also be discussed that are required to obtain a few extended types of Perov fixed-point theorem.

Keywords: fixed points; vector-valued metric space; Czerwik vector-valued metric space; Czerwik vector-valued $\mathcal{R}$-metric space

MSC: 47H10; 30L15

1. Introduction

The concept of metric space provides a significant contribution to research activities related to mathematical analysis. This meaningful concept was presented by Maurice Fréchet [1] who was a famous French mathematician. This concept was extended by many mathematicians according to their requirements: for example, b-metric space [2], partial metric space [3], cone metric space [4], vector-valued metric space [5], vector-valued b-metric space [6,7], order (ordered vector) metric space [8], order (ordered vector) pseudo-metric space [9], graphical metric space [10], and graphical b-metric space [11] etc.

The Banach contraction principle is the most basic result of the metric fixed-point theory, and it has been generalized by considering all the above-mentioned extended forms of metric space. The literature also contains several other generalizations of this famous result obtained through involving the concepts of partial order, graph, binary relation, or orthogonality relation associated with contraction mapping, see [12–14]. This technique of generalization raised the question: why not consider the concepts of partial order, graph, or binary relation to generalize the notion of metric space and then drive a generalization of the Banach contraction principle? The work presented in [10,11] is based on the answer to that question.

Perov [5] presented the matrix/vector version of the Banach contraction principle by introducing the notion of vector-valued metric spaces. This vector-valued metric space was extended to vector-valued b-metric space by Boriceanu [6], with a constant scalar multiple in the triangle inequality of vector-valued b-metric space. Ali and Kim [7] modified the triangle inequality of vector-valued b-metric space by replacing a constant scalar multiple with a constant matrix multiple. A couple of interesting results in the context of Perov have been derived by several researchers, for example, Bucur et al. [15] derived fixed-point theorems to generalize Perov's result that discuss the existence of fixed points of set-valued maps. Filip and Petrusel [16] modified the contraction-type inequality to generalize the

results of Perov and Bucur et al. [15]. Ali et al. [17] used the admissibility concept of single-valued maps to improve the result of Perov, Altun et al. [18] used the technique of θ-contraction to modify the result of Perov for single-valued maps. Guran et al. [19] used the concept of generalized w-distance and Hardy–Rogers-type contraction inequality to generalize the work of Perov. Guran et al. [20] extended the work of Perov for set-valued maps using a set-valued Hardy–Rogers-type contraction inequality. Martínez-Moreno and Gopal [21] defined the concept of Perov fuzzy metric space and studied the existence of common fixed points for compatible single-valued maps. The aim of this article is to introduce a notion of Czerwik vector-valued $\mathcal{R}$-metric space that is a generalized concept of vector-valued b-metric space. A few results confirming the existence of fixed points for certain types of maps are also derived using this notion. The idea of this article follows from the above-mentioned question.

2. Preliminaries

Throughout this article, we consider H as a nonempty set, $\mathbb{R}_+$ as the set of all non-negative real numbers, $M_{m,m}(\mathbb{R}_+)$ as a collection of all $m \times m$ matrices with non-negative real elements, $\bar{0}$ as an $m \times m$ zero matrix, I as $m \times m$ identity matrix, and $\mathbb{R}_m$ as the set of all $m \times 1$ real matrices. If $W, P \in \mathbb{R}_m$, that is $W = (w_1, w_2, \ldots, w_m)^T$ and $P = (p_1, p_2, \ldots, p_m)^T$, then

(i) $W \leq P$ means that $w_i \leq p_i$ for each $i \in \{1, 2, \ldots, m\}$,
(ii) $W < P$ means that $w_i < p_i$ for each $i \in \{1, 2, \ldots, m\}$,
(iii) $W \geq c \in \mathbb{R}_+$ means that $w_i \geq c$ for each $i \in \{1, 2, \ldots, m\}$.

A matrix $C \in M_{m,m}(\mathbb{R}_+)$ is called convergent to zero (or zero matrix) if $C^n \to \bar{0}$ as $n \to \infty$ (see Varga [22]). Also, note that $C^0 = I$. The following matrices are convergent to zero.

$$C := \begin{pmatrix} c & c \\ d & d \end{pmatrix}, \text{ where } c, d \in \mathbb{R}_+ \text{ and } c + d < 1;$$

$$D := \begin{pmatrix} c & d \\ 0 & e \end{pmatrix}, \text{ where } c, d, e \in \mathbb{R}_+ \text{ and } \max\{c, e\} < 1.$$

Czerwik vector-valued metric space was presented by Ali and Kim [7] in the following ways.

Definition 1. *A mapping $d_C : H \times H \to \mathbb{R}_m$ is called a Czerwik vector-valued metric on H, if for each $h_1, h_2, h_3 \in H$ the following axioms hold:*

(d_1) $d_C(h_1, h_2) \geq 0$;
$d_C(h_1, h_2) = 0$ if and only if $h_1 = h_2$;
(d_2) $d_C(h_1, h_2) = d_C(h_2, h_1)$;
(d_3) $d_C(h_1, h_3) \leq Q[d_C(h_1, h_2) + d_C(h_2, h_3)]$
where $Q = (q_{ij}) \in M_{m,m}(R_+)$ is a matrix with

$$q_{ij} = \begin{cases} q, & i = j \\ 0, & i \neq j \end{cases}$$

and $q \geq 1$. Then, the triple (H, d_C, Q) is called Czerwik vector-valued metric space, or Czerwik generalized metric space.

Note that the Cauchyness and convergence of a sequence in Czerwik vector-valued metric spaces are defined in a similar manner as in b-metric spaces/metric spaces.

If the matrix $Q = (q_{ij}) \in M_{m,m}(R_+)$ is defined by

$$q_{ij} = \begin{cases} 1, & i = j \\ 0, & i \neq j \end{cases}$$

then the Czerwik vector-valued metric space becomes a vector-valued metric space. Perov [5] presented the matrix/vector version of the Banach contraction principle on vector-valued metric space in the following way.

Theorem 1 ([5]). *Let (H, d_C) be a complete vector-valued metric space and $G: H \to H$ be a mapping such that*

$$d_C(Gh, Gk) \leq A d_C(h, k) \; \forall h, k \in H,$$

where $A \in M_{m,m}(R_+)$ is a matrix convergent to zero. Then, G has a unique fixed point.

The above result was generalized by Ali and Kim [7] in the following way.

Theorem 2. *Let (H, d_C, Q) be a complete Czerwik vector-valued metric space. Let $G: H \to H$ be a mapping such that*

$$d_C(Gh, Gk) \leq A d_C(h, k) + B d_C(k, Gh) \; \forall h, k \in H$$

where $A, B \in M_{m,m}(\mathbb{R}_+)$. Also assume that the matrix QA converges to zero. Then, G has a fixed point.

3. Main Results

This section begins with the definition of Czerwik vector-valued $\mathcal{R}$-metric space.

Definition 2. *Let H be a nonempty set equipped with an equivalence relation $\mathcal{R}$. A mapping $d_C \colon H \times H \to \mathbb{R}_m$ is called a Czerwik vector-valued $\mathcal{R}$-metric on H if for each $h_1, h_2, h_3 \in H$ the following axioms hold:*

(d_1) $d_C(h_1, h_2) \geq 0$;
  $d_C(h_1, h_2) = 0$ *if and only if* $h_1 = h_2$;
(d_2) $d_C(h_1, h_2) = d_C(h_2, h_1)$;
(d_3) $d_C(h_1, h_3) \leq Q[d_C(h_1, h_2) + d_C(h_2, h_3)]$ *provided that* $(h_1, h_2), (h_2, h_3) \in \mathcal{R}$
where $Q = (q_{ij}) \in M_{m,m}(R_+)$ is a matrix with

$$q_{ij} = \begin{cases} q, & i = j \\ 0, & i \neq j \end{cases}$$

and $q \geq 1$. Then, the $(H, \mathcal{R}, d_C, Q)$ is called a Czerwik vector-valued $\mathcal{R}$-metric space, or Czerwik generalized $\mathcal{R}$-metric space.

Remark 1. *It is important to note that the triangular property (d_3) of Definition 2 should hold for those elements of the set H that are related to each other under an equivalence relation $\mathcal{R}$. From this, an important question arises: why are the reflexive and symmetric conditions added along with the transitive condition on a binary relation involved in Definition 2? The answer is simple:*

(i) *The reflexive condition is required for the topology generated by d_C.*
(ii) *The symmetric condition is essential for the concept of $\mathcal{R}$-convergence of $\mathcal{R}$-sequence.*

Remark 2. *It is easy to see that Definition 2 reduces to Definition 1 by defining $\mathcal{R} = H \times H$. Thus, every Czerwik vector-valued metric space generates a Czerwik vector-valued $\mathcal{R}$-metric space. But the converse is not true in general.*

In the following, we present an example of Czerwik vector-valued $\mathcal{R}$-metric space.

Example 1. *Consider $H = \mathbb{N}$ and an equivalence relation $\mathcal{R} = \{(x,y) : x, y \in \{1,2,3\}\} \cup \{(x,x) : x \in \{4,5,\cdots\}\}$ on H. Define $d_C \colon H \times H \to \mathbb{R}_2$ by*

$$d_C(1,2) = d_C(2,1) = (2,2)^T$$
$$d_C(1,3) = d_C(3,1) = (2,2)^T$$
$$d_C(2,3) = d_C(3,2) = (5,5)^T$$
$$d_C(x,x) = (0,0)^T \forall x \in H$$
$$d_C(x,y) = d_C(y,x) = (1/|x-y|, 1/|x-y|)^T, \text{ if either } x \geq 4 \text{ or } y \geq 4 \text{ and } x \neq y.$$

One can check that $(H, \mathcal{R}, d_C, Q)$ is a Czerwik vector-valued $\mathcal{R}$-metric space with $Q = \begin{pmatrix} 2 & 0 \\ 0 & 2 \end{pmatrix}$.

Remark 3. *Note that the above-defined d_C is not a Czerwik vector-valued metric on H, because Axiom (d_3) of Definition 1 does not exist, for instance,*

$$d_C(2,3) > Q[d_C(2,4) + d_C(4,3)].$$

Example 2. *Consider $H = \mathbb{R}$, and an equivalence relation on H is defined by*

$$\mathcal{R} = \{(h_1, h_2) : h_1, h_2 \in [0, \infty)\} \cup \{(h,h) : h \in \mathbb{R}\}.$$

Define $d_C \colon H \times H \to \mathbb{R}_2$ by

$$d(h_1, h_2) = \begin{cases} \begin{pmatrix} |h_1 - h_2| \\ |h_1 - h_2| \end{pmatrix}, & \text{if } h_1, h_2 \geq 0 \\ \begin{pmatrix} \frac{|h_1 - h_2|}{1 + |h_1 - h_2|} \\ 0 \end{pmatrix}, & \text{otherwise.} \end{cases}$$

It is easy to check that $(H, \mathcal{R}, d_C, Q)$ is a Czerwik vector-valued $\mathcal{R}$-metric space with $Q = \begin{pmatrix} 1 & 0 \\ 0 & 1 \end{pmatrix}$.

Remark 4. *Note that the above-defined d_C does not satisfy Axiom (d_3) of Definition 1, for instance,*

$$d_C(1,5) \not\leq Q[d_C(1,-1) + d_C(-1,5)].$$

For any $\epsilon > 0$ and for any element h of the Czerwik vector-valued $\mathcal{R}$-metric space $(H, \mathcal{R}, d_C, Q)$, the d_C-open ball having center h and radius ϵ is defined by

$$B_{d_C}(h, \epsilon) = \{h_a \in H : (h, h_a) \in \mathcal{R}, d_C(h, h_a) < \epsilon\}.$$

$\mathcal{R}$ is a reflexive relation, thus $B_{d_C}(h, \epsilon) \neq \emptyset$ for each $h \in H$ and $\epsilon > 0$. Thus, the set $\{B_{d_C}(h, \epsilon) : h \in H, \epsilon > 0\}$ provides a neighbourhood system for the topology $\tau_\mathcal{R}$ on H induced by the Czerwik vector-valued $\mathcal{R}$-metric space.

Definition 3. *Let $(H, \mathcal{R}, d_C, Q)$ be Czerwik vector-valued $\mathcal{R}$-metric space. Then*
- *A sequence (h_n) in H is said to be an $\mathcal{R}$-sequence if $(h_n, h_{n+1}) \in \mathcal{R}$ for each $n \in \mathbb{N}$.*
- *An $\mathcal{R}$-sequence (h_n) in H is said to be $\mathcal{R}$-convergent to h in H if $\lim_{n\to\infty} d_C(h_n, h) = 0$ and $(h_n, h) \in \mathcal{R} \ \forall n \geq k$ for some natural number k.*
- *An $\mathcal{R}$-sequence (h_n) in H is said to be $\mathcal{R}$-Cauchy if $\lim_{n,m\to\infty} d_C(h_n, h_m) = 0$.*

- $(H, \mathcal{R}, d_C, Q)$ is said to be $\mathcal{R}$-complete if each $\mathcal{R}$-Cauchy sequence in H is $\mathcal{R}$-convergent in H.

Theorem 3. *Each $\mathcal{R}$-convergent sequence in $(H, \mathcal{R}, d_C, Q)$ has a unique limit point.*

Proof. Assume that the $\mathcal{R}$-sequence (h_n) is $\mathcal{R}$-convergent to h and l in H. That is,

$$\lim_{n\to\infty} d_C(h_n, h) = 0 \text{ and } (h_n, h) \in \mathcal{R} \ \forall n \geq k_1$$

and

$$\lim_{n\to\infty} d_C(h_n, l) = 0 \text{ and } (h_n, l) \in \mathcal{R} \ \forall n \geq k_2.$$

Then, for each $n \geq k = \max\{k_1, k_2\}$, we have $(h_n, h) \in \mathcal{R}$ and $(h_n, l) \in \mathcal{R} \ \forall n \geq k$. Thus, by (d_3), we obtain

$$d_C(h, l) \leq Q[d_C(h, h_n) + d_C(h_n, l)] \ \forall n \geq k.$$

Hence, by the above inequality, as $n \to \infty$, we conclude that $d_C(h, l) = 0$. That is, the limit point of the $\mathcal{R}$-convergent sequence is unique. □

Theorem 4. *Each $\mathcal{R}$-convergent sequence in $(H, \mathcal{R}, d_C, Q)$ is $\mathcal{R}$-Cauchy.*

Proof. Consider that an $\mathcal{R}$-sequence (h_n) is $\mathcal{R}$-convergent to h in H. That is,

$$\lim_{n\to\infty} d_C(h_n, h) = 0 \text{ and } (h_n, h) \in \mathcal{R} \ \forall n \geq k_1$$

Then, for each $n, k \geq k_1$, we have $(h_n, h) \in \mathcal{R}$, and $(h_k, h) \in \mathcal{R} \ \forall n, k \geq k_1$. Thus, by (d_3), we obtain

$$d_C(h_n, h_k) \leq Q[d_C(h_n, h) + d_C(h, h_k)] \ \forall n, k \geq k_1.$$

Hence, from the above inequality, we obtain $\lim_{n,k\to\infty} d_C(h_n, h_k) = 0$. □

We are now going to state and prove our first result that is a generalized form of the result presented by Perov [5].

Theorem 5. *Let $(H, \mathcal{R}, d_C, Q)$ be an $\mathcal{R}$-complete Czerwik vector-valued $\mathcal{R}$-metric space and let $G : H \to H$ be a mapping. Also, assume that*
(i) *There exists $h \in H$ with $(h, Gh) \in \mathcal{R}$;*
(ii) *$\mathcal{R}$ is G-closed, that is, for each $h_1, h_2 \in H$ with $(h_1, h_2) \in \mathcal{R}$, we have $(Gh_1, Gh_2) \in \mathcal{R}$;*
(iii) *Either*
   (a) *If $\{h_n\}$ is $\mathcal{R}$-convergent to $h \in H$, then $\{Gh_n\}$ is $\mathcal{R}$-convergent to Gh;*
   or
   (b) *For each $\mathcal{R}$-convergent sequence $\{h_n\}$ in H with $h_n \to h$, we have $d_C(h_n, \cdot) \to d_C(h, \cdot)$ as $n \to \infty$;*
(iv) *For each $(h, k) \in \mathcal{R}$, we have*

$$d_C(Gh, Gk) \leq A_1 d_C(h, k) + A_2 d_C(h, Gh) + A_3 d_C(k, Gk) + A_4 d_C(h, Gk) + B d_C(k, Gh) \quad (1)$$

where $A_1, A_2, A_3, A_4, B \in M_{m,m}(\mathbb{R}_+)$ such that $(I - (A_3 + A_4 Q))^{-1}$ exists and the matrix $Q[(I - (A_3 + A_4 Q))^{-1}(A_1 + A_2 + A_4 Q)]$ is convergent to zero.

Then, G has a fixed point.

Proof. Using hypothesis (i), we have $h_0 \in H$ with $(h_0, Gh_0) \in \mathcal{R}$. Starting from h_0, we can obtain an iterative sequence $\{h_n\}$, that is, $h_n = Gh_{n-1} = G^n h_0$ for each $n \in \mathbb{N}$. Since $\mathcal{R}$ is G-closed, thus, we conclude $(h_{n-1}, h_n) \in \mathcal{R}$ for all $n \in \mathbb{N}$. From (1), we obtain

$$d_C(Gh_{n-1}, Gh_n) \leq A_1 d_C(h_{n-1}, h_n) + A_2 d_C(h_{n-1}, Gh_{n-1}) + A_3 d_C(h_n, Gh_n)$$
$$+ A_4 d_C(h_{n-1}, Gh_n) + B d_C(h_n, Gh_{n-1}) \; \forall n \in \mathbb{N}. \tag{2}$$

That is,

$$d_C(h_n, h_{n+1}) \leq A_1 d_C(h_{n-1}, h_n) + A_2 d_C(h_{n-1}, h_n) + A_3 d_C(h_n, h_{n+1})$$
$$+ A_4 d_C(h_{n-1}, h_{n+1}) + B d_C(h_n, h_n) \; \forall n \in \mathbb{N}.$$

This implies that

$$(I - (A_3 + A_4 Q)) d_C(h_n, h_{n+1}) \leq (A_1 + A_2 + A_4 Q) d_C(h_{n-1}, h_n) \; \forall n \in \mathbb{N}.$$

The above inequality yields that

$$d_C(h_n, h_{n+1}) \leq (I - (A_3 + A_4 Q))^{-1} (A_1 + A_2 + A_4 Q) d_C(h_{n-1}, h_n) \; \forall n \in \mathbb{N}. \tag{3}$$

Putting $M = (I - (A_3 + A_4 Q))^{-1}(A_1 + A_2 + A_4 Q)$ in (3), we obtain

$$d_C(h_n, h_{n+1}) \leq M d_C(h_{n-1}, h_n) \; \forall n \in \mathbb{N}. \tag{4}$$

From (4), we conclude that

$$d_C(h_n, h_{n+1}) \leq M^n d_C(h_0, h_1) \; \forall n \in \mathbb{N}. \tag{5}$$

As $(h_{n-1}, h_n) \in \mathcal{R}$ for all $n \in \mathbb{N}$ and $\mathcal{R}$ is an equivalence relation, then by repeated application of the triangle inequality, i.e., Axiom (d_3), of Definition 2, we obtain

$$d_C(h_n, h_m) \leq \sum_{i=n}^{m-1} Q^i d_C(h_i, h_{i+1}) \; \forall m > n \in \mathbb{N}.$$

Thus, the above inequality and (5) yield the following inequality.

$$d_C(h_n, h_m) \leq \sum_{i=n}^{m-1} Q^i d_C(h_i, h_{i+1})$$
$$\leq \sum_{i=n}^{m-1} Q^i M^i d_C(h_0, h_1)$$
$$= \sum_{i=n}^{m-1} [QM]^i d_C(h_0, h_1) \; \forall m > n \; \text{(By Remark 5)}$$
$$\leq [QM]^n (I - QM)^{-1} d_C(h_0, h_1).$$

This proves that $\{h_n\}$ is an $\mathcal{R}$-Cauchy sequence in H. Considering the $\mathcal{R}$-completeness of H, we say that $\{h_n\}$ is an $\mathcal{R}$-convergent to $h_a \in H$, that is, $\lim_{n \to \infty} d_C(h_n, h_a) = 0$, and $(h_n, h_a) \in \mathcal{R}$ for all $n \geq k_0$, for some natural k_0. Now, consider Axiom (iii-a) exists, then we obtain $\lim_{n \to \infty} d_C(Gh_n, Gh_a) = 0$, and $(Gh_n, Gh_a) \in \mathcal{R}$, for all $n \geq k_0$.

Thus, through the triangle inequality, for each $n \geq k_0$, we obtain

$$d_C(h_a, Gh_a) \leq Q[d_C(h_a, h_{n+1}) + d_C(h_{n+1}, Gh_a)].$$

This yields $d_C(h_a, Gh_a) = 0$ as $n \to \infty$. That is, $h_a = Gh_a$. We now proceed with Axiom (iii-b). As $\{h_n\}$ is $\mathcal{R}$-convergent to $h_a \in H$, that is, $\lim_{n \to \infty} d_C(h_n, h_a) = 0$, and $(h_n, h_a) \in \mathcal{R}$ for all $n \geq k_0$ for some natural k_0. By (1), for each $n \geq k_0$, we obtain

$$\begin{aligned} d_C(Gh_n, Gh_a) &\leq A_1 d_C(h_n, h_a) + A_2 d_C(h_n, Gh_n) + A_3 d_C(h_a, Gh_a) \\ &\quad + A_4 d_C(h_n, Gh_a) + B d_C(h_a, Gh_n) \\ &\leq A_1 d_C(h_n, h_a) + A_2 d_C(h_n, Gh_n) + A_3 d_C(h_a, Gh_a) \\ &\quad + A_4 Q[d_C(h_n, h_{n+1}) + d_C(h_{n+1}, Gh_a)] + B d_C(h_a, Gh_n). \end{aligned}$$

That is,

$$\begin{aligned} d_C(h_{n+1}, Gh_a) &\leq A_1 d_C(h_n, h_a) + A_2 d_C(h_n, h_{n+1}) + A_3 d_C(h_a, Gh_a) \\ &\quad + A_4 Q[d_C(h_n, h_{n+1}) + d_C(h_{n+1}, Gh_a)] + B d_C(h_a, h_{n+1}). \end{aligned} \qquad (6)$$

Applying the limit $n \to \infty$ in (6) we obtain

$$d_C(h_a, Gh_a) \leq A_3 d_C(h_a, Gh_a) + A_4 Q d_C(h_a, Gh_a).$$

This gives $d_C(h_a, Gh_a) = 0$ because $(I - A_3 - A_4 Q)^{-1}$ exists. Hence, $h_a = Gh_a$. □

Remark 5. *If Q is a diagonal matrix and its nonzero elements are the same, then $Q^i M^i = (QM)^i$ $\forall i \in \mathbb{N}$.*

Example 3. *Consider $H = \mathbb{R}^2$, and the equivalence relation on H is defined by*

$$\mathcal{R} = \{((h_1, h_2), (k_1, k_2)) : h_1, h_2, k_1, k_2 \in [0, 3]\} \cup \{((h, k), (h, k)) : h, k \in \mathbb{R}\}.$$

Define a Czerwik vector-valued $\mathcal{R}$-metric on H by

$$d_C((h_1, h_2), (k_1, k_2)) = \begin{cases} \begin{pmatrix} (h_1 - k_1)^2 \\ (h_2 - k_2)^2 \end{pmatrix}, & \text{if } h_1, h_2, k_1, k_2 \in [0, 3] \\ \begin{pmatrix} \frac{|h_1 - k_1|}{1 + |h_1 - k_1|} \\ \frac{|h_2 - k_2|}{1 + |h_2 - k_2|} \end{pmatrix}, & \text{otherwise} \end{cases}$$

with $Q = \begin{pmatrix} 2 & 0 \\ 0 & 2 \end{pmatrix}$. Define a mapping $G : H \to H$ by

$$G(h_1, h_2) = \begin{cases} \left(\frac{h_1}{6} - \frac{h_2}{3} + 2, \frac{h_2}{3} + 2 \right), & \text{if } h_1, h_2 \geq 0 \\ ((h_1 + h_2)^2, (h_2)^2), & \text{otherwise.} \end{cases}$$

Readers can easily verify the following points:

- *For $h = (0, 0)$, we have $Gh = (2, 2)$, thus, we say that $(h, Gh) \in \mathcal{R}$.*
- *For each $h_1, h_2 \in [0, 3]$, we have $\frac{h_1}{6} - \frac{h_2}{3} + 2, \frac{h_2}{3} + 2 \in [0, 3]$.*
  Thus, we say that $(G(h_1, h_2), G(k_1, k_2)) \in \mathcal{R}$, provided $((h_1, h_2), (k_1, k_2)) \in \mathcal{R}$.
- *For each sequence $(h_n^1), (h_n^2)$ with $h_n^1, h_n^2 \in [0, 3]$ and $h_n^1 \to h^1, h_n^2 \to h^2$, it is obvious that $h^1, h^2 \in [0, 3]$, we say that $\frac{h_n^1}{6} - \frac{h_n^2}{3} + 2 \to \frac{h^1}{6} - \frac{h^2}{3} + 2$, and $\frac{h_n^2}{3} + 2 \to \frac{h^2}{3} + 2$. Thus, we conclude that if $\{h_n\}$ is $\mathcal{R}$-convergent to $h \in H$, then $\{Gh_n\}$ is $\mathcal{R}$-convergent to Gh.*

- For each $((h_1, h_2), (k_1, k_2)) \in \mathcal{R}$ with $(h_1, h_2) \neq (k_1, k_2)$, we have

$$d_C(G(h_1, h_2), G(k_1, k_2)) = d_C\left(\left(\frac{h_1}{6} - \frac{h_2}{3} + 2, \frac{h_2}{3} + 2\right), \left(\frac{k_1}{6} - \frac{k_2}{3} + 2, \frac{k_2}{3} + 2\right)\right)$$

$$= \begin{pmatrix} \left(\left(\frac{h_1}{6} - \frac{h_2}{3} + 2 - \frac{k_1}{6} + \frac{k_2}{3} - 2\right)^2 \\ \left(\frac{h_2}{3} + 2 - \frac{k_2}{3} - 2\right)^2 \end{pmatrix}$$

$$\leq \begin{pmatrix} 2/36 & 2/9 \\ 0 & 2/9 \end{pmatrix} \begin{pmatrix} (h_1 - k_1)^2 \\ (h_2 - k_2)^2 \end{pmatrix}$$

$$= \begin{pmatrix} 2/36 & 2/9 \\ 0 & 2/9 \end{pmatrix} d_C((h_1, h_2), (k_1, k_2)).$$

- For each $((h_1, h_2), (k_1, k_2)) \in \mathcal{R}$ with $(h_1, h_2) = (k_1, k_2)$, we have

$$d_C(G(h_1, h_2), G(k_1, k_2)) = \begin{pmatrix} 0 \\ 0 \end{pmatrix}$$

$$= \begin{pmatrix} 2/36 & 2/9 \\ 0 & 2/9 \end{pmatrix} d_C((h_1, h_2), (k_1, k_2)).$$

Thus, it can be concluded that the axioms of Theorem 5 exist. Therefore, G has a fixed point.

Remark 6. Note that the above-defined d_C is a Czerwik vector-valued $\mathcal{R}$-metric on H, but not a Czerwik vector-valued metric on H. Thus, the related fixed-point results on Czerwik vector-valued metric space from the existing literature are not applicable to this example.

The following corollary is an extended form of Theorem 2 given in the introduction of this article.

Corollary 1. Let (H, d_C, Q) be a complete Czerwik vector-valued metric space and let $G : H \to H$ be a mapping. Also, assume that

(i) For each $h, k \in H$, we have

$$d_C(Gh, Gk) \leq A_1 d_C(h, k) + A_2 d_C(h, Gh) + A_3 d_C(k, Gk) + A_4 d_C(h, Gk) + B d_C(k, Gh) \tag{7}$$

where $A_1, A_2, A_3, A_4, B \in M_{m,m}(\mathbb{R}_+)$ such that $(I - (A_3 + A_4 Q))^{-1}$ exists and the matrix $Q[(I - (A_3 + A_4 Q))^{-1}(A_1 + A_2 + A_4 Q)]$ is convergent to zero;

(ii) Either

(a) If $\{h_n\}$ is convergent to $h \in H$, then $\{Gh_n\}$ is convergent to Gh;

or

(b) For each convergent sequence $\{h_n\}$ in H with $h_n \to h$, we have $d_C(h_n, \cdot) \to d_C(h, \cdot)$ as $n \to \infty$.

Then, G has a fixed point.

The conclusion of this result follows from Theorem 5 by considering an equivalence relation on H by $\mathcal{R} = H \times H$.

If we define an equivalence relation on H by $\mathcal{R} = H \times H$, then the complete Czerwik vector-valued metric space will also be an $\mathcal{R}$-complete Czerwik vector-valued $\mathcal{R}$-metric space. As we consider $\mathcal{R} = H \times H$, then Axioms (i) and (ii) of Theorem 5 trivially hold. Also, Axioms (i) and (ii) of the above theorem imply the existence of Axioms (iv) and (iii) of Theorem 5, respectively. Hence, the conclusion of the above results follows from Theorem 5.

The following corollary is an extended form of Theorem 1 given in the Section 1.

Corollary 2. Let (H, d_C, Q) be a complete Czerwik vector-valued metric space and let $G : H \to H$ be a mapping such that for each $h, k \in H$, we have

$$d_C(Gh, Gk) \leq A_1 d_C(h, k) \tag{8}$$

where $A_1 \in M_{m,m}(\mathbb{R}_+)$ such that the matrix QA_1 is convergent to zero. Then, G has a fixed point.

The conclusion of this result follows from Corollary 1, since (8) implies the existence of (7) and implies the existence of (iii-a).

In the following results, we will study the existence of fixed points for multi-valued mappings. We denote by $N(H)$ the collection of all nonempty subsets of H.

Theorem 6. Let $(H, \mathcal{R}, d_C, Q)$ be an $\mathcal{R}$-complete Czerwik vector-valued $\mathcal{R}$-metric space and let $G : H \to N(H)$ be a mapping. Also, assume that
(i) There exist $h \in H$ and $h_* \in Gh$ with $(h, h_*) \in \mathcal{R}$;
(ii) $\mathcal{R}$ is G-closed, that is, for each $h, k \in H$ with $(h, k) \in \mathcal{R}$, we have $(q, w) \in \mathcal{R}$ $\forall q \in Gh$ and $w \in Gk$;
(iii) $Graph(G) = \{(h, k) : k \in Gh\}$ is $\mathcal{R}$-closed, that is, for all $\mathcal{R}$-convergent sequences $\{h_n\}$ and $\{k_n\}$ in H with $h_n \to h_* \in H$ and $k_n \to k_* \in H$, we have $(h_*, k_*) \in Graph(G)$, whenever $(h_n, k_n) \in Graph(G)$ $\forall n \geq k_0$ for some k_0;
(iv) For each $(h, k) \in \mathcal{R}$ and $q \in Gh$, there exists $w \in Gk$ with

$$d_C(q, w) \leq A_1 d_C(h, k) + A_2 d_C(h, q) + A_3 d_C(k, w) + A_4 d_C(h, w) + B d_C(k, q) \tag{9}$$

where $A_1, A_2, A_3, A_4, B \in M_{m,m}(\mathbb{R}_+)$ such that $(I - (A_3 + A_4 Q))^{-1}$ exists and the matrix $Q[(I - (A_3 + A_4 Q))^{-1}(A_1 + A_2 + A_4 Q)]$ is convergent to zero.
Then, G has a fixed point.

Proof. Assumption (i) of the theorem implies that there is some $h_0 \in H$ with $h_1 \in Gh_0$ and $(h_0, h_1) \in \mathcal{R}$. By using (9), for $(h_0, h_1) \in \mathcal{R}$ and $h_1 \in Gh_0$, there exists $h_2 \in Gh_1$ satisfying

$$d_C(h_1, h_2) \leq A_1 d_C(h_0, h_1) + A_2 d_C(h_0, h_1) + A_3 d_C(h_1, h_2) + A_4 d_C(h_0, h_2) + B d_C(h_1, h_1). \tag{10}$$

As $(h_0, h_1) \in \mathcal{R}$, then by assumption (ii), we obtain $(h_1, h_2) \in \mathcal{R}$. Now, (10) yields the following inequality:

$$d_C(h_1, h_2) \leq A_1 d_C(h_0, h_1) + A_2 d_C(h_0, h_1) + A_3 d_C(h_1, h_2) + A_4 Q[d_C(h_0, h_1) + d_C(h_1, h_2)].$$

That is,

$$d_C(h_1, h_2) \leq (I - A_3 - A_4 Q)^{-1}(A_1 + A_2 + A_4 Q) d_C(h_0, h_1).$$

By defining $M = (I - A_3 - A_4 Q)^{-1}(A_1 + A_2 + A_4 Q)$ in the above inequality, we obtain

$$d_C(h_1, h_2) \leq M d_C(h_0, h_1). \tag{11}$$

Again, by using (9), for $(h_1, h_2) \in \mathcal{R}$ and $h_2 \in Gh_1$, there exists $h_3 \in Gh_2$ with

$$d_C(h_2, h_3) \leq A_1 d_C(h_1, h_2) + A_2 d_C(h_1, h_2) + A_3 d_C(h_2, h_3) + A_4 d_C(h_1, h_3) + B d_C(h_2, h_2). \tag{12}$$

Since $(h_1, h_2) \in \mathcal{R}$, by assumption (ii), we obtain $(h_2, h_3) \in \mathcal{R}$. Now, (12) implies that

$$d_C(h_2, h_3) \leq A_1 d_C(h_1, h_2) + A_2 d_C(h_1, h_2) + A_3 d_C(h_2, h_3) + A_4 Q[d_C(h_1, h_2) + d_C(h_2, h_3)].$$

That is,

$$d_C(h_2, h_3) \leq M d_C(h_1, h_2) \tag{13}$$

where $M = (I - (A_3 + A_4Q))^{-1}(A_1 + A_2 + A_4Q)$. By (11) and (13), we obtain

$$d_C(h_2, h_3) \leq M^2 d_C(h_0, h_1). \tag{14}$$

Proceeding with the same methodology, we obtain a sequence $\{h_n\}$ such that $(h_{n-1}, h_n) \in \mathcal{R}$, $h_n \in Gh_{n-1}$ for all $n \in \mathbb{N}$ and

$$d_C(h_n, h_{n+1}) \leq M^n d_C(h_0, h_1) \; \forall n \in \mathbb{N}. \tag{15}$$

By using the triangular inequality and (15) we obtain

$$\begin{aligned} d_C(h_n, h_m) &\leq \sum_{i=n}^{m-1} Q^i d_C(h_i, h_{i+1}) \\ &\leq \sum_{i=n}^{m-1} [QM]^i d_C(h_0, h_1) \; \forall m > n. \end{aligned}$$

This yields that $\{h_n\}$ is an $\mathcal{R}$-Cauchy sequence in H. Thus, $\{h_n\}$ is $\mathcal{R}$-convergent to $h_a \in H$, that is $\lim_{n \to \infty} d_C(h_n, h_a) = 0$ and $(h_n, h_a) \in \mathcal{R}$, for all $n \geq k_0$ for some natural k_0. The construction of $\{h_n\}$ implies that $(h_n, h_{n+1}) \in Graph(G) \; \forall n \in \mathbb{N}$, since $Graph(G)$ is $\mathcal{R}$-closed, thus we obtain $(h_a, h_a) \in Graph(G)$, that is $h_a \in Gh_a$. This completes the proof of the result. $\square$

In the following result, we assume that $B(H)$ is the collection of all those subsets of H that are d_C-bounded with respect to $(H, \mathcal{R}, d_C, Q)$, that is, for $A \in B(H)$, $\delta_C(A) = \overline{\sup}\{d_C(a, b) : a, b \in A\}$ exists. Also, we define $\delta_C(A, B) = \overline{\sup}\{d_C(a, b) : a \in A, b \in B\}$ and $\delta_C(a, B) = \overline{\sup}\{d_C(a, b) : b \in B\}$. Note that for the set $W = \{(a_{11}^j, a_{21}^j, \cdots, a_{n1}^j)^T : j \in I\}$, for some index set I,

$$\overline{\sup} W = \left(\sup_{j \in I} a_{11}^j, \sup_{j \in I} a_{21}^j, \cdots, \sup_{j \in I} a_{n1}^j \right)^T.$$

Theorem 7. Let $(H, \mathcal{R}, d_C, Q)$ be an $\mathcal{R}$-complete Czerwik vector-valued $\mathcal{R}$-metric space and let $G : H \to B(H)$ be a mapping. Also, assume that

(i) There exist $h \in H$ and $h_* \in Gh$ with $(h, h_*) \in \mathcal{R}$;
(ii) $\mathcal{R}$ is G-closed, that is, for each $h, k \in H$ with $(h, k) \in \mathcal{R}$, we have $(q, w) \in \mathcal{R} \; \forall q \in Gh$ and $w \in Gk$;
(iii) $Graph(G) = \{(h, k) : k \in Gh\}$ is $\mathcal{R}$-closed, that is, for all $\mathcal{R}$-convergent sequences $\{h_n\}$ and $\{k_n\}$ in H with $h_n \to h_* \in H$ and $k_n \to k_* \in H$, we have $(h_*, k_*) \in Graph(G)$, whenever $(h_n, k_n) \in Graph(G) \; \forall n \geq k_0$ for some k_0;
(iv) For each $(h, k) \in \mathcal{R}$, we have

$$\delta_C(Gh, Gk) \leq A_1 d_C(h, k) + A_2 \delta_C(h, Gh) + A_3 \delta_C(k, Gk) \tag{16}$$

where $A_1, A_2, A_3 \in \mathbb{M}_m(\mathbb{R}_+)$ such that $(I - A_3)^{-1}$ exists and the matrix $Q[(I - A_3)^{-1}(A_1 + A_2)]$ is convergent to zero.
Then, G has a fixed point.

Proof. Using hypothesis (i), we have $h_0 \in H$ and $h_1 \in Gh_0$ such that $(h_0, h_1) \in \mathcal{R}$. Hypothesis (ii) now gives $(q, w) \in \mathcal{R} \; \forall q \in Gh_0$ and $w \in Gh_1$. Thus, we write $(h_1, h_2) \in \mathcal{R}$ with $h_1 \in Gh_0$ and $h_2 \in Gh_1$. Further, we can construct a sequence $\{h_n\}$ with $h_n \in Gh_{n-1}$, and $(h_{n-1}, h_n) \in \mathcal{R}$ for all $n \in \mathbb{N}$. By (16), we obtain

$$\delta_C(Gh_{n-1}, Gh_n) \leq A_1 d_C(h_{n-1}, h_n) + A_2 \delta_C(h_{n-1}, Gh_{n-1}) + A_3 \delta_C(h_n, Gh_n) \; \forall n \in \mathbb{N}. \tag{17}$$

That is,
$$\delta_C(h_n, Gh_n) \leq A_1 \delta_C(h_{n-1}, Gh_{n-1}) + A_2 \delta_C(h_{n-1}, Gh_{n-1}) + A_3 \delta_C(h_n, Gh_n) \, \forall n \in \mathbb{N}.$$

This implies that
$$(I - A_3)\delta_C(h_n, Gh_n) \leq (A_1 + A_2)\delta_C(h_{n-1}, Gh_{n-1}) \, \forall n \in \mathbb{N}.$$

This inequality yields that
$$\delta_C(h_n, Gh_n) \leq (I - A_3)^{-1}(A_1 + A_2)\delta_C(h_{n-1}, Gh_{n-1}) \, \forall n \in \mathbb{N}. \tag{18}$$

Letting $M = (I - A_3)^{-1}(A_1 + A_2)$ in (18), we obtain
$$\delta_C(h_n, Gh_n) \leq M \delta_C(h_{n-1}, Gh_{n-1}) \, \forall n \in \mathbb{N}. \tag{19}$$

From the above inequality, we conclude the following inequalities:
$$\delta_C(h_n, Gh_n) \leq M^n \delta_C(h_0, Gh_0) \, \forall n \in \mathbb{N} \tag{20}$$

and
$$d_C(h_n, h_{n+1}) \leq M^n \delta_C(h_0, Gh_0) \, \forall n \in \mathbb{N}. \tag{21}$$

By considering the triangular inequality and (21), we obtain the following inequality:
$$d_C(h_n, h_m) \leq \sum_{i=n}^{m-1} Q^i d_C(h_i, h_{i+1})$$
$$\leq \sum_{i=n}^{m-1} [QM]^i \delta_C(h_0, Gh_0) \, \forall m > n.$$

This proves that $\{h_n\}$ is an $\mathcal{R}$-Cauchy sequence in H. The $\mathcal{R}$-completeness of H ensures that $\{h_n\}$ is $\mathcal{R}$-convergent to $h_a \in H$, that is, $\lim_{n \to \infty} d_C(h_n, h_a) = 0$ and $(h_n, h_a) \in \mathcal{R}$, for all $n \geq k_0$ for some natural k_0. The construction of $\{h_n\}$ implies that $(h_n, h_{n+1}) \in Graph(G) \, \forall n \in \mathbb{N}$, since $Graph(G)$ is $\mathcal{R}$-closed, thus we obtain $(h_a, h_a) \in Graph(G)$, that is, $h_a \in Gh_a$. This completes the proof of the result. $\square$

Example 4. *Consider $H = \mathbb{R}$ and an equivalence relation on H is defined by*
$$\mathcal{R} = \{(h_1, h_2) : h_1, h_2 \in [0, \infty)\} \cup \{(h, h) : h \in \mathbb{R}\}.$$

Define the Czerwik vector-valued $\mathcal{R}$-metric $d_C : H \times H \to \mathbb{R}_2$ by
$$d_C(h_1, h_2) = \begin{cases} \begin{pmatrix} (h_1 - h_2)^2 \\ (h_1 - h_2)^2 \end{pmatrix}, & \text{if } h_1, h_2 \geq 0 \\ \begin{pmatrix} \frac{|h_1 - h_2|}{1 + |h_1 - h_2|} \\ 0 \end{pmatrix}, & \text{otherwise.} \end{cases}$$

with $Q = \begin{pmatrix} 2 & 0 \\ 0 & 2 \end{pmatrix}$. Define $G : H \to B(H)$ by
$$Gh = \begin{cases} \{(h+1)/2\}, & h \geq 0 \\ \{0\}, & h < 0. \end{cases}$$

The reader can easily verify that all the conditions of Theorem 7 are satisfied for this example. Hence, G has a fixed point.

4. Application

In this section, by the graph G we mean that $G = (V, E)$ is an undirected graph on a nonempty set H, such that $V = H$ and $E \subset H \times H$ contains all loops, that is, $(h, h) \in E$ for all $h \in H$, without any parallel edges. Define a path relation P_G on H equipped with the graph G: $(h, k) \in P_G$ if and only if there is a path from h to k in G. The relation P_G on H equipped with the graph G is reflexive, symmetric, and transitive, that is, $(h, h) \in P_G \; \forall h \in H$, $(h, k) \in P_G \implies (k, h) \in P_G$ and $(h, k), (k, l) \in P_G$ implies $(h, l) \in P_G$.

Definition 4. *Let H be a nonempty set and let G be the graph on H. A mapping $d_C \colon H \times H \to \mathbb{R}_m$ is called a Czerwik vector-valued graphical metric on H, if for each $h_1, h_2, h_3 \in H$ the following axioms hold:*

(d_1) $d_C(h_1, h_2) \geq 0$;
  $d_C(h_1, h_2) = 0$ *if and only if* $h_1 = h_2$;
(d_2) $d_C(h_1, h_2) = d_C(h_2, h_1)$;
(d_3) $d_C(h_1, h_3) \leq Q[d_C(h_1, h_2) + d_C(h_2, h_3)]$ *provided that* $(h_1, h_2), (h_2, h_3) \in P_G$,
where $Q = (q_{ij}) \in M_{m,m}(R_+)$ *is a matrix with*

$$q_{ij} = \begin{cases} q, & i = j \\ 0, & i \neq j \end{cases}$$

and $q \geq 1$. Then, (H, P_G, d_C, Q) is called a Czerwik vector-valued graphical metric space, or Czerwik generalized graphical metric space.

Remark 7. *Readers can note the following facts:*

(i) *Czerwik vector-valued graphical metric space is a particular case of Czerwik vector-valued $\mathcal{R}$-metric space.*
(ii) *Czerwik vector-valued graphical metric space provides an extended concept of graphical b-metric space [11] as well as graphical metric space [10] over an undirected graph.*

Definition 5. *Let (H, P_G, d_C, Q) be a Czerwik vector-valued graphical metric space. Then*

- *A sequence (h_n) in H is said to be P_G-sequence if $(h_n, h_{n+1}) \in E$ for each $n \in \mathbb{N}$.*
- *A P_G-sequence (h_n) in H is said to be P_G-convergent to h in H if $\lim_{n \to \infty} d_C(h_n, h) = 0$ and $(h_n, h) \in E \; \forall n \geq k$ for some natural number k.*
- *A P_G-sequence (h_n) in H is said to be P_G-Cauchy if $\lim_{n,m \to \infty} d_C(h_n, h_m) = 0$.*
- *(H, P_G, d_C, Q) is said to be P_G-complete if each P_G-Cauchy sequence in H is P_G-convergent in H.*

Theorem 8. *Let (H, P_G, d_C, Q) be a P_G-complete Czerwik vector-valued graphical metric space and let $T : H \to H$ be a mapping. Also, assume that*

(i) *There exists $h \in H$ with $(h, Th) \in E$;*
(ii) *For each $h_1, h_2 \in H$ with $(h_1, h_2) \in E$, we have $(Th_1, Th_2) \in E$;*
(iii) *Either*
  (a) *If $\{h_n\}$ is P_G-convergent to $h \in H$, then $\{Th_n\}$ is P_G-convergent to Th;*
  or
  (b) *For each P_G-convergent sequence $\{h_n\}$ in H with $h_n \to h$, we have $d_C(h_n, \cdot) \to d_C(h, \cdot)$ as $n \to \infty$;*
(iv) *For each $(h, k) \in E$, we have*

$$d_C(Gh, Gk) \leq A_1 d_C(h, k) + A_2 d_C(h, Gh) + A_3 d_C(k, Gk) + A_4 d_C(h, Gk) + B d_C(k, Gh) \quad (22)$$

where $A_1, A_2, A_3, A_4, B \in M_{m,m}(\mathbb{R}_+)$ such that $(I - (A_3 + A_4 Q))^{-1}$ exists and the matrix $Q[(I - (A_3 + A_4 Q))^{-1}(A_1 + A_2 + A_4 Q)]$ is convergent to zero.
Then, T has a fixed point.

The proof of this result is similar to the proof of Theorem 5.

5. Conclusions

This article presents the notion of Czerwik vector-valued $\mathcal{R}$-metric space, which is a generalized form of Czerwik vector-valued metric space. In Czerwik vector-valued $\mathcal{R}$-metric space, the triangle inequality is discussed only for comparable elements under an equivalence relation. The limit point of an $\mathcal{R}$-convergent sequence is unique in the Czerwik vector-valued $\mathcal{R}$-metric space. The set $\{B_{d_C}(h, \epsilon) : h \in H, \epsilon > 0\}$ provides a neighbourhood system for the topology on H induced by the Czerwik vector-valued $\mathcal{R}$-metric space. The existence of fixed points for single-valued and set-valued maps is also discussed using the Czerwik vector-valued $\mathcal{R}$-metric space.

Author Contributions: All authors contributed equally to this article. All authors have read and agreed to the published version of the manuscript.

Funding: This research work was funded by Institutional Fund Projects under the grant number IFPIP: 655-247-1443. The authors gracefully acknowledge technical and financial support provided by the Ministry of Education and King Abdulaziz University, DSR, Jeddah, Saudi Arabia.

Data Availability Statement: The data used to support the findings of this study are available from the corresponding author upon request.

Conflicts of Interest: The authors declare no conflict of interest.

References

1. Fréchet, M. Sur quelques points du calcul fonctionnel. *Rend. Circ. Mat. Palermo* **1906**, *22*, 1–74. [CrossRef]
2. Czerwik, S. The contraction mapping principle in quasimetric spaces. *Acta Math. Univ. Ostrav.* **1993**, *1*, 5–11.
3. Matthews, S.G. Partial metric topology, In: Proc. 8th Summer Conference on General Topology and Applications. *Ann. N. Y. Acad. Sci.* **1994**, *728*, 183–197. [CrossRef]
4. Huang, L.G.; Zhang, X. Cone metric spaces and fixed point theorems of contractive mappings. *J. Math. Anal. Appl.* **2007**, *332*, 1468–1476. [CrossRef]
5. Perov, A.I. On the Cauchy problem for a system of ordinary differential equations. *Pviblizhen. Met. Reshen. Differ. Uvavn.* **1964**, *2*, 115–134.
6. Boriceanu, M. Fixed point theory on spaces with vector-valued b-metrics. *Demonstratio Math.* **2009**, *42*, 831–841.
7. Ali, M.U.; Kim, J.K. An extension of vector-valued metric spaces and Perov's fixed point theorem. *Nonlinear Anal. Convex Anal. Rims* **2019**, *2114*, 12–20.
8. Li, J.L.; Zhang, C.J.; Chen, Q.Q. Fixed point theorems on ordered vector spaces. *Fixed Point Theory Appl.* **2014**, *2014*, 109. [CrossRef]
9. Ali, M.U.; Postolache, M. On vector valued pseudo metrics and applications. *Trans. Razmadze Math. Inst.* **2018**, *172*, 309–317. [CrossRef]
10. Shukla, S.; Radenovic, S.; Vetro, C. Graphical metric space: A generalized setting in fixed point theory. *RACSAM* **2017**, *111*, 641–655. [CrossRef]
11. Chuensupantharat, N.; Kumam, P.; Chauhan, V.; Singh, D.; Menon, R. Graphic contraction mappings via graphical b-metric spaces with applications. *Bull. Malays. Math. Sci. Soc.* **2019**, *42*, 3149–3165. [CrossRef]
12. Nieto, J.J.; Rodriguez-Lopez, R. Contractive mapping theorems in partially ordered sets and applications to ordinary differential equations. *Order* **2005**, *22*, 223–239. [CrossRef]
13. Jachymski, J. The contraction principle for mappings on a metric space with a graph. *Proc. Am. Math. Soc.* **2008**, *136*, 1359–1373. [CrossRef]
14. Alam, A.; Imdad, M. Relation-Theoretic contraction principle. *J. Fixed Point Theory Appl.* **2015**, *17*, 693–702. [CrossRef]
15. Bucur, A.; Guran, L.; Petrusel, A. Fixed points for multivalued operators on a set endowed with vector-valued metrics and applications. *Fixed Point Theory* **2009**, *10*, 19–34.
16. Filip, A.D.; Petrusel, A. Fixed point theorems on spaces endowed with vector-valued metrics. *Fixed Point Theory Appl.* **2010**, *2010*, 281381. [CrossRef]
17. Ali, M.U.; Tchier, F.; Vetro, C. On the existence of bounded solutions to a class of nonlinear initial value problems with delay. *Filomat* **2017**, *31*, 3125–3135. [CrossRef]

18. Altun, I.; Hussain, N.; Qasim, M.; Al-Sulami, H. H. A new fixed point result of Perov type and its application to a semilinear operator system. *Mathematics* **2019**, *7*, 1019. [CrossRef]
19. Guran, L.; Bota, M.; Naseem, A. Fixed point problems on generalized metric spaces in Perov's sense. *Symmetry* **2020**, *12*, 856. [CrossRef]
20. Guran, L.; Bota, M.; Naseem, A.; Mitrović, Z.D.; Sen, M.d.l.; Radenović, S. On some new multivalued results in the metric spaces of Perov's type. *Mathematics* **2020**, *8*, 438. [CrossRef]
21. Martínez-Moreno, J.; Gopal, D. A Perov version of fuzzy metric spaces and common fixed points for compatible mappings. *Mathematics* **2021**, *9*, 1290. [CrossRef]
22. Varga, R.S. *Matrix Iterative Analysis*; Springer Series in Computational Mathematics; Springer: Berlin/Heidelberg, Germany, 2000; Volume 27.

Disclaimer/Publisher's Note: The statements, opinions and data contained in all publications are solely those of the individual author(s) and contributor(s) and not of MDPI and/or the editor(s). MDPI and/or the editor(s) disclaim responsibility for any injury to people or property resulting from any ideas, methods, instructions or products referred to in the content.

Article

The Stability and Well-Posedness of Fixed Points for Relation-Theoretic Multi-Valued Maps

Isaac Karabo Letlhage [1], Deepak Khantwal [1], Rajendra Pant [1] and Manuel De la Sen [2,*]

[1] Department of Mathematics and Applied Mathematics, University of Johannesburg, Kingsway Campus, Auckland Park 2006, South Africa; karabol@uj.ac.za (I.K.L.); dkhantwal@uj.ac.za (D.K.); rpant@uj.ac.za (R.P.)
[2] Institute of Research and Development of Processes IIDP, Faculty of Science and Technology, University of the Basque Country, de Bilbao, Barrio Sarriena, 48940 Leioa, Bizkaia, Spain
* Correspondence: manuel.delasen@ehu.eus

Abstract: The purpose of this study is to present fixed-point results for Suzuki-type multi-valued maps using relation theory. We examine a range of implications that arise from our primary discovery. Furthermore, we present two substantial cases that illustrate the importance of our main theorem. In addition, we examine the stability of fixed-point sets for multi-valued maps and the concept of well-posedness. We present an application to a specific functional equation which arises in dynamic programming.

Keywords: metric space; binary relation; relation-theoretic contraction; fixed points

MSC: 47H10; 54H25

Citation: Letlhage, I.K.; Khantwal, D.; Pant, R.; Sen, M.D.I. The Stability and Well-Posedness of Fixed Points for Relation-Theoretic Multi-Valued Maps. *Mathematics* **2023**, *11*, 4271. https://doi.org/10.3390/math 11204271

Academic Editors: Timilehin Opeyemi Alakoya and Ioannis K. Argyros

Received: 3 September 2023
Revised: 8 October 2023
Accepted: 10 October 2023
Published: 13 October 2023

Copyright: © 2023 by the authors. Licensee MDPI, Basel, Switzerland. This article is an open access article distributed under the terms and conditions of the Creative Commons Attribution (CC BY) license (https://creativecommons.org/licenses/by/4.0/).

1. Introduction

Mathematical analysis has witnessed a significant surge in interest regarding the examination of fixed-point outcomes for diverse maps in recent times. The Banach contraction principle (BCP) is a fundamental theorem in classical mathematics. Drawing upon this initial framework, other scholars have expanded and broadened the concept of the BCP to incorporate a wide range of circumstances and maps (see [1–8]).

Suzuki's [9] generalization of the BCP introduced a new class of contractive maps that satisfy contraction conditions only for specific elements of the underlying space. Subsequently, Alam and Imdad [10] expanded the boundaries of the BCP by considering a complete metric space (CMS) equipped with a binary relation. They introduced the concept of relation-theoretic contraction, which applies to elements related under the binary relation rather than the entire space. Other researchers, such as Song-il Ri [11], further extended the BCP for a new class of contractive maps.

In 1969, Nadler Jr. [12] extended the BCP to multi-valued maps, yielding a fixed-point result for multi-valued contractions. This result was subsequently refined by Ciric [13] and led to a broader class of multi-valued contractions. Numerous mathematicians have contributed to the generalization of Nadler's theorem (see [4,5,13–18]), with Kikkawa and Suzuki [15] achieving significant progress in the study of generalized multi-valued maps.

Motivated by the works of Alam and Imdad [10], Kikkawa and Suzuki [15], and others, we present some new fixed-point results for multi-valued maps in relational metric spaces. These results extend and generalize the findings from previous studies by Alam and Imdad [10], Ciric [13], Kikkawa and Suzuki [15], Nadler [12], and others. Furthermore, the paper provides illustrative examples to support these findings and explores the stability of fixed-point sets for multi-valued maps within the framework of relational metric spaces. Lastly, by applying the presented results, the paper establishes the existence and uniqueness of solutions for a class of functional equations arising in dynamic programming.

2. Preliminaries

In this section, we recapitulate relevant notation, definitions, and results from the literature [12,13,18]. Throughout this paper, we denote a metric space (MS) as $(\mathcal{L}, \gamma)$, where $\mathcal{L}$ is a set and γ is a metric on $\mathcal{L}$. We use $\mathcal{CB}(\mathcal{L})$ to represent the collection of all nonempty closed and bounded subsets of $\mathcal{L}$, and $\mathcal{C}(\mathcal{L})$ to denote the collection of all nonempty compact subsets of $\mathcal{L}$. The Hausdorff metric $\Gamma_{\mathcal{H}}$ induced by γ is

$$\Gamma_{\mathcal{H}}(\mathcal{A}, \mathcal{B}) = \max\left\{ \sup_{\omega \in \mathcal{A}} \Gamma(\omega, \mathcal{B}), \sup_{\varpi \in \mathcal{B}} \Gamma(\varpi, \mathcal{A}) \right\},$$

for all $\mathcal{A}, \mathcal{B} \in \mathcal{CB}(\mathcal{L})$. Here, $\Gamma(\omega, \mathcal{B}) = \inf_{\varpi \in \mathcal{B}} \gamma(\omega, \varpi)$.

Let $\mathcal{F} : \mathcal{L} \to \mathcal{CB}(\mathcal{L})$ be a multi-valued map. A point $\vartheta \in \mathcal{L}$ is termed a fixed point of $\mathcal{F}$ if $\vartheta \in \mathcal{F}\vartheta$, and it is a strict fixed point of $\mathcal{F}$ if $\{\vartheta\} = \mathcal{F}\vartheta$. We denote the sets of fixed points and strict fixed points of $\mathcal{F}$ as $F(\mathcal{F})$ and $SF(\mathcal{F})$, respectively.

Theorem 1 ([12]). *Consider a CMS $(\mathcal{L}, \gamma)$ and a multi-valued map $\mathcal{F} : \mathcal{L} \to \mathcal{CB}(\mathcal{L})$. If for all $\omega, \varpi \in \mathcal{L}$*

$$\Gamma_{\mathcal{H}}(\mathcal{F}\omega, \mathcal{F}\varpi) \leq \kappa \gamma(\omega, \varpi), \tag{1}$$

where $\kappa \in [0, 1)$, then $\mathcal{F}$ possesses a fixed point.

Theorem 2 ([13]). *Suppose $(\mathcal{L}, \gamma)$ is a CMS and $\mathcal{F} : \mathcal{L} \to \mathcal{CB}(\mathcal{L})$ is a multi-valued map. If for all $\omega, \varpi \in \mathcal{L}$*

$$\Gamma_{\mathcal{H}}(\mathcal{F}\omega, \mathcal{F}\varpi) \leq \kappa m(\omega, \varpi), \tag{2}$$

where $\kappa \in [0, 1)$, and if

$$m(\omega, \varpi) = \max\left\{ \gamma(\omega, \varpi), \Gamma(\omega, \mathcal{F}\omega), \Gamma(\varpi, \mathcal{F}\varpi), \frac{\Gamma(\omega, \mathcal{F}\varpi) + \Gamma(\varpi, \mathcal{F}\omega)}{2} \right\},$$

then $\mathcal{F}$ has a fixed point.

Definition 1 ([15]). *Let $\phi : [0,1) \to (1/2, 1]$ be defined as $\phi(\kappa) = \frac{1}{1+\kappa}$. For an MS $(\mathcal{L}, \gamma)$ and a subset $\mathcal{M} \subseteq \mathcal{L}$, a map $\mathcal{F} : \mathcal{M} \to \mathcal{CB}(\mathcal{L})$ is called an a-KS multi-valued operator if $\kappa \in [0, 1)$ and*

$$\omega, \varpi \in \mathcal{M} \text{ with } \phi(\kappa)\Gamma(\omega, \mathcal{F}\omega) \leq \gamma(\omega, \varpi) \text{ implies } \Gamma_{\mathcal{H}}(\mathcal{F}\omega, \mathcal{F}\varpi) \leq \kappa \gamma(\omega, \varpi). \tag{3}$$

Theorem 3 ([15]). *Let $(\mathcal{L}, \gamma)$ be a CMS and $\mathcal{F}$ be an a-KS multi-valued operator from $\mathcal{L}$ into $\mathcal{CB}(\mathcal{L})$. Then, $\exists \vartheta \in \mathcal{L}$ such that $\vartheta \in \mathcal{F}\vartheta$.*

Definition 2 ([11]). *Let $\Phi = \left\{ \varphi : [0, \infty) \to [0, \infty) : \varphi(\omega) < \omega, \omega > 0 \text{ and } \limsup_{s \to \omega^+} \varphi(s) < \omega \right\}$.*

Now, we recall some relation-theoretic auxiliaries:

Definition 3 ([10,19]). *Let $\mathcal{L}$ be a nonempty set and $\aleph \subseteq \mathcal{L} \times \mathcal{L}$. Then, we say*

(1) *$\aleph$ is a binary relation on $\mathcal{L}$ and "ω relates to ϖ under $\aleph$" if and only if $(\omega, \varpi) \in \aleph$.*
(2) *ω and ϖ are $\aleph$-comparative, if either $(\omega, \varpi) \in \aleph$ or $(\varpi, \omega) \in \aleph$, and denoted by $[\omega, \varpi] \in \aleph$.*
(3) *$\aleph$ is complete, connected, or dichotomous if $[\omega, \varpi] \in \aleph$ for all $\omega, \varpi \in \mathcal{L}$.*
(4) *A sequence $\{\omega_\eta\}$ is called $\aleph$-preserving if $(\omega_\eta, \omega_{\eta+1}) \in \aleph$ for all $\eta \in \mathbb{N} \cup \{0\}$.*
(5) *$\aleph$ is γ-self-closed if whenever $\{\omega_\eta\}$ is $\aleph$-preserving sequence and $\omega_\eta \xrightarrow{\gamma} \omega$ then there exists a subsequence $\{\omega_{\eta_\kappa}\}$ of $\{\omega_\eta\}$ with $[\omega_{\eta_\kappa}, \omega] \in \aleph$ for all $\kappa \in \mathbb{N} \cup \{0\}$.*

Definition 4 ([20]). *Let $(\mathcal{L}, \gamma)$ be an MS and $\mathcal{F} : \mathcal{L} \to \mathcal{CB}(\mathcal{L})$ be a multi-valued map. Then, a binary relation $\aleph$ on $\mathcal{L}$ is called $\mathcal{F}$-γ-closed if for every*

$$(\omega, \varpi) \in \aleph,\ u \in \mathcal{F}\omega,\ v \in \mathcal{F}\varpi,\ \gamma(u,v) \leq \gamma(\omega, \varpi) \implies (u,v) \in \aleph.$$

Remark 1. *It we consider $\mathcal{F} := f$ as a single-valued map on $\mathcal{L}$, then $\aleph$ is called f-γ-closed if $(\omega, \varpi) \in \aleph, (f\omega, f\varpi) \leq \gamma(\omega, \varpi) \Rightarrow (f\omega, f\varpi) \in \aleph$.*

Definition 5 ([21]). *Consider an MS $(\mathcal{L}, \gamma)$ and $\aleph$ is a binary relation on $\mathcal{L}$. Let $\omega \in \mathcal{L}$, then a function $f : \mathcal{L} \to \mathbb{R} \cup \{+\infty, -\infty\}$ is said to be $\aleph$-lower semi-continuous at ω if, for any $\aleph$-preserving sequence $\{\omega_\eta\} \subseteq \mathcal{L}$ that converges to ω, the inequality $f(\omega) \leq \liminf_{\eta \to \infty} f(\omega_\eta)$ holds.*

Definition 6 ([19]). *Given a binary relation $\aleph$ defined on a nonempty set $\mathcal{L}$, the image of an element $a \in \mathcal{L}$ under the relation $\aleph$ is denoted as $Im(a, \aleph)$ and is defined as $\{\omega \in \mathcal{L} : (a, \omega) \in \aleph \text{ or } \omega = a\}$.*

3. Main Results

Theorem 4. *Consider a CMS $(\mathcal{L}, \gamma)$ equipped with a binary relation $\aleph$ on $\mathcal{L}$. Suppose $\mathcal{F} : \mathcal{L} \to \mathcal{CB}(\mathcal{L})$ is a multi-valued map that satisfies the following conditions:*

(a) *$\exists\, \omega_1 \in \mathcal{L}$ such that $\mathcal{F}\omega_1 \cap Im(\omega_1, \aleph) \neq \emptyset$;*
(b) *$\aleph$ is $\mathcal{F}$-γ-closed and transitive;*
(c) *either the function $f(\omega) := \Gamma(\omega, \mathcal{F}\omega)$ is $\aleph$-lower semi-continuous or*
(d) *for any trajectory $\{\omega_\eta\} \subset \mathcal{L}$ of $\mathcal{F}$, if $\{\omega_\eta\} \to \omega$ and $\omega_{\eta+1} \in \mathcal{F}\omega_\eta$ for all $\eta \in \mathbb{N}$, then the sequence $\{\omega_\eta\}$ has a subsequence (ω_{η_κ}) such that $[\omega_{\eta_\kappa}, \omega] \in \aleph$ for all $\kappa \in \mathbb{N}$;*
(e) *$\exists\, \varphi \in \Phi$ such that for any $\omega \in \mathcal{L}, \varpi \in \mathcal{F}\omega$ with $(\omega, \varpi) \in \aleph$*

$$\frac{1}{2}\Gamma(\omega, \mathcal{F}\omega) \leq \gamma(\omega, \varpi) \text{ implies } \Gamma_\mathcal{H}(\mathcal{F}\omega, \mathcal{F}\varpi) \leq \varphi(m(\omega, \varpi)), \qquad (4)$$

where $m(\omega, \varpi)$ is as in Theorem 2.
Then, $\mathcal{F}$ has a fixed point.

Proof. Since $\omega_1 \in \mathcal{L}$ then in view of assumption (a), let $\omega_2 \in \mathcal{F}\omega_1 \cap Im(\omega_1, \aleph)$, that is, $\omega_2 \in \mathcal{F}\omega_1$ and $(\omega_1, \omega_2) \in \aleph$. As $\frac{1}{2}\Gamma(\omega_1, \mathcal{F}\omega_1) \leq \Gamma(\omega_1, \mathcal{F}\omega_1) \leq \gamma(\omega_1, \omega_2)$, then condition (4) implies that

$$\begin{aligned} \Gamma(\omega_2, \mathcal{F}\omega_2) &\leq \Gamma_\mathcal{H}(\mathcal{F}\omega_1, \mathcal{F}\omega_2) \\ &\leq \varphi(m(\omega_1, \omega_2)) \end{aligned} \qquad (5)$$

where

$$m(\omega_1, \omega_2) = \max\left\{\gamma(\omega_1, \omega_2), \Gamma(\omega_1, \mathcal{F}\omega_1), \Gamma(\omega_2, \mathcal{F}\omega_2), \frac{\Gamma(\omega_1, \mathcal{F}\omega_2) + \Gamma(\omega_2, \mathcal{F}\omega_1)}{2}\right\}.$$

Here, it is easy to conclude from (5) that $m(\omega_1, \omega_2) = \gamma(\omega_1, \omega_2)$, otherwise we will obtain a contradiction. Thus,

$$\Gamma(\omega_2, \mathcal{F}\omega_2) \leq \varphi(\gamma(\omega_1, \omega_2)).$$

Since $\mathcal{F}\omega_2$ is a closed and bounded set, thus $\exists\, \omega_3 \in \mathcal{F}\omega_2$ such that

$$\gamma(\omega_2, \omega_3) \leq \varphi(\gamma(\omega_1, \omega_2)) < \gamma(\omega_1, \omega_2)$$

and from hypothesis (b), it follows that $(\omega_2, \omega_3) \in \aleph$. Now, continuing this process again and again, we can construct a sequence $\{\omega_\eta\} \subseteq \mathcal{L}$ such that $\omega_{\eta+1} \in \mathcal{F}\omega_\eta, (\omega_\eta, \omega_{\eta+1}) \in \aleph$ and

$$\gamma(\omega_{\eta+2}, \omega_{\eta+1}) \leq \varphi(\gamma(\omega_{\eta+1}, \omega_\eta)) < \gamma(\omega_{\eta+1}, \omega_\eta) \text{ for all } \eta \in \mathbb{N}.$$

Set $\gamma_\eta := \gamma(\omega_{\eta+1}, \omega_\eta)$. Thus, $\{\gamma_\eta\}$ is a monotonically decreasing and bounded-below sequence of non-negative numbers. This implies that $\lim_{\eta\to\infty} \gamma_\eta$ exists.

Suppose $\lim_{\eta\to\infty} \gamma_\eta = \gamma > 0$ and $\gamma_\eta = \gamma + \xi_\eta$ with $\xi_\eta > 0$. Since for all $t > 0$, $\limsup_{s \to t^+} \varphi(s) < t$ for (t_η) with $t_\eta \downarrow \gamma^+$, we have $\limsup_{t_\eta \to \gamma^+} \varphi(t_\eta) < \gamma$. Hence, we obtain

$$0 < \gamma = \lim_{\eta \to +\infty} \gamma_{\eta+1} \leq \lim_{\eta \to +\infty} \varphi(\gamma_\eta) \leq \lim_{\eta \to +\infty} \sup_{s \in (\gamma, \gamma_{\eta+1})} \varphi(s)$$
$$= \lim_{\gamma_{\eta+1} \to +0} \sup_{s \in (\gamma, \gamma+\xi_{\eta+1})} \varphi(s) \leq \lim_{\xi \to +0} \sup_{s \in (\gamma, \gamma+\xi)} \varphi(s) < \gamma,$$

a contradiction. Thus,

$$\lim_{\eta \to \infty} \gamma_\eta = 0 \text{ or } \lim_{\eta \to \infty} \gamma(\omega_\eta, \omega_{\eta+1}) = 0 \quad \text{for } \eta \in \mathbb{N}. \tag{6}$$

Therefore, for any $\varepsilon > 0$ there exists $\kappa \in \mathbb{N}$ such that

$$\gamma(\omega_{\eta_\kappa}, \omega_{\eta_\kappa+1}) < \varepsilon \quad \text{for } \eta_\kappa \geq \kappa. \tag{7}$$

Assume that (ω_η) is not a Cauchy sequence in $\mathcal{L}$. Then, for each positive integer κ, there exists an $\varepsilon > 0$ and sequences of positive integers $\{m_\kappa\}, \{\eta_\kappa\}$ such that $\kappa \leq m_\kappa < \eta_\kappa$ and the following assertions hold:

$$\gamma(\omega_{m_\kappa}, \omega_{\eta_\kappa}) \geq \varepsilon. \tag{8}$$

Without loss of generality, we may assume that η_κ is the smallest integer greater than m_κ satisfying the inequality (8) and

$$\gamma(\omega_{m_\kappa}, \omega_{\eta_\kappa - 1}) < \varepsilon. \tag{9}$$

Then, by triangle inequality and using inequality (9), we have

$$\gamma(\omega_{m_\kappa}, \omega_{\eta_\kappa}) \leq \gamma(\omega_{m_\kappa}, \omega_{\eta_\kappa - 1}) + \gamma(\omega_{\eta_\kappa - 1}, \omega_{\eta_\kappa})$$
$$< \gamma(\omega_{\eta_\kappa}, \omega_{\eta_\kappa - 1}) + \varepsilon.$$

Making $\kappa \to \infty$ and using (6), we obtain

$$\lim_{\kappa \to \infty} \gamma(\omega_{m_\kappa}, \omega_{\eta_\kappa}) = \varepsilon. \tag{10}$$

From (7) and (8), we have

$$\frac{1}{2}\gamma(\omega_{\eta_\kappa}, \omega_{\eta_\kappa+1}) \leq \gamma(\omega_{m_\kappa} \omega_{\eta_\kappa}) \quad \text{for all } \eta_\kappa > m_\kappa \geq \kappa. \tag{11}$$

Then, from condition (4) and by triangle inequality, we have

$$\begin{aligned}\gamma(\omega_{m_\kappa}, \omega_{\eta_\kappa}) &\leq \gamma(\omega_{m_\kappa}, \omega_{m_\kappa+1}) + \gamma(\omega_{m_\kappa+1}, \omega_{\eta_\kappa+1}) + \gamma(\omega_{\eta_\kappa+1}, \omega_{\eta_\kappa}) \\ &\leq \gamma(\omega_{m_\kappa}, \omega_{m_\kappa+1}) + \Gamma_{\mathcal{H}}(\mathcal{F}\omega_{m_\kappa}, \mathcal{F}\omega_{\eta_\kappa}) + \gamma(\omega_{\eta_\kappa+1}, \omega_{\eta_\kappa}) \\ &\leq \gamma(\omega_{m_\kappa}, \omega_{m_\kappa+1}) + \varphi\big(m(\omega_{m_\kappa}, \omega_{\eta_\kappa})\big) + \gamma(\omega_{\eta_\kappa+1}, \omega_{\eta_\kappa}).\end{aligned}$$

Making $\kappa \to \infty$ and using (6) and (10), we obtain

$$\varepsilon \leq \lim_{\kappa \to \infty} \varphi\big(m(\omega_{m_\kappa}, \omega_{\eta_\kappa})\big).$$

Since $\varepsilon = \lim\limits_{\kappa \to \infty} m(\omega_{m_\kappa}, \omega_{\eta_\kappa})$. Then, by $\limsup\limits_{s \to t^+} \varphi(s) < t$ for all $t > 0$, we obtain

$$\varepsilon \leq \lim\limits_{\kappa \to \infty} \varphi\big(m(\omega_{m_\kappa}, \omega_{\eta_\kappa})\big) \leq \lim\limits_{\delta \to +0} \sup\limits_{s \in (\varepsilon, \varepsilon + \delta)} \varphi(s) < \varepsilon,$$

which is a contradiction. Hence, the sequence $\{\omega_\eta\}$ is a Cauchy in $\mathcal{L}$. Since $\mathcal{L}$ is complete, $\{\omega_\eta\}$ converges to $\vartheta \in \mathcal{L}$.

Now, if $f(\omega) = \Gamma(\omega, \mathcal{F}\omega)$ is lower semi-continuous at the point ϑ, then we have

$$\Gamma(\vartheta, \mathcal{F}\vartheta) = f\vartheta \leq \liminf\limits_{\eta \to \infty} f(\omega_\eta) = \liminf\limits_{\eta \to \infty} \Gamma(\omega_\eta, \mathcal{F}\omega_\eta) = 0.$$

The closedness of $\mathcal{F}\vartheta$ implies $\vartheta \in \mathcal{F}\vartheta$.

On the other hand, if hypothesis (d) holds, then the sequence $\{\omega_\eta\}$ has a subsequence $\{\omega_{\eta_\kappa}\}$ such that $[\omega_{\eta_\kappa}, \vartheta] \in \aleph$ for all $\kappa \in \mathbb{N}$. Now, we show that

$$\text{either } \frac{1}{2}\gamma(\omega_{\eta_\kappa}, \omega_{\eta_\kappa + 1}) \leq \gamma(\omega_{\eta_\kappa}, \vartheta) \text{ or } \frac{1}{2}\gamma(\omega_{\eta_\kappa + 1}, \omega_{\eta_\kappa + 2}) \leq \gamma(\omega_{\eta_\kappa + 1}, \vartheta), \qquad (12)$$

for $\kappa \in \mathbb{N}$. By inference and contradiction, we assume that

$$\frac{1}{2}\gamma(\omega_{\eta_\kappa}, \omega_{\eta_\kappa + 1}) > \gamma(\omega_{\eta_\kappa}, \vartheta) \text{ and } \frac{1}{2}\gamma(\omega_{\eta_\kappa + 1}, \omega_{\eta_\kappa + 2}) > \gamma(\omega_{\eta_\kappa + 1}, \vartheta)$$

for each $\eta \in \mathbb{N}$. As a result of the triangle inequality, we have

$$\gamma(\omega_{\eta_\kappa}, \omega_{\eta_\kappa + 1}) \leq \gamma(\omega_{\eta_\kappa}, \vartheta) + \gamma(\vartheta, \omega_{\eta_\kappa + 1})$$
$$< \frac{1}{2}\gamma(\omega_{\eta_\kappa}, \omega_{\eta_\kappa + 1}) + \frac{1}{2}\gamma(\omega_{\eta_\kappa + 1}, \omega_{\eta_\kappa + 2})$$
$$< \frac{1}{2}\gamma(\omega_{\eta_\kappa}, \omega_{\eta_\kappa + 1}) + \frac{1}{2}\gamma(\omega_{\eta_\kappa}, \omega_{\eta_\kappa + 1}) = \gamma(\omega_{\eta_\kappa}, \omega_{\eta_\kappa + 1}).$$

This contradicts itself. The inequality (12) is valid for $\eta \in \mathbb{N}$. Since the first scenario,

$$\frac{1}{2}\Gamma(\omega_{\eta_\kappa}, \mathcal{F}\omega_{\eta_\kappa}) \leq \frac{1}{2}\gamma(\omega_{\eta_\kappa}, \omega_{\eta_\kappa + 1}) \leq \gamma(\omega_{\eta_\kappa}, \vartheta)$$

by (4), we have
$$\Gamma(\omega_{\eta_\kappa + 1}, \mathcal{F}\vartheta) \leq \Gamma_\mathcal{H}(\mathcal{F}\omega_{\eta_\kappa}, \mathcal{F}\vartheta) \leq \varphi\big(m(\omega_{\eta_\kappa}, \vartheta)\big).$$

We obtain by adding $\kappa \to \infty$,

$$\Gamma(\vartheta, \mathcal{F}\vartheta) \leq \lim\limits_{\kappa \to \infty} \varphi(m(\omega_{\eta_\kappa}, \vartheta))$$

Also, $\lim\limits_{\kappa \to \infty} m(\omega_{\eta_\kappa}, \vartheta) = \Gamma(\vartheta, \mathcal{F}\vartheta)$. Let $\Gamma = \Gamma(\vartheta, \mathcal{F}\vartheta)$. Then, by $\limsup\limits_{s \to t^+} \varphi(s) < t$ for all $t > 0$, we obtain

$$\Gamma \leq \lim\limits_{\kappa \to \infty} \varphi(m(\omega_{\eta_\kappa}, \vartheta)) \leq \lim\limits_{\delta \to +0} \sup\limits_{s \in (\Gamma, \Gamma + \delta)} \varphi(s) < \Gamma.$$

Therefore, unless $\Gamma = 0$ or $\Gamma(\vartheta, \mathcal{F}\vartheta) = 0$, is a contradiction. This suggests that $\vartheta \in \mathcal{F}\vartheta$. In the other scenario, we can conclude that $\vartheta \in \mathcal{F}\vartheta$. □

Considering $\mathcal{F} := f$ as a single-valued map, we obtain the following result:

Theorem 5. *Let $(\mathcal{L}, \gamma)$ be a CMS and $\aleph$ be a binary relation on $\mathcal{L}$. If $f: \mathcal{L} \to \mathcal{L}$ is a map and the following conditions are satisfied:*
(a) $\mathcal{L}(f, \aleph) \neq \varnothing$;
(b) $\aleph$ is f-γ-closed and transitive;

(c) either the function $f(\omega) := \gamma(\omega, f\omega)$ is $\aleph$-lower semi-continuous or
(d) $\aleph$ is γ-self closed;
(e) $\exists\, \varphi \in \Phi$ such that for any $\omega, \varpi \in \mathcal{L}$ with $(\omega, \varpi) \in \aleph$

$$\frac{1}{2}\gamma(\omega, f\omega) \leq \gamma(\omega, \varpi) \text{ implies } \Gamma_{\mathcal{H}}(f\omega, f\varpi) \leq \varphi(\eta(\omega, \varpi)),$$

where $\eta(\omega, \varpi) = \left\{ \gamma(\omega, \varpi), \gamma(\omega, f\omega), \gamma(\varpi, f\varpi), \dfrac{\gamma(\omega, f\varpi) + \gamma(\varpi, f\omega)}{2} \right\}$,

then, f has a fixed point.

If we assume $\aleph := \mathcal{L} \times \mathcal{L}$ as a universal relation on $\mathcal{L}$, then we obtain the following result:

Theorem 6. *Let $(\mathcal{L}, \gamma)$ be a CMS and $\mathcal{F} : \mathcal{L} \to \mathcal{CB}(\mathcal{L})$ a multi-valued map such that*

$$\frac{1}{2}\Gamma(\omega, \mathcal{F}\omega) \leq \gamma(\omega, \varpi) \text{ implies } \Gamma_{\mathcal{H}}(\mathcal{F}\omega, \mathcal{F}\varpi) \leq \varphi(m(\omega, \varpi)), \tag{13}$$

for any $\omega \in \mathcal{L}$, $\varpi \in \mathcal{F}\omega$, where $m(\omega, \varpi)$ is as in Theorem 2 and φ is as in Definition 2, then $\mathcal{F}$ has a fixed point in $\mathcal{L}$.

If we replace $m(\omega, \varpi) = \max\{\gamma(\omega, \varpi), \Gamma(\omega, \mathcal{F}\omega), \Gamma(\varpi, \mathcal{F}\varpi)\}$ in Theorem 4, then we obtain the following result.

Corollary 1. *Let $(\mathcal{L}, \gamma)$ be a CMS endowed with a binary relation $\aleph$ on $\mathcal{L}$. If $\mathcal{F} : \mathcal{L} \to \mathcal{CB}(\mathcal{L})$ is a multi-valued map and satisfying the following conditions:*
(a) $\exists\, \omega_1 \in \mathcal{L}$ such that $\mathcal{F}\omega_1 \cap Im(\omega_1, \aleph) \neq \varnothing$;
(b) $\aleph$ is $\mathcal{F}$-γ-closed and transitive;
(c) either the function $f(\omega) := \Gamma(\omega, \mathcal{F}\omega)$ is $\aleph$-lower semi-continuous or
(d) for any trajectory $\{\omega_\eta\} \subset \mathcal{L}$ of $\mathcal{F}$, if $\{\omega_\eta\} \to \omega$ and $\omega_{\eta+1} \in \mathcal{F}\omega_\eta$ for all $\eta \in \mathbb{N}$ then the sequence $\{\omega_\eta\}$ has a subsequence (ω_{η_κ}) such that $[\omega_{\eta_\kappa}, \omega] \in \aleph$ for all $\kappa \in \mathbb{N}$;
(e) $\exists\, \varphi \in \Phi$ such that for any $\omega \in \mathcal{L}, \varpi \in \mathcal{F}\omega$ with $(\omega, \varpi) \in \aleph$

$$\frac{1}{2}\Gamma(\omega, \mathcal{F}\omega) \leq \gamma(\omega, \varpi) \text{ implies } \Gamma_{\mathcal{H}}(\mathcal{F}\omega, \mathcal{F}\varpi) \leq \varphi(\max\{\gamma(\omega, \varpi), \Gamma(\omega, \mathcal{F}\omega), \Gamma(\varpi, \mathcal{F}\varpi)\}),$$

then $\mathcal{F}$ has a fixed point.

Similarly, if we replace $m(\omega, \varpi) = \gamma(\omega, \varpi)$ in Theorem 4, then we obtain the following result.

Corollary 2. *Let $(\mathcal{L}, \gamma)$ be a CMS endowed with a binary relation $\aleph$ on $\mathcal{L}$. If $\mathcal{F} : \mathcal{L} \to \mathcal{CB}(\mathcal{L})$ is a multi-valued map and satisfying the following conditions:*
(a) $\exists\, \omega_1 \in \mathcal{L}$ such that $\mathcal{F}\omega_1 \cap Im(\omega_1, \aleph) \neq \varnothing$;
(b) $\aleph$ is $\mathcal{F}$-γ-closed and transitive;
(c) either the function $f(\omega) := \Gamma(\omega, \mathcal{F}\omega)$ is $\aleph$-lower semi-continuous or
(d) for any trajectory $\{\omega_\eta\} \subset \mathcal{L}$ of $\mathcal{F}$, if $\{\omega_\eta\} \to \omega$ and $\omega_{\eta+1} \in \mathcal{F}\omega_\eta$ for all $\eta \in \mathbb{N}$ then the sequence $\{\omega_\eta\}$ has a subsequence (ω_{η_κ}) such that $[\omega_{\eta_\kappa}, \omega] \in \aleph$ for all $\kappa \in \mathbb{N}$;
(e) $\exists\, \varphi \in \Phi$ such that for any $\omega \in \mathcal{L}, \varpi \in \mathcal{F}\omega$ with $(\omega, \varpi) \in \aleph$

$$\frac{1}{2}\Gamma(\omega, \mathcal{F}\omega) \leq \gamma(\omega, \varpi) \text{ implies } \Gamma_{\mathcal{H}}(\mathcal{F}\omega, \mathcal{F}\varpi) \leq \varphi(\gamma(\omega, \varpi)),$$

then $\mathcal{F}$ has a fixed point.

Example 1. Let $\mathcal{L} = \{l, m, p, r, s\}$, $\aleph = \{(p,p), (p,r), (p,l), (p,m), (r,r), (r,l), (r,m),$
$(l,m), (l,r), (l,l), (m,r), (m,l), (m,m)\} \subset \mathcal{L} \times \mathcal{L}$ and γ is the metric on $\mathcal{L}$ defined by

$$\gamma(\omega, \omega) = 0, \gamma(\omega, \varpi) = \gamma(\varpi, \omega) \text{ for all } \omega, \varpi \in \mathcal{L},$$
$$\gamma(p,r) = \gamma(p,l) = \gamma(p,m) = 1,$$
$$\gamma(r,l) = \gamma(r,m) = \gamma(l,m) = \frac{3}{2},$$
$$\gamma(s,l) = \gamma(s,m) = \gamma(s,p) = \gamma(s,r) = 2.$$

Then, $(\mathcal{L}, \gamma)$ is a CMS. Define $\varphi : [0, \infty) \to [0, \infty)$ and $\mathcal{F} : \mathcal{L} \to \mathcal{CB}(\mathcal{L})$ by

$$\varphi(\omega) = \begin{cases} \frac{\omega^2}{2}, & \text{if } \omega \leq 1, \\ \omega - \frac{1}{4}, & \text{otherwise;} \end{cases} \quad \mathcal{F}\omega = \begin{cases} \{p\}, & \text{if } \omega \in \{p, r, m\}, \\ \{r, m\}, & \text{if } \omega = l, \\ \{s\}, & \text{if } \omega = s. \end{cases}$$

Then, $\aleph$ is $\mathcal{F}$-γ-closed, transitive and $f(\omega) = \Gamma(\omega, \mathcal{F}\omega)$ is a continuous map on $\mathcal{L}$ implying it is $\aleph$-lower semi-continuous on $\mathcal{L}$. Now, we consider the followings cases.

Case 1: $\omega, \varpi \in \{p, r, m\}$ or $\omega = \varpi = l$ and $(\omega, \varpi) \in \aleph$. Then,

$$\Gamma_{\mathcal{H}}(\mathcal{F}\omega, \mathcal{F}\varpi) = 0 \leq \varphi(\gamma(\omega, \varpi)).$$

Case 2: $(\omega, \varpi) = (p, l) \in \aleph$. Then,

$$\Gamma_{\mathcal{H}}(\mathcal{F}(p), \mathcal{F}(l)) = \Gamma_{\mathcal{H}}(\{p\}, \{r, m\}) = 1 < \frac{5}{4} = \varphi(\Gamma(l, \mathcal{F}(l))).$$

Case 3: $(\omega, \varpi) = (r, l)$ or $(l, r) \in \aleph$. Then,

$$\Gamma_{\mathcal{H}}(\mathcal{F}(r), \mathcal{F}(l)) = 1 < \frac{5}{4} = \varphi(\gamma(r, l)).$$

Case 4: $(\omega, \varpi) = (l, m)$ or $(m, l) \in \aleph$. Then,

$$\Gamma_{\mathcal{H}}(\mathcal{F}(l), \mathcal{F}(m)) = 1 < \frac{5}{4} = \varphi(\gamma(l, m)).$$

Thus, in all the cases, $\Gamma_{\mathcal{H}}(\mathcal{F}\omega, \mathcal{F}\varpi) \leq \varphi(m(\omega, \varpi))$, and (4) is satisfied. Further, all the conditions of Theorem 4 are satisfied and the mapping $\mathcal{F}$ has two fixed points at $p \in \mathcal{F}(p)$ and $s \in \mathcal{F}(s)$. However, for $\omega = p$ and $\varpi = s$, the mapping F does not satisfy contraction conditions (1), (2), and (3). Consequently, Theorems 1–3 cannot be applied to this particular example.

Example 2. Let $\mathcal{L} = [-3, 5]$, $\aleph = \mathcal{L} \times \mathcal{L}$ and γ be the usual metric $\mathcal{L}$. Then, $(\mathcal{L}, \gamma)$ is a CMS. Define $\varphi : [0, \infty) \to [0, \infty)$ and $\mathcal{F} : \mathcal{L} \to \mathcal{CB}(\mathcal{L})$ by

$$\varphi(\omega) = \begin{cases} \frac{\omega^2}{2}, & \text{if } \omega \leq 1, \\ \omega - \frac{1}{3}, & \text{otherwise;} \end{cases} \quad \mathcal{F}\omega = \begin{cases} \{\frac{\omega}{3}, 0\}, & \text{if } \omega < 0, \\ [0, \frac{\omega}{3}], & \text{if } \omega \geq 0. \end{cases}$$

We consider the followings cases.

Case 1: $\omega, \varpi < 0$. Then,

$$\begin{aligned} \Gamma_{\mathcal{H}}(\mathcal{F}\omega, \mathcal{F}\varpi) &= \Gamma_{\mathcal{H}}\left(\left\{\frac{\omega}{3}, 0\right\}, \left\{\frac{\varpi}{3}, 0\right\}\right) \\ &= \max\left\{\left|\frac{\omega}{3} - \frac{\varpi}{3}\right|, \left|\frac{\omega}{3}\right|, \left|\frac{\varpi}{3}\right|\right\} \\ &\leq \varphi(\max\{\gamma(\omega, \varpi), \Gamma(\omega, \mathcal{F}\omega), \Gamma(\varpi, \mathcal{F}\varpi)\}). \end{aligned}$$

Case 2: $\omega < 0$, $\varpi > 0$. Then,

$$\begin{aligned}\Gamma_{\mathcal{H}}(\mathcal{F}\omega, \mathcal{F}\varpi) &= \Gamma_{\mathcal{H}}\left(\left\{\frac{\omega}{3}, 0\right\}, \left[0, \frac{\varpi}{3}\right]\right) \\ &= \max\left\{\left|\frac{\omega}{3}\right|, \left|\frac{\varpi}{3}\right|\right\} \\ &\leq \varphi(\max\{\Gamma(\omega, \mathcal{F}\omega), \Gamma(\varpi, \mathcal{F}\varpi)\}).\end{aligned}$$

Case 3: $\omega, \varpi \geq 0$. Then,

$$\begin{aligned}\Gamma_{\mathcal{H}}(\mathcal{F}\omega, \mathcal{F}\varpi) &= \Gamma_{\mathcal{H}}\left(\left[0, \frac{\omega}{3}\right], \left[0, \frac{\varpi}{3}\right]\right) \\ &= \left|\frac{\omega}{3} - \frac{\varpi}{3}\right| \leq |\omega - \varpi|.\end{aligned}$$

Thus, in all the cases, $\Gamma_{\mathcal{H}}(\mathcal{F}\omega, \mathcal{F}\varpi) \leq \varphi(m(\omega, \varpi))$, and (4) is satisfied. Since under universal relation that is, $\aleph = \mathcal{L} \times \mathcal{L}$, conditions (b) and (d) both are obviously true. Thus, all the assertions of Theorem 4 are fulfilled, leading to the conclusion that $0 \in \mathcal{F}(0) \subset \mathcal{L}$ is a fixed point for the map $\mathcal{F}$.

4. Stability of Fixed-Point Sets and Well-Posedness

The stability of fixed points is concerned with understanding whether small deviations from a fixed point will lead the system's solutions to stay close to the fixed point or diverge away from it. This topic has been explored in various works; see [4–6,14,16,22–27]. Here, we delve into the stability of fixed-point sets for multi-valued maps. Our exploration begins with the following lemma.

Lemma 1 ([12]). *In an MS* $(\mathcal{L}, \gamma)$, *for every* $\omega \in \mathcal{L}$ $\exists \varpi \in B \in \mathcal{C}(\mathcal{L})$ *such that* $\gamma(\omega, \varpi) = \Gamma(\omega, B)$.

Theorem 7. *Let* $\aleph$ *be a binary relation on a CMS* $(\mathcal{L}, \gamma)$ *and* $\mathcal{F}_j : \mathcal{L} \to \mathcal{C}(\mathcal{L})$ $(j \in \{1,2\})$ *are two multi-valued maps satisfying all the assumptions of Theorem 4 with* $\sum_{\kappa=1}^{\infty} \varphi^\kappa(\omega) < \infty$ *for all* $\omega > 0$. *Then,*

(a) $F(\mathcal{F}_j) \neq \emptyset$ $(j \in \{1,2\})$.

(b) $\Gamma_{\mathcal{H}}(F(\mathcal{F}_1), F(\mathcal{F}_2)) \leq \Psi(L)$, *where* $L = \sup_{\omega \in \mathcal{L}} \Gamma_{\mathcal{H}}(\mathcal{F}_1(\omega), \mathcal{F}_2(\omega))$ *and* $\Psi(L) = \sum_{\kappa=1}^{\infty} \varphi^\kappa(L)$.

Proof. The validity of Theorem 4 guarantees the existence of nonempty fixed-point sets $F(\mathcal{F}_j) \neq \emptyset$ for $j \in \{1,2\}$, satisfying condition (a). Moving on, let us assume $\vartheta_1 \in F(\mathcal{F}_1)$, implying $\vartheta_1 \in \mathcal{F}_1\vartheta_1$. Using Lemma 1, since $\mathcal{F}_2\vartheta_1$ is a compact subset of $\mathcal{L}$, in view of Lemma 1, there exists $\vartheta_2 \in \mathcal{F}_2\vartheta_1$ such that $\gamma(\vartheta_1, \vartheta_2) = \Gamma(\vartheta_1, \mathcal{F}_2\vartheta_1)$. Repeating this process with Lemma 1, we determine $\vartheta_3 \in \mathcal{F}_2\vartheta_2$ such that $\gamma(\vartheta_2, \vartheta_3) = \Gamma(\vartheta_2, \mathcal{F}_2\vartheta_2)$. Continuing this iteration and following the proof strategy of Theorem 4, we generate an $\aleph$-preserving sequence $\{\vartheta_\eta\}$ that fulfills

$$\vartheta_{\eta+1} \in \mathcal{F}_2\vartheta_\eta \quad \text{and} \quad \gamma(\vartheta_{\eta+1}, \vartheta_{\eta+2}) \leq \varphi(\gamma(\vartheta_\eta, \vartheta_{\eta+1})) \leq \cdots \leq \varphi^\eta(\gamma(\vartheta_1, \vartheta_2)). \tag{14}$$

Now, as we follow the proof of Theorem 4, it becomes evident that the sequence $\{\vartheta_\eta\}$ is an $\aleph$-preserving Cauchy sequence. Thus, it inevitably converges to a point $w \in \mathcal{L}$. Furthermore, it can be established that w is a fixed point of $\mathcal{F}_2$ since

$$\gamma(\vartheta_1, \vartheta_2) = \Gamma(\vartheta_1, \mathcal{F}_2\vartheta_1) \leq \Gamma_{\mathcal{H}}(\mathcal{F}_1\vartheta_1, \mathcal{F}_2\vartheta_2).$$

Now, using the definition of L, we obtain

$$\gamma(\vartheta_1, \vartheta_2) \leq L = \sup_{\omega \in \mathcal{L}} \Gamma_{\mathcal{H}}(\mathcal{F}_1 \omega, \mathcal{F}_2 \omega). \tag{15}$$

With the triangle inequality and Equation (14), we obtain

$$\gamma(\vartheta_1, w) \leq \sum_{\kappa=1}^{\eta+1} \gamma(\vartheta_i, \vartheta_{i+1}) + \gamma(\vartheta_{\eta+2}, w) \leq \sum_{\kappa=1}^{\eta} \varphi^{\kappa}(\gamma(\vartheta_1, \vartheta_2)) + \gamma(\vartheta_{\eta+2}, w).$$

Taking the limit as $\eta \to \infty$ and utilizing Equation (15), we derive

$$\gamma(\vartheta_1, w) \leq \sum_{\kappa=1}^{\infty} \varphi^{\kappa}(\gamma(\vartheta_1, \vartheta_2)) + \gamma(\vartheta_{\eta+2}, w) \leq \sum_{\kappa=1}^{\infty} \varphi^{\kappa}(L) = \Psi(L).$$

Consequently, given $\vartheta_1 \in F(\mathcal{F}_1)$, we find $w \in F(\mathcal{F}_2)$ satisfying $\gamma(\vartheta_1, w) \leq \Psi(L)$. Similarly, it can be proven that for any $w_1 \in F(\mathcal{F}_2)$, $\exists u \in F(\mathcal{F}_1)$ such that $\gamma(w_1, u) \leq \Psi(L)$. This concludes the proof of condition (b). □

Lemma 2. *Assume that $(\mathcal{L}, \gamma)$ is a CMS, $\aleph$ is a binary relation on $\mathcal{L}$, and $\mathcal{F}_{\eta} : \mathcal{L} \to \mathcal{CB}(\mathcal{L})$ ($\eta \in \mathbb{N}$) is a sequence of multi-valued maps. If $(\mathcal{F}_{\eta})$ converges uniformly to $\mathcal{F} : \mathcal{L} \to \mathcal{CB}(\mathcal{L})$ for each $\eta \in \mathbb{N}$ and $\mathcal{F}_{\eta}$ satisfies all the conditions of Theorem 4, then $\mathcal{F}$ also satisfies (4) and has a fixed point in $\mathcal{L}$.*

Proof. Let $\omega \in \mathcal{L}$ and $\varpi \in \mathcal{F}\omega$ be such that $(\omega, \varpi) \in \aleph$. Since each $\mathcal{F}_{\eta}$ satisfies (4), we have

$$\frac{1}{2}\Gamma(\omega, \mathcal{F}_{\eta}\omega) \leq \gamma(\omega, \varpi) \text{ implies } \Gamma_{\mathcal{H}}(\mathcal{F}_{\eta}\omega, \mathcal{F}_{\eta}\varpi) \leq \varphi(m_{\eta}(\omega, \varpi))$$

for all $\omega \in \mathcal{L}, \varpi \in \mathcal{F}\omega$ with $(\omega, \varpi) \in \aleph$, where

$$m_{\eta}(\omega, \varpi) = \max\left\{\gamma(\omega, \varpi), \Gamma(\omega, \mathcal{F}_{\eta}\omega), \Gamma(\varpi, \mathcal{F}_{\eta}\varpi), \frac{\Gamma(\omega, \mathcal{F}_{\eta}\varpi) + \Gamma(\varpi, \mathcal{F}_{\eta}\omega)}{2}\right\}.$$

By letting $\eta \to \infty$ while maintaining uniform convergence, and following a similar argument as in the proof of Theorem 4, we conclude that

$$\frac{1}{2}\Gamma(\omega, \mathcal{F}\omega)) \leq \gamma(\omega, \varpi) \text{ implies } \Gamma_{\mathcal{H}}(\mathcal{F}\omega, \mathcal{F}\varpi) \leq \varphi(m(\omega, \varpi))$$

for all $\omega \in \mathcal{L}, \varpi \in \mathcal{F}\omega$ with $(\omega, \varpi) \in \aleph$, where $m(\omega, \varpi)$ is as defined in Theorem 4. This implies that $\mathcal{F}$ satisfies (4). Since $\mathcal{L}$ is complete and $\mathcal{F}$ satisfies (4), $\mathcal{F}$ has a fixed point in $\mathcal{L}$. □

Theorem 8. *Suppose $\aleph$ is a binary relation on a CMS $(\mathcal{L}, \gamma)$. If a sequence of maps $\{\mathcal{F}_{\eta}\}$, where $\mathcal{F}_{\eta} : \mathcal{L} \to \mathcal{CB}(\mathcal{L})$ for all $\eta \in \mathbb{N}$, converges uniformly to a function $\mathcal{F} : \mathcal{L} \to \mathcal{CB}(\mathcal{L})$ and for each $\eta \in \mathbb{N}$, $\mathcal{F}_{\eta}$ satisfies all the conditions of Theorem 4, then $F(\mathcal{F}_{\eta}) \neq \emptyset$ for all $\eta \in \mathbb{N}$ and $F(\mathcal{F}) \neq \emptyset$. Moreover, let $\Psi(\omega) = \sum_{\kappa=1}^{\infty} \varphi^{\kappa}(\omega)$ and $\lim_{\omega \to 0} \Psi(\omega) = 0$, then $\lim_{\eta \to \infty} \Gamma_{\mathcal{H}}(F(\mathcal{F}_{\eta}), F(\mathcal{F})) = 0$.*

Proof. By Lemma 2, $F(\mathcal{F}_{\eta}) \neq \emptyset$ for all $\eta \in \mathbb{N}$ and $F(\mathcal{F}) \neq \emptyset$. Suppose $L_{\eta} = \sup_{\omega \in \mathcal{L}} \Gamma_{\mathcal{H}}(\mathcal{F}_{\eta}\omega, \mathcal{F}\omega)$. For $(\mathcal{F}_{\eta})$ being uniformly convergent to $\mathcal{F}$, we obtain

$$\lim_{\eta \to \infty} \sup_{\omega \in \mathcal{L}} \Gamma_{\mathcal{H}}(\mathcal{F}_{\eta}\omega, \mathcal{F}\omega) = 0.$$

From Theorem 7, we have

$$\Gamma_{\mathcal{H}}(F_\eta(\mathcal{F}), F(\mathcal{F})) \leq \Psi(L_\eta) \text{ for all } \eta \in \mathbb{N}.$$

Further, $\lim_{\omega \to 0} \Psi(\omega) = 0$ implies

$$\lim_{\eta \to \infty} \Gamma_{\mathcal{H}}(F_\eta(\mathcal{F}), F(\mathcal{F})) \leq \lim_{\eta \to \infty} \Psi(L_\eta) = 0.$$

Therefore, sets of fixed points of $\mathcal{F}_\eta$ are stable. □

Now, we show that the fixed-point problem (fpp) is well-posed. We begin with the following definitions.

Definition 7. *Assume that $(\mathcal{L}, \gamma)$ is an MS, $\aleph$ is a binary relation, and $\mathcal{F} : \mathcal{L} \to \mathcal{CB}(\mathcal{L})$ is a multi-valued map. We say fpp is well-posed for $\mathcal{F}$ with respect to Γ if*
(i) $SF(\mathcal{F}) = \{\vartheta\}$;
(ii) *for any $\aleph$-preserving sequence (ω_η) in $\mathcal{L}$ with $\lim_{\eta \to \infty} \Gamma(\omega_\eta, \mathcal{F}\omega_\eta) = 0$, we have $\lim_{\eta \to \infty} \gamma(\omega_\eta, \vartheta) = 0$.*

Definition 8. *Assume that $(\mathcal{L}, \gamma)$ is an MS, $\aleph$ is a binary relation, and $\mathcal{F} : \mathcal{L} \to \mathcal{CB}(\mathcal{L})$ is a multi-valued map. We say fpp is well-posed for $\mathcal{F}$ with respect to $\Gamma_{\mathcal{H}}$ if*
(i) $SF(\mathcal{F}) = \{\vartheta\}$;
(ii) *for an $\aleph$-preserving sequence (ω_η) in $\mathcal{L}$ with $\lim_{\eta \to \infty} \Gamma_{\mathcal{H}}(\omega_\eta, \mathcal{F}\omega_\eta) = 0$, we have $\lim_{\eta \to \infty} \gamma(\omega_\eta, \vartheta) = 0$.*

Notice that when $F(\mathcal{F}) = SF(\mathcal{F})$ and fpp is well-posed for $\mathcal{F}$ with respect to Γ, then it is well-posed with respect to $\Gamma_{\mathcal{H}}$.

Theorem 9. *Let all the conditions of Corollary 1 be true along with assertions (i) $SF(\mathcal{F}) \neq \phi$ and (ii) all fixed points of F are comparative. Then,*
(a) $F(\mathcal{F}) = SF(\mathcal{F}) = \{\vartheta\}$;
(b) *the fpp is well-posed for $\mathcal{F}$ with respect to $\Gamma_{\mathcal{H}}$.*

Proof. (a) Let $u \in SF(\mathcal{F})$ and $\vartheta \in F(\mathcal{F})$ such that $u \neq \vartheta$. This leads to $0 = \frac{1}{2}\Gamma(u, \mathcal{F}u) < \gamma(u, \vartheta)$. As all fixed points of F are comparative, so we have $(u, \vartheta) \in \aleph$. Using (4) we find

$$\begin{aligned}\Gamma_{\mathcal{H}}(\mathcal{F}u, \mathcal{F}\vartheta) &\leq \varphi(\max\{\gamma(u, \vartheta), \Gamma(u, \mathcal{F}u), \Gamma(\vartheta, \mathcal{F}\vartheta)\}) \\ &= \varphi(\gamma(u, \vartheta)) < \gamma(u, \vartheta).\end{aligned}$$

This leads to

$$\gamma(u, \vartheta) = \Gamma(\vartheta, \mathcal{F}u) \leq \Gamma_{\mathcal{H}}(\mathcal{F}u, \mathcal{F}\vartheta) < \gamma(u, \vartheta),$$

which is contradictory unless $u = \vartheta$.

(b) Let $\{\omega_\eta\}$ be an $\aleph$-preserving sequence in $\mathcal{L}$ such that $\lim_{\eta \to \infty} \Gamma(\omega_\eta, \mathcal{F}\omega_\eta) = 0$. We aim to prove $\lim_{\eta \to \infty} \gamma(\omega_\eta, \vartheta) = 0$.

Assume for contradiction that $\lim_{\eta \to \infty} \gamma(\omega_\eta, \vartheta) \neq 0$. Then, $\exists \varepsilon > 0$ such that $\varepsilon < \gamma(\omega_\eta, \vartheta)$ for each $\eta \in \mathbb{N}$. As $\aleph$ is γ-self-closed and $\lim_{\eta \to \infty} \Gamma(\omega_\eta, \mathcal{F}\omega_\eta) = 0$, $\exists$ a subsequence $\{\omega_{\eta_\kappa}\}$ of $\{\omega_\eta\}$ with $[\omega_{\eta_\kappa}, \omega]$ and a number $\eta_0 \in \mathbb{N}$ such that

$$\Gamma(\omega_{\eta_\kappa}, \mathcal{F}\omega_{\eta_\kappa}) < \varepsilon \text{ for each } \eta_\kappa \geq \eta_0.$$

For $\eta_\kappa \geq \eta_0$, we have $\frac{1}{2}\Gamma(\omega_{\eta_\kappa}, \mathcal{F}\omega_{\eta_\kappa}) < \varepsilon < \gamma(\omega_{\eta_\kappa}, \vartheta)$. Utilizing (4), we obtain

$$\begin{aligned}
\gamma(\omega_{\eta_\kappa}, \vartheta) &= \Gamma(\omega_{\eta_\kappa}, \mathcal{F}\vartheta) \\
&\leq \Gamma(\omega_{\eta_\kappa}, \mathcal{F}\omega_{\eta_\kappa}) + \Gamma_{\mathcal{H}}(\mathcal{F}\omega_{\eta_\kappa}, \mathcal{F}\vartheta) \\
&\leq \Gamma(\omega_{\eta_\kappa}, \mathcal{F}\omega_{\eta_\kappa}) + \varphi(\max\{\gamma(\omega_{\eta_\kappa}, \vartheta), \Gamma(\omega_{\eta_\kappa}, \mathcal{F}\omega_{\eta_\kappa}), \Gamma(\vartheta, \mathcal{F}\vartheta)\}) \\
&= \Gamma(\omega_\eta, \mathcal{F}\omega_{\eta_\kappa}) + \varphi(\max\{\gamma(\omega_{\eta_\kappa}, \vartheta), \Gamma(\omega_{\eta_\kappa}, \mathcal{F}\omega_{\eta_\kappa})\}).
\end{aligned}$$

Taking $\kappa \to \infty$ and using the properties of φ, we derive

$$\varepsilon < \gamma(\omega_{\eta_\kappa}, \vartheta) \leq \varphi(\gamma(\omega_{\eta_\kappa}, \vartheta)) < \varepsilon,$$

which is a contradiction. Therefore, $\lim_{\eta \to \infty} \gamma(\omega_\eta, \vartheta) = 0$, and the fpp is well-posed for $\mathcal{F}$ concerning $\Gamma_{\mathcal{H}}$. □

5. An Application to Dynamic Programming

In the context of this section, we consider Banach spaces Ξ and Λ, with $\Pi \subset \Xi$ and $\mathcal{E} \subset \Lambda$, while $\mathbb{R}$ denotes the field of real numbers. We work with maps $\tau : \Pi \times \mathcal{E} \to \Pi$, $f : \Pi \times \mathcal{E} \to \mathbb{R}$, $F : \Pi \times \mathcal{E} \times \mathbb{R} \to \mathbb{R}$, and utilize the set $B(\Pi)$ to represent all bounded real-valued functions on Π.

Our focus in this section is on investigating the existence and uniqueness of a solution for the functional equation

$$p(\omega) = \sup_{\varpi \in \Gamma} f(\omega, \varpi) + F(\omega, \varpi, p(\tau(\omega, \varpi))), \quad \omega \in \Pi, \tag{16}$$

where f and F are bounded functions, ω and ϖ symbolize the state and decision vectors, respectively, τ denotes the process transformation, and $p(\omega)$ signifies the optimal return function given an initial state ω.

To facilitate our analysis, we introduce a map $\mathcal{F} : B(\Pi) \to B(\Pi)$, defined as:

$$\mathcal{F}(h(\omega)) = \sup_{\varpi \in \Gamma} \{f(\omega, \varpi) + F(\omega, \varpi, h(\tau(\omega, \varpi)))\}, \tag{17}$$

where h and κ belong to $B(\Pi)$. Additionally, we define a distance metric $\gamma : B(\Pi) \times B(\Pi) \to [0, \infty)$ as

$$\gamma(h, \kappa) = \sup_{\omega \in \Pi} |h(\omega) - \kappa(\omega)|. \tag{18}$$

Furthermore, we introduce the notation

$$\Gamma(h, \mathcal{F}(h)) = \inf_{\omega \in \Pi} |h(\omega) - \mathcal{F}(h(\omega))|.$$

Our aim is to establish the existence and uniqueness of a solution for the functional Equation (16) using the framework provided by Theorem 4.

Theorem 10. *Suppose that* $\exists \varphi \in \Phi$ *such that for every* $(\omega, \varpi) \in \Pi \times \mathcal{E}, \omega \in \Pi$ *and* $h, \kappa \in B(\Pi)$ *with* $h(\omega) \leq \kappa(\omega)$ *for all* ω, *we have*

$$\theta(r)|h(\omega) - \mathcal{F}(h(\omega))| \leq |h(\omega) - \kappa(\omega)| \tag{19}$$

implies

$$|F(\omega, \varpi, h(\omega)) - F(\omega, \varpi, \kappa(\omega))| \leq \varphi(M(h(\omega), \kappa(\omega))) \tag{20}$$

where $M(h(\omega), \kappa(\omega)) = \max\left\{\gamma(h, \kappa), \Gamma(h, \mathcal{F}(h)), \Gamma(\kappa, \mathcal{F}(\kappa)), \dfrac{\Gamma(h, \mathcal{F}(\kappa)) + \Gamma(\kappa, \mathcal{F}(h))}{2}\right\}.$
Then, the functional Equation (16) has a bounded solution in $B(\Pi)$.

Proof. Define $\aleph := B(\Pi) \times B(\Pi)$, a universal relation on $B(\Pi)$. Then, obviously $\aleph$ is $\mathcal{F}$-γ-closed, transitive, and γ-self-closed on $B(\Pi)$, where $\mathcal{F}$ is defined in (17). Also, $(B(\Pi), \gamma)$ is a CMS, where γ is defined by (18). Let λ be an arbitrary positive number and $h, \kappa \in B(\Pi)$. Let $\omega \in \Pi$ be arbitrary and choose $\varpi_1, \varpi_2 \in \Gamma$ such that

$$\mathcal{F}(h(\omega)) < f(\omega, \varpi_1) + F(\omega, \varpi_1, h(\tau_1)) + \lambda \qquad (21)$$

$$\mathcal{F}(\kappa(\omega)) < f(\omega, \varpi_2) + F(\omega, \varpi_2, \kappa(\tau_2)) + \lambda \qquad (22)$$

where $\tau_1 = \tau(\omega, \varpi_1)$ and $\tau_2 = \tau(\omega, \varpi_2)$. Further, by definition of $\mathcal{F}$, we know

$$\mathcal{F}(h(\omega)) \geq f(\omega, \varpi_2) + F(\omega, \varpi_2, h(\tau_2)) \qquad (23)$$

$$\mathcal{F}(\kappa(\omega)) \geq f(\omega, \varpi_1) + F(\omega, \varpi_1, \kappa(\tau_1)). \qquad (24)$$

Since (19) holds, thus from (21) and (24), we have

$$\begin{aligned}
\mathcal{F}(h(\omega)) - \mathcal{F}(\kappa(\omega)) &\leq F(\omega, \varpi_1, h(\tau_1)) - F(\omega, \varpi_1, \kappa(\tau_1)) + \lambda \\
&\leq |F(\omega, \varpi_1, h(\tau_1)) - F(\omega, \varpi_1, \kappa(\tau_1))| + \lambda \\
&\leq \varphi(M(h(\omega), \kappa(\omega))) + \lambda.
\end{aligned} \qquad (25)$$

Similarly, from (22) and (23), we obtain

$$\mathcal{F}(\kappa(\omega)) - \mathcal{F}(h(\omega)) \leq \varphi(M(h(\omega), \kappa(\omega))) + \lambda. \qquad (26)$$

Hence, from (25) and (26), we have

$$|\mathcal{F}(h(\omega)) - \mathcal{F}(\kappa(\omega))| \leq \varphi(M(h(\omega), \kappa(\omega))) + \lambda.$$

Since $\omega \in \Pi$ and $\lambda > 0$ is arbitrary, hence we find from inequality (19) that

$$\theta(r)\gamma(h(\omega), \mathcal{F}(h(\omega))) \leq \gamma(h(\omega), \kappa(\omega))$$

implies

$$\gamma(\mathcal{F}(h(\omega)), \mathcal{F}(\kappa(\omega))) \leq \varphi(M(h(\omega), \kappa(\omega))).$$

Therefore, all the conditions of Theorem 5 are fulfilled for the map $\mathcal{F}$. As a result, the map $\mathcal{F}$ possesses a fixed point denoted as $h(\omega)$, signifying that $h(\omega)$ is a bounded solution for the functional Equation (16). □

Author Contributions: Conceptualization, D.K. and R.P.; Methodology, I.K.L.; Validation, M.D.l.S. All authors have read and agreed to the published version of the manuscript.

Funding: This research received no external funding.

Acknowledgments: We are very thankful to the reviewers for their constructive comments and suggestions that have been useful for the improvement of this paper. The second author acknowledges the support from the URC/FRC fellowship, University of Johannesburg, South Africa.

Data Availability Statement: Not applicable.

Conflicts of Interest: The authors declare no conflict of interest.

References

1. Khantwal, D.; Aneja, S.; Gairola, U.C. A fixed point theorem for (ϕ, ψ)-convex contraction in metric spaces. *Adv. Theory Nonlinear Anal. Its Appl.* **2021**, *5*, 240–245.
2. Khantwal, D.; Aneja, S.; Prasad, G.; Gairola, U.C. A generalization of relation-theoretic contraction principle. *TWMS J. App. Eng. Math.* **2023**, *13*, 166–174.

3. Khantwal, D.; Aneja, S.; Prasad, G.; Joshi, B.C.; Gairola, U.C. Multivalued relation-theoretic graph contraction principle with applications. *Int. J. Nonlinear Anal. Appl.* **2022**, *13*, 2961–2971.
4. Lim, T.C. Fixed point stability for set valued contractive mappings with applications to generalized differential equations. *J. Math. Anal. Appl.* **1985**, *110*, 436–441. [CrossRef]
5. Markin, J.T. A fixed point stability theorem for nonexpansive set valued mappings. *J. Math. Anal. Appl.* **1976**, *54*, 441–443. [CrossRef]
6. Mishra, S.N.; Singh, S.L.; Pant, R. Some new results on stability of fixed points. *Chaos Solitons Fractals* **2012**, *45*, 1012–1016. [CrossRef]
7. Mizoguchi, N.; Takahashi, W. Fixed point theorems for multivalued mappings on complete metric spaces. *J. Math. Anal. Appl.* **1989**, *141*, 177–188. [CrossRef]
8. Pant, R.; Shukla, R. *New Fixed Point Results for Proinov–Suzuki Type Contractions in Metric Spaces*; Rendiconti del Circolo Matematico di Palermo Series 2; Springer: Berlin/Heidelberg, Germany, 2022; Volume 71, pp. 633–645.
9. Suzuki, T. A generalized Banach contraction principle that characterizes metric completeness. *Proc. Am. Math. Soc.* **2008**, *136*, 1861–1869. [CrossRef]
10. Alam, A.; Imdad, M. Relation-theoretic contraction principle. *J. Fixed Point Theory Appl.* **2015**, *17*, 693–702. [CrossRef]
11. Ri, S. A new fixed point theorem in the fractal space. *Indag. Math.* **2016**, *27*, 85–93. [CrossRef]
12. Nadler, S.B., Jr. Multivalued contraction mappings. *Pac. J. Math.* **1969**, *30*, 475–488. [CrossRef]
13. Ciric, L.B. Fixed Points Gen. Multivalued Contractions. *Mat. Vesn.* **1972**, *9*, 265–272.
14. Bose, R.K.; Mukherjee, R.N. Stability of fixed point sets and common fixed points of families of mappings. *Indian J. Pure Appl. Math.* **1980**, *11*, 1130–1138.
15. Kikkawa, M.; Suzuki, T. Three fixed point theorems for generalized contractions with constants in complete metric spaces. *Nonlinear Anal.* **2008**, *69*, 2942–2949. [CrossRef]
16. Mot, G.; Petrusel, A. Fixed point theory for a new type of contractive multivalued operators. *Nonlinear Anal.* **2009**, *70*, 3371–3377. [CrossRef]
17. Petrusel, A.; Rus, I.A.; Yao, J.-C. Well-posedness in the generalized sense of the fixed point problems for multivalued operators. *Taiwan. J. Math.* **2007**, *11*, 903–914. [CrossRef]
18. Singh, S.L.; Mishra, S.N.; Pant, R. New fixed point theorems for asymptotically regular multi-valued maps. *Nonlinear Anal.* **2009**, *71*, 3299–3304. [CrossRef]
19. Alam, A.; Imdad, M.; Asim, M.; Sessa, S. A relation-theoretic formulation of Browder–Gohde fixed point theorem. *Axioms* **2021**, *10*, 285. [CrossRef]
20. Shukla, S.; Rodrıguez-Lopez, R. Fixed points of multi-valued relation-theoretic contractions in metric spaces and application. *Quaest. Math.* **2020**, *43*, 409–424. [CrossRef]
21. Senapati, T.; Dey, L.K. Relation-theoretic metrical fixed-point results via w-distance with applications. *J. Fixed Point Theory Appl.* **2017**, *19*, 2945–2961. [CrossRef]
22. Nadler, S.B., Jr. Sequences of contractions and fixed points. *Pacific J. Math.* **1968**, *27*, 579–585. [CrossRef]
23. Bonsall, F.F. *Lectures on Some Fixed Point Theorems of Functional Analysis*; Tata Institute of Fundamental Research: Bombay, India, 1962.
24. Dey, D.; Fierro, R.; Saha, M. Well-posedness of fixed point theorems. *J. Fixed Point Theory Appl.* **2018**, 20–57.
25. Pant, R.; Mishra, S.N. Stability results for Suzuki contractions with an application to initial value problems. *Filomat* **2018**, *32*, 3297–3304. [CrossRef]
26. Robinson, C. *Dynamical Systems: Stability, Symbolic Dynamics and Chaos*, 2nd ed.; CRC Press: Boca Raton, FL, USA, 1998.
27. Singh, S.L.; Mishra, S.N.; Sinkala, W. A note on fixed point stability for generalized multivalued contractions. *Appl. Math. Lett.* **2012**, *25*, 1708–1710. [CrossRef]

Disclaimer/Publisher's Note: The statements, opinions and data contained in all publications are solely those of the individual author(s) and contributor(s) and not of MDPI and/or the editor(s). MDPI and/or the editor(s) disclaim responsibility for any injury to people or property resulting from any ideas, methods, instructions or products referred to in the content.

Article

Solving Integral Equation and Homotopy Result via Fixed Point Method

Badriah Alamri

Department of Mathematics and Statistics, College of Science, University of Jeddah, Jeddah 23218, Saudi Arabia; baalamri@uj.edu.sa

Abstract: The aim of the present research article is to investigate the existence and uniqueness of a solution to the integral equation and homotopy result. To achieve our objective, we introduce the notion of (α, η, ψ)-contraction in the framework of $\mathfrak{F}$-bipolar metric space and prove some fixed point results for covariant and contravariant mappings. Some coupled fixed point results in $\mathfrak{F}$-bipolar metric space are derived as outcomes of our principal theorems. A non-trivial example is also provided to validate the authenticity of the established results.

Keywords: fixed point; generalized contractions; $\mathfrak{F}$-bipolar metric space; integral equation; homotopy

MSC: 47H10; 46S40; 54H25

Citation: Alamri, B. Solving Integral Equation and Homotopy Result via Fixed Point Method. *Mathematics* **2023**, *11*, 4408. https://doi.org/10.3390/math11214408

Academic Editor: Timilehin Opeyemi Alakoya

Received: 15 September 2023
Revised: 9 October 2023
Accepted: 11 October 2023
Published: 24 October 2023

Copyright: © 2023 by the author. Licensee MDPI, Basel, Switzerland. This article is an open access article distributed under the terms and conditions of the Creative Commons Attribution (CC BY) license (https://creativecommons.org/licenses/by/4.0/).

1. Introduction

In pure mathematics, one of the most well-known and classical theories is fixed point theory, which has vast applications in various fields. The fundamental and inaugural result in the aforementioned theory is the Banach fixed point theorem [1], which is an attractive and effective tool in investigating existence problems. Over the years, it has been generalized in different directions by several mathematicians. Recently, Samet et al. [2] initiated the conception of α-admissibility and α-ψ-contractions in complete metric spaces and presented some fixed point problems for the aforementioned mappings. Subsequently, Salimi et al. [3] modified these ideas of α-admissibility and α-ψ-contractions and established new fixed point theorems for such mappings in complete metric space.

In all the above outcomes, the idea of metric space represents a crucial and significant aspect, which was introduced by Frechet [4] in 1906. Later on, various researchers extended the notion of metric space by considering the metric postulates or changing its range and domain (see [5–8]). Jleli et al. [9] introduced a fascinating generalization of classical metric space, b-metric space and Branciari metric space, which is well known as an $\mathfrak{F}$-metric space. Subsequently, Hussain et al. [10] employed the idea of $\mathfrak{F}$-metric space ($\mathfrak{F}$-MS) and demonstrated a number of results for (β, ψ)-contractions.

We take the distance between members of only one set in all these generalizations of metric space. Thus, a question arises: how can the distance between members of two different sets be analyzed? Such questions of computing the distance can be considered in different fields. Mutlu et al. [11] presented the idea of bipolar metric space (bip MS) to address such matters. Moreover, this up-to-date conception of bip MS leads to the evolution and advancement of fixed point theorems. In due course, Mutlu et al. [12] established coupled fixed point results in the framework of bip MS. Kishore et al. [13] extended the concept of coupled fixed point to common coupled fixed point and presented an application of it. Rao et al. [14] proved common coupled fixed point results for Geraghty-type contractions and applied their result to homotopy theory. Gürdal et al. [15] utilized the notion of bip MS to obtain fixed point theorems for (α, ψ)-contractions. A significant task relates to the existence of fixed points in the setting of bip MS (see [16–20]). Rawat et al. [21]

unified the above two important notions, specifically $\mathfrak{F}$-MS and bip MS, and introduced the notion of $\mathfrak{F}$-bipolar metric space ($\mathfrak{F}$-bip MS) and presented some results.

In the present research article, we introduce the notion of (α, η, ψ)-contraction against the background of $\mathfrak{F}$-bipolar metric space and establish fixed point results for covariant and contravariant mappings. As a consequence, we derive some coupled fixed point results in $\mathfrak{F}$-bipolar metric spaces. An integral equation is explored as an application of our principal result.

2. Preliminaries

The conventional Banach fixed point theorem [1] is given in the following way.

Theorem 1 ([1]). *Let $(\mathcal{S}, \eth)$ be a complete metric space (CMS) and let $\mathcal{B} : \mathcal{S} \to \mathcal{S}$. If there exists $\lambda \in [0, 1)$ such that*
$$\eth(\mathcal{B}\mathfrak{w}, \mathcal{B}\hbar) \leq \lambda \eth(\mathfrak{w}, \hbar),$$
for all $\mathfrak{w}, \hbar \in \mathcal{S}$, then $\mathcal{B}$ has a unique fixed point.

Samet et al. [2] initiated the following concepts.

Definition 1. *Let Ψ be a family of mappings $\psi : [0, +\infty) \to [0, +\infty)$ satisfying the following conditions:*
(ψ_1) ψ is nondecreasing,
(ψ_2) $\sum_{\imath=1}^{\infty} \psi^\imath(t) < +\infty$, for all $t > 0$, where $\psi^\imath$ is the $\imath$-th iterate of ψ.

Lemma 1. *If $\psi \in \Psi$, then, for each $t > 0$, $\psi(t) < t$ and $\psi(0) = 0$.*

Definition 2 ([2]). *Let $\alpha : \mathcal{S} \times \mathcal{S} \to [0, +\infty)$ be any function. A mapping $\mathcal{B} : \mathcal{S} \to \mathcal{S}$ is said to be an α-admissible if*
$$\alpha(\mathfrak{w}, \hbar) \geq 1 \implies \alpha(\mathcal{B}\mathfrak{w}, \mathcal{B}\hbar) \geq 1,$$
for all $\mathfrak{w}, \hbar \in \mathcal{S}$.

Definition 3 ([2]). *Let $(\mathcal{S}, \eth)$ be a metric space. A mapping $\mathcal{B} : \mathcal{S} \to \mathcal{S}$ is said to be (α, ψ)-contraction if there exist some $\alpha : \mathcal{S} \times \mathcal{S} \to [0, +\infty)$ and $\psi \in \Psi$ such that*
$$\alpha(\mathfrak{w}, \hbar)\eth(\mathcal{B}\mathfrak{w}, \mathcal{B}\hbar) \leq \psi(\eth(\mathfrak{w}, \hbar)),$$
for all $\mathfrak{w}, \hbar \in \mathcal{S}$.

Jleli et al. [9] presented an impressive extension of MS as follows.
Let $\mathfrak{F}$ be the class of mappings $f : (0, +\infty) \to \mathbb{R}$ fulfilling the following assertions:
($\mathcal{F}_1$) $f(t) < f(s)$, for $t < s$,
($\mathcal{F}_2$) for each sequence $\{t_\imath\} \subseteq \mathbb{R}^+$, $\lim_{\imath \to \infty} t_\imath = 0 \iff \lim_{\imath \to \infty} f(t_\imath) = -\infty$.

Definition 4 ([9]). *Let $\mathcal{S} \neq \varnothing$ and let $\eth : \mathcal{S} \times \mathcal{S} \to [0, +\infty)$. Assume that there exist $(f, \kappa) \in \mathfrak{F} \times [0, +\infty)$ such that for all $(\mathfrak{w}, \hbar) \in \mathcal{S} \times \mathcal{S}$,*
(i) $\eth(\mathfrak{w}, \hbar) = 0 \iff \mathfrak{w} = \hbar$,
(ii) $\eth(\mathfrak{w}, \hbar) = \eth(\hbar, \mathfrak{w})$,
(iii) for every $(u_\imath)_{\imath=1}^{p} \subset \mathcal{S}$ with $(u_1, u_p) = (\mathfrak{w}, \hbar)$, we have
$$\eth(\mathfrak{w}, \hbar) > 0 \Rightarrow f(\eth(\mathfrak{w}, \hbar)) \leq f\left(\sum_{\imath=1}^{p-1} \eth(u_\imath, u_{\imath+1})\right) + \kappa,$$
for $p \geq 2$ and $p \in \mathbb{N}$. Then, $\eth$ is said to be an $\mathfrak{F}$-metric on $\mathcal{S}$ and $(\mathcal{S}, \eth)$ is said to be an $\mathfrak{F}$-MS.

Example 1 ([9]). *Let* $\mathcal{S}=\mathbb{R}$, $f(t) = \ln(t)$ *and* $\kappa = \ln(3)$. *Define* $\eth : \mathcal{S} \times \mathcal{S} \to [0, +\infty)$ *by*

$$\eth(\mathrm{w}, \hbar) = \begin{cases} (\mathrm{w} - \hbar)^2 & \text{if } (\mathrm{w}, \hbar) \in [0,3] \times [0,3] \\ |\mathrm{w} - \hbar| & \text{if } (\mathrm{w}, \hbar) \notin [0,3] \times [0,3] \end{cases},$$

and $(\mathcal{S}, \eth)$ *is an* $\mathfrak{F}$-*MS*.

Mutlu et al. [11] introduced the idea of bipolar metric space (bip MS) in the following manner.

Definition 5 ([11]). *Let* $\mathcal{S} \neq \emptyset$ *and* $\mathcal{T} \neq \emptyset$ *and let* $\eth : \mathcal{S} \times \mathcal{T} \to [0, +\infty)$ *satisfy*

(bi_1) $\eth(\mathrm{w}, \hbar) = 0 \iff \mathrm{w} = \hbar$,
(bi_2) $\eth(\mathrm{w}, \hbar) = \eth(\hbar, \mathrm{w})$, *if* $\mathrm{w}, \hbar \in \mathcal{S} \cap \mathcal{T}$,
(bi_3) $\eth(\mathrm{w}, \hbar) \leq \eth(\mathrm{w}, \hbar') + \eth(\mathrm{w}', \hbar') + \eth(\mathrm{w}', \hbar)$,

for all $(\mathrm{w}, \hbar), (\mathrm{w}', \hbar') \in \mathcal{S} \times \mathcal{T}$. *Then, the triple* $(\mathcal{S}, \mathcal{T}, \eth)$ *is called a bip MS*.

Example 2 ([11]). *Let* $\mathcal{S}$ *and* $\mathcal{T}$ *be the set of all compact and singleton subsets of* $\mathbb{R}$ *independently. Define* $\eth : \mathcal{S} \times \mathcal{T} \to [0, +\infty)$ *by*

$$\eth(\mathrm{w}, \Xi) = |\mathrm{w} - \inf(\Xi)| + |\mathrm{w} - \sup(\Xi)|,$$

for $\{\mathrm{w}\} \subseteq \mathcal{S}$ *and* $\Xi \subseteq \mathcal{T}$, *and then* $(\mathcal{S}, \mathcal{T}, \eth)$ *is a complete bip MS*.

Definition 6. *Let* $(\mathcal{S}_1, \mathcal{T}_1, \eth_1)$ *and* $(\mathcal{S}_2, \mathcal{T}_2, \eth_2)$ *be two bip MSs. A mapping* $\mathcal{B} : \mathcal{S}_1 \cup \mathcal{T}_1 \rightrightarrows \mathcal{S}_2 \cup \mathcal{T}_2$ *is said to be a covariant mapping, if* $\mathcal{B}(\mathcal{S}_1) \subseteq \mathcal{S}_2$ *and* $\mathcal{B}(\mathcal{T}_1) \subseteq \mathcal{T}_2$. *Similarly, a mapping* $\mathcal{B} : \mathcal{S}_1 \cup \mathcal{T}_1 \rightrightarrows \mathcal{S}_2 \cup \mathcal{T}_2$ *is called a contravariant mapping, if* $\mathcal{B}(\mathcal{S}_1) \subseteq \mathcal{T}_2$ *and* $\mathcal{B}(\mathcal{S}_2) \subseteq \mathcal{T}_1$.

We will symbolize the covariant mapping as $\mathcal{B} : (\mathcal{S}_1, \mathcal{T}_1) \rightrightarrows (\mathcal{S}_2, \mathcal{T}_2)$ and the contravariant mapping as $\mathcal{B} : (\mathcal{S}_1, \mathcal{T}_1) \rightleftarrows (\mathcal{S}_2, \mathcal{T}_2)$.

Rawat et al. [21] unified the above two novel notions, $\mathfrak{F}$-MS and bip MS, and introduced the notion of $\mathfrak{F}$-bipolar metric space ($\mathfrak{F}$-bip MS) in the following way.

Definition 7 ([21]). *Let* $\mathcal{S}$ *and* $\mathcal{T}$ *be nonempty sets and let* $\eth : \mathcal{S} \times \mathcal{T} \to [0, +\infty)$. *Suppose that there exist* $(f, \kappa) \in \mathfrak{F} \times [0, +\infty)$ *such that, for all* $(\mathrm{w}, \hbar) \in \mathcal{S} \times \mathcal{T}$,

(D_1) $\eth(\mathrm{w}, \hbar) = 0 \iff \mathrm{w} = \hbar$,
(D_2) $\eth(\mathrm{w}, \hbar) = \eth(\hbar, \mathrm{w})$, *if* $\mathrm{w}, \hbar \in \mathcal{S} \cap \mathcal{T}$,
(D_3) *for every* $(u_\iota)_{\iota=1}^p \subset \mathcal{S}$ *and* $(v_\iota)_{\iota=1}^p \subset \mathcal{T}$ *with* $(u_1, v_p) = (\mathrm{w}, \hbar)$, *we have*

$$\eth(\mathrm{w}, \hbar) > 0 \Rightarrow f(\eth(\mathrm{w}, \hbar)) \leq f\left(\sum_{\iota=1}^{p-1} \eth(u_{\iota+1}, v_\iota) + \sum_{\iota=1}^{p} \eth(u_\iota, v_\iota)\right) + \kappa,$$

for $p \geq 2$ *and* $p \in \mathbb{N}$. *Then,* $(\mathcal{S}, \mathcal{T}, \eth)$ *is called an* $\mathfrak{F}$-*bip MS*.

Example 3. *Let* $\mathcal{S} = \{1, 2\}$ *and* $\mathcal{T} = \{2, 7\}$. *Define* $\eth : \mathcal{S} \times \mathcal{T} \to [0, +\infty)$ *by*

$$\eth(1, 2) = 6, \eth(1, 7) = 10, \eth(2, 7) = 2, \eth(2, 2) = 0,$$

and then $\eth$ *satisfies all the conditions of an* $\mathfrak{F}$-*bip metric with* $\kappa = 0$ *and* $f(t) = \ln t$, *for* $t > 0$. *Thus,* $(\mathcal{S}, \mathcal{T}, \eth)$ *is an* $\mathfrak{F}$-*bip MS but not a bip MS*.

Remark 1 ([21]). *Taking* $\mathcal{T} = \mathcal{S}$, $p = 2\iota$, $u_j = u_{2j-1}$ *and* $v_j = u_{2j}$ *in the above definition (7), we obtain a sequence* $(u_j)_{j=1}^{2\iota} \in \mathcal{S}$ *with* $(u_1, u_{2\iota}) = (\mathrm{w}, \hbar)$ *such that condition (iii) of Definition 4 holds. Thus, every* $\mathfrak{F}$-*MS is an* $\mathfrak{F}$-*bip MS but the converse is not true in general*.

Definition 8 ([21]). *Let $(\mathcal{S}, \mathcal{T}, \eth)$ be an $\mathfrak{F}$-bip MS.*

(i) *An element $\mathfrak{w} \in \mathcal{S} \cup \mathcal{T}$ is called a left point if $\mathfrak{w} \in \mathcal{S}$ and $\mathfrak{w} \in \mathcal{S} \cup \mathcal{T}$ is called a right point if $\mathfrak{w} \in \mathcal{T}$. Moreover, $\mathfrak{w}$ is called a central point if it is both a left and right point.*

(ii) *A sequence $(\mathfrak{w}_\iota)$ on $\mathcal{S}$ is said to be a left sequence and $(\hbar_\iota)$ on $\mathcal{T}$ is called a right sequence. A left sequence or a right sequence is called a sequence in an $\mathfrak{F}$-bip MS.*

(iii) *The sequence $(\mathfrak{w}_\iota)$ converges to a point $\mathfrak{w}$, if and only if $(\mathfrak{w}_\iota)$ is a left sequence, $\mathfrak{w}$ is a right point and $\lim_{\iota \to \infty} \eth(\mathfrak{w}_\iota, \mathfrak{w}) = 0$ or $(\mathfrak{w}_\iota)$ is a right sequence, $\mathfrak{w}$ is a left point and $\lim_{\iota \to \infty} \eth(\mathfrak{w}, \mathfrak{w}_\iota) = 0$. A bisequence $(\mathfrak{w}_\iota, \hbar_\iota)$ on $(\mathcal{S}, \mathcal{T}, \eth)$ is a sequence on the set $\mathcal{S} \times \mathcal{T}$. If $(\mathfrak{w}_\iota)$ and $(\hbar_\iota)$ are convergent, then the bisequence $(\mathfrak{w}_\iota, \hbar_\iota)$ is also convergent, and if $(\mathfrak{w}_\iota)$ and $(\hbar_\iota)$ converge to a common element, then the bisequence $(\mathfrak{w}_\iota, \hbar_\iota)$ is said to be biconvergent.*

(iv) *A bisequence $(\mathfrak{w}_\iota, \hbar_\iota)$ in an $\mathfrak{F}$-bip MS $(\mathcal{S}, \mathcal{T}, \eth)$ is called a Cauchy bisequence if, for each $\epsilon > 0$, there exists $\iota_0 \in \mathbb{N}$, such that $\eth(\mathfrak{w}_\iota, \hbar_p) < \epsilon$, for all $\iota, p \geq \iota_0$.*

Definition 9 ([21]). *An $\mathfrak{F}$-bip MS $(\mathcal{S}, \mathcal{T}, \eth)$ is said to be complete, if every Cauchy bisequence in $(\mathcal{S}, \mathcal{T}, \eth)$ is convergent.*

3. Fixed Point Results for Covariant Mappings

Definition 10. *Let $\alpha : \mathcal{S} \times \mathcal{T} \to [0, +\infty)$ be any function. A mapping $\mathcal{B} : (\mathcal{S}, \mathcal{T}, \eth) \rightrightarrows (\mathcal{S}, \mathcal{T}, \eth)$ is said to be covariant α-admissible if*

$$\alpha(\mathfrak{w}, \hbar) \geq 1 \implies \alpha(\mathcal{B}\mathfrak{w}, \mathcal{B}\hbar) \geq 1, \tag{1}$$

for all $(\mathfrak{w}, \hbar) \in \mathcal{S} \times \mathcal{T}$.

Example 4. *Let $\mathcal{S} = [0, +\infty)$ and $\mathcal{T} = (-\infty, 0]$ and $\alpha : \mathcal{S} \times \mathcal{T} \to [0, +\infty)$ is defined as*

$$\alpha(\mathfrak{w}, \hbar) = \begin{cases} 1, & \text{if } \mathfrak{w} \neq \hbar, \\ 0, & \text{if } \mathfrak{w} = \hbar. \end{cases}$$

A covariant mapping $\mathcal{B} : (\mathcal{S}, \mathcal{T}, \eth) \rightrightarrows (\mathcal{S}, \mathcal{T}, \eth)$ defined by $\mathcal{B}(\mathfrak{w}) = \mathfrak{w}$ is covariant α-admissible.

Definition 11. *Let $(\mathcal{S}, \mathcal{T}, \eth)$ be an $\mathfrak{F}$-bip MS and $\mathcal{B} : (\mathcal{S}, \mathcal{T}, \eth) \rightleftarrows (\mathcal{S}, \mathcal{T}, \eth)$ is a covariant mapping. A mapping $\mathcal{B} : (\mathcal{S}, \mathcal{T}, \eth) \rightrightarrows (\mathcal{S}, \mathcal{T}, \eth)$ is said to be covariant α-admissible with respect to η if there exist the functions $\alpha, \eta : \mathcal{S} \times \mathcal{T} \to [0, +\infty)$ such that*

$$\alpha(\mathfrak{w}, \hbar) \geq \eta(\mathfrak{w}, \hbar) \text{ implies } \alpha(\mathcal{B}\mathfrak{w}, \mathcal{B}\hbar) \geq \eta(\mathcal{B}\mathfrak{w}, \mathcal{B}\hbar),$$

for all $(\mathfrak{w}, \hbar) \in \mathcal{S} \times \mathcal{T}$.

Remark 2. *If we take $\eta(\mathfrak{w}, \hbar) = 1$, then this Definition 14 reduces to Definition 13. Moreover, if we take $\alpha(\mathfrak{w}, \hbar) = 1$, then we can say that $\mathcal{B}$ is an η-subadmissible mapping.*

Definition 12. *Let $(\mathcal{S}, \mathcal{T}, \eth)$ be an $\mathfrak{F}$-bip MS. A mapping $\mathcal{B} : (\mathcal{S}, \mathcal{T}, \eth) \rightrightarrows (\mathcal{S}, \mathcal{T}, \eth)$ is said to be a covariant (α, η, ψ)-contraction if $\mathcal{B}$ is covariant and there exist two functions $\alpha, \eta : \mathcal{S} \times \mathcal{T} \to [0, +\infty)$ and $\psi \in \Psi$ such that*

$$\alpha(\mathfrak{w}, \hbar) \geq \eta(\mathfrak{w}, \hbar) \implies \eth(\mathcal{B}\hbar, \mathcal{B}\mathfrak{w}) \leq \psi(\eth(\mathfrak{w}, \hbar)), \tag{2}$$

for all $(\mathfrak{w}, \hbar) \in \mathcal{S} \times \mathcal{T}$.

Remark 3. *A mapping $\mathcal{B} : (\mathcal{S}, \mathcal{T}, \eth) \rightrightarrows (\mathcal{S}, \mathcal{T}, \eth)$ satisfying the Banach contraction in $\mathfrak{F}$-bipolar metric space $(\mathcal{S}, \mathcal{T}, \eth)$ is a covariant (α, η, ψ)-contraction with*

$$\alpha(\mathfrak{w}, \hbar) = \eta(\mathfrak{w}, \hbar) = 1,$$

for all $(\mathfrak{w}, \hbar) \in \mathcal{S} \times \mathcal{T}$ and $\psi(t) = kt$, for some $k \in [0, 1)$ and for $t \geq 1$.

(P) there exists $z \in \mathcal{S} \cap \mathcal{T}$ such that $\alpha(\mathfrak{w}, z) \geq 1$ and $\alpha(z, \hbar) \geq 1$ for all $(\mathfrak{w}, \hbar) \in \mathcal{S} \times \mathcal{T}$.

Theorem 2. *Let $(\mathcal{S}, \mathcal{T}, \eth)$ be a complete $\mathfrak{F}$-bip MS and let $\mathcal{B} : (\mathcal{S}, \mathcal{T}, \eth) \rightrightarrows (\mathcal{S}, \mathcal{T}, \eth)$ be a covariant (α, η, ψ)-contraction. Assume that the following assertions hold:*

(i) $\mathcal{B}$ is covariant α-admissible with respect to η,
(ii) there exists $\mathfrak{w}_0 \in \mathcal{S}, \hbar_0 \in \mathcal{T}$ such that $\alpha(\mathfrak{w}_0, \hbar_0) \geq \eta(\mathfrak{w}_0, \hbar_0)$ and $\alpha(\mathfrak{w}_0, \mathcal{B}\hbar_0) \geq \eta(\mathfrak{w}_0, \mathcal{B}\hbar_0)$,
(iii) $\mathcal{B}$ is continuous or, if $(\mathfrak{w}_\iota, \hbar_\iota)$ is a bisequence in $(\mathcal{S}, \mathcal{T}, \eth)$ such that $\alpha(\mathfrak{w}_\iota, \hbar_\iota) \geq \eta(\mathfrak{w}_\iota, \hbar_\iota)$, for all $\iota \in \mathbb{N}$ with $\mathfrak{w}_\iota \to \omega$ and $\hbar_\iota \to \omega$, as $\iota \to \infty$ for $\omega \in \mathcal{S} \cap \mathcal{T}$, then $\alpha(\omega, \hbar_\iota) \geq \eta(\omega, \hbar_\iota)$, for all $\iota \in \mathbb{N}$.

Then, the mapping $\mathcal{B} : (\mathcal{S}, \mathcal{T}, \eth) \rightrightarrows (\mathcal{S}, \mathcal{T}, \eth)$ has a fixed point. Furthermore, if the property (P) holds, then the fixed point is unique.

Proof. Let $\mathfrak{w}_0$ and $\hbar_0$ be arbitrary points in $\mathcal{S}$ and $\mathcal{T}$, respectively, and suppose that $\alpha(\mathfrak{w}_0, \hbar_0) \geq \eta(\mathfrak{w}_0, \hbar_0)$ and $\alpha(\mathfrak{w}_0, \mathcal{B}\hbar_0) \geq \eta(\mathfrak{w}_0, \mathcal{B}\hbar_0)$. Define the bisequence $(\mathfrak{w}_\iota, \hbar_\iota)$ in $(\mathcal{S}, \mathcal{T}, \eth)$ by

$$\mathfrak{w}_{\iota+1} = \mathcal{B}\mathfrak{w}_\iota \text{ and } \hbar_{\iota+1} = \mathcal{B}\hbar_\iota,$$

for all $\iota \in \mathbb{N}$. As $\mathcal{B}$ is a covariant α-admissible mapping with respect to η, we have

$$\alpha(\mathfrak{w}_0, \hbar_0) \geq \eta(\mathfrak{w}_0, \hbar_0),$$

which implies

$$\alpha(\mathfrak{w}_1, \hbar_1) = \alpha(\mathcal{B}\mathfrak{w}_0, \mathcal{B}\hbar_0) \geq \eta(\mathcal{B}\mathfrak{w}_0, \mathcal{B}\hbar_0) = \eta(\mathfrak{w}_1, \hbar_1).$$

and

$$\alpha(\mathfrak{w}_0, \hbar_1) = \alpha(\mathfrak{w}_0, \mathcal{B}\hbar_0) \geq \eta(\mathfrak{w}_0, \mathcal{B}\hbar_0) = \eta(\mathfrak{w}_0, \hbar_1),$$

which implies

$$\alpha(\mathfrak{w}_1, \hbar_2) = \alpha(\mathcal{B}\mathfrak{w}_0, \mathcal{B}\hbar_1) \geq \eta(\mathcal{B}\mathfrak{w}_0, \mathcal{B}\hbar_1) = \eta(\mathfrak{w}_1, \hbar_2).$$

Similarly,

$$\alpha(\mathfrak{w}_1, \hbar_1) = \alpha(\mathcal{B}\mathfrak{w}_0, \mathcal{B}\hbar_0) \geq \eta(\mathcal{B}\mathfrak{w}_0, \mathcal{B}\hbar_0) = \eta(\mathfrak{w}_1, \hbar_1),$$

which implies

$$\alpha(\mathfrak{w}_2, \hbar_2) = \alpha(\mathcal{B}\mathfrak{w}_1, \mathcal{B}\hbar_1) \geq \eta(\mathcal{B}\mathfrak{w}_1, \mathcal{B}\hbar_1) = \eta(\mathfrak{w}_2, \hbar_2),$$

and

$$\alpha(\mathfrak{w}_1, \hbar_2) = \alpha(\mathcal{B}\mathfrak{w}_0, \mathcal{B}\hbar_1) \geq \eta(\mathcal{B}\mathfrak{w}_0, \mathcal{B}\hbar_1) = \eta(\mathfrak{w}_1, \hbar_2),$$

which implies

$$\alpha(\mathfrak{w}_2, \hbar_3) = \alpha(\mathcal{B}\mathfrak{w}_1, \mathcal{B}\hbar_2) \geq \eta(\mathcal{B}\mathfrak{w}_1, \mathcal{B}\hbar_2) = \eta(\mathfrak{w}_2, \hbar_3).$$

Likewise,

$$\alpha(\mathfrak{w}_2, \hbar_2) = \alpha(\mathcal{B}\mathfrak{w}_1, \mathcal{B}\hbar_1) \geq \eta(\mathcal{B}\mathfrak{w}_1, \mathcal{B}\hbar_1) = \eta(\mathfrak{w}_2, \hbar_2),$$

which implies

$$\alpha(\mathfrak{w}_3, \hbar_3) = \alpha(\mathcal{B}\mathfrak{w}_2, \mathcal{B}\hbar_2) \geq \eta(\mathcal{B}\mathfrak{w}_2, \mathcal{B}\hbar_2) = \eta(\mathfrak{w}_3, \hbar_3).$$

Continuing in this way, we have

$$\alpha(\mathfrak{w}_{\iota+1}, \hbar_\iota) \geq \eta(\mathfrak{w}_{\iota+1}, \hbar_\iota) \text{ and } \alpha(\mathfrak{w}_{\iota+1}, \hbar_{\iota+1}) \geq \eta(\mathfrak{w}_{\iota+1}, \hbar_{\iota+1}), \qquad (3)$$

for all $\imath \in \mathbb{N}$. Now, by (2) and (3), we have

$$\eth(\mathfrak{w}_\imath, \hbar_{\imath+1}) = \eth(\mathcal{B}\mathfrak{w}_{\imath-1}, \mathcal{B}\hbar_\imath) \leq \eth(\mathcal{B}\mathfrak{w}_{\imath-1}, \mathcal{B}\hbar_\imath) \leq \psi(\eth(\mathfrak{w}_{\imath-1}, \hbar_\imath)) \qquad (4)$$

for all $\imath \in \mathbb{N}$. Additionally,

$$\eth(\mathfrak{w}_{\imath+1}, \hbar_{\imath+1}) = \eth(\mathcal{B}\mathfrak{w}_\imath, \mathcal{B}\hbar_\imath) \leq \eth(\mathcal{B}\mathfrak{w}_\imath, \mathcal{B}\hbar_\imath) \leq \psi(\eth(\mathfrak{w}_\imath, \hbar_\imath)), \qquad (5)$$

for all $\imath \in \mathbb{N}$. By (4) and mathematical induction, we obtain

$$\eth(\mathfrak{w}_\imath, \hbar_{\imath+1}) \leq \psi(\eth(\mathfrak{w}_{\imath-1}, \hbar_\imath)) \leq \psi(\psi(\eth(\mathfrak{w}_{\imath-2}, \hbar_{\imath-1}))) \leq \ldots \leq \psi^\imath(\eth(\mathfrak{w}_0, \hbar_1)). \qquad (6)$$

Similarly, by (5) and mathematical induction, we obtain

$$\eth(\mathfrak{w}_{\imath+1}, \hbar_{\imath+1}) \leq \psi(\eth(\mathfrak{w}_\imath, \hbar_\imath)) \leq \psi(\psi(\eth(\mathfrak{w}_{\imath-1}, \hbar_{\imath-1}))) \leq \ldots \leq \psi^{\imath+1}(\eth(\mathfrak{w}_0, \hbar_0)), \qquad (7)$$

for all $\imath \in \mathbb{N}$. Let $(f, \kappa) \in \mathfrak{F} \times [0, \infty)$ be such that (D_3) is satisfied. Let $\epsilon > 0$ be fixed. By $(\mathfrak{F}_2)$, there exists $\delta > 0$ such that

$$0 < t < \delta \implies f(t) < f(\epsilon) - \kappa. \qquad (8)$$

Let there exist $\epsilon > 0$ and $\imath(\epsilon) \in \mathbb{N}$ such that

$$\sum_{\imath \geq \imath(\epsilon)} \psi^\imath(\eth(\mathfrak{w}_0, \hbar_1)) < \frac{\epsilon}{2},$$

and

$$\sum_{\imath \geq \imath(\epsilon)} \psi^{\imath+1}(\eth(\mathfrak{w}_0, \hbar_0)) < \frac{\epsilon}{2}.$$

Now, for $p > \imath \geq \imath(\epsilon)$, by applying (D_3), we have that $\eth(\mathfrak{w}_\imath, \hbar_p) > 0$ implies

$$\begin{aligned}
f(\eth(\mathfrak{w}_\imath, \hbar_p)) &\leq f\left(\begin{array}{c}\eth(\mathfrak{w}_\imath, \hbar_{\imath+1}) + \eth(\mathfrak{w}_{\imath+1}, \hbar_{\imath+1}) + \eth(\mathfrak{w}_{\imath+1}, \hbar_{\imath+2}) + \\ \ldots + \eth(\mathfrak{w}_{p-1}, \hbar_{p-1}) + \eth(\mathfrak{w}_{p-1}, \hbar_p)\end{array}\right) + \kappa \\
&\leq f\left(\sum_{j=\imath}^{p-1} \eth(\mathfrak{w}_j, \hbar_{j+1}) + \sum_{j=\imath}^{p-2} \eth(\mathfrak{w}_{j+1}, \hbar_{j+1})\right) + \kappa \\
&\leq f\left(\sum_{j=\imath}^{p-1} \psi^j(\eth(\mathfrak{w}_0, \hbar_1)) + \sum_{j=\imath}^{p-2} \psi^{\imath+1}(\eth(\mathfrak{w}_0, \hbar_0))\right) + \kappa \\
&\leq f\left(\sum_{\imath \geq \imath(\epsilon)} \psi^\imath(\eth(\mathfrak{w}_0, \hbar_1)) + \sum_{\imath \geq \imath(\epsilon)} \psi^{\imath+1}(\eth(\mathfrak{w}_0, \hbar_0))\right) + \kappa \\
&< f(\epsilon).
\end{aligned}$$

for all $j \in \mathbb{N}$. Similarly, for $\iota > p \geq \iota(\epsilon)$, by applying (D_3), we have that $\mathfrak{d}(\mathfrak{w}_\iota, \hbar_p) > 0$ implies

$$\begin{aligned}
f(\mathfrak{d}(\mathfrak{w}_\iota, \hbar_p)) &\leq f\left(\begin{array}{c}\mathfrak{d}(\mathfrak{w}_p, \hbar_p) + \mathfrak{d}(\mathfrak{w}_p, \hbar_{p+1}) + \mathfrak{d}(\mathfrak{w}_{p+1}, \hbar_{p+1}) + \\ \ldots + \mathfrak{d}(\mathfrak{w}_\iota, \hbar_{\iota+1}) + \mathfrak{d}(\mathfrak{w}_\iota, \hbar_\iota)\end{array}\right) + \kappa \\
&\leq f\left(\sum_{j=p}^{\iota} \mathfrak{d}(\mathfrak{w}_j, \hbar_j) + \sum_{j=\iota}^{\iota} \mathfrak{d}(\mathfrak{w}_j, \hbar_{j+1})\right) + \kappa \\
&\leq f\left(\sum_{j=p}^{\iota} \psi^j(\mathfrak{d}(\mathfrak{w}_0, \hbar_0)) + \sum_{j=p}^{\iota} \psi^{\iota+1}(\mathfrak{d}(\mathfrak{w}_0, \hbar_1))\right) + \kappa \\
&\leq f\left(\sum_{\iota \geq \iota(\epsilon)} \psi^\iota(\mathfrak{d}(\mathfrak{w}_0, \hbar_0)) + \sum_{\iota \geq \iota(\epsilon)} \psi^{\iota+1}(\mathfrak{d}(\mathfrak{w}_0, \hbar_1))\right) + \kappa, \\
&< f(\epsilon)
\end{aligned}$$

for all $j \in \mathbb{N}$. Then, by $(\mathfrak{F}_1)$, $\mathfrak{d}(\mathfrak{w}_\iota, \hbar_p) < \epsilon$, for all $p, \iota \geq \iota_0$. Thus, $(\mathfrak{w}_\iota, \hbar_\iota)$ is a Cauchy bisequence in $(\mathcal{S}, \mathcal{T}, \mathfrak{d})$. As $(\mathcal{S}, \mathcal{T}, \mathfrak{d})$ is complete, $(\mathfrak{w}_\iota, \hbar_\iota)$ biconverges to a point $\omega \in \mathcal{S} \cap \mathcal{T}$. Thus, $(\mathfrak{w}_\iota) \to \omega$, $(\hbar_\iota) \to \omega$. Moreover, as $\mathcal{B}$ is continuous, we obtain

$$(\mathfrak{w}_\iota) \to \omega \implies (\mathfrak{w}_{\iota+1}) = (\mathcal{B}\mathfrak{w}_\iota) \to \mathcal{B}\omega.$$

Additionally, since $(\hbar_\iota)$ has a limit ω in $\mathcal{S} \cap \mathcal{T}$. Since the limit is unique in $\mathfrak{F}$-bip MS, $\mathcal{B}\omega = \omega$. Thus, $\mathcal{B}$ has a fixed point.

As a bisequence $(\mathfrak{w}_\iota, \hbar_\iota)$ in $(\mathcal{S}, \mathcal{T}, \mathfrak{d})$ is such that $\alpha(\mathfrak{w}_\iota, \hbar_\iota) \geq \eta(\mathfrak{w}_\iota, \hbar_\iota)$, for all $\iota \in \mathbb{N}$ with $\mathfrak{w}_\iota \to \omega$ and $\hbar_\iota \to \omega$, as $\iota \to \infty$ for $\omega \in \mathcal{S} \cap \mathcal{T}$, then, by hypothesis (iii), we have $\alpha(\omega, \hbar_\iota) \geq \alpha(\omega, \hbar_\iota)$, for all $\iota \in \mathbb{N}$. Now, by (19), we have

$$\begin{aligned}
f(\mathfrak{d}(\mathcal{B}\omega, \omega)) &\leq f(\mathfrak{d}(\mathcal{B}\omega, \mathcal{B}\hbar_\iota) + \mathfrak{d}(\mathcal{B}\mathfrak{w}_\iota, \mathcal{B}\hbar_\iota) + \mathfrak{d}(\mathcal{B}\mathfrak{w}_\iota, \omega)) + \kappa \\
&\leq f(\alpha(\omega, \hbar_\iota)\mathfrak{d}(\mathcal{B}\omega, \mathcal{B}\hbar_\iota) + (\mathcal{B}\mathfrak{w}_\iota, \mathcal{B}\hbar_\iota) + \mathfrak{d}(\mathfrak{w}_{\iota+1}, \omega)) + \kappa \\
&\leq f(\psi(\mathfrak{d}(\omega, \hbar_\iota)) + \psi(\mathfrak{d}(\mathfrak{w}_\iota, \hbar_\iota)) + \mathfrak{d}(\mathfrak{w}_{\iota+1}, \omega)) + \kappa \\
&\leq f\left(\begin{array}{c}\psi(\mathfrak{d}(\omega, \hbar_\iota)) \\ +\psi\left(\begin{array}{c}\mathfrak{d}(\mathfrak{w}_\iota, \omega) \\ +\mathfrak{d}(\omega, \omega) + \mathfrak{d}(\omega, \hbar_\iota)\end{array}\right) + \mathfrak{d}(\mathfrak{w}_{\iota+1}, \omega)\end{array}\right) + \kappa.
\end{aligned}$$

Taking the limit as $\iota \to \infty$ and using the continuity of f and ψ at $t = 0$, we have $\mathfrak{d}(\mathcal{B}\omega, \omega) = 0$. Thus, $\mathcal{B}\omega = \omega$. Hence, $\mathcal{B}$ has a fixed point.

Now, if ϖ is another fixed point of $\mathcal{B}$, then $\mathcal{B}\varpi = \varpi$ implies that $\varpi \in \mathcal{S} \cap \mathcal{T}$ such that $\omega \neq \varpi$. Then, by the property (P), there exists $z \in \mathcal{S} \cap \mathcal{T}$ such that

$$\alpha(\omega, z) \geq \eta(\omega, z) \text{ and } \alpha(z, \varpi) \geq \eta(z, \varpi). \tag{9}$$

Since $\mathcal{B}$ is a covariant α-admissible mapping with respect to η, by (9), we have

$$\alpha(\omega, \mathcal{B}^\iota z) \geq \eta(\omega, \mathcal{B}^\iota z) \text{ and } \alpha(\mathcal{B}^\iota z, \varpi) \geq \eta(\mathcal{B}^\iota z, \varpi), \tag{10}$$

for all $\iota \in \mathbb{N}$. Now, by $(\mathfrak{F}_1)$ and (2), we have

$$\begin{aligned}
f(\mathfrak{d}(\omega, \mathcal{B}^\iota z)) &\leq f\left(\mathfrak{d}\left(\mathcal{B}\omega, \mathcal{B}\left(\mathcal{B}^{\iota-1} z\right)\right)\right) \\
&\leq f\left(\mathfrak{d}\left(\mathcal{B}\omega, \mathcal{B}\mathcal{B}^{\iota-1} z\right)\right) \\
&\leq f\left(\psi\left(\mathfrak{d}\left(\omega, \mathcal{B}^{\iota-1} z\right)\right)\right) \\
&\leq \ldots \leq f(\psi^\iota(\mathfrak{d}(\omega, z))). \tag{11}
\end{aligned}$$

Similarly, we have

$$\begin{aligned} f(\eth(\mathcal{B}^\imath z,\varpi)) &\leq f\left(\eth\left(\mathcal{B}\left(\mathcal{B}^{\imath-1}z\right),\mathcal{B}\varpi\right)\right) \\ &\leq f\left(\eth\left(\mathcal{B}\left(\mathcal{B}^{\imath-1}z\right),\mathcal{B}\varpi\right)\right) \\ &\leq f\left(\psi\left(\eth\left(\mathcal{B}^{\imath-1}z,\varpi\right)\right)\right) \\ &\leq \ldots \leq f\left(\psi^\imath\left(\eth\left(\mathcal{B}^{\imath-1}z,\varpi\right)\right)\right). \end{aligned} \quad (12)$$

Letting $\imath \to +\infty$ in (11) and (12) and using the continuity of f and ψ, we have

$$\lim_{\imath \to \infty} f(\eth(\omega, \mathcal{B}^\imath z)) = -\infty, \quad (13)$$

and

$$\lim_{\imath \to \infty} f(\eth(\mathcal{B}^\imath z, \varpi)) = -\infty. \quad (14)$$

Thus, from (13) and (14) by $(\mathfrak{F}_2)$, we have

$$\mathcal{B}^\imath z \to \omega \text{ and } \mathcal{B}^\imath z \to \varpi,$$

which is a contradiction because the limit is unique. Hence, $\omega = \varpi \in \mathcal{S} \cap \mathcal{T}$. □

Example 5. *Let $\mathcal{S} = \{9, 10, 18, 20\}$ and $\mathcal{T} = \{3, 5, 11, 18\}$. Define the usual metric $\eth : \mathcal{S} \times \mathcal{T} \to [0, \infty)$ by*

$$\eth(\mathfrak{w}, \hbar) = 2^{|\mathfrak{w} - \hbar|}.$$

Then, $(\mathcal{S}, \mathcal{T}, \eth)$ is a complete $\mathfrak{F}$-bip MS. Define the covariant mapping $\mathcal{B} : \mathcal{S} \cup \mathcal{T} \to \mathcal{S} \cup \mathcal{T}$ by

$$\mathcal{B}(\mathfrak{w}) = \begin{cases} 18, & \text{if } \mathfrak{w} \in \mathcal{S} \cup \{11\} \\ 9, & \text{otherwise.} \end{cases}$$

Then, all the conditions of Theorem 2 are satisfied with $\psi(\mathfrak{t}) = \frac{3}{4}\mathfrak{t}$. Hence, by Theorem 2, $\mathcal{B}$ must have a unique fixed point, which is $18 \in \mathcal{S} \cap \mathcal{T}$.

By taking $\eta(\mathfrak{w}, \hbar) = 1$ in Theorem 2, we have the following result.

Corollary 1. *Let $(\mathcal{S}, \mathcal{T}, \eth)$ be a complete $\mathfrak{F}$-bip MS and let $\mathcal{B} : (\mathcal{S}, \mathcal{T}, \eth) \rightrightarrows (\mathcal{S}, \mathcal{T}, \eth)$ be a covariant mapping. Assume that there exists $\psi \in \Psi$ and $\alpha : \mathcal{S} \times \mathcal{S} \to [0, +\infty)$ such that*

$$\alpha(\mathfrak{w}, \hbar) \geq 1 \implies \eth(\mathcal{B}\mathfrak{w}, \mathcal{B}\hbar) \leq \psi(\eth(\mathfrak{w}, \hbar)),$$

for all $(\mathfrak{w}, \hbar) \in \mathcal{S} \times \mathcal{T}$.

Moreover, suppose that the following postulations hold:
(i) $\mathcal{B}$ is covariant α-admissible,
(ii) there exists $\mathfrak{w}_0 \in \mathcal{S}, \hbar_0 \in \mathcal{T}$ such that $\alpha(\mathfrak{w}_0, \hbar_0) \geq 1$ and $\alpha(\mathfrak{w}_0, \mathcal{B}\hbar_0) \geq 1$,
(iii) $\mathcal{B}$ is continuous or, if $(\mathfrak{w}_\imath, \hbar_\imath)$ is a bisequence in $(\mathcal{S}, \mathcal{T}, \eth)$ such that $\alpha(\mathfrak{w}_\imath, \hbar_\imath) \geq 1$, for $\imath \in \mathbb{N}$ with $\mathfrak{w}_\imath \to \omega$ and $\hbar_\imath \to \omega$, as $\imath \to \infty$ for $\omega \in \mathcal{S} \cap \mathcal{T}$, then $\alpha(\omega, \hbar_\imath) \geq 1$, for $\imath \in \mathbb{N}$.
Then, the mapping $\mathcal{B} : (\mathcal{S}, \mathcal{T}, \eth) \rightrightarrows (\mathcal{S}, \mathcal{T}, \eth)$ has a fixed point.

By taking $\alpha(\mathfrak{w}, \hbar) = 1$ in Theorem 2, we have the following result.

Corollary 2. *Let $(\mathcal{S}, \mathcal{T}, \eth)$ be a complete $\mathfrak{F}$-bip MS and let $\mathcal{B} : (\mathcal{S}, \mathcal{T}, \eth) \rightrightarrows (\mathcal{S}, \mathcal{T}, \eth)$ be a covariant mapping. Assume that there exists $\psi \in \Psi$ and $\eta : \mathcal{S} \times \mathcal{S} \to [0, +\infty)$ such that*

$$\eta(\mathfrak{w}, \hbar) \leq 1 \implies \eth(\mathcal{B}\mathfrak{w}, \mathcal{B}\hbar) \leq \psi(\eth(\mathfrak{w}, \hbar)),$$

for all $(\mathfrak{w}, \hbar) \in \mathcal{S} \times \mathcal{T}$.

Moreover, suppose that the following postulations hold:

(i) $\mathcal{B}$ is covariant η-subadmissible,
(ii) there exists $\mathfrak{w}_0 \in \mathcal{S}, \hbar_0 \in \mathcal{T}$ such that $\eta(\mathfrak{w}_0, \hbar_0) \leq 1$ and $\eta(\mathfrak{w}_0, \mathcal{B}\hbar_0) \leq 1$,
(iii) $\mathcal{B}$ is continuous or, if $(\mathfrak{w}_\imath, \hbar_\imath)$ is a bisequence in $(\mathcal{S}, \mathcal{T}, \eth)$ such that $\eta(\mathfrak{w}_\imath, \hbar_\imath) \leq 1$, for all $\imath \in \mathbb{N}$ with $\mathfrak{w}_\imath \to \omega$ and $\hbar_\imath \to \omega$, as $\imath \to \infty$ for $\omega \in \mathcal{S} \cap \mathcal{T}$, then $\eta(\omega, \hbar_\imath) \leq 1$, for all $\imath \in \mathbb{N}$.

Then, the mapping $\mathcal{B} : (\mathcal{S}, \mathcal{T}, \eth) \rightrightarrows (\mathcal{S}, \mathcal{T}, \eth)$ has a fixed point.

The following result is a direct consequence of Corollary 1.

Corollary 3. Let $(\mathcal{S}, \mathcal{T}, \eth)$ be a complete $\mathfrak{F}$-bip MS and let $\mathcal{B} : (\mathcal{S}, \mathcal{T}, \eth) \rightrightarrows (\mathcal{S}, \mathcal{T}, \eth)$ be a covariant mapping. Assume that there exists $\psi \in \Psi$ and $\alpha : \mathcal{S} \times \mathcal{S} \to [0, +\infty)$ such that

$$\alpha(\mathfrak{w}, \hbar)\eth(\mathcal{B}\mathfrak{w}, \mathcal{B}\hbar) \leq \psi(\eth(\mathfrak{w}, \hbar)),$$

for all $(\mathfrak{w}, \hbar) \in \mathcal{S} \times \mathcal{T}$.

Moreover, suppose that the following postulations hold:

(i) $\mathcal{B}$ is covariant α-admissible,
(ii) there exists $\mathfrak{w}_0 \in \mathcal{S}, \hbar_0 \in \mathcal{T}$ such that $\alpha(\mathfrak{w}_0, \hbar_0) \geq 1$ and $\alpha(\mathfrak{w}_0, \mathcal{B}\hbar_0) \geq 1$,
(ii) $\mathcal{B}$ is continuous or, if $(\mathfrak{w}_\imath, \hbar_\imath)$ is a bisequence in $(\mathcal{S}, \mathcal{T}, \eth)$ such that $\alpha(\mathfrak{w}_\imath, \hbar_\imath) \geq 1$, for $\imath \in \mathbb{N}$ with $\mathfrak{w}_\imath \to \omega$ and $\hbar_\imath \to \omega$, as $\imath \to \infty$ for $\omega \in \mathcal{S} \cap \mathcal{T}$, then $\alpha(\omega, \hbar_\imath) \geq 1$, for all $\imath \in \mathbb{N}$.

Then, the mapping $\mathcal{B} : (\mathcal{S}, \mathcal{T}, \eth) \rightrightarrows (\mathcal{S}, \mathcal{T}, \eth)$ has a fixed point.

Remark 4. If we define $\alpha : \mathcal{S} \times \mathcal{S} \to [0, +\infty)$ by $\alpha(\mathfrak{w}, \hbar) = 1$ and $\psi(t) = kt$, where $0 < k < 1$ in Corollary 3, then we deduce the principal result of Rawat et al. [21].

Remark 5. Taking $f(t) = \ln(t)$, for $t > 0$ and $\kappa = 0$ in Definition 7, then $\mathfrak{F}$-bip MS is reduced to bip MS. Thus, the main result of Gürdal et al. [15] is a direct consequence of the above result.

Remark 6. If we take $\mathcal{S} = \mathcal{T}$ in Definition 7, then the $\mathfrak{F}$-bip MS is reduced to $\mathfrak{F}$-MS and we derive the leading result of Hussain et al. [10] from the above corollary.

Corollary 4. Let $(\mathcal{S}, \mathcal{T}, \eth)$ be a complete $\mathfrak{F}$-bip MS and let $\mathcal{B} : (\mathcal{S}, \mathcal{T}, \eth) \rightrightarrows (\mathcal{S}, \mathcal{T}, \eth)$. Assume that there exist $\psi \in \Psi$, $\alpha : \mathcal{S} \times \mathcal{S} \to [0, +\infty)$ and $\ell > 0$ such that

$$(\alpha(\mathfrak{w}, \hbar) + \ell)^{\eth(\mathcal{B}\mathfrak{w}, \mathcal{B}\hbar)} \leq (1 + \ell)^{\psi(\eth(\mathfrak{w}, \hbar))}, \tag{15}$$

for all $(\mathfrak{w}, \hbar) \in \mathcal{S} \times \mathcal{T}$.

Moreover, suppose that the following postulations hold:

(i) $\mathcal{B}$ is covariant α-admissible,
(ii) there exists $\mathfrak{w}_0 \in \mathcal{S}, \hbar_0 \in \mathcal{T}$ such that $\alpha(\mathfrak{w}_0, \hbar_0) \geq 1$ and $\alpha(\mathfrak{w}_0, \mathcal{B}\hbar_0) \geq 1$,
(iii) $\mathcal{B}$ is continuous or, if $(\mathfrak{w}_\imath, \hbar_\imath)$ is a bisequence in $(\mathcal{S}, \mathcal{T}, \eth)$ such that $\alpha(\mathfrak{w}_\imath, \hbar_\imath) \geq 1$, for all $\imath \in \mathbb{N}$ with $\mathfrak{w}_\imath \to \omega$ and $\hbar_\imath \to \omega$, as $\imath \to \infty$ for $\omega \in \mathcal{S} \cap \mathcal{T}$, then $\alpha(\omega, \hbar_\imath) \geq 1$, for $\imath \in \mathbb{N}$.

Then, the mapping $\mathcal{B} : (\mathcal{S}, \mathcal{T}, \eth) \rightrightarrows (\mathcal{S}, \mathcal{T}, \eth)$ has a fixed point.

Proof. Let $\alpha(\mathfrak{w}, \hbar) \geq 1$. Then, by (15), we have

$$(1 + \ell)^{\eth(\mathcal{B}\mathfrak{w}, \mathcal{B}\hbar)} \leq (\alpha(\mathfrak{w}, \hbar) + \ell)^{\eth(\mathcal{B}\mathfrak{w}, \mathcal{B}\hbar)} \leq (1 + \ell)^{\psi(\eth(\mathfrak{w}, \hbar))},$$

which implies $\eth(\mathcal{B}\mathfrak{w}, \mathcal{B}\hbar) \leq \psi(\eth(\mathfrak{w}, \hbar))$, and all the conditions of Corollary 1 are satisfied and $\mathcal{B} : (\mathcal{S}, \mathcal{T}, \eth) \rightrightarrows (\mathcal{S}, \mathcal{T}, \eth)$ has a fixed point. □

Similarly, we have the following corollary.

Corollary 5. Let $(\mathcal{S}, \mathcal{T}, \eth)$ be a complete $\mathfrak{F}$-bip MS and let $\mathcal{B} : (\mathcal{S}, \mathcal{T}, \eth) \rightrightarrows (\mathcal{S}, \mathcal{T}, \eth)$. Assume that there exist $\psi \in \Psi$, $\alpha : \mathcal{S} \times \mathcal{S} \to [0, +\infty)$ and $\ell > 0$ such that

$$(\eth(\mathcal{B}\mathfrak{w}, \mathcal{B}\hbar) + \ell)^{\alpha(\mathfrak{w}, \hbar)} \leq \psi(\eth(\mathfrak{w}, \hbar)) + \ell, \tag{16}$$

for all $(\mathfrak{w}, \hbar) \in \mathcal{S} \times \mathcal{T}$.

Moreover, suppose that the following postulations hold:
(i) $\mathcal{B}$ is covariant α-admissible,
(ii) there exists $\mathfrak{w}_0 \in \mathcal{S}$, $\hbar_0 \in \mathcal{T}$ such that $\alpha(\mathfrak{w}_0, \hbar_0) \geq 1$ and $\alpha(\mathfrak{w}_0, \mathcal{B}\hbar_0) \geq 1$,
(iii) $\mathcal{B}$ is continuous or, if $(\mathfrak{w}_\imath, \hbar_\imath)$ is a bisequence in $(\mathcal{S}, \mathcal{T}, \eth)$ such that $\alpha(\mathfrak{w}_\imath, \hbar_\imath) \geq 1$, for $\imath \in \mathbb{N}$ with $\mathfrak{w}_\imath \to \omega$ and $\hbar_\imath \to \omega$, as $\imath \to \infty$ for $\omega \in \mathcal{S} \cap \mathcal{T}$, then $\alpha(\omega, \hbar_\imath) \geq 1$, for $\imath \in \mathbb{N}$.

Then, the mapping $\mathcal{B} : (\mathcal{S}, \mathcal{T}, \eth) \rightrightarrows (\mathcal{S}, \mathcal{T}, \eth)$ has a fixed point.

Proof. Let $\alpha(\mathfrak{w}, \hbar) \geq 1$. Then, by (16), we have

$$(\eth(\mathcal{B}\mathfrak{w}, \mathcal{B}\hbar) + \ell) \leq (\eth(\mathcal{B}\mathfrak{w}, \mathcal{B}\hbar) + \ell)^{\alpha(\mathfrak{w}, \hbar)} \leq \psi(\eth(\mathfrak{w}, \hbar)) + \ell,$$

which implies $\eth(\mathcal{B}\mathfrak{w}, \mathcal{B}\hbar) \leq \psi(\eth(\mathfrak{w}, \hbar))$, and all the conditions of Corollary 1 are satisfied and $\mathcal{B} : (\mathcal{S}, \mathcal{T}, \eth) \rightrightarrows (\mathcal{S}, \mathcal{T}, \eth)$ has a fixed point. □

Corollary 6. Let $(\mathcal{S}, \mathcal{T}, \eth)$ be a complete $\mathfrak{F}$-bip MS and let $\mathcal{B} : (\mathcal{S}, \mathcal{T}, \eth) \rightrightarrows (\mathcal{S}, \mathcal{T}, \eth)$ be a covariant and continuous mapping. Assume that there exists $\psi \in \Psi$ such that

$$\eth(\mathcal{B}\mathfrak{w}, \mathcal{B}\hbar) \leq \psi(\eth(\mathfrak{w}, \hbar)),$$

for all $(\mathfrak{w}, \hbar) \in \mathcal{S} \times \mathcal{T}$.

Then, the mapping $\mathcal{B} : (\mathcal{S}, \mathcal{T}, \eth) \rightrightarrows (\mathcal{S}, \mathcal{T}, \eth)$ has a unique fixed point.

Proof. Take $\alpha, \eta : \mathcal{S} \times \mathcal{T} \to [0, +\infty)$ by $\alpha(\mathfrak{w}, \hbar) = \eta(\mathfrak{w}, \hbar) = 1$, for $\mathfrak{w} \in \mathcal{S}$ and $\hbar \in \mathcal{T}$ in Theorem 2. □

Corollary 7. Let $(\mathcal{S}, \mathcal{T}, \eth)$ be a complete $\mathfrak{F}$-bip MS and let $\mathcal{B} : (\mathcal{S}, \mathcal{T}, \eth) \rightrightarrows (\mathcal{S}, \mathcal{T}, \eth)$ be a covariant and continuous mapping. Assume that there exists $0 < k < 1$ such that

$$\eth(\mathcal{B}\mathfrak{w}, \mathcal{B}\hbar) \leq k\eth(\mathfrak{w}, \hbar),$$

for all $(\mathfrak{w}, \hbar) \in \mathcal{S} \times \mathcal{T}$.

Then, the mapping $\mathcal{B} : (\mathcal{S}, \mathcal{T}, \eth) \rightrightarrows (\mathcal{S}, \mathcal{T}, \eth)$ has a unique fixed point.

Proof. Define $\psi : [0, +\infty) \to [0, +\infty)$ by $\psi(t) = kt$, where $0 < k < 1$ and $\alpha, \eta : \mathcal{S} \times \mathcal{T} \to [0, +\infty)$ by $\alpha(\mathfrak{w}, \hbar) = \eta(\mathfrak{w}, \hbar) = 1$, for $\mathfrak{w} \in \mathcal{S}$ and $\hbar \in \mathcal{T}$ in Theorem 2. □

4. Fixed Point Results for Contravariant Mappings

Definition 13. Let $(\mathcal{S}, \mathcal{T}, \eth)$ be an $\mathfrak{F}$-bip MS and $\mathcal{B} : (\mathcal{S}, \mathcal{T}, \eth) \rightleftarrows (\mathcal{S}, \mathcal{T}, \eth)$ is a contravariant mapping. A mapping $\mathcal{B} : (\mathcal{S}, \mathcal{T}, \eth) \rightleftarrows (\mathcal{S}, \mathcal{T}, \eth)$ is said to be contravariant α-admissible if there exists a function $\alpha : \mathcal{S} \times \mathcal{T} \to [0, +\infty)$ such that

$$\alpha(\mathfrak{w}, \hbar) \geq 1 \implies \alpha(\mathcal{B}\hbar, \mathcal{B}\mathfrak{w}) \geq 1, \tag{17}$$

for all $(\mathfrak{w}, \hbar) \in \mathcal{S} \times \mathcal{T}$.

Example 6. Let $\mathcal{S} = [0, +\infty)$ and $\mathcal{T} = (-\infty, 0]$ and $\alpha : \mathcal{S} \times \mathcal{T} \to [0, +\infty)$ is defined as

$$\alpha(\mathfrak{w}, \hbar) = \begin{cases} 1, & \text{if } \mathfrak{w} \neq \hbar, \\ 0, & \text{if } \mathfrak{w} = \hbar. \end{cases}$$

A contravariant mapping $\mathcal{B} : (\mathcal{S}, \mathcal{T}, \eth) \rightleftarrows (\mathcal{S}, \mathcal{T}, \eth)$ *defined by* $\mathcal{B}(\mathfrak{w}) = -\mathfrak{w}$ *is contravariant* α-*admissible.*

Definition 14. *Let* $(\mathcal{S}, \mathcal{T}, \eth)$ *be an* $\mathfrak{F}$-*bip MS and* $\mathcal{B} : (\mathcal{S}, \mathcal{T}, \eth) \rightleftarrows (\mathcal{S}, \mathcal{T}, \eth)$ *is a contravariant mapping. A mapping* $\mathcal{B} : (\mathcal{S}, \mathcal{T}, \eth) \rightleftarrows (\mathcal{S}, \mathcal{T}, \eth)$ *is said to be contravariant* α-*admissible with respect to* η *if there exist two functions* $\alpha, \eta : \mathcal{S} \times \mathcal{T} \to [0, +\infty)$ *such that*

$$\alpha(\mathfrak{w}, \hbar) \geq \eta(\mathfrak{w}, \hbar) \implies \alpha(\mathcal{B}\hbar, \mathcal{B}\mathfrak{w}) \geq \eta(\mathcal{B}\hbar, \mathcal{B}\mathfrak{w}), \tag{18}$$

for all $(\mathfrak{w}, \hbar) \in \mathcal{S} \times \mathcal{T}$.

Definition 15. *Let* $(\mathcal{S}, \mathcal{T}, \eth)$ *be an* $\mathfrak{F}$-*bip MS. A mapping* $\mathcal{B} : (\mathcal{S}, \mathcal{T}, \eth) \rightleftarrows (\mathcal{S}, \mathcal{T}, \eth)$ *is said to be a contravariant* (α, η, ψ)-*contraction if* $\mathcal{B}$ *is contravariant and there exist some* $\alpha, \eta : \mathcal{S} \times \mathcal{T} \to [0, +\infty)$ *and* $\psi \in \Psi$ *such that*

$$\alpha(\mathfrak{w}, \hbar) \eth(\mathcal{B}\hbar, \mathcal{B}\mathfrak{w}) \leq \psi(\eth(\mathfrak{w}, \hbar)), \tag{19}$$

for all $(\mathfrak{w}, \hbar) \in \mathcal{S} \times \mathcal{T}$.

Remark 7. *A mapping* $\mathcal{B} : (\mathcal{S}, \mathcal{T}, \eth) \rightleftarrows (\mathcal{S}, \mathcal{T}, \eth)$ *satisfying the Banach contraction in a* $\mathfrak{F}$-*bip MS* $(\mathcal{S}, \mathcal{T}, \eth)$ *is a contravariant* (α, η, ψ)-*contraction with*

$$\alpha(\mathfrak{w}, \hbar) = \eta(\mathfrak{w}, \hbar) = 1,$$

for all $(\mathfrak{w}, \hbar) \in \mathcal{S} \times \mathcal{T}$ *and* $\psi(t) = kt$, *for some* $k \in [0, 1)$ *and for* $t \geq 1$.

Theorem 3. *Let* $(\mathcal{S}, \mathcal{T}, \eth)$ *be a complete* $\mathfrak{F}$-*bip MS and let* $\mathcal{B} : (\mathcal{S}, \mathcal{T}, \eth) \rightleftarrows (\mathcal{S}, \mathcal{T}, \eth)$ *be a contravariant* (α, η, ψ)-*contraction. Assume that the following postulations hold:*
(i) $\mathcal{B}$ *is contravariant* α-*admissible with respect to* η,
(ii) *there exists* $\mathfrak{w}_0 \in \mathcal{S}$ *such that* $\alpha(\mathfrak{w}_0, \mathcal{B}\mathfrak{w}_0) \geq \eta(\mathfrak{w}_0, \mathcal{B}\mathfrak{w}_0)$,
(iii) $\mathcal{B}$ *is continuous or, if* $(\mathfrak{w}_\imath, \hbar_\imath)$ *is a bisequence in* $(\mathcal{S}, \mathcal{T}, \eth)$ *such that* $\alpha(\mathfrak{w}_\imath, \hbar_\imath) \geq \eta(\mathfrak{w}_\imath, \hbar_\imath)$, *for* $\imath \in \mathbb{N}$ *with* $\mathfrak{w}_\imath \to \omega$ *and* $\hbar_\imath \to \omega$, *as* $\imath \to \infty$ *for* $\omega \in \mathcal{S} \cap \mathcal{T}$, *then* $\alpha(\mathfrak{w}_\imath, \omega) \geq \eta(\mathfrak{w}_\imath, \omega)$, *for* $\imath \in \mathbb{N}$.

Then, the mapping $\mathcal{B} : \mathcal{S} \cup \mathcal{T} \to \mathcal{S} \cup \mathcal{T}$ *has a fixed point. Furthermore, if the property* (P) *holds, then the fixed point is unique.*

Proof. Let $\mathfrak{w}_0$ and $\hbar_0$ be arbitrary points in $\mathcal{S}$ and $\mathcal{T}$, respectively, and suppose that $\alpha(\mathfrak{w}_0, \mathcal{B}\mathfrak{w}_0) \geq \eta(\mathfrak{w}_0, \mathcal{B}\mathfrak{w}_0)$. Define the bisequence $(\mathfrak{w}_\imath, \hbar_\imath)$ in $(\mathcal{S}, \mathcal{T}, \eth)$ by

$$\hbar_\imath = \mathcal{B}\mathfrak{w}_\imath \text{ and } \mathfrak{w}_{\imath+1} = \mathcal{B}\hbar_\imath$$

for all $\imath \in \mathbb{N}$. As $\mathcal{B}$ is a contravariant α-admissible mapping with respect to η, we have

$$\alpha(\mathfrak{w}_0, \hbar_0) = \alpha(\mathfrak{w}_0, \mathcal{B}\mathfrak{w}_0) \geq \eta(\mathfrak{w}_0, \mathcal{B}\mathfrak{w}_0) = \eta(\mathfrak{w}_0, \hbar_0),$$

which implies

$$\alpha(\mathfrak{w}_1, \hbar_0) = \alpha(\mathcal{B}\hbar_0, \mathcal{B}\mathfrak{w}_0) \geq \eta(\mathcal{B}\hbar_0, \mathcal{B}\mathfrak{w}_0) = \eta(\mathfrak{w}_1, \hbar_0),$$

and $\alpha(\mathfrak{w}_1, \hbar_0) \geq \eta(\mathfrak{w}_1, \hbar_0)$ implies

$$\alpha(\mathfrak{w}_1, \hbar_1) = \alpha(\mathcal{B}\hbar_0, \mathcal{B}\mathfrak{w}_1) \geq \eta(\mathcal{B}\hbar_0, \mathcal{B}\mathfrak{w}_1) = \eta(\mathfrak{w}_1, \hbar_1).$$

Similarly, $\alpha(\mathfrak{w}_1, \hbar_1) \geq \eta(\mathfrak{w}_1, \hbar_1)$ implies

$$\alpha(\mathfrak{w}_2, \hbar_1) = \alpha(\mathcal{B}\hbar_1, \mathcal{B}\mathfrak{w}_1) \geq \eta(\mathcal{B}\hbar_1, \mathcal{B}\mathfrak{w}_1) = \eta(\mathfrak{w}_2, \hbar_1),$$

and $\alpha(\mathfrak{w}_2, \hbar_1) \geq \eta(\mathfrak{w}_2, \hbar_1)$ implies

$$\alpha(\mathfrak{w}_2, \hbar_2) = \alpha(\mathcal{B}\hbar_1, \mathcal{B}\mathfrak{w}_2) \geq \eta(\mathcal{B}\hbar_1, \mathcal{B}\mathfrak{w}_2) = \eta(\mathfrak{w}_2, \hbar_2).$$

Continuing in this way, we have

$$\alpha(\mathfrak{w}_\iota, \hbar_\iota) \geq \eta(\mathfrak{w}_\iota, \hbar_\iota) \text{ and } \alpha(\mathfrak{w}_{\iota+1}, \hbar_\iota) \geq \eta(\mathfrak{w}_{\iota+1}, \hbar_\iota), \tag{20}$$

for all $\iota \in \mathbb{N}$. Now, by (19) and (20), we have

$$\eth(\mathfrak{w}_\iota, \hbar_\iota) = \eth(\mathcal{B}\hbar_{\iota-1}, \mathcal{B}\mathfrak{w}_\iota) \leq \psi(\eth(\mathfrak{w}_\iota, \hbar_{\iota-1})), \tag{21}$$

for all $\iota \in \mathbb{N}$. Moreover,

$$\eth(\mathfrak{w}_{\iota+1}, \hbar_\iota) = \eth(\mathcal{B}\hbar_\iota, \mathcal{B}\mathfrak{w}_\iota) \leq \psi(\eth(\mathfrak{w}_\iota, \hbar_\iota)), \tag{22}$$

for all $\iota \in \mathbb{N}$. By (21) and mathematical induction, we obtain

$$\eth(\mathfrak{w}_\iota, \hbar_\iota) \leq \psi(\eth(\mathfrak{w}_\iota, \hbar_{\iota-1})) \leq \psi(\psi(\eth(\mathfrak{w}_{\iota-1}, \hbar_{\iota-2}))) \leq \ldots \leq \psi^\iota(\eth(\mathfrak{w}_1, \hbar_0)). \tag{23}$$

Similarly, by (22) and mathematical induction, we obtain

$$\eth(\mathfrak{w}_{\iota+1}, \hbar_\iota) \leq \psi(\eth(\mathfrak{w}_\iota, \hbar_\iota)) \leq \psi(\psi(\eth(\mathfrak{w}_{\iota-1}, \hbar_{\iota-1}))) \leq \ldots \leq \psi^{\iota+1}(\eth(\mathfrak{w}_0, \hbar_0)), \tag{24}$$

for all $\iota \in \mathbb{N}$. Let $(f, \kappa) \in \mathfrak{F} \times [0, \infty)$ be such that (D_3) is satisfied. Let $\epsilon > 0$ be fixed. By $(\mathfrak{F}_2)$, there exists $\delta > 0$ such that

$$0 < t < \delta \implies f(t) < f(\epsilon) - \kappa. \tag{25}$$

Let there exist $\epsilon > 0$ and $\iota(\epsilon) \in \mathbb{N}$ such that

$$\sum_{\iota \geq \iota(\epsilon)} \psi^\iota(\eth(\mathfrak{w}_1, \hbar_0)) < \frac{\epsilon}{2},$$

and

$$\sum_{\iota \geq \iota(\epsilon)} \psi^{\iota+1}(\eth(\mathfrak{w}_0, \hbar_0)) < \frac{\epsilon}{2}.$$

Now, for $p > \iota \geq \iota(\epsilon)$, by applying (D_3), we have that $\eth(\mathfrak{w}_\iota, \hbar_p) > 0$ implies

$$\begin{aligned}
f(\eth(\mathfrak{w}_\iota, \hbar_p)) &\leq f\left(\begin{array}{c}\eth(\mathfrak{w}_\iota, \hbar_\iota) + \eth(\mathfrak{w}_{\iota+1}, \hbar_\iota) + \eth(\mathfrak{w}_{\iota+1}, \hbar_{\iota+1}) + \\ \ldots + \eth(\mathfrak{w}_p, \hbar_{p-1}) + \eth(\mathfrak{w}_p, \hbar_p)\end{array}\right) + \kappa \\
&\leq f\left(\sum_{j=\iota}^{p} \eth(\mathfrak{w}_j, \hbar_j) + \sum_{j=\iota}^{p-1} \eth(\mathfrak{w}_{j+1}, \hbar_j)\right) + \kappa \\
&\leq f\left(\sum_{j=\iota}^{p} \psi^j(\eth(\mathfrak{w}_1, \hbar_0)) + \sum_{j=\iota}^{p-1} \psi^{\iota+1}(\eth(\mathfrak{w}_0, \hbar_0))\right) + \kappa \\
&\leq f\left(\sum_{\iota \geq \iota(\epsilon)} \psi^\iota(\eth(\mathfrak{w}_1, \hbar_0)) + \sum_{\iota \geq \iota(\epsilon)} \psi^{\iota+1}(\eth(\mathfrak{w}_0, \hbar_0))\right) + \kappa \\
&< f(\epsilon),
\end{aligned}$$

for all $j \in \mathbb{N}$. Similarly, for $\imath > p \geq \imath(\epsilon)$, by applying (D_3), we have that $\eth(\mathfrak{w}_\imath, \hbar_p) > 0$ implies

$$\begin{aligned}
f(\eth(\mathfrak{w}_\imath, \hbar_p)) &\leq f\left(\begin{array}{c}\eth(\mathfrak{w}_\imath, \hbar_{\imath-1}) + \eth(\mathfrak{w}_{\imath-1}, \hbar_{\imath-1}) + \eth(\mathfrak{w}_{\imath-1}, \hbar_{\imath-2}) + \\ \ldots + \eth(\mathfrak{w}_p, \hbar_{p-1}) + \eth(\mathfrak{w}_p, \hbar_p)\end{array}\right) + \kappa \\
&\leq f\left(\sum_{j=p}^{\imath-1} \eth(\mathfrak{w}_j, \hbar_j) + \sum_{j=\imath}^{\imath} \eth(\mathfrak{w}_j, \hbar_{j-1})\right) + \kappa \\
&\leq f\left(\sum_{j=p}^{\imath-1} \psi^j(\eth(\mathfrak{w}_1, \hbar_0)) + \sum_{j=p}^{\imath} \psi^{\imath+1}(\eth(\mathfrak{w}_0, \hbar_0))\right) + \kappa \\
&\leq f\left(\sum_{\imath \geq \imath(\epsilon)} \psi^{j+1}(\eth(\mathfrak{w}_0, \hbar_0)) + \sum_{\imath \geq \imath(\epsilon)} \psi^\imath(\eth(\mathfrak{w}_1, \hbar_0))\right) + \kappa \\
&< f(\epsilon),
\end{aligned}$$

for all $j \in \mathbb{N}$. Then, by $(\mathfrak{F}_1)$, $\eth(\mathfrak{w}_\imath, \hbar_p) < \epsilon$, for all $p, \imath \geq \imath_0$. Thus, $(\mathfrak{w}_\imath, \hbar_\imath)$ is a Cauchy bisequence in $(\mathcal{S}, \mathcal{T}, \eth)$. As $(\mathcal{S}, \mathcal{T}, \eth)$ is complete, $(\mathfrak{w}_\imath, \hbar_\imath)$ biconverges to a point $\omega \in \mathcal{S} \cap \mathcal{T}$. Thus, $(\mathfrak{w}_\imath) \to \omega$, $(\hbar_\imath) \to \omega$. Additionally, since $\mathcal{B}$ is continuous, we obtain

$$(\mathfrak{w}_\imath) \to \omega \implies (\hbar_\imath) = (\mathcal{B}\mathfrak{w}_\imath) \to \mathcal{B}\omega.$$

Moreover, since $(\hbar_\imath)$ has a limit ω in $\mathcal{S} \cap \mathcal{T}$ and the limit is unique, $\mathcal{B}\omega = \omega$. Thus, $\mathcal{B}$ has a fixed point. Now, since a bisequence $(\mathfrak{w}_\imath, \hbar_\imath)$ in $(\mathcal{S}, \mathcal{T}, \eth)$ is such that $\alpha(\mathfrak{w}_\imath, \hbar_\imath) \geq \eta(\mathfrak{w}_\imath, \hbar_\imath)$, for all $\imath \in \mathbb{N}$ with $\mathfrak{w}_\imath \to \omega$ and $\hbar_\imath \to \omega$, as $\imath \to \infty$ for $\omega \in \mathcal{S} \cap \mathcal{T}$, then, by hypothesis (iii), we have $\alpha(\mathfrak{w}_\imath, \omega) \geq \eta(\mathfrak{w}_\imath, \omega)$, for $\imath \in \mathbb{N}$. Now, by (19), we have

$$\begin{aligned}
f(\eth(\mathcal{B}\omega, \omega)) &\leq f(\eth(\mathcal{B}\omega, \mathcal{B}\mathfrak{w}_\imath) + \eth(\mathcal{B}\hbar_\imath, \mathcal{B}\mathfrak{w}_\imath) + \eth(\mathcal{B}\hbar_\imath, \omega)) + \kappa \\
&\leq f(\psi(\eth(\mathfrak{w}_\imath, \omega)) + \psi(\eth(\mathfrak{w}_\imath, \hbar_\imath)) + \eth(\mathfrak{w}_{\imath+1}, \omega)) + \kappa \\
&\leq f\left(\begin{array}{c}\psi(\eth(\mathfrak{w}_\imath, \omega)) \\ +\psi\left(\begin{array}{c}\eth(\mathfrak{w}_\imath, \omega) + \eth(\omega, \omega) \\ +\eth(\omega, \hbar_\imath)\end{array}\right) + \eth(\mathfrak{w}_{\imath+1}, \omega)\end{array}\right) + \kappa.
\end{aligned}$$

Taking the limit as $\imath \to \infty$ and using the continuity of f and ψ at $t = 0$, we have $\eth(\mathcal{B}\omega, \omega) = 0$. Thus, $\mathcal{B}\omega = \omega$. Hence, $\mathcal{B}$ has a fixed point. □

The uniqueness of the fixed point is the same as given in Theorem 2.

5. Coupled Fixed Point Theorems

In the present section, we obtain coupled fixed point results from our established results.

Definition 16. *Let $(\mathcal{S}, \mathcal{T}, \eth)$ be a complete $\mathfrak{F}$-bip MS and let $\mathcal{F} : (\mathcal{S} \times \mathcal{T}, \mathcal{T} \times \mathcal{S}) \rightrightarrows (\mathcal{S}, \mathcal{T})$ be a convariant mapping. A point $(a, b) \in \mathcal{S} \times \mathcal{T}$ is alleged to be a coupled fixed point of $\mathcal{F}$ if*

$$\mathcal{F}(a, b) = a \text{ and } \mathcal{F}(b, a) = b.$$

Lemma 2. *Let $\mathcal{F} : (\mathcal{S} \times \mathcal{T}, \mathcal{T} \times \mathcal{S}) \rightrightarrows (\mathcal{S}, \mathcal{T})$ be a convariant mapping. If we define a convariant mapping $\aleph : (\mathcal{S} \times \mathcal{T}, \mathcal{T} \times \mathcal{S}) \rightrightarrows (\mathcal{S} \times \mathcal{T}, \mathcal{T} \times \mathcal{S})$ by*

$$\aleph(\mathfrak{w}, \hbar) = (\mathcal{F}(\mathfrak{w}, \hbar), \mathcal{F}(\hbar, \mathfrak{w})),$$

for all $(\mathfrak{w}, \hbar) \in \mathcal{S} \times \mathcal{T}$, then $(\mathfrak{w}, \hbar)$ is a coupled fixed point of $\mathcal{F}$ if only if $(\mathfrak{w}, \hbar)$ is a fixed point of $\aleph$.

We state a property (P$'$) that is required in our result.

(P$'$) there exists $(z_1, z_2) \in (\mathcal{S} \times \mathcal{T}) \cap (\mathcal{T} \times \mathcal{S})$ such that

$$\alpha((\mathfrak{w}, \hbar), (z_1, z_2)) \geq 1, \ \alpha((z_2, z_1), (\hbar, \mathfrak{w})) \geq 1,$$

and
$$\alpha((u,v),(z_1,z_2)) \geq 1, \ \alpha((z_2,z_1),(u,v)) \geq 1,$$
for all $(\mathfrak{w},\hbar) \in \mathcal{S} \times \mathcal{T}$ and $(u,v) \in \mathcal{T} \times \mathcal{S}$.

Theorem 4. *Let $(\mathcal{S}, \mathcal{T}, \mathfrak{d})$ be a complete $\mathfrak{F}$-bip MS and let $\mathcal{F} : (\mathcal{S} \times \mathcal{T}, \mathcal{T} \times \mathcal{S}) \rightrightarrows (\mathcal{S}, \mathcal{T})$ be a convariant mapping. Assume that there exist $\alpha : (\mathcal{S} \times \mathcal{T}) \times (\mathcal{T} \times \mathcal{S}) \to [0, +\infty)$ and $\psi \in \Psi$ such that*

$$\alpha((\mathfrak{w},\hbar),(u,v))\mathfrak{d}(\mathcal{F}(\mathfrak{w},\hbar),\mathcal{F}(u,v)) \leq \psi\left(\frac{\mathfrak{d}(\mathfrak{w},u)+\mathfrak{d}(v,\hbar)}{2}\right), \quad (26)$$

for all $(\mathfrak{w},\hbar), (u,v) \in \mathcal{S} \times \mathcal{T}$, and the following hypotheses also hold:
(i) $\alpha((\mathfrak{w},\hbar),(u,v)) \geq 1$ *implies* $\alpha((\mathcal{F}(\mathfrak{w},\hbar),\mathcal{F}(\hbar,\mathfrak{w})),(\mathcal{F}(u,v),\mathcal{F}(v,u))) \geq 1$,
(ii) *there exists $(\mathfrak{w}_0,\hbar_0) \in \mathcal{S} \times \mathcal{T}$ such that*

$$\alpha((\mathfrak{w}_0,\hbar_0),(\mathcal{F}(\hbar_0,\mathfrak{w}_0),\mathcal{F}(\mathfrak{w}_0,\hbar_0))) \geq 1,$$

and
$$\alpha((\mathcal{F}(\mathfrak{w}_0,\hbar_0),\mathcal{F}(\hbar_0,\mathfrak{w}_0)),(\mathfrak{w}_0,\hbar_0)) \geq 1,$$

(iii) *$\mathcal{F}$ is continuous or, if $(\mathfrak{w}_\imath, \hbar_\imath)$ is a bisequence in $(\mathcal{S}, \mathcal{T}, \mathfrak{d})$ such that $\alpha((\mathfrak{w}_\imath, \hbar_\imath),(\hbar_{\imath+1}, \mathfrak{w}_{\imath+1})) \geq 1$ and $\alpha((\hbar_{\imath+1}, \mathfrak{w}_{\imath+1}),(\mathfrak{w}_\imath, \hbar_\imath)) \geq 1$, for all $\imath \in \mathbb{N}$ with $\mathfrak{w}_\imath \to \mathfrak{w}$ and $\hbar_\imath \to \hbar$, as $\imath \to \infty$ for $(\mathfrak{w},\hbar) \in \mathcal{S} \cap \mathcal{T}$, then*

$$\alpha((\mathfrak{w}_\imath,\hbar_\imath),(\mathfrak{w},\hbar)) \geq 1 \text{ and } \alpha((\mathfrak{w},\hbar),(\mathfrak{w}_\imath,\hbar_\imath)) \geq 1,$$

for all $\imath \in \mathbb{N}$.

Then, $\mathcal{F}$ has a coupled fixed point. Furthermore, if the property (P') holds, then the coupled fixed point is unique.

Proof. Let $L = \mathcal{S} \times \mathcal{T}$ and $H = \mathcal{T} \times \mathcal{S}$ and

$$\delta((\mathfrak{w},\hbar),(u,v)) = \mathfrak{d}(\mathfrak{w},u) + \mathfrak{d}(v,\hbar),$$

for all $(\mathfrak{w},\hbar) \in L$ and $(u,v) \in H$. Then, (L, H, δ) is a complete $\mathfrak{F}$-bipolar metric space. By (26), we have

$$\alpha((\mathfrak{w},\hbar),(u,v))\mathfrak{d}(\mathcal{F}(\mathfrak{w},\hbar),\mathcal{F}(u,v)) \leq \psi\left(\frac{\mathfrak{d}(\mathfrak{w},u)+\mathfrak{d}(v,\hbar)}{2}\right), \quad (27)$$

and
$$\alpha((\mathfrak{w},\hbar),(u,v))\mathfrak{d}(\mathcal{F}(\mathfrak{w},\hbar),\mathcal{F}(u,v)) \leq \psi\left(\frac{\mathfrak{d}(\mathfrak{w},u)+\mathfrak{d}(v,\hbar)}{2}\right). \quad (28)$$

Combining (27) and (28), we obtain

$$\beta(\varkappa,\varrho)\mathfrak{d}(\mathcal{F}\varkappa,\mathcal{F}\varrho) \leq \psi(\delta(\varkappa,\varrho)),$$

for all $\varkappa = (\varkappa_1, \varkappa_2) \in L$ and $\varrho = (\varrho_1, \varrho_2) \in H$. Moreover, the function $\beta : L \times H \to [0, +\infty)$ is defined as

$$\beta(\varkappa,\varrho) = \min\{\alpha((\varkappa_1,\varkappa_2),(\varrho_1,\varrho_2)), \alpha((\varrho_2,\varrho_1),(\varkappa_2,\varkappa_1))\},$$

and $\aleph : (L, H) \rightrightarrows (L, H)$ is defined by

$$\aleph(\mathfrak{w},\hbar) = (\mathcal{F}(\mathfrak{w},\hbar), \mathcal{F}(\hbar,\mathfrak{w})).$$

Then, $\aleph$ is a continuous and covariant (β, ψ)-contraction. Now, we suppose that $\beta(\varkappa, \varrho) \geq 1$. Then, by (i), we have $\beta(\aleph\varkappa, \aleph\varrho) \geq 1$. By condition (ii), there exists $(\mathfrak{w}_0, \hbar_0) \in L$ (or $(\hbar_0, \mathfrak{w}_0) \in H$) such that

$$\beta((\mathfrak{w}_0, \hbar_0), \aleph(\mathfrak{w}_0, \hbar_0)) \geq 1,$$

(or $\beta(\aleph(\mathfrak{w}_0, \hbar_0), (\hbar_0, \mathfrak{w}_0,)) \geq 1$). Since $\aleph$ is continuous, $\aleph$ has a fixed point. Now, if $(\mathfrak{w}_l, \hbar_l)$ is a bisequence in $L = \mathcal{S} \times \mathcal{T}$ and $(\hbar_l, \mathfrak{w}_l)$ is a bisequence in $H = \mathcal{T} \times \mathcal{S}$ such that $\alpha((\mathfrak{w}_l, \hbar_l), (\hbar_{l+1}, \mathfrak{w}_{l+1})) \geq 1$ and $(\mathfrak{w}_l, \hbar_l) \to (\mathfrak{w}, \hbar)$ as $n \to \infty$. Then, by (iii), we have $\alpha((\mathfrak{w}_l, \hbar_l), (\hbar, \mathfrak{w})) \geq 1$. Thus, all the conditions of Corollary 3 are satisfied and $\aleph$ has a fixed point. Hence, by Lemma 2, $\mathcal{F}$ has a coupled fixed point. Now, since the property (P$'$) holds, $\mathcal{F}$ has a unique coupled fixed point. □

Remark 8. *Taking $\alpha((\mathfrak{w}, \hbar), (u, v)) = 1$ and $\psi(t) = kt$, where $0 < k < 1$ in Theorem 4, we can obtain the leading result of Mutlu et al. [12].*

6. Application
6.1. Integral Equations

Fixed point theory is a valuable tool used to solve differential and integral equations, which are used to investigate the solutions of various mathematical models, as well as in game theory, dynamical systems, physics, engineering, computer science, neural networks and many other domains (see [22–24]). In the present section, we discuss the uniqueness and existence of an integral equation.

$$\varphi(\mathfrak{w}) = g(\mathfrak{w}) + \int_{\mathcal{S} \cup \mathcal{T}} K(\mathfrak{w}, \hbar, \varphi(\mathfrak{w})) \partial\hbar, \tag{29}$$

where $\mathcal{S} \cup \mathcal{T}$ is a Lebesgue measurable set and g is real-valued continuous function.

Theorem 5. *Suppose that the following conditions hold:*
(i) $K : (\mathcal{S}^2 \cup \mathcal{T}^2) \times [0, \infty) \to [0, \infty)$ *and* $f \in \mathcal{L}^\infty(\mathcal{S}) \cup \mathcal{L}^\infty(\mathcal{T})$,
(ii) *there exists a continuous function* $Y : \mathcal{S}^2 \cup \mathcal{T}^2 \to [0, \infty)$ *such that*

$$|K(\mathfrak{w}, \hbar, \varphi(\hbar)) - K(\mathfrak{w}, \hbar, \phi(\hbar))| \leq \frac{1}{2} Y(\mathfrak{w}, \hbar) |\phi(\hbar) - \varphi(\hbar)|,$$

for all $\mathfrak{w}, \hbar \in (\mathcal{S}^2 \cup \mathcal{T}^2)$,
(iii) $\left\| \int_{\mathcal{S} \cup \mathcal{T}} Y(\mathfrak{w}, \hbar) \partial\hbar \right\| \leq 1$, *that is,* $\sup_{\mathfrak{w} \in \mathcal{S} \cup \mathcal{T}} \int_{\mathcal{S} \cup \mathcal{T}} |Y(\mathfrak{w}, \hbar)| \partial\hbar \leq 1$.

Then, the integral Equation (29) has a unique solution in $\mathcal{L}^\infty(\mathcal{S}) \cup \mathcal{L}^\infty(\mathcal{T})$.

Proof. Let $\Xi = \mathcal{L}^\infty(\mathcal{S})$ and $\Theta = \mathcal{L}^\infty(\mathcal{T})$ be two normed linear spaces, where $\mathcal{S}$ and $\mathcal{T}$ are Lebesgue measurable sets and $m(\mathcal{S} \cup \mathcal{T}) < \infty$. Consider $\partial : \Xi \times \Theta \to [0, \infty)$ to be defined by

$$\partial(\xi, \zeta) = \|\xi - \zeta\|_\infty$$

for all $\xi, \zeta \in \Xi \times \Theta$. Then, (Ξ, Θ, ∂) is a complete $\mathfrak{F}$-bip MS. Define the mapping $I : \Xi \cup \Theta \to \Xi \cup \Theta$ by

$$I(\varphi(\mathfrak{w})) = g(\mathfrak{w}) + \int_{\mathcal{S} \cup \mathcal{T}} K(\mathfrak{w}, \hbar, \varphi(\mathfrak{w})) \partial\hbar,$$

for $\mathfrak{w} \in \mathcal{S} \cup \mathcal{T}$ and $\alpha, \eta : \Xi \times \Theta \to [0, +\infty)$ by

$$\alpha(\varphi(\mathfrak{w}), \phi(\mathfrak{w})) = \eta(\varphi(\mathfrak{w}), \phi(\mathfrak{w})) = 1.$$

Now, we have

$$\begin{aligned}
\eth(I(\varphi(\mathfrak{w})), I(\phi(\mathfrak{w}))) &= \|I(\varphi(\mathfrak{w})) - I(\phi(\mathfrak{w}))\| \\
&= \left| \int_{\mathcal{S}\cup\mathcal{T}} K(\mathfrak{w},\hbar,\varphi(\mathfrak{w}))\partial\hbar - \int_{\mathcal{S}\cup\mathcal{T}} K(\mathfrak{w},\hbar,\phi(\mathfrak{w}))\partial\hbar \right| \\
&\leq \int_{\mathcal{S}\cup\mathcal{T}} |K(\mathfrak{w},\hbar,\varphi(\mathfrak{w})) - K(\mathfrak{w},\hbar,\phi(\mathfrak{w}))|\partial\hbar \\
&\leq \int_{\mathcal{S}\cup\mathcal{T}} \frac{1}{2} Y(\mathfrak{w},\hbar)|\phi(\hbar) - \varphi(\hbar)|\partial\hbar \\
&\leq \frac{1}{2}\|\phi(\hbar) - \varphi(\hbar)\| \int_{\mathcal{S}\cup\mathcal{T}} |Y(\mathfrak{w},\hbar)|\partial\hbar \\
&\leq \frac{1}{2}\|\phi - \varphi\| \sup_{\mathfrak{w}\in\mathcal{S}\cup\mathcal{T}} \int_{\mathcal{S}\cup\mathcal{T}} |Y(\mathfrak{w},\hbar)|\partial\hbar \\
&\leq \frac{1}{2}\|\phi - \varphi\| \\
&= \psi(\eth(\phi,\varphi)).
\end{aligned}$$

Define $\psi : [0,+\infty) \to [0,+\infty)$ by $\psi(t) = \frac{1}{2}t$, for $t > 0$. Thus, by result 2, I has a unique fixed point in $\Xi \cup \Theta$. □

6.2. Homotopy Result

Theorem 6. *Let $(\mathcal{S},\mathcal{T},\eth)$ be a complete $\mathfrak{F}$-bip MS and let (Ξ,Θ) be an open subset of $(\mathcal{S},\mathcal{T})$ and $(\overline{\Xi},\overline{\Theta})$ be a closed subset of $(\mathcal{S},\mathcal{T})$ and $(\Xi,\Theta) \subseteq (\overline{\Xi},\overline{\Theta})$. Suppose that $\mathcal{L} : (\overline{\Xi}\cup\overline{\Theta}) \times [0,1] \to \mathcal{S}\cup\mathcal{T}$ satisfies the following conditions:*
(hom1) $\mathfrak{w} \neq \mathcal{L}(\mathfrak{w},q)$ for each $\mathfrak{w} \in \partial\Xi \cup \partial\Theta$ and $q \in [0,1]$,
(hom2) for all $\mathfrak{w} \in \overline{\Xi}, \hbar \in \overline{\Theta}$ and $q \in [0,1]$

$$\eth(\mathcal{L}(\hbar,q), \mathcal{L}(\mathfrak{w},q)) \leq \psi(\eth(\mathfrak{w},\hbar)),$$

where $\psi \in \Psi$,
(hom3) there exists $M \geq 0$ such that

$$\eth(\mathcal{L}(\mathfrak{w},r), \mathcal{L}(\hbar,o)) \leq M|r - o|,$$

for all $\mathfrak{w} \in \overline{\Xi}, \hbar \in \overline{\Theta}$ and $r,o \in [0,1]$.
Then, the mapping $\mathcal{L}(\cdot,0)$ has a fixed point if and only if $\mathcal{L}(\cdot,1)$ has a fixed point.

Proof. Let

$$\Re_1 = \{\tau \in [0,1] : \mathfrak{w} = \mathcal{L}(\mathfrak{w},\tau), \mathfrak{w} \in \Xi\}$$

and

$$\Re_1 = \{o \in [0,1] : \hbar = \mathcal{L}(\hbar,o), \hbar \in \Theta\}.$$

Since $\mathcal{L}(\cdot,0)$ has a fixed point in $\Xi \cup \Theta$, then we get $0 \in \Re_1 \cap \Re_2$. Thus $\Re_1 \cap \Re_2 \neq \emptyset$. Now, we shall prove that $\Re_1 \cap \Re_2$ is both open and closed in $[0,1]$ and so, by connetedness, $\Re_1 = \Re_2 = [0,1]$. Let $(\{\tau_\imath\}_{\imath=1}^\infty), (\{o_\imath\}_{\imath=1}^\infty) \subseteq (\Re_1,\Re_2)$ with $(\tau_\imath, o_\imath) \to (\rho,\rho) \in [0,1]$ as $\imath \to \infty$. We also claim that $\rho \in \Re_1 \cap \Re_2$. Since $(\tau_\imath, o_\imath) \in \Re_1 \cap \Re_2$, for $\imath \in \mathbb{N} \cup \{0\}$. Hence there exists a bisequence $(\mathfrak{w}_\imath, \hbar_\imath) \in (\Xi,\Theta)$ such that $\hbar_\imath = \mathcal{L}(\mathfrak{w}_\imath, \tau_\imath)$ and $\mathfrak{w}_{\imath+1} = \mathcal{L}(\hbar_\imath, o_\imath)$. Also, we get

$$\begin{aligned}
\eth(\mathfrak{w}_{\imath+1}, \hbar_\imath) &= \eth(\mathcal{L}(\hbar_\imath, o_\imath), \mathcal{L}(\mathfrak{w}_\imath, \tau_\imath)) \\
&\leq \psi(\eth(\mathfrak{w}_\imath, \hbar_\imath)).
\end{aligned}$$

And,

$$\begin{aligned}\mathfrak{d}(\mathfrak{w}_\iota,\hbar_\iota) &= \mathfrak{d}(\mathcal{L}(\hbar_{\iota-1},o_{\iota-1}),\mathcal{L}(\mathfrak{w}_\iota,\tau_\iota)) \\ &\leq \psi(\mathfrak{d}(\mathfrak{w}_\iota,\hbar_{\iota-1})).\end{aligned}$$

Following the proof of Theorem 2, one can easily show that $(\mathfrak{w}_\iota,\hbar_\iota)$ is a Cauchy bisequence in (Ξ,Θ). Since (Ξ,Θ) is complete, so there exists $\rho_1 \in \Xi \cap \Theta$ such that $\lim_{\iota \to \infty}(\mathfrak{w}_\iota) = \lim_{\iota \to \infty}(\hbar_\iota) = \rho_1$. Now, we have

$$\begin{aligned}f(\mathfrak{d}(\mathcal{L}(\rho_1,o),\hbar_\iota)) &= f(\mathfrak{d}(\mathcal{L}(\rho_1,o),\mathcal{L}(\mathfrak{w}_\iota,\tau_\iota))) \\ &\leq f(\psi(\mathfrak{d}(\mathfrak{w}_\iota,\rho_1))) = -\infty,\end{aligned}$$

whenever $\iota \to \infty$. Hence by $(\mathfrak{F}_2)$, we get $\mathfrak{d}(\mathcal{L}(\rho_1,o),\rho_1) = 0$, which implies that $\mathcal{L}(\rho_1,o) = \rho_1$. Similarly, $\mathcal{L}(\rho_1,\tau) = v_1$. Thus $\tau = o \in \Re_1 \cap \Re_2$, and evidently $\Re_1 \cap \Re_2$ is closed set in $[0,1]$. Next, we have to prove that $\Re_1 \cap \Re_2$ is open in $[0,1]$. Suppose $(\tau_0,o_0) \in (\Re_1,\Re_2)$, then there is a bisequence $(\mathfrak{w}_0,\hbar_0)$ so that

$$\mathfrak{w}_0 = \mathcal{L}(\mathfrak{w}_0,\tau_0), \hbar_0 = \mathcal{L}(\hbar_0,o_0).$$

Since $\Xi \cup \Theta$ is open, so there exists $r > 0$ so that $B_\mathfrak{d}(\mathfrak{w}_0,r) \subseteq \Xi \cup \Theta$ and $B_\mathfrak{d}(r,\hbar_0) \subseteq \Xi \cup \Theta$. Choose $\tau \in (o_0 - \epsilon, o_0 + \epsilon)$ and $o \in (\tau_0 - \epsilon, \tau_0 + \epsilon)$ such that

$$|\tau - o_0| \leq \frac{1}{M^\iota} < \frac{\epsilon}{2}$$

$$|o - \tau_0| \leq \frac{1}{M^\iota} < \frac{\epsilon}{2},$$

and

$$|\tau_0 - o_0| \leq \frac{1}{M^\iota} < \frac{\epsilon}{2}.$$

Hence, we have

$$\hbar \in \overline{B_{\Re_1 \cup \Re_2}(\mathfrak{w}_0,r)} = \left\{ \begin{array}{c} \hbar : \hbar_0 \in \Theta : \\ \mathfrak{d}(\mathfrak{w}_0,\hbar) \leq r + \mathfrak{d}(\mathfrak{w}_0,\hbar_0) \end{array} \right\}$$

and

$$\mathfrak{w} \in \overline{B_{\Re_1 \cup \Re_2}(r,\hbar_0)} = \left\{ \begin{array}{c} \mathfrak{w} : \mathfrak{w}_0 \in \Xi : \\ \mathfrak{d}(\mathfrak{w},\hbar_0) \leq r + \mathfrak{d}(\mathfrak{w}_0,\hbar_0) \end{array} \right\}.$$

Moreover, we have

$$\begin{aligned}\mathfrak{d}(\mathcal{L}(\mathfrak{w},\tau),\hbar_0) &= \mathfrak{d}(\mathcal{L}(\mathfrak{w},\tau),\mathcal{L}(\hbar_0,o_0)) \\ &\leq \mathfrak{d}(\mathcal{L}(\mathfrak{w},\tau),\mathcal{L}(\hbar,o_0)) \\ &\quad + \mathfrak{d}(\mathcal{L}(\mathfrak{w}_0,\tau),\mathcal{L}(\hbar,o_0)) \\ &\quad + \mathfrak{d}(\mathcal{L}(\mathfrak{w}_0,\tau),\mathcal{L}(\hbar_0,o_0)) \\ &\leq 2M|\tau - o_0| + \mathfrak{d}(\mathcal{L}(\mathfrak{w}_0,\tau),\mathcal{L}(\hbar,o_0)) \\ &\leq \frac{2}{M^\iota - 1} + \psi(\mathfrak{d}(\mathfrak{w}_0,\hbar)) \\ &\leq \frac{2}{M^\iota - 1} + \mathfrak{d}(\mathfrak{w}_0,\hbar).\end{aligned}$$

Letting $\iota \to \infty$, we get

$$\mathfrak{d}(\mathcal{L}(\mathfrak{w},\tau),\hbar_0) \leq \mathfrak{d}(\mathfrak{w}_0,\hbar) \leq r + \mathfrak{d}(\mathfrak{w}_0,\hbar_0).$$

By corresponding fashion, we get

$$\eth(\mathfrak{w}_0, \mathcal{L}(\hbar, o)) \leq \eth(\mathfrak{w}, \hbar_0) \leq r + \eth(\mathfrak{w}_0, \hbar_0).$$

But

$$\begin{aligned}\eth(\mathfrak{w}_0, \hbar_0) &= \eth(\mathcal{L}(\mathfrak{w}_0, \tau_0), \mathcal{L}(\hbar_0, o_0)) \\ &\leq M|\tau_0 - o_0| \leq \frac{1}{M^{\iota-1}} \to 0,\end{aligned}$$

as $\iota \to \infty$, which yields that $\mathfrak{w}_0 = \hbar_0$. As a result, $o = \tau \in (o_0 - \epsilon, o_0 + \epsilon)$ for each fixed o and $\mathcal{L}(\cdot, \tau) : \overline{B_{\Re_1 \cup \Re_2}(\mathfrak{w}_0, r)} \to \overline{B_{\Re_1 \cup \Re_2}(\mathfrak{w}_0, r)}$. Since all the conditions of Corollary 3 hold, $\mathcal{L}(\cdot, \tau)$ has a fixed point in $\overline{\Xi} \cap \overline{\Theta}$, which certainly exists in $\Xi \cap \Theta$. Then $\tau = o \in \Re_1 \cap \Re_2$ for each $o \in (o_0 - \epsilon, o_0 + \epsilon)$. Hence $(o_0 - \epsilon, o_0 + \epsilon) \in \Re_1 \cap \Re_2$ which gives $\Re_1 \cap \Re_2$ is open in $[0, 1]$. Similarly, we can prove the converse of it. □

7. Conclusions

In this research article, we have defined (α, η, ψ)-contractions against the background of $\mathfrak{F}$-bip MS and established fixed point results. Some coupled fixed point results in $\mathfrak{F}$-bip MS are also derived as a result of our main theorems. An important example is also provided to validate the authenticity of the established theorems. We have explored the existence and uniqueness of a solution of an integral equation by applying our main result. Additionally, we have explored the unique solution of the homotopy result.

The given results in this research work can be extended to some multivalued mappings and fuzzy mappings in the framework of $\mathfrak{F}$-bip MS. In addition, a number of common fixed point results for these contractions can be obtained. As applications of these outcomes against the background of $\mathfrak{F}$-bip MS, some differential and integral inclusions can be explored.

Funding: This research received no external funding.

Data Availability Statement: Not applicable.

Conflicts of Interest: The author declares no conflict of interest.

References

1. Banach, S. Sur les operations dans les ensembles abstracts ET leur applications aux equations integrals. *Fund. Math.* **1922**, *3*, 133–181. [CrossRef]
2. Samet, B.; Vetro, C.; Vetro, P. Fixed point theorem for $\alpha - \psi$ contractive type mappings. *Nonlinear Anal.* **2012**, *75*, 2154–2165. [CrossRef]
3. Salimi, P.; Latif, A.; Hussain, N. Modified α-ψ-contractive mappings with applications. *Fixed Point Theory Appl.* **2013**, *151*, 1–19. [CrossRef]
4. Frechet, M. Sur quelques points du calcul fonctionnel. *Rend. Circ. Mat. Palermo* **1906**, *22*, 1–72. [CrossRef]
5. Czerwik, S. Contraction mappings in b-metric spaces. *Acta Math. Inform. Univ. Ostra.* **1993**, *1*, 5–11.
6. Matthews, S.G. Partial metric topology. *Ann. N. Y. Acad. Sci.* **1994**, *1994*, 183–197. [CrossRef]
7. Khamsi, M.A.; Hussain, N. KKM mappings in metric type spaces, *Nonlinear Anal.* **2010**, *7*, 3123–3129.
8. Branciari, A. A fixed point theorem of Banach-Caccioppoli type on a class of generalized metric spaces. *Publ. Math. Debr.* **2000**, *57*, 31–37. [CrossRef]
9. Jleli, M.; Samet, B. On a new generalization of metric spaces, *J. Fixed Point Theory Appl.* **2018**, *20*, 128. [CrossRef]
10. Hussain, A.; Kanwal, T. Existence and uniqueness for a neutral differential problem with unbounded delay via fixed point results. *Trans. Razmadze Math. Inst.* **2018**, *172*, 481–490. [CrossRef]
11. Mutlu, A.; Gürdal, U. Bipolar metric spaces and some fixed point theorems. *J. Nonlinear Sci. Appl.* **2016**, *9*, 5362–5373. [CrossRef]
12. Mutlu, A.; Ozkan, K.; Gürdal, U. Coupled fixed point theorems on bipolar metric spaces. *Eur. J. Pure Appl. Math.* **2017**, *10*, 655–667.
13. Kishore, G.N.V.; Prasad, D.R.; Rao, B.S.; Baghavan, V.S. Some applications via common coupled fixed point theorems in bipolar metric spaces. *J. Crit. Rev.* **2019**, *7*, 601–607.
14. Rao, B.S.; Kishore, G.N.V.; Kumar, G.K. Geraghty type contraction and common coupled fixed point theorems in bipolar metric spaces with applications to homotopy. *Int. J. Math. Technol.* **2018**, *63*, 1–10.

15. Gürdal, U.; Mutlu, A.; Ozkan, K. Fixed point results for α-ψ-contractive mappings in bipolar metric spaces. *J. Inequal. Spec. Funct.* **2020**, *11*, 64–75.
16. Gaba, Y.U.; Aphane, M.; Aydi, H. (α, BK) -contractions in bipolar metric spaces. *J. Math.* **2021**, *2021*, 1–6. [CrossRef]
17. Kishore, G.N.V.; Rao, K.P.R.; Sombabu, A.; Rao, R.V.N.S. Related results to hybrid pair of mappings and applications in bipolar metric spaces. *J. Math.* **2019**, *2019*, 1–7. [CrossRef]
18. Kishore, G.N.V.; Rao, K.P.R.; Isik,H.; Rao, B.S.; Sombabu, A. Covariant mappings and coupled fixed point results in bipolar metric spaces. *Int. J. Nonlinear Anal. Appl.* **2021**, *12*, 1–15.
19. Kishore, G.N.V.; Isik, H.; Aydi, H.; Rao, B.S.; Prasad, D.R. On new types of contraction mappings in bipolar metric spaces and applications. *J. Linear Topol. Algebra* **2020** , *9*, 253–266.
20. Mutlu, A.; Ozkan, K.; Gürdal, U. Some common fixed point theorems in bipolar metric spaces. *Turk. J. Math. Comput. Sci.* **2022**, *14*, 346–354. [CrossRef]
21. Rawat, S.; Dimri, R.C.; Bartwal, A. $\mathfrak{F}$-Bipolar metric spaces and fixed point theorems with applications. *J. Math. Computer Sci.* **2022**, *26*, 184–195. [CrossRef]
22. Yang, X.; Wu, L.; Zhang, H. A space-time spectral order sinc-collocation method for the fourth-order nonlocal heat model arising in viscoelasticity. *Appl. Math. Comput.* **2023**, *457*, 128192. [CrossRef]
23. Yang, X.; Zhang, Q.; Yuan, G.; Sheng, Z. On positivity preservation in nonlinear finite volume method for multi-term fractional subdiffusion equation on polygonal meshes. *Nonlinear Dyn.* **2018**, *92*, 595–612. [CrossRef]
24. Gu, X.-M.; Sun, H.-W.; Zhang, Y.; Zhao, Y.-L. Fast implicit difference schemes for time-space fractional diffusion equations with the integral fractional Laplacian. *Math. Meth. Appl. Sci.* **2021**, *44*, 441–463. [CrossRef]

Disclaimer/Publisher's Note: The statements, opinions and data contained in all publications are solely those of the individual author(s) and contributor(s) and not of MDPI and/or the editor(s). MDPI and/or the editor(s) disclaim responsibility for any injury to people or property resulting from any ideas, methods, instructions or products referred to in the content.

 mathematics

Article

An Algorithm That Adjusts the Stepsize to Be Self-Adaptive with an Inertial Term Aimed for Solving Split Variational Inclusion and Common Fixed Point Problems

Matlhatsi Dorah Ngwepe [1], Lateef Olakunle Jolaoso [1,*], Maggie Aphane [1] and Ibrahim Oyeyemi Adenekan [2]

[1] Department of Mathematics and Applied Mathematics, Sefako Makgatho Health Sciences University, Pretoria 0204, South Africa
[2] Department of Mathematics, University of Louisiana at Lafayette, Lafayette, LA 70504, USA; ibrahim.adenekan1@louisiana.edu
* Correspondence: l.o.jolaoso@soton.ac.uk

Abstract: In this research paper, we present a new inertial method with a self-adaptive technique for solving the split variational inclusion and fixed point problems in real Hilbert spaces. The algorithm is designed to choose the optimal choice of the inertial term at every iteration, and the stepsize is defined self-adaptively without a prior estimate of the Lipschitz constant. A convergence theorem is demonstrated to be strong even under lenient conditions and to showcase the suggested method's efficiency and precision. Some numerical tests are given. Moreover, the significance of the proposed method is demonstrated through its application to an image reconstruction issue.

Keywords: split variational inclusion; inertial term; self-adaptive algorithm; maximal monotone; Hilbert spaces

MSC: 65K15; 47J25; 65J15; 90C33

1. Introduction

In this paper, we consider the Split Variational Inclusion Problem (SVIP) introduced by Moudafi [1], which is the problem of finding the null point of a monotone operator in a Hilbert space whose image under a bounded linear operator belongs to another Hilbert space. Mathematically, the problem is defined as follows: find

$$a^* \in H_1 \quad \text{such that} \quad 0 \in m_1(a^*) \tag{1}$$

and

$$b^* = Ba^* \quad \text{solves} \quad 0 \in m_2(b^*), \tag{2}$$

where 0 is called the zero vector, with H_1 and H_2 being both real Hilbert spaces together with the multivalued maximal monotone mappings, $m_i : H_i \to 2^{H_i}$ where $i = 1, 2$. Furthermore, the bounded linear operator is denoted by $B : H_1 \to H_2$. We denote the solution set of (1) and (2) by Γ.

An operator $m : H \to 2^H$ is called:

(i) Monotone if

$$\langle k - x, a - b \rangle \geq 0 \quad \forall \quad k \in m(a), x \in m(b) \quad \forall a, b \in H.$$

(ii) Maximal monotone if the graph of any monotone mapping does not properly contain graph $G(m)$ of m, where:

$$G(m) = \{(a, k) \in H_1 \times H_1 \mid k \in m(a)\}.$$

(iii) The symbol used to represent the solution of m when a certain value λ greater than zero is used as a parameter is called the resolvent, which is denoted by J_λ^m:

$$J_\lambda^m(a) = (I + \lambda m)^{-1}(a) \quad \forall a \in H.$$

Other nonlinear optimization problems, such as split feasibility problems, split minimization problems, split variational inequality, split zero problems, and split equilibrium problems, can all be generalized by the SVIP; see [2–4]. Reducing SVIPs to split feasibility problems is important when modeling the intensity-modulating radiation therapy (IMRT) treatment planning. Moreso, the SVIPs play important roles in formulating many problems arising from engineering, economics, medicine, data compression, and sensor networks [5,6].

Recently, several authors have introduced some iterative methods for solving SVIPs, which have improved over time. In 2002, Byrne et al. [7] first introduced a weak convergence method for solving SVIPs as follows:

$$a_{n+1} = J_\lambda^{m_1}(a_n + \gamma B^*(J_\lambda^{m_2} - I)Ba_n), \tag{3}$$

for some parameter $\lambda > 0$, we have B^* representing the adjoint of B together with $L = ||B^*B||$, $\gamma \in (0, \frac{2}{L})$ and $J_\lambda^{m_i} = (I + \lambda m_i)^{-1}$ known as the resolvent operator for m_i (with $i = 1, 2$). The sequence $\{a_n\}$ generated by (3) was proved to converge weakly to a^* under some certain conditions. Moudafi [1] proposed an iterative method that helps to solve SVIP with inverse strongly monotone operators; he also obtained weak convergence results using the following iteration:

$$a_{n+1} = U(a_n + \gamma B^*(F - I)Ba_n) \quad \forall n \in N, \tag{4}$$

where $\lambda > 0, \gamma \in (0, \frac{2}{L})$ with L being the largest absolute value of the operator B^*B, $U = J_\lambda^{m_1}(I - \lambda\phi)$ and $F = J_\lambda^{m_2}(I - \lambda\varphi)$, and $J_\lambda^{m_1}$ together with $J_\lambda^{m_2}$ are the resolvent operators of m_1 and m_2, respectively. Lastly, let $\phi : H_1 \to H_1$ and $\varphi : H_2 \to H_2$ be single-valued operators. Marino and Xu [8] presented an iterative scheme that considers the strong convergence of the viscosity approximation method introduced by Moudafi [9]:

$$a_{n+1} = (I - \alpha_n G)Fa_n + \alpha_n G\beta f(a_n) \quad n \geq 0, \tag{5}$$

f is a function that contracts on the set H with the contraction coefficient $\alpha \in (0,1)$. G is a linear operator that is strongly positive and bounded on H with a constant μ. The parameter is defined in a way that $0 < \beta < \frac{\mu}{\alpha}$, exclusive. There exists a nonexpansive mapping F and a sequence $\{\alpha_n\}$ that takes values in $(0,1)$. The strong convergence of the sequence $\{a_n\}$ obtained from (5) to the fixed point $a^* \in Fix(F) := \{a^* : F(a^*) = a^*\}$ has been proven. Furthermore, a^* serves as the unique solution of the variational inequality:

$$\langle (G - \beta f)a^*, a - a^* \rangle \geq 0, a \in C. \tag{6}$$

The presentation of the optimality condition for the minimization problem is included as follows:

$$\min_{a \in C} \frac{1}{2}\langle Ga, a \rangle - h(a),$$

the function h is a potential function for βf, i.e.,

$$h(a) = \{\beta f(a) \quad for \quad a \in H\}.$$

In 2014, Kazmi and Rizvi [10] were inspired by the work of Byrne et al. (3) to propose the following iteration for solving SVIPs. For a given $a_1 \in H_1$,

$$\begin{cases} k_n = J_\lambda^{m_1}(a_n + \gamma B^*(J_\lambda^{m_2} - I)Ba_n), \\ a_{n+1} = \alpha_n f(a_n) + (1 - \alpha_n)Sk_n \quad n \geq 1, \end{cases} \quad (7)$$

where $\alpha > 0, \gamma \in (0, \frac{1}{L})$, L is the spectral radius of the operator B^*B and sequence $\{\alpha_n\}$ satisfies the conditions: $\lim_{n\to\infty} \alpha_n = 0$, $\sum_{n=0}^\infty \alpha_n = \infty$, and $\sum_{n=0}^\infty |\alpha_n - \alpha_{n-1}| < \infty$. The sequences $\{k_n\}, \{a_n\}$ generated by (7) converges strongly to $z \in Fix(S) \cap \Gamma$. Note that algorithms (3), (4), and (7) contain a stepsize γ, which requires the computation of the norm of the bounded linear operator; this computation is not easy to compute making these algorithms difficult to compute. The inertial technique has been gaining attention from researchers to enhance the accuracy and performance of various algorithms. This technique plays a vital role in the convergence rate of the algorithms and is based on a discrete version of a second-order dissipative dynamical system; see, for instance [11–20]. In Hilbert spaces, Chuang [21] introduced a hybrid inertial proximal algorithm for solving SVIPs in 2017:

The proof of this proposed algorithm establishes that if $\{\lambda_n\} \subset [\lambda, \frac{\delta}{\|B\|^2}]$ and $\{a_n\}$ meets a specific requirement, then sequence $\{a_n\}$ from Algorithm 1 weakly converges to an SVIP solution:

$$\sum_{n=1}^\infty \|a_n - a_{n-1}\|^2 < \infty. \quad (8)$$

Algorithm 1 Hybrid inertial proximal algorithm.

Initialization: Choose $\{\theta_n\} \subset [0,1), \{\beta_n\} \subset (0,1)$. Let $a_0, a_1 \in H_1$ be arbitrary. Set $n = 1$.
Iterative steps: Calculate a_{n+1} as follows:
Step 1. Set $v_n = a_n + \theta_n(a_n - a_{n-1})$ and compute

$$b_n = J_{\beta_n}^{m_1}[v_n - \lambda_n B^*(I - J_{\beta_n}^{m_2})Bv_n],$$

where $\lambda_n > 0$ satisfies

$$\lambda_n \|B^*(I - J_{\beta_n}^{m_2})Bv_n - B^*(I - J_{\beta_n}^{m_2})Bb_n\| \leq \delta \|v_n - b_n\| \quad 0 < \delta < 1$$

if $b_n = v_n$ then stop and b_n is a solution of the SVIP. Otherwise,
Step 2. Compute

$$a_{n+1} = J_{\beta_n}^{m_1}(v_n - \alpha_n d(v_n, b_n)),$$

where

$$d(v_n, b_n) = v_n - b_n - \lambda_n[B^*(I - J_{\beta_n}^{m_2})Bv_n - B^*(I - J_{\beta_n}^{m_2})Bb_n],$$

$$\alpha_n = \frac{\langle v_n - b_n, d(v_n, b_n)\rangle}{\|d(v_n, b_n)\|^2}.$$

Set $n = n + 1$ and go to step 1.

It is easy to see that Algorithm 1 depends on a prior estimate of the norm of the bounded operator, and the Condition (8) is too strong to verify before computation.

Furthermore, Kesornprom and Cholamjiak [22] improved the contraction step in Algorithm 2 and introduced the following algorithm for solving the SVIP:

Algorithm 2 Proximal type algorithms with linesearch and inertial methods.

Let $\zeta, \lambda \in (0,1), \delta > 0$, and sequences $\{\beta_n\}_{n\in\mathbb{N}} \in (0,\infty)$, $\{\theta_n\}_{n\in\mathbb{N}} \in [0,\theta) \subseteq [0,1)$. Take arbitrarily $a_1 \in H_1$ and compute

$$\begin{aligned} k_n &= a_n + \theta_n(a_n - a_{n-1}) \\ b_n &= J_{\beta_n}^{m_1}(k_n - \rho_n B^*(I - J_{\beta_n}^{m_2})Bk_n), \end{aligned} \qquad (9)$$

where $\zeta_n = \delta \zeta^{r_n}$ and r_n is considered as the smallest possible non-negative integer such that

$$\rho_n \|B^*(I - J_{\beta_n}^{m_2})Bk_n - B^*(I - J_{\beta_n}^{m_2})Bb_n\| \leq \lambda \|k_n - b_n\|.$$

Define

$$a_{n+1} = k_n - \phi \alpha_n d(k_n, \rho_n)$$

where $\phi \in (0,2)$,

$$d(k_n, \rho_n) = k_n - b_n - \rho_n(B^*(I - J_{\beta_n}^{m_2})Bk_n - B^*(I - J_{\beta_n}^{m_2})Bb_n)$$

and

$$\alpha_n = \frac{\langle k_n - b_n, d(k_n, \rho_n)\rangle + \rho_n\|(I - J_{\beta_n}^{m_2})Bb_n\|^2}{\|d(k_n, \rho_n)\|^2}.$$

They also proved a weak convergence result under similar conditions as in Algorithm 1. Let us mention that both Algorithms 1 and 2 involve a line search procedure, which consumes extra computation time and memory during implementation. As a way to overcome this setback, Tang [23] recently introduced a self-adaptive technique for selecting the stepsize without a prior estimate of the Lipschitz constant nor a line search procedure as follows (Algorithm 3):

Algorithm 3 Self-adaptive technique method.

Initialization: Choose a sequence $\{\zeta_n\}$ that is non-negative and satisfies conditions $0 < \zeta_n < 4, inf\zeta_n(4 - \zeta_n) > 0$. Select starting points arbitrarily a_0 and set $n = 0$.
Iterative step: Given the current iterate $a_n (n \geq 0)$. Compute

$$\tau_n = \frac{\zeta_n f(a_n)}{\|T(a_n)\|^2 + \|H(a_n)\|^2}$$

and calculate the next iteration as

$$a_{n+1} = J_\lambda^{m_1}(I - \tau_n B^*(I - J_\lambda^{m_2})B)a_n.$$

Stop criterion: If $a_{n+1} = a_n$, then stop the iteration. Otherwise, set $n = n + 1$ and go back to the iterative step.

where $f(a) = \frac{1}{2}\|(I - J_\lambda^{m_2})Ba\|^2$, $T(a) = B^*(I - J_\lambda^{m_2})Ba$ and $H(a) = (I - J_\lambda^{m_1})x$. The author proved that the sequence generated by Algorithm 3 converges weakly to a solution of the SVIP. Tan, Qin, and Yao [24] introduced four self-adaptive iterative algorithms with inertial effects to solve SVIPs in real Hilbert spaces. This algorithm does not need any prior information about the operator norm. This means that their stepsize is self-adaptive. The conditions assumed in performing the strong convergences of the four algorithms are as follows:

(C1) Let the solution set of (SVIP) be nonempty, i.e., $\Omega \neq \emptyset$.
(C2) Let H_1 and H_2 be assumed to be two real Hilbert spaces with a bounded linear operator and its adjoint denoted by $B : H_1 \to H_2$ and $B^* : H_2 \to H_1$, respectively.

(C3) Let $T_i : H_i \to H_i, i = 1, 2$ be the set-valued maximal monotone mappings and $f : H_1 \to H_2$ is a mapping which satisfies the p-contractive property with a constant $p \in [0, 1)$.

(C4) Let the sequence $\{\tilde{\omega}_n\}$ be positive such that $\lim_{n\to\infty} \frac{\tilde{\omega}_n}{\sigma_n} = 0$ where $\{\sigma_n\} \subset (0, 1)$ satisfies $\lim_{n\to\infty} \sigma_n = 0$ and $\sum_{n=1}^{\infty} \sigma_n = \infty$.

Various methods inspired the first iterative algorithm. Namely, Byrne et al.'s [7] method, the viscosity-type method, and the projection and contraction method. An iterative method called the self-adaptive inertial projection and contraction method is utilized for solving the SVIP. A description of the initial iterative method is provided below (Algorithm 4):

Algorithm 4 Viscocity type with projection and contraction method.

Initialization: Set $\lambda, x, \zeta > 0$, $\chi, \delta \in (0, 1)$, $\kappa \in (0, 2)$, and let $a_0, a_1 \in H$.
Iterative steps: Calculate a_{n+1} as follows:
Step 1: Given the iterates a_{n-1} and $a_n (n \geq 1)$, set $k_n = a_n + x_n(a_n - a_{n-1})$ where

$$x_n = \begin{cases} \min\{\frac{\tilde{\omega}}{\|a_n - a_{n-1}\|}, x\} & \text{if } a_n \neq a_{n-1}, \\ x & \text{otherwise.} \end{cases} \quad (10)$$

Step 2. Compute $q_n = J_{\lambda T_1}[k_n - \gamma_n B^*(I - J_{\lambda T_2})Bk_n]$ where $\gamma_n = \zeta \chi^{w_n}$ and w_n is the smallest non-negative integer such that

$$\gamma_n \|B^*(I - J_{\lambda T_2})Bk_n - B^*(I - J_{\lambda T_2})Bq_n\| \leq \delta \|k_n - q_n\|. \quad (11)$$

If $k_n = q_n$, stop the process and consider q_n a valid solution for the problem (SVIP). Otherwise, proceed to step 3.

Step 3. Compute $g_n = k_n - \kappa \mu_n c_n$ where

$$c_n = k_n - q_n - \gamma_n[B^*(I - J_{\lambda T_2})Bk_n - B^*(I - J_{\lambda T_2})Bq_n],$$

$$\mu_n = \frac{\langle k_n - q_n, c_n \rangle}{\|c_n\|^2}. \quad (12)$$

Step 4. Compute $a_{n+1} = \eta_n f(a_n) + (1 - \eta_n)g_n$.
Go to step 1 after setting $n = n + 1$.

Strong convergence was obtained. The second proposed algorithm is an inertial Mann-type projection and contraction algorithm to solve the SVIP, which is presented as follows (Algorithm 5):

Algorithm 5 Mann-type with projection and contraction method.

Initialization: Set $\lambda, x, \zeta > 0$, $\chi, \delta \in (0, 1)$, $\kappa \in (0, 2)$ and let $a_0, a_1 \in H$.
Iterative steps: To determine the upcoming iteration point a_{n+1}, follow these steps:

$$\begin{cases} k_n = a_n + k_n(a_n - a_{n-1}), \\ q_n = J_{\lambda T_1}[k_n - \gamma_n B^*(I - J_{\lambda T_2})Bk_n], \\ g_n = k_n - \kappa \mu_n c_n, \\ a_{n+1} = (1 - \eta_n - \tau_n)k_n + \tau_n g_n, \end{cases} \quad (13)$$

where $\{x_n\}, \{\gamma_n\}$, and $\{c_n\}$ are defined in (10), (11), and (12), respectively.

Strong convergence was obtained. The third proposed algorithm is an inertial Mann-type algorithm whereby the new stepsize does not require any line search process, making it a self-adaptive algorithm. The details of the iterative scheme are described below (Algorithm 6):

Algorithm 6 Inertial Mann-type with self-adaptive method.

Initialization: Set $\lambda, x > 0$, $\phi \in (0,2)$ and let $a_0, a_1 \in H$.
Iterative steps: To determine the upcoming iteration point a_{n+1}, follow these steps:

$$\begin{cases} k_n = a_n + x_n(a_n - a_{n-1}), \\ g_n = J_{\lambda T_1}[k_n - \gamma_n B^*(I - J_{\lambda T_2})Bk_n], \\ a_{n+1} = (1 - \eta_n - \tau_n)k_n + \tau_n g_n, \end{cases} \quad (14)$$

The sequence $\{x_n\}$ is given in Equation (10) and the value of the stepsize γ_n is modified using the subsequent formula below:

$$\gamma_n = \begin{cases} \frac{\phi_n \|(I - J_{\lambda T_2})Bk_n\|^2}{\|B^*(I - J_{\lambda T_2})Bk_n\|^2} & if \quad \|B(I - J_{\lambda T_2})Bk_n\| \neq 0, \\ 0 & otherwise. \end{cases} \quad (15)$$

Strong convergence was obtained. The algorithm proposed fourthly is a variation of Algorithm 6, which leverages the viscosity-type approach to prove the robust convergence of the proposed method. We present the algorithm as follows (Algorithm 7):

Algorithm 7 New inertial viscocity method.

Initialization: Set $\lambda, x > 0$, $\phi \in (0,2)$ and let $a_0, a_1 \in H$.
Iterative steps: To determine the upcoming iteration point a_{n+1}, follow these steps:

$$\begin{cases} k_n = a_n + x_n(a_n - a_{n-1}), \\ g_n = J_{\lambda T_1}[k_n - \gamma_n B^*(I - J_{\lambda T_2})Bk_n], \\ a_{n+1} = \eta_n f(a_n) + (1 - \eta_n)g_n, \end{cases} \quad (16)$$

where $\{x_n\}$ and $\{\gamma_n\}$ are defined in (10) and (15), respectively.

Strong convergence was obtained. The four algorithms contain an inertial term that plays a role at the rate of the convergence of Algorithms 4–7. Note that the strong convergence theorems proved for Algorithms 4–7 proposed by Tan, Qin, and Yan were obtained under some weaker conditions. Zhou, Tan, and Li [25] proposed a pair of adaptive hybrid steepest descent algorithms with an inertial extrapolation term for split monotone variational inclusion problems in infinite-dimensional Hilbert spaces. These algorithms benefit from combining two methods, the hybrid steepest descent method and the inertial method, ensuring and achieving strong convergence theorems. Secondly, the stepsizes of the two proposed algorithms are self-adaptive, which overcomes the difficulty of the computation of the operator norm. The details of the first algorithm are presented as follows (Algorithm 8):

Algorithm 8 Inertial hyrbid steepest descent algorithm.

Requirements: Take arbitrary starting points $a_0; a_1 \in H_1$. Choose sequences $\{\alpha_n\} \subset [0,1), \{\eta_n\}$ and $\{\beta_n\}$ in $(0,1)$ and $\gamma, \tau, \mu > 0$.
1. Set $n = 1$ and compute $k_n = a_n + \alpha_n(a_n - a_{n-1})$ and adaptive stepsize

$$\lambda_n = \begin{cases} \frac{\eta_n \|(I - W_2)Bk_n\|^2}{\|B^*(I - W_2)Bk_n\|^2} & Bk_n \notin Fix(W_2), \\ 0 & otherwise. \end{cases} \quad (17)$$

2. Compute $b_n = W_1(k_n - \lambda_n B^*(I - W_2)Bk_n)$.
3. If $b_n = k_n$, then stop. Otherwise, compute $a_{n+1} = \beta_n \tau_n h(b_n) + (I - \beta_n \mu D)b_n$.
4. Set $n = n + 1$ and return to 1.

Strong convergence was obtained. The second proposed algorithm is presented as follows (Algorithm 9):

Algorithm 9 Self-adaptive hybrid steepest descnt method.

Requirements: Two arbitrary starting points $a_0; a_1 \in H_1$. Choose sequences $\{\alpha_n\} \subset [0,1), \{\eta_n\}$ and $\{\beta_n\}$ in $(0,1)$ and $\gamma, \tau, \mu > 0$.
1. Set $n = 1$ and compute $k_n = a_n + \alpha_n(a_n - a_{n-1}), z_n = W_1(k_n)$ and adaptive stepsize

$$\alpha_n = \begin{cases} \frac{\eta_n \|(I-W_2)Bz_n\|^2}{\|B^*(I-W_2)Bz_n\|^2} & Bz_n \notin Fix(W_2), \\ 0 & otherwise. \end{cases} \quad (18)$$

2. Compute $b_n = z_n - \lambda_n B^*(I - W_2)Bz_n$.
3. If $b_n = z_n = k_n$, then stop. Otherwise, compute $a_{n+1} = \beta_n \tau_n h(b_n) + (I - \beta_n \mu D)b_n$.
4. Set $n = n + 1$ and return to 1.

Strong convergence was obtained. The assumptions applied to Algorithms 8 and 9 are as follows: Let H_1 and H_2 denote two Hilbert spaces, and suppose that $B: H_1 \to H_2$ is a linear operator that is bounded. Additionally, let B^* be the adjoint operator of B. Let $f_i : H_i \to H_i$ be a v_i-inverse strongly monotone mapping with $i = 1, 2$ and $m_i : H_i \to 2^{H_i}$ be set-valued maximal monotone mappings with $i = 1, 2$. $D : H_1 \to H_1$ is L_2-Lipschitz continuous and η-strongly mapping with $L_2, \eta > 0$. Let $h : H_1 \to H_1$ be L_1-Lipschitz continuous mapping with $L_1 > 0$. Moreover, Alakoya et al. [26] introduced a method with an inertial extrapolation technique, viscosity approximation, and contains a stepsize that is self-adaptive; thus, the method is known as an inertial self-adaptive algorithm for solving the SVIP (Algorithm 10):

Algorithm 10 General viscosity with self-adaptive and inertial method.

Step 0: Select $a_0, a_1 \in H_1, \{\rho_n\} \in (0,4), \{\beta_n\}, \{\alpha_n\} \subset (0,1), \{\theta_n\} \subset [0,\theta)$ for some $\theta > 0$. Set $n = 1$.
Step 1: Given the $(n-1)$-th and n-th iterates, set

$$v_n = a_n + \theta_n(a_n - a_{n-1}).$$

Step 2: Compute

$$k_n = J_\lambda^{m_1}(v_n - \tau_n B^*(I - J_\lambda^{m_2}))$$

where

$$\tau_n = \begin{cases} \frac{\rho_n g(v_n)}{\|T(v_n)\|^2 + \|H(v_n)\|^2} & \text{if } \|T(v_n)\|^2 + \|H(v_n)\|^2 \neq 0, \\ 0 & otherwise. \end{cases} \quad (19)$$

Step 3: Compute

$$a_{n+1} = \alpha_n f(a_n) + \beta_n a_n + ((1-\beta_n)I - \alpha_n G)Sk_n.$$

Set $n = n + 1$ and return to Step 1.

---

where $S : H_1 \to H_1$ is a quasi-nonexpansive mapping, $G : H_1 \to H_1$ is a strongly positive mapping, and $f : H_1 \to H_1$ is a contraction mapping. The convergence of a common solution for the sequence $\{a_n\}$ generated by Algorithm 10 was established by the authors through proof of its strong convergence $z \in \Gamma \cap Fix(S)$ provided that $\{\alpha_n\}$ and $\{\theta_n\}$ satisfy $\lim_{n \to \infty} \frac{\theta_n}{\alpha_n}\|a_n - a_{n-1}\| = 0$. It is clear that Algorithm 10 performs better than Algorithms 1–3 and other related methods. However, there is a need to improve the performance of Algorithm 10 by using an optimal choice of parameters for the inertial extrapolation term.

Based on the outcomes above, our paper presents a novel approach that utilizes an optimal selection of inertial term and self-adaptive techniques for solving the SVIP and fixed point problems by employing multivalued demicontractive mappings in actual Hilbert spaces. Our algorithm enhances the results of Algorithms 1–3 and 10, and other associated findings in the literature. We demonstrate a robust convergence outcome, subject to certain mild conditions, and provide relevant numerical experiments to showcase the efficiency of the proposed method. We also consider an application of our algorithm to solving image deblurring problems to demonstrate the applicability of our results.

2. Preliminaries

In this section, we present certain definitions and fundamental outcomes that will be employed in our ensuing analysis. Suppose that H is a real Hilbert space, and C is a subset of H that is closed, nonempty, and convex. We use $a_n \to p$ and $a_n \rightharpoonup p$ to denote the strong and weak convergences, respectively, of a sequence $\{a_n\} \subseteq H$ to a point $p \in H$.

For every vector $\bar{k} \in H$, there exists a unique element $P_C\bar{k}$ in the subspace C such that

$$||P_C(\bar{k}) - \bar{k}|| = \min\{||z - \bar{k}|| : z \in C\}.$$

The metric projection from H onto C is denoted as P_C and can be defined by the subsequent expression:

(i) For $\bar{k} \in H$ and $z \in C$,

$$z = P_C(\bar{k}) \Leftrightarrow \langle \bar{k} - z, z - b \rangle \geq 0, \quad \forall b \in C; \tag{20}$$

(ii) $\langle \bar{k} - b, P_C(\bar{k}) - P_C(b) \rangle \geq ||P_C(\bar{k}) - P_C(b)||^2 \quad \forall \bar{k}, b \in H$;

(iii) For each $\bar{k} \in H$ and $b \in C$

$$||b - P_C(\bar{k})||^2 + ||\bar{k} - P_C(\bar{k})||^2 \leq ||\bar{k} - b||^2.$$

An operator $F : H \to H$ is called:

(i) α-Lipschitz if there is a positive value of α such that

$$||Fb - Fa|| \leq \alpha ||b - a|| \quad \forall b, a \in H$$

and a contraction if $\alpha \in (0, 1)$;

(ii) Nonexpansive if F is 1-Lipschitz;

(iii) Quasi-nonexpansive when its fixed point set is not empty and

$$||Fb - p|| \leq ||b - p|| \quad \forall b \in H, p \in Fix(F);$$

(iv) k-demicontractive if $Fix(F) \neq \emptyset$ and there exists a constant $k \in [0, 1)$ such that

$$||Fa - p||^2 \leq ||a - p||^2 + k||a - Fa||^2 \quad \forall a \in H, \quad p \in Fix(F).$$

Note that the nonexpansive and quasi-nonexpansive mappings are contained in the class of k-demicontractive mapping; we also follow the same conditions for the Hausdorff mapping, $S : H \to 2^H$.

Suppose we have a metric space (X, d) and a family of subsets $CB(X)$ that are both closed and bounded. We can induce the Hausdorff metric using the metric d on any two subsets $X, Y \in CB(X)$. This metric is defined as follows:

$$\mathcal{H}(X,Y) = \max\left\{\sup_{x \in X} d(x,Y), \sup_{y \in Y} d(X,y)\right\},$$

where $d(x,Y) = \inf_{y \in Y} d(x,y)$. A fixed point of a multivalued mapping $S : H \to CB(H)$ is a point $a \in H$ that belongs to Sa. If $S(a)$ only contains a, then we refer to a as a strict fixed point of S. The study of strictly fixed points for a specific type of contractive mappings was first conducted by Aubin and Siegel [27]. Since then, this condition has been rapidly applied to various multivalued mappings, such as those in [28–30].

Lemma 1. *The inequalities stated below are valid in a Hilbert space denoted by H.:*
(i) $||b-a||^2 = ||b||^2 - 2\langle b,a\rangle + ||a||^2 \quad \forall b,a \in H$;
(ii) $||b+a||^2 \leq ||b||^2 + 2\langle a, b+a\rangle \quad \forall b,a \in H$.

We also use the following Lemmas to achieve our goal in the section on the main results; Lemmas [31–33].

3. Main Results

In this section, we introduce our algorithm and provide its convergence analysis. First, we prove the state of our algorithm as follows:

Let H_1, H_2 be two real Hilbert spaces, and the multivalued maximal monotone operators are denoted by $m_i : H_i \to 2^{H_i}$, where $i = 1,2$. We denote the bounded linear operator with its adjoint as $B : H_1 \to H_2$ and $B^* : H_2 \to H_1$, respectively. For $i = 1,\ldots,m$ define $S_i : H_1 \to CB(H_1)$ be a finite family of k_i-demicontractive mappings such that $I - S_i$ is demiclosed at the point zero with $S_i(q) = \{q\} \quad \forall q \in Fix(S_i)$ and $k = \max\{k_i\}$. Suppose that the solution set:

$$\Gamma = \{a^* \in H_1 : 0 \in m_1(a^*), 0 \in m_2(Ba^*)\} \cap \bigcap_{i=1}^{r} Fix(S_i) \neq \emptyset. \tag{21}$$

Let our contraction mapping be $g : H_1 \to H_1$ with a constant of $\sigma \in (0,1)$ and $D : H_1 \to H_1$ be a strongly non-negative operator with $\eta > 0$ being its coefficient where this condition, $0 < \xi < \frac{\eta}{\sigma}$, is satisfied. Moreover, let $\{\epsilon_n\}, \{\rho_{n,i}\}, \{\lambda_n\}$ be non-negative sequences such that $0 < y \leq \epsilon_n, \rho_{n,i}, \lambda_n \leq u < 1$. Define the following functions:

$$f(a) = \frac{1}{2}||(I - J_\sigma^{m_2})Ba||^2 \tag{22}$$

and

$$T(a) = B^*(I - J_\lambda^{m_2})Ba, \quad H(a) = (I - J_\lambda^{m_1})a. \tag{23}$$

Now, we present our algorithm as follows (Algorithm 11):

Algorithm 11 Proposed new inertial and self-adaptive method.

Step 0: Choose $\alpha > 3, \eta_n \in (0,4)$ and select initial guess $a_0, a_1 \in H_1$. Set $n = 1$.
Step 1: Choose θ_n such that $0 \leq \theta_n \leq \bar{\theta}_n$, where $\bar{\theta}_n$ is defined below, given the $(n-1)$th and nth iterates:

$$\bar{\theta}_n = \begin{cases} \min\left\{\frac{n-1}{n+\alpha-1}, \frac{\epsilon_n}{\max\{\|a_n - a_{n-1}\|, n^2\|a_n - a_{n-1}\|^2\}}\right\} & \text{if } a_n \neq a_{n-1}, \\ \frac{n-1}{n+\alpha-1} & \text{otherwise.} \end{cases} \quad (24)$$

Set
$$v_n = a_n + \theta_n(a_n - a_{n-1}).$$

Step 2: Compute
$$\tau_n = \frac{\eta_n f(v_n)}{\|T(v_n)\|^2 + \|H(v_n)\|^2}$$

and
$$b_n = J_\sigma^{m_1}(I - \tau_n B^*(I - J_\sigma^{m_2})B)v_n$$

Step 3: Compute the next iterate via
$$\begin{cases} z_n = \rho_{n,0} b_n + \sum_{i=1}^r \rho_{n,i} \chi_{n,i}, \\ a_{n+1} = \lambda_n \xi g(a_n) + (1 - \lambda_n D)z_n, \end{cases} \quad (25)$$

where $\chi_{n,i} \in S_i b_n$ and $\sum_{i=1}^r \rho_{n,i} = 1$. Set $n = n + 1$ and go back to **Step 1**.

To ensure our convergence outcomes, we have made assumptions on the control parameters $\lambda_n, \epsilon_n, \rho_{n,i}$ that must meet certain conditions:
(C1) $\lim_{n \to \infty} \lambda_n = 0$ and $\sum_{n=0}^\infty \lambda_n = \infty$,
(C2) $\liminf_{n \to \infty}(\rho_{n,0} - k)\rho_{n,i} > 0 \quad \forall i = 1, 2, \ldots, r$,
(C3) $\epsilon_n = o(\lambda_n)$, i.e., $\lim_{n \to \infty} \frac{\epsilon_n}{\lambda_n} = 0$.

Remark 1. *It is clear from (24) and Assumptions (C3), that*

$$\lim_{n \to \infty} \frac{\theta_n}{\lambda_n} \|a_n - a_{n-1}\|^2 \leq \lim_{n \to \infty} \frac{\bar{\theta}_n}{\lambda_n} \|a_n - a_{n-1}\|^2 \leq \lim_{n \to \infty} \frac{\epsilon_n}{\lambda_n} \cdot \frac{1}{n^2} = 0$$

and

$$\lim_{n \to \infty} \frac{\theta_n}{\lambda_n} \|a_n - a_{n-1}\| \leq \lim_{n \to \infty} \frac{\bar{\theta}_n}{\lambda_n} \|a_n - a_{n-1}\| \leq \lim_{n \to \infty} \frac{\epsilon_n}{\lambda_n} = 0.$$

Convergence Analysis

We begin the convergence of Algorithm 11 by proving the following results.

Lemma 2. *Consider the function $f : H_2 \to \mathbb{R}$ and $h : H_1 \to \mathbb{R}$ defined in (22); then, the functions T and H defined on (23) are Lipschitz continuous.*

Proof. Since $T(a) = B^*(I - J_\sigma^{m_2})Ba$, therefore

$$\begin{aligned} \|T(a) - T(b)\|^2 &= \langle B^*((I - J_\sigma^{m_2})Ba - (I - J_\sigma^{m_2})Bb), B^*((I - J_\sigma^{m_2})Ba - (I - J_\sigma^{m_2})Bb)\rangle \\ &= \langle (I - J_\sigma^{m_2})(Ba - Bb), BB^*((I - J_\sigma^{m_2})Ba - (I - J_\sigma^{m_2})Bb)\rangle \\ &\leq L\|(I - J_\sigma^{m_2})Ba - (I - J_\sigma^{m_2})Bb\|^2, \end{aligned} \quad (26)$$

where $L = ||B^*B||$. On the other hand,

$$\begin{aligned}
\langle T(a) - T(b), a - b \rangle &= \langle B^*((I - J_\sigma^{m_2})Ba - (I - J_\sigma^{m_2})Bb), a - b \rangle \\
&= \langle (I - J_\sigma^{m_2})Ba - (I - J_\sigma^{m_2})Bb, Ba - Bb \rangle \\
&\geq ||(I - J_\sigma^{m_2})Ba - (I - J_\sigma^{m_2})Bb||^2.
\end{aligned} \qquad (27)$$

Combining the above formulas, we have:

$$\langle T(a) - T(b), a - b \rangle \geq \frac{1}{L}||T(a) - T(b)||^2,$$

T being $\frac{1}{L}$ inverse strong monotone implies that its inverse is L-Lipschitz continuous. Furthermore,

$$\langle T(a) - T(b), a - b \rangle \leq ||T(a) - T(b)|| ||a - b||,$$

hence

$$||T(a) - T(b)|| \leq L||a - b||.$$

Likewise, it can be observed that the function H exhibits Lipschitz continuity. □

Lemma 3. *The sequence $\{a_n\}$, which was generated by Algorithm 11 is bounded.*

Proof. Given $q \in \Gamma$, then

$$\begin{aligned}
||v_n - q|| &= ||a_n + \theta_n(a_n - a_{n-1}) - q|| \\
&\leq ||a_n - q|| + \theta_n||a_n - a_{n-1}||.
\end{aligned} \qquad (28)$$

Since $\Gamma \neq \emptyset$, then $q = J_\sigma^{m_1}(q)$, $Bp = J_\sigma^{m_2}(Bq)$, and $(I - J_\sigma^{m_2})Bq = Bq - Bq = 0$. Note that $T(v_n) = B^*(I - J_\sigma^{m_2})Bv_n$, $I - J_\sigma^{m_2}$ is firmly nonexpansive, therefore we obtain the following:

$$\begin{aligned}
\langle T(v_n), v_n - q \rangle &= \langle B^*(I - J_\sigma^{m_2})Bv_n, v_n - q \rangle \\
&= \langle (I - J_\sigma^{m_2})Bv_n - (I - J_\sigma^{m_2})Bq, Bv_n - Bq \rangle \\
&\geq ||(I - J_\sigma^{m_2})Bv_n||^2 \\
&= 2f(v_n)
\end{aligned} \qquad (29)$$

and

$$\begin{aligned}
||b_n - q||^2 &= ||J_\sigma^{m_1}(I - \tau_n B^*(I - J_\sigma^{m_2})B)v_n - q||^2 \\
&\leq ||(I - \tau_n B^*(I - J_\sigma^{m_2})B)v_n - q||^2 \\
&= ||v_n - q - \tau_n T(v_n)||^2 \\
&= ||v_n - q||^2 + \tau_n^2 ||T(v_n)||^2 - 2\tau_n \langle T(v_n), v_n - q \rangle \\
&\leq ||v_n - q||^2 + \tau_n^2 ||T(v_n)||^2 - 4\tau_n f(v_n) \\
&\leq ||v_n - q||^2 - \eta_n(4 - \eta_n) \frac{f^2(v_n)}{||T(v_n)||^2 + ||H(v_n)||^2}.
\end{aligned} \qquad (30)$$

Since $0 < \eta_n < 4$, then $||b_n - q|| \leq ||v_n - q||$. We use Lemma [31] to obtain the following results:

$$||z_n - q||^2 = ||\rho_{n,0} b_n + \sum_{i=1}^{r} \rho_{n,i} \chi_{n,i} - q||^2$$

$$\leq \rho_{n,0}||b_n - q||^2 + \sum_{i=1}^{r} \rho_{n,i}||\chi_{n,i} - q||^2 - \sum_{i=1}^{r} \rho_{n,0}\rho_{n,i}||b_n - \chi_{n,i}||^2$$

$$= \rho_{n,0}||b_n - q||^2 + \sum_{i=1}^{r} \rho_{n,i} d(\chi_{n,i}, S_i q)^2 - \sum_{i=1}^{r} \rho_{n,0}\rho_{n,i}||b_n - \chi_{n,i}||^2$$

$$\leq \rho_{n,0}||b_n - q||^2 + \sum_{i=1}^{r} \rho_{n,i} \mathcal{H}(S_i b_n, S_i q)^2 - \sum_{i=1}^{r} \rho_{n,0}\rho_{n,i}||b_n - \chi_{n,i}||^2$$

$$\leq \rho_{n,0}||b_n - q||^2 + \sum_{i=1}^{r} \rho_{n,i}(||b_n - q||^2 + \kappa_i d(b_n, S_i b_n)^2) - \sum_{i=1}^{r} \rho_{n,0}\rho_{n,i}||b_n - \chi_{n,i}||^2$$

$$\leq ||b_n - q||^2 - \sum_{i=1}^{r}(\rho_{n,0} - \kappa)\rho_{n,i}||b_n - \chi_{n,i}||^2, \tag{31}$$

thus, we apply condition (C2) and have the following:

$$||z_n - q||^2 \leq ||b_n - q||^2. \tag{32}$$

Follow from (28), (30), and (31) to obtain:

$$||a_{n+1} - q|| = ||\lambda_n(\xi g(a_n) Dq) + (1 - \lambda_n D)(z_n - q)||$$

$$\leq \lambda_n ||\xi g(a_n) - Dq|| + (1 - \lambda_n \eta)||z_n - q||$$

$$\leq \lambda_n \big[||\xi(g(a_n) - g(q)) + (\xi g(q) - Dq)||\big] + (1 - \lambda_n \eta)||z_n - q||$$

$$\leq \lambda_n \xi \sigma ||a_n - q|| + \lambda_n ||\xi g(q) - Dq|| + (1 - \lambda_n \eta)[||a_n - q|| + \theta_n ||a_n - a_{n-1}||]$$

$$= (1 - \lambda_n(\eta - \xi \sigma))||a_n - q|| + \lambda_n ||\xi g(q) - Dq|| + (1 - \lambda_n \eta)\sigma_n ||a_n - a_{n-1}||$$

$$= (1 - \lambda_n(\eta - \xi \sigma))||a_n - q|| +$$

$$(\eta - \xi \sigma)\lambda_n \left\{ \frac{||\xi g(q) - Dq||}{\eta - \xi \sigma} + \left(\frac{1 - \lambda_n \eta}{\eta - \xi \sigma}\right) \frac{\theta_n}{\lambda_n} ||a_n - a_{n-1}|| \right\}. \tag{33}$$

Note that $\sup_{n \geq 1} \left(\frac{1-\lambda_n \eta}{\eta - \xi \sigma}\right) \frac{\theta_n}{\lambda_n} ||a_n - a_{n-1}||$ exists by Remark 1 and let

$$M = \max \left\{ \frac{||\xi g(q) - Dq||}{\eta - \xi \sigma}, \sup_{n \geq 1} \left(\frac{1 - \lambda_n \eta}{\eta - \xi \sigma}\right) \frac{\theta_n}{\lambda_n} ||a_n - a_{n-1}|| \right\}.$$

Therefore, we have the following:

$$||a_{n+1} - q|| \leq (1 - \lambda_n(\eta - \xi \sigma))||a_n - q|| + \lambda_n(\eta - \xi \sigma)M.$$

We continue and use Lemma [32] (i) to imply that $\{||a_n - p||\}$ is bounded and therefore, $\{a_n\}$ is also bounded. Consequently, sequences $\{v_n\}, \{z_n\}$, and $\{b_n\}$ are bounded. □

Lemma 4. *Given $\{a_n\}$ as the sequence generated by the proposed Algorithm 5, put $s_n = ||a_n - q||^2$, $\tilde{a}_n = \frac{2\lambda_n(\eta - \xi \sigma)}{1 - \lambda_n \xi \sigma}$, $u_n = \frac{1}{2(\eta - \xi \sigma)}(2\langle \xi g(q) - Dq, a_{n+1} - q\rangle + \lambda_n M_1)$, for some $M_1 > 0$ and $c_n = \frac{\theta_n ||a_n - a_{n-1}||}{1 - \lambda_n \xi \sigma} M_2$ where $M_2 = \sup_{n \geq 1}((1 - \lambda_n q)^2(||a_n - q|| + ||a_{n-1} - q||) + 2(1 - \lambda_n q)^2 ||a_n - a_{n-1}||)$ and $q \in \Gamma$.*

Then, the following conclusions hold:

(i) $s_{n+1} \leq (1 - \tilde{y}_n) s_n + c_n + \tilde{y}_n u_n$.
(ii) $-1 \leq \limsup_{n \to \infty} u_n < +\infty$.

Proof. From Algorithm 11, we have

$$\begin{aligned}||v_n - q||^2 &= ||a_n + \theta_n(a_n - a_{n-1}) - q||^2 \\ &= ||a_n - q||^2 + 2\theta_n\langle a_n - q, a_n - a_{n-1}\rangle + \theta_n^2||a_n - a_{n-1}||^2.\end{aligned} \quad (34)$$

Let us use Lemma 1(i) in order to determine the following results:

$$2\langle a_n - q, a_n - a_{n-1}\rangle = -||a_{n-1} - q||^2 + ||a_n - q||^2 + ||a_n - a_{n-1}||^2 \quad (35)$$

thus, substituting (35) into (34), we obtain

$$\begin{aligned}||v_n - q||^2 &= ||a_n - q||^2 + \theta_n(-||a_{n-1} - q||^2 + ||a_n - q||^2 + ||a_n - a_{n-1}||^2) + \theta_n^2||a_n - a_{n-1}||^2 \\ &\leq ||a_n - q||^2 + \theta_n(||a_n - q||^2 - ||a_{n-1} - q||^2 + 2\theta_n||a_n - a_{n-1}||^2).\end{aligned} \quad (36)$$

Now, we follow from Lemma 1(ii) and have that

$$\begin{aligned}||a_{n+1} - q||^2 &= ||\lambda_n(\xi g(a_n) - Dq) + (1 - \lambda_n D)(z_n - q)||^2 \\ &\leq (1 - \lambda_n \eta)^2||z_n - q||^2 + 2\lambda_n\langle \xi g(a_n) - Dq, a_{n+1} - q\rangle.\end{aligned} \quad (37)$$

Follow from (30), (32), and (34) to obtain

$$\begin{aligned}||a_{n+1} - q||^2 &\leq (1 - \lambda_n\eta)^2||v_n - q||^2 + 2\lambda_n\langle \xi g(a_n) - Dq, a_{n+1} - q\rangle \\ &= (1 - \lambda_n\eta)^2(||a_n - q||^2 + \theta_n(||a_n - q||^2 - ||a_{n-1} - q||^2) + 2\theta_n||a_n - a_{n-1}||^2) + \\ &\quad 2\lambda_n\langle \xi g(a_n) - Dq, a_{n+1} - q\rangle \\ &= (1 - \lambda_n\eta)^2||a_n - q||^2 + \theta_n(1 - \lambda_n\eta)^2(||a_n - q||^2 - ||a_{n-1} - q||^2) + \\ &\quad 2\theta_n(1 - \lambda_n\eta)^2||a_n - a_{n-1}||^2 + 2\lambda_n\langle \xi g(a_n) - Dq, a_{n+1} - q\rangle \\ &\leq (1 - \lambda_n\eta)^2||a_n - q||^2 + \theta_n(1 - \lambda_n\eta)^2(||a_n - q|| + ||a_{n-1} - q||)||a_n - a_{n-1}|| + \\ &\quad 2\theta_n(1 - \lambda_n\eta)^2||a_n - a_{n-1}||^2 + 2\lambda_n\langle \xi g(a_n) - Dq, a_{n+1} - q\rangle.\end{aligned} \quad (38)$$

Also,

$$\begin{aligned}2\langle \xi g(a_n) - Dq, a_{n+1} - q\rangle &= 2\langle \xi(g(a_n) - g(q)) + \xi g(q) - Dq, a_{n+1} - q\rangle \\ &\leq 2\xi\sigma||a_n - q||\,||a_{n+1} - q|| + 2\langle \xi g(q) - Dq, a_{n+1} - q\rangle \\ &\leq \xi\sigma(||a_n - q||^2 + ||a_{n+1} - q||^2) + 2\langle \xi g(q) - Dq, a_{n+1} - q\rangle.\end{aligned} \quad (39)$$

Furthermore, substitute (39) into (38) and have that

$$\begin{aligned}||a_{n+1} - q||^2 &\leq [(1 - \lambda_n\eta)^2 + \lambda_n\xi\sigma]||a_n - q||^2 + \theta_n(1 - \lambda_n\eta)^2(||a_n - q|| + ||a_{n-1} - q||)||a_n - a_{n-1}|| + \\ &\quad 2\theta_n(1 - \lambda_n\eta)^2||a_n - a_{n-1}||^2 + \lambda_n\xi\sigma||a_{n+1} - q||^2 + 2\lambda_n\langle \xi g(q) - Dq, a_{n+1} - q\rangle \\ &= (1 - \lambda_n(2q - \xi\sigma))||a_n - q||^2 + (\lambda_n\eta)^2||a_n - q||^2 + \theta_n[(1 - \lambda_n\eta)^2(||a_n - q|| + ||a_{n-1} - q||) + \\ &\quad 2(1 - \lambda_n\eta)^2||a_n - a_{n-1}||]||a_n - a_{n-1}|| + \lambda_n\xi\sigma||a_{n+1} - q||^2 + 2\lambda_n\langle \xi g(q) - Dq, a_{n+1} - q\rangle \\ &\leq (1 - \lambda_n(2q - \xi\sigma))||a_n - q||^2 + \lambda_n\xi\sigma||a_{n+1} - q||^2 + \theta_n[(1 - \lambda_n\eta)^2(||a_n - q|| + ||a_{n-1} - q||) + \\ &\quad 2(1 - \lambda_n)^2||a_n - a_{n-1}||]||a_n - a_{n-1}|| + \lambda_n(2\langle \xi g(q) - Dq, a_{n+1} - q\rangle + \lambda_n M_1)\end{aligned} \quad (40)$$

for some $M_1 \geq 0$, we have that

$$\begin{aligned}
||a_{n+1} - q||^2 &\leq \frac{(1 - \lambda_n(2q - \xi\sigma))}{1 - \lambda_n\xi\sigma}||a_n - q||^2 + \frac{\theta_n}{1 - \lambda_n\xi\sigma}||a_n - a_{n-1}||M_2 + \\
&\quad \frac{\lambda_n(2\langle \xi g(q) - Dq, a_{n+1} - q\rangle + \lambda_n M_1)}{1 - \lambda_n\xi\sigma} \\
&= \left(1 - \frac{2\lambda_n(\eta - \xi\sigma)}{1 - \lambda_n\xi\sigma}\right)||a_n - q||^2 + \frac{\theta_n}{1 - \lambda_n\xi\sigma}||a_n - a_{n-1}||M_2 \\
&\quad + \frac{2\lambda_n(\eta - \xi\sigma)}{1 - \lambda_n\xi\sigma} \frac{(2\langle \xi g(q) - Dq, a_{n+1} - q\rangle + \lambda_n M_1)}{2(\eta - \xi\sigma)}.
\end{aligned} \quad (41)$$

Furthermore, from the boundedness of $\{a_n\}$, it is easy to see that

$$\sup_{n \geq 0} u_n \leq \sup_{n \geq 0} \frac{1}{2(\rho - \xi\sigma)}(2||\xi g(q) - Da^*||||a_{n+1} - q|| + M_1) < \infty.$$

Our next objective is to demonstrate that $\limsup_{n\to\infty} u_n \geq -1$. To do so, we will assume the opposite and suppose that $\limsup_{n\to\infty} u_n < -1$, which implies that there exists $n_0 \in \mathbb{N}$ where $u_n \leq -1 \quad \forall n \geq n_0$. Therefore, according to (i), we can conclude that

$$\begin{aligned}
s_{n+1} &\leq (1 - \tilde{y}_n)s_n + c_n + \tilde{y}_n u_n \\
&< (1 - \tilde{y}_n)s_n + c_n - \tilde{y}_n \\
&= c_n + s_n - \tilde{y}_n(s_n + 1) \\
&\leq c_n + s_n - 2(\eta - \xi\sigma)\lambda_n.
\end{aligned} \quad (42)$$

By induction, we obtain

$$s_{n+1} \leq s_{n_0} + \sum_{i=n_0}^{r} c_i - 2(\eta - \xi\sigma)\sum_{i=n_0}^{r} \lambda_i \quad \forall n \geq n_0.$$

Taking the limit superior of both sides of the last inequality and noting that c_i approaches 0, we obtain

$$\limsup_{n\to\infty} s_n \leq s_{n_0} - \lim_{n\to\infty} 2(\eta - \xi\sigma)\sum_{i=n_0}^{r} \lambda_i = -\infty.$$

This is a contradiction of $\{s_n\}$ being a non-negative real sequence. Therefore, we can conclude that $\limsup_{n\to\infty} u_n \geq -1$. □

Remark 2. *Given that the $\lim_{n\to\infty} \lambda_n \to 0$, it becomes easier to confirm that $\tilde{y}_n$ also approaches zero. In addition, according to Remark 1, c_n approaches zero with an increasing n value.*

Now, we present our strong convergence theorem.

Theorem 1. *Given $\{a_n\}$ as the sequence generated by the proposed Algorithm 11 and suppose that Assumption (C1)–(C3) are satisfied. Then, $\{a_n\}$ strongly converges to a unique point $p = P_\Gamma(I - D + \xi g)(p)$, which solves the variational inequality*

$$\langle (D - \xi g)p, p - a\rangle \leq 0, a \in \Gamma. \quad (43)$$

Proof. Given $q \in \Gamma$. We will use Φ_n to denote $||a_n - q||^2$. Below are the possible cases we are considering.

CASE A: We start by assuming that there exists a $n_0 \in \mathbb{N}$ such that Φ_n is monotonically decreasing $\forall n \geq n_0$. Then, $\lim_{n \to \infty} \Phi_n - \Phi_{n+1} \to 0$. Our first aim is to demonstrate that $\lim_{n \to \infty} \{||b_n - v_n||, ||\chi_{n,i} - b_n||, ||a_{n+1} - a_n||\} \to 0$.

$$\begin{aligned} ||v_n - a_n|| &= ||a_n - a_n + \theta_n(a_n - a_{n-1})|| \\ &= \theta_n ||a_n - a_{n-1}|| \to 0 \quad as \quad n \to \infty, \end{aligned} \quad (44)$$

thus, $\lim_{n \to \infty} ||v_n - a_n|| = 0$. From Equations (30) and (37) we have that:

$$\begin{aligned} \eta_n(4 - \eta_n) \frac{f^2(v_n)}{||T(v_n)||^2 + ||H(v_n)||^2} &\leq ||v_n - q||^2 - ||b_n - q||^2 \\ &\leq ||v_n - q||^2 - ||a_{n+1} - q||^2 + ||a_{n+1} - q||^2 - ||b_n - q||^2 \\ &\leq ||a_n - q||^2 + \theta_n M(||a_n - a_{n-1}||) - ||a_{n+1} - q||^2 + (1 - \lambda_n \tau)||z_n - q||^2 + \\ &\quad 2\lambda_n \langle \xi g(a_n) - Dq, a_{n+1} - q \rangle - ||b_n - q||^2 \\ &\leq \Phi_n - \Phi_{n+1} + \theta_n M ||a_n - a_{n+1}|| + ||b_n - q||^2 - \lambda_n \tau ||b_n - q||^2 + \\ &\quad 2\lambda_n \langle \xi g(a_n) - Dq, a_{n+1} - q \rangle - ||b_n - q||^2 \to 0 \quad as \quad n \to \infty. \end{aligned} \quad (45)$$

Note that $\inf \eta_n(4 - \eta_n) > 0$ and T together with H are Lipschitz continuous, so we obtain that:

$$\lim_{n \to \infty} f^2(v_n) = 0.$$

Therefore, $f(v_n) \to 0$ and $||b_n - v_n|| \to 0$ as $n \to \infty$. From (30), (31), (36), and (37), we obtain the following results:

$$\begin{aligned} ||a_{n+1} - q||^2 &\leq (1 - \lambda_n \eta)^2 ||z_n - q||^2 + 2\lambda_n \langle \xi g(a_n) - Dq, a_{n+1} - q \rangle \\ &\leq (1 - \lambda_n \eta)^2 \left\{ ||b_n - q||^2 - \sum_{i=1}^{r}(\rho_{n,0} - k)\rho_{n,i}||b_n - \chi_{n,i}||^2 \right\} + 2\lambda_n \langle \xi g(a_n) - Dq, a_{n+1} - q \rangle \\ &\leq (1 - \lambda_n \eta)^2 \left\{ ||a_n - q||^2 + \theta_n(||a_n - q||^2 - ||a_{n-1} - q||^2) \right\} + (1 - \lambda_n \eta)^2 \\ &\quad \left\{ 2\theta_n ||a_n - a_{n-1}||^2 - \sum_{i=1}^{r}(\rho_{n,0} - k)\rho_{n,i}||b_n - \chi_{n,i}||^2 \right\} + 2\lambda_n \langle \xi g(a_n) - Dq, a_{n+1} - q \rangle. \end{aligned} \quad (46)$$

Hence,

$$\begin{aligned} (1 - \lambda_n \eta)^2 \sum_{i=1}^{r}(\rho_{n,0} - k)\rho_{n,i}||b_n - \chi_{n,i}||^2 &\leq (1 - \lambda_n \eta)^2 ||a_n - q||^2 + \theta_n(1 - \lambda_n \eta)^2(||a_n - q||^2 \\ &\quad -||a_{n-1} - q||^2) + 2\theta_n(1 - \lambda_n \eta)||a_n - a_{n-1}||^2 \\ &\quad +2\lambda_n \langle \xi g(a_n) - Dq, a_{n+1} - q \rangle - ||a_{n+1} - q||^2 \\ &\leq \Phi_n - \Phi_{n+1} + \lambda_n M_3 + \theta_n(1 - \lambda_n \eta)^2(\Phi_n - \Phi_{n+1}) \\ &\quad +\theta_n(1 - \lambda_n \eta)^2 ||a_n - a_{n-1}||^2 \\ &\quad +2\lambda_n \langle \xi g(a_n) - Dq, a_{n+1} - q \rangle \to 0 \quad as \quad n \to \infty. \end{aligned} \quad (47)$$

Thus, by applying condition (C2), we obtain

$$\lim_{n \to \infty} ||b_n - \chi_{n,i}|| = 0. \quad (48)$$

We also have that

$$\begin{aligned} ||z_n - b_n|| &= ||\rho_{n,0} b_n + \sum_{i=1}^{r} \rho_{n,i} \chi_{n,i} - b_n|| \\ &\leq \rho_{n,0} ||b_n - b_n|| + \sum_{i=1}^{r} \rho_{n,i} ||\chi_{n,i} - b_n|| \to 0, n \to \infty, \end{aligned} \quad (49)$$

thus $\lim_{n\to\infty} ||z_n - b_n|| = 0$. Therefore,
$$\lim_{n\to\infty} ||z_n - a_n|| = \lim_{n\to\infty}(||z_n - b_n|| + ||b_n - a_n||) = 0.$$

Finally,
$$\begin{aligned}||a_{n+1} - z_n|| &= ||\lambda_n \xi g(a_n) + (1 - \lambda_n D)z_n - z_n|| \\ &= \lambda_n ||\xi g(a_n) - Dz_n|| \to 0, n \to \infty,\end{aligned} \quad (50)$$

which results in the following:
$$||a_{n+1} - a_n|| \leq ||a_{n+1} - z_n|| + ||z_n - a_n|| \to 0 \quad as \quad n \to \infty.$$

As $k \to \infty$, the subsequence $\{a_{n_k}\}$ weakly converges to a^*. Denote $F_{n_k} = I - \tau_{n_k} B^*(I - J_\sigma^{m_2})B$, since $J_\sigma^{m_2}$ is firmly nonexpansive, hence F_{n_k} and $J_\sigma^{m_1}(I - \tau_{n_k} B^*(I - J_\sigma^{m_2})B)$ are averaged and nonexpansive. So the subsequence $\{v_{n_k}\}$ converges weakly to a fixed point a^* of the operator $J_\sigma^{m_1} F_n$. We now show that $a^* \in \Gamma$ that is $a^* \in m_1^{-1}(0)$ with $Ba^* \in m_2^{-1}(0)$ and $a^* \in \cap_{i=1}^r Fix(S_i)$. From (30) we have

$$\eta_n(4 - \eta_n) \frac{f^2(v_n)}{||T(v_n)||^2 + ||H(v_n)||^2} \leq ||v_n - q||^2 - ||b_n - q||^2,$$

since T and H are Lipschitz continuous, thus $T(v_n)$ and $H(v_n)$ are bounded. In addition, $\inf \eta_n(4 - \eta_n) > 0$, hence $f(v_n) \to 0$ as $n \to 0$. Since the subsequence $\{a_{n_k}\}$ converges weakly to a^*, therefore, the function f is lower semi-continuous and $||v_n - a_n|| \to 0$ as $n \to \infty$, then we can determine

$$0 \leq f(a^*) \leq \liminf_{k\to\infty} f(v_{n_k}) = \lim_{n\to\infty} f(v_n) = 0.$$

That is,
$$f(a^*) = \frac{1}{2}||(I - J_\sigma^{m_2})Ba^*||^2 = 0.$$

This implies that Ba^* is a fixed point of $J_\sigma^{B_2}$ or $(I - J_\sigma^{B_2})Ba^* = 0$, then we can have $Ba^* \in m_2^{-1}(0)$ or $0 \in m_2(Ba^*)$. Moreover, the point a^* is a fixed point of the operator $J_\sigma^{m_1}(I - \tau_n B^*(I - J_\sigma^{m_2})B)$, which means that $a^* = J_\sigma^{m_1}(I - \tau_n B^*(I - J_\sigma^{m_2})B)a^*$. Since $(I - J_\sigma^{m_2})Ba^* = 0$, hence $(I - \tau_n B^*(I - J_\sigma^{m_2})B)a^* = a^*$, consequently $a^* = J_\sigma^{m_1} a^*$, This implies that a^* is a stationary (fixed) point of $J_\sigma^{m_1}$, in fact, $a^* \in m_1^{-1}(0)$. Furthermore, from (48) and the fact that $I - S_i$ is demiclosed at zero, then $a^* \in Fix(S_i)$ for $i = 1, \ldots, r$. Hence $a^* \in \Gamma$.

First, we show that $\{a_n\}$ strongly converges to a^*, where $a^* = P_\Gamma(I - D + \xi g)a^*$ is the unique solution of the variational inequality (VI):

$$\langle (D - \xi g)a^*, a^* - a \rangle \leq 0, a \in \Gamma.$$

For us to achieve our goal, we prove that $\limsup_{n\to\infty} \langle (D - \xi g)a^*, a^* - a_n \rangle \leq 0$. Choose a subsequence $\{a_{n_j}\}$ of $\{a_n\}$ such that $\limsup_{j\to\infty} \langle (D - \xi g)a^*, a^* - a_n \rangle = \lim_{j\to\infty} \langle (D - \xi g)a^*, a^* - a_{n_j} \rangle$. Since $a_{n_j} \rightharpoonup \bar{a}$ and using (10), we have

$$\begin{aligned}\limsup_{j\to\infty} \langle (D - \xi g)a^*, a^* - a_n \rangle &= \lim_{j\to\infty} \langle (D - \xi g)a^*, a^* - a_{n_j} \rangle \\ &= \langle (D - \xi g)a^*, a^* - \bar{a} \rangle \\ &= \langle a^* - (I - (D - \xi g))a^*, a^* - \bar{a} \rangle \leq 0.\end{aligned} \quad (51)$$

Furthermore, we make use of Lemma 4, Lemma 4(i), and (51) to obtain that $||a_n - a^*|| \to 0$, implying that sequence $\{a_n\}$ strongly converges to a^*. Case A is concluded.

CASE B: Now we assume that $\{||a_n - q||\}$ is not monotonically decreasing. Then for some n_0 and $\forall n \geq n_0$, we define $\phi : \mathbb{N} \to \mathbb{N}$ by the following:

$$\phi(n) = max\{t \in \mathbb{N} : t \leq n : \phi_t \leq \phi_{t+1}\}.$$

Moreover, ϕ is increasing with $\lim_{n\to\infty} \phi(n) \to \infty$ and

$$0 \leq ||a_{\phi(n)} - q|| \leq ||a_{\phi(n)+1} - q||, \quad \forall \ n \geq n_0.$$

We can apply a similar argument to the one used in Case A and conclude that

$$\lim_{n\to\infty} ||b_{\phi(n)} - v_{\phi(n)}|| = \lim_{n\to\infty} ||x_{\phi(n),i} - b_{\phi(n)}|| = \lim_{n\to\infty} ||a_{\phi(n)+1} - a_{\phi(n)}|| = 0.$$

Thus, $\Omega_v(a_{\phi(n)}) \in \Gamma$, where $\Omega_v(a_{\phi(n)})$ is the weak subsequential limit of $\{a_{\phi(n)}\}$. Also, we have

$$\limsup_{n\to\infty} \langle (D - \xi g)q, q - a_{\phi(n)}\rangle \leq 0. \tag{52}$$

Thus, we follow from Lemma 4(i) and we have

$$||a_{\phi(n)+1} - q||^2 \leq \left(1 - \frac{2\lambda_{\phi(n)}(\eta - \xi\sigma)}{1 - \lambda_{\phi(n)}\xi\sigma}\right)||a_{\phi(n)} - q||^2 + \frac{2\lambda_{\phi(n)}(\eta - \xi\sigma)}{1 - \lambda_{\phi(n)}\xi\sigma}(2\langle\xi g(q) - Dq, a_{\phi(n)+1} - q\rangle + \lambda_{\phi(n)}M) + \frac{\alpha_{\phi(n)}M_2||a_{\phi(n)} - a_{\phi(n)-1}||}{1 - \lambda_{\phi(n)}\xi\sigma} \tag{53}$$

for some $M > 0$ and where

$$M_2 = \sup_{n \geq 1}((1 - \lambda_{\phi(n)}q)^2(||a_{\phi(n)} - q|| + ||a_{\phi(n)-1} - q||) + 2(1 - \lambda_{\phi(n)}q)^2||a_{\phi(n)} - a_{\phi(n)-1}||).$$

Since $||a_{\phi(n)} - q||^2 \leq ||a_{\phi(n)+1} - q||^2$ then from (??), we obtain the following results:

$$0 \leq \left(1 - \frac{2\lambda_{\phi(n)}(\eta - \xi\sigma)}{1 - \lambda_{\phi(n)}\xi\sigma}\right)||a_{\phi(n)} - q||^2 + \frac{2\lambda_{\phi(n)}(\eta - \xi\sigma)}{1 - \lambda_{\phi(n)}\xi\sigma}(2\langle\xi g(q) - Dq, a_{\phi(n)+1} - q\rangle + \lambda_{\phi(n)}M) + \frac{\alpha_{\phi(n)}M_2||a_{\phi(n)} - a_{\phi(n)-1}||}{1 - \lambda_{\phi(n)}\xi\sigma} - ||a_{\phi(n)} - q||^2. \tag{54}$$

Hence, we obtain:

$$\frac{2\lambda_{\phi(n)}(\eta - \xi\sigma)}{1 - \lambda_{\phi(n)}\xi\sigma}||a_{\phi(n)} - q||^2 \leq \frac{2\lambda_{\phi(n)}(\eta - \xi\sigma)}{1 - \lambda_{\phi(n)}\xi\sigma}(2\langle\xi g(q) - Dq, a_{\phi(n)+1} - q\rangle + \lambda_{\phi(n)}M) + \frac{\alpha_{\phi(n)}M_2||a_{\phi(n)} - a_{\phi(n)-1}||}{1 - \lambda_{\phi(n)}\xi\sigma}. \tag{55}$$

Therefore, we obtain the results below:

$$||a_{\phi(n)} - q||^2 \leq 2\langle\xi g(q) - Dq, a_{\phi(n)+1} - q\rangle + \lambda_{\phi(n)}M_4 + \frac{\alpha_{\phi(n)}M_2||a_{\phi(n)} - a_{\phi(n)-1}||}{2\lambda_{\phi(n)}(\eta - \xi\sigma)}. \tag{56}$$

Since the sequence $\{a_{\phi(n)}\}$ is bounded and $\lim_{n\to\infty}\lambda_{\phi(n)} \to 0$, it follows from Equation (52) and Remark 1.

$$\lim_{n\to\infty} ||a_{\phi(n)} - q|| = 0. \tag{57}$$

We can conclude that $\forall n \geq n_o$, the following statement holds:

$$0 \leq ||a_n - q||^2 \leq max\{||a_{\phi(n)} - q||^2, ||a_{\phi(n)+1} - q||^2\} = ||a_{\phi(n)+1} - q||^2.$$

Hence, $\lim_{n\to\infty} ||a_n - q|| = 0$. Therefore, we imply that sequence $\{a_n\}$ converges strongly to q. This completes the proof. □

The result presented in Theorem 1 can lead to an improvement when compared to the findings of [26]. It is important to recall that the set of quasi-nonexpansive mappings can be classified as 0-demicontractive. Therefore, we can utilize the same discoveries to obtain outcomes when approximating a common solution for the SVIP, together with a restricted number of multivalued quasi-nonexpansive mappings. The following remark highlights our contributions to this paper:

Remark 3.
(i) *A new optimal choice of the inertial extrapolation technique is introduced. This can also be adapted for other iterative algorithms to perform better.*
(ii) *The algorithm obtained a strong convergence result without necessarily imposing a solid condition on the control parameters.*
(iii) *The self-adaptive technique prevents the need to calculate a prior estimate of the norm of the bounded linear operator at every iteration.*
(iv) *The algorithm produces suitable solutions that approximate the entire set of solutions Γ as stated in (1), using appropriate starting points. This feature sets it apart from Tikhonov-type regularization methods, which always converge to the same solution sequence. We find this attribute particularly intriguing.*

4. Numerical Illustrations

Let us provide some numerical examples that demonstrate the effectiveness and efficiency of the suggested algorithms. We will compare the performance of Algorithm 11 (also known as Algorithm 11) with Algorithms 1, 2, 3 and 10 (also known as Algorithms 1, 2, 3, and 10, respectively). Kindly note that the renumbering of the article occurred due to the change in the numbering style in the template. All codes were written in MATLAB R2020b and performed on a PC Desktop. Intel(R) Core(TM) i7-6600U CPU @ 3.00 GHz 3.00 GHz, RAM 32.00 GB.

Example 1. *Let $H_1 = H_2 = \mathbb{R}^3$ and $B, m_1, m_2 : \mathbb{R}^3 \to \mathbb{R}^3$ be defined by*

$$B = \begin{pmatrix} 1 & -1 & 0 \\ 1 & 2 & 0 \\ 0 & 0 & 3 \end{pmatrix}, \quad m_1 = \begin{pmatrix} 4 & 0 & 0 \\ 0 & 3 & 0 \\ 0 & 0 & 2 \end{pmatrix} \quad \text{and} \quad m_2 = \begin{pmatrix} 6 & 0 & 0 \\ 0 & 5 & 0 \\ 0 & 0 & 4 \end{pmatrix}. \tag{58}$$

It is easy to check that the resolvent operators concerning m_1 and m_2 are defined by

$$J_\sigma^{m_1}(a) = \left(\frac{a_1}{1+4\sigma}, \frac{a_2}{1+3\sigma}, \frac{a_3}{1+2\sigma}\right)^\top \quad \text{and} \quad J_\sigma^{m_2}(a) = \left(\frac{a_1}{1+5\sigma}, \frac{a_2}{1+5\sigma}, \frac{a_3}{1+4\sigma}\right)^\top$$

for $\sigma > 0$ and $a \in \mathbb{R}^3$. Also, let $F_j : \mathbb{R}^3 \to 2^{\mathbb{R}^3}$ be defined by

$$F_j a = \begin{cases} \frac{-(3j+1)x}{3}, \quad -(j+1)a & \text{if} \quad a \leq 0 \\ -(j+1)a, \quad \frac{-(3j+1)a}{3} & \text{if} \quad a > 0 \end{cases} \tag{59}$$

It is clear that $T(F) = \{0\}$ and $\mathcal{H}(F_j a, F_j 0) = (j+1)^2 |z|^2$. Thus,

$$\begin{aligned}
d(a, F_j a)^2 &= \left| a + \frac{(3j+1)}{3} a \right|^2 \\
&= \left| \frac{(3j+4)}{3} a \right|^2 \\
&= \left(\frac{9j^2 + 24j + 16}{9} \right) |a|^2.
\end{aligned}$$

Furthermore,

$$\begin{aligned}
\mathcal{H}(F_j a, F_j 0)^2 &= (j+1)^2 |a|^2 \\
&= |a - 0|^2 + (j^2 + 2j)|a - 0|^2 \\
&= |a - 0|^2 + \frac{9j^2 + 2j}{9j^2 + 24j + 16} d^2(a, F_j a). \tag{60}
\end{aligned}$$

Hence, F_j is k-demicontractive with $k = \frac{(9j^2+2j)}{9j^2+24j+16} \in (0.1)$. Moreover, the solution set $\Gamma = \{0\}$. We choose the following choice of parameters for Algorithm 11: $\theta_n = \frac{1}{(n+1)^2}$, $\eta_n = \frac{2n}{5n+4}$, $\beta_n = \frac{1}{m+1}$, $\lambda_n = \frac{1}{n+1}$, $\xi = 1, \alpha = 0.2$ $g(a) = \frac{a}{4}$ $D(a) = a$. For Algorithm 1, we take $\theta_n = \frac{2n}{5n+4}, \delta = 0.03$; for Algorithm 2, we take $\theta_n = \frac{1}{(n+1)^2}, \delta = 0.04, \lambda = 0.03$; for Algorithm 3, we take $\eta_n = 0.04$; and for Algorithm 10, we take $\theta_n = \frac{2n}{5n+3}, \alpha_n = \frac{1}{n+1}, \sigma_n = \frac{1}{2\|B^*B\|^2}$. We test the algorithms using the following initial points:

([Case I:]) $a_0 = \text{eye}(3,1)$ and $a_1 = \text{rand}(3,1)$,

([Case II:]) $a_0 = \text{rand}(3,1)$ and $a_1 = \text{rand}(3,1)$,

([Case III:]) $a_0 = \text{randn}(3,1)$ and $a_1 = \text{randn}(3,1)$,

([Case IV:]) $a_0 = \text{ones}(3,1)$ and $a_1 = \text{rand}(3,1)$,

where "eye", "randn", "rand", and "ones" are MATLAB functions. We used $\|a_{n+1} - a_n\| < 10^{-6}$ as the stopping criterion for all the implementation. The numerical results are shown in Table 1 and Figure 1. Furthermore, we run the algorithms for 100 randomly generated starting points to check the performance of the algorithms using the performance profile metric introduced by Dolan and More [34], which is widely accepted as a benchmark for comparing the performance of algorithms. The details of the setup of the performance profile can be found in [34]. In particular, for each algorithm $s \in \mathcal{S} = \{1, 2, \ldots, 5\}$ and case $p \in \mathcal{P} = \{1, \ldots, 100\}$, we defined a parameter $t_{p,s}$ which is the computation value of algorithm $s \in \mathcal{S}$ for solving problem case $p \in \mathcal{P}$ such as the number of iterations, time of execution, or error value of Algorithm $s \in \mathcal{S}$ to solve problem $p \in \mathcal{P}$. The performance of each algorithm is scaled concerning the best performance of any other algorithm in $\mathcal{S}$, which yields the performance ratio

$$\eta_{p,s} = \frac{t_{p,s}}{\min\{t_{p,s} : s \in \mathcal{S}\}}.$$

We select a parameter η_r such that $\eta_r \geq \eta_{p,s}$ for all p and s, and $\eta_{p,s} = \eta_r$ only if solver s is unable to solve problem p. It is worth noting that the choice of η_r does not affect the performance evaluation, as explained in [34]. To determine an overall assessment of each solver's performance, we use the following measurement:

$$P_s(t) = \frac{1}{n_p} \text{size}\{p \in \mathcal{P} : \eta_{p,s} \leq t\},$$

the probability $P_s(t)$ represents the likelihood of solver $s \in \mathcal{S}$ to achieve a performance ratio $\eta_{p,s}$ within a factor $t \in \mathbb{R}$ of the best possible ratio. The performance profile $P_s : \mathbb{R} \to [0,1]$ for a solver is a non-decreasing function that is piecewise continuous from the right at each breakpoint when P_s is defined as the cumulative distribution function of the performance ratio. The probability $P_s(1)$ denotes the chance of the solver achieving the best performance among all solvers. The performance profile results (Figure 2 show that Algorithm 11 has the best performance for 100% of the cases considered in terms of the number of iterations. In contrast, Algorithm 3 has the worst performance. Moreover, Algorithm 10 performs better than Algorithms 1–3 even in worst senerios. Also, Algorithm 11 has the best performance for about 82% of the cases in terms of the time of execution, followed by Algorithm 10 for about 18% of the cases. In contrast, Algorithm 3 has the worst performance in terms of the time of execution. It is good to note that despite the self-adaptive technique used in selecting the stepsize for Algorithm 3, its performance is relatively worse than other methods.

Table 1. Numerical results for Example 1.

		Case I	Case II	Case III	Case IV
Algorithm 11	No of L.	13	15	17	14
	CPU time (s)	0.0013	0.0076	0.0090	0.0018
Algorithm 1	No of L.	43	50	63	48
	CPU time (s)	0.0282	0.0223	0.0114	0.0156
Algorithm 2	No of L.	41	48	59	46
	CPU time (s)	0.0270	0.0191	0.0137	0.0166
Algorithm 3	No of L.	104	140	160	73
	CPU time (s)	0.0305	0.0425	0.0278	0.0194
Algorithm 10	No of L.	28	32	37	28
	CPU time (s)	0.0167	0.0161	0.0148	0.0034

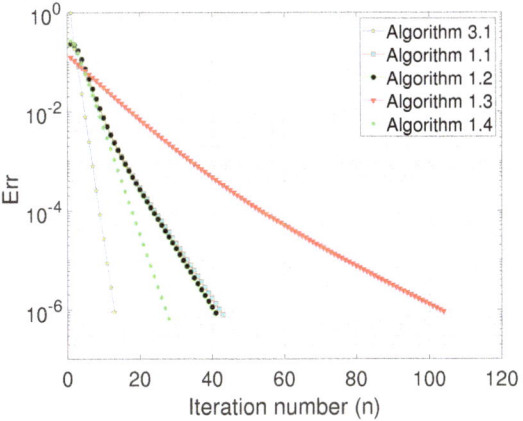

Figure 1. Cont.

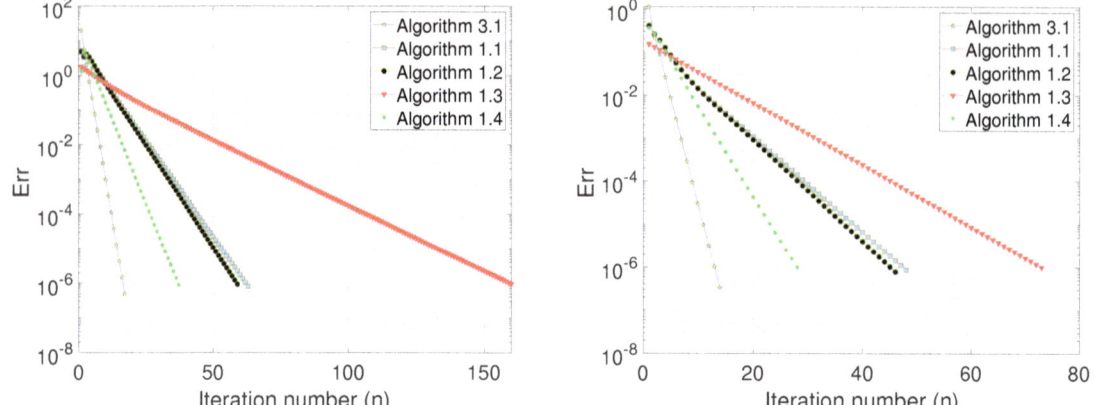

Figure 1. Example 1, (**Top Left**): Case I; (**Top Right**): Case II, (**Bottom Left**): Case III; (**Bottom Right**): Case IV.

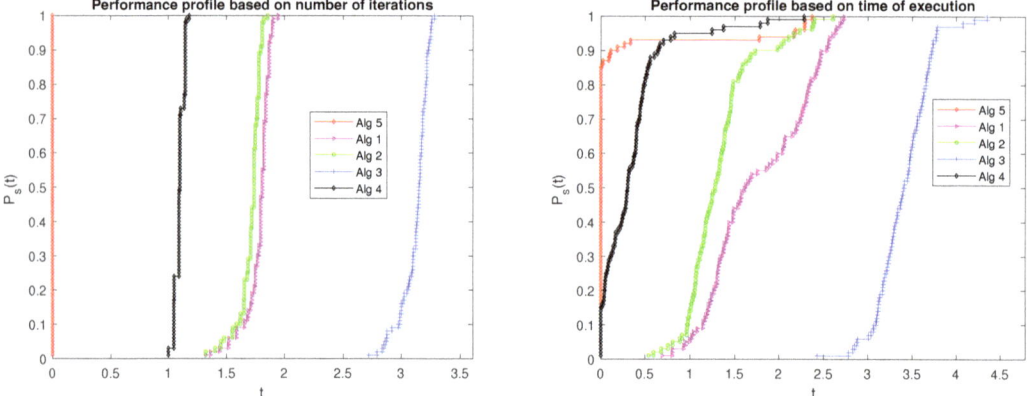

Figure 2. Performance profile results for Example 1 in terms of number of iterations (**left**) and time of execution (**right**).

Example 2. *Our algorithms are utilized to solve an image reconstruction problem that can be modeled as the Least Absolute Selection and Shrinkage Operator (LASSO) problem described in Tibshirani's work [35]. Alternatively, it can be modeled as an underdetermined linear system given by*

$$z = ma + \epsilon, \tag{61}$$

where a is the original image in $\mathbb{R}^M$, m is the blurring operator in $M \times N (M << N)$, ϵ is noise, and z is the degraded or blurred data which must be recovered. Typically, this can be reformulated as a convex unconstrained minimization problem given by

$$\min_{a \in \mathbb{R}^N} \left\{ \frac{1}{2} \|ma - z\|_2^2 + \lambda \|a\|_1 \right\}, \tag{62}$$

where $\lambda > 0$, $\|a\|_2$ is the Euclidean norm of a and $\|a\|_1 = \sum_{i=1}^{N} |y_i|$ is the l_1-norm of a. Various scientific and engineering fields have found the problem to be a valuable tool. Over the years, several iterative techniques have been developed to solve Equation (62), with the earliest being the projection approach introduced by Figureido et al. [36]. Equivalently, the LASSO problem (62) can be expressed as an SVIP when $C = \{a \in \mathbb{R}^k : \|a\|_1 \leq t\}$ and $Q = \{z\}$, $m_1 = \partial i_C$, $m_2 = \partial i_Q$, where i_C and i_Q are the indicator functions on C and Q, respectively. We aim to reconstruct the initial image a based on the information the blurred image z provides. The image is in greyscale and has a width of M pixels and a height of N pixels, with each pixel value within the $[0, 255]$ range. The total number of pixels in the image is $D = M \times N$. The signal-to-noise ratio, which is determined by the amount of noise present in the restored image, is used to evaluate the quality of the resulting image, and it is defined by

$$SNR = 20 \times \log_{10}\left(\frac{\|a\|_2}{\|a - a^*\|_2}\right),$$

with a and a^* being the original and restored images, respectively. In image restoration, the quality of the restored image is typically measured by its signal-to-noise ratio (SNR), where a higher SNR indicates better quality. To evaluate the effectiveness of our approach, we conducted experiments using three test images: Cameraman (256×256), Medical Resonance Imaging (MRI) (128×128), and Pout (400×318), all of which were obtained from the Image Processing Toolbox in MATLAB. Specifically, we degraded each test image using a Gaussian 7×7 blur kernel with a standard deviation of 4. We processed the algorithms using the following control parameters: Algorithm 11: $\theta_n = \frac{1}{n^2}$, $\eta_n = \frac{2n-1}{8n+7}$, $\beta_n = \frac{1}{r+1}$, $\lambda_n = \frac{1}{100n+1}$, $\xi = 1, \alpha = 0.4$ $g(a) = \frac{a}{8}$ $D(a) = 2a$. For Algorithm 1, we take $\theta_n = \frac{n}{7n+3}, \lambda = 0.05$; for Algorithm 2, we take $\theta_n = \frac{1}{n^2}, \delta = 0.06, \lambda = 0.09$; for Algorithm 3, we take $\eta_n = 0.05$; and for Algorithm 10, we take $\theta_n = \frac{n}{7n+3}, \alpha_n = \frac{1}{100n+1}, \sigma_n = \frac{1}{2\|B^*B\|^2}$. We also choose the initial values as $a_0 = \mathbf{0} \in \mathbb{R}^{M \times N}$ and $a_1 = \mathbf{1} \in \mathbb{R}^{M \times N}$. The numerical results are shown in Figures 3–6 and Table 2. It is easy to see that all the algorithms efficiently reconstruct the blurred image. Though the performance of the algorithms varies in terms of the quality of the reconstructed image, we note that Algorithm 11 was able to reconstruct the images faster than other algorithms used in the experiments. This also emphasizes the importance of the proposed algorithm.

Figure 3. Cont.

Figure 3. Image reconstruction using cameraman (256 × 256) image.

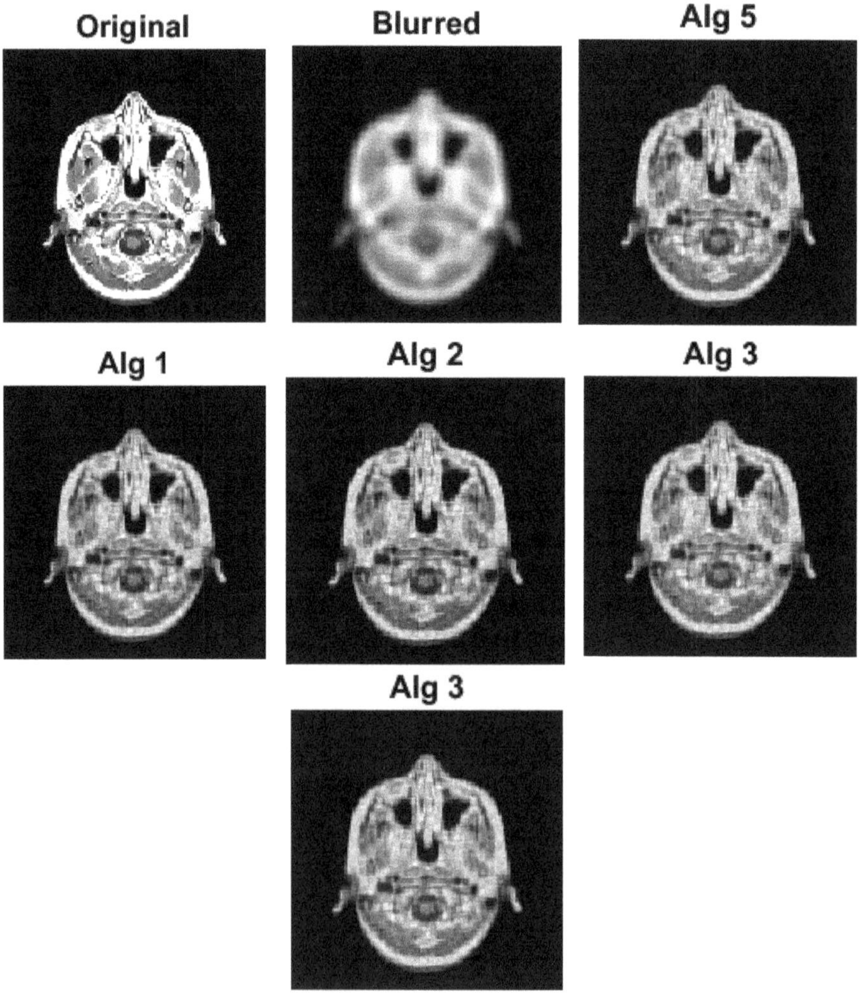

Figure 4. Image reconstruction using MRI (128 × 128) image.

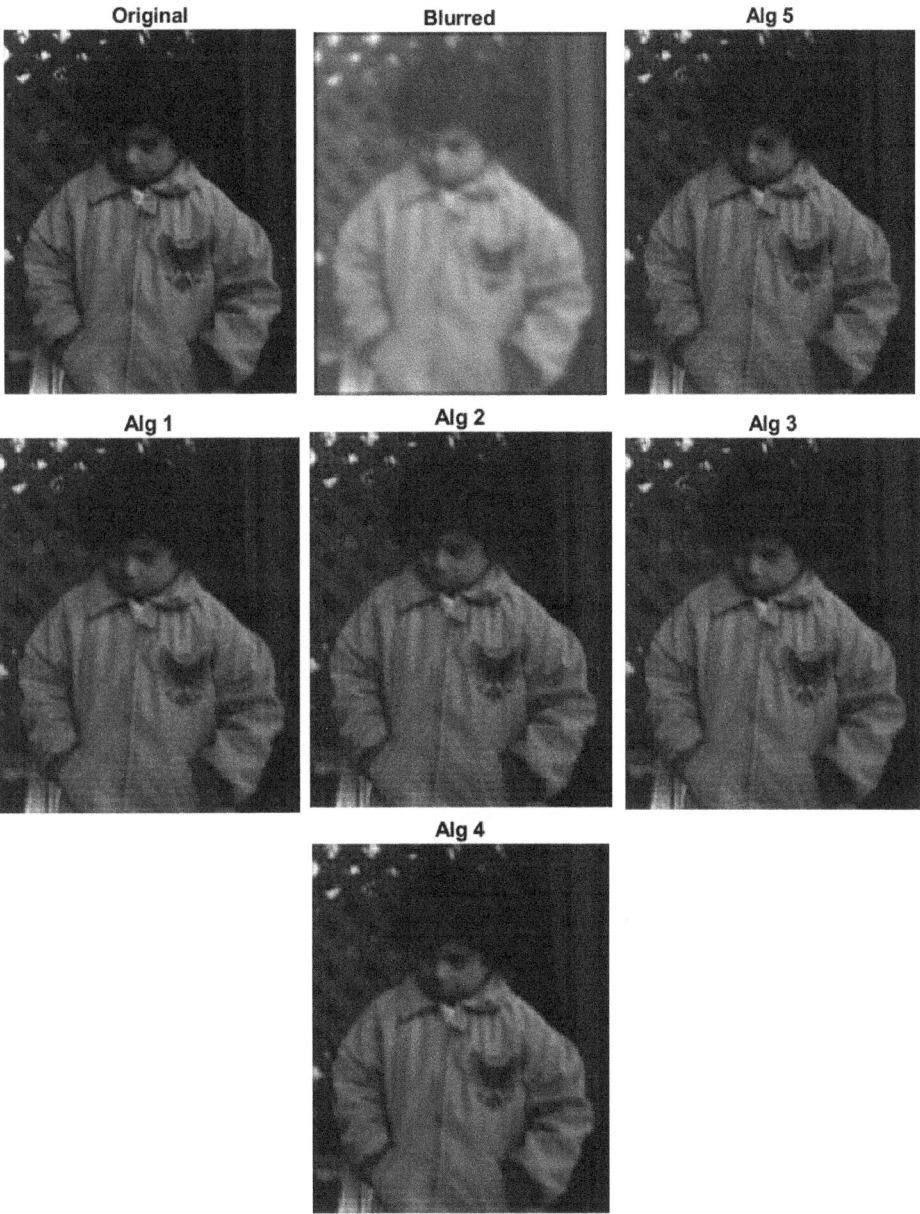

Figure 5. Image construction using Pout image (291 × 240).

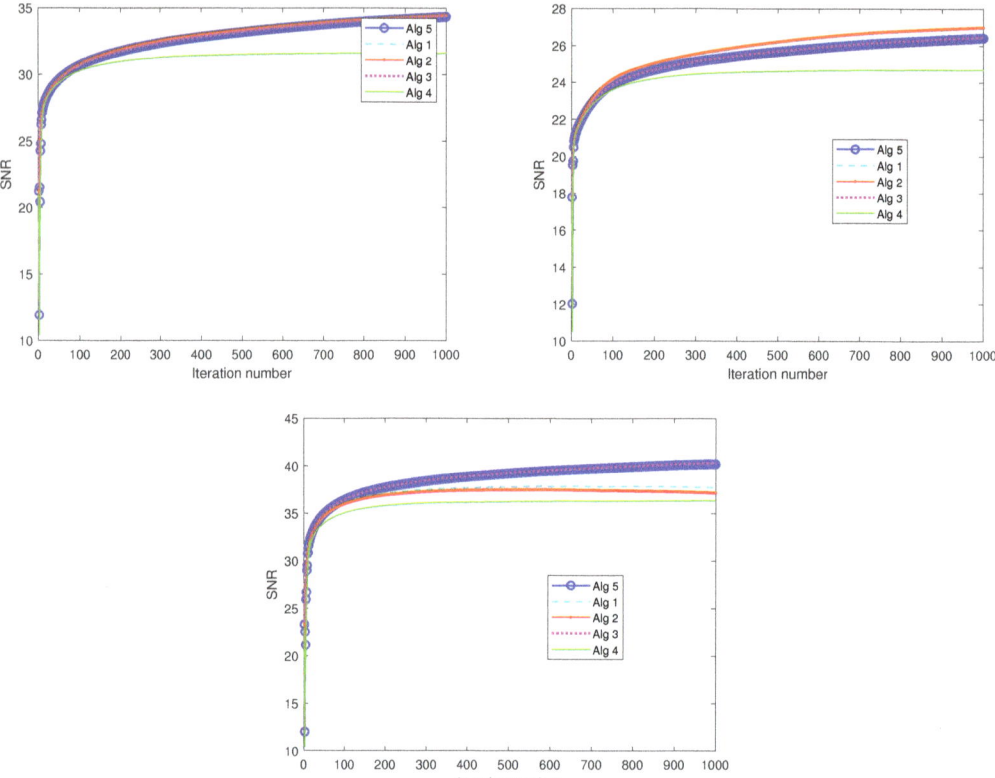

Figure 6. Graphs of SNR against iteration number. **Top Left**: Cameraman; **Top Right**: MRI; and **Bottom**: Pout.

Table 2. Computational result for Example 2.

Algorithms	Cameraman		MRI		Pout	
	Time (s)	SNR	Time (s)	SNR	Time (s)	SNR
Algorithm 11	14.2169	34.3580	2.3627	26.4215	11.3969	40.2075
Algorithm 1	16.9989	34.3517	2.7461	26.9565	12.5370	37.7244
Algorithm 2	19.6273	34.3468	2.8171	25.8976	12.3931	40.9870
Algorithm 3	18.8111	34.4365	2.7333	26.4675	13.5479	40.3109
Algorithm 10	17.3022	31.5974	2.7074	24.6775	12.3144	36.2867

5. Conclusions

Our paper proposes a novel inertial self-adaptive iterative technique that utilizes viscosity approximation to obtain a common solution for split variational inclusion problems and fixed point problems in real Hilbert spaces. We have selected an optimal inertial extrapolation term to enhance the algorithm's accuracy. Additionally, we incorporated a self-adaptive technique that allows for stepsize adjustment without relying on prior knowledge of the norm of the bounded linear operator. Our method has been proven to converge strongly, and we have included numerical implementations to demonstrate its efficiency and effectiveness.

Author Contributions: Conceptualization, M.D.N. and L.O.J.; methodology, M.D.N. and L.O.J.; software, I.O.A.; validation, M.A. and L.O.J.; formal analysis, M.D.N. and L.O.J.; investigation, M.D.N.; resources, M.A.; data curation, I.O.A.; writing—original draft preparation, M.D.N.; writing—review and editing, L.O.J.; visualization, L.O.J. and I.O.A.; supervision, M.A. and L.O.J.; project administration, M.D.N.; funding acquisition, M.A. All authors have read and agreed to the published version of the manuscript.

Funding: This research received no external funding

Data Availability Statement: Data are contained within the article.

Conflicts of Interest: The authors declare no conflict of interest.

References

1. Moudafi, A. Split monotone variational inclusions. *J. Optim. Theory Appl.* **2011**, *150*, 275–283. [CrossRef]
2. Censor, Y.; Elfving, T. A multiprojection algorithms using Bregman projection in a product space. *Numer. Algorithms* **1994**, *8*, 221–239. [CrossRef]
3. Censor, Y.; Bortfeld, T.; Martin, B.; Trofimov, A. A unified approach for inversion problems in intensity-modulated radiation therapy. *Phys. Med. Biol.* **2006**, *51*, 2353–2365. [CrossRef] [PubMed]
4. Censor, Y.; Gibali, A.; Reich, S. Algorithms for the split variational inequality problem. *Numer. Algorithms* **2012**, *59*, 301–323. [CrossRef]
5. Byrne, C. Iterative oblique projection onto convex subsets and the split feasibility problem. *Inverse Probl.* **2002**, *18*, 441–453. [CrossRef]
6. Combettes, P.L. The convex feasibility problem in image recovery. In *Advances in Imaging and Electron Physics*; Hawkes, P., Ed.; Academic Press: New York, NY, USA, 1996; pp. 155–270.
7. Byrne, C.; Censor, Y.; Gibali, A.; Reich, S. Weak and strong convergence of algorithms for the split common null point problem. *J. Nonlinear Convex. Anal.* **2012**, *13*, 759–775.
8. Marino, G.; Xu, H.K. A general iterative method for nonexpansive mapping in Hilbert spaces. *J. Math. Anal. Appl.* **2006**, *318*, 43–52. [CrossRef]
9. Moudafi, A. Viscosity approximation methods for fixed-points problems. *J. Math. Anal. Appl.* **2000**, *241*, 46–55. [CrossRef]
10. Kazmi, K.R.; Rizvi, S.H. An iterative method for split variational inclusion problem and fixed point problem for a nonexpansive mapping. *Optim. Lett.* **2014**, *8*, 1113–1124. [CrossRef]
11. Alvarez, F.; Attouch, H. An inertial proximal method for maximal monotone operators via discretization of a nonlinear oscillator with damping. *Set-Valued Anal.* **2001**, *9*, 3–11. [CrossRef]
12. Polyak, B.T. Some methods of speeding up the convergence of iterarive methods. *Z. Vychisl. Mat. Mat. Fiz.* **1964**, *4*, 1–17.
13. Moudafi, A.; Oliny, M. Convergence of a splitting inertial proximal method for monotone operators. *J. Comput. Appl. Math.* **2003**, *155*, 447–454. [CrossRef]
14. Deepho, J.; Kumam, P. The hybrid steepest descent method for split variational inclusion and constrained convex minimization problem. *Abstr. Appl. Anal.* **2014**, *2014*, 365203. [CrossRef]
15. Anh, P.K.; Thong, D.V.; Dung, V.T. A strongly convergent Mann-type inertial algorithm for solving split variational inclusion problems. *Optim. Eng.* **2021**, *22*, 159–185. [CrossRef]
16. Maingé, P.E. Regularized and inertial algorithms for common fixed points of nonlinear operators. *J. Math. Anal. Appl.* **2008**, *34*, 876–887. [CrossRef]
17. Wangkeeree, R.; Rattanaseeha, K. The general iterative methods for split variational inclusion problem and fixed point problem in Hilbert spaces. *J. Comput. Anal. Appl.* **2018**, *25*, 19–31.
18. Long, L.V.; Thong, D.V.; Dung, V.T. New algorithms for the split variational inclusion problems and application to split feasibility problems. *Optimization* **2019**, *68*, 2339–2367. [CrossRef]
19. Dong, Q.L.; Lu, Y.Y.; Yang, J. The extragradient algorithm with inertial effects for solving the variational inequality. *Optimization* **2016**, *65*, 2217–2226. [CrossRef]
20. Alakoya, T.O.; Jolaoso, L.O.; Mewomo, O.T. Modified inertial subgradient extragradient method with self-adaptive stepsize for solving monotone variational inequality and fixed point problems. *Optimization* **2020**, 545–574. [CrossRef]
21. Chuang, C.S. Hybrid inertial proximal algorithm for the split variational inclusion problem in Hilbert spaces with applications. *Optimization* **2017**, *66*, 777–792. [CrossRef]
22. Kesornprom, S.; Cholamjiak, P. Proximal type algorithms involving linesearch and inertial technique for split variational inclusion problem in hilbert spaces with applications. *Optimization* **2019**, *68*, 2369–2395. [CrossRef]
23. Tang, Y. Convergence analysis of a new iterative algorithm for solving split variational inclusion problem. *J. Ind. Manag. Optim.* **2020**, *16*, 235–259. [CrossRef]
24. Tan, B.; Qin, X.; Yao, J.C. Strong convergence of self-adaptive inertial algorithms for solving split variational inclusion problems with applications. *J. Sci. Comput.* **2021**, *87*, 20. [CrossRef]

25. Zhou, Z.; Tan, B.; Li, S. Adaptive hybrid steepest descent algorithms involving an inertial extrapolation term for split monotone variational inclusion problems. *Math. Methods Appl. Sci.* **2022**, *45*, 8835–8853. [CrossRef]
26. Alakoya, T.O.; Jolaoso, L.O.; Mewomo, O.T. A self adaptive inertial algorithm for solving split variational inclusion and fixed point problems with applications. *J. Ind. Manag. Optim.* **2022**, *18*, 239–265. [CrossRef]
27. Aubin, J.P.; Siegel, J. Fixed points and stationary points of dissipative multivalued maps. *Proc. Am. Math. Soc.* **1989**, *78*, 391–398. [CrossRef]
28. Panyanak, B. Endpoints of multivalued nonexpansive mappings in geodesic spaces. *Fixed Point Theory Appl.* **2015**, *2015*, 147. [CrossRef]
29. Kahn, M.S.; Rao, K.R.; Cho, Y.J. Common stationary points for set-valued mappings. *Int. J. Math. Math. Sci.* **1993**, *16*, 733–736. [CrossRef]
30. Jailoka, P.; Suantai, S. The split common fixed point problem for multivalued demicontractive mappings and its applications. *RACSAM* **2019**, *113*, 689–706. [CrossRef]
31. Chidume, C.E.; Ezeora, J.N. Krasnoselskii-type algorithm for family of multi-valued strictly pseudo-contractive mappings. *Fixed Point Theory Appl.* **2014**, *2014*, 111. [CrossRef]
32. Mainge, P.E. Convergence theorems for inertial KM-type algorithms. *J. Comput. Appl. Math.* **2008**, *219*, 223–236. [CrossRef]
33. Mainge, P.E. A hybrid extragradient viscosity method for monotone operators and fixed point problems. *SIAM J. Control Optim.* **2008**, *49*, 1499–1515. [CrossRef]
34. Dolan, E.D.; Moré, J.J. Benchmarking optimization software with performance profiles. *Math. Program* **2002**, *91*, 201–213. [CrossRef]
35. Tibshirani, R. Regression Shrinkage and Selection via the Lasso. *J. R. Stat. Soc. Ser. B* **1996**, *58*, 267–288. [CrossRef]
36. Figueiredo, M.A.T.; Nowak, R.D.; Wright, S.J. Gradient projection for sparse reconstruction: Application to compressed sensing and other inverse problems. *IEEE J. Sel. Top. Signal Process.* **2007** *1*, 586–597. [CrossRef]

Disclaimer/Publisher's Note: The statements, opinions and data contained in all publications are solely those of the individual author(s) and contributor(s) and not of MDPI and/or the editor(s). MDPI and/or the editor(s) disclaim responsibility for any injury to people or property resulting from any ideas, methods, instructions or products referred to in the content.

MDPI AG
Grosspeteranlage 5
4052 Basel
Switzerland
Tel.: +41 61 683 77 34

Mathematics Editorial Office
E-mail: mathematics@mdpi.com
www.mdpi.com/journal/mathematics

Disclaimer/Publisher's Note: The statements, opinions and data contained in all publications are solely those of the individual author(s) and contributor(s) and not of MDPI and/or the editor(s). MDPI and/or the editor(s) disclaim responsibility for any injury to people or property resulting from any ideas, methods, instructions or products referred to in the content.

www.ingramcontent.com/pod-product-compliance
Lightning Source LLC
LaVergne TN
LVHW070508100526
838202LV00014B/1812